THE JAPANESE COLONIAL EMPIRE, 1895–1945

This book is based on a conference sponsored
by the Joint Committee on Japanese Studies
of the American Council of Learned Societies
and the Social Science Research Council

THE JAPANESE COLONIAL EMPIRE, 1895–1945

Edited by Ramon H. Myers *and* Mark R. Peattie

CONTRIBUTORS

Ching-chih Chen
Edward I-te Chen
Bruce Cumings
Peter Duus
Lewis H. Gann
Samuel Pao-San Ho
Marius B. Jansen

Mizoguchi Toshiyuki
Ramon H. Myers
Mark R. Peattie
Michael E. Robinson
E. Patricia Tsurumi
Yamada Saburō
Yamamoto Yūzō

Princeton University Press / Princeton, N. J.

Copyright © 1984 by Princeton University Press
Published by Princeton University Press,
41 William Street, Princeton, New Jersey 08540
In the United Kingdom: Princeton University Press,
Guildford, Surrey

All Rights Reserved
Library of Congress Cataloging in Publication Data
will be found on the last printed page of this book

ISBN 0-691-05398-7

This book has been composed in Linotron Bembo
Clothbound editions of Princeton University Press books
are printed on acid-free paper, and binding materials are
chosen for strength and durability.
Paperbacks, although satisfactory for personal collections,
are not usually suitable for library rebinding

Printed in the United States of America by
Princeton University Press, Princeton, New Jersey

*This book is dedicated to the memory of
Yanaihara Tadao (1893-1961)
Scholar, teacher, Christian, and pioneer
in Japanese colonial studies*

Table of Contents

PART IV / The Japanese Empire in Historical and
  Global Perspective

Preface

While much has been written in Japanese and Western languages about Japanese overseas expansionism in the late nineteenth and the first half of the twentieth centuries, this scholarship has rarely treated the issues related to the founding, management, and development of the colonial territories acquired by Japan between the Sino-Japanese war of 1894–1895 and the end of World War II.

The focus of this volume is therefore the formal colonial empire of Japan: Taiwan, Korea, Karafuto (southern Sakhalin), the Kwantung Leased Territory on the Liaotung peninsula, and the Nan'yō (the Japanese mandate islands of Micronesia). We have thus set aside Japan's informal empire in China, including its settlements in the treaty ports and railway "zones" in Manchuria, as well as the wartime conquests in China, Southeast Asia, and the South Pacific from 1931 to 1945, topics which each deserve separate treatment elsewhere. As editors, we have encouraged a comparative perspective in the drafting of these essays. By and large, the contributors have tried to examine particular problems of Japanese colonial rule from the vantage point of two or more colonies within the empire and, where appropriate, have drawn comparisons with Western colonial systems.

The genesis of these studies on the Japanese empire was a conference on that topic held in August 1979 at the Hoover Institution on War, Revolution, and Peace, Stanford University, sponsored by the Social Science Research Council. Both of these institutions provided funds to help us prepare this volume for publication. We wish to express our thanks for their generous support.

Noel Diaz, cartographic illustrator, prepared the six maps contained in the volume. Mark Peattie researched and selected the photographs. Ronald Aqua of the Joint Committee on Japanese Studies and the Joint Committee on Korean Studies of the Social Science Research Council proved to be extraordinarily helpful and supportive in staging our conference and encouraging the publication of this volume. Maxine Douglas, secretary of the East Asian Collection of the Hoover Institution, carried on our voluminous correspondence with contributors and interested parties. She also planned and managed our conference. Finally, we are extremely grateful to Princeton

University Press for publishing this volume, which we sincerely hope will encourage future scholars to address the problems and issues raised in this collection of essays.

Ramon H. Myers
Mark R. Peattie

THE JAPANESE COLONIAL EMPIRE, 1895-1945

Introduction

Mark R. Peattie

Colonialism, one of the "five ideas that changed the world," in the words of Barbara Ward, is a human activity both very old and very modern. While the instincts underlying colonialism may be traced to the beginnings of human society, the modern colonial era is a recent historical phenomenon. Generally speaking, the formal colonial systems which were eroded by movements for national independence by the mid-twentieth century were the products of a late-nineteenth-century spasm of imperial expansion remarkable for its global dimensions and its brief duration. In less than thirty years—from the mid 1880's to World War I—a surge of aggrandizement by the older European powers, as well as by newer imperial aspirants, had almost entirely partitioned the African continent and had, except for China, Japan, and Siam, occupied the remaining unclaimed portions of Asia and the Pacific.

The older mercantilist imperialism of maritime powers, Spain and Portugal in the sixteenth century, and Holland, Britain, and France in the seventeenth and eighteenth centuries, had been largely a process of colonization, the settlement abroad of peoples from European mother countries, which unfolded for the most part in the temperate zones (India and the East Indies being the most notable exceptions to this pattern). The settlement colonies which gradually evolved over this three-hundred-year period were remarkably diverse in form and character, reflecting the contrasts in European civilization. In contrast, the "new imperialism," as the late-nineteenth-century burst of imperial activity by the industrial West has come to be called, created modern colonial systems notable for the rapidity with which they were assembled and the degree to which they were similar in arrangement, structure, and evolution. Indeed, if we allow for important exceptions in all these categories, modern colonial empires can be seen as a type. Geographically, they were tropical territories composed of broad expanses of jungle, great stretches of desert, or scattered islands in the torrid zones. Dispersed over the globe at great distance from the European mother countries, these tropic territories had been dispersed and opened by explorers, adventurers, traders, missionaries, or merchants often acting on their own and on the fringe of national interest, but ultimately backed by the full political or military weight of their home governments. The modern tropical colony, moreover, was typically a colony of occupation, in which a European elite minority ruled over a large indigenous population whose racial origins and cultural traditions were entirely distinct from those of the conquerors and whose material conditions were vastly inferior.

The administrative structures of such colonies were, moreover, significantly similar. Bureaucratically administered, with effective power concentrated at the center by highly efficient executive institutions, they were managed by an elite corps of civil servants reasonably well trained, well paid, and honest. Despite individual differences in degree, territories within modern colonial systems were administered autocratically and, because of this, lacked demonstrable public support. This led to the common defect of overly cautious conservatism, which, far from attempting radical programs to transform colonial peoples in the European image, tended to perpetuate indigenous social and economic systems, isolating them from the contemporary industrial world. In the economic sphere, modern tropical empires included enterprises, state or private, designed to extract and exploit the wealth of their colonial territories with a success and rigor which varied from colony to colony.

Finally, in the view of David Fieldhouse, modern tropical colonies, from their formation to their dissolution, passed through a series of recognizable phases, beginning with the initial chaos involved in colonial conquests, proceeding to a period of conscious attention to the interests of the subject peoples, adulterated in the 1900's by the racialist assumptions of Social Darwinism. In the 1930's growing universalist assumptions of the perfectibility of all peoples encouraged the idea of colonial trusteeship and, by implication, the possibility of autonomy within the imperial system some time in the future. In the last stage, the rush of decolonization between 1945 and the 1960's, previous assumptions of indefinite colonial rule had to be abandoned and preparations quickly begun for a complete transfer of power to nationalist forces.[1]

All of these attributes came to form the configurations of what we know as modern colonialism: the establishment and maintenance for an extended time of rule by alien minorities who represented, among other things, machine-oriented civilization, powerful economies,

[1] David Fieldhouse, *The Colonial Empires: A Comparative Survey from the Eighteenth Century* (New York: Delacourt Press, 1966), pp. 377-378.

Christian origins, rapid pace of life, and who asserted feelings of racial and cultural superiority over indigenous majorities who were separate from and subordinate to the ruling colonial race.[2]

But while colonialism displayed a common pattern of arrangement and structure, the character and avowed purpose of colonial rule among various tropical empires was often strikingly different. For colonialism was as much a state of mind—a constellation of attitudes and assumptions—as it was a system of bureaucratic mechanisms, legal institutions, and economic enterprises. This outlook on the rationale of empire and the governing of alien peoples in overseas territories was itself the sum of national history and of imperial circumstances which stamped the characters and thus the policies of individual European empires of the late nineteenth and early twentieth centuries. Thus the globe-girdling British imperium—composed as it was of older white settlement territories, a vast Indian empire, latter-day tropical territories of occupation—by its very diversity of origin and function allowed the possibility of autonomous development of its various components, while still bearing the common "burden" of trusteeship. France, on the other hand, drawing on the republican principles of 1789, which its statesmen and thinkers believed were applicable in all times and places, held to the theory (though less in practice) that her colonies were parts of an indivisible republic whose global purpose was a *mission civilisatrice*, the propagation of French civilization. Germany, to offer a third example, though disdaining an overseas mission as such, brought to its colonial tasks the accomplishments of nineteenth-century German science and rationalism and thus prided itself on the creation of a "scientific colonialism." This approach was based on the contemporary German passion for methodical research and investigation, both of which were seen as prerequisites for economically sound administration and maximum efficiency in the extraction of wealth from colonial territories.

Though all of the modern European colonial systems, in ethos and policy, reflected the diverse cultural and historical conditions of their metropolitan countries, most were created amid the ideological gusts of the "new imperialism." Their individual acquisitions were rapidly assembled for a variety of reasons: prestige, trade, missionary zeal, strategic location, comparative advantage vis-à-vis some other colonial power, and sometimes—as in the case of some British colonial territories—for no immediately discernible reason at all. But justifications for the formation of these late-nineteenth-century colonial

[2] Georges Balandier, "La situation coloniale: Approche theorique," *Cahiers Internationaux de Sociologie*, XI: 51 (1951), pp. 75-76.

systems were often made after the initial impetus of their creation and often on grounds that had dramatic appeal. Statesmen took the lead in providing new theories for empire which would quicken the imperial appetites of the mass electorates of Europe. Leaders like Jules Ferry in France, Joseph Chamberlain and Cecil Rhodes in Britain, and writers like Friederich Fabri in Germany, offered neo-mercantilistic arguments and pseudo-scientific logic to the call to enter the scramble for colonies abroad. They trumpeted the needs of a new industrial system—outlets for surplus capital, markets for surplus production, and secure sources for raw materials—as well as the importance of colonies as new living space for "surplus" populations at a time when nations and races were supposedly locked in a struggle for survival.

THE JAPANESE COLONIAL EMPIRE AS AN ANOMALY

As the only non-Western imperium of recent times, the Japanese colonial empire★ stands as an anomaly of modern history. Because it was assembled at the apogee of the "new imperialism" by a nation which was assiduously striving to emulate Western organizational models, it is not surprising that it was formally patterned after the tropical empires of modern Europe. Yet the historical and geographic circumstances of the overseas Japanese empire set it apart from its European counterparts and gave it a character and purpose scarcely duplicated elsewhere.[3]

There was, to begin with, the fact that Japan itself had only narrowly avoided colonial subjugation during the advance of Western power in East Asia during the nineteenth century and had been saved from that fate largely because of the pull of other Asian opportunities on aggressive Western energies. As it was, Japan's emergence as a colonial power in the 1890's coincided with its extraction from a humiliating period of diplomatic inferiority imposed three decades earlier under the unequal treaty system. Indeed, the revolutionary transformation of Japan from a weak, feudal, and agrarian country into a modern industrial power, economically and militarily capable

★ I deal here only with the formal colonial territories acquired by Japan between 1895 and 1914 whose status under Japanese authority was given international recognition: Taiwan, Korea, Karafuto (the southern half of Sakhalin), the Kwantung Leased Territory (on the Liaotung peninsula), and the former German islands of Micronesia.

[3] A number of the characteristics of the Japanese colonial regime which I enumerate in the following paragraphs were first identified by Hyman Kublin in his pioneering article, "The Evolution of Japanese Colonialism," in *Comparative Studies in Society and History*, II (1959), pp. 67-84.

of resisting foreign domination, had been due to a collective recognition of the nation's vulnerability.

Given the self-evident connection between power and territorial expansion, it was not surprising that Japan rapidly moved from concern with national survival toward national assertiveness beyond its own shoreline. But Japan paid the price for its laggard entry on the world scene. Sealed up for two and a half centuries of self-imposed isolation, the nation had been a passive spectator to the advance of Western power in Asia and the West Pacific. By the time of its re-emergence into the turbulent stream of modern history Japan had lost the opportunity to preempt a dominant position in either of those areas. Certainly, the limited political, military, and economic resources of the fledgling government did not allow an assertion of national power of far-distant shores, even had the Meiji leaders so wished. To maximize its strength, the effort to assert its presence in Asia—the creation of empire—would have to begin with the domination over neighboring areas close to home, essentially those on the northeast Asian continent. Thus, despite the fact that Japan was an island nation and its possessions lay literally overseas, the thrust and ultimately the purpose of this empire was both regional and continent-directed.

The regional dimensions of the empire created their own singularities. Because it was an Asian empire, except for its Pacific territories, its most important colonies, Taiwan and Korea, were well-populated lands whose inhabitants were racially akin to their Japanese rulers with whom they shared a common cultural heritage. This sense of cultural affinity with its subject peoples made Japan unique among the colonial powers of modern times and profoundly shaped Japanese attitudes toward colonial governance once the empire was assembled.

The historical timing of the empire, coupled with its Asian provenance, meant that the metropolitan homeland encountered singular difficulties as well as unique opportunities in establishing its rule. Since the near-at-hand territories, which were the object of Japan's imperial ambitions, were not empty stretches of jungle or desert as yet unclaimed, but were controlled outright by other nations or were within their sphere of influence, Japan was obliged, by force of arms, to pry each of these territories out of the grasp of other powers. Yet, in each case, the successful outcome for Japan was determined by its proximity to the theater of combat, enabling Japan to bring sufficient military and political strength to bear for the seizure of the territory in question and, once it had been occupied, to have available such military and police power as to make Japanese rule unchallengeable from within or without.

The regional configuration of the Japanese empire also gave Japan a unique economic advantage over Western colonial powers in the development of its empire. The economic historian James Nakamura has pointed out that the proximity of Japan to its colonies, as well as the Asian provenance of the empire, meant that lower transportation costs, more rapid communication between home government and colony, as well as the fact that Japan and its two major colonial territories shared a basic and traditional agricultural commodity—rice—made it possible for Japan to aim toward the integration of its colonial economies with that of the metropole, whereas most tropical European colonies could evolve only as export-oriented enclaves.[4]

The circumscribed location and dimensions of the empire were also the result of the overriding concern for Japan's insular security. Indeed, no colonial empire of modern times was as clearly shaped by strategic considerations, carefully weighed and widely agreed upon by those in authority in the metropolitan homeland. With the exception of Taiwan, which was acquired largely for reasons of prestige, each of Japan's colonies was obtained after a deliberate decision at the highest levels that the territory would meet the strategic interests of Japan. Largely continental in dimension, these interests were more akin to the traditional link which Britain drew between her own security and the neutrality of the Lowlands across the English Channel than they were to the advantages sought and enjoyed by European powers on more distant shores.[5] For that reason, as Marius Jansen points out, Japanese imperialism was reactive, in the sense that Japan's expansion on the continent was in large part undertaken to guarantee the nation's strategic frontiers at the flood tide of Western advance in Asia. As early as the 1880's the compass of Japan's strategic concerns had placed them within concentric circles radiating from the home islands: the "cordon of sovereignty" encompassing territory vital to the nation's survival and under formal occupation, and the "cordon of advantage" an outer limit of informal Japanese dominion, seen as necessary to protect and guarantee the inner line.[6]

[4] James Nakamura, "Incentives, Productivity Gaps, and Agricultural Growth Rates in Prewar Japan, Taiwan, and Korea," in *Japan in Crisis: Essays in Taisho Democracy*, Bernard Silberman and Harry Harootunian, eds. (Princeton, N.J.: Princeton University Press, 1974), p. 350.

[5] This parallel was first drawn by Peter Duus in his unpublished paper, "The Abacus and the Sword: Japanese Business and Imperialist Expansion," presented at the Colloquium of the Center for Japanese and Korean Studies, University of California, Berkeley, December 10, 1975.

[6] Marius Jansen, "Modernization and Foreign Policy in Meiji Japan," in *Political Development in Modern Japan*, Robert Ward, ed. (Princeton, N.J.: Princeton University Press, 1968), p. 182.

But the obsession of successive Japanese governments with the strategic security of the empire's borders played a pernicious role in the ultimate downfall of the empire itself. The initial rationale for Japan's imperial expansion—the need to control adjacent continental or insular territories on the way to near-at-hand formal empire— made it impossible to give finite limits to Japan's imperial ambitions even after the formal empire had been put together. In the Japanese perspective, each new imperial acquisition required the control of a buffer territory adjacent to it. Ever subject to expanding redefinition of national interest, the perimeters of the empire thus came to involve Japan in a successive series of strategic problems which tortured Japan's domestic politics and imperilled its foreign relations: the "Korean problem" in the late 1870's, the "Manchurian-Mongolian problem" in the 1920's, the "China problem" in the 1930's, and the "southern advance problem" which led Japan into Southeast Asia and world conflict in the 1940's.[7]

If security—or rather insecurity—in relation to the advance of Western power in Asia seems, by the evidence, to have been the dominant concern in the acquisition of the component territories of the Japanese empire, there were other impulses as well behind Japan's drive for empire. Idealism played at least a peripheral role. While Meiji Japan lacked a missionary spirit akin to Christian evangelism, the political and social reformism of the Meiji liberal movement found an outlet for its energies and frustrations on the Asian continent and fired some Meiji activists with dreams of transforming "corrupted" and "decaying" Asian civilizations through reform, a vision which they sought to realize through their own dramatic efforts. An officially sponsored sense of national destiny to inspire reform from above and to guide Asian peoples along the path of modernity pioneered by Japan did not appear until the third decade of the empire. Yet individual propagandists for imperial expansion in late Meiji did speak of a Japanese "mission" in Asia to bring about development and progress, just as Greece and Rome had brought Western civilization to the Mediterranean.[8]

To a degree, elements of excitement and adventure were also there. The prospects of overseas activity after centuries of national isolation and inertia spurred individual Japanese to lone exploits on the Asian continent or to peregrinations in the South Seas in the 1880's and

---

[7] Yamabe Kentarō, "Nihon teikokushugi to shokuminchi" [Japanese Imperialism and Colonies], in *Iwanami kōza: Nihon rekishi* [Iwanami Lectures: Japanese History], Vol. 19, Iwanami Kōza, eds. (Tokyo: Iwanami Shōten, 1963), pp. 207-208.

[8] Kenneth Pyle, *The New Generation in Meiji Japan: Problems in Cultural Identity, 1885-1895* (Stanford, CA: Stanford University Press, 1969), p. 181.

1890's. Accounts of such activities helped to quicken the imagination of the reading public about Japanese courage and vigor on far frontiers.[9]

But the flag seldom followed the wanderings of these single adventurers. More influential were matters of pride and prestige which involved the nation as a whole. Just as steel navies, constitutions, machine guns, rationalized tax structures, and steam locomotives seemed part of modernity and efficiency, acquisition of a colonial empire in the late nineteenth century was a mark of national eminence, the ultimate status symbol upon the world scene. Starting late in the scramble for colonies, Edward Chen has pointed out, Japan viewed its victory over China in 1894-1895 and its consequent acquisition of Taiwan as the shortest distance to a place in the sun, much in the same way that Bismark had seen that victory over France in 1870-1871 and the subsequent annexation of Alsace-Lorraine would bring pride and power to a united Germany.[10] In this Itō Hirobumi and his associates were reinforced by public appetite for military triumph and territorial reward. Donald Keene has elsewhere described how a sensationalist press, relaying euphoric, jingoist accounts of the nation's armies and navies in its short victorious conflict, whipped up enthusiasm for war and colonial conquest, creating in the process a lurid pictorial and literary genre in the mass media.[11]

But public excitement about the empire hardly lasted beyond the easy victories of the Sino-Japanese War. The conflict with Russia was too costly in human life, too somber in tone, to allow a spirit of exhilaration when it ended. Thereafter, there was too little drama to stir patriotic or romantic interest in the colonies (though other motivations to which I have alluded maintained public support for expansion in general). No tales of explorer's discoveries of great mountain ranges or vast river systems thrilled an expectant public and no colonial campaigns continued to fill the columns of Japanese newspapers in the way that clashes in the Sahara or the Khyber Pass enlivened the pages of the French and British press, keeping the colonies alive before the eyes of the reading publics of those countries.

[9] Hanzawa Hiroshi, *Ajia e no yume* [Dream of Asia] (Tokyo: San'ichi Shobō, 1970); Kaneko Tamio, *Chūō Ajia ni haitta Nihonjin* [Japanese Who Entered Central Asia] (Tokyo: Shinjimbutsu Ōrai sha, 1973); and Yano Tōru, *Nihon no Nan'yō shikan* [Japan's Historical View of the South Seas] (Tokyo: Chūō Shinsho, 1979).

[10] Edward I-te Chen, "Japan's Decision to Annex Taiwan: A Sudy of Itō-Mutsu Diplomacy," in *Journal of Asian Studies*, XXXVII: 1 (November 1977), p. 71.

[11] Donald Keene, "The Sino-Japanese War of 1894-95 and Its Cultural Effects in Japan," in *Tradition and Modernization in Japanese Culture*, Donald Shively, ed. (Princeton, N.J.: Princeton University Press), pp. 121-175.

Initially at least, the justifications for the acquisition of empire were couched in the language of the "new imperialism" of late-nineteenth-century Europe. Some Japanese colonial publicists came to speak of overseas territory as new living area for the vigorous diffusion and augmentation of the Japanese race in its struggle for survival—Social Darwinist justifications similar to those which sought to buttress German and Italian colonial expansion in Africa. But colonization—the overseas settlement of Japanese—never became the dominant activity of the Japanese colonial empire. With the exception of Karafuto and a few of the large islands in Micronesia during the 1930's, Japan's overseas territories were essentially occupation colonies where a minority of Japanese colonials existed amid a sea of indigenous peoples. Other arguments for empire alluded to the needs of a new industrial system—outlets for surplus capital, markets for surplus production, and secure sources for raw materials—arguments common in French and British imperial literature of the late nineteenth century.

These last assertions bring us, inevitably, to the question of economic interest in the formation of the Japanese colonial empire. A quicksand problem, it has consumed an inordinate amount of argument, good and bad, so I shall be quick in clarifying those elements of the problem which concern Ramon Myers and myself as co-editors of this volume. In acknowledging the existence of Japanese economic imperialism and its role in the formation and evolution in the Japanese empire we are, like Peter Duus, less interested in economic imperialism as a stage of historical development or a particular arrangement of socio-economic relationships, as used by Marxist scholarship, than we are in deliberate state policy directed toward the exploitation of less-developed peoples and territories for continuing material and economic advantage by an economically advanced power.[12]

If one accepts this definition and relates it to the processes by which the empire was acquired, several things become clear from the historical evidence. As Duus's essay in this volume demonstrates, it is obvious that Meiji statesmen clearly perceived that Japan had economic interests abroad, specifically in Asia, and that this belief, frequently shaped in the language of the "new imperialism," affected their conception of foreign policy. These interests included opportunities for trade and investment, access to sources of foodstuffs and strategic materials, as well as to markets for manufactured goods.

[12] Peter Duus, "Economic Aspects of Meiji Imperialism" (*Occasional Papers*, No. 1, East Asia Institute, Free University of Berlin, 1980), p. 1.

But Duus reminds us that, while the late Meiji leadership was well aware of the economic opportunities presented by territorial expansion and clearly and openly sought economic rights and concessions, it did so as an adjunct to strategic advantage and that in the creation of the empire, in the final analysis, politics was still in command.

This acknowledgment of economic interest by the state in overseas expansion is, of course, rather different from the Leninist emphasis on the dominating financial interests of a capitalist class seeking outlets for congested domestic capital overseas. Indeed, the Leninist model does not fare well when applied to the Japanese situation in the late nineteenth century, since a shortage, not an excess, of private capital was one of Japan's main economic problems at the beginning of Japanese imperialistic expansion. Indeed, the Japanese government, like that of Wilhelmian Germany, had difficulty in luring domestic capital into colonial investment at the outset of the nation's imperial venture. Hence, it is not apparent that the acquisition of Japanese colonial territories derived from the schemes of bankers or merchants manipulating the Mejii leadership.[13]

Of course, private economic interests of an often rapacious sort did indeed become active in the empire, but these emerged after the initial steps were taken on the road to colonial conquest, not before, and their main thrust was directed less toward the formal colonial territories than it was to Japan's "informal empire" in Manchuria and mainland China, which existed as a formidable commercial and strategic extension of the formal empire.

In any event, after pondering the relative importance of the various drives and motivations which have been ascribed to the origins of the Japanese colonial empire, I am compelled to agree with the late William Lockwood when he wrote, over a quarter century ago: "The quest for empire in East Asia was impelled by no single motive, except as most Japanese were indoctrinated in varying degrees with a mystical faith in the Imperial Destiny. It drew support from various interest groups and for differing reasons. Its momentum and direc-

[13] For a discussion of the relative importance of economic interests in the acquisition of Japan's empire, see Hilary Conroy, *Japan's Seizure of Korea: 1868-1910: A Study of Realism and Idealism in International Relations* (Philadelphia: University of Pennsylvania Press, 1960), pp. 442-491. For opposing Marxist interpretations see Fujii Shōichi, "Capitalism, International Politics and the Emperor System," in *The Emergence of Imperial Japan: Self-Defense or Calculated Aggression?* Marlene Mayo, ed. (Lexington, Mass.: D. C. Heath and Co., 1970), pp. 75-82 and Inoue Kiyoshi, "Nihon teikokushugi no keisei" [The Administration of Japanese Imperialism], in *Kindai Nihon no keisei* [Modern Japanese Administration], Rekishigaku Kenkyūkai, eds. (Tokyo: Iwanami Shōten, 1953), pp. 51-130.

tion reflected the political struggle at home, as well as the resistance it met abroad."[14]

Lockwood's last statement brings us back to the question of circumstance rather than of motivation. Japan's precarious position in Asia in the late nineteenth century makes one hesitant, of course, about flatly asserting that Japan's rise as a colonial power was inevitable. Yet the probability exists that Japan would have come to dominate adjacent portions of the decaying Chinese empire, regardless of motivation. In this sense, as Marius Jansen has noted, Japanese imperialism was less deliberate than situational in origin. The aggressive movement of Japanese forces into Korea, China, and Micronesia was as much due to the absence of effective power to resist it as it was to specific policies and planning.

Historical circumstance and geographical location also had much to do with inherently inconsistent Japanese attitudes toward empire in general and toward their own in particular. On the one hand, the Japanese empire resembled its European counterparts in that its authority was based on an assumption of the superiority of the colonial rulers over their subject peoples. To a degree this basic perspective stemmed from the fact, common to all colonial systems, that the empire had been imposed by conquest or force by a stronger, more materially advanced race upon weaker, more materially retarded peoples. Yet, in part, this assumption also derived from credos that were uniquely Japanese. These included Japanese beliefs in the mythic origins of the Japanese race, the divine creation and inherent virtue of the Japanese Imperial House, and the mystical link between the emperor and his people. The relative isolation of the country throughout most of its history, as well as the cultural deference toward China, had in centuries past prevented these beliefs of racial uniqueness from being transmogrified into a theory of racial supremacy. But a few decades of expanding dominion over neighboring Asian peoples, reinforced by racial notions of Social Darwinism, inevitably released the virus of racial assertiveness into the Japanese ideological bloodstream and quickened the Japanese sense of superiority to the rest of Asia.

As I have pointed out in my essay on Japanese colonial ideology, these contrasting Western and Asian—Japanese—patterns of empire thus formed the perimeters for an evolving and contrasting set of Japanese attitudes toward colonialism, their own and that of other nations. As such they provoked two quite dissimilar Japanese approaches to the relations of colonial ruler and ruled.

[14] William Lockwood, *The Economic Development of Japan: Growth and Structural Change, 1868-1938* (Princeton, N.J.: Princeton University Press, 1954), p. 534.

The first of these, essentially Western in concept and manifestation, drew its inspiration from the overseas tropical empires of modern Europe. Similar to the paternalist and racially exclusive colonial doctrines of British colonialism in particular, this Japanese view of empire held that Japan and its subject territories were distinct and separate entities, with distinct and separate destinies. Firm guidance and enlightened colonial administration could and should "civilize" the subordinate peoples over time, of course, but for decades into the future Japan and its colonies were to proceed on parallel, but not converging, paths.

The contrasting theory of Japanese colonial rule was distinctly more Asian in its frame of reference. Continent-oriented, it stressed the apparent racial and cultural affinities between the Japanese and their colonial subjects. These similarities of origins and values seemed, in this view, to open the way to an integration of rulers and ruled to an extent hardly possible within European colonial systems.

In this respect Japanese colonial doctrine had less in common with the overseas colonial empires of Western Europe than it had with "continental imperialism," which Hannah Arendt identified in her discussion of the emotional appeals to common race and culture which stirred Germanic and Slavic peoples in late nineteenth- and early twentieth-century Europe.[15] For many Japanese concerned with the empire such a fusion of race and culture, "an enlarged tribal consciousness," in Arendt's words, made Japanese overseas dominion seem distinct from and ultimately superior to European colonial rule. As the empire matured and developed an ideological framework, the opportunities, limits, and implications of such an integration became a central issue in Japanese colonial policy.

Arendt's distinction between "overseas" imperialism, of geographically and racially separated colonial territories, and "continental" imperialism, of a geographically and racially more contiguous sort, cannot precisely define nor fully explain the dichotomies in the evolution of Japanese colonial policy from 1895 to 1945, of course. Yet it does seem of help in sorting out the various arguments—broadly Western or Asian in their inspiration—in the changing Japanese approaches to colonialism described in my essay.

Certainly a caveat is needed. Whereas Hannah Arendt used the notion of "continental imperialism" to help to explain the origins of totalitarianism, it is not clear, from the Japanese case, at least, that either continental or overseas patterns of imperial control are *inher-*

---

[15] Hannah Arendt, *The Origins of Totalitarianism* (New York: Harcourt, Brace and World, 1966), pp. 223-224.

ently more or less oppressive than the other. A paternalistic, racially separatist approach to colonial rule, which made racial distinctions within an empire, such as manifested by a number of modern European overseas empires, could lead, as in the case of British colonial doctrine in Africa, to concepts of indirect rule and imperial trusteeship, which themselves opened the way to the possibility of autonomy and independence of colonial territories. Yet a "continental" perspective, which insisted on the homogeneity of races and interests within an empire and which tightened rather than loosened the bonds between peoples of the homeland and the colonies, could also have served to diffuse throughout the empire the political rights and civil liberties which existed in the mother country. The irony and tragedy of the Japanese case was that the colonial empire ultimately came to include the worst and most contradictory racial assumptions of both patterns. As a result the Japanese were not able to form a consistent theory of racial relations within the empire, and because of this they were unable to shape a coherent colonial doctrine which might justify the empire to themselves, to their subjects, and to the rest of the world.

PLANTING THE FLAG, 1895-1922

Japan's turn toward the Korean peninsula marked its first step on the road to empire. While, in a formal sense, Korea was the next to last addition to the colonial empire, it was the first alien overseas territory to provoke aggressive Japanese attention. The Meiji leadership viewed Korea as both a problem and an opportunity. "A dagger thrust at the heart of Japan," Major Meckel, Prussian advisor to the Meiji army, had called it. Dangerous enough as a satellite of China, Korea in the hands of Russia might prove fatal to Japan. The peninsula's very accessibility and vulnerability had attracted the romantic ambitions of the free-booting element of the former samurai class, who very nearly dragged the nation into an ill-considered attempt to conquer Korea outright in the early 1870's. Such reckless adventurism had been swiftly rejected by the central leadership, conscious of the nation's weakness and determined to act only within the framework of a carefully deliberated national policy. That policy had as its initial objective the neutralization of the Chinese presence on the Korean peninsula. But throughout the 1880's, as the Japanese government gathered strength, an array of diplomats, garrison commanders, traders, and adventurers represented an increasingly aggressive Japanese presence in the country, working to undermine the influence of China and the authority of the stubbornly traditional Korean government.[16]

When war came, the success of the Japanese armies was as rapid as it was unexpected. A tub-thumping dementia seized the Japanese public at the news of the first imperial victories, proclaimed by military bands and illustrated in vividly colored contemporary battle prints, hawked from every street corner. A public at full cry and a jingo press caught up in the excitement of the struggle insisted on territorial spoils. With the Chinese shadow banished from the peninsula, the outright annexation of Korea was neither planned nor necessary and, in any event, would have risked the active opposition of the Powers. But at Shimonoseki Itō Hirobumi and his co-negotiators pressed their demands on the stubborn and uncomprehending Chinese delegation: cession of the Liaotung peninsula and the island of Taiwan, as well as payment of a huge indemnity. The Chinese government had little recourse and yielded to Japanese pressure. But within a short time, however, the notorious "Triple Intervention" of Russia, Germany, and France had forced the retrocession of Liaotung, to the suppressed fury of patriots like Tokutomi Sohō, who, visiting Liaotung, scooped up its earth and took it home as an emotion-laden souvenir of Japan's first bid for a place on the Asian continent.[17] But with Taiwan in its possession, Japan had its first colonial territory, a proud first step on the way to empire, and a place among the nations of the world.[18]

Yet, Taiwan was an imperial accessory, a laboratory where the "new boy" among the colonial powers could show off his modernizing skills, not the heart of Japan's strategic concerns. Those interests were on the continent, in Korea. As a result of its victory over China, Japan had inexorably tightened its grip on the peninsula. Japanese "advisors" forced a growing number of modernizing reforms upon a weak but obdurate Korean government, at the same time that it deepened its economic stake in Korea with the construction of railways and a rapid increase in commercial activity throughout the country. Between 1898 and 1904 the agents of the Czar countered

[16] The best overview in English of Japan's growing involvement in Korea in the nineteenth century is still Conroy's *The Japanese Seizure of Korea*. A briefer, but useful summary is Andrew Nahm's introduction to *Korea under Japanese Colonial Rule: Studies of the Policy and Techniques of Japanese Colonialism*, Andrew Nahm, ed. (Kalamazoo, Mich.: The Center for Korean Studies, Institute of International and Area Studies, Western Michigan University, 1973), pp. 17-38.

[17] Pyle, *The New Generation in Meiji Japan,* p. 108.

[18] The processes by which Japan acquired Taiwan are analyzed in Chen's "Japan's Decision to Annex Taiwan."

with an expansion of Russian influence southward from Manchuria into Korea. The advance of Japanese power temporarily checked, the emperor's ministers offered St. Petersburg a compromise: a recognition of Russian primacy in Manchuria for a free hand for Japan in Korea. When Russia, confident in its own imperial designs, flicked the proposal aside, Japan drew the sword. The bloody struggles of the Russo-Japanese War, 1904–1905, were a measure of how badly Russia had slipped and how Japan had risen as military and imperial powers. In frightful combat and at terrible cost Japanese armies reconquered the Liaotung peninsula and the strategic ports of Dairen and Port Arthur, driving Russia from South Manchuria. To the northeast the Japanese stormed onto the southern end of Sakhalin, so that the island might be used as a bargaining chip when the two combatants sat down to talk at Portsmouth, New Hampshire, under the watchful eye of Theodore Roosevelt.

The Portsmouth Treaty gave Japan her next imperial acquisitions: a long-term lease on the Liaotung peninsula—now renamed the Kwantung Leased Territory; the southern half of Sakhalin—to which the Japanese gave the name Karafuto; and all Russian rights and privileges in South Manchuria. With the Rising Sun flag rippling over Port Arthur and Dairen, Japan now held the finest naval base and one of the best ice-free ports on the coast of northeast Asia.[19]

These acquisitions hardly lessened Japanese pressure on Korea. Indeed, Korea's lingering pretensions to independence were now short-lived. With the elimination of Japan's last effective rival to the control of that unhappy country, it was not long before it was swallowed whole into the Japanese empire. That process took place in two stages: the first saw the establishment of a Japanese protectorate, 1905–1910, during which a civilian Resident General, the Meiji oligarch Itō Hirobumi, attempted a series of well-intentioned reforms while at the same time systematically liquidating Korean political institutions and substituting Japanese ones; the second phase took place in 1910 when Korea, with the helpless acquiescence of the Korean monarch, was formally annexed as a colony—Chōsen—under the iron-fisted rule of General Terauchi Masatake, its first governor-general. In Korea itself, the bitter protest of Korean patriots of every class and calling

[19] The Japanese conquest and annexation of Karafuto is surveyed in John Stephan's *Sakhalin: A History* (Oxford University Press, 1971). For the early administration of the Kwantung Leased Territory, see Ōyama Azusa, *Nichi-Ro sensō no gunsei shiroku* [Historical Record of Military Administration during the Russo-Japanese War] (Tokyo: Fuyō Shobō, 1973).

had swelled into open rebellion between 1908 and 1910, but was suppressed with the overwhelming military force which Japan now had available on the peninsula. Every act of resistance met ever more savage reprisal by a colonial government determined to impose its law and its order upon a recalcitrant people. "I will whip you with scorpions," Terauchi is alleged to have raged, and if the remark is apochryphal, the sentiment was not, for the next decade of what came to be known as the period of "military rule" (*budan seiji*) in Korea was draconian and vindictive, at the same time that it saw the expansion of Japanese institutional reform and economic development.[20]

Four years after the annexation of Korea, Japan made the final addition to its formal empire. Exploiting the outbreak of global hostilities in 1914, Japan joined the Allied powers as a sunshine combatant, in order to snap up Germany's colonial territories in Asia and the South Pacific: Tsingtao on the Shantung peninsula and the German-held islands in Micronesia—the Marshalls, the Carolines, and the Marianas (excluding Guam), all of which were weakly defended. While Japanese expansionists had long sought a territorial foothold on the China coast, the South Pacific had hardly been an area of traditional Japanese interest. But with the emergence of American-Japanese naval rivalry in the Pacific, the Japanese navy suddenly saw the advantage of acquiring bases in those seas. Between the Versailles Conference and the subsequent Washington nine-power treaty Japan was forced to relinquish all claims to Shantung, but was awarded mandatory control over the German islands in Micronesia already in her possession, an arrangement which I discuss in some detail in my essay on *Japan in the South Pacific*. With the acquisition of these "South Seas islands"—the Nan'yō guntō—the formal empire was completed.[21]

EVOLUTION OF THE EMPIRE, 1895-1945

The first phase of Japanese colonialism, like that of most European colonial empires, began with the initial chaos of colonial conquest. It

[20] For discussion of the Japanese domination of Korea during the first two decades of the twentieth century, see Yamabe Kentarō, *Nihon tōjika no Chōsen* [Korea under Japanese Rule] (Tokyo: Iwanami Shoten, 1971), pp. 1-100, and David Brudnoy, "Japan's Experiment in Korea," in *Monumenta Nipponica*, XXX:1-2 (1970), pp. 155-156.

[21] At present, the most detailed discussion concerning the Japanese acquisition of its Micronesian territories is David C. Purcell, Jr., *Japanese Expansion in the South Pacific, 1895-1934*, unpublished Ph.D. dissertation, University of Pennsylvania, 1967.

was initiated by the military pacification of Taiwan, an effort not unlike that undertaken by French military and naval forces against the Black Flag rebels in Tonkin in the 1880's or the United States Army against Filipino insurgents after the conclusion of the Spanish-American War.[22] No more or less ruthless than the average colonial pacification campaign, the Japanese effort soon brought the island under effective control, except for the mountainous interior, where resistance by aboriginal tribesmen smouldered on for decades.[23] But pacification did not quickly bring progress to Japan's first colony. Lacking any tradition or experience as a colonial power, Japan had acquired Taiwan without long-range objectives for its management, and this administrative vacuum was at first filled by military men untrained for the new colonial tasks and civilian incompetents and carpet-baggers from the home islands, eager for quick profit.

Conscious as always of foreign scrutiny of its modernizing efforts, the Meiji government moved to end this chaotic environment and to give its first colony pride, purpose, and efficiency. General Kodama Gentarō, fourth governor-general of the island, largely aided by his brilliant civil administrator, Gotō Shimpei, within a decade transformed the territory from an embarrassment to a colonial showcase through the massive restructuring of the political, social, and economic order. Gotō's "scientific" approach to colonial governance and development, which emphasized extensive research as the basis of colonial policy, resulted in a series of well-planned and coordinated efforts which collectively changed a backward, economically fragmented, and debt-ridden territory into a modern, economically self-sufficient colony.[24]

In the development of Taiwan, Japan's colonial authorities were fortunate to have the passive acquiescence of a thoroughly submissive population. Such was not the case in Korea, where the vehement protest and occasionally active resistance of a fearful, obstinate, and antagonized colonial people made reform a matter of harsh enforcement by an openly oppressive military administration. Under the essentially civilian administration of the Japanese protectorate, the

[22] Harry Lamley, "The 1895 Taiwan War of Resistance: Local Chinese Efforts Against a Foreign Power," in *Taiwan: Studies in Local Chinese History*, Leonard Gordon, ed. (New York: Columbia University Press, 1970), pp. 23-77.

[23] Yamabe Kentarō, ed. *Taiwan*, II (*Gendaishi shiryō* [Documents on Modern History], Vol. XX, Misuzu Shobō, 1971), pp. 3-79.

[24] Chang Han-yu and Ramon Myers, "Japanese Colonial Development Policy in Taiwan, 1895-1906: A Case of Bureaucratic Entrepreneurship," in *Journal of Studies*, XXII:2 (August 1963), pp. 433-449.

residency-general had already taken over all the institutions of Korean government, including the Korean army and police. During the subsequent decade the government-general under Terauchi developed into a powerful bureaucratic machine which was able to undertake the ruthless political, educational, and social transformation of Korea, while in the process it attempted to liquidate Korean national identity. Gregory Henderson's term "development shock" is an apt term for the trauma undergone by the Korean people during this period in their history.[25]

Elsewhere in the empire the lesser colonial administrations—the Kwantung government (Kantō-chō), the Karafuto government (Karafuto-chō), and the South Seas government (Nan'yō-chō)—suffered initial periods of administrative uncertainty and economic instability under military rule. But, small in size and in population, without problems of indigenous resistance, these colonies hardly needed military garrisons of the scale which Japan required in Korea or even in Taiwan.

The Kwantung garrison and its successor, the famed Kwantung army, were created not for the purpose of suppressing any internal resistance to Japanese rule in the Leased Territory, but rather to defend the territory and Japanese interests in South Manchuria from external threats. For these reasons military administration in these colonial territories soon gave way to rule by civilian governors who presided over the peaceful development of their territories undisturbed by political turmoil.[26]

In the decade between 1914 and 1924 powerful currents of political change in the Japanese homeland began to nudge colonial authorities in all the colonies toward a more liberal administration. In Japan these trends were marked by an erosion of the influence of both the genrō and the military, parallelled by a rise in the power of political parties and the Diet, which were more accommodative to the interests of the nation's colonial populations. Abroad, the emergence of Wilsonian idealism, particularly the principle of the self-determination of peoples, gave heart to Taiwanese and Koreans who sought autonomy for their homelands and placed Japanese colonialism increasingly on the defensive. In Taiwan, these ideas encouraged moderate "assimilation" and home-rule movements designed to extend to Taiwan certain basic civil rights enjoyed by Japanese in the home country, while keeping Taiwan within the empire. Supported by liberals in Japan, but blocked by the colonial government and unable to

[25] Gregory Henderson, "Japan's Chōsen: Immigrants, Ruthlessness and Development Shock," in Nahm, pp. 261-269.

[26] Yamabe, "Nihon teikokushugi to shokuminchi," p. 209.

enlist the support of a generally docile population, these political initiatives evaporated by the 1920's.[27]

In Korea, the rigor of General Terauchi's procrustean efforts to make the populace conform to Japanese values and institutions created violent antagonisms which could not long be contained and which finally burst forth in an explosion of national resentment in March 1919. The March First Movement, which brought together over two million Koreans in a call for national liberation, demonstrated the depth of Korean sentiment.[28] The brutality of the colonial response, launched against a generally unresisting population, showed the rigor with which Japan was determined to maintain its presence undiminished upon the peninsula.

The spasm of colonial repression in Korea in 1919 served one progressive purpose. The horrified protests around the world, as well as in Japan, against the Korea government-general encouraged those political forces in the home islands which sought to moderate Japanese colonial policy. To Prime Minister Hara Kei, who believed that colonial administration should be guided by the same sort of bureaucratic reform which had recently evolved in Japan, the March 1919 crisis in Korea and the death of the incumbent military governor-general in Taiwan provided opportunities to announce administrative changes which would modify Japanese rule throughout the empire in general, but in Korea in particular. Had not Hara been assassinated in office, it is just possible that the transformation of these symbolic pronouncements into substantive advances for Korean national aspirations might have been undertaken with greater vigor. Certainly, the feeble administrative and social reforms of the decade of "cultural rule" (bunka seiji) in Korea hardly realized Hara's objective of extending Japanese liberties and rights to Korea, let alone satisfied the demands of Korean patriots for political, social, and economic independence, though, for a time, they did moderate the more overtly arbitrary and oppressive aspects of Japanese rule.[29]

In any event, even the pretensions to liberal reform in the Japanese colonial empire did not outlast the 1920's. In the succeeding decade, social and economic dislocations in the home islands and uncertainties and instabilities abroad—particularly in East Asia—contributed to the shift in Japan and in the colonies toward domestic authoritarianism

[27] Harry Lamley, "Assimilation Efforts in Taiwan: The Fate of the 1914 Movement," in Monumenta Serica, Vol. XXIX (17-71), pp. 496-520.

[28] See Frank Baldwin, The March First Movement: Korean Challenge and Japanese Response, unpublished Ph.D. dissertation, Columbia University, 1969.

[29] For an evaluation of the "cultural rule" decade in Korea, see Brudnoy, pp. 172-179, and Yamabe, Nihon tōjika no Chōsen, pp. 102-119.

and the resurgent influence of the military in shaping policy. In consequence, the Japanese empire was re-militarized, and its component territories were transformed into regimented and exploited base areas for aggressive Japanese expansion into East Asia, spearheaded on more than one occasion by the arbitrary initiatives of Japan's field armies abroad.

Had Japan been content with the modest colonial empire which she had assembled by the end of World War I and abjured the reckless adventurism in Asia which spilled beyond its boundaries, the course of history would have been profoundly different for Japan, for the empire, and for the rest of Asia. But upon the completion of the formal empire in 1922 neither Japan's strategic insecurities nor its imperial ambitions had been substantially lessened, and the decade of the 1920's had seen Japan pressing forward once more into Asia. The consequent risk to the empire, which had won grudging acceptance from the West by World War I, was hardly recognized by those Japanese in and out of government who pressed most aggressively for its geographic extension. Heedless of the passing of the old imperialist world order which had tolerated the growth of Japanese imperialism, or of the new tide of nationalism abroad in Asia, Japan pressed ahead on the continent in an illusory quest for final security and economic autonomy. Fatally linked to these ever-receding goals, the formal empire became a base and an arsenal for the increasingly dangerous effort to dominate adjacent territories.

Central to the concerns of Japanese colonial policy in this aggressive decade were the economic consolidation of the empire and the integration of its colonial economies to meet the wartime requirements of the home islands. In the new geopolitical perspective which obsessed the national leadership, the colonies were seen as productive parts of a central economic engine, geared to the creation of a self-sufficient garrison state.[30] In this final militarized, exploited, and regimented condition the empire was harnessed to Japan's headlong collision with the West, 1941-1945, and was shattered in the process. At war's end the victors dismembered the empire completely: Taiwan was returned to Chinese sovereignty, only to find itself once again set apart from the mainland after 1949; Korea emerged in its mutant form of independence—two bitterly antagonistic half-countries locked by geography onto a single peninsula; the Liaotung peninsula became Chinese territory once again (though Port Arthur was jointly administered by the Peoples' Republic and the Soviet Union until 1955);

[30] Yamabe, "Nihon teikokushugi to shokuminchi," pp. 205-209.

the Soviet Union simply absorbed Karafuto into its administration of Sakhalin; and the United States succeeded Japan in Micronesia, which it held as a trusteeship but ruled as a military base.

THE MEIJI STRATEGIES FOR MODERNIZATION

I have spoken of the maritime tropical empires of the West as the pattern for the overseas empire which Japan assembled between 1895 and 1922. In a general as well as in a symbolic sense, this is true, for the trappings of the Japanese colonial presence and life-style were indeed Western in appearance. But the framework of colonial *policy* as it was formed in the first half of the empire was less modelled on direct European precedents than on the superbly successful modernization effort which Japan itself had undertaken in the three decades after the Meiji leadership had overthrown the Tokugawa feudal order, a reform program based in large part, of course, on Western experience. It is not too much to say that Japanese colonialism in its formative stage cannot be understood outside the perimeters of *fukoku kyōhei*—that collective exhortation of early Meiji that bound all of Japan's modernizing reforms to the twin goals of a strong and prosperous Japan. All that Japan undertook in its colonies during the first quarter century of the empire was based upon Meiji experience in domestic reform.

In its two largest colonies, certainly, Japan was confronted with problems of the kind which had challenged the young leadership at the outset of Meiji rule: a peasant society whose response to the new administration ranged from dull acquiescence to active hostility; the resistance of large segments of the traditional elite who occupied positions of wealth, privilege, and prestige; an agrarian bureaucracy which had become progressively weakened, corrupt and inefficient; an underdeveloped and relatively stagnant agrarian economy whose uncertain harvests were a poor base for rationalized tax structure; an arbitrary and uncertain land tenure system for which up-to-date and accurate data was lacking; and a Confucian-oriented educational structure which was ill-suited to the requirements of a modernizing state.

To meet these problems the Meiji modernization effort in Japan had concentrated on three main tasks: consolidation of military and political power at the center; creation of economic self-sufficiency through the expansion and exploitation of an agricultural base; and the transformation of society through basic education and a variety of innovations in social engineering in order to develop new skills and attitudes among the people and to shape their loyalty and obedience to the new state. In carrying out these strategies, the Meiji leaders, concerned for the well-being of their nation and convinced of the rectitude of their policies, had ruled by fiat, undeterred by political critics or by popular protest. In doing so, they acted within the *kanson mimpi* tradition of Japanese bureaucracy—the exaltation of government over the people it ruled—formed and hardened during two hundred and fifty years of Tokugawa feudal administration.

Lacking a colonial tradition or colonial expertise, Japan, not surprisingly, in modernizing its newly acquired territories, set out with vigor, confidence, and determination to apply those strategies, so recently successful in the homeland, to the administration and development of its empire. Yet, obviously, there were major differences between the situation faced at home by the early Meiji modernizers and those which challenged Japanese colonial authorities in the colonies overseas, particularly in the two larger colonies, Taiwan and Korea. Critical among these was the fact that the new rulers and the subjects they ruled, despite their common cultural heritage, were not of the same nationality, nor able to speak the same tongue. Nor, in its approach to its colonial subjects, could Japanese colonial government appeal to a common historical past, to a common interest, or to common necessity. These differences point up the difficulties involved in externally imposed modernization, as compared to modernization from within a particular society. In Taiwan such differences meant that Japan's modernizing efforts generally met with grudging if not enthusiastic public acceptance. In Korea they were exacerbated by mutual antagonisms—Korean indignation at the record of Japanese interference and misconduct on the peninsula, on the one hand, and Japanese contempt for the derelict nature of Korean government and society, on the other—as well as by the emergence of a sense of Korean national identity just at the time when Japan chose to impose its rule. Together with the Japanese bureaucratic style we have mentioned, such resistance made externally imposed modernization in Korea a matter of ruthless enforcement. As Marius Jansen has noted, many of the Japanese reform measures in Korea—termination of elite privileges, changes in dress and hair, changes in land tenure—which had aroused difficulty in Japan but had ultimately been accepted as necessary, were bitterly resisted in Korea as the work of a hated foreign oppressor.[31] Insensitive to Korean sentiments and impatient with Korean conservatism, Japan's

[31] Marius Jansen, *Japan and China: From War to Peace, 1894-1972* (Chicago: Rand McNally, 1975), p. 126.

colonial agents kicked and dragged Korea into conformity with Japan's modern values and institutions, rather than explaining the objectives or rewards of modernization. Yet the ruthlessness and insensitivity with which Japan set about applying the Meiji domestic strategies overseas should not cloud our judgments about their purpose, work, or effectiveness. To an evaluation of each of those strategies in their new colonial settings I now turn.

CONSOLIDATING CONTROL

For the new colonial administration in Taiwan and Korea, as for the new regime in the early decades of Meiji Japan, the liquidation of effective oppositional resistance and consolidation of military and political power was the first priority. In Taiwan this objective was behind the initial six-month pacification campaign on the island; in Korea it meant taking over important "advisory" posts within the independent Korean army, then reducing it in size, and finally, in 1907, disbanding it altogether and incorporating its best officers into the Japanese army. Just as early reform in the home islands had provoked resistance among an important segment of Japan's traditional elite in 1877, these moves by the Japanese had sparked mutiny within the Korean army, but this upheaval was as effectively and totally suppressed as had been the Satsuma Rebellion.[32] Once organized resistance came to an end, the colonial administrators in Japan had sufficient military and police power to compel instant obedience to the new authority.

Part of the task of consolidating political control, based upon Meiji policy, was the creation of a rationalized central administrative system which could promptly and effectively carry out reform and insure uniform compliance with colonial policy. The Japanese colonial administrations in both colonies may have faltered in their effort at first, but the determination of the home government to bring about order and progress soon led to the creation of powerful colonial bureaucracies, centered in the capital and housed in impressively modern buildings of sufficient size and splendor to convey the idea of imperial power. From these bastions of colonial authority in Keijō (Seoul) and Taihoku (Taipei) the governors-general of Korea and Taiwan directed colonial governments that were semi-autonomous and highly authoritarian. They possessed enormous executive, judicial, and even legislative powers, far greater indeed than any single

[32] C. I. Eugene Kim, "Japan's Rule in Korea (1905-1910): A Case Study," in *Proceedings of the American Philosophical Society*, CVI (February 1962), pp. 53-59.

office in the home government, that of the prime minister's office included.

Of these two colonial administrations, that in Korea was the most awesome in its powers. While appointments to the position of governor-general were in theory open to civilians after 1919, only in Taiwan was such a change actually made. In Korea, at the steely insistence of the Japanese army, the rule of military commanders continued unbroken. Given the power and prestige of the Japanese military generally, as well as its independence from civil control, it is not to be wondered that the governors-general of Korea functioned as imperial pro-consuls, rather than as mere agents of civil government. From their capitals the governors-general of Taiwan and Korea presided over a large cadre of trusted, hard-working bureaucrats, products of the outstanding Japanese civil service. Placed in local colonial administrations and empowered to govern according to a uniform system of legal codes and statutes, they worked through compliant indigenous elites to carry out Japanese colonial policy.[33]

Whatever else may be said about Japanese administration in the overseas territories, one must give Japanese colonial administrators high marks as a group. Indeed, the competence and quality of the average Japanese colonial bureaucrat is remarkable when one considers that he had little of the professional tradition or experience of his counterparts in the British or French colonial systems. As Japan tightened its administrative grip on the colonies, the few undesirables of the early years of Japanese rule were shaken out of the system, and by the second decade of the empire foreign visitors to Taiwan and Korea were bringing back highly favorable impressions of the intelligence, dedication, and integrity of the Japanese colonial bureaucracy they saw there. This general rule of competence is largely explained by the fact that senior and middle-level officials serving in the colonies were drawn from the various ministries and bureaus of civil government in metropolitan Japan and were, for the most part, graduates of Japan's imperial universities who had passed the rigorous civil-service examinations and who met the exacting and uniform standards of the Japanese bureaucracy. Generally aloof and isolated from the indigenous peoples whom they administered, they were nevertheless imbued with a vigorous sense of public service typical of Japanese civil government and took their jobs seriously. Because of these qualities and because they were openly given preferential

[33] For a comparison of the powers of the governors-general of Korea and Taiwan see Edward I-te Chen, "Japanese Colonialism in Korea and Formosa: A Comparison of the Systems of Political Control," in *Harvard Journal of Asiatic Studies*, XXX (1970), pp. 126-159.

1. *Jaluit district headquarters, Nan'yō-chō (South Seas Agency)*

2. Taihoku (Taipei) circa 1910

3. Central Keijo (Seoul) circa 1940

4. Gotō Shimpei

5. *General Akashi Motojirō, Governor General of Taiwan, with his administrative staff in front of the old Governor General's residence, Taihoku, circa 1918*

6. *Visit of Prince Chichibu to a forestry experimental station, Taiwan, circa 1925*

7. *Japanese emigrants debarking off Saipan, circa 1935*

8. *Korean farmers executed by a Japanese firing squad for protesting Japanese seizure of Korean land, circa 1905*

9. *Japanese colonial schoolroom for Micronesian children, Yap, circa 1930*

10. *U.S. naval aircraft bombarding Wotje Atoll, Marshall Islands, February 1942*

treatment and reward (a point of bitter resentment by their Korean and Taiwanese coworkers) they were rarely tainted with corruption or malfeasance.

A key element in the general effectiveness of Japanese colonial administration was the availability of military and police power in such scale and pervasiveness as to insure obedience to Japanese authority. In the most sensitive and trouble-prone colony, Korea, Japan kept its greatest military strength at hand. Korea had been subdued and its army disbanded by one division and several infantry regiments; after 1920 the Japanese army permanently stationed two of its best divisions on the northern half of the peninsula, along with a wide distribution of gendarmerie (*kempeitai*) units throughout the colony. In Taiwan, considering the smaller size of the colony and the smaller potential for civil unrest, the military strength maintained by the Japanese was considerable, though not on the same scale as that in Korea. In the lesser colonies, however, Japanese military and naval forces in the first half of Japanese colonial rule were negligible, except for elements of the Kwantung army which were on station largely to protect the Kwantung Leased Territory and Japanese interests in South Manchuria from external threat.[34]

Yet, when one considers the diminutive size of garrisons providing security for Britain's vast African territories, the military forces that Japan maintained in the colonies or had available nearby in the home islands seem massive for the modest size of her empire. Undoubtedly, this preponderance of military power influenced the attitude of Japanese colonial officialdom, which knew that it could count on instant, loyal, and overwhelming military support and was therefore much less likely to temporize in dealing with colonial populations.

Yet, rarely did Japanese colonial governments have to call upon regular military forces to preserve order. As Ching-chih Chen's essay shows, the first line of internal security in the empire was the double weave of two systems of law enforcement employed by the Japanese: modern and superbly efficient police forces, supplemented by the clever exploitation of indigenous systems of community control.

As the first Japanese colony, Taiwan became the precedent for Japan's system of law enforcement throughout the empire. The immediate problem after the acquisition of the island was the suppression of continuing anti-Japanese activities. The regular units of the Japanese army being too expensive to maintain as permanent local security forces, the government-general created a modern police force

[34] The Kwantung army did not become a really sizeable military force until the 1930's. See Shimada Toshihiko, *Kantōgun* [The Kwantung Army] (Tokyo: Chūō Shinsho, 1964), pp. 2-11.

patterned after the police system in the home islands, but adapted it to suit the conditions in Taiwan. Carefully recruited, rigorously trained, and distributed throughout the island, except in the wildest areas of the aboriginal interior, the Japanese police in Taiwan were placed in every village, ready to punish any resistance to Japanese authority.

In addition to its primary duty of law enforcement, the police became the backbone of local administration in Taiwan. Assigned a wide range of functions—tax collection, enforcement of sanitary regulations, public information, superintendence of local public works programs, and other supervisory tasks—the Japanese policeman became a colonial functionary, not unlike the district officer in British Africa.

During the next several decades the structure and function of this police system was perfected and extended to the other colonies, though adaptations were made to conform to regional circumstances. To Japanese colonial authorities the wide-ranging functions of Japanese police were a continuing source of pride and an indication of the efficiency of Japanese colonial government (though Western visitors to the empire often found them officious and inquisitorial). In this perspective the predominant place of the Japanese policeman in colonial affairs gave evidence of law, order, and material progress in the empire.

Modern police forces were expensive, and by themselves would have been inadequate to maintain both local order and bureaucratic control throughout the empire. To supplement and support the uniformed police in their various functions, the Japanese were quick to exploit traditional systems of village security and leadership. Here again, Ching-chih Chen tells us, Taiwan provided valuable precedents. Using his rapidly acquired knowledge of local customs, Civil Administrator Gotō Shimpei was quick to adopt the ancient *pao-chia* system of collective responsibility for maintaining law and order in the village. This mechanism for community control had for centuries contributed to the stability of rural China, but had fallen into disuse in Taiwan. Under Gotō's direction the *pao-chia* (*hokō* in Japanese) system became a crushingly effective mechanism for information gathering, militia mobilization, and search and seizure of suspected dissidents, as well as for general administrative purposes which required the use of local manpower. While varying circumstances elsewhere in the empire prevented the extension of the *pao-chia* system to other colonies, Japanese colonial authorities, building on their experience in community control on Taiwan, learned how to manipulate traditional leadership mechanisms on the local level in all their territories. Thus, using Japanese police power in combination with these indigenous institutions, Japan was able to extend tight bureaucratic control even to the remotest parts of the empire.

Occasionally, Japanese concern for security and control obstructed other Japanese colonial objectives. The problem of extending Japanese law to all the colonies is a case in point. At the outset, Japan had intended to bring all its colonies under one legal system, consistent with that of the home islands. Yet, as Edward Chen's essay in this volume shows us, that objective foundered on the ambiguities of Japan's colonial purpose: on the one hand, the Japanese home government did not deviate in its determination to bind the colonies to the political, legal, and economic requirements of the metropole, and, on the other hand, it wished to retain its authority undiminished in all the colonies, an impossibility should Japanese law be applied uniformly throughout the empire. The crux of the problem was the extension to Taiwanese and Koreans (in particular) the political rights enjoyed under the Constitution by Japanese citizens in the home islands, specifically the right to participate, through the ballot box, in the decisions which affected them, a grant of autonomy which would inevitably lead to a loss of political authority by Japan. Had Japan chosen to extend Japanese law to the empire without exception, the right of suffrage might have been granted to Japan's colonial peoples through either of two means: the creation of elected colonial assemblies with power to initiate legislation, or participation by colonial representatives in the Diet in Tokyo. As Edward Chen notes, the former idea was never entertained by any Japanese government and the latter did not outlive its sponsor, Hara Kei.

Eventually, in order to provide a degree of legal uniformity for the empire, while at the same time avoiding any possibility of autonomy or interference by colonial peoples, the central government worked out a pernicious compromise. While continuing to hold that the provisions of the Meiji Constitution, including rights of suffrage, did not apply to the colonies (a subject on which Japanese legal specialists were divided), the central government passed (in 1918) a law providing for a uniform legal system for the colonies themselves covering civil, criminal, and commercial matters, as well as military conscription. Thus, as the empire evolved, Japan increasingly came to speak of the uniform *obligations* of all its *subjects* and less and less of the specific *rights* enjoyed only by Japanese *citizens* in the home islands.

Thus, unimpeded by any barriers to arbitrary and authoritarian rule and able to subject their colonial populations to constant police surveillance and to various systems of rigorous community control, Japanese colonial governments assured an unprecedented degree of law, order and stability throughout the empire. In the process they created bureaucracies more centralized and more authoritarian than any that existed in Japan itself, a fact which accounts for the vigor and force with which Japan was able to carry out its colonial policies.

ECONOMIC RELATIONS WITHIN THE EMPIRE:
DEVELOPMENT AND EXPLOITATION

After the consolidation of military and political control, no aspect of the Meiji strategy had been more important in the modernization of Japan than the creation of a sound economic base for the nation, one which would not only make it economically self-sufficient, but would also provide sufficient growth for the new state to pay for the extraordinary costs of a wide range of modernizing programs and institutions. The accomplishment of this task had been achieved by the only practical means available: the mobilization of the slack resources—principally land and labor—of agriculture, the primary sector of the traditional economy. The success of this boot-strap operation, in which the rural sector was made to bear the financial burden of modernization during the initial stages of an emerging industrial sector, is too well known to be recounted here. What is important to highlight is the fact that the Japanese government used the same general approach toward the colonial empire, specifically toward its two largest colonies, to deal with a majority of problems—a lagging agricultural sector, balance of payments deficits, new costs of creating modern infrastructures—not dissimilar to those which had faced the early Meiji state.

As Ramon Myers and Yamada Saburō demonstrate, one of the first concerns of the colonial regimes, beginning with that in Taiwan, was to establish a rationalized agricultural tax base which could provide a regular source of revenue. Just as the Meiji modernizers had recognized that this could only be achieved through the clarification of land ownership, so too did Japanese colonial governments undertake a series of land survey and registration programs (in Taiwan, 1898-1903, in Korea, 1912-1918, in the Kwantung Leased Territory, 1914-1924, in Karafuto, and in the Nan'yō, 1922-1923) in order to classify land, identify and measure property ownership, simplify the sale and purchase of land, promote land utilization, and most of all provide accurate assessments for tax purposes. There is no doubt that all Japanese colonial governments achieved these objectives, but there remains considerable dispute concerning the equity of the land-tenure arrangements which followed, particularly those in Korea. In general, postwar Korean and Japanese scholars have forcefully condemned Japanese land policy on the peninsula as favoring land-hungry Japanese settlers and as socially and economically destabilizing in that it resulted in the dispossession of large numbers of Korean cultivators and a consequent upsurge in tenancy. Yet a small but growing number of Japanese and American scholars, Yamada and Myers among them, have argued that the surveys and registration programs were scrupulously honest and not originally intended to redistribute land to Japanese at the expense of Korean cultivators, though a good deal of land did come under Japanese ownership eventually. While avoiding final judgments on these matters, one can assert that the land-tax reforms, particularly in Taiwan and Korea, provided a strong incentive for new and old landowners to increase the productivity of their land, since colonial governments now began to collect taxes with scrupulous honesty and firm regularity.

Once the colonial governments had rationalized the land tenure and agricultural tax systems of their territories, they exercised their massive authority to direct agricultural development by using special tax revenues to influence the behavior of agricultural producers, to disseminate modern agricultural technology, and to establish monopolies in certain agriculturally based industries which were expected to provide substantial revenue. These programs had been particularly important at the beginning of the empire when Taiwan, in its first years as a Japanese possession, proved to be a drain on the resources of the home government which Japan could not long afford, no matter what its values as a status symbol. Determined to make the island economically self-sufficient and, more than that, to ease the balance of payments problem for the metropolitan country, the Taiwan colonial government devoted intensive research and planning to the development of commodities which offered the best prospects for a quick return on investment and which at the same time would meet Japan's domestic needs. These efforts laid the foundations for a highly successful sugar industry between 1900 and 1910, heavily subsidized at first, but which, within a decade, became the leading industry of the colony and helped to reduce Japan's dependence on outside sources for this important commodity and thus improved its overall trade balance.

From the outset of the empire Japan looked to its colonial territories to provide more than revenue and their own economic self-sufficiency (which, in fact, was really achieved only by Taiwan and the Nan'yō). It also aimed at making them contribute to the economic well-being of the home islands. Taiwan and Korea, in particular, were increasingly seen as alleviating a growing problem in Japan's domestic economy. By the period in which both colonies were acquired, it had become apparent that the agricultural production of the home islands were insufficient to meet the domestic requirements of a growing Japanese population. Because of its continuing balance of payments problem the nation could not afford to import large amounts of food, nor did it seem wise to make large investments in domestic agriculture at the expense of the still fragile modern sector. It was for these reasons that Japan looked to its two largest colonies to make up the gap. Since the principal Japanese food requirement was rice, it was, as I have noted, the nation's good fortune that this traditional staple was also basic to the agrarian economies of Taiwan and Korea, so that Japan was able to devote its efforts at agricultural development in those colonies primarily to increasing the output of a long-familiar crop.

In this volume Myers and Yamada have charted the institutional developments and technological measure involved in this effort. Taken together these amounted to what they call a "biological revolution" in agricultural production in both countries. Indeed, as James Nakamura has elsewhere noted, the unprecedented success of these efforts to develop small-scale traditional agriculture in a relatively short time produced agricultural growth rates in Taiwan and Korea which surpassed those of early Meiji Japan.[35]

From a structural point of view, however, what is important about the economic relationship between Japan and its two major colonies is that they became, in Samuel Ho's words, agricultural appendages which functioned to solve Japan's domestic food problems. This marked the beginning of an ever-closer integration of colonial economies with that of the metropolitan country, so that the economic evolution of Taiwan, Korea, and to a lesser extent the other colonies cannot be understood apart from the shifting economic circumstances of Japan's domestic economy during the lifetime of the empire.

By the end of the 1920's, in any event, both Taiwan and Korea had been molded into docile colonial economies, linked to the colonial power by a trade cycle—a triangular model, as Samuel Ho explains it—of raw materials and foodstuffs, export and import of manufactured goods. All economic activities, such as the development of non-agricultural industries, were not only neglected but were positively restricted by Japan's colonial governments, which sought to prevent the emergence of competition in the colonies with industrial enterprises in Japan. To this end Japanese colonial governments actually discouraged the great *zaibatsu* from extending their activities

[35] Nakamura, "Incentives, Productivity Gaps, and Agricultural Growth Rates in Prewar Japan, Taiwan, and Korea," pp. 330-350.

to the colonies. But at the outset of the 1930's a dramatic shift in the economic circumstance of Japan ushered in the second phase of Japan's colonial economic policy and sharply redirected the colonial economies of Taiwan and Korea.

As Japan moved toward a semi-war economy and the parallel decision to create a self-sufficient industrial base, the two major colonies were seen as strategic areas for a contribution to this endeavor. During the first half of the decade, plans were drawn up for major industrialization programs by the colonial governments of Korea and Taiwan, while agricultural production was sharply downgraded as an economic priority. Other economic trends in Japan had already pointed toward this shift. Foundering in the world crisis of 1929, Japan needed profitable investment opportunities to contend with these difficulties, and Korea, with its rich mineral resources, abundant hydroelectric power, and cheap labor, was suddenly seen by the Japanese business community as an attractive market, a view encouraged by the government-general of Korea. There was, moreover, the fact of agricultural depression in Japan, manifested particularly in the plummeting price of rice. In both Taiwan and Korea, therefore, agricultural expansion programs were curtailed, while industrial facilities were created to produce the raw materials—petro-chemicals, ores, and metals—needed by Japanese heavy industry. For reasons explored by Samuel Ho in his essay, these efforts were a good deal more successful in Korea than in Taiwan, although by 1939 industry and agriculture occupied almost equal proportions of the total production of Taiwan. With the outbreak of Japan's war in China, Korea was increasingly pressed into the role of a logistical base for Japanese military operations on the continent and its industrial plants converted to the task of keeping Japan's armies in China supplied with the sinews of war. (At the same time, rice shipments from Korea continued to flow toward the home islands, to the considerable hardship of the Korean people.)[36]

Consideration of the application of the Meiji economic strategy to the colonies and the subsequent integration of the colonial economies with those of the metropolitan country inevitably leads to the consideration of two quite different questions about the Japanese economic effort in the colonies. The first of these is concerned with the economic value of the empire from the point of view of Japan itself. In brief, one may legitimately ask, to what extent did Japan's efforts in the economic modernization of its colonies, particularly Taiwan

[36] Yamabe, *Nihon tōjika no Chōsen*, pp. 187-203.

and Korea, contribute to the economic well-being of the home islands?

The initial judgments of Ho, Myers, and Yamada is that the Japanese colonial economic policies were, on the whole, of considerable benefit to Japan. Certainly, the remarkable agricultural growth in both major colonies, generated by careful Japanese planning and the introduction of the latest technology, produced sufficient foodstuffs to meet the growing needs of the population in the home islands and eased the Japanese balance of payments. In the latter half of the empire, Taiwan and Korea became important sources of industrial raw materials, particularly those which were energy-intensive. The smaller colonial territories provided fewer vital products, but nevertheless contributed to the remarkable overall growth of the empire in the period between the wars. The colonies provided an export market for Japanese domestic manufactures, particularly consumer items, as income levels rose in the colonies over time, as well as offering increased white-collar employment for Japanese from the home islands. In the second half of the empire, moreover, private Japanese business interests—the Oriental Development Company in Korea, the Taiwan Electrical Company, the Ōji Paper Company in Karafuto, and the South Seas Development Company, to name a few—also found economic participation to be quite profitable.

Yet, at the same time, the empire entailed economic costs and disadvantages to Japan, some hidden and some more apparent. Obviously, in a strict debit and loss sense, it is impossible to determine whether the empire was a net asset or liability to Japan. There is no accounting system which can calculate the "costs" of maintaining a colonial establishment—military expenditures, government subsidies, administrative outlays and such—and can match them against "returns"—volume of trade, reductions in foreign exchange disbursements, repatriated capital, and so on. What is more realistic is to note that the economic benefits of empire accruing to Japan were very mixed, the advantages of one group often being the costs of another. Because of imports of rice from Korea, for example, the Japanese city dweller paid less for rice than would otherwise have been the case, but, on the other hand the Japanese rice farmer had reduced earning power. Similarly, while the importance of sugar from Taiwan reduced pressure on Japan's foreign exchange and was a source of considerable profit to Japanese entrepreneurs involved in sugar manufacture, the long-standing tariff against importation of foreign sugar into Japan meant that the Japanese consumer paid more for that commodity.

In considering the contribution of the empire to the economic requirements of the home islands, moreover, one must also understand that the colonies collectively occupied only a moderately important position in the total economy of Japan, and in terms of strategic imports never enabled Japan to become economically self-sufficient. While Korea and Taiwan, in the late 1920's supplied the colonial power with four-fifths of its rice imports, two-thirds of its sugar imports, and lesser amounts of minerals, lumber, and other items, Japan was never able to obtain from her colonies her chief requirements for a whole range of strategic products, including textile fibers, metals, petroleum, and fertilizers, which she was forced to seek abroad. During the lifetime of the empire, moreover, the colonies provided Japan with no more than a modest export market for her manufactures (about twenty percent of Japan's industrial exports and about ten percent of her textile exports in 1930). Japan's colonial trade, while it grew far more rapidly than that with foreign countries, counted for only about one quarter of the nation's total overseas trade.[37] Even if these problems did not exist, conclusions about the economic record of Japanese colonialism depend greatly on the departure points for specific research. This essay and others in this volume have stressed national interest and the modernizing experience of the metropole as central to the shaping of Japanese colonial policy. Yet, as Ramon Myers demonstrates in his historiographical survey of Japanese colonialism, much of postwar Japanese scholarship on the empire has concentrated on key socio-economic class relationships within the empire and has viewed Japanese colonial policy as the result of a complex mix between Japanese colonial bureaucracy and a local elite which controlled the resources and means of production in the colonies. Different questions obviously lead to different answers.

These facts considered, one is led to agree with the late William Lockwood when he concluded that the main asset of the Japanese colonial empire to Japan was more strategic than economic in nature since it provided the metropolitan country with control over an enlarged food base, created a ring of defensive barriers around Japan proper, and afforded bases for further expansion into East Asia.[38] And yet, as we have noted, the exploitation of those strategic assets led to the over-extension of Japanese power, confrontation with the West, and the collapse of the empire altogether.

Economic value and benefit must, of course, be also considered from the viewpoint of Japan's colonial peoples. Here the results of

---

[37] Yamabe, "Nihon teikokushugi to shokuminchi," pp. 205-207.
[38] Lockwood, *The Economic Development of Japan*, p. 51.

Japan's colonial rule are very mixed. Indeed, no aspect of Japanese colonial history is more complex or more subject to disagreement than the impact of Japanese economic policy within the empire itself. The controversy is between those scholars who concentrate on Japanese economic activities in the empire which collectively merit the term "exploitation"—the harsh demands of the metropole upon the colonial territories, the economic inequities between the Japanese and their colonial charges, the distortions and imbalances wrought by Japanese policies in the economic structures of the colonies—and those who emphasize the creation of modern economic infrastructures in the colonies, the promotion of dramatic increases in both agricultural and industrial production, the consequent improvement of the economic conditions of the indigenous colonial peoples in terms of health, education, and increased opportunity and purchasing power, conditions which can be collectively termed "development." That the debate has come to involve emotional recrimination, incomplete or disputed data, and highly specialized analytical methodology, in almost equal proportions, has made its resolution in the near future all the more unlikely.

From the essays in this volume, however, as well as from other studies of the economic structure of the Japanese colonial empire, one can draw a few conclusions on which most might agree and which, not surprisingly, add up to a mixed pattern of development *and* exploitation. Generally applicable to the empire as a whole, they apply specifically to Taiwan and Korea, the colonies which figured largest in Japan's economic policies.

Since the economies of the principal territories of the empire were essentially agricultural, any change in the broadly based traditional agriculture—rice—would have the greatest impact on the economic conditions of the empire's indigenous peoples. Evidence from various studies attests to the remarkable growth of agriculture during the Japanese colonial period. Thus, the majority of Taiwanese and Koreans were drawn into "the creative process of agricultural productivity" (Samuel Ho's phrase) and shared widely in the benefits of that productivity, largely in increased purchasing power.

At the same time it appears also true that, because of the dominant place of Japanese in colonial agriculture and their disproportionate control of not only land, but the mechanisms of the export market, the indigenous share of the increase in agricultural output was far smaller than that of the Japanese themselves. The question of the material benefit accruing from Japanese rule must thus include consideration of the inequities in economic condition. Moreover, Japanese policy, by shaping the colonial economies so drastically to the needs of the home islands, often worked against the interests of the colonial peoples. Despite the remarkable increases in rice production in Taiwan and Korea, for example, consumption of rice by Taiwanese and Koreans actually dropped because of the substantial shipments of rice to Japan, so that the indigenous population were forced to consume less desirable cereals, such as barley and millet.

It is far less clear that the later emphasis on industrial productivity had substantial direct impact, positive or negative, on the indigenous peoples of the empire, since relatively few indigenes were drawn into the industrial sector. Those who did enter the industrial labor force did so mostly as unskilled labor, though they appear to have gained some increase in income, thereby.

On the plus side it is also clear that the colonial peoples benefited from ambitious Japanese programs to create modern facilities and institutions essential to economic growth. Modern transportation and communications networks, banking and monetary systems, educational and health facilities, were enjoyed by colonizer and colonized alike. It is a matter of historical record that Japanese investment in public health care in all the colonies caused remarkable decreases in mortality, and a general increase in the health of its colonial peoples, for example. When the colonial rulers built a bridge over a Korean river or connected two Taiwanese towns by rail, all benefited. Yet even in an institutional sense inequities existed not only between Japanese colonials and colonial indigenes, but also between component territories of the empire, exemplified by disparities in consumer services, wage differentials, and employment rates. Despite the fact that hydroclectric production in Korca nearly tripled that of Taiwan, less than 12 percent of Korean families enjoyed electric lighting, as compared to 36.3 percent by Taiwanese households (and as compared to over 90 percent by Japanese families in the home islands). Not only did Taiwanese tend to receive higher wages than their counterparts in Korea, but wage differentials between Japanese and indigenes in the same jobs were far greater in Korea than in Taiwan, where employment rates were almost twice those of Korea.[39]

Lastly, one must consider the economic legacy of Japanese colonial rule for her former colonial peoples. Here again, the record is mixed. Whatever inequities existed in income distribution between Japanese colonials and indigenous peasants, and despite the distinct advantages that the Japanese consumer may have gained at the time from the modernization and expansion of the agricultural sectors of Taiwan

[39] Kim Kwan-suk, "An Analysis of Economic Change in Korea," in Nahm, pp. 107-110.

and Korea, it cannot be denied that both countries emerged from Japanese rule with efficient and productive agricultural systems. Yet recent studies have come to cast doubt on the other long-range economic contributions of Japanese colonialism to the former colonial territories. Despite the fact that Taiwan and Korea evinced industrial expansion during their colonial periods, it has been argued that Japan did not provide the necessary elements for sustained industrial growth in either colony. In large part this was due to the discriminatory elements in Japanese economic policy. Because Japan kept economic power out of the hands of Taiwanese and Koreans, a modern entrepreneurial class failed to develop in Korea and grew only marginally in Taiwan. Since, in both countries, industrial and administrative positions which required technical or managerial skills were so often filled by Japanese during the colonial period, few indigenous technicians or managers were available to either country, a fact which resulted in massive dislocations in the economic machinery of Taiwan and Korea when the Japanese withdrew.[40]

THE TRANSFORMATION OF SOCIETY

No task facing the young leadership in early Meiji Japan had been more essential to the creation of a new state than the transformation of Japanese society. In the long run, all other innovations attempted by the Meiji modernizers to promote national security and prosperity would depend upon the social and intellectual transformation of the people as a whole, so as to shape their loyalty and obedience to the new state, as well as to develop new attitudes and new skills among the people so as to meet the challenges and opportunities of modernity. The fledgling government thus sought to introduce new ideas and new technologies in order to create a truly "modern" people, while at the same time assuring a conformism and uniformity of outlook seen as essential to national cohesion and strength.

As Patricia Tsurumi explains, the principal vehicle for accomplishing these objectives was a modern educational system, essentially dual in purpose: first, to provide basic schooling for the entire population, as well as large doses of social and political indoctrination to inculcate loyalty for the new state, and, second, to offer advanced education

[40] Suh Chang-chul, *Growth and Structural Changes in the Korean Economy, 1910-1940* (Cambridge, Mass.: Council on East Asian Studies, Harvard University, 1978), pp. 143-156, and Samuel P.-S. Ho, "The Development Policy of the Japanese Colonial Government in Taiwan, 1895-1945," in Gustav Ranis, ed., *Government and Economic Development* (New Haven, Ct.: Yale University Press, 1971), p. 328.

to those Japanese of superior ability to whom the future guidance of the nation would be entrusted.

In undertaking this social transformation, ambitious as it was, the Japanese government was fortunate that its policies were directed toward an homogenous society. No profound regional, ethnic, or linguistic divisions served to complicate the task of developing a uniform, unified, and enlightened citizenry, or to create sectional jealousies and enmity as a new elite emerged based upon education and merit. By 1895, as Japan stood at the edge of its imperial advance, the success of this effort was obvious: the creation of a basically skilled and literate mass of people, increasingly uniform in dedication to emperor and state, and a corps of superbly trained young professionals, ready to assume the political and economic management of a modern nation.

From the beginning of its imperial responsibilities it was obvious, however, that Japan could not and would not apply its Meiji education strategy to the colonial empire without pronounced alterations to meet both the circumstances of the colonial environment and the subordinate role which the Japanese rulers expected of the colonial peoples in their charge. Complicating the original goals of creating a uniform, enlightened, and loyal society throughout the empire was the fact that, except for Karafuto, the colonial peoples of the empire were racially, historically, and linguistically different, not only in relation to the Japanese themselves, but within the empire as a whole. And yet, the Asian provenance of the empire meant that its two largest colonies, Taiwan and Korea, contained peoples not utterly alien to their conquerors in race and cultural tradition. It was the conflicting Japanese perceptions to this basic ambiguity which clouded the purposes and policies of Japan's social transformation of the empire.

If one believed, as did the majority of Japanese colonial administrators, educators, and publicists in the first half of the empire, in a racially separated approach to colonial rule which accepted the current Social Darwinist idea that "biological"—that is, racial—differences determined the political capacities of various peoples, a number of conclusions could be drawn: that races should evolve separately, according to their inherent capacities to modernize; that superior races had a moral right, indeed a responsibility, to guide the destinies of "lesser" peoples; and that "civilizing" these peoples would take an infinite time in order for the benefits of colonial rule to work their good. Thus, in this perspective, Taiwanese and Koreans, Chinese and Micronesians, as alien peoples, were to retain a separate identity and to be governed pragmatically, with due respect to their own institutions. As "lesser" races, however, they would be kept indefinitely in a subordinate position to the colonizing race, without either the political rights or responsibilities of their rulers.

Yet, as I have noted earlier, it was possible for Japanese to view their colonial charges in quite a different light. If one stressed affinities of race and culture between Japan and the peoples of its two most populous colonies, one could believe that the latter were, in Tsurumi's words, "not quite Japanese, but capable of becoming Japanese." From this conception emerged the doctrine of assimilation (dōka) which incorporated a cluster of assumptions: the supposedly indissoluble bond between Japan and the other countries of the Chinese culture area, the Confucian faith in the benevolence of the emperor toward all his subjects, and the mystical linkage which Japanese had for centuries drawn between the emperor and his people. The central purpose behind the Japanese version of assimilation was thus "Japanization" of her colonial subjects, Taiwanese and Koreans in particular, and their transformation into diligent, loyal, law-abiding "imperial peoples" (kōmin), imbued with the same values, bearing the same responsibilities, and sharing the same life-styles of Japanese in the same islands.

The most accommodating interpretation of assimilation, one articulated by liberal Japanese politicians and journalists in the Taishō period, perceived that the indigenous majorities in the colonies, particularly in the two largest colonies, through education and encouragement, could be made fully Japanese, with the same claims to liberties and economic opportunities as the citizens of metropolitan Japan. Such an alternative would indeed have contributed to the development of a truly assimilated empire, one in which the responsibilities of all subjects would be balanced by their rights.

But that view was transient, and, in any event, never represented that of responsible Japanese authority, which intended from the outset that the enlightenment and progress of the indigenes were to be consistent with the limited and distinctly inferior position which they were to occupy within the empire. For this reason the application of the Meiji educational strategy to the colonies was sharply amended to concentrate on shaping the loyalties and outlook of indigenous peoples toward Japan through moral education and Japanese language training and to limit their educational advancement to the acquisition of vocational and practical skills. In that view, the uncontrolled dissemination of knowledge beyond that needed for the household or the vocations could only breed discontent and subvert a social order in which Taiwanese and Koreans were to be content to have a bottom place. As Tsurumi puts it, the goal of Japanese educational policies in the colonies was to duplicate the lower track of the two-track Meiji education system, the upper being reserved for Japanese colonials.

In general outline, that educational configuration was not dissimilar to the racially segregated colonial education systems of the West. But by the 1920's forces both within and without the empire had driven Japan to adopt social and educational policies which fused the most oppressive and restrictive of the two contrasting perspectives on racial relations within the empire. On the one hand, the pace of assimilation—the Japanization—of Taiwanese, Koreans, Chinese, and Micronesians in thought and appearance was to be accelerated, lest they be tainted with notions of liberalism and individualism, and, on the other, all thought that they might become Japanese in terms of rights and opportunities was rigorously suppressed. While colonial governments spoke with increasing fervor about a merger of colonizers and colonized under the "impartiality and equal favor" (isshi dōjin) of the Japanese emperor, the discriminatory environment of Japanese colonialism rarely permitted the realization of such an ideal anywhere in the empire. What emerged instead was an assimilation effort of a most mechanical sort designed to reinforce the physical identities of indigenous populations with their rulers and thus to serve as a vehicle for social control.[41] But even the pace of this artificial transformation of society was judged insufficient by Japanese colonial authority and by the 1930's assimilation had given way to a more intensified concept—"imperialization" (kōminka)—the forced draft regimentation of all aspects of colonial life.[42] During the last decade and a half of the empire Japan's colonial peoples were constantly admonished that they shared with all Japanese subjects the common sacrifices and obligations to the Japanese state, burdens which became increasingly heavy as Japan dragooned material support from its colonies.

Michael Robinson, in his contribution to this volume, reminds us that social control in the empire was not limited to matters of educational policy, but extended to Japanese direction of the printed word. Despite a number of circumventions by Korean writers and editors, Robinson tells us, censorship and press controls enabled the colonial authority to limit the spread of radical ideas and to shape the content of Korean publications to its satisfaction. In this perspective, it appears that flexibility of colonial authority in applying control measures, rather than simple brutality, were effective in structuring the

[41] Lamley, "Assimilation Efforts in Taiwan," pp. 498-499.
[42] For a discussion in English of the Kōminka movement, see William Kirk, "Social Change in Formosa," Sociology and Social Research, XXVI (1941-1942), pp. 18-22.

Korean mass media to conform to Japanese policies. Here again, the strategy employed seems to have been remarkably similar to precedents undertaken in the metropole, in which a number of methods were selected to limit the scope of dissent and to reinforce a unity of thought and outlook. As in Japan, rigorous suppression had been balanced by limited toleration of more moderate dissent, so in Korea harsh treatment of radical left-wing expression was parallelled by less exacting restrictions applied to moderate nationalist publications.

In molding her colonial peoples to her own image Japan was only partially successful. From Sakhalin to the Marshall Islands there was certainly a superficial attainment of Japanese objectives in terms of acceptance of the Japanese language, custom, and dress, but not the fundamental transformation of colonial society which had been sought by Japanese colonial authority. Given the internal contradictions in Japanese racial attitudes within the empire and the obvious inequities in political status and economic opportunity between Japanese colonials and the indigenous majorities in which they existed, the stunted results of Japanese assimilation efforts were inevitable.

In Taiwan, the Japanese came the closest to their objectives and attained a modest progress in shaping the values and loyalties of the colonial population. In the Kwantung Leased Territory and Micronesia the results were more superficial, and in Korea, the Japanese efforts to "imperialize" the indigenous majority fell on bitter ground. Both in this volume and elsewhere Tsurumi and Edward Chen have enumerated the reasons for the stark contrast in the results of Japanese efforts to transform the societies of Taiwan and Korea: the differing evolution and nature of the two peoples, the separate and distinct processes by which they fell under Japanese colonial rule, and the contrasting treatment they were accorded by Japanese colonial authority.[43] It suffices, at this juncture, only to note the bleak results of the Meiji strategy in Korea, seen from the Japanese perspective, despite the similarity of Japanese aims in both Taiwan and Korea. Whereas, through Japanese efforts, the Taiwanese acquired a certain identification with their colonial rulers, for Koreans the Japanese remained foreign oppressors and exploiters. Indeed, Japanese efforts in education and socialization in Korea, as Tsurumi explains, were actually counter-productive; to be educated in Korea was to be anti-Japanese, so bitter was Korean resentment toward the Japanese educational efforts to separate Koreans from their own cultural and historical identity.

[43] See also Patricia Tsurumi, *Japanese Colonial Education in Taiwan, 1895-1945* (Cambridge, Mass.: Harvard University Press, 1977), pp. 172-176, and Edward I-te Chen, "Japan: Oppressor or Modernizer?" in Nahm, pp. 251-260.

What of the values of this Meiji strategy from the perspective of the colonial peoples themselves? At one level one cannot deny the positive advances in aptitudes and skills made by the peoples of the empire under the stimulus of the Japanese educational effort, not only in the schoolroom, but in other areas of colonial life. An increasing number of indigenes did enter the formal colonial educational system, where the broad mass of the people were exposed to new ideas. As Samuel Ho puts it, the average Taiwanese or Korean at the end of the Japanese colonial period was a far different person in terms of skills and knowledge than his parents at the beginning of Japanese colonial rule. The problem, Ho notes and Tsurumi outlines in detail, again centers on the inequities of opportunity. These were wrought at the outset by the fundamental revision of the Meiji strategy, one designed to restrict the intellectual growth of Japan's colonial peoples. By admitting indigenous populations only to the lower of the two-track educational system and assimilating them only at the bottom of the Japanese social order, Japan failed in the truest sense to provide them with modern education.

THE JAPANESE COLONIAL EMPIRE IN HISTORICAL PERSPECTIVE

The extension of the Meiji pattern of national development to the overseas Japanese empire was not a unique phenomenon, of course. Western colonial systems, too, tended to reflect the political and social structures of the colonial powers. Michel Crozier, in his book *The Bureaucratic Phenomenon*, has written that "political and social organization brought by a western country to the territories it has colonized—its methods of imposing and maintaining that organization, the aims it pursues—all of these reflect closely as in an enlarged sketch, its own patterns of social organization."[44] During the conference at which the papers included in this volume were presented, Albert Craig noted the relevance of Crozier's comment to the Japanese colonial situation and went on to point out the similarities between the highly centralized styles of French and Japanese bureaucratic assimilation in the two empires, mirroring the transformations of the French and Japanese nations. In both cases colonial rule and the attempt to assimilate colonial peoples brought peace, order, and development, but the rigidity of the structures imposed allowed no room for the evolution of colonial societies, nor any possibility of collective response from those societies other than violent resistance.

[44] Michel Crozier, *The Bureaucratic Phenomenon* (Chicago: University of Chicago Press, 1963), pp. 263-264.

In his essay in this volume, Lewis Gann has placed the Japanese colonial empire in comparative perspective and has charted with considerable insight both similarity and difference between the Japanese colonial empire and the empires of the Western powers. Yet, if we are speaking of what Craig calls the "transformative dynamic" of the colonial systems, it would seem that in its intensity of impact and change the Japanese imperium stands alone. Taken together, the Meiji strategies employed in the Japanese colonies comprised one of the most intensive programs for colonial development, exploitation, and change ever undertaken by a colonial power. Whatever else may be said in defense or criticism of Japan's colonial policies it cannot be said that they were wanting in organization or effort. Where Lewis Gann and Peter Duignan, in their re-evaluation of sub-Saharan Africa, could speak of ignorance and neglect as among the worst evils of Western colonialism, Hyman Kublin has written that, far from having been neglected, Japan's colonies suffered from the excessive attention of a colonial power whose traditions of cultural and social conformity, whose fervent conviction in the superiority of its own way of life, and whose boundless energy insured the imposition of drastic change among its colonial societies.[45] Year by year, the Japanese census taker, the health inspector, the teacher, and, most ubiquitously, the policeman, went earnestly, humorlessly, and sometimes mercilessly about their tasks of order, improvement, regimentation, and those activities which we may collectively call modernizing.

A just apportionment of good or evil in the results achieved by these relentless efforts defies the most objective observer of Japanese colonialism. As I have implied in my discussion of economic dynamics in the empire, it is difficult to draw up a balance sheet of benefits and injuries on which all would agree. To a greater or lesser extent this is a problem which hinders the assessment of any colonial regime. In noting the complexity of such a task Gann and Duignan have noted the dangers of

> . . . what might be called the "scenic railway" approach to writing history, in which the visitor is taken along a pre-ordained route which never varies. The tourist on the pro-colonial track goes past hospitals and housing schemes, schools, cattle dips and wells, and massive government buildings. Sitting in his compartment, he talks to former colonial administrators; he reads statistics about rising population figures and percentile production increases; he returns from his journey as an enthusiastic advocate of empire in retrospect. The rival train takes him on a very different trip. He travels

[45] Kublin, "The Evolution of Japanese Colonialism," p. 80.

past city slums, slag heaps, and refuse dumps; the train continues through eroded reserves. On the way, the traveler talks to pessimistic economists and angry "prison graduates"; he reads statistics about social evils, property, and crimes; he may return a convinced opponent of . . . colonialism in all its forms.[46]

Much of the same could be said of the contrasting views of Japan's colonial record. How does one balance the creation of a modern educational system in Korea with the attempt to eradicate the Korean language and culture? What is the trade-off between the establishment of modern administrative structures against the difficulty of a Taiwanese gaining responsible positions within them?

It is more useful perhaps to take note of the transforming effects—for good or ill—of Japanese rule among its colonies. About these the present state of Japanese colonial studies does not permit us to be very precise in terms of degree, but it is possible to enumerate broad categories of change which could be termed "modernizing." Prime among these would be what Karl Deutsch has termed "social mobilization," the erosion of old social, economic, and psychological relationships and behavior through exposure to the various aspects of modern life, growth in literacy, response to mass media, urbanization, and so on.[47] Equally important in the transformation of Japan's colonial peoples was the introduction of industrial activity, particularly in the two larger colonies, involving high-level technology, more specialized economic functions, and a growth in the scope and complexity of various markets. It is most difficult to generalize about the nature of the last category—political change in the colonial empire—since, except for Korea, special circumstances in each of the former colonies prevented the colonial populations from forming independent national regimes in the post-colonial period which would allow us to make judgments about the relationship between Japanese colonial rule and political change in the empire. As far as Korea is concerned, the Japanese political legacy, as described by Bruce Cumings in this volume, seems Janus-faced. On the one hand, it cannot be denied that the introduction of the centralized bureaucratic state, with its powerful coercive and integrative mechanisms to maintain control, crush opposition, and foster economic progress, was a development of profound importance not only to colonial Korea, but to

[46] Lewis Gann and Peter Duignan, *The Burden of Empire: An Appraisal of Western Colonialism in Africa South of the Sahara* (Stanford, CA: Hoover Institution Press, 1971), pp. 373-374.

[47] Karl Deutsch, "Social Mobilization and Political Development," in *American Political Science Review*, 55 (September 1961), pp. 494-495.

the two mutually hostile postwar Korean regimes which inherited it. Yet, at the same time, it is apparent that Japanese rule was politically disintegrative in that it fractured potential nationalist leadership. Through manipulation and pressure Japanese colonial authority separated Korean moderate nationalists from radicals, the former being eventually stigmatized as collaborators, the latter being driven from the country and, once scattered abroad, coming to hold very different and very ideological viewpoints on the nature of a Korea liberated from Japanese control.

The acuteness of change wrought in the colonies by the Meiji strategies that I have discussed is all the more remarkable when one considers the relative brevity of Japanese rule in those areas. In this, of course, it shared the fate of all modern colonial systems. One of the remarkable features of the empires created by the "new imperialism" of the late nineteenth century was the shortness of their span, generally less than a century and, in the case of Germany, Italy, and Japan, not much more than a generation. In Korea, this was just long enough for Koreans to recall the national injury suffered at the hands of the Japanese and too short for the effects of Japanese education and assimilation to have taken hold on the loyalties and interests of a younger generation of Koreans. To a degree, the inadequacy of time to legitimize colonial rule worked against Japanese colonialism in all the colonies. In this sense, it can be said that basis to the failure of Japanese colonialism to bequeath a legacy of specifically Japanese values to its former colonial subjects was the failure of the empire to mature. Had Japan continued to devote its efforts to the modest overseas empire that it had acquired by the 1920's, it is possible that the positive effects of its colonial strategies would have been more enduring and the memories of its presence less bitter. One can imagine that, given time and the full attention of a home government unencumbered by the pull of other, wider imperial interests, Japan might have molded a different sort of empire. To be sure, it would inevitably have been an authoritarian system, geared to the interests of the metropole, but it might well have been one which increasingly took into account the material well-being of its colonial peoples, a growing proportion of whom, through education and indoctrination, thought of themselves as Japanese. There were indications, certainly, that the empire was moving, if ever so slightly, in that direction in the early 1920's. But, as we have seen, largely through the unchecked ambitions of the home government, the empire was overtaken by disaster before making real progress along these lines.

Finally, in assessing the place of the Japanese empire in the history of modern colonialism, one must keep in mind the distortion of our view of the longer history of that empire because of its transmogrification during the last decade and a half of its existence. By the beginning of World War II in the minds of most Americans certainly, the outlines of Japan as a conventional and accepted colonial power had become blurred with the image of ceaseless and unbridled aggression in East Asia and the brutal efforts of Japan to dragoon support from conquered Asian peoples for further military aggression. When one adds to this the release of the long pent-up bitterness of Japan's former colonial subjects in the years immediately following the war, it is understandable that Japan gained a malodorous reputation as the worst of all the world's colonial powers. Yet, if one looks at the Japanese colonial record during the first thirty-five years of the empire, a rather different picture emerges, one which is a good deal more recognizable in Western terms and one which quite often earned high praise from numerous foreign observers and visitors for its efficiency, administrative integrity, and stability. If it was an empire in which the blessings of colonial rule accrued in far greater measure to the rulers than to the ruled, certainly much the same could be said about other colonial systems. In terms of general trade-offs between the benefits to colonial peoples of foreign rule—improvements in health and education, in the creation of modern facilities and institutions—and the injuries done to those same peoples—the humiliations, the inequities, the absence of adequate means to express the popular will—Japanese colonialism in the first half of its existence compares favorably with most other colonial empires. Certainly, it was as responsible in its policies toward its colonial populations during those years as was Belgium in the Congo, France in Indochina, Holland in the East Indies, or Germany, Italy, Spain, or Portugal in Africa. And in all fairness, it can be argued, it is against these other colonial situations, rather than against some theoretical utopia, that Japan's colonial efforts should be judged.

PROBLEMS AND POSSIBILITIES FOR FURTHER RESEARCH

What these reflections and the essays which follow them suggest is a need to take a fresh look at Japanese colonialism in its entirety, seeking less to justify or to condemn than to understand. With a wealth of written record to draw upon and the techniques of comparative history and modern social science analysis to employ, it should be possible to push scholarly inquiry along on several different levels: the placement of the evolution and character of Japanese colonialism within the broader, comparative context of colonial studies in general; the evaluation of the role and influence of the colonial empire in the growth and dilemmas of the modern Japanese state up until 1945; and, lastly, the treatment of significant institutions and dynamics within the empire.

In considering these categories I feel it important to recognize how isolated at present is research on the Japanese empire. Writing some years ago, Akira Iriye noted the existence of a "gap between imperial historians who pay little attention to East Asia and East Asian historians who are ignorant of the incessant reinterpretations of imperialism."[48] Much the same sort of discrepancy could be said to exist between the study of colonialism—the concrete manifestation of imperialism—and the study of Japanese history. The burden of this neglect seems to be shared equally by historians of modern colonialism and by specialists in the history of modern Japan. It is worth noting, for example, that, on the one hand, the excellent survey *The Colonial Empires*, by David Fieldhouse, gives virtually no space to the Japanese empire and, on the other, that the many monographs and conference volumes on Japan's modernization give almost no attention to Japan's overseas possessions or to their interrelation with metropolitan Japan. To this extent an understanding of both colonialism as a world phenomenon and Japan as a modern state are incomplete.

One might begin to close this gap with a more detailed and comprehensive comparison than we have attempted here between the Japanese colonial empire and a more general colonial typology of Western colonial systems. The model sketched by David Fieldhouse supposes that modern colonial empires, for all their dissimilarities, have a number of common qualities: effective power concentrated at the center, the professional character of colonial administration, the integrative techniques of centralization, and the fact that colonial economies are rarely the closed monopolistic systems that the colonial authorities had originally planned.[49] A study of the adherence or deviation of Japanese colonialism in relation to this general pattern, at the very least, might help to place research on the Japanese colonial empire within the framework of more general studies on imperialism and colonialism.

Comparison might be even more useful on specific levels. No one has thought to extend the interesting generalizations made by Hyman Kublin nearly twenty years ago, which touched upon the similarities between the Japanese and German colonial empires.[50] Beyond the

[48] Akira Iriye, "Imperialism in East Asian," in *Modern East Asia: Essays in Interpretation*, James Crowley, ed. (New York: Harcourt, Brace, and World, 1970), p. 123.

[49] Fieldhouse, *The Colonial Empires: A Comparative Survey from the Eighteenth Century*, pp. 375-380.

[50] Kublin, "The Evolution of Japanese Colonialism," pp. 82-84.

reference in this volume to Gotō Shimpei's scientific training in Berlin and the similarity of the Japanese and German approaches to "scientific colonialism" we need to have a better understanding of whether Germanic ideas helped to shape early Japanese colonial policy in the same way that they contributed to the formation of Japanese medicine, the modern Japanese army, and to the drafting of the Meiji Constitution.

Another example of the potential for an imaginative use of the comparative approach to a case study of Japanese colonial history was provided some years ago by Gregory Henderson when he suggested that the influx into Korea of impoverished lower-class Japanese from rural Kyūshū at the beginning of this century parallelled the wave of *pieds noirs*—poor French and Italian farmers—into North Africa, particularly Tunisia, in the nineteenth century.[51] (In both cases, Henderson noted, the newly arriving immigrants, aggressively shoving their way into the colonies, were of lower economic, social, and cultural status than much of the indigenous population, a fact which, in both situations, added the bitter taste of contempt to the poisonous relationship which developed between ruler and ruled.) The patterns of Japanese immigration into Korea and Taiwan from 1900 to 1920 have never really been traced in detail in Western literature, let alone discussed from a comparative standpoint.

Turning to the relationship between the empire and Japan's modern history, we need a more detailed explanation of the place of the overseas territories in the inter-war economy of the home islands than the contributors of this volume have been able to provide, since understandably their focus has been on development within the colonies themselves. While I have already asserted my doubts as to the practicality of any accounting system of imperial debits and credits in determining the net economic value of the empire, further research into the scale and dimensions of trade, investment, and manpower utilization in the empire would provide a better understanding of the ways in which the metropolitan economy was linked to the colonies. If one thinks in terms of imperial costs, it would be useful, also, to have some better correlation between the Japanese investment in human talent and physical resources, as well as in actual capital, in the colonies and the availability of those elements in the home islands. This would enable us to perceive somewhat more accurately the burden of empire to Japan.

I have stressed the importance of strategic considerations in the acquisition of the Japanese empire and the fact that Japan eventually

[51] Henderson, "Japan's Chōsen," p. 264.

used its overseas possessions as stepping stones to ill-considered expansion beyond the boundaries of the formal empire. No one has as yet surveyed the relevant archival sources to determine the place of the empire in the evolution of Japan's overall strategies in Asia and the Pacific. It would be interesting to know, for example, how the various overseas territories were related to the opposing arguments of the "advance north"—"advance south" debate that emerged by the second decade of the empire.

It is the exploration of the specific institutions and dynamics of the Japanese colonial empire which provide the most immediate opportunities for fruitful research. Investigation in these areas may also offer the relation of Japan's overseas venture to the general studies of colonialism and to the history of modern Japan.

Obviously, the economic dynamics of the empire will continue to be a central problem in the investigation of Japanese colonialism. While one cannot say that the question of economic motivation in the acquisition of the empire has been put to rest, it is perhaps time to advance the debate into the period after the formal empire was put together. The various activities of the business boom in the colonies beginning in the 1920's—the flow of investment, where it came from and where it went, the role of banking, the relationship of parent corporations based in Japan and branch firms in colonial areas, and the relationship of business and government in the effort to maintain closed economic systems in the overseas territories—all deserve a closer look. Business, in the form of the larger corporations operating overseas by the 1920's began to exert pressure on Japanese colonial policy in ways which English language studies have only begun to assess. Karl Moskowitz, in his interesting investigation of Korean interests of the Oriental Development Company, has shown the way for other studies of these formidable economic lobbies.[52] An assessment of the role and influence of the various colonization and emigration associations in the formation of economic policy in the colonies is also overdue.

The study of Japanese colonial history, which has dealt almost exclusively with the operation of specific territorial regimes, could also be enriched by looking at its evolution from a Tokyo perspective. Only in this way can we get a better understanding of both the formal institutions and the informal pressure groups which guided the acquisition of colonies and then shaped their development. The role

[52] Karl Moskowitz, "The Creation of the Oriental Development Company: Japanese Illusions Meet Korean Reality" (*Occasional Papers on Korea:* No. 2, Joint Committee on Korean Studies of the American Council of Learned Societies and the Social Science Research Council, March 1974).

of the Japanese military in the evolution of the empire, for example, merits greater attention than we or any other scholars have given it so far. Given the fact of the military domination of Japan's colonies—perpetual in the case of Korea, extended in the cases of Taiwan and the Nan'yō—the influence in colonial policy of the general staffs in Tokyo is an important question. To look in another direction: the relationship of the Japanese Colonial Ministry (Takumushō) and the various colonial territories, as well as those between the ministry and other governmental agencies concerned with the empire, seem worthy of study.

Finally, we need to expand our awareness of the colonial experience of the Japanese themselves. History, political science, and economics have given us an increased understanding of the means by which Japan gained an overseas empire, of the techniques of Japanese colonial administration, of the institutions of Japanese colonial education and police control, of the growth patterns of agriculture under Japanese direction, of the nature of development programs in Taiwan and Korea, and the impact of all of these for good or ill upon the subject peoples of the empire. But it is odd how fleetingly the Japanese themselves have figured in research on Japanese colonialism so far. Studies abound of Japanese emigrants to the Western hemisphere, but we do not know very much about overseas Japanese in Asia and the South Pacific—their regional origins, their motives for emigration, their life-styles in a colonial setting, and little that is concrete about the attitudes of the average Japanese colonial toward the indigenous peoples around him. The perspectives of social psychology might be useful here, and in this connection one recalls Dominique Mannoni's psychological model for colonialism. Mannoni, it will be remembered, used the symbolism of Shakespeare's *Tempest* to shape what he called the "Prospero complex," a psycholgical condition of the "paternalist colonial with his pride, his neurotic impatience, his desire to dominate."[53] An effort to test Mannoni's thesis that the inherent inferiority complex of persons from advanced, competitive societies finds balm in the homage of dependent native peoples might itself lead us to know more about the kind of Japanese who went to the colonies and why. The perspectives of cultural anthropology might also help us to learn more about the position and outlook of the Japanese in the colonies, to understand in which situations they regarded themselves as settlers with a sense of permanence in a colonial territory and a commitment to its development, and in which their

[53] Dominique Mannoni, *Prospero and Caliban: The Psychology of Colonization* (New York: Praeger, 1964), p. 32.

roles as merchants, traders, and administrators reinforced their ties to the home country.

The human dimension to Japanese colonialism will not be as easily traced as the other problems that we have touched upon. As yet it lies fragmented, we suspect in the biographical data provided in individual colonial surveys; in the files of such colonial newspapers as have survived the ravages of war, time, and the transfer of power; in the recollections of now elderly colonial expatriates.[54] Yet, in seeking it out, scholars might not only move beyond the limiting perspectives of impersonal "forces" in the evolution of Japanese colonialism, but will abandon the sterotypical image of Japanese in the empire. For the Japanese in their colonies were not a faceless elite of uniformed oppressors, no more than they were all marble exemplars of progress and civilization, but were earnest administrators and calculating speculators, wealthy landlords and tenant farmers, teachers and ruffians, housewives and prostitutes, doctors and adventurers, who collectively embodied Japanese visions and prejudices, plans and passions, knowledge and ignorance, altruism and greed. When contemporary scholarship begins to populate the Japanese colonial landscape with living, acting individuals, Japanese colonialism will at last begin to take on a humanity, if not a humaneness, which it does not yet possess.

[54] A wealth of insights into the Japanese colonial experience are provided, for example, in the memoirs of Urao Bunzō, a long-time Japanese resident in Korea. See Muramatsu Takeji, "Shokuminsha no kaisō" [Recollections of a Colonialist] in *Chōsen Kenkyū* (September 1957 to December 1968).

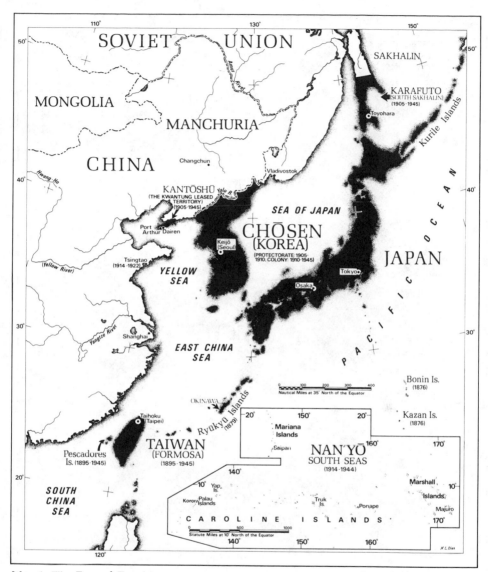

MAP 1: The Formal Empire

MAP 2: Taiwan

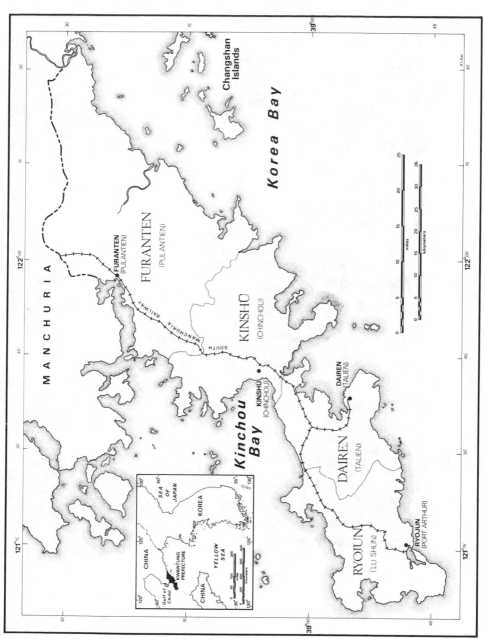

MAP 3: Kwantung Leared Territory and South Manchuria Railway

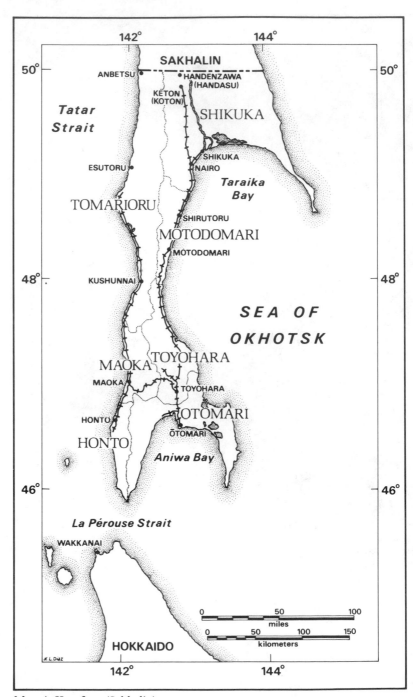

MAP 4: Karafuto (Sakhalin)

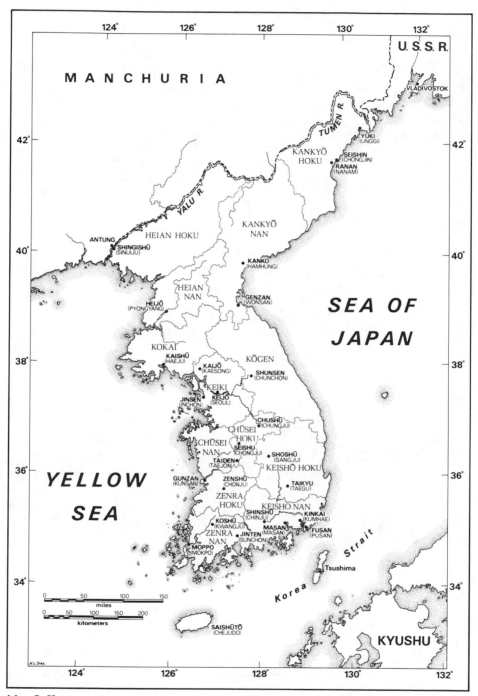

MAP 5: Korea

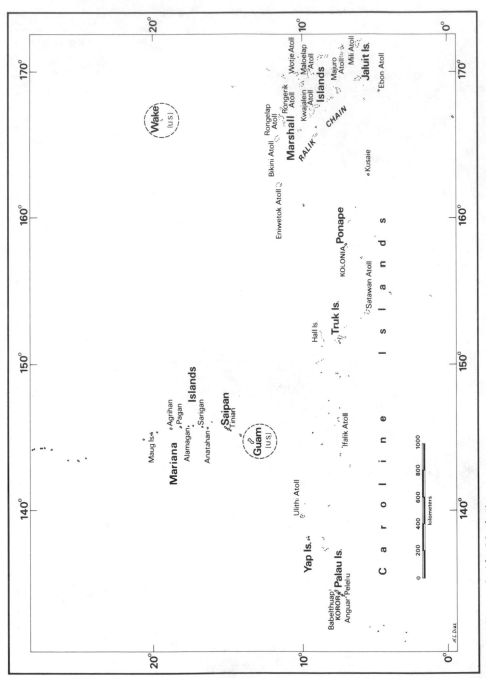

MAP 6: Micronesia (the Nan'yō)

PART I

The Origins and Meaning of Japan's Colonial Empire

CHAPTER 1

Japanese Imperialism: Late Meiji Perspectives

Marius B. Jansen

The four decades since Japan came to be a major concern for American scholarship have seen several shifts of focus. During the first decade or more, problems centered around the origins and course of twentieth-century expansion by the Japanese empire in northeast and southeast Asia. By the third decade of scholarship, Japan's postwar recovery had posed new problems that centered on the background of Japanese stability and economic growth, and as a result the discussion turned to the process and potential for modernization. This period brought a concentration on the nineteenth-century period of nation building. The most recent decade has seen a larger community of scholars pursuing a greater variety of topics, which range from long-neglected treatment of early and medieval Japan to the nature of contemporary Japanese society. On the whole, attention has shifted from Japan as aggressor and Japan as modernizer to a recognition of the complexities and ambiguities of the historical process. Patterns of dissension and protest, counter-productive aspects of Japanese modernization, and the maladies common to post-industrial societies, have all come to receive attention.

In this process the early stages of empire in Japan have not received the attention one might expect. There has been generous attention to the mid-twentieth century Japanese empire, whose expansionist drive is treated as pathological, and the Meiji process of statecraft, which has received more respectful attention, but the late Meiji process of empire building has yet to receive its due. The same is true of late-Meiji ideology and conservatism. Several studies are now underway of the conservatism and of state-imposed curbs on freedom of expression in literature and politics, but these essays are among the first to take up the themes of empire and imperialism.

Even a casual review of postwar Japanese discussions of the origins of Meiji imperialism shows that they are usually set in terms of condemnation and regret. Japan, writers point out, benefited throughout its history from a favorable international environment in which its neighbors were peaceful agriculturalists, only to repay good with evil when once modern tools of aggression were available.[1] In earlier years the threatening international setting of late-nineteenth-century imperialism was usually invoked to stress the defensive and reactive nature of Japanese imperial expansion, which was described as a movement to preempt European control of areas essential to Japanese stability and strength. In addition, the instability of northeast Asia, where a defenseless and inept Korea and China tempted Western aggressors, could be cited as explanation for the Japanese leaders' determination to expand. Implicit for the many writers who addressed themselves to these problems has been the assumption that the imperial developments of late Meiji Japan were somehow aberrant and require censure or defense.

It is the purpose of these pages to suggest that the problem posed in this fashion is wrongly stated, and that it leads to unrewarding apologetics or accusations. Almost all writers have proceeded on the assumption that Japan, as an Asian country, was morally bound to behave differently from Western powers that had fewer scruples or different racial sensibilities. On the contrary: it is equally valid to argue that in the climate of the times Meiji Japan had every reason to pursue an imperialist path, and that there were no real inhibitions against doing so in Japanese tradition or social thought.

1. NINETEENTH-CENTURY JAPAN'S SEARCH FOR WEALTH AND POWER

The leaders and would-be leaders of the Meiji state saw their problem as one of building strength in a competetive and possibly dangerous setting. Meiji period clichés about Western powers as "ravenous wolves" need no repetition or documentation. In the 1850's Japan found itself saddled with the same network of unequal treaties that European powers had devised for other non-European states. Treaty ports, fixed tariffs, most-favored-nation clause, and extraterritoriality constituted a set of rules worked out by the West for the non-West in a pattern that had been applied to Persia in 1836 and 1857, to Turkey in 1838 and 1861, to Siam in 1855, and, most importantly, to China in 1842 and 1858.[2] Japanese nationalists railed against these as an insulting infringement of national sovereignty, and the revision or abolition of those treaties, a process that was complete only at the

---

[1] For one example, Irokawa Daikichi, *Meiji no bunka* [Meiji Culture] (Tokyo, 1970), p. 4.

[2] Nakamura Satoru, "Kaikokugo no bōeki to sekai ichiba" [Trade after the opening of Japan and the World Market], *Iwanami kōza Nihon rekishi* 13 (*kinsei* 5, Tokyo 1977), pp. 95-96.

very end of the Meiji period in 1911, was the most pressing and explosive issue in domestic politics.

Direct resistance to the West was quickly seen to be futile and dangerous, as it could lead only to shattering defeat. The remaining option was to emulate Western techniques, and the unappetizing aspects of that were usually sugared over with the promise of future equality and even superiority. Similar notes are struck time after time in late Tokugawa days. Thus Etō Shimpei, a Saga samurai, wrote a long memorandum in 1856 to record his conversion from policies of exclusion to those of opening. He contrasted the feasibility of exclusion in the seventeenth century with the far greater power of the contemporary West. Japan, as an island country, faced particularly severe difficulties in preparing its coast defense. What was required, he concluded, was a long-range plan to utilize the talents, not merely of all Japanese, but of talent wherever it might be found throughout the world. Whatever excellence might be found in tools, in arms, in medicine, in land development, in astronomy, and so on, should be utilized for the development of national wealth and strength. Such policies, when brought to fruition, would promise a Japan able to defeat any enemy and strong enough to expand. In former days Westerners had compared Japan's position to that of England; yet today England was strong and wealthy, with numerous dependencies around the world, despite the fact that it was smaller, located in northern latitudes with an uninviting climate, and with agricultural products in no way comparable to those of Japan. England had become strong and wealthy through its ability to navigate the seas to Asia; let Japan similarly develop its navigation and trade, and it would "truly be the greatest country of the world." Emulation, in short, would produce even better results in Japan. The Western strength had prompted the need to compete.[3]

The great era of imperialist aggrandizement came almost a half century later, but the Japanese response could be anticipated in the prospects for future growth and importance that were sketched out by late Tokugawa *shishi* like Etō. By the 1880's European empires were closing the ring around possible Japanese expansion points in eastern Asia, and a memorandum of Foreign Minister Inoue Kaoru in 1887 showed his awareness of this. Inoue called to his colleagues' attention the fact that European powers were competing ruthlessly for the few areas of Asia and Africa that still remained. Asian countries with the exception of China were to a greater or lesser degree already taken by the West. Moreover, those colonies were adding

[3] Matono Hansuke, *Etō Nampaku*, Vol. 1 (1914), p. 126 foll.

daily to the power of their imperialist masters; with improved communications and administration and growing populations, they would become an ever larger element in the mother countries' power. No one could doubt that this would continue. "In my opinion," Inoue concluded, "what we must do is to transform our empire and our people, make the empire like the countries of Europe and our people like the peoples of Europe. To put it differently, we have to establish a new, European-style empire on the edge of Asia."[4]

National policies premised on the necessity of emulating the countries that were Japan's problem could not have been expected to overlook the expansive drive that was such a prominent feature of all modernizing states in the last decades of the nineteenth century. Even in the West, it must be remembered, voices critical of these new developments were relatively few, for the "moral" face of imperialism's expansive urge was the promise of bringing civilization and Christianity to backward races. Recent writers point out that few in England used "imperialism" or "imperial" with pejorative connotations in the mid-century decades; by the 1870's "imperial interests" became a popular slogan in Britain. By century's end Britain became self-consciously "imperialist" with a self-congratulatory awareness; there were comparisons with the greatness of Rome as well as professions of Britain's duty to take up the task of civilization.[5] So too in the United States, the vigorous debate that attended the United States decision to annex the Philippines in 1899 found as many churchmen as industrialists supporting that annexation, and the export of scripture was as prominent a goal as the import of sugar. Where, then, would Meiji men have found denunciations of the idea of adding territory to build upon the greatness of Japan? Even doubters had to grant that annexations rescued Asians from a faltering Manchu or, in Korea, *yangban* rule. Similarly, most Americans were prepared to grant that their institutions were superior to those of Spain in the Caribbean and South Pacific.

To be sure, the turn of the century produced some critical comments in Japan as in the West. In England J. Hobson (*Imperialism,*

[4] Quoted and discussed in Marius B. Jansen, "Modernization and Foreign Policy in Meiji Japan," in Robert E. Ward, ed., *Political Development in Modern Japan* (Princeton, N.J.: Princeton University Press, 1968), p. 175.

[5] Richard Koebner and Helmut Dan Schmidt, *Imperialism: The Story and Significance of a Political Word, 1840-1960* (New York: Cambridge University Press, 1964). "At the end of the nineteenth century the late Victorians and Edwardians could, and did, identify their society with that of Periclean Athens in its ideals and its constitutional arrangements, and with Augustan Rome in its sense of imperial mission," Lawrence Stone and Marius B. Jansen, "Education and Modernization in Japan and England," in *Comparative Studies in Society and History* IX, 2 (January 1967), p. 231.

1902) was moved by his aversion to the Boer War to blame the development on capitalism and especially on capitalists. He charged that great industrialists and banking houses instigated imperialist adventures in order to provide profitable, high interest-bearing investments for surplus capital. In 1916 Lenin would build on Hobson to make imperialist competition and war an inevitable working out of monopoly capital.[6] And in 1901, a year before Hobson, Kōtoku Shūsui wrote *Imperialism: The Specter of the Twentieth Century*, to focus on the amorality of imperialist expansion. Kōtoku described Japan's nascent imperialism as the product of militarism and jingoism, emotions based on the least admirable characteristics of selfish man. His standards were in good part Confucian. The goals of civilization, he argued, should be humanism, justice, and righteousness, but instead nationalism had liberated men from feudalism only to lead them into new forms of slavery. Japan's government was using imagined foreign glory to distract its citizens from domestic ills. Moreover, the dangers of this process were even greater in Japan than in European countries because the possibilities of repression were greater where democratic standards were still so poorly developed.[7]

Nevertheless, such criticism was unusual. A far more widely read author was the journalist Tokutomi Sohō, a product of the early Christian movement, best-selling author and founder of the first mass circulation journal *The Nation's Friend* (*Kokumin no tomo*) and publisher of *Kokumin Shinbun*. Tokutomi began as advocate of pacifism and parliamentarianism and hailed the work of Herbert Spencer. By the mid-1890's he recognized the currents of Darwinism abroad in international behavior, and abandoned his pacifism for the advocacy of imperialism. He explained that shift in a letter to a friend by pointing out that "it should be remembered that my conversion is closely related to the following facts: first, the change in Japan's international standing after the Sino-Japanese War, and, second, the trend throughout the world toward imperialism." By 1913, when he wrote *A Tract for the Times* (*Jimmu ikkagen*), he was prepared to list the heavy costs that Japan had incurred through its wars and expansion. From the Taiwan expedition of 1874 through the Russo-Japanese War the costs had been heavy. Nor had it been a succession of glorious victories; the West had denied Japan the advantages of the Treaty of Shimonoseki

[6] For a convenient summary of literature, Akira Iriye, "Imperialism in East Asia," in James B. Crowley, ed., *Modern East Asia: Essays in Interpretation* (New York: Harcourt Brace, 1970), p. 122 foll.

[7] *Teikoku shugi* Iwanami reprint, 1966. See also F. G. Notehelfer, *Kōtoku Shūsui: Portrait of a Japanese Radical* (New York: Cambridge University Press, 1971), p. 82 foll.

in the Triple Intervention, and Russian recovery after 1905 had been so rapid that one might well think that Russia, not Japan, had won the war. Japan's position had been achieved at staggering costs with frightful burdens for the taxpayers, and more lay ahead. Nevertheless, Tokutomi argued, that was simply the price and the condition of national greatness. What the country had to do was adopt "social democracy" at home and imperialism abroad. "There are two courses open for our country—self-reliance or dependency. The first course requires imperialism as our aim, whereas the second means that we will have to be prepared to accept the fate of annexation." And again, "Japanese imperialism is not based on momentary whims; it is neither a pleasurable pastime, nor something that is to be undertaken in a spirit of lightheartedness. It is a policy born out of necessity if we are to exist as a nation and survive as a race."[8]

We still lack adequate surveys of press and popular opinion during these years.[9] But it seems clear that during the last decade of the Meiji period, the years in which Japanese imperialism was being established, most articulate Japanese were prepared to accept the argument that Darwinian selection and competition in the international order made imperialist expansion the expected path for a vigorous and healthy polity that expected to compete. Small countries might not have the means, and undeveloped, non-modernized countries might not have the wit for this competition, but the struggle for equality that Japan had pursued since 1868 left no doubt that Japan belonged in that race. That being so, it requires no search for some special center of political, military, or economic conniving on which to fasten the blame. The expansion of Japan seemed in line with world historical currents. It was parallel with courses followed by autocratic and democratic countries alike. There was in fact not a case to be found of a major state that was not a participant in that competition. To expect deviation from a Japan that was explicitly modelling its international behavior on that of its peers is unreasonable.

Nevertheless, there does not seem to have been a single, persistent plan by policy makers. The 1895 decision to press for cession of Taiwan was, as Edward Chen describes, a product of jockeying and

[8] *Jimmu ikkagen* (Tokyo, 1913), p. 265 foll; and John D. Pierson, *Tokutomi Sohō 1863-1957: A Journalist for Modern Japan* (Princeton, N.J: Princeton University Press, 1980), pp. 264, 318.

[9] In addition to the titles suggested in Iriye, *loc. cit.*, and also by him in *Nihon no gaikō* [*The Diplomacy of Japan*] (Tokyo, 1966), mention should be made of a pioneering essay by Oka Yoshitake, "Kokuminteaki dokuritsu to kokka risei" [National Independence and the Logic of Nation] *Kindai Nihon shisōshi kōza*, VIII (Tokyo, 1961), pp. 9-38.

influence within the leadership that produced a decision by Itō Hirobumi for cession as less dangerous and less consequential than larger
plans nurtured by others.[10] The decision for annexation of Korea was
preceded by repeated assertions of lesser goals by Itō and his followers in the face of more sweeping requirements demanded by the military.[11] The trend was expansive and outward, but its timing and
articulation were the product of competing pressures at every point.

When one considers the principal advocates of imperial expansion,
army leaders probably have to be given first place. Yamagata Aritomo, the founder of the modern army, was particularly explicit in
memoranda he wrote for his colleagues in the late 1880's. These documents have been much quoted and discussed, and they do not require extensive exposition here.[12] Yamagata saw Japan's problem caused
by the rival imperialisms of Russia and England, each of which was
advancing toward Japan: the Russians by the Trans-Siberian route,
the English via the Trans-Canada Railroad. Japan would have to choose
between them, he thought, for the two were certain to come to blows.
Their interests would compete in Korea and in Afghanistan, and yet
neither country was in a state to defend its own interests. Yamagata
went on to distinguish between Japan's line of sovereignty, the home
islands, and its line of advantage or interest, which included Korea.
Its ally would have to be chosen with that line of interest in mind,
and that consideration predisposed him toward alignment with England against Russia in the defense of Japanese interests in Korea. Within
a few years the Sino-Japanese War made possible Japanese probings
for Liaotung in South Manchuria. By the time of the Russo-Japanese
War Yamagata was convinced that Manchuria itself was Japan's "life
line," the only possible area for expansion and an essential buffer
against Russian revenge.

While Japan's military masters interpreted security in ever more

[10] Edward I-Te Chen, "Japan's Decision to Annex Taiwan: A Study of Itō-Mutsu
Diplomacy, 1894-95," *Journal of Asian Studies*, XXXVII, 1 (November 1977), pp. 61-
72. See also, on Mutsu, Marius B. Jansen, "Mutsu Munemitsu," in Albert M. Craig
and Donald H. Shively, eds., *Personality in Japanese History* (Berkeley, CA: University
of California Press, 1970), pp. 328-329, and most recently Mutsu's memoirs, *Kenken-
roku*, tr. Gordon Berger (Princeton, N.J.: Princeton University Press, 1982).

[11] The basic works in English are Hilary Conroy, *The Japanese Seizure of Korea 1868-
1910: A Study of Realism and Idealism in International Relations* (Philadelphia: University
of Pennsylvania Press, 1960) and Shumpei Okamoto, *The Japanese Oligarchy and the
Russo-Japanese War* (New York: Columbia University Press, 1970). I have also profited
from an unpublished essay by Professor Okamoto entitled "Komura and Japan's Advance into South Manchuria" (1972).

[12] See above, Jansen, "Modernization and Foreign Policy," and Roger F. Hackett,
Yamagata Aritomo in the Rise of Modern Japan, 1838-1922 (Cambridge, Mass., Harvard
University Press, 1971), p. 156.

generous territorial terms, however, it should be remembered that this was by no means the only possible interpretation to be drawn from Japan's military victory over China. Kitaoka Shin'ichi points out that while the army's victory in that war had been foreseen, the navy's sweeping victories over the larger ships of the Peiyang Fleet exceeded expectations and brought on a radical reassessment of security needs by navy leaders. Admiral Yamamoto Gon'nohyoei tried to revise the government's "army first" mentality and policy with a "navy first" substitute, culminating in a proposed policy statement of 1899 to the effect that the strategic significance of Japan as an island country, dependent on foreign trade, was that the Japanese navy had to be given the capability of attacking enemy forces at a great distance from the home islands in order to protect Japanese shipping. Defining Japan as an "island empire," Yamamoto put forth the striking proposition that even Korea was not essential to the security of Japan; defense of the home islands would suffice.[13] Army leaders, although they rejected this formulation, conciliated Yamamoto by granting the navy more status and responsibility in the command structure. Even so the Russo-Japanese War found the army dissatisfied with the navy's cooperation in operations against North Korea and Sakhalin. Ironically, the outcome of the war found the navy disadvantaged because its overwhelming victory had deprived it of a putative enemy in Northeast Asia while the army had reason to be worried about a Russian attempt for revenge. This meant a commitment to land strength and strategy which was reflected in defense plans drawn up by Tanaka Gi'ichi for Yamagata in 1906 and adopted by the high command early in 1907. Under these the maintenance and expansion of Japanese rights on the continent that had been established by the sacrifice of "tens of thousands in lives and treasure" were declared the highest priority of national policy.[14]

Hitherto Japan had felt itself a disadvantaged latecomer to modernization; it now began to style itself a disadvantaged latecomer to empire. While deploring unequal treatment and injustice to Japanese nationals, Japanese leaders utilized such complaints to secure other basic interests. The skill with which the late Meiji leadership carried this out received the fullest admiration of Karl Haushofer, the voice of inter-war geopolitics in Germany. Haushofer wrote that when "weighing . . . the forces behind Japan's expansion drive, we must admit that they did not develop out of the need of the moment but out of concern for the distant future. They grew out of a space far-

[13] Kitaoka Shin'ichi, *Nihon rikugun to tairiku seisaku* [The Japanese Army and Continental Policy] (Tokyo, 1978), p. 11.

[14] *Ibid.*, p. 12.

sightedness rare in political life. . . . This noble race, sheltered in its growth by an unusually favorable geographical situation and spoiled by the quality of its soil and the mildness of its climate, is much more exacting than the average nation."[15]

An important figure in this development, who received Haushofer's highest praise, was the Harvard-trained diplomat Komura Jutarō. Komura served in Washington during the early stages of American-Japanese difficulties over immigration, and concluded that America's Japanese immigrants, who were drawn from farming and laboring classes, were detrimental to the Japanese image in the United States. Service in Peking convinced him of the weakness of the Ch'ing polity; by 1901, when he became Foreign Minister in the Katsura cabinet, he became the principal figure in the move toward war and the definition of war aims. It fell to him to negotiate these at Portsmouth in 1905. Komura returned to Japan determined to squash moves toward international control of or access to Manchuria, and he served as the statesman of Japanese empire in negotiations with China over the transfer of Russian rights in South Manchuria.

Komura's skill is particularly apparent in his handling of questions relating to Japanese immigration to the United States. The middle decades of the Meiji period saw numerous commercial companies formed to expedite the emigration of Japanese farmers to Hawaii, the United States, and even Southeast Asia. In his Washington days Komura had concluded that immigrants were a source of unprofitable diplomatic difficulty. (Though, one suspects, he saw them of some value for capitalizing on the "underprivileged latecomer" theme in negotiations like the Taft-Katsura agreement.) In his foreign policy speech as Foreign Minister of the second Katsura cabinet in February of 1909, Komura reassured the Diet that immigration difficulties were limited to the area of California, and that Japan was in contact with the central government of the United States. "But in any case," he went on, "what has to be noted is that as a result of the Russo-Japanese War the status of the empire has changed and the area under its administration has grown larger; we should avoid scattering our people in the foreign countries where they are lost. It has become necessary that as far as possible we should direct our people to one area and avail ourselves of their collective strength."[16] Thus the solution of a growing expansionist need in Korea and Manchuria contained the answer to a growing diplomatic problem with the United

[15] Haushofer quotations are conveniently brought together in Andreas Dorpalen, *The World of General Haushofer* (New York: Farrar and Rinehart, 1942), p. 34 foll.

[16] Text of speech from *Dai Nihon teikoku gikai shi*, Vol. 7 [History of the Imperial Diet of Great Japan] (Tokyo, 1928), pp. 578-579, proceedings of February 6, 1909.

States. During the same years, of course, discussions of Japan's crowded islands and disadvantaged position began to strike home to domestic and to foreign opinion, easing the response to quiet steps of territorial expansion.

2. POSSIBLE SOURCES OF DISSENSION

I have asserted that Japan's slide into imperialism was a logical response to Japanese perceptions of world trends. In many ways the perceptions were accurate. If the problem is phrased in this way, it then becomes more appropriate to ask who might have opposed, than to ask who might have advocated, the path of imperialist expansion in late Meiji Japan.

The Meiji decades provide little promise for study along these lines. The narrow samurai elite of the first Meiji decade certainly holds no hope for such a search. Not that one should make much of the exuberant proposals for expansion in late Tokugawa days, for little connection can be drawn between the proposals for advance and the implementation of such plans four decades or more later. Tokugawa expansionists were reacting against a long period of seclusion and torpor, and there was little likelihood that they would be called upon to implement their suggestions. To a considerable degree they were only legitimating their proposals for opening the country to trade and proving that their patriotism should not be questioned. At another level, an underdeveloped sense of nationality may have combined with an overdeveloped particularism of domain to make Korea or Peking seem only slightly less distant and "foreign" than Edo to those who advocated expansion. Such sentiments are, I suspect, best dismissed as overblown rhetoric.

These considerations extend to the rhetoric of the first decade of the Meiji period. Samurai advocates of punishment of Korea or of Taiwanese aborigines were expressing long-pent-up aspirations to greatness and action, and the urgency of their advocacy was the greater because hopes that had been raised in late Tokugawa rhetoric were not being realized. In terms of regional concentration, expansionist or Korean enthusiasm was greatest in the southwestern domains that had led in Restoration politics. The areas whose samurai had had the highest hopes and which had contributed most to the Tokugawa fall were in the van of calls for war with Korea. There was also an element of class urgency; some advocates of the Korean expedition envisaged it as a palliative for disappointed hopes held by theretofore "loyal" samurai.

The 1880's were years of the movement for democratic rights, but on the whole there was little more opposition to expansionist policies to be found among the leaders of the *jiyū minken* persuasion than there had been among the samurai malcontents of the previous decade. There was of course a substantial overlap between the two groups. The social base of the new movement was broader, its numbers larger, and its sophistication far greater, than had been true of the simple calls for punishment of Korean insults in 1873. A few liberal leaders—Nakae Chōmin and Ueki Emori—were quite free of chauvinist rhetoric, and one need not doubt that a foreign policy they controlled would have been quite different.[17] But from the first the liberal leaders found that calls for a strong foreign policy were among their best weapons against the government they challenged. Treaty reform proposals punctuated the political rhetoric of the 1880's. Some liberals proposed to stage independent efforts for reform in Korea, optimistic that success there would help to bring about political reforms in Japan. The educator-publisher Fukuzawa Yukichi made his own contribution to private attempts at influencing reform in Korea through his students, but upon the failure of those attempts with the incidents of 1882 and 1884 he withdrew from the effort with his much-quoted editorial on "Parting with Asia." Japan seemed powerless to speed and affect reform in an Asia that was unable or unwilling to respond, he concluded, and further association with its neighbors of Asia would only impede Japan's own reputation and efforts to secure equality with the West. The only policy for the time being was to treat Asia the same way that the West did.[18]

"Liberal" and political party calls for a strong and "positive" foreign policy in Asia echoed through the early Diets after the implementation of the Meiji Constitution in 1890. Early cabinets found themselves hard-pressed by parliamentarians who deplored insults from the West, resisted the idea of unrestricted foreign residence that was a condition of treaty reform, and called for action against the dominance that China seemed to be asserting in Korea in the early 1890's. The Sino-Japanese War was so popular with the Diet, which convened in Hiroshima to be closer to the headquarters of the war effort, that some historians have speculated on the possibility that the war

[17] Note particularly Nakae's sentiments in *Sansuijin keirin mondō*, translated by Margaret Dardess as *A Discourse on Government* (Western Washington State College, Program in East Asian Studies, Occasional Paper No. 10, 1977).

[18] Discussed in Kimitada Miwa, "Fukuzawa Yukichi's 'Departure from Asia': A Prelude to the Sino-Japanese War," in Edmund Skzypczak, ed., *Japan's Modern Century* (Tokyo, 1968), pp. 1-26.

decision represented a deliberate tactical maneuver by the government of Prime Minister Itō and Foreign Minister Mutsu to solve their problems with a refractory legislature. Certainly for some years to follow, the military's need of gearing up for the struggle with Russia was usually sufficient to send budgets speeding through to enactment. The only sense in which the 1895 cession of Liaotung to Japan by China was controversial was in its revocation after warnings delivered by Germany, France, and Russia in the "Triple Intervention." Fresh evidence that Japan was not yet the equal of the Western powers was sufficient to justify a new round of sacrifices for military expansion at cost to domestic benefits. Clearly, expansion and the costs involved in calls to greatness were popular; they would have been more difficult for a government to brake than they were to accelerate.

Religious groups in Meiji Japan also held out little hope of anti-imperialist leadership. Certainly not Shintō. Newly appropriated by the state through the cult of the divine ruler, State Shintō made it possible to describe the extension of Japan's perfect governance to its neighbors as an act of generosity. The civil role of State Shintō also helped to make Japanese imperial control unusually suffocating and overbearing for the populations that came under Japanese sway. Buddhism in the Meiji period was long in recovering from the shock of the anti-Buddhist Shintō prejudice of the early years, and it tended to emphasize its nationality and patriotism in contrast to Christianity, which it saw as its principal problem. On at least some occasions it was in the service of the Meiji state in working for the extension of Japanese influence in China.[19] In the 1890's Meiji Christianity came under attack as unpatriotic and pro-foreign. Uchimura Kanzō's refusal to bow to the Imperial Rescript on Education in 1891, his displeasure with the seizure of Chinese territory in 1895, and his pacifist stand at the time of the Russo-Japanese War combined to make his the leading voice in opposition to imperialist expansion. But Uchimura's was also an isolated voice, for the Christian leaders tended to take a very cautious position on political concerns. Consequently, opposition to Japanese expansion was limited to isolated voices in the Meiji religious establishments. Moreover, with the establishment of

[19] Iriye Akira, "Chūgoku ni okeru Nihon Bukyō fukyō mondai" [The Problem of Japanese Propagation of Buddhism in China] in *Nihon gaikō no shomondai* [Problems of Japanese Diplomacy], ed. Kokusai gakkai (Tokyo, 1965), pp. 86-100, describes late Meiji issues of protection for Buddhist missionaries in which a largely indifferent government wanted only equal treatment. In Boxer times, however, Honganji missionaries precipitated Japanese occupation of Amoy.

Japanese suzerainty in Taiwan and, to a lesser extent, in Korea, Meiji religious groups could see opportunities for themselves in a ministry of modernization, the lure that drew many of their American counterparts to endorse opportunities for mission in the Philippines. To some extent Korea was an exception to this, for Christianity had a firm start under American auspices there; in consequence it assumed a nationalistic cast in defiance of Japanese efforts, and Shintō efforts there were particularly distasteful to a resentful populace.

With the establishment of the Imperial Diet under the Meiji Constitution one might have expected critical discussion of imperialist trends from exponents of middle-class democracy, but such was not the case. With the release of the contents of the Treaty of Shimonoseki in 1895 its provisions for the cession of Chinese territory drew criticism from the crusty Tosa general Tani Kanjō in the House of Peers, but not in the lower house. On the contrary: the contemporary trend toward imperialism in Western democracies brought supporting sentiments from some of the outstanding spokesmen of late Meiji / early Taishō bourgeois democracy.

One influential voice was that of Ukita Kazutami (1859-1945). In a series of articles he wrote for *Kokumin Shimbun* in 1902, in his *Imperialism and Education* [*Teikokushugi to kyōiku*, 1901] and in *Logical Imperialism* [*Ronriteki teikokushugi*, 1909], Ukita described imperialism as a tide of the times. It had already been adopted by Russia, England, Germany, and the United States, and it seemed likely to become the leitmotif of the twentieth century. Imperialism, he went on, should be seen as a superior way to build national strength. It was in fact an inevitable working out of Darwinian principles of natural selection and progress. Ukita was anything but a "militarist" or ideologue of state power. He had begun (like Tokutomi) as one of the charter members of Captain Janes's "Kumamoto Band" of student Christians in 1876; he went on to study at Dōshisha and Yale, taught at Dōshisha and Waseda before becoming editor of the influential *Taiyō* in 1909, and he maintained his standing as a leading Christian and scholarly analyst and advocate of constitutional government throughout his career. Ukita held that choice was possible within imperialism, as it was within modernization; Japan should avoid the militarist imperialism of Germany, which would one day be doomed, and see its task as one of civilizing abroad and becoming more cosmopolitan at home. He grouped the imperialist urge with constitutionalism, and saw the latter as an essential device for increasing popular participation in government, and the former as a related means for increasing cosmopolitanism and participation abroad. His goal was an imperialism of industry and of goods, though he recognized that instances of resistance by less developed races might require the application of force for Japan to play its role in regional development.[20] It goes without saying that an emphasis *Taiyō* writers utilized for the advocacy of constitutional government could also be slanted for the advocacy of a strong foreign policy. "Constitutional Government at Home, Imperialism Abroad!" was also used for the opening pronouncement of the Kokumin Kurabu in 1905 in protest against the Portsmouth Treaty of Peace.[21]

One group from which opposition might have been expected was the considerable number of "Asia firsters" in Meiji society. These ranged in social status and importance from private activists like the Miyazaki brothers to Prince Konoe Atsumaro, who was at the very top of the Meiji establishment.[22] Men of this persuasion devoted their lives and energies to redressing their government's determined "Europe first" policies of Westernization and Western orientation. They argued that Japan's future lay in Asia, and that it was tied to its Asian neighbors by traditions of culture, language, and race and could expect no final home in a West that was increasingly obsessed with racial distinction and fear of a "yellow peril." In particular, Japan and China had both been the objects of Western imperialism in the treaty port phase, and should stand together in efforts to withstand the Western threat.

The Miyazaki brothers (Tamizō, Yazō, and especially Tōten [Torazō] came through the liberal movement with its idealism of human betterment, democracy, and social reform. Born to a gōshi landlord family in Kyushu's Kumamoto Prefecture, they had intimate knowledge of the hardships of tenant life under the Meiji provisions for a regular monetized tax. They associated the human problem of hunger with the Asian problem of reform and of independence, and held

---

[20] Eizawa Kōji, "Teikokushugi seiritsuki ni okeru Ukita Kazutami no shisōteki tokushitsu" [The Special Characteristics of Ukita Kazutami's Thought at the Time Japan's Imperialism Was Established], *Rekishigaku kenkyū* 332 (January, 1968), pp. 33-46.

[21] Sakeda Masatoshi, *Kindai Nihon ni okeru taigai kō undō no kenkyū* [Studies on Movements for an Aggressive Foreign Policy in Modern Japan] (Tokyo, 1978), pp. 3, 304.

[22] Marius B. Jansen, "Konoe Atsumaro," in Akira Iriye, ed., *The Chinese and the Japanese: Essays in Political and Cultural Interactions* (Princeton, N.J.: Princeton University Press, 1980), pp. 107-123; *The Japanese and Sun Yat-sen* (Cambridge, Mass.: Harvard University Press, 1954), and tr. with Etō Shinkichi, *My Thirty-Three Years' Dream: The Autobiography of Miyazaki Tōten* (Princeton, N.J.: Princeton University Press, 1982).

that the problem of China was central to a solution of the problem of Asia and, indeed, of all mankind. In the end the two younger brothers resolved to seek for a "hero" who might be able to overthrow the old order and solve its social and political problems. By this means revolution in China would speed reform in Japan as well. The autobiography of Miyazaki Tōten (Torazō, 1871-1922) is full of convincing demonstrations of intensity and sincerity. Resolved to infiltrate Chinese society and work closely with his "hero," he tried to approach China through Korea, through Siam, where he led a group of immigrant farmers, through the Philippines, where Aguinaldo was resisting the new American overlords, and finally through service with Sun Yat-sen, whose cause he served throughout the rest of his life.

Miyazaki and some of his fellows were critical and distrustful of Japanese imperialism, but they did not provide a successful critique of that development. Because of their intensity and indigence they were occasionally welcomed by their social and political betters, helped in their plans, and utilized for their contacts. Without such assistance in their own society they were quite powerless, unless they were working under the subsidy of their refugee guests from China. They constituted a welcome change from the self-serving and often disingenuous rhetoric of their countrymen, but they never became a significant counterforce to the stronger imperialist trends around them. Even they, moreover, tended to make a distinction between their own country's errors of policy and those of Western imperialists.

To sum up: nowhere in Meiji society, except among the miniscule number of genuine social revolutionaries and critics like Kōtoku and Uchimura on the fringe of the social democratic and Christian movements, was there to be found a genuine, thoroughgoing critique of the imperialist course that Meiji Japan was following. After World War I and the advent of Taishō democracy, on the other hand, the international *jisei* changed, and with it Japanese liberal consciousness as well. Thus there are significant differences between the attitudes on imperialism adopted by Yoshino Sakuzō, teacher and commentator, and his predecessor Ukita Kazutami. It required a change in the international setting to produce that change in Japan. In Meiji Japan, however, imperialism developed virtually without challenge.

3. SOME OBSERVATIONS

I have suggested that Japanese imperialism was readily explicable as the response to international examples by a generation that was modelling its behavior and polity on those of the world's leading countries and that the sources for opposition to such a response in domestic opinion or tradition were few. In many respects Japan's drive for colonial control was an entirely reasonable approach to security in an era when much of the world and most of Asia seemed divided up between the powers. Japanese access to essential resources and markets was uncertain, and a desire for security in access to food supply and raw materials that would permit competition in world markets under any conditions was to be anticipated. With the disappearance of Western imperialism in postwar Asia, on the other hand, the problems to which Japanese imperialism seemed a partial solution disappeared, and so also Japanese desires for regional autarchy. Much of this can be described as entirely logical, but there were also ways in which Japanese imperialism was rather special.

One is that with the exception of a few highly placed, though not very articulate, government leaders like Komura Jutarō and Gotō Shimpei, Japanese expansionism does not seem to have been so much a deliberate, thought-out plan, as a response to opportunities in the international setting and environment. Japan reacted to dangers and opportunities more than it tried to create such opportunities. As a result it can probably be said that imperialism never became a very important part of the national consciousness. There were no Japanese Kiplings, there was little popular mystique about Japanese overlordship and relatively little national self-congratulation. The Colonial Ministry never became an important part of the national bureaucracy; it was seldom the base for major figures, and as the period of military expansion neared in the 1930's Korea, the most important dependency, was withdrawn from the Colonial Ministry administration altogether. The passing of empire in Japan evoked little trauma and few regrets. It has in fact scarcely been discussed at all. In this a comparison would be drawn with the United States, whose imperialist era was, like that of Japan, a half century in length, and the contrast would be with England. Like the Americans, and unlike the English, Japanese have not looked back.

Japan's imperial control was unique in that Japan was itself an Asian country that began with the same disadvantages its neighbors did. It managed to join the circle of foreign oppressors, first in Korea and then in China, and finally entered the imperialist camp as a full partner. Despite this, throughout this process Japanese writers and leaders continued to talk about Japan's fraternal relationships with its neighbors. The result was a pattern of contradictions that are at the core of the strong tone of moral indignation with which the process of imperialism is discussed in postwar Japan. Slogans like *Dōbun-dōshu* (common culture, common race), that were aimed particularly at China did little to prepare the Chinese for the substance of Japanese policy. Strong statements about historical ties with Korea jarred with the *Mainichi*'s smug editorial statement on the occasion of the annexation of Korea that "The world can enjoy peace only when all countries reach the same level of civilization. It cannot permit such a thing as countries with low civilization."[23] The particularity of Shintō nationalism gave the lie to assertions of brotherhood with Korea, where Japan came to combine a bland insistence on full assimilation with the virtual extinction of Korean nationality. The Korean ruling house was absorbed into that of Japan, and the Japanese sovereign graciously extended fatherly sway to a people declared to be Japanese. In 1942 Korea was formally declared an integral part of Japan, and its administration was transferred from the Colonial to the Home Ministry. Instruction in the Korean language had already been abolished in lower schools, and the study of Korean history forbidden. State Shintō was forced on Koreans, who were furthermore required to adopt Japanese readings for their surnames. Yet the administrative force remained overwhelmingly Japanese; at higher levels, over 80 percent. This prepares one for the fact that An Chung-gun, who assassinated Japanese Resident General Itō Hirobumi in 1909, immediately became a post-independent national hero memorialized by a statue in front of Itō's former residence. There are probably few cases in which a country's national hero is such by reason of his assassination of a neighboring country's national hero. The contradictions inherent in an Asian imperialism that was avowedly designed to protect Japan's Asian neighbors from Western imperialism persisted throughout the years of the Pacific War and were reflected in ratiocinations of some Japanese intellectuals, who sought meaning for that war as ending a Western era in Asian history. Their formulations have more credibility in 1982 than they did in 1941, though that credibility is based upon the end of Japanese as well as of Western imperialism.

Another difference relates to the imagery that was common between "mother country" and colony. In many cases it was colonial control that gave the colony a clear-cut sense of national identity; the more modernized, developed "mother country" was granted, reluctantly or not, higher status as somehow more advanced. In Korea, however, the Japanese occupied a land whose sense of self, national

---

[23] Quoted in Conroy, *op.cit.*, p. 391.

identity, borders, and history were fully as established as their own. It required no unification brought about by colonial administration to make that area a nation, and it would under the best of conditions have required an unusually long time for Japanese administration to produce a significant class that oriented itself toward Japan and Japanese culture.

Our thinking about imperial country and "colony" is typically a compound of distance and numbers. Distance normally prevented great numbers of carpetbaggers from going to the dependency, and in the great majority of cases there was relatively little to encourage Europeans—except the managerial classes—to do so. The dependency was densely populated and often difficult climatically as well, and European workers and shopkeepers had little chance to live better lives there than those they knew. But the Japanese dependencies were nearby; Japanese of all classes could go, and in considerable numbers. They could compete at many levels; colonial officials encouraged agricultural settlement as well as administrative guidance, and as a result Japan established an unusual intensity of occupation. Korea, again, is the best example, from land-holding patterns to commerce to administration. By the 1930's there was one policeman for 1,150 Koreans; if the gendarmerie is included, the count rises to one policeman per 400 Koreans. This, too, has left its mark on Korean-Japanese relations.

A further point, too complex to argue here in detail, is that Japan's imperial expansion began before its industrial growth. Japanese expansion cannot by any means be explained as a result of that growth in terms of the "monopoly capital" that it produced, as the Leninist formulation would have it. Of course it cannot be denied that industrial growth accompanied the imperial expansion and profited from it, and it follows that Japanese planners saw the colonies as important to their economic stability. In successive stages they represented additional sources of food in rice and sugar, markets for inexpensive manufacturers, and, toward the end, off-shore locations for light and medium manufacturing activities. A world of open commerce in which these advantages are attainable without political competition or control, however, has produced a radically different Japanese approach toward imperialism.

In sum, although Japan's territorial expansion was temporarily stabilizing and profitable for Japan, the problems to which it led soon contributed to a destructive tug-of-war within the Japanese establishment to produce policies that closed foreign doors to Japan, in turn encouraging ever more aggressive policies. The Japanese empire became destabilizing for Northeast Asia, and a destabilizing force within Japanese politics. The even tenor of policy and growth in postwar Japan owes much to the absence of the kind of sources for divisive arguments and interests that were spawned by the creation of the twentieth-century empire. A final irony is that the term "emperor," renounced by the Imperial government as an inappropriate translation for its sovereign in the 1930's, is now in standard use by the government of Japan decades after its empire has come to an end in name and in fact.

CHAPTER 2

Japanese Attitudes Toward Colonialism, 1895-1945

Mark R. Peattie[1]

Without an empire until the twentieth century, it was hardly possible for Japan to have had a clearly articulated set of attitudes concerning the purpose and function of colonial rule up to that time. Two and a half centuries of stern isolation under the Tokugawa shogunate had done little to prepare the nation intellectually for the challenges of expansion in general, or for the management of alien peoples in particular. What did exist prior to 1895 was acquaintance with colonization, as distinct from colonialism, though even here Japanese experience was shallow. Indeed, while the long history of colonization in Europe since ancient times had provided Europeans with a rich vocabulary dealing with this activity, adequate terminology to encompass the concept of a "colony" hardly existed in Japanese until the mid-nineteenth century.[2] Then, in the 1870's the implications of colonization rapidly impinged on the Japanese consciousness. There was, to begin with, the Japanese effort in the development, exploration, and colonization of Hokkaido, 1873-1883, which provided

[1] I wish to thank the Institute for Arts and Humanistic Studies at The Pennsylvania State University, as well as the Joint Committee on Japanese Studies of the American Council of Learned Societies and the Social Science Research Council, for financial support of the research for this paper.

[2] Nitobe Inazō, in his comprehensive study of colonialism, noted that pre-nineteenth-century Japanese concepts of colonizing activities were limited to Chinese terms which were inadequate to deal with the multiple implications behind the English word "colony," since the Chinese language lacked a single term to encompass at once the ideas of opening new land and the emigration and transplantation of peoples to new territories. In the 1860's Doeff's Dutch-Japanese dictionary used the Dutch word *volk-plannting* for colony without explaining it. The term *shokumin*, a wholly Japanese construction, meaning "colonization" or "settlement" and later broadened to include the sense of colonial rule, was first used in an English-Japanese dictionary in 1862, but did not come into vogue until the 1870's. Nitobe Inazō, *Zenshū* [Collected Works], IV (Iwanami Shoten, 1943), pp. 49-50. In contrast, overseas settlement activity in the classical, medieval, and modern West provided a wealth of terminology to be defined, classified, and sorted out by Western writers on the subject. See, for example, Albert Keller, *Colonization: A Study of the Founding of New Societies* (Boston, 1908).

practical experience in the creation of a settlement colony, not unlike the British colonization of Australia and New Zealand, wherein a government settles its own lands with its own peoples. But such colonizing—as opposed to colonial—activities never became the dominant activity in the larger empire, though colonization as an ideal continued to inspire propagandists for Japanese expansion in the decades to come.

Intellectually, too, Japanese began to explore the meaning and value of colonies, though the Japanese frame of reference was almost entirely within the context of Western economic theory, rather than related to colonial administration as such. Along with Fukuzawa Yukichi, Meiji writers like Kanda Kōhei, Amano Tamesuke, and Taguchi Ukichi, reacting against the state orthodoxy of the Tokugawa, were diligent in translating and propagating works of liberal economic thinkers in the West, especially those colonial theorists in Britain like Adam Smith who stressed the ideas of free competition.[3] Thus, it is an odd fact that the first intellectual speculations in Japan on colonial matters were inspired by Western theories which were in essence anti-colonial, or at least deprecated earlier mercantilist beliefs in the economic value of formal colonies. Admittedly, certain Japanese writers of the time were initially more influenced by the protectionist ideas of Georg Friedrich List and were thus concerned with problems of formal colonial rule, but again more in terms of political economy than of governmental administration.[4]

On the eve of Japan's entry into the colonial lists, more aggressive urges for the acquisition of territories beyond the Japanese islands had been expressed in vague terms by different groups. Those responsible for the nation's military policies, concerned with the Korean "dagger" pointed at Japan, sought to sheath it with some sort of Japanese presence on the peninsula; for a number of expansionist writers the South Pacific was a magnet for their hazy dreams of Japanese living space or Japanese claims to lands as yet unspoken for; and to Tokutomi Sohō, taking pride in the political vigor of his countrymen, it was possible to speak of a Japanese imperial mission "to extend the blessings of political organization throughout the rest of East Asia

[3] Kuroda Ken'ichi, *Nihon shokumin shisōshi* [Japanese Colonial Thought] (Kōbundo, 1942), pp. 184-193 and 211-224. Taguchi, in particular, wrote extensively on colonial theory from the perspective of political economy and criticized the administration of Hokkaido as too oppressive and restrictive of economic activities in the island.

[4] The nationalistic and protectionist ideas of Wakayama Giichi and Sata Kaiseki, for example, stood in direct opposition to the laissez-faire beliefs of liberal colonial theory. Wakayama advocated the application of a rigorous program of protectionism in Hokkaido as part of an effort to give employment to the economically deprived samurai class. *Ibid.*, pp. 187, 224, and 227.

and the South Pacific, just as the Romans had once done for Europe and the Mediterranean.''[5] For the leadership of Meiji Japan, however, territorial expansion, once decided upon, involved pragmatic and particularistic concerns. Taiwan was acquired in 1895 for reasons that in fact had more to do with opportunism, diplomatic pressures, and matters of international prestige than those ex-post-facto justifications for its occupation which were couched in the language of the new imperialism.[6]

If there was little consistency in these aspirations and nothing as yet resembling a doctrine of Japanese imperial expansion, this was partly due to the jumble of ideas in the West concerning the nature and value of colonies. The great nineteenth-century treatises on imperial purpose, such as Henry Leroy-Beaulieu's *De la colonisation chez les peuples modernes* (1874) and J. R. Seeley's *The Expansion of England* (1883), representing concerns with the older mercantilist imperialism and the expansion of peoples in overseas colonization, had been written on the very eve of the new imperialism which now proclaimed the virtues of Social Darwinism, protectionism, and the advantages of industrial capitalism. As for colonial rule itself, with the major exceptions of India, Algeria, and the East Indies, the administration of alien races was so recent an imperial task that colonialism was a concept whose implications had only just begun to be explored. It is small wonder, then, that the first Japanese speculations on colonial mission proceeded from no common theoretical point of departure and that Japanese writers on the subject tended initially to use terms like expansion, imperialism, emigration, and colonization, without fine distinction.[7]

THE EUROPEAN IMPRESS 1895-1920

By 1895, however, one thing was certain: Japan had acquired a colonial territory and had thus joined the ranks of the colonial—the civilized—powers; the new territory, once the government decided to keep it, became a source of common pride, a symbol of the nation's equality with the West and of its participation in the great work of modern civilization. "Western nations," the politician and journalist

[5] Kenneth Pyle, *The New Generation of Meiji Japan: Problems of Cultural Identity 1885-1895* (Stanford, 1969), p. 181.

[6] Edward I-te Chen, "Japan's Decision to Annex Taiwan: A Study of Mutō-Itō Diplomacy," in *Journal of Asian Studies* XXXVII: 1 (Nov. 1977), 62.

[7] For the diversity of viewpoint of Japanese expansionist thinking prior to 1895 see Akira Iriye, *Pacific Estrangement: Japanese and American Expansion, 1897-1911* (Cambridge, Mass.), 1972.

Takekoshi Yosaburō declared, "have long believed that on their shoulders alone rested the responsibility of colonizing the yet-unopened portions of the globe and extending to the inhabitants the benefits of civilization; but now we Japanese, rising from the ocean in the extreme Orient, which as a nation to take part in this great and glorious work."[8] Yet, without a colonial tradition, literature, or policy, or a corps of trained administrators, it was difficult to translate self-satisfied pronouncements into effective colonial policy, as the first chaotic and haphazard attempts to govern Taiwan quite dismally revealed. Lacking civil administrative experience, high-level policy to guide them, or personal vision to inspire them, and forced to concentrate on the military pacification of a stubbornly resistant population, the first few governors general were ill-equipped to develop the arts of colonial government.[9]

Yet, waiting in the wings, stood the first of a steady stream of competently trained civil bureaucrats, able to guide their superiors, the military governors general, in the complexities of modern management. With the arrival of Kodama Gentarō and his civil administrator Gotō Shimpei, the Japanese presence in Taiwan at last found a policy and a purpose. Superbly trained in the medical profession in Germany, widely read in the contemporary literature of colonialism, Gotō combined outstanding organizational talent with a quick and searching mind. Working under an influential and trusting superior and reinforced by important political connections at home, moreover, he had the benefit of operating in an underdeveloped territory with a broad latitude of authority. In the future there would be honest and competent, but somewhat unimaginative, colonial administrators, like Den Kenjirō, acting within narrower limits of authority, and a few scholars like Yanaihara Tadao, who were profoundly informed on colonial affairs, but out of touch and out of favor with colonial authority. But never again would knowledge, ability, and

[8] Takekoshi Yosaburō, *Japanese Rule in Formosa* (London, 1907), p. vii.

[9] The outlook of the war hero Nogi Maresuke, third of the military governors-general, was typical of their rather simplistic approach toward colonial rule. A moralist but not an administrator, he was convinced that the key to successful colonial administration was to "mix severity with generosity, to deal justice and mercy at the proper time, and to make [colonial peoples] obedient to moral authority." Such an outlook hardly aided him in the formation of concrete policy to bring about the colony's stability and progress. While believing, for example, in the prime importance of education as a civilizing force, he could think no further than having the Imperial Rescript on Education translated and distributed throughout the island. Cited in Mark Peattie, "The Last Samurai: The Military Career of Nogi Maresuke," in *Princeton Papers on East Asia: Japan*, I (Princeton, 1972), pp. 99-100.

scope be so brilliantly combined in one office of Japanese colonial administration.

Gotō's accomplishments in restructuring the political, social, and economic order in Taiwan, successes which transformed the territory from an embarrassment to a colonial showcase, have long since been documented[10] and need no recapitulation, but the outlook which he brought to his tasks deserves renewed attention. For if Gotō stands alone in the sum of his capacities and accomplishments, his approach to colonial rule reflected an emerging outlook of the Japanese bureaucrats, politicians, and journalists concerned with Japan's pioneer efforts as a colonial power. This opinion, in turn, was closely identified with contemporary European concepts.

To begin with, colonial order and efficiency were prized because they supposedly contributed to the universal civilizing task in which Japanese felt they now participated. Convinced, like others in the late Meiji bureaucracy, that these goals were best attained through the techniques of modern science, the reformist officialdom in Taiwan sought to take a "scientific" approach to the solution of a wide range of problems—social, political, economic, and sanitary—which Japan faced in the colony. More than anything else, this meant obtaining sound and relevant information on which to base policy, information to be derived from careful research. Here Gotō, with his professional training, took the lead. The various research centers and organizations that he established, of which the "Commission for the Investigation of Traditional Customs in Taiwan," so influential in the formation of social policy, was only the most famous, were concrete manifestations of Gotō's perception of Taiwan as a "laboratory" for Japan's experiment in colonial rule. A voracious reader, he also amassed a collection of works at his official residence which represented the best of contemporary European commentary on colonial affairs. When Takekoshi Yosaburō once called upon him in his study Gotō expansively announced, "You know, we look upon the Governor General's office as a sort of university where one may study the theories and principles of colonization, in which branch we, Japanese, are not overly well posted. The Governor General is the president, I am the

<hr />

[10] See, for example, Chang Han-yu and Ramon H. Myers, "Japanese Colonial Development Policy in Taiwan, 1895-1906: A Case of Bureaucratic Entrepreneurship," in *Journal of Asian Studies*, XXII: 2 (Aug. 1963), pp. 443-449; Ramon H. Myers, "Taiwan as an Imperial Colony of Japan, 1895-1945," in *Journal of the Institute of Chinese Studies*, Chinese University of Hong Kong, Vol. VI (Dec. 1973), pp. 425-451; and Yukiko Hayase, "The Career of Gotō Shimpei: Japan's Statesman of Research, 1857-1929," unpublished Ph.D. dissertation, The Florida State University, 1974, pp. 40-90.

manager, and this room we are now in is the library of this colonization university."[11]

It seems likely that it was Gotō's wide reading in contemporary Western colonial thought, buttressed, perhaps, by his own professional training in Berlin, which brought him to adopt current European—particularly German—notions about colonial policy. In particular, his systematic and research-oriented approach to the development of Taiwan and his perception of the island as a "laboratory," wherein experiments to control its social and political environment could supposedly determine the course of social change and evolution in the colony, reflected the pseudo-scientific passion of the time for the application of "biological laws" to political and social institutions.[12] In the realm of colonial affairs such ideas had come to be exalted in Europe as "scientific colonialism," a term particularly favored in Wilhelmian Germany, where it had been promoted by the energetic colonial reformer Bernhard Dernberg.[13]

But to Gotō and his colleagues in Taiwan "scientific colonialism" meant more than just research to rationalize colonial policy or social engineering as an aid to colonial development. In its Social Darwinist obsession with "biological politics" it also implied a way of looking at supposed differences in political capacity between ruler and ruled, differences seen to be shaped by biological principles. As Takekoshi Yosaburō insisted, ". . . biological laws prevail in politics as well as in the human body. . . . We of the latter-day school of the science of government firmly believe that the government of a colony cannot go beyond biological laws. . . ."[14]

[11] Takekoshi, *Formosa*, pp. 21-22.

[12] For Gotō's rather murky statement on the way by which biological "principles" supposedly related to colonial administration, see Ramon Myers, p. 435.

[13] Peter Duignan and Lewis Gann, *The Rulers of German Africa, 1884-1914* (Stanford, 1972), pp. 179 and 189. There are interesting parallels between Dernburg and Gotō as colonial administrators, as there are between the general colonial ideas of Wilhelmian Germany and late Meiji Japan. Both Dernburg and Gotō received medical training in Germany, and both saw medical training and research as an essential part of colonial reform. Improvements in public health came to be a paramount advertisement for success claimed by the colonial authorities in both German and Japanese empires. In more general terms no two colonial powers devoted as much attention to research as part of the colonial task. In Germany this effort resulted in the huge encyclopedias on the colonies, like Heinrich Schnee's *Deutches Kolonial Lexicon*, published after Germany has lost its colonies. In the case of Japan it materialized in the vast amount of information on colonial territories collected and published by various Japanese agencies, an activity begun by Gotō in Taiwan, continued in Korea, and perfected by the South Manchuria Railway Company in its research on Manchuria and China.

[14] Takekoshi Yosaburō, "Japan's Colonial Policy" in *Japan to America*, Naoichi Masaoka, ed. (Putman, 1915), p. 97.

These Japanese attitudes concerning the overseas empire that took shape in the near decade and a half after the conclusion of the Gotō era in Taiwan were a strange combination of continuing detachment and gathering interest. Despite the seeming public neglect of colonial matters, a growing body of knowledge and informed opinion on the subject emerged between 1905 and 1920. It was shaped by a group of publicists—ex-administrators, scholars, politicians, journalists—who were widely read in modern colonial theory, but who also possessed a first-hand knowledge of colonial affairs from extensive service or observation in the colonies, particularly in Taiwan. Prominent in their own right, men like Nitobe Inazō, Tōgō Minoru, Mochiji Rokusaburō, Takekoshi Yosaburō, and Nagai Ryūtarō began to produce a steady flow of commentary on the Japanese colonial empire.

It is difficult to measure in precise terms the influence of these men. One cannot say that they necessarily represented an unofficial expression of official views, nor indeed that of any particular interest group or segment of Japanese opinion. Yet, given the government background of most of these men and the influential positions which they had come to hold in politics, academe, or journalism, they can be said to have expressed collectively the most informed, most articulate, and most frequently voiced Japanese attitudes toward colonial matters during the first quarter century of the empire.

It was not long before this growing expertise in colonial affairs began to acquire institutional support. In 1908, at the initiative of Gotō Shimpei (now president of the South Manchuria Railway Company), Tokyo University established a chair in colonial studies, and Nitobe Inazō, who had been one of Gotō's brilliant young brain trust in Taiwan, was named its first occupant. Nitobe's meticulous and wide-ranging study of colonialism marked a major chapter in the evolution of Japanese colonial thought. In particular, his lectures on colonial policy which he delivered in 1916-1917 at his university collated and synthesized a great mass of information and commentary regarding colonial institutions around the globe and constituted the first systematic study of the subject in Japan.[15] Similar initiatives followed. A year after Nitobe assumed the chair at Tōdai, Nagai Ryūtarō was appointed to an equivalent position at Waseda, and other less prestigious institutions began to offer courses in colonial studies.

What is important about the efforts of Nitobe, and other commentators perhaps less exhaustive in their investigations, is that their writings on the Japanese colonial empire now placed the empire within

[15] See Nitobe's "Shokumin seisaku kōgi oyobi ronbunshū" [Collected Lectures and Essays on Colonial Policy], Nitobe, Zenshū, Vol. IV.

the context of colonialism as a global phenomenon and began to strengthen Japanese understanding of colonial affairs in the broadest sense, not just as an offshoot of economic theory. Drawing attention to the circumstances of Japan's own colonies, they raised questions about the nature and purpose of Japanese rule over foreign peoples. Conveying the commentaries of foreign thinkers and specialists like J. R. Seeley, Paul Reisch, and Jules Harmand, they began to ponder the relative merits of particular European colonial systems for the Japanese situation.

In comparison with writers or commentators of later decades who were either more liberal or more radically authoritarian in their attitudes, the Japanese specialists on colonial affairs between 1905 and 1920 might be called both moderate and conservative. Their outlook on the issues of colonial rule mixed hard national interest, cautious humanitarianism, racially oriented pseudo-science, paternalism, and complacent assumptions about the status quo in almost equal proportions. In this it was at one with much of contemporary colonial thought in Europe, which was not surprising in view of their deep immersion in the growing corpus of Western literature on colonial affairs.

The new Japanese expertise on colonial matters flourished within a growing confidence in imperial success following the nation's victory over Russia which not only augmented the territorial limits of the empire (with acquisition of southern Sakhalin and the Liaotung peninsula) but, in terms of status, raised Japan to the ranks of the major colonial powers. With an increased understanding of other colonial systems the Japanese were better able to match their qualifications against the generally acknowledged requisites in colonial rulership and to note with satisfaction that they measured up to the demanding standards imposed by Western specialists in colonial policy.[16]

Such self-congratulation was buttressed by the plaudits of foreign observers concerning Japan's accomplishments in her first decade as a colonial power. Initial foreign commentary of Japanese talents for the management of alien territory had been skeptical or patronizing.

[16] Bureaucrat, politician, and colonial publicist, Tōgō Minoru expressed the confidence of many Japanese in the nation's historic capacities for overseas dominion, but brought in Western theory to confirm it. Citing the six prerequisites ascribed by Sir Charles Lucas, the prominent British geographer, for success as a colonial race—entrepreneurial spirit, commercial acumen, ability as emigrants to establish a new society, military prowess, administrative skill, and the power of assimilation—Tōgō, after scanning Japan's history, concluded that it gave ample proof of all these attributes. Tōgō Minoru, *Nihon shokuminron* [On Japanese Colonialism], 1906, pp. 358-359.

"Whether they possess the mystic faculty or not only time can tell," sniffed one British writer at the opening of the century, but after the success of the Gotō era in Taiwan doubts had turned to enthusiastic praise. In a short decade Japan turned from a colonial "new boy" to "a colonizing power worthy of study and attention."[17]

Basic also to Japan's growing confidence in colonial rule was the increasing identification with European colonialism in form, as well as in idea. For Gotō, the British example served as the starting point for much of his revitalizing effort in Taiwan. Having read widely in the literature of British colonialism, he encouraged his subordinates to do the same, an activity which he initiated by having Sir Charles Lucas' *Historical Geography of the British Colonies* translated into Japanese. Convinced that the secret of British administrative success lay in the self-confidence engendered by British education, Gotō attempted the novel and ultimately abortive scheme of establishing a character-building institution for upper-class Japanese youth in Taiwan not unlike a British public school.[18] More effectively, he adopted to the Japanese colonial scene British concepts of physical grandeur to reinforce colonial authority. Taking his cue from the role of the public edifice in British India, he undertook the transformation of the decaying jumble of Chinese Taipei into the stately European-style capital of Taihoku. At its center he placed the imposing Government General Building, whose viceregal proportions were meant to symbolize the authority and permanence of the Japanese presence. Other Japanese empire builders approved. "Colonial rulers should take care to maintain pride in themselves," declared Nitobe, commenting on the new structure. "Merely being kind to [colonial subjects] is insufficient. Primitive peoples are motivated by awe."[19] Lord Curzon and Earl Cromer would have agreed.

Yet if material pomp and circumstance provided the pride and glitter of empire for a handful of civil servants and residents in Taiwan, subsequent territorial annexations seemed to offer the prospect that

[17] Archibald Colquhon, *The Mastery of the Pacific* (New York, 1902), p. 398, and Alfred Stead, *Great Japan: A Study of National Efficiency* (New York, 1906), p. 426.

[18] E. Patricia Tsurumi, *Japanese Colonial Education in Taiwan, 1895-1945* (Cambridge, Mass.), 1977, pp. 74–77.

[19] Nitobe, *Zenshū*, IV, 144. To Takekoshi Yosaburō the idea of architectural pomp was Chinese as well. Quoting a T'ang poet—"How shall the people recognize the Emperor's majesty if the palace be not stately?"—he declared that "In order to establish the national prestige in the island and eradicate the native yearnings after the past it is fitting that the authorities should erect substantial and imposing buildings and thus show that it is their determination to rule the country permanently." Takekoshi, *Formosa*, p. 16.

the Japanese people as a whole might participate in and contribute to the great work of imperial expansion. With the acquisition of Karafuto and eventually Korea, hopes were raised that the empire might somehow develop as an outlet for overseas settlement where the "surplus" portion of the Japanese population could find new living space under the Japanese flag and where the energies and resourcefulness of Japanese agriculturalists could create "new Japans" which would strengthen and increase the Japanese race in its world struggle for survival, as well as furnish foodstuffs for the health and vigor of the homeland.[20] Initially, some Japanese publicists had placed hopes on Taiwan and Sakhalin as territories for such mass emigration, but recognition of difficult conditions of climate and topography on both islands ultimately channeled Japanese expectations toward the direct agricultural colonization of Korea. From faulty population statistics and from wishful thinking colonial propagandists derived heady visions of large tracts of underdeveloped Korean land available for Japanese settlement. Nagai Ryūtarō spoke glowingly of the peninsula as a splendid haven for Japanese immigrants, and in 1912 Takekoshi Yosaburō, noting that Japan, prior to 1895, had colonists but no colonies, joyfully reported that "now Korea has room for ten million immigrants and Formosa two million."[21]

But circumstances and the predispositions of Japanese immigrants into Korea undercut the tidy assumptions of Japanese colonial theorists. By the time of Korea's annexation, Karl Moskowitz tells us, the incredible illusions about Korea's sparse population and available land had been dispelled and Japanese aspirations to direct agricultural colonization of the peninsula had foundered on the hard fact that Korea was already filled—with Koreans. Nor had those Japanese colonists, who had indeed emigrated to Korea in considerable numbers by 1910, conformed to the cherished notions of those specialists concerned with colonial policy. Gregory Henderson has likened the Japanese immigrants who entered Korea to the impoverished *pieds noirs* who poured in massive numbers into the North African maghreb in the late nineteenth century. Tinkers, peddlers, failed shopkeepers, rough adventurers, they represented the marginal elements of Japanese society and, far from being hardy pioneers of the soil, willing to till the Korean hillsides into paddy land, they were profit-seekers

[20] Tōgō Minoru and Satō Shirō, *Taiwan shokumin hattatsu shi* [History of Colonial Development in Taiwan], Kōbunkan (Taipei, 1916), pp. 1-7.

[21] Nagai Ryūtarō, *Shakai mondai to shokumin mondai* [Social and Colonial Problems] (Shinkōsha, 1912), pp. 397-400; and Takekoshi, "Japan's Colonial Policy," *Japan to America*, p. 98.

who naturally gravitated to the cities, or buying up land already cultivated, eventually became the new landlords of Korea.[22]

With the diminished prospects for a continued and massive outflow of Japan's population to Korea the emigrationist element in Japanese colonialism began to fade. Nevertheless, demands for "living space" for Japan's "surplus" population remained a powerful argument in the 1920's for Japanese expansionists who pressed for the occupation of Manchuria, and to a lesser extent it provided the impetus for the ballooning Japanese immigration in the island territories of Micronesia in the 1930's. Yet, in fact, by 1920, all overseas Japanese territories, save Karafuto and a number of the Micronesian islands, were colonies of occupation rather than settlement.

Diminished expectations for the enlargement of the Japanese race in overseas territories under the national flag did not affect the basic expansionist assumptions imbedded in Japanese attitudes toward empire since the acquisition of Japan's first colony. It is not necessary to subscribe to unsubstantiated devil theories about Japanese conspiracies for conquest in order to recognize that Japan came to regard its colonies as bases for the extension of Japanese trade, influence, and power in Asia and the West Pacific. Once in Japanese hands, Taiwan, in particular, came to be valued for the economic and political penetration of South China and Southeast Asia. Katsura Tarō, the colony's second governor, had readily connected Japan's colonial presence in Taiwan with Japanese ambitions in those regions, and, while the authenticity of the sensational "Kodama Report of 1902" and its alleged discussion of Taiwan as a military base for the conquest of Southeast Asia remains as dubious as that of the Tanaka Memorial of two decades later, it is true that over the years, as the hazy notions of a "southern advance" (nanshin) evolved in the minds of Japanese expansionists, Taiwan retained its importance as a "stone aiming at the southeast" (Tōnan no seki).[23] In 1918, Akashi Motojirō, then governor general of Taiwan, underscored the importance of the island as a pivot for Japanese expansion in an address to colonial subordinates, during which he referred to Taiwan as "the essential hinge in the

[22] Karl Moskowitz, "The Creation of the Oriental Development Company: Japanese Illusions Meet Korean Reality," in *Occasional Papers on Korea* No. 2. New York, 1974, pp. 77-102, and Gregory Henderson, "Japan's Chōsen: Immigrants, Ruthlessness and Developmental Shock," in *Korea Under Japanese Colonial Rule: Studies of the Policy and Techniques of Japanese Colonialism*, Andrew C. Nahm, ed. (Kalamazoo, 1973), pp. 263-265.

[23] Chang and Myers, p. 434; George Kerr, "The Kodama Report: Plan for Conquest," in *Far Eastern Survey*, XIV: 14 (July 18, 1945), pp. 185-190; and A. J. Grajdanzev, *Formosa Today: An Analysis of the Economic Development and Strategic Importance of Japan's Tropical Colony* (New York, 1942), p. 183.

Empire's southern gate."[24] Similar, though less frequent, appraisals of the position of each of the colonial territories and of expansionism as an inherent element of Japan's colonial purpose were made by civilian as well as military spokesmen for the empire.[25]

It needs to be re-emphasized, however, that while expansion of commerce and influence appears to have been an integral part of Japan's views on the value of empire, there was little consistent pressure between 1910 and 1920 for the territorial augmentation of the formal empire. True, the former German territories in Shantung and Micronesia were occupied in 1914, but those windfall acquisitions were due less to Japanese planning than to a sudden and fortuitous turn in international events. Most who spoke and wrote on colonial themes stressed the idea of colonial development rather than territorial aggrandizement. "We do not need more colonies than we already have," declared Takekoshi Yosaburō in 1912. "Anyone who attempts to acquire more would act contrary to sound imperial policy and for his own private venture. Japan's imperial policy today calls for the development of Korea and Manchuria, as well as of Formosa, and Japan's colonial policy should not be otherwise than to fulfull her responsibility to those lands."[26]

Takekoshi's reference to Japan's colonial "responsibility" is of interest in light of the impression, in Western commentary, that Japan never developed a colonial ethos which included a sense of obligation to its colonial peoples. Much has been made, indeed, of Japan's overriding concern with economic profit and the Japanese tendency to judge the colonial successes and failures according to the principles of the accountant.[27] To a large extent this is true. Japanese self-satisfaction at having managed Taiwan so skillfully that it was economically self-sufficient within a decade was a recurrent theme in early Japanese literature on colonial affairs. As Japanese imperial propagandists became caught up in the spurious economic arguments of the "new imperialism," moreover, the material advantages of colonies

[24] Komori Tokuji, *Akashi Motojirō*, II. Hara Shobō, pp. 54–56.

[25] The humanist Nitobe Inazō, for example, viewed the penetration of Southeast Asia and the South Pacific as the future mission of the Japanese. Nitobe was careful to emphasize, however, that he referred only to the extension of Japanese economic leadership in these areas and cautioned that even in this function Japanese policies would have to be cooperative and humane: "If we treat the peoples of these areas harshly; if we are unfair to the whites in commercial rivalry; if, in competing with Chinese labor, we treat the Chinese badly; if, in a word, we neglect humanitarianism, then our great mission will have little success." Nitobe, *Zenshū*, IV, 474–478.

[26] Takekoshi Yosaburō, "Japan's Colonial Policy," in *Japan to America*, p. 98.

[27] Kublin, "The Evolution of Japanese Colonialism," pp. 77–78.

to the Japanese homeland came to occupy a prominent place in Japanese colonial thinking.

Yet the implication that the Japanese, from the beginning of their empire, were singularly blatant in their concern with economic profit and material advantage is both unwarranted and indiscriminate. In all European colonial systems, attitudes toward colonial rule have included the basic presumption that overseas territories exist or ought to exist for the benefit of the metropolitan nation. In the Japanese case, justifications evolved which proclaimed a moral responsibility toward subject peoples and which cloaked, yet in many cases modified, this naked self-interest. These arguments usually embraced the ideas of a civilizing mission and the obligation for the welfare of dependent peoples. Leaving aside the labyrinthian question of the relative proportions of hypocrisy and idealism in such vindications of empire, it is important to understand that, like colonial thought in the West, the range of Japanese attitudes toward colonialism during the first half of the fifty-year history of the empire included those which recognized the nation's responsibility to protect the interests of its colonial peoples.

Such opinions were articulated between 1905 and 1920 by those in the emerging community of Japanese specialists in colonial problems. Taken together their arguments represented a theory of colonial governance which was paternalistic and gradualist, and which viewed the colonies as entities distinct from the mother country and thus deserving policies separate from it. It was a perspective which had much in common with European theorizing on colonial policy during those years and was, at the same time, an approach to colonial policy framed within a growing sense of Japanese rights and responsibilities toward Asia as a whole. As Akira Iriye has noted, this emerging sense of "mission" to enlighten and to reform a decaying Asia was still directed toward the modernization of Asia in the Western mode and thus must be seen as distinct from the Pan-Asianism of the 1920's and 1930's with its strident call for the union of Asian peoples and for the ejection of Western imperialism from Asia.[28]

Basic to this view was the recognition that the welfare and happiness of colonized peoples were linked to a nation's reputation as a responsible colonial power, and thus the pursuit of material advantage in any colony required moderation and compromise on the part of the conquering race. This realization contained the implicit admission that the early years of Japanese rule in Taiwan and Korea had

[28] Akira Iriye, *Pacific Estrangement*, p. 92, and Akira Iriye, "Japan's Policies Toward the United States," in *Japan's Foreign Policy, 1868-1941, A Research Guide*, James Morley, ed. (New York, 1974), p. 425.

involved shameful abuses of the interests of the indigenous peoples by freebooting colonists (a common bane at the outset of many colonial regimes). Economic advantage pursued at the expense of the colonized, insisted ex-bureaucrat Mochiji Rokusaburō, was but temporary advantage, since the ruin of Japan's colonial subjects could only injure the wider interests of Japan as a whole. "The conquered stand before the conquerors like sheep before a tiger," wrote Mochiji in 1912. "Those who bear heavy responsibility for public government in the colonies must keep this ever in mind; if they do not, the progress of Japan as a civilized nation will be jeopardized."[29] Nitobe Inazō, drawing on a wealth of personal experience in colonial administration and a broad understanding of colonial theory, spoke to the essential problem in the management of alien peoples overseas:

> What is vital in any colonial scheme seems to me to be the right answer to this question: Do we govern an unwilling people for their sake or for our own? As to the general unwillingness of any colony . . . to be governed by a power alien to it, there is little doubt. A colonial government has received no consent of the governed. Nor is there much reason to believe that a colonial power, white or brown, bears the sacrifice simply to better the lot of the people placed in its charge. The history of colonization is the history of national egotism. But even egotism can attain its end by following the simple law of human intercourse—"give and take." Mutual advantage must be the rule.[30]

As in most modern colonial systems it often turned out, of course, that in terms of effecting a humane policy toward colonized peoples, reforming bureaucrats and theoreticians in Japan proposed, while overbearing officials, callous policemen, and rapacious traders in the colonies disposed. The record of Japan's viciousness in Korea and frequent insensitivity in Taiwan and the Pacific territories is too clear to deny that Japanese colonials on the scene often had little regard for the interests of Taiwanese, Koreans, or Micronesians. Yet there did exist in Japan, and to a lesser extent in the colonies, persons of influence who were genuinely concerned with Japan's colonial responsibilities and whose opinions on the subject were a good deal more liberal and humane than those occasionally voiced by European colonial spokesmen.[31]

[29] Mochiji Rokusaburō, *Taiwan shokumin seisaku* [Colonial Policy in Taiwan] (Fuzambō, 1912), p. 407.

[30] Nitobe Inazō, "Japanese Colonization," in *Asian Review*, Series 4, Vol. 16 (Jan. 1920), pp. 120-121.

[31] It is instructive to juxtapose Nitobe's statement quoted above with that of Theo-

In part such perceptions stemmed from the recognition that while colonized peoples could be conquered by force they could not be permanently held by it. Ultimately, their docility toward alien rule would best be assured if they came to identify their security and welfare with the civilizing efforts of Japan. Thus, argued those in the mainstream of Japanese colonial thought, Japan's subject peoples should be introduced to the benefits of modern civilization—hospitals, railways, the telegraph, basic schooling—under the careful scrutiny of colonial authority. Typically, Mochiji spoke of a policy of "reassurance and guidance" (*suibu keidō*) for the Taiwanese, one which linked humanitarian protection of their rights and interests with paternalistic supervision of their progress toward modernity.[32]

But underlying this view was the assumption that the tempo and direction of the advance of dependent peoples would in large part be determined by the nature and status of their own societies. This, many Japanese colonial theorists insisted, was particularly true in the case of the Taiwanese and Koreans, races of ancient cultural traditions. To attempt abrupt changes in such societies was morally reprehensible, as it could only lead to the disintegration of their social and cultural order. Such forced-draft modernization would also be a self-defeating policy for Japan, in that it would merely generate hostility to colonial rule among traditional elements in those populations and would exaggerate the expectations of freedom among those more disposed to modern ideas. Thus, Japan should move cautiously in its civilizing mission, always respectful of the separate (and subordinate) cultural identities of their colonial peoples.[33]

To the moderate and conservative colonial theorists of late Meiji and early Taishō, therefore, one of the most important elements in the formulation of sound and lasting colonial policy was time. Colo-

---

dore Leutwein, governor of German Southwest Africa, 1894-1905, who concluded that "the final objective of all colonization is to make money. The colonizing race has no intention of bringing happiness to the aboriginal people, the kind of happiness that the latter perhaps expects. In the first instance, the conquerors seek their own advantage. Such objectives correspond to human egotism and therefore accord with nature. Colonial policy must, therefore, be determined by the expected profits." Gann and Duignan, p. 44. Recognizing that there were those in Japan who were far less humane than Nitobe in their attitudes toward Japan's dependent peoples and theorists in Germany (like Dernburg) who would have agreed with Nitobe's statement quoted here, Nitobe's judgment nevertheless demonstrates that there were Japanese in these years whose views were a good deal more liberal than those sometimes found in European colonial systems.

[32] Mochiji, *Taiwan shokumin seisaku*, pp. 431-432.
[33] Nitobe, *Zenshū*, IV, 165, and Takekoshi, pp. 33-34.

nial peoples could be guided toward the higher civilization of the metropolitan country at only the most gradual pace. Gotō Shimpei, while in Taiwan, had spoken of a "hundred-year plan" for the gradual evolution of Taiwanese society; Nitobe Inazō thought eight hundred years a reasonable period for the evolution of certain colonial peoples. Here again, "biological principles" were invoked to support this extreme gradualism. Since human communities evolved over a long period of time, Gotō argued, any attempt to force sudden change in Taiwanese society would contradict the principles of evolution and civilization. The same arguments were applied to Korea following its annexation. "Success in our policy (of gradualism) in Formosa," wrote Takekoshi Yosaburō in 1912, "made us extend the principle to Korea. . . . The Koreans can be slowly and gradually led in the direction of progress, but it is against all laws of sociology and biology to make them enter a new life at once. . . ."[34] Naturally, such contentions, which dealt from alleged differences in the capacities of races to modernize, evoked powerful arguments for preservation of the status quo, for the subordinate position of dependent peoples, and the superior place of their alien rulers. In a sense, this element in Japanese colonial thought of the 1905-1920 period which implied the biological inferiority of colonized peoples bore some resemblance to the racial doctrines of colonial bureaucrats and theorists in the Italian colonial empire of the 1930's.[35]

These were the ideas, then, of the most articulate elements of Japanese colonial opinion between 1905 and 1920. These commentators took cognizance of the welfare of Japan's dependent peoples and balanced them against the national interests of Japan, though they assumed the moral right of "advanced" colonial races like Japan to establish dominion over "lesser" indigenous peoples. Confident in these assumptions, they presumed the availability of an infinite amount of time for the benefits of colonial rule to work their good, unhurried either by international challenges to the status quo or by violent pressures from the colonial peoples themselves. Finally, they perceived the Japanese colonies to be separate territories, distinct from the homeland and not merely extensions of it. In this sense theirs was an approach not unlike the French doctrine of association, which held that colonies should retain a separate identity and be governed prag-

[34] Tsurumi, pp. 51 and 81; Takekoshi Yosaburō, "Japan's Colonial Policy," in *Oriental Review*, III:2 (Dec. 1912), 102-103.

[35] See Dennis Mack Smith, *Mussolini's Roman Empire* (New York, 1976), pp. 112-115.

matically, with due regard to the institutions and traditions of their native peoples.[36]

In sum, the impulse behind the moderate-conservative Japanese colonial policy derived largely from the example of European colonial empires whose overseas territories were geographically dispersed and racially diverse. "The island of Formosa," Takekoshi declared, "where Japanese have come to establish power over the native population of three million people differing widely from us in tradition, customs, language, race and physical conditions, can only be regarded as a colony and therefore the island can only be governed in accord with the example and precedents furnished by other colonial powers."[37]

ASSIMILATION AND ITS CRITICS, 1905-1920

And yet, as they evolved, Japanese perspectives also contained assumptions about relations between homeland and colonial peoples which ran counter to principles established within European colonial empires. Affinities of race and culture between Japan and her colonial peoples (excepting the islanders of the South Pacific) made possible the idea of a fusion of the two and suggested that ultimately Japanese colonial territories had no separate, autonomous identities of their own, but only a destiny which was entirely Japanese. This concept found its expression in the doctrine of assimilation—dōka in Japanese—which came to be the central issue in Japanese colonial affairs.

Assimilation as a general concept, of course, was not uniquely Japanese. Best defined as "that system which tends to efface all differences between the colonies and the motherland and which views the colonies simply as a prolongation of the mother country beyond the seas,"[38] it found its most enthusiastic and articulate expression in French colonial theory. But while Japanese who wrote and acted on colonial matters were aware of French assimilationist doctrine there is scant evidence that French concepts, based as they were on the republican ideals of 1789, had much influence in the formation of Japanese assimilationist ideas, which were distinctly Asian in origin and character. Nor was the maturation of Japanese assimilationist theory similar to that of France. The French colonial empire began the nineteenth

---

[36] D. K. Fieldhouse, *The Colonial Empires: A Comparative Survey from the Eighteenth Century* (New York, 1966), p. 319.

[37] Takekoshi, *Formosa*, p. 33.

[38] S. H. Roberts, *A History of French Colonial Policy, 1870-1925*, I (London, 1929), p. 67.

century dedicated to the ideal of assimilation, but by the century's end had made a pragmatic adjustment toward the principle of association. In effect, Japanese colonial policy during the half century of the empire moved in exactly the opposite direction.

At least four assumptions about Japan's cultural heritage appear to have been central to Japanese ideas of assimilation. The *dōbun dōshū* (same script, same race) formula of cultural and racial affinity with the Chinese cultural area were basic to these concepts, of course. But, more than this, Japanese ideas of assimilation contained a strongly moralistic tone, derived from the Chinese Confucian tradition and expressed in the endlessly-repeated phrase *isshi dōjin*—"impartiality and equal favor"—which conveyed the idea that all who came under the sway of the sovereign shared equally in his benevolence.[39] Applied to modern administration, it implied, at least to some, that in the colonies, Japanese and the native populations were to be treated equally, subject to the same obligations and invested with the same rights. But like the "Three Peoples' Principles" of Republican China, *isshi dōjin* was sufficiently nebulous that it could encompass a variety of meanings to suit quite disparate political purposes. It could be given the most liberal construction, stressing equal rights, or the most authoritarian interpretation, emphasizing equal obligations. A rhetorical device rather than a practical guide to colonial policy, it nevertheless became an incantation for numerous Japanese involved in colonial affairs, since, unlike the more prosaic and contentious term *dōka*, it appeared sanctified by its implied reference to the Imperial will.

This link to the Japanese emperor as head of the Japanese race and state came to be the third distinguishing feature of Japanese ideas on assimilation. The origins of the Japanese race were held to be mystically linked to the Imperial house and thus to constitute an Imperial "family," a principle which could be extended outward to include new populations brought under Japanese dominion, so that these too could become "imperial peoples" (*kōmin*). Yet here again, the concept was so murky as to defy any precise application of rights and responsibilities to such "imperialized"—that is, Japanized—nationalities, a vagueness which made it less a policy than a dogma. Touched upon infrequently in the initial decades of Japanese colonialism, the

[39] The phrase had its origins in the Chinese *i-shih t'ung-jen*, meaning to be equally merciful to all, granting an impartial kindness or favor. It is mentioned in the *Han-yu yuan-jin* by a famous T'ang poet and sage: "Therefore, the sage treats everyone equally and impartially." See Miao T'ien-hua, ed., *Ch'eng yü-t'ien* [Dictionary of terms and phrases], Fu-hsing shu-chu (Taipei, 1973).

idea of "imperialization" by the 1930's came to sanctify the increasing regimentation and subordination forced on Japan's colonial peoples.[40]

Lastly, some Japanese thinking about assimilation was colored by a conviction that Japanese historical experience had provided the race with unique talents for the assimilation of foreign peoples and ideas. Such a belief based its claims on various examples of semi-mythical, as well as of a factual, nature: the emergence of the Yamato people, Japan's assimilation of Chinese culture in ancient times, and its adaption of Western forms in the modern period. The idea not only rested on a simplistic view of Japanese history, but represented an ill-conceived attempt to fit the "facts" of Japan's pre-modern past to a modern colonial setting where, in fact, a minority of Japanese existed amidst alien majorities. But such realities did not prevent the idea's frequent appearance among the battery of arguments for assimilation.[41]

Despite the rhetoric of *isshi dōjin*, of course, the actual environment of Japanese colonialism was hostile to any true merger of the Japanese with their dependent peoples on the basis of familiarity or mutual respect. Largely subordinate in position and treatment under separate colonial law, the indigenous populations had no representation in the Japanese Diet, nor any effective legislative bodies of their own. Japanese occupied the overwhelming portion of influential positions in government. Active Japanese discouragement of racial intermarriage and the isolation of colonial Japanese in their tight and exclusive urban communities hardly contributed to easy intercourse between the races. Above all, the attitudes of resident Japanese in the colonies, not dissimilar to those of most colonial elites, undercut the possibilities of real assimilation. Their feelings of superiority, their jealous grip on privilege and position, were insurmountable barriers to mutually responsive communications between colonizers and colonized, and their obvious fear of being swamped culturally and politically by native majorities mocked Japanese assertions of the historic capacity of their race to assimilate foreign peoples.

Yet assimilation as a theory came to have a powerful appeal for a wide spectrum of Japanese. At its most idealized level—the mystic of *isshi dōjin*—assimilation was central to the idea of a civilizing mission and thus a widely accepted perspective within the range of Japanese

[40] Gotō Shimpei, in an address to a group of Japanese educators in Taiwan in 1903, spoke of the "inherent benefits to the Taiwanese on becoming part of 'our imperial race' (*waga kō no min*)." Shirai Asakichi and Ema Tsunekichi, *Kōminka undō* [The Japanization Movement] (Taipei, 1939), pp. 10-11.

[41] See, for example, Akashi Motojirō's views on the assimilation of the Yamato and Izumo races, in Komori, pp. 50-51.

attitudes toward colonialism. This was in large part because the vagueness of its ideas meant that it could be perceived in quite different ways by different people and thus espoused by bureaucrats, politicians, scholars, and reformers for reasons that were often quite contradictory. Undoubtedly, moreover, because assimilation in any colonial system has always implied one-directional change by "inferior" colonized peoples toward the culture of the "superior" colonizing race, it found wide favor among Japanese of all persuasions.

As an ultimate and ideal goal, therefore, assimilation might even be said to have been accepted by those Japanese who had adopted a gradualist position in colonial affairs. In their view, Japan's colonial peoples, under the proper guidance and over sufficient time, could be "lifted up" to the superior culture of Japan and in this way, over a long period, become part of that higher plane of civilization. Such a process could not be forced or rushed, but only "influenced by enlightenment" (kanka kaigō), as Mochiji Rokusaburō put it.[42] In this sense, as Harry Lamley has noted, isshi dōjin sentiments reflected a certain humanitarianism, a Meiji belief in progress, coupled with feelings of superiority common to all colonial elites.[43] Education, closely supervised and with carefully tailored objectives, was to be the vehicle for the gradual enlightenment of the colonized. Thus, in a sense, Gotō Shimpei in his program of Japanese language training at the mass level had worked toward long-range assimilationist goals in Taiwan. Gotō's limited effort can be seen as the initial step in a fifty-year attempt by the colonial authorities in Taiwan to use education as a device to incorporate the Taiwanese as an obedient, subordinate element in the Japanese race, a process charted in detail by Patricia Tsurumi's splendid monograph on colonial education in Taiwan.[44]

In Nitobe Inazō's view, the progress toward assimilation in any particular colony was necessarily determined by the extent to which cultural differences already existed between colonizer and colonized. (From this point of view Nitobe considered assimilation more possible in Korea than in Taiwan.) Nitobe cited, by European example, the painful consequences when colonial powers failed to recognize these differences and attempted hasty and ill-considered efforts to immerse dependent alien peoples in the advanced cultures of their

[42] Harry J. Lamley, "Assimilation Efforts in Colonial Taiwan: The Fate of the 1914 Movement," in Monumenta Serica, XXIX (1970-71), pp. 498-499; and Tsurumi, pp. 23-25.

[43] Mochiji, Taiwan shokumin seisaku, p. 400.

[44] Lamley, "The 1895 Taiwan War of Resistance: Local Chinese Efforts Against a Foreign Power" and Tsurumi, "Japanese Colonial Education in Taiwan 1895-1945," pp. 38-45.

colonial masters. He concluded that at present assimilation was only "an idealistic concept and [thought] all arguments in its favor stem from lofty ideas"; its realization could only be brought about by small, incremental advances over a great span of time.[45]

If some Japanese colonial thinkers were willing to accept assimilation in theory as a distant objective of colonial policy, Japanese colonial officialdom viewed assimilation of a very limited, mundane sort as an immediately useful administrative concept. As a restricted mechanical means to "Japanize" the appearance and lifestyles of Japan's colonial peoples and thus to remold them outwardly as loyal, law-abiding Japanese, it was seized upon by the colonial bureaucracy at the outset of Japanese rule in Taiwan. Concerned primarily with the problem of control, the Japanese colonial bureaucrat was delighted with programs which induced Taiwanese, Koreans, Chinese, and Micronesians to speak Japanese, live in Japanese style houses, dress in modern Japanese (Western) clothing, and reinforce their physical identity with the ruling elite.[46] Ultimately, because Japanese authorities in the colonial empire failed to come to grips with the contradictions inherent in Japanese attitudes toward colonialism, official policies supporting assimilation were reduced to this mechanical level and generally achieved results among colonial populations that were similarly limited and superficial.

But, in 1912, to a more thoughtful observer of the colonial scene like Mochiji, it seemed possible to achieve greater integration between Japan and her colonial peoples than merely their "material assimilation" (keijika dōka). Concerned essentially with Taiwan, Mochiji believed that it was essential to transform the entire mental and spiritual outlook of the Taiwanese to make them susceptible to the "Japanese spirit," which, for Mochiji, a man of late Meiji outlook, was undoubtedly a blend of modern Western and traditional Japanese values. But these deeper attitudinal changes among the Taiwanese could be brought about only through a more direct contact between the two races, and this in turn, depended largely upon a change of attitude by the Japanese in Taiwan. Criticizing his fellow countrymen for their cliquishness and their concentration in cities and larger towns apart from the Taiwanese, he called upon the home government to encourage Japanese agricultural settlement in Taiwan, not for economic reasons alone, but to stimulate conditions of "accommodative assimilation" (yūwa dōka) whereby Japanese agriculturalists, living closely and harmoniously amongst their Taiwanese neighbors, would

[45] Nitobe, Zenshū, IV, 158-160 and 163-164.
[46] Lamley, "The 1895 Taiwan War of Resistance," p. 498, 5.

inspire them through example and amity to become Japanese in out-look as well as lifestyle. (Mochiji also urged the promotion of Japa-nese missionary activity—Buddhist and Christian—among the Tai-wanese as an important and underdeveloped means to their assimilation.) While these well-intentioned prescriptions for racial co-operation were both paternalistic and naive, what is interesting is that Mochiji placed them in a wider framework of national destiny and imperial purpose. While Japan had proved itself capable of the me-chanics of colonial administration and development, he argued, the amalgamation of colonial peoples, particularly of Chinese racial stock, was the great challenge of the future, one for which nothing from the Western colonial past would serve as adequate example or guide. "But on the solution of this profound problem," Mochiji concluded, "lies the fate and direction of an expanding Japanese empire." By linking cooperation among Asian races with Japanese expansionism Mochiji's view foreshadowed Pan-Asianist views of succeeding dec-ades.[47]

None of these speculations on assimilation touched upon the sen-sitive question of the political relationship between metropolitan Ja-pan and the colonies, particularly in terms of the Meiji Constitution. This was a critical problem, for if it were accepted that the provisions of the Constitution applied to all territory under formal Japanese ju-risdiction, the authority of Japanese colonial governments would be reduced and the position of Japan's colonial peoples elevated to some-thing approaching equality with the Japanese, a true political assim-ilation of colonizers and colonized. The impetus for this most con-troversial aspect of assimilation theory had come from liberal politicians in the Diet who were concerned about the creation of arbitrary bu-reaucratic power in Japanese territory overseas. Specifically, their criticism focused on the notorious Law 63 (Rokusan hō) of 1896, which had granted the Governor General of Taiwan authority to pass leg-islation for the colony. The one colonial issue which perennially stirred political debate in Japan, Law 63, was repeatedly attacked in the Diet as illegal, on the ground that, under the Constitution, the Diet had sole law-making power. The law was eventually modified,[48] though the arbitrary authority of the government-general in Korea remained undented. Working, in any event, from the basic premise that the Meiji Constitution must apply to all Japanese territories, Japanese

[47] Mochiji, Taiwan shokumin seisaku, pp. 15, 398-403.

[48] For a thorough discussion of Japanese administrative law in Taiwan and Korea, including the problem of Law 63, see Edward I-te Chen, "Japanese Colonialism in Korea and Formosa: A Comparison of the Systems of Political Control," in Harvard Journal of Asiatic Studies, XXX (1970), pp. 126-159.

liberals in early Taishō increasingly voiced concern that Japan's colonial populations did not possess the same political rights and liberties under the Constitution enjoyed by Japanese in the home islands. Their objective was therefore to "extend the homeland" (*naichi enchō*), a favored term almost as nebulous as *isshi dōjin*, in order to apply the provisions of the Constitution in all Japanese territories. In this way, they believed, the colonies would be more rapidly and directly assimilated into the political, social, and economic structure of Japan through at least modest provisions for civil liberties, political responsibility, and advanced education, as well as through the dissolution of restrictions hindering such union. Many of these concepts were incorporated into the program of the ill-fated assimilation movement of 1914 in Taiwan, which received wide support among liberals in Japan.[49]

It was the furious response to these provocative and liberal ideas which shaped the ideas of the gradualists already discussed. Reacting heatedly to both the proposals for assimilation in a political and legal sense and to suggestions for liberalization of colonial policy in general cultural and educational terms, they cited the Western colonial example to argue that such ideas undermined colonial authority on the one hand and agitated colonial peoples on the other. Taking note of French and American assimilationist policies, Takekoshi concluded that "those nations which have considered their colonies as part and parcel of the home country have almost always failed in their system of [colonial] government; while, as a rule those nations have succeeded which have looked upon their colonies as a special kind of body politic quite distinct from the mother country."[50] Tōgō Minoru, writing in the official government monthly in Taiwan, not only cited Algeria and Indochina as examples of the failures of French assimilationist theory, but went on to portray the hazards of rebellion and disorder invited by the British in India in their provision of advanced Western education and "almost unlimited freedom" (Tōgō's phrase) to the upper Indian elite.[51]

While assimilation as a theory drew vigorous opposition from those concerned with colonial affairs who questioned its underlying assumptions and analyzed its failures as a concrete policy, these were by and large measured responses of an intellectual sort. Much more visceral and unenlightened was the outcry by Japanese bureaucrats

---

[49] Such groups and individuals included Ōzaki Yukio, Inukai Tsuyoshi, a number of university presidents, ranking figures in all three major political parties, a number of ministers in the Ōkuma cabinet, as well as a number of major newspapers. Lamley, pp. 510-511, and Tsurumi, p. 295, note 41.

[50] Takekoshi, *Formosa*, pp. 24-25.

[51] Tsurumi, "Japanese Colonial Education in Taiwan 1895-1954," p. 48.

and residents in Taiwan against Itagaki Taisuke's abortive assimilation movement of 1914. Aghast at Itagaki's suggestion of extending basic liberties in Japan to the Taiwanese, Japanese bureaucrats and colonists in Taiwan, like all colonial elites, reacted vehemently to the prospect of any diminution of their power and privilege. The local Japanese press had shouted down the idea and finally the government-general, resentful of Itagaki and his fellow assimilationists as meddlesome outsiders, had simply banned the movement. Raw self-interest and jealous privilege of Japanese colonials ultimately doomed the single most substantive effort in the history of Japanese colonialism to provide a relatively egalitarian integration of a colonized people with the metropolitan country.[52]

And yet, the ambiguity of its implications meant that, for quite different reasons, assimilation came to be espoused by conservatives, liberals, and expansionists alike. Not the least of its appeals was its emotional and somewhat hazy identification with emerging Pan-Asianist ideals of many Japanese. By demonstrating in Taiwan, initially, how members of the Japanese and Chinese races could co-exist and prosper together, Japan could display its lofty purpose of Asian prosperity and union in contrast with divisive and self-serving designs of Western colonialism in Asia. Itagaki, believing that the ideal of racial harmony could be an important element in Japan's expanding influence in Asia, had given voice to this idea in his support of the 1914 assimilation movement.[53]

Within a few years others took up the theme more vigorously. Kumamoto Shigekichi, a colonial educator in Taiwan writing in the *Taiwan jihō* in 1920, called for Pan-Asian unity among the yellow races in the face of consolidation by the white race and announced that the basis of Pan-Asianism must be the assimilation by Japan of the peoples within its colonial empire in language, customs, and outlook. To accomplish this, Kumamoto urged redoubled efforts to provide a common education, particularly through the diffusion of the Japanese language, the abolition of discriminatory practices, the establishment of museums and libraries to foster the idea of a common cultural heritage, and above all a commitment to the idea of assimilation by Japanese colonists, whom he called upon to work more closely and generously with their Taiwanese neighbors in establishing a common loyalty. Just as the United States had "Americanized" its immigrants, Japan must, in a reverse process, make one national people out of the racial components of the empire by Japan-

[52] Lamley, "The 1895 Taiwan War of Resistance," pp. 514-515.
[53] *Ibid.*, p. 499, and Tsurumi, p. 66.

izing its newly acquired populations. With the commonplace inconsistency of most Pan-Asianists of the day, Kumamoto concluded that such assimilation efforts would contribute simultaneously to strengthening Japanese power and influence in Asia and to peaceful cooperation between white and yellow races.[54]

LIBERAL ALTERNATIVES, 1920-1930

It was the powerful currents of change in the Japanese homeland and abroad from 1914 to 1920, however, that did most to invigorate assimilation as an issue in Japanese colonial thought and to reinforce, at least temporarily, its liberal and accommodative form. In Japan, the erosion of the influence of the elder statesmen and the high tide of political party power had brought Hara Kei to the premiership and had strengthened support for more liberal administration for the colonies. Abroad, the emergence of Wilsonian idealism, particularly the principles of self-determination of peoples, gave heart to Taiwanese and Koreans who sought autonomy for their homelands and, in an international atmosphere less disposed to empires and colonial privilege, placed Japan's imperial propagandists on the defensive.

Not surprisingly, the first reaction by Japanese colonial officialdom to the liberalizing trends abroad had been both harsh and reactionary. In Taiwan, Akashi Motojirō, a professional officer of sinister reputation, brought from his previous colonial positions in Korea a record of ruthlessness as a military policeman and administrator. As governor general he pursued with vigor an assimilationist policy, not as a gradual program of cultural amalgamation, or as an accommodation to Taiwanese pleas for a share of Japanese civil and political liberties, but as an immediate attempt to tighten Japan's political and ideological control over the colony. For Akashi, assimilation meant an accelerated effort, through the police system as well as the schools, to cement Japan's grip on Taiwan before the appeals of Wilson's principles of self-determination could weaken Taiwanese loyalties. Thus, while he could speak of *isshi dōjin* and "mutual cooperation" (*kyōshin ritsuryoku*,[55] it is clear that Akashi's ideas of assimilation, like that of Japanese military administrators of later decades, had little to do with Taiwanese aspirations for political equality and shared responsibility.

In Korea, the rigor with which Japan-centered assimilation was pursued by the military administration had created violent antago-

---

[54] Kumamoto Shigekichi, "Dai naru Nihon to dōka mondai" [The Great Problem of Assimilation], in *Taiwan jihō* (Jan. 1920), pp. 55-63.
[55] Komori, *Akashi Motojirō*, II, p. 60.

nisms which could not have been permanently contained. To Terauchi Masatake, Japan's first pro-consul on the peninsula and symbol of the oppressive era of *budan seiji* (military [dictatorial] rule), complete assimilation of the Korean people meant their total subjugation. To justify a policy of enforced conformity to Japanese institutions and values, Terauchi marshalled all the classic arguments of Meiji times for Japanese rule over Korea: geographic proximity between the two countries, shared ethnic origin, Japanese "special understanding" of Korea's history and character, as well as the need to protect Korea from the corrosive influence of Western liberal ideas.[56]

Yet a few Japanese civilian observers had begun to question some of the assumptions of Japanese colonialism in both Taiwan and Korea. Liberal journalist and educator Yoshino Sakuzō, at the forefront of the new democratic drift in Taishō Japan, smelled the acrid smoke of popular indignation while on a trip through the peninsula in 1916. To Yoshino the ponderous bureaucratism and mountainous arrogance of the government-general seemed to suggest what relations between officials and people must have been like under the feudal tyranny of the Tokugawa shogunate. In his view, the mindless rhetoric of Terauchi's administration, which spoke of the racial and cultural affinities between Koreans and Japanese, was fatally compromised by the racial and cultural contempt with which the Korean people were viewed by their colonial masters. Assimilation of a people of a relatively advanced and distinctive culture—and Yoshino considered the Koreans to be such people—would be difficult in any event. But denial of social or legal equality to a colonized people in their own land not only made the task impossible, but made their resistance inevitable. Under these circumstances, education, the cherished means of colonial administrators to dispense Japanism, could only increase the white-hot sense of racial and national identity among the Korean people. Indeed, in Korea, Yoshino reported to Japanese readers, to be educated was to be anti-Japanese.[57]

The explosion of Korean national resentment on March 1, 1919 rocked all segments of informed opinion in Japan. The wrath of the

[56] Wonmo Dong, "Assimilation and Social Mobilization in Korea: A Study of Japanese Colonial Policy and Political Integration Effects," in Nahm, pp. 152-153. For a critical analysis of Japanese assimilation policy in Korea, see Hatada Takashi, "Nihonjin no Chōsenkan" [Japanese Attitudes toward Korea), in *Nihon to Chōsen* [Japan and Korea], Vol. III of *Ajia-Afurika kōza* [Lectures on Asia and Africa] (Keisō Shobō, 1965), pp. 5-10.

[57] Yoshino Sakuzō, "Mankan o shisatsu shite" [A Tour of Manchuria and Korea], in *Chūō kōron*, XXXI:6 (June, 1916), 43-44.

Japanese military was manifest in the bloody-handedness with which it crushed the movement. Yet the depth of the Korean protest and the brutality of the Japanese colonial response combined to open the way to more liberal assimilationist alternatives, not only in Korea, but in all the Japanese colonial territories. In large part the modest administrative reforms which followed were generated by Japan's anxiety for its reputation as a responsible colonial power. Writing less than a month after the March demonstration, Yoshino had sounded this concern: "The uprising in Korea," he declared, "is a great stain upon the history of the Taishō period, which we must exert every effort to wipe away. Unless we do so successfully it will not only reflect upon the honor of the most advanced country in East Asia, but will have a serious impact upon our national destiny." Yet Yoshino's remedies to deal with the crisis also serve to illustrate the perimeters of the liberal approach to Japan's colonial policies. The immediate need, he averred, was rigorous suppression of the uprising, punishment of its instigators, and provision of relief measures for Koreans made destitute by the ensuing violence. Yoshino saw the long-range amelioration of Japan's troubled policy in the colony in a basic rearrangement of Japanese-Korean relations. Assimilation—and here Yoshino used the term *isshi dōjin*—must mean that "impartiality and equal favor" become a political, social, and economic reality by the abolition of all discriminatory practices against Koreans. Equal opportunity would create new and closer bonds of loyalty between the two peoples. At the same time, outright Korean independence was obviously unthinkable. As an alternative, Japan must grant Korea a greater degree of autonomy and the Korean people a larger role in the management of their own destiny, all within the framework of the empire.[58]

To Premier Hara Kei, long a foe of autocratic rule in the colonies, yet an early advocate of the rapid and complete integration of Taiwan with the mother country, the March 1919 crisis in Korea and the sudden demise of Akashi Motojirō in Taiwan signalled new opportunities for administrative reform in both colonies, as well as in the newly awarded mandate in the South Pacific.[59] The first step was to abolish or limit military rule in those colonies where it still existed. Successful in attaining his objective in Taiwan and the Japanese mandated islands, he was turned aside by the military in trying to apply the principle of civilian rule in Korea. He pushed ahead, nonetheless,

[58] Yoshino Sakuzō, "Chōsen bōdō zengosaku" [Our Policy in Korea Before and After the Uprising], in *Chūō kōron*, XXXIV:4 (April, 1919), pp. 121-122.

[59] Tsurumi, "Japanese Colonial Education in Taiwan 1895-1945," p. 91.

for a liberalization of colonial administration in all Japan's overseas possessions, believing that colonial reforms should proceed along the same channels which bureaucratic reform had followed in Japan. Korea posed the most immediate and difficult problem, of course. Its population, in a state of near revolt, seemed capable of turning Korea into the Ireland of the Japanese empire, while the Japanese military administration there seemed prepared to scourge the length of the peninsula to stamp out the fires of Korean unrest. In Hara's view, the ultimate solution to these problems lay in binding Korea closer to an administratively liberalized and reformed Japan. He rejected the idea that Korea be governed as a colony in the same way that Britons or Americans administered peoples of different races, religions, and histories. Admitting that dissimilar levels of civilization and living standards between Korea and Japan meant that equality must be attained by gradual stages, Hara nevertheless argued that Japan must develop a common administrative policy for both the home islands and the peninsula.[60] Above all, Koreans must eventually be granted the same political rights as Japanese, chief among which should be the right to send representatives to the Imperial Diet. To a visiting American journalist he insisted: "The desire of most Koreans is not for independence, but to be treated as equals of the Japanese. I intend to see to it that the Koreans have such equal opportunities in education, industry, and government position, as well as to undertake reform of local government along the same lines it has proceeded in Japan."[61]

Had Hara not been assassinated in office it is possible that such changes in Japan's colonial administration might have been pursued with greater vigor. Certainly, the pale administrative and social reforms that comprised the ensuing decade or more of the *bunka seiji* (cultural rule) period of Japanese administration in Korea hardly realized Hara's objectives, let alone satisfied Korean demands for justice and autonomy. Filtered as it was through a colonial administration which still held Korean political aspirations and capacities in contempt, liberalization of Japanese rule in Korea quickly evaporated into lofty slogans empty of any solid reform. "Co-existence and co-prosperity" (*kyōzon kyōei*), for example, far from ushering in a new era of economic justice for the Koreans, came to mean economic development of Korea largely to promote Japanese interest. "Assimilation of Japan and Korea" (*naisen dōka*) had nothing to do with

[60] Hara Kei, *Hara Kei nikki* [The Diary of Hara Kei], VIII (Kangensha, 1950-1955), pp. 216-217.

[61] *Ibid.*, p. 563.

extending Japanese civil liberties and political rights to Korea, but was merely an accelerated effort to inculcate Japanese values among the Koreans. Yet, if neither the depth nor the tempo of colonial reform went far in meeting the legitimate demands of Korean patriots, the more overt and arbitrary aspects of Japanese oppression were at least muted for a time and respect for Korean culture retrieved by extensive Japanese scholarly research into Korea's past.[62]

In Taiwan, where Hara was able to shunt aside military control of the colonial administration, his ideas were given voice by his old political colleague, Den Kenjirō, whom he appointed as the island's first civilian governor-general. Believing, like Hara, that Taiwan, as a territory of the empire, must eventually come within the jurisdiction of the Meiji Constitution, Den was committed to advancing the possibilities for political equality in Taiwan through a program of "acculturation" (kyōka). As Patricia Tsurumi tells us, this particular approach to assimilation, with its connotations of enlightening, civilizing, and evangelizing of a colonized people, was directed toward education of the Taiwanese in the broadest sense. For Den, acculturation extended beyond the classroom to include, inter alia, education of the Taiwanese toward greater political responsibilities, provision of equal employment opportunities for Taiwanese and Japanese, and social and racial integration of the two peoples through diffusion of the Japanese language and official encouragement of intermarriage.[63] Den believed that these measures would ultimately lead to the extension to Taiwan of the full political rights enjoyed by Japanese in the home islands.

To see Den as a liberal innovator, ready to bring about greatly enhanced Taiwanese independence or a radical equalization of Japanese and Taiwanese opportunities in the colony would be a mistake, of course. His commitment to the inculcation of Taiwanese loyalty to the Japanese Imperial family, his stress on "appropriate social status" (mibun sōō) as the basis for association between the two races, and his denunciation of the Taiwanese home-rule movement place him well within the outlook of the Japanese colonial establishment.[64] Nevertheless, within the range of official Japanese attitudes toward colonial empire, his views and those of his immediate civilian suc-

---

[62] For an overview of the bunka seiji period and the fate of its highly publicized reforms see David Brudnoy, "Japan's Experiment in Korea," in Monumenta Nipponica, XXV:2 (1970), pp. 172-216.

[63] Tsurumi, p. 146; Kuroda Kokurō, ed., Den Kenjirō den [The Biography of Den Kenjiro] (Den Kenjirō Denki Hensankai, 1932), pp. 384-385.

[64] Ibid., pp. 389-392; Tsurumi, p. 189.

cessors were among the most accommodative and enlightened in Japan's entire colonial history.

A Conservative Critique of Japanese Colonialism: Aoyagi Tsunatarō and Tōgō Minoru, 1925

To unreconstructed Japanese colonialists the liberal drift of both world events and Japan's colonial policy seemed intolerable. The barrage of angry criticism with which they responded constitutes a considerable portion of Japanese writings on colonialism. The commentary of Seoul newspaper editor Aoyagi Tsunatarō may, I think, be taken as typical of this view. Writing in 1923, Aoyagi filled the pages of his *Chōsen tōchi ron* (On the administration of Korea) with the florid rhetoric of justification and denunciation in an attempt to rouse his countrymen against the dangerous tides of liberalism which threatened, he believed, to sweep away all that Japan had done to lift Korea from material and spiritual morass. Contrasting the "moral degeneracy" and "material greed" of the Korean people with the "unique spiritual qualities of Japan" he saw the annexation of Korea by Japan as both moral and inevitable and ridiculed the idea of Korean independence. Without any history of real independence, Aoyagi insisted, the Koreans were a people without a concept of the state. Such a people were destined to be ruled by others. To advocate any advance in the autonomy of Korea was to press chaos on its people, for they were incapable of the complexities of modern administration.[65]

Yet, paradoxically, despite the contempt which Aoyagi endlessly poured out upon Korean civilization and attainments, he was capable, like other commentators of his persuasion, of indulging in the worst flummery of Pan-Asian arguments about racial and cultural affinities between Koreans and Japanese, even to the point of repeating Marshal Terauchi's pronouncement that Japan's annexation of Korea was like "the re-union of two long-separated brothers." For Aoyagi the "facts" of Korean and Japanese affinity argued for redoubled efforts to bind Korea more closely to Japan. The most important spiritual task of Japan in Korea was to assimilate the Korean people by "eradicating their more 'indecent' characteristics" and by "raising their cultural level to that of the Japanese." Oblivious to the contradictions inherent in this thesis, Aoyagi repeatedly returned to the theme that, given the wide differences in racial characteristics and customs be-

---

[65] Aoyagi Tsunatarō, *Chōsen tōchiron* [On the Administration of Korea] (Seoul, 1923), pp. 139, 480-481, and 782.

tween Japan and Korea, passive efforts to assimilate the Koreans were futile. Instead, aggressive assimilation policies, including abolition of the Korean language and enforced use of Japanese, must be undertaken to *compel* Koreans to adhere to Japanese values and institutions.[66] Above all, Aoyagi warned his Japanese readers, Japan should prevent the spread into Korea of the infection of nationalism generated by radical ideas from abroad: "If President Wilson's principles of the self-determination of peoples, voiced at the Versailles Peace Conference, are realized and the Koreans come to agitate for equal participation in such self-determination, then in Korea, made frivolous by ignorance and filled with a morally relapsed people, Japan's civilizing mission of the decade past will be undone."[67]

Within the spectrum of contemporary Japanese colonial thought, Aoyagi's ideas, while not uncommon, were markedly bigoted and unyielding. Other colonial publicists, also striving against the liberal assaults on colonialism in general and Japan's colonial autocracy in particular, were more thoughtful and better informed. In 1925, Tōgō Minoru, as part of his ongoing criticism of the theory and practice of assimilation, completed his most ambitious work, *Colonial Policy and Racial Consciousness (Shokumin seisaku to minzoku shinri)*, which placed his critique of assimilation as a colonial policy within the larger questions of race, the nation state, and the emergence of multi-racial empires. In so doing he attempted a theoretical framework from which to defend the assumptions of the pre-World War I colonial order from the ideological attacks upon it at home and abroad.

Tōgō's critique took note of the differences between "natural races" (*shizen minzoku*), which had common physical and anatomical characteristics, but which did not necessarily belong to one state or share a common historical or cultural heritage; "historical races" (*rekishi minzoku*), whose members shared a common historical experience and cultural outlook; and a "people" or "nation" (*kokumin*), who belonged to one state, but who did not necessarily possess common physical characteristics or a common cultural heritage.[68]

The ideal political structure for any state, Tōgō assumed, would be that of "one race, one nation" (*ichi minzoku ikkoku*), but he recognized that since ancient times only a few states had been uni-racial and that in modern times advanced countries were composed of complex mixtures of "historical races." The great powers of the modern world, moreover, were not only compelled to administer various

[66] *Ibid.*, pp. 127-128 and 139.

[67] *Ibid.*, pp. 422-423.

[68] Tōgō Minoru, *Shokumin seisaku to minzoku shinri* [Colonial Policy and Racial Consciousness] (Tokyo, Iwanami Shoten, 1925), pp. 56-58.

historical races within their own boundaries, but with the acquisition of far flung colonial territories had taken charge of a welter of different racial groupings. This situation would not have become a problem, had there not emerged within the past century a surge of racial consciousness which had taken the form of demands for national identity. Among the great powers of Europe, racial nationalism had begun to manifest itself in the great "pan" movements, which, along with British imperialism, aimed at the creation of racial consciousness, had spread to lesser countries and eventually, through the increase of modern education and communications, to indigenous colonial peoples, whose struggle to find their own national identity now threatened the peace and stability of modern colonial empires. Japan now faced these problems as well. In the distant past the Japanese had comprised an homogeneous race with few racial tensions and conflicts, but with the acquisition of overseas colonial territories, in particular Taiwan and Korea, both of which had significant populations, economic organization, and cultural attainments, racial nationalism had come to present a distinct challenge to Japan's colonial policy.[69]

Tōgō believed that the movements among colonial peoples for national and racial identity derived from a natural instinct for races to express their individual qualities. The general aim of colonial peoples, Tōgō freely admitted, was to become independent. Colonized peoples, furthermore, had no inclination to thank their colonial masters for the material benefits of foreign rule, no matter how generous those might be. "More than anything else they wish to satisfy their claims to their own countries, no matter what price might be paid in stability and prosperity for that independence."[70]

Yet, in Tōgō's view, this natural instinct for self-determination of colonial peoples, agitated within the last decade by Wilson's call for its realization, ran counter to an equally natural trend of modern times: the great power drive to acquire colonial territory. Citing Leroy-Beaulieu, Tōgō underscored the theme that only strong countries would survive in the future, that strength derived from national self-sufficiency, and that self-sufficiency derived from control of vast amounts of territory, either contiguous in position or in the form of transoceanic colonies. Hence, it was foolish, Tōgō argued, to expect, as Wilson had, that colonial powers should sacrifice their own survival and set their colonies free in order to satisfy the demands of their colonial peoples for self-determination.[71]

[69] *Ibid.*, pp. 1-2, 279-284, and 293-303.
[70] *Ibid.*, p. 325.
[71] *Ibid.*, pp. 326-330.

What was to be done to resolve this dilemma which pitted the "natural instincts" of colonized and colonizer against each other? The solution, as Tōgō perceived it, was for colonized peoples to take part in the management of their own destinies to the extent that they were able, yet within the framework of the larger—colonial—nation. But colonial governments could persuade them to do so only if they were satisfied that their racial and cultural identities would be preserved and allowed to develop. Too often, Tōgō thought, colonial rulers had treated movements for self-determination as purely political problems and had attempted to suppress them by coercive measures, either through a policy of colonial autocracy exercised without restraint by colonial governors on behalf of the metropolitan power, or by assimilation, essentially a policy designed to break down the institutions and racial consciousness of a colonized people. The results in either case were usually counterproductive, but enforced assimilation, in Tōgō's view, particularly served to fan the flames of national resistance to colonial rule.[72]

As an alternative to these coercive policies, Tōgō proposed an approach which he termed "differentiation" (*bunka seisaku*), by which he meant a policy which permitted indigenous colonial peoples to determine their own political levels through the full exercise of their individual temperaments and institutions. Thus, in Tōgō's view, Japanese colonial policy should accept as natural, indeed as desirable, distinction among the racial components of the empire, accommodating itself to the distinctive needs of each colony, which was to be regarded as a unit separate from the mother country. To this extent differentiation would be assimilation in reverse, the civilization of the colonizer being adjusted to that of the colonized. Since indigenous colonial people would be minimally disturbed in the expression of their racial and cultural talents, they would have little reason to oppose the political management and economic utilization of the colony by the colonial power. Once colonial systems recognized the mutual advantages of a policy of differentiation, the dilemma of conflicting needs would be resolved. Colonial territories in the future would neither become fully independent, nor compelled to conform to the values and institutions of another country, but would exist as separate but subordinate political entities, shaped by a symbiotic accommodation between their needs and the needs of the colonial power.[73] "In other words," Tōgō concluded, "the highest purpose in the administration of colonial peoples is not the eradication of the [cul-

[72] *Ibid.*, pp. 293-303, 305-307, and 330.
[73] *Ibid.*, pp. 307, 323, and 326-327.

tural] essence of those peoples, but leadership. It is to provide them with new cultural opportunities and beneficent politics, and to assist them in achieving the greatest happiness as part of a greater nation. To do so means avoiding the extremes of assimilation and emphasizing instead a policy of accommodation."[74]

Basic to Tōgō's theory of colonial rule was his concern with what he called "ethno-psychology," by which he apparently meant a sensitivity to the cultural, anthropological, and psychological characteristics of different races. These characteristics, which served to categorize racial talents and qualities, Tōgō believed, undercut the very assumptions on which assimilation theory was built. While assimilation assumed that all races were moving toward a common path of rationality, nineteenth-century science had demonstrated, on the contrary, that men were swayed by inherited religious belief, custom, and instinct. "Any policy which neglects these differences in the psychological composition of races, or which is based on an assumption of equality between individual races, is, from the standpoint of ethno-psychology, utterly unreasonable."[75] What Tōgō was saying, of course, was that there were "superior" races, like the Japanese, and "inferior" races, like their colonial peoples, and that assimilationist efforts to equalize relations between the two would founder on their inequalities. Implied in his argument, moreover, was the belief that, left to their own devices, colonial peoples would never be able to demonstrate their capacities for complete independence, since even the fullest expression of their political talents would still fall far short of demonstrating their ability to take complete control of their own affairs.

Tōgō Minoru's *Colonial Policy and Racial Consciousness*, which up to 1937 went through four separate printings, represented the last real defense of late-nineteenth-century colonialism in the range of Japanese colonial theory. As such, it was moderate in the demands that it made of colonial peoples to identify themselves with Japan, yet distinctly racist in its attitudes toward them. If it spoke of tolerance by Japan toward "native sentiment" and of granting colonial peoples their own racial identity, it nevertheless had little to say about equal opportunity in education, employment, economic well-being, or social contact between colonized peoples and the colonizing race; indeed, it most emphatically denied such equalization. For Tōgō, Taiwan and Korea were to be ruled as colonies, not as extensions of Japan; they were to be separate, but definitely not equal.

[74] *Ibid.*, p. 311.
[75] *Ibid.*, pp. 90-91, and 310-311.

A Liberal Critique of Japanese Colonialism: Yanaihara Tadao, 1924-1937

If Tōgō Minoru's work represented a refutation of what he perceived to be the liberal drift of colonial policy in the 1920's it was left to a young scholar, Yanaihara Tadao, to provide the most profound liberal critique of the reactionary inertia of Japanese colonialism.[76] A student of Nitobe Inazō, Yanaihara had attended Nitobe's famous lectures on colonial policy while studying at Tokyo University. After his mentor had become too involved with a distinguished career at the League of Nations to continue his research in colonial studies, Yanaihara had begun to collate and edit the lectures, a task which he did not complete until he himself assumed Nitobe's chair in colonial policy at the university in 1937. In the meantime, Yanaihara had embarked on his own wide-ranging study of colonial systems, building on the work begun by his teacher. He shared a number of traits with Nitobe: both men were devout Christians, both were superbly trained scholars, and both were interested in the study of colonialism in comparative perspective. Yet, as an intellectual and scholar, Yanaihara's place in the evolution of Japanese colonial thought is undoubtedly higher than Nitobe's, his concern with the moral implications of policy was far less adulterated with the justifications of Japanese nationalism, and Yanaihara's encyclopedic studies of colonial problems surpass Nitobe's work in depth and breadth.[77]

Yanaihara's scholarship in the field of colonial affairs centered on both detailed institutional studies and broad theoretical problems. In institutional terms Yanaihara minutely examined the mechanisms of colonial administration not only of Japan but of other colonial systems, devoting particular attention to comparing and contrasting Japan's position in Taiwan and Korea with Britain's imperial policies in Canada and Ireland. On a broader plane Yanaihara's interests dealt with imperialism as a theory and with its particular function in the Japanese case. His perspective was economic, though this had less to do with Marx than it had to do with a reconsideration of the theories

[76] For the details of Yanaihara's career, see Ubukata Naokichi, "Profile of an Asian-minded man: Yadao Yanaihara," in *The Developing Economies*, IV:1 (March, 1966), pp. 91-105.

[77] Yanaihara's major works on colonialism and imperialism include *Shokumin seisaku kōgian* [Lectures on Colonial Policy, a Draft], 1924; *Shokumin oyobi shokumin seisaku* [Colonization and Colonial policy], 1926; *Teikokushugika no Taiwan* [Taiwan under Imperialism], 1929; *Manshū mondai* [The Manchurian Problem], 1934; *Nan'yō guntō no kenkyū* [Studies on the South Sea Islands], 1935; and *Teikokushugi kenkyū* [Studies in Imperialism], 1948. All of these are to be found in *Yanaihara Tadao zenshū* [Collected works of Yanaihara Tadao], 29 vols. (Tokyo, Iwanami Shoten, 1963-1965).

of Adam Smith and with the concerns of his own Christian humanism. While his best-known economic studies of colonialism were his
critique of the Japanese effort to increase rice production in Korea
and his analysis of the sugar industry in Taiwan, Yanaihara was interested in the entire spectrum of economic, political, and social
problems in the Japanese empire, and his research, supported by extensive travel and observation, covered each and all of Japan's colonial territories.[78]

At the same time, Yanaihara's erudition supported his vigorously
expressed moral concern with Japanese colonial policy. Drawing upon
a profound knowledge of the conditions of each of Japan's overseas
territories, Yanaihara, over the years, compiled an indictment of what
he perceived to be the degraded situation of Japan's colonial peoples
and a passionate brief for the augmentation of their political rights
and the reduction of their economic exploitation. "Should I be asked
to express my feelings about the colonial question," he declared, "I
would say from the bottom of my heart, 'the liberation of those who
are downtrodden, the raising up of those who would sink, and a
peaceful union of those who are independent.' "[79]

To Yanaihara one of the worst aspects of Japanese colonialism was
the arbitrary authoritarianism of individual colonial governments. Such
autonomy of colonial administrations was all very well in the Ko-
dama-Gotō era in Taiwan, he believed, but in recent decades it had
not only become an obstacle to reform, but had also led to corruption
and malfeasance. Such a situation stemmed from the lack of a central
direction to Japanese colonial policy which, while technically in the
hands of the prime minister, in actual fact devolved upon the individual governors-general, who were able to act without restraint to
suppress the liberties of colonial peoples. It was essential, he therefore
believed, to curtail the authority of colonial governments and to increase the leadership and guidance of the central government through
the creation of a colonial ministry and the provision of clear responsibilities of the Diet in the field of colonial affairs.[80]

It was Yanaihara's startling and consistent advocacy of home rule
for the more advanced of Japan's colonial territories, however, which
set him apart from even the most liberal of Japan's colonial theorists
and policy-makers, most of whom had gone no further than to suggest colonial representation in the Japanese Diet. Yanaihara, on the
contrary, urged that Taiwanese and Koreans be granted their own
legislative assemblies. While in 1921 he had supported the movement

[78] Ubukata, pp. 90-92; *Yanaihara zenshū*, vol. XXVI, p. 36.
[79] Cited in Ubukata, p. 90.
[80] *Yanaihara zenshū* (in *Shokuminchi kenkyū*, pp. 327-329).

for the establishment of a Taiwanese parliament, his most vigorous prose was devoted to the cause of a Korean national assembly. Given the population, cultural advancement, and aspirations of the Korean people, Yanaihara argued, there was no excuse for denying them the right to manage their own political affairs. Ticking off the list of insignificant and backward colonial possessions of the British empire which had no legislative assemblies of their own, Yanaihara charged that "the political status that has been granted to our own Korea is no higher than those of small, uncivilized Negro regions or fleet bases" and that, since even Java, the Philippines, and many French colonies had been granted degrees of legislative autonomy, "there exists no positive reason for not granting the people of Korea political rights, except that the government simply doesn't want to do so."[81]

To Yanaihara, assimilation, the Japanese government's official response toward political restlessness in the two colonies, was a mistaken policy. Certainly, without the abundant information about the colonial environment and an appreciation of the indigenous culture of the sort provided a quarter of a century before by Gotō's Commission for the Investigation of Traditional Customs in Taiwan, assimilation as a uniform policy would inevitably collapse.[82] Nor was he impressed with official efforts to provide basic communications between the ruling Japanese and their dependent peoples. In 1929 he noted that, despite all the talk of the Japanese language as an aid in assimilation, there did not even exist a Japanese–Taiwanese dictionary; nearly a decade later he charged that in thirty years no more than three percent of the Korean population possessed more than a rudimentary knowledge of Japanese.[83] But assimilation "policies" in Yanaihara's view were themselves the problem. Essentially, assimilation as a regimented government program represented interference in human affairs. Accommodative assimilation (*yūwa dōka*), the only lasting integration of two races or cultures, required centuries of natural, unmonitored contact, not mechanical enforcement over a few years. Indeed, a *policy* of assimilation, Yanaihara insisted, merely got in the way of assimilation as a natural process.[84]

Yanaihara gave all these criticisms their sharpest focus in his extensive writings on Korea. The main problem with his country's "cultural policy" in Korea, he argued, was that, through empty sloganeering, Japan had stimulated the aspirations of the Korean people

[81] *Yanaihara zenshū*, I, 739–740. Translation of the statement cited here is to be found in Ubukata, p. 93.
[82] *Yanaihara zenshū*, I, 315–318.
[83] *Ibid.*, IV, 324.
[84] *Ibid.*, I, 314.

without giving them the means to fulfill them. Consequently, insecurity, desperation, hopelessness had become their lot. "Co-existence and co-prosperity" between Japan and Korea raised questions as to how Japan planned to make this a reality, given its exploitation of the Korean economy. "Assimilation of Koreans and Japanese" was just as meaningless. How could such a policy, as it was currently conceived, provide social equality for Koreans, who, in fact, constituted an historically different society? "Assimilation by fiat," Yanaihara flatly declared, "is impossible. Korea cannot form a single society with Japan."[85] Why, he asked, could not his country realize that what Koreans wanted was not to become a pale copy of Japan, but the right to their own political destiny. "Go to Korea and look!" he demanded, "Every pebble by the roadside cries out for freedom."[86]

It was obvious to Yanaihara, moreover, that continuation of an assimilation policy which concentrated on limited material advances for the Korean people, while depriving them of the basic political rights as subjects of the empire until some distant day when they were sufficiently "Japanized," was merely to borrow trouble for the future. In an essay on colonial policy for Korea which he wrote in 1938, Yanaihara pointed out that:

> With the gradual modernization and advancement of the social life and productive powers of the Koreans their political aspirations and demands will grow and increase, regardless of how popular the Japanese language may become. This is bound to lead to a conflict between the two phases of the government's assimilation policy—paternalistic protection and encouragement on the one hand and bureaucratic oppression on the other.[87]

Such bureaucratic oppression, Yanaihara warned, would require increasingly heavy expenditures to maintain a military garrison on the peninsula capable of dealing with any threat to Japanese authority. In this way Korea, far from contributing to the economic prosperity of the empire, could only become a serious financial drain on the Japanese government.

On the other hand, granting the people of Korea the right of political participation in their own administation would reduce the pressures within the colony for independence from Japan and would reinforce their feeling of solidarity with the empire. Thus, after an extended

[85] *Ibid.*, I, 729-737.
[86] *Ibid.*, I, 740. Translation from Ubukata, p. 93.
[87] Yanaihara Tadao, "Problems of Japanese Administration in Korea." in *Pacific Affairs*, XI:II (June, 1938), pp. 206-207.

period of Japanese guidance in which the Koreans were led toward the responsibilities of home rule, Korea might assume a stable and useful position in the Japanese empire not unlike that of Canada within the British Commonwealth. Indeed, while he hoped and assumed that Korea would stay within the empire in some capacity, Yanaihara had expressed the opinion over a decade before that it should not be unthinkable for arrangements to be worked out which would allow the colony to become completely separated from Japan, while still retaining informal ties of friendship between the two countries. For Korea to gain her independence after a period of responsible political tutelage by Japan, Yanaihara had concluded, would be an honorable destiny for both countries.[88]

Yanaihara Tadao was thus one of the few Japanese colonial theorists to develop the idea of colonial trusteeship in the British and American sense. Had such an idea been given breathing room in official policy toward Korea before 1919, Japan's reputation as a colonial power might have been salvaged and the present relationship between the two countries less haunted by memories of a repressive past. But Yanaihara's hopes for Korean autonomy within the colonial empire, particularly his idea of a Korean parliament, were doomed from the outset. For all his liberalism and sympathy with Korean aspirations, he lacked a profound understanding of Korean nationalism. In the eyes of most Korean patriots after 1919, his failure to provide continued and active support for outright Korean independence fatally undermined his proposals for a gradual advance to home rule. His moderate recommendations were thus too fragile to have served as a bridge between Korean nationalism and Japanese colonial policy. More importantly, not only were they utterly rejected by the Japanese government as the futile arguments of an academic doctrinaire, but by 1937 they had also brought about his own professional eclipse. In that year Yanaihara was dismissed from his lectureship in colonial studies at Tokyo University, and in 1938 his works were banned and he was purged from public life, though, with considerable courage, he continued to speak out against Japan's colonial abuses. Only with the collapse of the empire in 1945 were the ideas of Japan's foremost colonial scholar vindicated.[89]

[88] *Yanaihara zenshū*, I, 284 and 741-742.

[89] Ubukata, p. 94, and Kusubara Yoshiharu, "Yanaihara Tadao Chōsen kankei ronbun ni tsuite" [Yanaihara Tadao's Essays Relating to Korea], in *Chōsen kenkyū*, XLII (August, 1965), II. After the war, Yanaihara, now a prophet with honor, became renowned for his public lectures on Christianity, peace, democracy, and education. President of Tokyo University from 1951 to 1957, Yanaihara died in 1961.

THE EMPIRE UNDER FORCED DRAFT, 1931-1945:
REJECTION OF THE EUROPEAN PATTERN

In any event, Yanaihara was the last colonial specialist to advocate a
liberal alternative to an increasingly authoritarian colonial policy.[90]
The decade of the 1920's, still open to the winds of Taishō liberalism,
had seen a good deal of discussion and debate on colonial affairs.[91]
As late as the autumn of 1930, when controversy erupted in the Diet
over responsibility for the Musha Rebellion in Taiwan, it was possible to debate the nature and purpose of Japanese colonial policy.[92]
But after 1931, amid the growing sense of national crisis and mili-
tancy, Japanese colonial thought assumed a doctrinaire orthodoxy
which supported a policy of exploitation, regimentation, and forced-
draft assimilation in Japan's overseas possessions. The pale wash of
liberal reform and modest accommodation to the interests of Japan's
colonial peoples during the earlier decade was soon dissolved in the
acids of aggressive nationalism and military necessity. In the over-
heated political atmosphere of the times the empire once again became expansive, though less by design from its metropolitan center
than by the arbitrary initiatives of its military agencies abroad. Moving first from the Liaotung peninsula and Korea into Manchuria, and
from there into North China, Japanese garrisons on the continent,
acting largely on their own, ushered in an era of military expansion
outside the boundaries of the formal empire through *faits de guerre*
not unlike the forward sweep of late nineteenth-century French mil-

[90] Marxist scholars in Japan and those who applied Marxist analyses to modern
Japanese expansion endeavored to offer a critique of Japanese imperialism, of course,
though most of their work was banned by the end of the 1930's. Among these, the
historian and social critic Hosokawa Karoku (1888-1962) devoted the greatest attention
to colonial affairs per se. While his frame of reference was derived from the broader
generalizations of Hobson and Lenin, he was also interested in the workings of policy
in the colonies, particularly in Taiwan and in Korea. See his *Shokuminshi* (Colonial
History), Vol. II of the *Hosokawa Karoku chosakushū* (Rironsha, 1972). Along with
Yanaihara, Hosokawa was jailed during World War II for his pacifist views.

[91] An interesting example of the fairly open discussion of Japanese colonial policy
during this period is a collection of essays on Japanese administrative policy in Korea,
Chōsen tōchi ronbunshū, edited by Imoto Ikujirō and published in Seoul in 1929. The
viewpoints expressed in the collection are surprisingly disparate.

[92] The Musha rebellion was a bloody spasm of resistance by the aborigines in the
mountains of central Taiwan in mid-autumn of 1930, provoked by Japanese encroach-
ments and abuses. Nearly two hundred Japanese died in the initial uprising, which
took place during a public ceremony to dedicate new administrative buildings in Musha village, a regional headquarters in the province of Taichung. Both the origins of
the rebellion and its violent suppression by colonial authorities were subjects of heated
debate in the Japanese Diet.

itary imperialism in West Africa.[93] At the same time, as the decade progressed, the Japanese leadership, both civilian and military, came to perceive the component territories of the empire, and, to a degree, those newly occupied zones adjoining it, to be one undifferentiated unit, Asian in composition, uncompromisingly Japanese in outlook and purpose.

Thus did Japan's colonial empire increasingly reflect the "continental imperialism" of Hannah Arendt's typology referred to in the introduction of this volume: a "cohesive expansion" into territories contiguous to the formal empire, justified in the name of racial solidarity, and linked to the conviction that the empire must be regarded as a political and racial whole. As it did so, the empire moved rapidly and purposefully away from any identification with the European pattern of "overseas" colonialism.

Central to the concerns of Japanese colonial policy in the new decade were the economic consolidation of the empire and the integration of its colonial economies to meet the requirements of the home islands, now under semi-wartime conditions. Official pronouncements heralded the new direction of Japan's colonial purpose. In an introduction to a huge compendium on the Japanese colonial empire published by a Japanese scholarly association in 1934, Koriyama Satoru, bureau chief in the Colonial Ministry, took note of the inability of the nations to develop an interdependent economic order after the World War and the consequent trend toward autarky. Inevitably, Koriyama declared, these developments required Japan to build her own economic bloc, centered on her colonial empire, to which the nation had to look for its own economic survival.[94] In this perspective colonies were seen chiefly as productive elements of a central economic engine, geared to the creation of a self-sufficient garrison state. Increasingly, military necessity dictated that the economic interests of individual colonies be subordinated to the semi-wartime, and after 1937, to the wartime needs of metropolitan Japan.

But economic integration of the empire was only part of the policy of regimentation which overtook all of Japan's colonies. By mid-decade the colonial governments of both Taiwan and Korea were

[93] To a surprising degree the unauthorized activities of French military commanders in the Sudan, which led to the creation of a vast military empire in that portion of West Africa in the 1890's, parallel the field initiatives of the Kwantung Army in Manchuria, Mongolia, and North China in the 1930's. See Alexander Kanya-Forstner, *The Conquest of the Western Sudan: A Study in French Military Imperialism* (London, 1969), pp. 266-268.

[94] Nihon Gyōsei Gakkai, ed., *Bankin Dai Nippon takushokushi* [The Recent Colonial History of Japan] (Tokyo, Nihon Gyōsei Gakkai, 1934), introduction, pp. 3-4.

under military commanders and the mandated islands in Micronesia placed under de facto control of the Japanese navy by 1940. No longer open to debate, assimilation became the guideline for all colonial policy. But increasingly directed toward the inculcation of aggressive Japanese patriotism among Japan's colonial peoples, assimilation was now stripped of all considerations of accommodation or equal opportunity for colonizer and colonized. Used in public by colonial officialdom, *isshi dōjin* decreasingly bore any connotations of common rights and increasingly became freighted with the idea of common obligations toward the Japanese state. Gone too were the assumptions held by Gotō and Nitobe that assimilation would be a process of centuries. Under the pressures of national and international crisis the tempering of colonial races to the institutions and value systems of Japan was now to proceed at white heat.

By 1937 these increasingly coercive efforts pushed assimilation to its final stage, a movement for the "imperialization of subject peoples"—*Kōminka*—which aimed at the complete regimentation and Japanization of Japan's colonial races, and justified these goals through endless moral platitudes couched in Confucian phraseology and centered on inculcation of a sense of obligation to the Japanese Emperor.[95] "Without this sense of profound gratitude for the limitless benevolence of our Emperor," intoned one commentator on the subject, "provisional subjects [like the colonial peoples] cannot grasp the true meaning of what it is to be Japanese." And for those who failed to get the point, he noted that "while *Kōminka* as a concept may seem abstract and difficult to grasp, its fundamental principles are the same as those in the Imperial Rescript on Education; to understand the one is to understand the other."[96]

The *Kōminka* movement involved frenetically paced efforts along two lines, seen by Japanese authorities as mutually supportive: the further Japanization of the alien races of the empire and the mobilization of their energies for the Japanese war effort. It thus involved programs of "spiritual mobilization"—mass campaigns to harness "voluntary" public commitment to the most stringent wartime duties; accelerated efforts to diffuse the Japanese language throughout the colonies; efforts to abolish lingering patterns of indigenous culture in the colonies; and government–sponsored youth movements to inculcate loyalty to the Japanese Emperor and to instill a spirit of

[95] The origins of the term *Kōminka* are not clear. While Gotō Shimpei had spoken in 1903 of the "imperialization" of the Taiwanese, the word itself appears to have been fashioned by Japanese journalists about 1937. Washisu Atsuya, *Taiwan tōji kaikodan* [Recollections of Government in Taiwan] (Taipei, 1943), p. 339.

[96] *Ibid.*, pp. 342 and 346.

public service.[97] The oppressive measures of the *Kōminka* movement fell most heavily on Korea, where the efforts to blot out an entire culture and to dragoon economic and military support from the Korean people amounted to "colonial totalitarianism" (Gregory Henderson's phrase). By 1941, however, it was felt even to the outer reaches of the mandated islands, where the colonial government attempted to institute among the contented Micronesians the aggressive industriousness and patriotism of wartime Japan, an effort which met with only partial success, despite the rigor with which it was undertaken.[98]

Yet, if Japanese colonial policy was increasingly subservient to military needs and wartime exigencies, it was increasingly justified and publicized with the mystical rhetoric of Japanese ultra-nationalism, which preached the divine origins and unique attributes of the race. An official publication of the government–general in Taiwan in 1938 attributed the results of Japan's "unique colonial record" to "the spirit of the Imperial Way" (*Kōdō seishin*), which, the editor explained, meant "the maternal love of Japan for her children." The introduction to the 1940 edition of the Colonial Ministry's annual survey was studded with references to the Japanese "national essence" (*kokutai*), "the world under eight corners of one roof" (*hakkō ichiu*), and other incantations which obsessed Japanese nationalistic propaganda of the time.[99]

Incorporated more than ever into this rhetoric, was the language of a reinvigorated Pan-Asianism which entered the ideological bloodstream of Japan in the 1930's. At its mildest, Pan-Asianism still spoke of the capacity of the Japanese empire to "harmonize" international relations, exemplified by Nagai Ryūtarō's statement in 1932 that Taiwan, with its Chinese cultural heritage, could serve as a bridge to restore friendly relations to Japan (an argument so filled with incongruities as to verge on the bizarre).[100] In its more virulent form, however, the new Pan-Asianist outlook in Japanese colonial policy, especially when combined with military considerations, took on the overtly expansionist character associated with the announcement of

[97] William Kirk, "Social Change in Formosa," in *Sociology and Social Research*, XXVI (1941-1942), 18-26.

[98] Alexander Spoehr, "Saipan: The Ethnology of a War-Devastated Island," in *Fieldiana: Anthropology*, XLI (Chicago, 1954), p. 139.

[99] Naito Hideo, ed., *Taiwan, A Unique Colonial Record* (Kokusai Nippon Kyōkai, 1938), p. 21, and Takumushō [Colonial Ministry], ed., *Takumu yōran* [Colonial Survey], 1940, p. 1.

[100] Nagai Ryūtarō, "Taiheiyō heiwa no kagi o nigiru Taiwan" [Taiwan as the Key to Peace in the Pacific] in *Taiwan taikan* [A Comprehensive View of Taiwan], Tokyo, Nihon Gōdō Tsūshinsha, editors and publishers (1932), p. 332.

a "New Order" in East Asia and with the designs of the Greater East Asia Co-Prosperity Sphere. An article in the *Kōminka* movement appearing in 1941 in the official journal, *Taiwan jihō*, declared that Japan's assimilationist policies recognized that "total war included not just military strategy, but political, economic, cultural, and ideological elements" and asserted that, through the experience gained from the *Kōminka* movement, Taiwan could become "extremely valuable in the construction of East Asia."[101]

Increasingly, therefore, the idea of *Kōminka*, with its implications of Japanese superiority based on the supposedly divine origins of the race, was linked to the appeals of Pan-Asianism, which professed the racial brotherhood and union of all Asian peoples. If this contradiction was soon apparent to other Asians, it seems to have been lost upon military and civilian authorities in Tokyo, for whom Pan-Asian ideas took on the sanctity of holy writ. In this sense, the claims of Japan's emerging Pan-Asianism of the 1930's are recognizable as a variant of Hannah Arendt's explanation of the ideology of the pan-movements of Europe, which "offered a new religious theory and a new concept of holiness [which] preached the divine origins of their peoples. . . ."[102]

By mid-decade the Japanese colonial empire had come to be seen by its officials as a staging area for the economic, political, and military domination of East and Southeast Asia. In 1936, Colonial Minister Nagata Hidejirō declared in the Diet that "the historical mission of Taiwan lies in the south, because of Taiwan's geographic position," and in a public address that same year Admiral Takahashi Sankichi, commander of the Imperial Japanese Navy's Combined Fleet, argued that "Japan's economic advantage must be directed southward, with either Formosa or the South Sea Islands as a foothold," adding that "the cruising radius of the Japanese navy must be expanded suddenly as far as New Guinea, Borneo, and the Celebes."[103]

By 1941, therefore, Japanese colonial policy was exploitative, regimented, and expansionist. It was, moreover, avowedly "anti-colonial." Within the empire itself this meant efforts to maintain the fiction that Japanese colonialism did not exist. The European-style trappings of empire were down-graded. Gone, for example, were the colonial white uniforms and pith helmets of the past, their place taken by the drab serge of the *kokuminfuku*, the national tunic of wartime

[101] Cited in A. J. Grajdanzev, *Formosa Today: The Development and Strategic Importance of Japan's Tropical Colony* (New York, 1942), pp. 358–359.

[102] Arendt, *The Origins of Totalitarianism*, pp. 232–233.

[103] *Ibid.*, p. 188, and James K. Eyre Jr., "Formosa, Japan's Southern Naval Bastion," U.S. Naval Institute *Proceedings*, LXIX:3 (March, 1943), p. 332.

Japan. References to the *shokuminchi*—colonies—were no longer in favor. Now there were only the *naichi*—"the inner area" (the Japanese home islands)—and the *gaichi*—"the outer area" (Japan overseas)[104]—which were held to comprise a single expanding, Pan-Asian bloc. As the Pacific war deepened, wartime conditions hardened these concepts into a reorganization of the colonial administrative structure. The Colonial Ministry was abolished in 1942 and succeeded by the more ideologically oriented Greater East Asia Ministry, which handled relations with all Japanese-occupied territory in Asia except Taiwan, Korea, and Karafuto. The administration of Korea was brought under the control of the Home Ministry in 1942, and in 1944 Karafuto was transformed into just another Japanese prefecture.

Externally, Japan's Pan-Asian, expansionist, and "anti-colonial" perspectives made possible a self-righteous assault on colonialism in general and on Western colonial regimes in Asia in particular. Far from being accepted as the modern standard against which to measure Japanese progress in the art of administering alien races abroad, Western colonialism was now pictured by Japanese propagandists as venal, decadent, and unjust. A corrupt and outmoded system, it was to be swept away by the "co-prosperous" forces of the "New Asian Order."

As Japanese armies swept into Western colonial territories in Southeast Asia, official propaganda endlessly repeated these ideas as a matter of course. But those scholars and specialists still permitted to publish also sounded the new anti-colonial themes. In a series of lectures delivered in the spring and summer of 1942, economist Nagao Sakurō, attempting to give Japanese expansion in Asia a philosophical and theoretical underpinning, seized on the work of J. R. Seeley to give focus to his ideas. Just as Seeley's *Expansion of England* had sought to rouse the late-nineteenth-century British public to a renewed sense of imperial greatness, Nagao asserted he aimed to educate the Japanese people in the "spiritual meaning" of Japanese aggrandizement within the context of a regenerated Asia. But, to Nagao, Seeley's British empire, like other Western colonial systems, was played out, a victim of its internal weaknesses and injustice. Moreover, its very structure no longer made sense in view of the new realities of world power. Whereas control of colonial territory had once been the hallmark of great power status, an asset which Japan had been late in acquiring, "colonies" were now a liability, as the decline and recent collapse of a number of the old colonial sys-

[104] Muramatsu Takeshi, ed., "Shokuminsha no kaisō" [Recollections of a Colonialist], in *Chōsen kenkyū*, XII, p. 48.

tems had amply demonstrated. The new locus of international power, Nagao concluded, was the racially linked, "co-prosperous" economic blocs. Thus, Japan's recent territorial expansion made possible by Japan's position within the Greater East Asia Co-Prosperity Sphere had already more than compensated for the nation's tardy colonial development earlier in the century.[105]

While Nagao, as a scholar, was not uninformed as to comparative colonial history, nor his studies lacking in solid analysis of past colonial institutions, his general line of argument naturally strikes one as unconvincing today. To skim the pages of his collected lectures (which are somewhat incongruously titled *Trends in Japanese Colonial Policy*) is to recognize all the inconsistencies and self-serving arguments of Japanese wartime expansion. Nebulous speculations like Nagao's— and they were legion in the 1930's and 1940's—on the "post-colonial" nature of Japanese overseas dominion never explored the actual status of Japan's possessions within any fraternal union of East Asian races and nations, nor even explained the way in which "co-prosperity" related to unidirectional exploitation of the resources of the Japanese empire. Yanaihara Tadao's questions were thus never answered, merely bypassed.

Nor did the proclamations of racial harmony within the greatly expanded Japanese imperium ever resolve the problem of racial status in the colonies, which had remained ambiguous from the outset. Indeed, wartime planning by the military for the political reorganization of Asia seemed to cloud Japan's public commitment to Asian equality. A 1942 Army General Staff memorandum for "nationality policy" within the Greater East Asia Co-Prosperity Sphere spoke of "master peoples" (*shūjin minzoku*), meaning the Japanese, who would take the lead in the sphere but who were cautioned to maintain "the purity of the blood"; "friendly peoples" (*yūjin minzoku*), like the Koreans, who held similar rights and duties but were in a reduced status commensurate with their capabilities; and "guest peoples" (*kigū minzoku*), presumably Occidental nationalities whose presence was to be tolerated, if they behaved themselves. The lesser races were to be shifted about Asia at the bidding of the "master people" as military and economic necessity dictated.[106]

Thus, what had become Asia's most slavish colonial system, an empire of the lash, ended by denying that there was anything colonial

[105] Nagao Sakurō, *Nihon shokumin seisaku no dōkō* [Trends in Japanese Colonial Policy] (Tokyo, Yūhikaku, 1944), pp. 1-8, 29, and 457-459.

[106] Cited in *Japan's East Asia Co-Prosperity Sphere in World War II; Selected Readings and Documents*, edited and introduced by Joyce C. Lebra (New York, 1975), pp. 120-121.

in its motivations or structure. While "liberated" colonial territories of the West were given some independent identity within the Japanese-controlled sphere, Japan's own colonial territories were bound ever more tightly to a nation which staggered toward defeat. Linked to the image of Asian conquest and to the horrors of the China and Pacific wars, this mutant form of Japanese colonial theory quickly shriveled in the holocaust that consumed the colonial empire by 1945. Nor, unlike the phoenix of Japanese national recovery, was it likely to rise from the ashes of war. For it would seem that, as Akira Iriye has said of Japanese imperialism as a whole, Japanese colonial rule was in the end ill-served by ideas which could justify it to the Japanese themselves, to their colonial peoples, or to the nation's victorious enemies.[107] Without even a feeble commitment to the principle of trusteeship, without indeed any sort of legitimization of rule over alien peoples beyond Japan's own interests, Japanese colonial theory, as it evolved in its final stage, could not provide the nation with any pride in tutelary accomplishment when the empire was liquidated at war's end. The transfer of power from colonizer to colonized, unlike most Western de-colonization in the post-war era, came not as a gift bestowed by a gracefully departing colonial officialdom amid independence ceremonies marked by sentiments of mutual confidence and respect, but decreed by triumphant enemies of the colonial power, dispensed by their military or naval garrisons of occupation, and received by peoples bitterly resentful of their recent colonial past.

And yet, we have seen that within the range of Japanese opinion concerning the nature and purpose of colonialism during the fifty-year history of the empire, there were ideas as enlightened and constructive as many which had motivated Western colonial practice. Had the more open domestic and international atmosphere of the 1920's been perpetuated, such accommodative attitudes, shared by a number of bureaucrats and politicians, might possibly have led to a greater sense of responsibility by Japan's colonial stewards toward their colonial charges and opened the way for political arrangements which could have increased in those peoples a sense of participation in a Japanese system. Given time in which to instill Japanese values and loyalties among the indigenous majorities, the empire would have undoubtedly commanded stronger acceptance from its overseas subjects, in whom some sense of gratitude and respect might have remained after the Japanese imperium disappeared.

[107] Akira Iriye, "The Ideology of Japanese Imperialism: Imperial Japan and China," in *Imperial Japan and Asia: A Reassessment*, Grant K. Goodman, compiler. *Occasional Papers of the East Asian Institute* (New York, Columbia University Press, 1967), pp. 44-45.

As it was, the ethos of Japanese colonialism bequeathed no legacy of cultural deference nor forged any bonds of mutual affection, particularly among the peoples of the largest colonies. What did remain behind after the colonial rulers had departed were the standards of success set by Japan in meeting the challenge of modernity. In provoking among its colonial peoples an appreciation, indeed an outraged envy, of Japanese organization, diligence, and competitiveness, Japan's colonial rulers wrought more than they knew.

CHAPTER 3

Economic Dimensions of Meiji Imperialism: The Case of Korea, 1895-1910

Peter Duus

Since the late 1920's Japanese intellectuals and scholars have argued over the relationship between Japan's socio-economic development at home and its policies of expansion abroad. Most parties to the debate, under the influence of Marxist-Leninist theories of imperialism, have assumed that there is a necessary and intrinsic relationship between the two, and that the term "imperialism" describes not only a type of foreign policy but also a particular stage of capitalist development. Much of the controversy has focussed on the question of just when "modern imperialism" (i.e., territorial expansion at the service of "finance capital" or "monopoly capital") really began. The problem is particularly vexing since Japan began to acquire its colonial empire at a time when its economy was much less advanced than those of the Western imperialist powers. The theoretical and definitional calisthenics generated often are of little interest to the uncommitted, but the debate has raised many questions and produced a large body of empirical research on the economic aspects of Japanese expansion.[1]

Few Western scholars have paid much attention to this literature, especially the diplomatic historians, possibly because they suffer the same occupational disease as diplomats: tunnel vision induced by overlong immersion in the dispatches. While "cultural" or "psychological" influences often seem important to Western writers, the socio-economic context of political expansion is either taken for granted, ignored, or regarded as irrelevant. There are, of course, exceptions.

---

[1] Three useful bibliographical essays on the study of Japanese imperialism are Fujimura Michio, "Nihon teikokushugi no seiritsu [The Establishment of Japanese Imperialism]," in Rekishigaku Kenkyūkai (ed.), *Nihon shi no mondaiten* [Issues in Japanese History] (Tokyo: Yoshikawa Kobunkan, 1965), pp. 332-349; Fujii Shōichi (ed.), *Shimpojium Nihon rekishi 19: Nihon teikokushugi* [Symposium on Japanese History 19: Japanese Imperialism] (Tokyo: Gakuseisha, 1975), pp. 9-43; Shinobu Seisaburō and Nakayama Jiichi, *Nichi-Rō sensō no kenkyū* [A Study of the Russo-Japanese War] (Tokyo: Kawade shobō shinsha, 1972), pp. 12-34.

Among them is Hilary Conroy's provocative monograph on the Japanese seizure of Korea, which directly addresses the question of whether "the economic factor" influenced the decision to make a colony out of Korea. Conroy argues emphatically that it did not. As he observes in his conclusion, "Economic matters . . . had no important effect in determining the Japanese course toward the annexation of Korea." Writing in the late 1950's he found that the general thrust of Japanese scholarship supported this view: "It is now generally accepted that the causes of the Sino-Japanese War were *not* economic, to be found neither in the search for expanding markets on the mainland of an expanding Japanese capitalism nor in economic-based class struggle in Japan."[2] Among Western scholars there have been few if any murmurs of dissent from Conroy's conclusions, even though in Japan the continuing analysis of imperialist expansion in socio-economic terms has produced refinements to the debates of the 1950's. Perhaps it is time to reopen the question of what role, if any, "economic matters" played in Japanese expansion into Korea.

At the outset, let us set aside the question that Conroy addressed: whether expansion into Korea was "caused" by the political pressure of private capitalists, the emergence of class contradictions, or the development of structural economic needs for overseas territories. It is fairly clear, as Conroy and others have shown, that the most compelling impulses behind the earliest Japanese decisions to expand are to be found in the flow of immediate political events, the emergence of strategic anxieties, and the interplay of misguided idealism and simple opportunism. The primary goal of the advance into Korea was to deny control to any other power lest Japan's own strategic position in the region be weakened. There is little evidence in the diplomatic documents or in the papers of the statesmen to indicate that economic advantage was the *primary* concern of the decision makers or that they were heavily influenced by the lobbying of private business interests. Had markets, resources, or the interests of private capitalists been the only questions at stake, it is doubtful that the oligarchs would have fought the Chinese in 1894, the Russians in 1904, or the Korean resistance after 1905. But to admit this does not mean that we can brush aside the question of economic impulses entirely or that we can ignore the economic context of expansion. There are other issues to be raised about the economic dimensions of Japanese expansion.

There is the problem, first of all, of whether or not the govern-

[2] Hilary Conroy, *The Japanese Seizure of Korea* (Philadelphia: University of Pennsylvania Press, 1960), pp. 485, 491.

ment and its leaders thought that expansion would bring economic advantages as well as political-strategic advantages to the state. As Mark Peattie and others have shown, more secure access to the economic resources of Northeast China was an important consideration in the minds of the military expansionists of the late 1920's and 1930's, and their conception of the national interest included "economic matters." Could the same considerations have played a role in the minds of the late Meiji leaders as well? One of the most interesting developments in recent Japanese scholarship on Meiji imperialism is the greater attention given to the importance of "state capital" (as opposed to private "surplus capital") in explaining the development of the empire. If the government was willing to invest its resources in the economic exploitation of the newly acquired territories, what were they trying to accomplish? Perhaps we need to look more closely at how the national leadership perceived the country's economic situation in relationship to the policy of expansion.

We should also take another look at the perceived interests of private businessmen and their views on the policy of expansion. To be sure, business leaders at the turn of the century often complained, with some justice, that their impact on national policies was limited, and certainly not congruent with their importance in society, but at the same time they were singularly vocal on a wide range of public issues, from education through foreign policy. It is not difficult to find them making pronouncements on the economic advantages of expansion. Were they speaking as good patriotic Japanese, no less enthusiastic for promoting national security than national political leaders, or did the prospect of profit play a significant role in their view of foreign policy? Were their views on the economic value of expansion congruent with those of government leaders, and if so did private business play a synergistic function in expansion, facilitating and accelerating the penetration of political interests in Korea? Does one need to find business present at the highest deliberations of state policy in order to establish a role for them in the process of expansion?

Finally, if we move from the realm of perceived or real economic interests to that of concrete activity, we can raise the question of how the general state of the economy affected the ability of private businessmen or public officials to exploit the opportunities provided by the expansion of Japanese political influence in Korea. To be sure, this sounds very much like the question that Japanese Marxist scholars ask: to what extent did structural imperatives require or make inevitable political expansion into Korea? In fact, however, it is more fruitful to put the question the other way: namely, to what extent did the relatively retarded level of Japanese development inhibit the ability of the Japanese to exploit their opportunities to the fullest? What kinds of economic activity were most suitable, given the fact that modern economic growth had only just begun in Japan, and to a large extent coincided with initial expansion into the Asian continent? To raise the question of the relationship between economic development and expansion is not to suggest that the relationship is constant, however. As a number of recent Japanese studies have argued, changes in the structure of the domestic economy may have brought changes in the character of economic activities in colonial and other overseas areas.

The Oligarchs and the International Economy

Let us begin our exploration of these questions by looking at the leaders who created the empire: the oligarchs and their lieutenants. We usually think of them as they appear in the official portraits of the 1890's, as masters of realpolitik bedecked in serge and gold braid, contemptuous of those who pursued private profit or mere wealth. To a degree this image is an accurate reflection of their political style, their essential concern for the maximization and manipulation of state power, and their relative aloofness from the pressures of domestic political interests. Yet it is wise to remember that whatever their style or rhetoric may have been, it was the oligarchs and their lieutenants who had created a capitalist political economy in Japan. Indeed, had they not developed a sophisticated understanding of capitalism, neither they nor the nation would have prospered in the decades since the Restoration. Whatever else they were, the oligarchs were "economic animals," perhaps less aggressively or exclusively so than the leaders of post-Occupation Japan, but no less determined to build Japan as a modern economic power with a strong role in the world market.

While the oligarchs often expressed contempt for the profit motive, and placed it far below service to the state in their hierarchy of values, they recognized that the economic strength of the country ultimately depended on it, and that the economy revolved around the entrepreneurs, financiers, and managers who lived by its commands. Itō Hirobumi, Matsukata Masayoshi, Inoue Kaoru, and Ōkuma Shigenobu had all been centrally involved in the *shokusan kōgyō* policies of the 1870's. As we are often told, early on they had come to appreciate the intimate connection between national wealth (*fukoku*) and national strength (*kyōhei*). It was only natural that they continued to do so. On his speaking tours throughout the country in the late

1890's, Itō Hirobumi, the future resident-general of Korea, stressed the central role that economic development played in building national power. The "foundation of national independence and self-defense" lay in economic strength, he told an audience in 1897. "Promoting the progress of the state is the same as nurturing national strength," he said, "and national strength springs from nothing more or less than the nurturing of the people's wealth."[3] For him as for the other Meiji leaders, politics and economics, government and business, were therefore difficult if not impossible to separate. It was perhaps for this reason that Itō took special care to include representatives of the business world in his plans for organizing the Seiyūkai.

If anything, the importance that the Meiji leaders attached to industrial development grew stronger in the 1890's. During the early Meiji period, the government had followed a policy of taxing agricultural production and exporting agricultural surpluses in order to build up a modern sector of military industries or import substitute industries. In other words, the Meiji leaders had used agriculture to finance the development of modern manufacturing. By the 1890's that policy had succeeded so well that agriculture had receded in relative importance, while manufacturing, especially in textiles and other light industry, grew at an accelerated rate. With increasing frequency after the 1894-1895 war, government officials spoke of "building Japan as a commercial and manufacturing country (shōkō rikkoku)." What they meant by this was a deliberate shift of Japan's world economic role from that of an agricultural goods exporting nation to that of a manufactured goods exporting nation. This reassessment rested on a rational consideration of Japan's international comparative advantage. As Kaneko Kentarō pointed out in 1904, "Japan as an agricultural country cannot stand against Russia, Australia, Canada, or America."[4] If Japan were to compete in the world market, it would have to do so on the basis of its manufactures.

The circumstances that led to this new orientation in external economic policy were varied and complex, but it is possible to single out several influences at work. In the first place, the oligarchs were well aware that international political competition was beginning to assume new forms in the 1890's. National strength was not measured simply by the strength of a country's army, the size of its fleet, or even the extent of its colonies. It was also measured by the economic integuments that knit a sphere of influence together. The Western

[3] Itō Hirobumi, "Tai-Shin shōsaku [Policy Toward China]," in *Jitsugyō no Nihon* (hereafter *JNN*), 1.19 (1897), p. 7.

[4] Alfred Stead (ed.), *Japan by the Japanese* (London: W. Heinemann, 1904), p. 96.

powers appeared to be more intensely on the hunt for concessions and profit in East Asia than ever before. The Meiji leaders feared that unless Japan was more active abroad economically as well as politically, opportunities for trade and investment available to Japan in the region would slip into the hands of competitors. It was important that Japanese rather than Russians or Frenchmen build railroads in Korea, that Japanese as well as Englishmen set up cotton mills in Shanghai, that Japanese rather than Americans control the textiles market in Manchuria, or that Japanese rather than Chinese carry foreign goods to Taiwan.

The post-1896 European race for concessions in China, and the rumors of that country's imminent partition, intensified these feelings. As Prime Minister Ōkuma told a group of businessmen and high officials in 1898: "If you ask what international interests are most fought over today, it is commerce. . . . Foreign trade has the largest connection with a country's national interests. It is so important that success or failure in foreign trade establishes a nation's success or failure."[5] Foreign Minister Komura Jutarō summarized the new vision of international competition, as well as the anxiety it generated, in a memorial to the cabinet in late 1902:[6]

> Competition through commercial and industrial activity and through overseas enterprises is a phenomenon of grave importance in recent international relations. Its emergence has been most prominent in the Far East. For a number of years the Western countries . . . have been zealous in expanding their rights in mining, or in railroads, or in internal waterways, and in various other directions on the Asian continent, especially in China. . . . However, when we look at the measures [taken by] our own empire, which has the most important ties of interest in the area, separated by only a thin stretch of water, there is not much to be seen yet. Both those in government and those outside it regard this as highly regrettable.

A policy of *shokusan kōgyō* abroad was as intimately linked to international status and influence in the 1890's and 1900's as it had been in the 1870's.

The late Meiji leadership had also come to realize that the maintenance of economic growth as well as of international prestige de-

---

[5] *Dai-sankai nōshōkō kōtō kaigiroku* [Record of the Proceedings of the Third Conference on Agriculture, Commerce, and Manufacturing], n.p., n.d., p. 42.

[6] Gaimushō (ed.), *Nihon gaikō nempyō oyobi shūyō monjo* [A Chronology and Principal Documents of Japan's Foreign Diplomacy] (hereafter *NGNSM*), Vol. I (Tokyo: Gaimushō, 1955), p. 206.

pended on the active growth of foreign trade. The expansion of foreign exports was particularly important in order to avoid a long-term balance-of-payments problem. While the development of a domestic cotton-spinning industry had reduced dependence on outside imports by the mid-1890's, there was a growing demand for industrial raw materials (principally raw cotton), producer durables (spinning and metal working machinery) and armaments (naval vessels, steel, and heavy ordinance). To pay for these imports, the Japanese had to earn foreign exchange abroad. Owing to the long-term decline in the relative value of silver vis-à-vis gold, imported goods had grown steadily more expensive from the 1880s into the 1890's. The pressure of imports on the trade balance was alleviated to some extent by the shift from a *de facto* silver standard to a gold standard in 1897, and the Chinese indemnity, paid in British pounds, provided Japan with an instant specie reserve to draw upon. But over the long run, exports were needed to balance trade.[7]

By the late 1890's there was also concern that the country might become more dependent on agricultural imports. Domestic agriculture might not be capable of providing the foodstuffs required by the Japanese. The demands for agricultural products such as sugar, wheat, soy beans, and even rice were growing as the population expanded and consumer tastes changed. While Japan remained a net exporter of rice, the import of foreign rice rose steadily from the early 1890's. As an official report observed in 1904, ". . . the inland production of rice is sufficient for the present, but the consumption of rice shows a tendency quickly to extend itself to wider classes as the standard of living rises, and it will not be long before Japan has to complain more or less of the want of food supply, if she neglects to take due care for the increase of the production of rice."[8] This created fears, not of a starving population, but of depleted foreign exchange balances and inflated consumer prices. The continued growth of food imports was likely to create as serious pressures on the balance of payments as the import of manufacturer's goods and armaments.

Export expansion was linked in the official mind with the realization that the burgeoning economy and requirements of a great power status meant heavy economic dependence on the outside world. Quite simply, an aggressive export policy was required if the political economy was to continue advancing. It might be objected that the Meiji leaders had been conscious of this problem since the early 1870's. To

[7] Cf. Ishii Kanji, "Nisshin sengo kei'ei [Post Sino-Japanese War Policy]," in *Iwanami kōza Nihon rekishi* [Iwanami Lectures on Japanese History], Vol. 16, (Tokyo: Iwanami shoten, 1976), pp. 47-88.

[8] Stead, *op.cit.*, p. 419

be sure, they had, but in the 1890's they began thinking of new ways to deal with it. Their new vision of how and in what direction Japan should advance in world markets assumed that since the economic base of the country had shifted from agriculture to manufacturing, Japan could begin to compete in the world market as an exporter of manufactured goods.

This view was most succinctly presented by Kaneko Kentarō, a protégé of Itō, and a key figure in the Commerce–Agriculture Ministry in the late 1890's. Kaneko constantly stressed Japan's assets as a manufacturing power: it was blessed with ample supplies of coal needed for power generation; its labor force was superior in dexterity and mental power to workers in neighboring countries; and as a result it had ample opportunities to expand into overseas markets. Significantly, however, as Kaneko and others saw it, those markets were of two distinct sorts, each requiring a different trading strategy. In the markets of Europe and the United States, where manufacturing was more highly advanced than in Japan, it made little sense to compete in the sale of machine-made goods. Instead Japan should advance in these markets through the sale of raw silk, habutae, ceramics, lacquerware, paper, and straw goods—in short, artistic or craft goods produced in the traditional sector. By contrast, in Asia and the Pacific, where there was no indigenous modern industry, but a growing demand for foreign manufactures, Japan should attempt to sell the products of its light industry—cotton yarn, cotton cloth, flannel, matches, canned goods, cement, and the like. Given Japan's proximity to Asia, as well as its other advantages, its traders could deliver these products at prices competitive with Western goods.[9]

During the late 1890's the notion of Asia, and especially of China, as the most promising future market for Japanese manufactured goods had become conventional wisdom among government leaders. In March 1895 Komura Jutarō, then chief of the Political Affairs Bureau of the Foreign Ministry, presented Mutsū Munemitsu with a memorial fairly saturated with a "myth of the China market":[10]

> The territory of China is vast, her people are numerous, and her resources not inconsiderable. If our marine products and manufactured products are to have one great market in the future, then we must take this opportunity to expand our commercial privileges [in China].

[9] Kaneko Kentarō, "Taigai kōgyō no hōshin [Goals for Overseas Manufacturing]," in *JNN*, 2.6 (6/1898), pp. 5-8; 2.7 (7/1898), pp. 6-10.

[10] Quoted in Nasu Hiroshi, *Teikokushugi seiritsuki no tennōsei* [The Emperor System During the Formation of Imperialism] (Tokyo: Fūbaisha, 1974), pp. 97-98.

Two years later, Sakatani Yoshirō, a key figure in the Ministry of Finance, observed, "If one looks at the whole world today, there is no place for Japan to secure commercial and industrial profit but Asia . . . if one asks where the products of our country are preferred and welcomed, the answer is China and Korea." He even argued to business leaders that the Sino-Japanese War had been fought to that end: "I may be expressing myself a little too grandly, but let me ask why it was that we fought the Sino-Japanese War. The reason we fought it . . . was to provide permanently for the commercial and manufacturing interests in China and Korea, was it not?"[11] In 1904 Itō also pointed to the shift in Japan's external markets:[12]

> The foreign trade of Japan has made considerable progress since the Restoration of 1868, with the United States as her best customer. But we must not rest contented with this, but try to make China a great market for our products. . . . In my opinion, China is a country likely to demand our products to a much greater extent, and to become our best customer in the future.

The late 1890's, usually seen as a period of military and naval build-up in preparation for a new war with Russia, was also a period when the government, through legislation or administrative decision, worked to facilitate the outflow of exports. While many of the measures adopted are well known, it will be useful to recapitulate them briefly. First of all, there were legislative efforts to promote the development of a native merchant marine through the passage in January 1896 of laws to promote long-distance shipping lines and the development of a domestic ship construction industry. These laws granted subsidies, based on the tonnage and speed of vessels, to private shipping firms employing modern iron-clad steam vessels. Second, there were measures intended to reduce overseas prices of Japanese manufactures, particularly textile goods: the abolition of export duties on cotton yarn (July 1894), the abolition of import duties on raw cotton (April 1896), and the granting of subsidies to exporters of silk yarn (March 1897). It could also be argued that resistance to the passage of factory legislation reflected a policy of keeping manufacturing costs down. Finally, there were a whole series of measures to facilitate foreign trade transactions—the establishment of a bonded warehouse system (March 1897), laws permitting and encouraging the formation of export associations or export cartels (1896), the opening up of 22 new ports to foreign trade (July 1899), and the establishment

[11] *Daisankai nōshōkō kōtō kaigiroku*, pp. 652-653.
[12] Stead, *op.cit.*, p. 71.

of new Asian branches of the Yokohama Specie Bank (Bombay, 1894; Hong Kong, 1896; Tientsin, 1899; Chefoo, 1900; Peking, 1902).[13] This rush of activity did not cease at the end of the 1890's, but its sudden inception underlines the obsessive new concern for expanding exports, the central focus of economic foreign policy for the next generation.

If one looks not at foreign policy debates among the late Meiji leaders but at the context of economic thinking within which they took place, it becomes clear that "economic matters" were very much on their minds. Quite obviously there is considerable evidence that acquisition of economic advantages and interests overseas was an important goal of the national leadership in the late 1890's. While in and of itself the existence of such a goal does not provide a sufficient explanation for decisions to expand politically, it underlines the persistent drive for a weightier Japanese economic position in the regional markets of East Asia. The late Meiji leadership expressed clear desires to acquire economic rights and concessions as an adjunct of strategic advantage, and an equally strong concern to expand exports in order to finance economic and military expansion at home. In other words, the oligarchs and their lieutenants were well aware of the economic opportunities presented by political/military expansion and of the economic value of colonial possessions. They wanted to promote Japanese economic interests abroad through the expansion of trade, the promotion of shipping lines, the establishment of overseas banking and credit networks, the acquisition of mining and railroad concessions, and the export of domestic capital. They were as alert as they had ever been to the economic interests of the state.

ECONOMIC POLICIES TOWARD KOREA

Such considerations played a key role in the formulation of Japanese policies toward Korea from the time of the Sino-Japanese War until formal annexation. The primary goals of Japanese policy were the expulsion of Chinese and Russian influence, the initiation of modernizing reforms, and the establishment of Korean independence under Japanese protection. But the Japanese government also exerted continuous pressure on the Korean court for economic privileges. As Japanese influence in Korea expanded, the government's economic goals grew more substantial, until finally its leaders came to the conclusion that the Korean economy should be developed for the advan-

---

[13] Miyamoto Mataji, *Meiji zenki keizaishi no kenkyū* [Studies on Early Meiji Economic History] (Osaka: Seibundo, 1971), pp. 260-288.

tage of Japan. The benefits of this development, as the Meiji leaders well knew, would be shared by private business interests. Indeed, private business was one of the chief instruments through which they hoped to achieve their goals.

For some Meiji leaders the expansion of Japanese economic interests in Korea was from the beginning a primary goal. On the eve of the Sino-Japanese War, in June 1894, Matsukata Masayoshi urged the government to push for "real rights and interests" in Korea instead of forcing internal reforms on the Korean court, a tactic he feared would invite a hostile Chinese reaction. In a memorial to Kuroda Kiyotaka, he wrote, "We have already sent troops to Korea. . . . [They are there] only to secure [Korea's] independence. But we must not forget to work for our national advantage in other respects too. . . . There are four ways of doing so. The first is to take advantage of this opportunity to make Korea open three more ports and establish foreign settlement zones. The second is to secure rights to mine coal in Korea. The third is to monopolize the concession to build telegraph lines. The fourth is to secure rights to construct a railroad line between Fusan and Seoul. These will truly be to the advantage of both countries."[14] In other words, Matsukata proposed to use the crisis in Korea to expand Japan's trading privileges and to develop and control a modern transportation/communication infrastructure there.

While the government did not press for all the items on Matsukata's shopping list, Foreign Minister Mutsū Munemitsu was very anxious to secure "material advantage" in negotiations with the Korean court. He told the Japanese minister in Seoul to negotiate for treaty guaranteed rights to build railroad lines, to control telegraph lines, and to develop mines. Such rights would endure even if a pro-Ch'ing regime were to come to power in Korea once more. A provisional agreement concluded on August 20 provided for the eventual construction of railway lines between Seoul-Fusan and Seoul-Inchon, the maintenance of telegraph lines laid down by the Japanese between Seoul-Fusan and Seoul-Inchon, and the opening of a new port on the coast of Cholla Do.[15]

The motives for seeking these economic concessions were several. First, there was a strong army interest in railroad construction. Pre-

[14] Tokutomi Ichiro, *Kōshaku Matsukata Masayoshi den* [Biography of Matsukata Masayoshi], Vol. II (Tokyo: Kōshaku Matsukata Masayoshi denki hakkō-jo, 1935), p. 499.

[15] Fujimura Michio, *Nisshin sensō* [The Sino-Japanese War] (Tokyo: Iwanami shoten, 1973), pp. 104-105; Shinobu Seisaburō, *Nisshin sensō* [The Sino-Japanese War] (Tokyo: Nansōsha, 1970), pp. 233, 590-591.

liminary surveys for a Seoul-Fusan line had been completed even before the war broke out. Yamagata Aritomo was a strong advocate of building a line from Fusan through Seoul to Uiju on the Manchurian border. He saw it as the beginning of a "great thoroughfare across the Asian continent," which someday might stretch through China to India, enabling Japan to exercise hegemony in the Far East and to assume a place among the ranks of the powers. He thought of railroad lines as sinews of political empire, instruments for political domination of territory.[16] Second, from mid-summer 1894 the popular press in Japan had been clamoring for all kinds of economic privileges in Korea. The *Kokumin no tomo*, for example, had a list of fourteen demands, including Japanese rights to establish a postal service, build railroad lines, participate in coastal shipping, fish in coastal waters, and own land—in short, the right to transact business in Korea without any major restrictions. In order to placate this public clamor, and in order to justify the dispatch of troops and the expenditure of public funds, Mutsū sought the concessions embodied in the August agreement.[17] Finally, one can speculate that the Japanese government was anxious to secure economic rights in order to prevent other foreigners from getting them. Concession hunters had been drifting into Korea since the middle of the 1880's—among them Thomas Edison with a proposal to obtain exclusive rights for electric light and telephone systems. It was inevitable that they would eventually seek railroad concessions. Indeed, in May 1895 four diplomatic representatives in Seoul (United States, Great Britain, Germany, and Russia) protested that it was unfair to give Japan monopoly in railroad rights and other concessions in Korea.[18]

After the war with China ended, Japanese pressure to expand its economic privileges in Korea was stalemated by the sudden decline of Japanese influence over the Korean court. To counter the penetration of Japanese economic influence, the Korean court tried to bring in businessmen from other countries, in effect, playing barbarian against barbarian. In 1896, it sold the concession for the Seoul-Inchon line to James A. Morse, an American promoter, and began negotiating the sale of the Seoul-Fusan concession to a French businessman. These actions violated previous agreements with Japan, but

[16] Oka Yoshitake, *Yamagata Aritomo* [Yamagata Aritomo] (Tokyo: Iwanami shoten, 1959), pp. 61-62.

[17] Natatsuka Akira, *Nisshin sensō no kenkyū* [A Study of the Sino-Japanese War] (Tokyo: Aoki shoten, 1968), pp. 164-176.

[18] Cf. Spencer J. Palmer (ed.), *Korean-American Relations: Documents Pertaining to the Far Eastern Diplomacy of the United States*, Vol. II (Berkeley: University of California, 1963), pp. 260-261.

within the oligarchic leadership the Itō–Inoue faction was reluctant to pressure the Korean government to comply with their original promises. Itō did not wish to antagonize the Russians by pursuing too aggressive a policy of economic penetration of Korea, although eventually he was persuaded to change his mind.[19] As we shall see, by the turn of the century the Japanese had secured a concession for the Seoul-Fusan line and were trying to raise the capital for it.

As the tension between Japan and Russia grew after 1900, the top government leadership felt even more poignantly the need for extending economic influence into Korea. In the fall of 1902 Foreign Minister Komura urged the appropriation of funds to subsidize the building of a railroad line in Korea, to establish a Sino-Japanese bank, to set up commercial exhibitions in Shanghai and Tientsin, and to carry out commercial surveys in China. "The position of our empire, which rose dramatically as a result of the Sino-Japanese War, has advanced yet again as the result of the North China Incident (i.e., the Boxer Rebellion)," he argued. "At the same time, the Anglo-Japanese Alliance has increased our authority in the Far East. . . . Among the most urgent business facing us is to augment our empire's present position by using this opportunity to expand the operations of our business enterprises in China and Korea. . . ."[20]

It was not until after the outbreak of the war with Russia that the genro and the cabinet formulated an explicit definition of its future goals in Korea. A cabinet decision on May 31, 1904 asserted the contradictory goal of maintaining "Korea's independence and territorial security" by turning it into a protectorate of Japan, which would assume responsibility for Korea's defense, its foreign relations, and its finances. But the decision also made clear the government's intention to dominate Korea's economic infrastructure. A summary of the concrete goals is instructive:[21]

1. Rapid completion of the Seoul-Fusan line.
2. Construction by the military of a Seoul-Uiju line, the postwar operation of which was to be determined by consultation with the Korean court.
3. Securing of rights to build a railroad line from Kyongsan and Gensan to Unggi Bay.
4. Indirect or direct control over the Masan-Samlangjin line.

[19] Ryūmonsha (ed.), *Shibusawa Eiichi denki shiryō* [Materials for the Biography of Shibusawa Eiichi] (hereafter *SEDS*), Vol. 16 (Tokyo: Shibusawa Eiichi Denki Shiryō Kankōkai, 1955-65), pp. 355-356.

[20] *NGNSM*, Vol. I, pp. 206-210.

[21] *NGNSM*, Vol. I, pp. 224-228.

5. Direct control over postal service, telegraph lines, and telephone lines and merging with the Japanese domestic systems.

In other words, the Japanese government aimed at total domination over Korea's transportation and communication system.

Rather more interesting, however, is the fact that the cabinet now committed itself to "developing" the country to Japan's economic advantage. They defined the future economic relationship between the two countries as follows:[22]

> The most promising business for our nationals in Korea is to engage in agriculture. In the past Korea as an agricultural country has supplied our country principally with foodstuffs and raw materials, and from our country they have received supplies of manufactured goods (*kōgeihin*). We believe that the future economic relations between the two countries must develop in accordance with this principle.
>
> Moreover, the population of Korea is small in comparison with its land area. If many of our nationals are able to move into Korean territory . . . we will acquire an immigration colony for our excess population on the one hand, and on the other will be able to augment our insufficient supplies of foodstuffs.

In other words, the highest leadership had decided that Korea was essentially to serve as a purchaser of Japanese manufactured goods, a supplier of agricultural products, and as an emigration territory. These goals, of course, meshed perfectly with the larger vision of Japan's position in the world economy. To achieve them, the government proposed to enable "reliable men of capital" to develop agriculture by securing the right of Japanese to lease public lands or to buy and sell private land; to secure lumbering rights along the Yalu River; to carry out surveys of potential mineral deposits and resources; and to expand the right of Japanese to fish in coastal waters.

The May 31 cabinet decision should remove any doubts that "economic matters" were very much part of the Meiji leadership's interest in Korea. It would be difficult to discover a smokier gun. To be sure, the content of the government's economic goals had enlarged between 1895 and 1905, and the proximate causes of the war with Russia lay in strategic concerns. But to neglect or to ignore the quite avid and explicit economic ambitions of the government in Korea distorts an understanding of how the Japanese empire took shape.

[22] *Ibid.*

THE BUSINESS COMMUNITY AND EXPANSIONIST FOREIGN POLICY

Having explored the attitudes of the oligarchic leadership toward overseas economic expansion, let us now turn to the attitudes of the business community toward overseas political expansion. While this might seem an academic question, the position taken by the business was a matter of considerable practical importance to the oligarchs and their lieutenants. The cooperation, experience, and knowledge of business leaders, especially genro like Shibusawa Eichi (Dai-Ichi Bank), Masuda Takashi (Mitsui Bussan), and Ōkura Kihachirō (Ōkura-gumi), was critical to the success of economic expansion abroad. Business leaders themselves were well aware of this. Time and time again, they pointed out that business had a central role to play in the international competition: first, by increasing national wealth and production, business generated the new tax revenues needed to finance the government's military and naval build-up; and, second, by exploiting in peacetime what the soldier had won in battle, the trader, the banker, and the manufacturer could secure and protect Japanese political influence abroad.[23]

For the most part the rhetoric and interests of the business community meshed with those of the government. Top business leaders fell into line behind the government's imperialist foreign policy. No voices of doubt were raised about the wisdom of going to war either in 1894 or in 1904. On the contrary, there was hearty and sometimes effusive support from top business leaders. During both the Sino-Japanese and Russo-Japanese Wars senior business leaders helped to raise large sums of money needed on short notice to cover war costs by promoting public bonds or loans in domestic and foreign money markets. Shortly after the outbreak of hostilities with China in August 1894, Fukuzawa Yūkichi joined forces with several business leaders—Shibusawa Eiichi, Iwasaki Hisaya, and Mitsui Hachirozaemon—to organize the Hōkokukai (Patriotic Service Association), a group intended to solicit private financial contributions for the war effort from businessmen and other persons of wealth.[24] When Ito heard of the project, he called Shibusawa in to tell him that the government intended to raise funds through the role of public bonds, and Shibusawa agreed that this method was more likely to succeed. Similarly, on the eve of the Russo-Japanese War in December 1903, General Kodama Gentarō made a visit to Shibusawa, asking him to lend his influence in lining up support among the banking commu-

---

[23] Cf. Masuda Takashi, "Keizaikai no futatsu daikyūmu [Two Urgent Matters for the Business World]," *JNN*, 1.8 (1897), pp. 10-12.

[24] *SEDS*, Vol. 28, pp. 440-450; Shinobu Seisaburō, *op.cit.*, p. 427.

nity, a service he performed willingly.[25] As a follow-up, in late January 1904, Prime Minister Katsura called in leading bankers and businessmen to his Nagata-chō residence to enjoin their cooperation in underwriting public bond issues, and after the war had begun he dispatched Takahashi Korekiyo to raise loans in the money markets of New York and London.[26]

While one can argue that government bonds were as safe and profitable an investment for the buyers as any—the bonds issued in 1894-1895 paid 5 percent, while those in 1904-1905 paid 5-6 percent—it should be emphasized that big business did not back these wars from such narrowly defined motives of profit. They saw military expansion as compatible with their long-term interests—or, at least, not destructive of them. In the midst of the race for concessions in China, the *Jitsugyō no Nihon* declared that a "great economic war" was underway in the Far East—"a war in manufacturing, in trade, and in economics—a war to be won not by armies but by businessmen."[27]

The victory in 1895 was important in suggesting the profitability of military expansion. Although some businessmen had feared that the war would be disruptive of trade, and might even cut off raw cotton supplies from China, it proved to have no major negative impact on the economy. The China trade did come to a standstill, but Japanese traders found that it was easy enough to send their goods to Hong Kong instead of to Shanghai for transshipment by British or American merchant houses into the interior.[28] The treaty settlement left business leaders relatively optimistic about the possible consequence of future conflicts. The victory not only secured "unequal treaty" privileges giving greater access to the China market; it also boosted Japanese trade with Taiwan and Korea. At the same time, the Chinese indemnity (¥364,510,000) was more than half again as large as the actual war costs (¥200,476,000), and amounted to nearly one third of the national GNP (though no one at the time knew how to calculate that). Business leaders were not entirely happy that a major portion of the indemnity was used to finance a renewed build-up of armaments instead of retiring public bond issues, but the fact remained that on the public balance sheet the war had earned a healthy profit. As Shibusawa later reminisced, "The Sino-Japanese War gave great strength to our economy. . . . We got a large indemnity from China, and it was very useful both for the government and the mil-

---

[25] *SEDS*, Vol. 28, pp. 472-477.

[26] Shinobu and Nakayama, *op.cit.*, pp. 331-338.

[27] "Jitsugyōkoku to shite no Nihon [Japan as a Business Nation]," *JNN*, 1.11 (11/1897), p. 1-3.

[28] *Sakatani Yoshirō den* [Biography of Sakatani Yoshirō], 1951, pp. 154-155.

itary . . . if we had not undergone the experience of that war, I think the advance of our economy would have been much inferior. If that is the case, it is safe to say that war is a very effective helper for the economy."[29]

These lessons continued to inform business views on foreign policy for the next decade. When the Boxer Incident broke out in 1899–1900, business leaders polled by the *Jitsugyō no Nihon* all minimized the likelihood that it would have any major impact on trade with China or on general business conditions. On the contrary, some felt that the disturbance might prove good fortune for Japan. Disruption of production in China might lead to increased demand for Japanese exports abroad, both in Western markets and in the Chinese market.[30] Settlement of the disturbances might produce another indemnity, and beyond that provide an opportunity to force the Ch'ing government to end *likin* and internal transport taxes, to loosen restrictions on the export of rice and other foodstuffs, and to standardize currency and weights. Some even suggested that the powers might reward Japan's participation in the relief expedition by putting an immediate end to treaty tariffs in Japan.[31] Takahashi Shinkichi, president of the Bank of Japan, summed up the prevailing view: "In sum, the influence of the China incident on our economic world is extremely slight. This being the case, the incident should not cause grave concern. Rather, our people should take every advantage of it to shape bold plans for increasing our national wealth."[32]

Military confrontation with Russia was far more risk-laden than either the Sino-Japanese War or the Boxer Incident, but few if any business leaders spoke of the dangers publicly. Instead, they stressed the need to secure greater influence over Korea, or at least deny it to the Russians. If Russia took over Manchuria, warned Morimura Ichizaemon, a leading foreign trader, it would then want Korea, and that would be a disaster both politically and economically for Japan. He argued:[33]

Korea and China are excellent markets at present, and will be in the future. The vast populations of both countries like the excellent

[29] *SEDS*, Vol. 10, p. 481–482.
[30] "Shinkoku jihen waga keizaikai ni oyobosu eikyō [The Impact of the China Incident on Our Financial World]," *JNN*, 3.11 (1899), pp. 38–41.
[31] *JNN*, 3.14 (1899), p. 8–10; 3.15 (1899), p. 12.
[32] Takahashi Shinkichi, "Shinkoku jihen no keizaiteki kansatsu [Economic Observations on the China Incident]," *JNN*, 3.12 (1899), pp. 4–6.
[33] Morimura Ichizaemon, "Keizai zaiseijō yori mitaru Nichirō sensō [The Russo-Japanese War Viewed from an Economic and Financial Perspective]," *JNN*, 8 (1903), pp. 5–8.

products we make in imitation of European and American goods. But it is absolutely clear that if we give in to Russia, our goods ultimately will be thrown out of those markets. It is often said that "Trade follows the flag." I feel this to be strongly true in the case of China and Korea.

Horikoshi Zenjurō, another prominent figure in foreign trade, put the argument more strongly:[34]

Look at how the amount of our trade with China, Korea, and other countries expanded after the Sino-Japanese War. Think how the pusillanimous attitude of our government toward the Manchurian problem hinders the advance of trade in Korea and China. How should we go about expanding our trade and increasing our national wealth? Only by developing a new empire through the acquisition of new territory and by using tariff rights to exclude the products of other countries.

While Horikoshi was an extremist—like Professor Tomizu, he wanted Japan to seize Siberia east of Lake Baikal—his sentiment that Japan should use political and military force to expand its markets was widely shared. When war finally broke out, Ikeda Kenzō (15th Bank) called it the "raising of the curtain on a great commercial advance in the continent"; Morimura welcomed it as a "great stimulus for the development of our business world"; and Hatano Shōgorō (Mitsui Bank) said it was being fought not simply for national defense but to "establish Japan's economic rights in Korea."[35]

Neither the size of the adversary nor the cost of the war daunted business leaders—or, if it did, they expressed no public qualms. The general anticipation was that the war would be short. The scene of battle was far from the Russian heartland, and the Japanese were likely to dominate the sea. More important, there was general optimism about the ability of the country to finance the war. The conventional guess was that war expenses would run as high as ¥300,000,000-400,000,000, about twice as much as the Sino-Japanese War. In 1894-1895 the financial world had been able to absorb the bonds (¥17,000,000) issued to cover half the war costs. Since the economy had grown in size, and the financial community was much

[34] Horikoshi Zenjirō, "Nichi-Rō Kaisenron [Essay on the Outbreak of the Russo-Japanese War]," in *JNN*, 8.12 (1903), pp. 196-200.

[35] Ikeda Kenzō, "Senji ni okeru taigai bōeki [Foreign Trade During the War]," in *JNN*, 7.7 (3/15/1904), pp. 7-8; Morimura Ichizaemon, "Senso to jitsugyo [War and Business]," in *JNN*, 7.4 (2/15/1904), p. 68; Hatano Shōgorō, "Ko tai-Kan kei'ei no ichi yōten [One Essential Point About Management of Korea]," in *Tōyō keizai shimpō* (hereafter *TKS*), 298 (3/15/1904), pp. 355-356.

stronger than it had been then, there were some who felt that it would be possible to defray the whole cost of the war in this way. There was general reluctance to finance the war by raising taxes, but if public bond issues did not supplement regular revenues, some suggested a mix of other measures—increase in existing taxes, imposition of new consumer taxes, or the buying of hoarded gold with new issues of paper currency.[36]

The war proved to be far more expensive than anticipated. In mid-April 1904 the government announced an annual military budget of ¥580,000,000, which meant that war costs might reach ¥1,200,000,000 if it continued for as long as two years. But this did not deter business leaders from expressing strongly positive views. Ōkura Kihachirō warned businessmen against pessimism, and even against frugality, in the midst of war. Asano Sōichirō pointed out that the Russian economy was beginning to show signs of strain—factory shutdowns had risen and confidence among banking circles had declined—while the Japanese economy held firm even in the face of heavy war costs. Even if the war continued, he said, business was unlikely to experience distress, since the economy was continuing to grow, the bulk of military procurements were domestic, external trade was on the increase, and the harvest was good. Asabuki Eiji expressed similar sentiments. While a small number of businesses in trouble before the war were suffering, he said, business conditions were very solid, and there was no likelihood of any major problems even if the government had to issue more public bonds or raise new public loans.[37] Disenchantment with the profitability of war settled in only after the peace treaty was signed, for the Russians paid no indemnity, and Japan was left burdened with a huge national war debt.

In sum, until the end of the Russo-Japanese War big business leaders and the highest echelons of government were moving on parallel tracks in their assessments of the economic future, their evaluation of an expansionist foreign policy, and their sense of economic promise in Asia. It is difficult, and perhaps unnecessary, to understand who was influencing whom. The more important point to consider is that both government leaders and businessmen were responding to the same situation with shared attitudes. Both groups felt that Japan

[36] Cf. *JNN*, 7.4 (2/15/1904), pp. 68-71; 7.7 (3/15/1904), pp. 5-6.

[37] Ōkura Kihachirō, "Senji jitsugyōjō no chū'i [Warning About Wartime Business Conditions]," in *JNN*, 7.12 (6/1/1904), pp. 5-6; Asano Sōichi, "Senki no sen'en to zaikai [The Business World and the Prolongation of the War]," in *JNN*, 7.23 (11/15/1904), pp. 5-7; Asabuki Eiji, "Yo ga senkyoku no sen'en o ureezaru yuen [Why I Am Not Upset by Prolongation of the War]," in *JNN*, 7.21 (10/15/1904), pp. 8-10.

needed to expand its external trade, that it had to finance the purchase of Western manufactures by selling its own manufactures in Asia and its agricultural products in North America, and that the costs of military and political expansion were well worth the money. This by no means implies the existence of a "capitalist plot" to promote imperialism. As Jon Halliday has observed, ". . . a group in essential agreement does not have to 'plot' to exploit their workers; they agree on this without having to discuss."[38] The same comment can be applied to assessments of the impact of "economic factors" on political expansion. One does not have to find business leaders manipulating the Meiji leadership to establish the existence of economic impulses at work in expansion. One has only to root out the unspoken assumptions at work in the minds of both.

Yet it should be added that while business leaders supported political expansion, they did not regard the acquisition of new territory as necessary for the expansion of private business interests abroad. The prevailing view among business leaders was that the most promising business opportunities in East Asia lay not in Korea but in China, where there was no possibility of extending political control. The vast population, size, and well-developed commercial economy of China made its market larger, more penetrable, and more easily exploited than those of Taiwan or Korea. "Korea is our political territory, but China is our economic territory," wrote Katō Masayoshi (president, NYK Shipping Company) in 1903. "In terms of economic value . . . one cannot speak of Korea in the same breath as China. In Korea we must make arrangements to buttress our national security, but in China we must make arrangements to facilitate the increase of our economic profit."[39] The lure of China rested on historical experience. Until the end of the Meiji period, the volume of Japanese exports there exceeded that of exports to Taiwan, Korea, and the Kwantung territories together (Table 1). The leading foreign trade firm, Mitsui Bussan, did far more business there than elsewhere in Asia (Table 2). In a sense the "political territory" of Korea lay deep in the shadow of the China market, and its economic value was not ranked as high as its political value, even among businessmen. On the other hand, the China market was dominated by the Westerners, particularly the British, who were powerful competitors, while

[38] Jon Halliday, *The Political History of Japanese Capitalism* (New York: Pantheon, 1975), p. 343, n. 53.

[39] Katō Masayoshi, "Shinkoku ni oite kei'ei subeki jigyō [Enterprises that Ought to be Undertaken in China]," in *JNN*, (1903), pp. 5-6. Cf. also the remarks of Masuda Takashi, "Tai-Shin Kei'ei [Policy Toward China]," in *JNN*, 9.1 (1/1/1906), pp. 19-24.

in Korea it was possible to build a privileged market, or at least one in which the Japanese had easier access than did the Western businessmen.

THE ECONOMIC PENETRATION OF KOREA, 1895-1910

Consensus on economic foreign policy, especially the promotion of manufactured goods exports, did not assure that economic expansion in East Asia, in Korea, and elsewhere would be a smooth and easy process. It is important to underline the difficulties facing the Japanese lest one fall into easy arguments about the "inevitability" or "profitability" of expansion. While there were compelling political reasons for an aggressive export policy and the acquisition of special economic rights in Korea, domestic economic conditions in Japan were not entirely conducive to rapid exploitation of new opportunities. Certain factors or disincentives hindered Japanese business activities abroad. The country, unlike the Western imperialist powers with whom it was trying to compete, was still at the early stages of modern economic growth, encumbered by obstacles that limited the range of activities that private business interests were willing or able to undertake. At times, despite their shared outlook, government and business leaders found themselves at odds over foreign economic activities. During a series of high-level conferences convened by the government in 1896, 1897, and 1898, leading officials expressed frustration at the lack of private business initiatives abroad, and business leaders argued that such initiatives could be undertaken only if there was adequate promise of profit. The disadvantages of being a late-developing imperialist power were obvious to all.[40]

To begin with, most Japanese businessmen, including those at the highest levels of management, often lacked knowledge, experience, and familiarity with business conditions overseas. The "unequal treaty" systems had worked to their disadvantage. For much of the Meiji period, the external trade of Japan had been in the hands of foreign trading firms. Even in 1896 foreign merchants handled 74 percent (by value) of the country's non-official exports and 70 percent (by value) of the non-official imports (Table 3). Hence, opportunities for Japanese businessmen to gain a firsthand knowledge of foreign markets and of investment conditions were limited. "Who among our present-day businessmen is going to get the idea of going to live in Europe or the United States, where he cannot speak the language and where life is so radically different, in order to promote foreign

[40] A transcript of these discussions may be found in *Meiji zenki sangyō hattatsushi shiryō* [Materials on the History of Industrial Development in Early Meiji], Supplementary series, Vols. 27, 28, 29, 30, 31 (Tokyo: Meiji bunken shiryō kankōkai, 1973).

trade?" asked Kaneko Kentarō. "It is only human nature to avoid what is difficult, and this is especially true in the business world."[41] Despite frequent talk about the advantage of *dōgo dōbun* (similar language, similar writing system), there were few Japanese qualified to carry on business transactions in China or able to understand Chinese commercial customs, and much of the Sino-Japanese trade was handled by Chinese merchant houses operating in Japanese treaty ports. During and after the Russo-Japanese War, *Jitsugyō no Nihon*, a magazine normally devoted to encouraging young men to move upward and onward in the world of business, also carried warnings for those who thought they could make their fortunes in Korea. Amaharu Matasaburō (Inchon Grain Association), an old Korean hand, pointed out that no quick profits awaited the carpet-baggers who arrived in the van of the Japanese military forces in 1904 and that many found no useful employment: there were simply too many pitfalls for the would-be entrepreneurs.[42] The manpower and information problems were an important constraint on expansion of business activities abroad.

Since the economy was in a period of expansion at home, there were still considerable opportunities for lucrative investment at home. The rate of return on risk venture capital at home was extremely high, and successful firms paid high dividends, often more than they could afford, in order to attract buyers of stock. Table 4 illustrates the profitability of cotton manufacturing and shipping, both growth industries in the 1890's. These high rates of return, as well as a relatively high rate of bank interest, underline the fact that the Japanese economy suffered from capital scarcity, or at least a scarcity of risk capital. The problem was exacerbated by periodic business recessions from 1890 onward. By the late 1890's government officials, as well as financial and business leaders, began to call for the importation of foreign capital. In 1904 Soeda Ju'ichi (president, Japan Industrial Bank), observed: ". . . the desire for capital is keenly felt, while the supply is limited, because the habit of saving, or rather making the proper use of savings, is not fully developed among our people. The result is a dearth of money and a high rate of interest, which on average has been oscillating somewhere about 10 percent on loans throughout

---

[41] Miyamoto Mataji, "Nisshin sensōgo no sangyō kei'ei to bōeki kakuchō saku [Production Policy and Foreign Trade Expansion After the Sino-Japanese War]," in *Keizaigaku kenkyū*, 13.2 (1940), p. 59.

[42] Amaharu Matasaburō, "Kankoku hōshi kibōsha no chū'i [A Warning to Hopeful Persons Going to Korea]," in *JNN*, 7.9 (4/15/1904), pp. 68-71; cf. also "Sengo tō-kan Nihonjin shippai no gen'in [Why Japanese Fail in Post-War Korea]," in *JNN*, 9.16 (8/1/1906), pp. 33-36; "Nisshin bōeki jijo [The State of Sino-Japanese Trade]," *JNN*, 1.19 (1897), pp. 33-38.

the country, and a little over 7 percent according to the present official rate of the Bank of Japan, although the discount rate is much lower."[43]

There were frequent complaints about the rentier psychology of investors too, particularly the rural well-to-do and the wealthy heirs of the daimyo aristocracy. In 1899 Masuda Takashi, head of Mitsui Bussan, complained that "those who possess wealth do not attempt at all to put it into new ventures. Instead there is a tendency for them to follow the conservative and passive course of buying land or subscribing to public bonds and certificates, thinking only of the security of their property and planning for their descendents. Those with wealth . . . cling to this conservatism."[44] The public equity market was still comparatively limited, and the habit of investing in stocks relatively new. Large amounts of capital for overseas investment were most readily available from large concerns, banks or consortia of banks, but investment had to be induced by guarantees of a rate of return comparable to those at home. Most early attempts to raise money for large-scale enterprises in Taiwan and Korea met with considerable sales resistance. Often it was necessary to break this by mobilizing a few key investors to create confidence—a major kazoku family like the Mori or Shimazu or even the Imperial household—or by official guarantees of returns.

In addition to these domestic restraints on overseas expansion, there was considerable doubt about the political stability of Taiwan, Korea, and China. Investors and entrepreneurs were all the more hesitant if they thought the time, energy, and capital invested overseas might be lost as a result of riot, war, or rebellion. Ironically, during the late 1890's, the one area under direct Japanese control, Taiwan, was probably less attractive in this respect than either Korea or China. As late as 1899 colonial officials admitted that it was not possible to leave either Taipei or Tainan unarmed, and that business in the interior was extremely hazardous.[45] By contrast, in China, Western gunboats guaranteed the security of the treaty ports, and in Korea the traditional administrative system continued to function. But even in Korea the future was not entirely certain until the Japanese victory in

[43] Stead, op.cit., p. 100.

[44] Masuda Takashi, "Shigyoka no chi'i [The Position of Businessmen]," in JNN, 3.3 (1899), pp. 1-3.

[45] Kaneko Yūhei, "Taiwan no tōchi to jitsugyō kankei [The Relation Between Business and the Control of Taiwan]," in TKS, 18 (1896), pp. 9-12; "Taiwan dan [A Talk About Taiwan]," in TKS, 113 (1899), pp. 14-17.

the Russo-Japanese War, when Japanese armies assumed responsibility for the peninsula's defense.

The lack of institutional modernization also hindered the exploitation of areas like Korea and Taiwan. While trade with Korea was possible and even lucrative under existing conditions in the 1890's, the reform of the currency system, the establishment of reliable legal avenues of redress, and other similar changes were constantly called for by business leaders. Even at the end of the Russo-Japanese War, there were those who argued that the advance of Japanese business activities in Korea depended on the creation of an institutional infrastructure to assure stability of business conditions. The alternative was to accept a reluctance by Japanese to do business in Korea. "If conditions continue as they presently are," wrote one observer, "then even though Japanese residents in Korea will not be in as precarious a position as the Korean people, it is still not possible to say that their lives and property are truly secure. However, ordinary people will hesitate to invest capital or do business in such a precarious place."[46]

All these obstacles were surmountable in the long run, but in the decade and a half before the formal annexation of Korea, they had important implications for the types and timing of enterprises carried on there. Generally speaking, business activities related to foreign trade were the least difficult to undertake, while those requiring large-scale capital intensive investment were the most difficult. The flow of business activities was also very much affected by changing political conditions, and only after the establishment of the Japanese protectorate, which brought about increased dependence on Japan, did full-scale exploitation of Korea begin at an accelerated rate. Trade seemed to follow the flag rather than vice versa. The government often took the lead as it had in promoting the development of the domestic economy in the 1870's. To illustrate these statements, let us look at some key areas of Japanese business activity during the period in question.

a. Trade: cotton manufactures

Initially big business saw its main economic opportunities in terms of expanded trade. This made sense in a capital-poor country like Japan. The costs of entry were relatively low compared with direct

[46] Cf. "Kankoku jitsugyō kei'ei no saikyūmu [The Most Urgent Matters for the Business Management in Korea]," in *JNN*, 8.14 (7/1/1905), pp. 1-6; Nakahashi Tokugorō, "Nikkan bōekijo no ichidai shogai [One Hindrance to Korean-Japanese Trade]," in *JNN*, 7.2 (1/15/1904), pp. 8-10.

investment. Little or no fixed capital was required, and commercial activities could flourish with relatively small amounts of operating capital, supplied either from private resources or from bank loans. Japanese traders rather quickly penetrated the Korean market in the late 1870's, and while trade fell off abruptly after the emeute of 1884 it slowly recovered over the next decade. The striking phenomenon is a sudden spurt in the volume of exports to Korea from 1894 onward (Tables 5 and 6), especially in manufactured goods. In 1896 the structure of Japanese exports to Korea was as follows: cotton tissues (29 percent), cotton yarn (13 percent), metal goods (6 percent), sake (4 percent), matches (3 percent), and assorted sundry goods. The upsurge in trade can be attributed directly to the increase of Japanese military and political influence in the wake of the 1894 victory. Chinese merchants and traders retreated from the country, leaving it wide open to the Japanese and to other foreign traders. Under pressure from the Japanese, the Korean government accepted Bank of Japan notes as convertible currency in 1902, much facilitating the trade with Japan. But essentially the increase in trade resulted from increased confidence in the political atmosphere.

The mechanism by which trade expanded can best be illustrated by the export of cotton manufactures. These had constituted the bulk of Japanese export goods to Korea in the 1880's, but the Japanese had then been engaged in third-country carrying trade, buying foreign cotton manufactures in Shanghai and re-exporting them to Korea. The ability of the Chinese merchants to do this better may have accounted in part for the downturn in Japanese trade in the mid-1880's. Japanese cotton manufactures made rather dramatic inroads into the Korean market after 1896. In contrast to the China market, where the Japanese sold cotton yarn, in Korea they sold mainly cotton tissues, especially machine-made sheeting (fashioned from the coarser Japanese yarns) and traditional homespuns (woven in narrow widths by cottage production). Between 1895 and 1900 approximately 50 percent of Japan's total machine made cotton exports, or approximately 3 percent of its total cotton textiles production, went to Korea. (Cf. Table 7.) On the whole, the level of cotton tissues exports to Korea was higher than to China.

The Japanese, however, were unable to monopolize the cotton textile market since the Koreans continued to buy most of their high-quality textile goods from England. The competitive situation for the Japanese, in other words, was the same as in the cotton yarn market in China, where British and Indian manufactures dominated the market for higher count yarns. The cotton manufacturers were well aware of this situation. In less-developed areas, where price competition was more important than quality competition, Japanese goods were relatively successful. The coarser cotton yarns made by the Japanese, for example, sold better in north China, where living standards and buying power were lower than in south China and where there was a demand for goods regardless of quality.

With the establishment of the protectorate at the end of 1905, a coalition of manufacturing, trading, and banking interests organized themselves to drive Western cotton textiles completely out of the Korean market. While Japanese domination of the country's central economic and political institutions doubtlessly facilitated the effort, the main tactic was the organization of an export association to capture control of the market through combination. In 1906 as the result of negotiations between Shibusawa Eiichi (Dai-Ichi Bank) and Iida Giichi (Mitsui Bussan), three major Osaka cotton firms (Osaka Spinning Company, Mie Spinning Company, and Kanakin Weaving Company) organized the San'ei Cotton Textiles Association, a joint marketing arrangement using Mitsui Bussan as it sales agency in Korea. The purpose was to strengthen their position relative to the Western exports by reducing competition among the three companies in the Korean market. For Mitsui the goal was to stabilize its marketing activities by maintaining a steady volume of business. In 1907, Kanegafuchi Spinning Company and Fuji Gauze Company attempted to reorganize a similar association, though with less success.[47]

The main point to note is that expansion of the cotton textile market in Korea resulted from business initiative. It required no government help or backing. The structure of the domestic manufacturing industry and the resources of the trading company like Mitsui Bussan were sufficient to the purpose. If anything, the cotton manufacturers came to feel that their interests were not fully served by colonial policy in Korea. After annexation in 1910 the government, mainly out of a concern not to offend the powers, chose not to turn Korea into a privileged market by erecting tariff barriers against non-Japanese goods. The change in Korea's political status brought no change in marketing conditions for cotton manufactures. Despite this, the

[47] On the advance of Japanese cotton manufacturers in Korea, see Murakami Katsuhiko, "Shokuminchi [Colonial Territories]," in Ōishi Kaichirō, Nihon sangyō kakumei no kenkyū [Studies on the Japanese Industrial Revolution], Vol. 1 (Tokyo: Gakuseisha, 1972), pp. 232-250; Takamura Naosuke, Nihon bōsekigyōshi josetsu [An Introduction to the History of the Japanese Cotton Industry], Vol. 2 (Tokyo: Hanawa shobō 1971), pp. 184-187; SEDS, Vol. 10, pp. 497-504.

Japanese share of the cotton textile market continued to grow, until 1920, when it dominated 92 percent of all Korean cotton textile imports.

b. Trade: banking

The financing of Japanese trade in Korea was handled mainly by Japanese banks. The Dai-Ichi Bank, the most powerful Japanese banking interest in Korea until annexation, began operations there in 1878, with the specific purpose of facilitating trade. Assisted by a government loan of ¥100,000, Shibusawa Eichi and Ōkura Kihachirō set up shop in a two-storey Western-style house brought to Fusan from Nagasaki. The fortunes of the bank followed those of Japanese trade. As trade fell off in the late 1880's, the Korean branch handled only a modest amount of the bank's total deposits and loans, producing a steady but only modest proportion of the bank's total profits. Indeed, the operation was sufficiently marginal that in 1893 it was rumored that the bank intended to close down its Seoul branch.[48] Alarmed at this, Foreign Minister Mutsū and Finance Minister Watanabe urged Shibusawa Eichi not to do so lest it endanger Japanese trade with Korea. As has been frequently noted, the Dai-Ichi Bank expanded its activities after the Sino-Japanese War, shifting toward more political operations, and from 1905 it functioned more or less as a central bank for Korea. During this period, the position of Korean branches of the bank grew enormously important in the total operation. The share of profits produced by the Korean branch rose from an average of 10.9 percent in 1896–1899 to an astonishing 37.1 percent in 1906–1909.

Yet the bank continued to serve as a trade bank, and it was able to do so without a substantial investment of Japanese capital. Much of the bank's deposits were official Korean government funds. From 1895 onward at least 40 percent of the deposits came from this source, and in some years the proportion reached as high as 60 percent. The deposit of customs receipts, which the bank had acquired in 1884, was particularly important as a source of operating funds. The bank paid no interest on the customs receipts, and on the contrary charged the Korean government a handling fee. This was a particularly lucrative line of operations since it assured a steady source of deposits and increased public confidence in the bank. The bulk of the bank's loans,

---

[48] SEDS, Vol. 16, pp. 46–47. On the development of the Dai-Ichi Bank operations in Korea, see SEDS, Vol. 16, passim; Murakami, op.cit., pp. 226–289; Daiichi ginkō shi [History of the Dai Ichi Bank], Vol. 1 (Tokyo: 1959), pp. 525–543, 675–706.

by contrast, went toward the financing of Japanese commerce and trade in Korea. Indeed, so important was the link between the deposit of the customs and the financing of trade, that when the Russo-Korean Bank was established after the Sino-Japanese War, local Japanese merchants in Fusan, Inchon, and Gensan urged the government to assure that the Dai-Ichi Bank continue to be a bank of deposit for the Korean government since these deposits ultimately provided working capital for Japanese trade.

The Dai-Ichi Bank did not function as an investment or development bank. Its concern was not with building factories or opening mines or even building railroads. According to a study of the bank's loans in 1909, the bulk went toward financing of commercial activities; specifically, 89 percent of its loans went for commerce, 3 percent went for manufacturing, and none went for agriculture. Loans to Japanese far exceeded deposits from Japanese, whereas deposits from Koreans and non-Japanese foreigners far exceeded loans to them.[49] This suggests that in effect the Dai-Ichi Bank was funneling capital acquired from Korean nationals and others to finance the trading operations of the Japanese. In this fashion, private business interests were able to promote Japanese trade without resort to domestic sources of capital.

c. Direct investment: railroads

If trade was the central interest of big business in Korea before annexation, it is also true that business leaders were vitally interested in the development of an institutional infrastructure to promote trade. They wanted establishment of stable currency systems, uniform systems of weights and measures, the improvement of harbors, the construction of railway lines, accessible credit and banking facilities, insurance companies, regular shipping routes, warehousing facilities, and the like.[50] Some of this infrastructure required public investment. In the case of Korea before 1905, this meant investment by the Korean government. But there were also efforts to create infrastructure through private initiative and private capital. The most salient example was the building of railroad lines, the major form of Japanese private investment overseas before the Russo-Japanese War.

As we have already seen, the government had been interested in the construction of a Seoul-Fusan line before the Sino-Japanese War.

[49] Murakami, op.cit., pp. 281-282.
[50] Cf. Asabuki Eiji, "Waga kokumin no kakugo [The Determination of Our People]," in JNN, 7.9 (4/15/1904), p. 71.

In time of war such a railroad line could move troops and supplies quickly northward from the main southern port. From the perspective of business, however, the line was important because it opened up new markets, brought down the cost of moving Japanese goods into the interior, and facilitated the rice trade. The line ran through the most populous agricultural sections of southern Korea. As Shibusawa Eiichi observed in 1900: "Last year 1,000,000 koku of Korean rice was sold in this country. If the price of agricultural products is made cheaper in Korea, it will increase the wealth of Korea. If you ask what profit there is in that, the answer is: more Japanese manufactures will be sold there. . . . Making their agricultural goods cheaper is a way of selling more of our manufactures there. If you ask how to make Korean agricultural goods cheaper, the answer lies in convenient transportation and communication."[51] In short, railroad construction was likely to stimulate general economic development.

The main economic obstacle to a Seoul-Fusan line was financial. In the late 1890's the Korean government did not have the resources, and the Japanese government was reluctant to undertake the task, so the initiative fell to private business. In June 1896 a group of promoters approached Itō and Mutsū to persuade them to ask the Korean government to let the Japanese have the Seoul-Fusan line concession. For the reasons already mentioned, Itō was reluctant to do so but finally agreed to lend his support if responsible business leaders like Shibusawa Eiichi, Masuda Takashi, Nakano Buei, and Ōe Taku (*riji* of the Tokyo Stock Exchange) became involved. After two years of private negotiations and diplomatic pressure, the Korean court finally agreed in 1898 to let the Japanese have the concession on the condition that construction begin within three years. In August 1899 a group of promoters under the leadership of Shibusawa organized the Seoul-Fusan Railway Company, capitalized at ¥25,000,000 (¥5,000,000 in stock and ¥20,000,000 in bonds).

The promoters faced two problems—to persuade the government to back the project with financial guarantees, and to raise the capital required. The problems were interlinked. Given general investor caution, it would be difficult to raise the necessary capital without the government guarantees. The Itō-Inoue faction, still reluctant to embark on a project that might antagonize the Russians, proposed instead that the line be financed by an international consortium on the model of the Ottoman Bank. The advent of anti-Russian Yamagata to power in 1899, however, enabled the promoters to surmount this

[51] *SEDS*, Vol. 56, p. 600.

difficulty: his Army Minister, Katsura Tarō, advanced ¥50,000 from army secret service funds to begin preliminary construction work; the government agreed to subsidize profits; and it issued regulations guaranteeing 6 percent return on both company stock and company bonds for a period of fifteen years. In effect this meant that (at simple interest) investors could recover 90 percent of their investment at the end of the fifteen years.

The government guarantees, of course, reduced the risk for investors considerably. Money invested in stock or bonds of Seoul-Fusan Railroad Company was less like venture capital than like money put into a loan at a fixed rate of interest. Such terms were helpful in overcoming the rentier psychology of many investors. The government backed the project in other ways. The Home Minister assigned each prefectural governor a quota of stock to sell, a practice followed in the sale of government bonds during the Sino-Japanese War. The main appeal to raise capital was the "national worth" of the line. The promoters emphasized not only the economic value of the line, but also its political significance. If the line were not built, they said, the lives and money expended in the Sino-Japanese War would be for nought; Korea would fall under the control of another power; and the independence of Japan would be jeopardized. "If you are concerned about devoting yourself to the country," they argued, "then buy what you can."[52] Investing in the stock, in other words, was promoted as a patriotic act.

There are two aspects about the raising of capital that bear some attention. First, although the stock was oversubscribed substantially, indicating a high degree of public interest, there were considerable difficulties in collecting subscriptions, so much so that construction was slowed down for want of funds. In other words, capital shortage plagued the venture even with the government guarantees. Second, the sale of bonds was much slower than that of stocks, even though bonds were more secure. Early plans to raise capital in foreign money markets were abandoned. Since Prime Minister Katsura was anxious to expedite the construction of the line for military purposes, in 1903 he persuaded the Bank of Japan to mobilize the banking community. In August a syndicate of twelve private and public banks agreed to buy ¥4,000,000 worth of bonds. Once again, capital shortages had their impact. When the Russo-Japanese War finally broke out, the Katsura government stepped into the venture more directly. It pro-

---

[52] *SEDS*, Vol. 56, pp. 401-402. Cf. also the argument of the Diet resolution cited on p. 396.

vided ¥1,750,000 in direct construction subsidies, authorized an issue of ¥10,000,000 government guaranteed bonds, and dispatched government technicians to help to complete construction. The price exacted was increased government control over company management. Top managerial officers were nominated by the government, and the Seoul-Fusan Railway Company became a quasi-governmental enterprise.[53]

Investors had been reluctant to put money into the project because of capital shorages, but they were also uncertain about the long-term fate of Korea, and once Japan established the protectorate the capital flowed in more readily. During 1905-1906 the remaining bonds were underwritten and the rest of the stock was subscribed. Eventually, however, the company was bought out by the government when the domestic railway system was nationalized, and the Seoul-Fusan line became a public enterprise. The point to emphasize is that large capital intensive ventures like the Seoul-Fusan line were beyond the capacity of the private sector to undertake. The only alternative was to fall back on indirect government support, and eventually on direct government involvement. The creation of a basic developmental infrastructure, though of central concern to business leaders, was a task that business could not accomplish on its own, no matter how enthusiastic it was for expansion or how much expansion served its interests.

d. Direct investment: agriculture

Before the end of the Russo-Japanese War, the Dai-Ichi Bank and the Seoul-Fusan Railway Company were the only large-scale Japanese business ventures in Korea. There were a handful of small-scale manufacturing enterprises, tiny factories or workshops producing leather goods, tinned goods, milled rice and the like; and there was also a good deal of small-scale speculation, sometimes in money-lending, sometimes in quasi-legal activities, and sometimes in smuggling, mostly of a profiteering sort with no very great stability or large capital reserves. There were also a host of small enterprises—restaurants, inns, tea shops, whorehouses, and the like—to provide services for Japanese residents in the Korean treaty ports (Table 8). Even in 1908 the average company in Korea had a paid-in capital of only

[53] On the development of the Seoul-Fusan railway line, see SEDS, Vol. 56, pp. 355-515, 570-576; Chōsen tetsudō shi [History of the Korean Railroad], Vol. 1 (Seoul: Chōsen Sōtokufu, 1929), pp. 1-59.

¥37,000, and the average manufacturing firm was smaller, capitalized at only ¥26,000.[54]

The end of the war brought a change in the situation. The economic infrastructure assumed a more visible shape, and the prospects for a long-term investment became more promising. But it is striking to note that there was very little new investment in large-scale manufacturing enterprises. In part this was because big business regarded the Korean market as quite limited, and sales were not likely to justify fixed capital investment. Equally important, certain manufacturing interests, the cotton textile industry in particular, were reluctant to build factories for fear of undercutting Japanese exports to the Korean market. It made little sense to build a cotton spinning or weaving mill in Korea, if the final effect was to reduct the thriving export trade in cotton manufactures. Even in 1918 the cotton manufacturers protested efforts by the colonial government to subsidize the construction of a cotton mill in Korea.[55]

The main opportunities for investment were seen to lie in agriculture or agriculture-related enterprise. An active rice trade with Japan had developed since the end of the 1880's (Table 9). While Korean rice was more expensive than rice imported from Southeast Asia (principally Indo-China and India), it was better suited to Japanese taste, and it was cheaper than domestic rice. The import of Korean rice was important to Japan, especially in poor harvest years, and there was a ready market for it in the urbanized sectors of the Kansai region. But rice exports served mainly to balance trade with Japan. Consequently, there was a widespread feeling that a good way to increase the export of manufactures to Korea was by increasing the buying power of the rural population by increasing agricultural production. "It goes without saying that in [Korea], a country without manufacturing or mining, the primary way to develop national wealth is through agriculture," observed the *Jitsugyō no Nihon*.[56] In other words, from the vantage point of big business, the primary thrust of direct investment in Korea should be to make the Koreans better customers. Investment in agriculture, moreover, was likely to produce immediate returns, since it was relatively easy and inexpensive to set up a rice mill or to purchase a small plot of land. The *Jitsugyō*

[54] Okurashō (ed.), *Nihonjin no kaigai katsudō ni kansuru rekishiteki chōsa* [A Historical Investigation of Overseas Activities of the Japanese], Vol. 5, n.p., n.d., p. 34.

[55] *Dai Nihon bōseki rengōkai geppō*, 294 (2/25/1917), p. 1; 318 (2/25/1919), pp. 1-2.

[56] *JNN*, 8.13 (6/15/1905), p. 2. For similar comments, see "Nan-Kan ni mikomi aru jigyō [Enterprises With Good Prospects in South Korea]," *JNN*, 7.24 (12/1/1904), pp. 22-25.

no Nihon estimated that the safest and most profitable industry that Japanese investors could venture into was rice milling.[57]

Trading concerns like the Ōkura and Murai interests, as well as a few aristocratic rentier families (such as the Okabe and Nabeshima), had already begun to buy up land while the country was at war with Russia. Between 1906 and 1907 several company promotions—often with overlapping management and directors, including, of course, Shibusawa Eiichi—were launched to exploit agricultural opportunities in Korea: Kankoku Kogyō Kabushiki Kaisha (capitalized at ¥1,000,000) to purchase and reclaim marginal land; the Kankoku Kaitaku Kabushiki Kaisha (capitalized at ¥1,000,000) to purchase both reclaimed and unreclaimed land; and the Kankoku Seito Kabushiki Kaisha (capitalized at ¥800,000) to develop a sugar-beet industry. The basic idea behind all these ventures was to combine Japanese capital and farm technology with Korean labor and land to boost agricultural production. For example, the Kankoku Kogyō Kabushiki Kaisha, backed mainly by the Dai-Ichi Bank, planned to lend money against land as collateral, to buy land and farm it with tenants, and to introduce the most advanced agricultural techniques.[58]

Significantly, however, the largest venture established to exploit Korean agriculture was a quasi-public corporation, the Oriental Development Company (capitalized at ¥2,500,000), initiated within the bureaucracy and backed by government guarantee. Although Shibusawa Eiichi, Toyokawa Ryōhei, Nakano Buei, and other business leaders were nominally involved in the organization, the real planning took place in the Ministry of Finance. The main purpose was to promote Japanese immigration to Korea, a way of relieving potential population pressure as opportunities for migration to North America were closed off. The company was to provide Japanese settlers with immigration costs, to purchase land for them to farm, and to finance their agricultural activities by long-term, low-interest loans. The hope was that eventually a group of independent self-cultivating farmers could be established in Korea. The management was to be appointed by the residency-general, stock was to be held by both Korean and Japanese nationals, company bonds were to be underwritten by a consortium of Japanese banks, and the Japanese government agreed to guarantee the interest on bonds up to ¥2,000,000 and to provide annual subsidies of ¥300,000. With such heavy government backing the initial issue of stock was oversubscribed as dra-

57 *JNN*, 8.13 (6/15/1905), pp. 1-5.

58 "Kankoku ni okeru hōjin no shin jigyō to sono kei'eisha [New Japanese Enterprises in Korea and Their Operation]," in *JNN* (5/15/1907), pp. 3ff; *SEDS*, Vol. 16, pp. 589-600.

matically as that of the Fusan-Seoul line. While plans to promote migration to Korea ultimately had to be abandoned for want of takers, the company eventually became one of the principal landholders in Korea.[59]

CONCLUSION

The central argument of this paper has been that, during the decade and a half before annexation, government leaders and businessmen saw Korea as having economic value because it could become part of Japan's expanding market network in East Asia. Even enterprises initiated to exploit Korean agriculture often were thought of as a possible stimulus to Korean buying power. By contrast, there was far less interest in investment in manufacturing or in the development of non-agricultural resources. One can argue perhaps that Japan was driven by a sort of economic "necessity" to expand its economic activities in the peninsula. If the Japanese economy were to continue expanding, it had to find markets for its exports. These markets could serve as outlets for "surplus production" in the cotton industry, but, more important, they were seen as a way to solve the balance of payments problems created by expansion of the military establishment and by a growing manufacturing sector. This does not mean, however, that Japan assumed political control over Korea to control it as a market, nor that business interests lobbied toward this end. As we have seen, there was a considerable ambiguity in their views of Korea's economic value.

It is interesting to note that once Japan had formally annexed Korea, it made no immediate move to turn the colony into a privileged market, i.e., one that could trade only with the metropolis. Existing tariff duties fixed by earlier "unequal treaties" were to remain in force for ten years; all the existing ports, with the exception of one that was converted into a naval base, remained open; foreign vessels were permitted to engage in coastal trade between open ports in Korea; and foreign vessels were permitted to engage in trade between Korea and open ports in Japan. The one treaty right that the foreigners lost was extraterritoriality. Instead they were enjoying the same rights as foreigners resident in Japan. No protective tariff barriers were established until 1920. The only discernibly "protective" meas-

[59] On the organization of the Oriental Development Company, see Kurose Yūji, "Nichi-Rō sengo no Chōsen kei'ei to Tōyō takushoku kabushiki kaisha [The Oriental Development Company and the Management of Korea After the Russo-Japanese War]," in Chōsen shi kenkyūkai rombunshū [Collected Essays on the Study of Korean History], 12 (3/1975), pp. 99-111.

ure was the issuance of regulations requiring the licensing of newly established companies by the colonial government, which gave it the power to exclude foreign concerns.

This seeming anomaly is not difficult to explain. Although Japan had become an imperialist power, as a second-rank nation its leaders continued to be solicitous of the opinions of other imperialists. Had the Japanese government attempted to shut off Korea to foreign trade, doubtless an outcry would have arisen from the foreign powers, particularly the United States and Great Britain. The "open door" principle, after all, was still more or less intact as the modality by which the imperialist powers forestalled international rivalries in East Asia. The Japanese continued to be mindful of foreign sensitivities. They no longer feared Western gunboats, but they did not wish to upset an international status quo from which they had begun to benefit. Furthermore, the Japanese were also beholden to foreign bankers and investors for help in financing their overseas business and economic operations. Foreign investors had bought the public bonds that made possible the Russo-Japanese War, and after the war they had bought stocks and bonds in enterprises like the South Manchurian Railway Company and the Oriental Development Company. Much of Japan's overseas economic expansion, in other words, depended on recycled foreign capital, again an indication of capital shortages within Japan.

This willingness to subordinate the interests of Japanese businessmen to diplomatic necessity illustrates an important point. In the final analysis, politics was still in command in the creation of the Japanese empire. While the economic potential of a territory like Korea was very much in the minds of the expansionists, economic exploitation of this potential was not allowed to jeopardize or to compromise the political objectives of expansion. In the late 1890's, for example, Itō was reluctant to push the Seoul-Fusan Railroad project too forcefully for fear of antagonizing the Russians, and the project succeeded in winning government support only because the Yamagata faction found that it suited their political and diplomatic purposes. Despite agreement on the desirability of economic expansion, tensions continued to be generated by the tug of the government's interests against those of business. One can speculate that usually the bureaucrats had their way, but the problem is one that deserves further exploration.

In the long run, of course, perception of the economic value of Korea began to change. Trade continued to grow after annexation, from 4 percent of Japan's total foreign trade in 1910 to 16 percent in 1930, but other economic functions of the colony began to assume importance. From the end of the First World War, in response to the rice riots, attempts were made to increase the agricultural production of Korea in order to increase rice exports to Japan, and after 1920 Japanese firms showed greater interest in making direct investment in manufacturing. Exploitation of the colony became more multi-faceted and complex. It became especially so after 1931, when Japan attempted to build a self-sufficient, or nearly self-sufficient, yen bloc in East Asia. But it would be a mistake to read these developments as evidence for the original motives behind annexation. Rather, they provide evidence for the contention that the economic exploitation of Japan's colonial possessions was dependent on the state of its domestic economy and that only as Japan became more fully industrialized did it begin to reap the full economic benefits of being a colonial power.

TABLE 1
Annual Japanese Exports to East Asia, 1897-1915 (1,000 YEN)

Year	Korea	Taiwan	Kwantung	Total Colonial	China	Colonial as % of China	Total East Asia	Colonial as % of East Asia
1897-1902	8,964	7,747		16,717	38,217	43.8	49,772	33.8
1903-1907	23,374	14,044		37,418	87,012	43.0	139,428	26.8
1908-1911	29,102	26,936	18,912	74,950	77,946	96.1	153,616	48.8
1912-1915	43,179	41,654	25,463	110,296	143,245	77.1	278,329	49.6

Source: Takahashi Kamekichi, Nihon kindai keizai hattatsu shi [History of Modern Japanese Economic Development], Vol. III (Tokyo: Tōyō Keizai Shimpōsha, 1973), p. 213.

TABLE 2
Volume of Business Handled by Mitsui Bussan (1,000 Yen) Branch Offices, 1904-1909

Year	Domestic	Korea	Taiwan	Manchuria	China	Br. Malaya	South Seas	India	(Worldwide) TOTAL
1904	79,357	479	4,011		29,213	2,874	1,258	249	127,621
1905	117,312	555	2,296		44,390	2,290	989	202	180,895
1906	115,869	2,160	4,065	4,854	52,663	1,817	514	266	199,502
1907	138,911	3,252	5,089	10,672	36,077	3,063	1,648	1,290	235,164
1908	146,386	5,459	5,041	7,147	36,416	4,330	1,432	3,931	242,771
1909	113,450	3,583	4,279	8,581	34,139	3,079	1,462	2,229	223,742

Source: Kohon Mitsui Bussan Kabushiki Kaisha 100 nen shi [Draft of the One Hundred Year History of Mitsui Corporation], Vol. I (Date of publication unknown; for company circulation only), pp. 285-286.

TABLE 3

Value of Trade Handled by Foreign and Japanese Trading Firms, 1874-1900 (percent)

	Exports handled by:		Imports handled by:	
Year	Japanese Traders	Foreign Traders	Japanese Traders	Foreign Traders
1874	.55	99.45	.03	99.97
1883	14.59	85.41	4.89	95.11
1887	12.97	87.03	11.87	88.13
1893	15.49	84.50	19.06	80.94
1900	35.9	61.0	39.3	60.4

Source: Miyamoto Mataji, Meiji zenki keizaishi no kenkyū [Studies of Early Meiji Economic History] (Osaka Seibundō, 1971), pp. 224-227.

TABLE 4

Company Dividend Rates, 1890-1900 (percent)

	(Average)	Cotton Spinning Co. Dividend Rate		Nihon Yūsen Co. Dividend Rate		Osaka Shōsen Co. Dividend Rate
Year		1st half	2nd half			
1890		5.7	4.5	11		2
1891		5.7	7.7	9		5
1892		12.1	14.3	8		5
1893		11.9	14.6	8		8
1894		11.3	11.3	10		12
				1st half	2nd half	
1895		9.6	13.4	10	30	18
1896		9.9	11.2	18	33	16
1897		10.1	6.2	10	—	3
1898		5.3	2.7	—	—	7
1899		6.1	10.6	9	10	7
1900		5.8	4.3	10	12	9.5

Source: (1) Takamura Naosuke, Nihon bōsekigyōshi josetsu [An Introduction to the History of the Japanese Cotton Industry], Vol. I (Tokyo: Hanawa Shōbo, 1971), p. 206.

(2) Nihon Yūsen Kabushiki Kaisha, Shichijūnen-shi [Seventy Year History] (Tokyo: 1956), p. 705.

(3) Ōsaka Shōsen Kabushiki Kaisha, Gojūnenshi [Fifty Year History] (Osaka, 1934), Appendices.

TABLE 5
Japan–Korea Trade, 1890–1911

	Exports		Imports	
Year	Value (1,000 Yen)	Percentage of Total Exports	Value (1,000 Yen)	Percentage of Total Exports
1890	1,251	2.2	4,364	5.3
1891	1,466	1.8	4,033	6.4
1892	1,411	1.5	3,046	4.3
1893	1,301	1.5	1,999	2.3
1894	2,365	2.1	2,183	1.9
1895	3,831	2.8	2,925	2.3
1896	3,368	2.9	5,119	3.0
1897	5,197	3.2	8,864	4.0
1898	5,844	3.6	4,796	1.8
1899	6,996	3.3	4,976	2.3
1900	9,953	5.0	8,806	3.4
1901	11,373	4.5	10,052	3.9
1902	10,554	4.1	7,958	2.9
1903	11,761	4.1	8,912	2.8
1904	20,390	6.4	6,401	1.7
1905	26,619	8.3	6,151	1.3
1906	25,210	5.9	8,206	2.0
1907	32,792	7.6	16,372	3.3
1908	30,273	8.0	13,718	3.1
1909	26,998	6.5	14,139	3.6
1910	31,450	6.7	16,902	3.6
1911	41,688	8.5	15,802	3.0

Source: Ōishi Kaichirō, Nihon sangyō kakumei no kenkyū [Studies of the Japanese Industrial Revolution], Vol. II (Tokyo: Tōkyō Daigaku Shuppankai, 1975), p. 233.

TABLE 6

Structure of Japanese Exports to Korea: 1885, 1896, 1908 (percent)

Type of Product	1885 Japan made	1885 Foreign made	1896 Japan made	1896 Foreign made	1908 Japan made
Rice/foodstuffs	31.8	9.58	10.97	16.57	15.25
Tobacco	1.54	.33	2.08	1.52	3.03
Oil, fats, wax	0.45	9.71	0.94	26.31	0.50
Drugs, cosmetics	1.45	15.24	0.04	11.84	1.51
Coal, coke	1.4	0.0	1.03	0.0	3.93
Metals, metal products	24.42	7.22	8.81	21.60	5.53
Watches, machinery, etc.	0.0	0.72	0.29	1.09	2.60
Ceramics, glass, brick	2.10	0.11	1.92	1.59	2.26
Lumber	0.86	0.0	0.77	0.04	6.57
Paper, paper products	0.96	1.0	0.63	0.24	3.62
Rope, baskets, straw goods	—	—	—	—	3.66
Matches	1.20	0.0	3.35	0.0	1.51
Cotton yarn, textiles, raw cotton	22.75	51.40	53.29	14.53	35.40
Other	3.65	4.17	2.22	1.74	6.13
Uncertain	8.83	0.50	13.17	2.37	8.33
Total	100.00	100.00	100.00	100.00	100.00
Total Value (1,000 Yen)	233.3	227.4	3,065.3	302.4	29,569.0

Source: Ōishi Kaichirō, Nihon sangyō kakumei no kenkyū [Studies of the Japanese Industrial Revolution], Vol. II (Tokyo: Tōkyō Daigaku Shuppankai, 1975), p. 237.

TABLE 7
Export of Cotton Tissues, 1887–1912 (1,000 Yen)

Year	Total Production	Total Exported	Export to Korea	Export to China	Export to Hong Kong	Export to Kwantung
1887	12,025	170	13	150	—	—
1888	12,345	153	11	134	—	—
1889	19,945	147	9	12	113	—
1890	13,564	173	40	10	101	—
1891	16,927	243	70	39	100	—
1892	19,113	544	27	153	252	—
1893	22,310	1,109	18	337	430	—
1894	27,168	1,861	238	387	620	—
1895	37,084	2,315	966	404	506	—
1896	39,084	2,224	876	546	547	—
1897	42,453	2,512	1,195	603	413	—
1898	48,728	2,597	1,236	524	664	—

TABLE 7 (cont.)

Year	Total Production	Total Exported	Export to Korea	Export to China	Export to Hong Kong	Export to Kwantung
1899	52,857	3,910	1,620	1,070	951	—
1900	61,326	5,723	3,615	820	935	—
1901	—	—	—	—	—	—
1902	—	—	—	—	—	—
1903	51,326	6,875	2,409	2,983	1,113	—
1904	51,828	7,743	3,331	3,068	871	—
1905	72,845	11,492	5,235	4,606	1,087	—
1906	86,474	15,619	5,010	8,161	1,395	—
1907	103,590	16,345	6,385	4,718	1,083	2,730
1908	101,186	14,611	5,523	4,534	424	2,109
1909	116,412	17,672	4,509	6,727	522	3,583
1910	122,151	20,462	2,528	10,078	865	4,979
1911	140,024	27,062	7,383	10,128	561	6,756
1912	152,748	35,528	9,767	12,717	873	9,169

Source: Takamura Naosuke, Nihon bōseki shi josetsu [An Introduction to the History of the Japanese Spinning Industry], Vol. I, p. 212; Vol. II, p. 151 (Tokyo: Hanawa Shōbo, 1971).

TABLE 8
Japanese Resident in Korea by Occupation, 1908

Occupation	Number	Percent
Commerce	47,000	41.0
Miscellaneous	17,000	14.8
Officials	15,000	13.1
Manufacturing	18,000	15.7
Agriculture	4,800	4.2
Unemployed	4,400	3.8
Prostitutes, etc.	4,200	3.7
Fishing	3,000	2.6
Physicians, Midwives	1,100	1.0
Total	114,500	100.0

Source: Lim Byon-yun, *Shokuminchi ni okern shōgyōteki nōgyō no tenkai* [Development of Colonial Commercial Agriculture] (Tokyo: Tokyō Daigaku Shuppankai, 1971), pp. 90-91.

TABLE 9

Rice Imports to Japan by Origin, 1895–1912 (1,000 piculs)

Year	Total Imports	Imports from China	Percent	Imports from Korea	Percent	Imports from Taiwan	Percent
1895	1,685	66	(4)	305	(18)	—	—
1896	1,862	393	(21)	945	(51)	387	(21)
1897	6,301	1,323	(21)	1,793	(28)	738	(12)
1898	11,696	767	(7)	650	(6)	750	(6)
1899	1,651	60	(4)	437	(26)	401	(24)
1900	2,287	84	(4)	1,132	(49)	760	(33)
1901	3,112	227	(7)	1,457	(47)	398	(13)
1902	4,509	90	(2)	891	(20)	633	(14)
1903	12,162	432	(4)	1,044	(9)	255	(2)
1904	14,732	191	(1)	328	(2)	535	(4)
1905	11,596	361	(3)	259	(2)	196	(2)
1906	6,101	64	(1)	314	(5)	78	(1)
1907	6,770	94	(1)	1,531	(23)	42	(1)
1908	4,854	63	(1)	1,116	(23)	124	(3)
1909	3,313	24	(1)	998	(30)	46	(1)
1910	2,297	15	(1)	370	(16)	37	(2)
1911	4,299	44	(1)	—	—	8	(–)
1912	5,586	69	(1)	—	—	0	(–)

Source: Yokohama-shi shi: Shiryō-hen II: Nihon bōeki tōkei [Collected Materials on the History of Yokohama City: Japanese Trade Statistics] (Yokohama: Yokohamashi 1958–), p. 220. (1) Excluding Taiwan imports.

CHAPTER 4

The Nan'yō: Japan in the South Pacific, 1885-1945

Mark R. Peattie

The Japanese occupation of Micronesia from 1914 to 1944 was an anomaly within the nation's modern colonial experience. Where the rest of the empire was generally compact and at close distance to the metropole, the Nan'yō—the South Seas—as Japan came to call its Micronesian islands collectively,[1] lay dispersed over an expanse of ocean stretching from the arcuate islands of the Marianas in the western Pacific, across the widely separated "high islands" of the western and eastern Carolines, to the remote atolls of the Marshalls to the east. Yet together they comprised the smallest land area in the empire, eight hundred and sixty square miles in all. Inhabited by technologically primitive, comparatively docile, and widely scattered peoples who were far less culturally advanced than those of Taiwan or Korea and far less prepared to resist the imposition of foreign rule, the islands posed no difficult administrative problem for Japanese authority, except perhaps that of distance. Nevertheless, Japanese stewardship of its Micronesian territories under a League of Nations mandate represented the sole case in which an overseas Japanese territory was at least minimally subject to administrative standards established by authority external to the empire.

In keeping with the Japanese imperial pattern, the prime value of the islands was initially perceived as strategic, and it was for strategic reasons that the Japanese occupied the islands when the opportunity

[1] In its historical context. Nan'yō—the South Seas—is at once an ambiguous and a precise term. In its most general application, it includes not only the South Pacific, but also the South China Sea, and Southeast Asia. In this widest sense, the word gained official as well as popular currency during the 1930's and early 1940's. But, in addition, in pre-war Japanese parlance, the word had specific reference to the islands of Micronesia, and in this sense was used in connection with the Japanese naval occupation of the islands from 1914 to 1920 and the subsequent Japanese mandate over the islands (minus the American territory of Guam) established in 1920. My use of the word "Nan'yō" in this essay pertains to this narrower geographic definition. There also existed a precise geographical but slightly less popular term: Nan'yō guntō—South Sea islands—which pertains strictly to Micronesia.

to do so presented itself in 1914. Economic justifications for their acquisition followed soon afterward and, once placed under the Japanese flag, the islands were more intensively developed and exploited than the Pacific island territories of any other power, a policy which also followed other Japanese colonial precedents. The beginning and end of the Japanese presence in the South Pacific contrasted with the rest of the empire, however. Occupied swiftly and quietly in the first stage of World War I by Japanese naval landing parties with far less effort than that expended to acquire any other Japanese colonial territory, thirty years later the islands were the scene of some of the most terrible combat of the Pacific War, as American marines fought their way across their coral reefs to annihilate the Japanese defenses, strong point by strong point.

Perhaps the most singular characteristic of the Nan'yō was that, alone among overseas territories, it stood outside the Asian provenance of the empire. To acknowledge that fact is to reflect upon the tension throughout the history of Japan between its two physical configurations: the Asian nation, integrally linked with the continent, and the maritime nation, one of the countries of the Pacific rim. The basic orientation in pre-modern Japanese history, backed by culture and politics, if not economics, was essentially continental, demonstrated by the clear influence of China in ancient and feudal times, as well as by Toyotomi Hideyoshi's invasion of Korea in the late sixteenth century.

At the same time, the maritime orientation proved compelling. Indeed, it helps to explain the vigorous advance of Japanese influence south into tropic seas by private persons—traders, pirates, and even colonists—from the fifteenth into the sixteenth centuries. The seclusion policy of the Tokugawa feudal government suppressed both these impulses for two and a half centuries, but within several decades after the opening of Japan in the nineteenth century they were once again released and given even greater force by the dynamic environment of world imperialism.

THE LURE OF TROPIC SEAS: JAPANESE IN THE NAN'YŌ, CA. 1885-1914

As I have noted in the introduction to this volume, the major thrust of Japan's modern expansionism in the nineteenth century was continent-directed, more akin to the advance of Russian power in Europe and Asia than to the creation of the overseas empires of western Europe. Yet, slighted by most historians of modern Japan was the fact that soon after the reopening of the country, a considerable number of Japanese revived the notion that Japan had a maritime destiny which, almost by definition, appeared to lie in southern seas.

As early as the 1800's, even before Japan had established a foothold on the Asian continent, a varied group of individual Japanese—traders, journalists, politicians, and adventurers—began to express the vague idea that the nation would find glory, prosperity, and new territory for its expanding population by advancing into southern lands and oceans.

There seem to have been a number of impulses behind this sudden interest in the South Pacific. There was the obvious fact, first of all, that after two hundred and fifty years of self-imposed isolation Japan had once again begun to act as a maritime nation, had begun to recognize the importance of the high seas and sea lanes, and had begun to send its vessels of commerce and war abroad upon them. That initial phase of Meiji expansion which Marius Jansen has seen as clarifying national boundaries, an effort to establish clear Japanese authority over neighboring insular territories in the Pacific—the Kuriles, Sakhalin, the Ryūkyūs, and the Bonins—was also part of that interest.[2] The impulse to recover the Bonins, farthest out in the Pacific, had inevitably stirred the interest of the curious and the adventurous about lands farther to the south.

But clarifying the national unit was not just a matter of boundaries or of sticking pins on a map. Akira Iriye has reminded us how the indigenous tradition of overseas emigration had, by early Meiji, been reinvigorated by the introduction of Malthusian fears of population growth and by a general admiration for western overseas expansion.[3] By the 1880's these ideas had moved expansionist thought in Japan beyond the colonization of Hokkaido to the idea of settlement outside Japan. While, by the end of the century, these concerns were to pull Japan toward Korea and China, in the early Meiji years, when Japanese expansionism was not yet rivetted to matters of national security, they were directed to more distant lands and seas. Their appearance in the 1880's in connection with the South Pacific and Southeast Asia marks the beginning of modern Japanese interest in the "South Seas" which, in various forms, was to magnetize Japanese imaginations and ambitions intermittently up to the nation's defeat in 1945.[4] In its earliest stage this interest was infused with arguments

[2] Marius Jansen, "Modernization and Foreign Policy in Meiji Japan," in *Political Development in Modern Japan*, Robert E. Ward, ed. (Princeton, N.J.: Princeton University Press, 1968), p. 164.

[3] Akira Iriye, *Pacific Estrangement, 1897-1911* (Cambridge, Mass.: Harvard University Press, 1972), pp. 18-19.

[4] Professor Yano Tōru's two books, *Nanshin no keifu* [Geneology of the Southward

which are customarily linked by historians to the motives behind continental expansionism in Meiji Japan: the problem of employment for a huge samurai class, the often symbiotic relationship between Meiji liberalism and chauvinism, the political romanticism which colored much of Japanese democratic thought in these years—all of which were expressed in the pronouncements of those Japanese who urged their nation to extend its influence into tropic waters. In the 1880's and 1890's, indeed, readership in Japan was provided with a flood of political novels based in the South Seas. *The Rising Sun Flag, The Great King of the Islands,* and *Great Exploits in Southern Seas* are but some of the works whose titles convey something of the fevered romanticism with which their authors, most of whom had never travelled abroad, conjured the South Pacific and the opportunities which awaited there for the adventurous and the idealisic.[5]

Interestingly, while notions of southern expansion in this period had little to do with naval strategy and even less with the use of naval force, it was through the Imperial Japanese Navy that the first personal accounts of the South Seas reached Japan. Beginning with the voyage of the screw sloop *Tsukuba* in 1875, the early Meiji navy, spreading its sails and pressing on steam, began a series of training missions in the South Pacific for its cadets. In 1884 the corvette *Ryūjo,* stopping at Kusaie in the eastern Carolines, was the first Japanese vessel to probe Micronesian waters, and by the end of the decade the navy's newest warships were being used for these training voyages.[6]

But it is not the logs and official reports of these warships that are of interest to us, but rather the written observations of certain civilians who, under arrangements that are not entirely clear today, were often able to board these ships for their entire voyages. It was these extra-complement civilians—men like Shiga Shigetaka, Suzuki Keikun (Tsunenori) and Miyake Setsurei—who later rose to positions of literary or political prominence who evoked a compelling vision of the South Pacific for the reading public. Shiga's *Nan'yō jiji* (Conditions in the South Seas 1887), an account of his voyage through the South Pacific in 1886 aboard the *Tsukuba,* not only established him in the world of Japanese letters, but marked the appearance of the first persuasive, firsthand report of the South Pacific for the reading

---

Advance] (Tokyo: Chūō Shinsho, 1975) and *Nihon no Nan'yō shikan* [Japanese Historical View of the South Seas] (Tokyo: Chūō Shinsho, 1979) represent the most interesting and important works of recent scholarship on the subject of southward expansion in modern Japanese history. They have greatly influenced my whole approach to the problem.

[5] Yano, *Nihon no Nan'yō shikan,* pp. 18–20.

[6] *Ibid.,* pp. 14–15.

public. Suzuki Keikun, in three major works, *Nan'yō tanken jikki* (A True Account of Exploration in the South Seas), 1892, *Nantō junkōki* (Journal of a Cruise to the South Sea Islands), 1893, and *Nan'yō fūbūtsūshi* (An Account of the Landscapes of the South Seas), 1893, provided detailed descriptions of life and nature in the South Pacific. Miyake Setsurei, on his way to a distinguished career as literary critic, wrote of his Pacific travels in a number of works.

What appealed to these first Japanese to cruise the Pacific, as well as to their readers at home, was the thought that the islands of the South Pacific were not yet entirely spoken for by other nations, though the German annexation of the Marshall Islands in 1884 made it obvious that the Pacific was rapidly filling up. The hope existed that Japan might yet find some small unclaimed land mass in that equatorial world where the Japanese flag might be planted and Japanese trade and settlement might follow. In the mid-1880's Japan was a decade away from its scramble to compete in the imperial contest for lands and spheres of interest on the continent, yet Japanese abroad on the high seas, standing on a warship's deck beneath a rippling ensign of their nation's young navy, understandably felt the first stirrings of imperial acquisitiveness. Miyake, who had boarded a navy training ship for a South Pacific cruise in 1891, remembered years later that so strong had been the desire for colonies in the Pacific that the ship's officers had searched their navigational charts for any unclaimed islands.[7] Some years earlier, his literary and political colleague, Shiga Shigetaka, had sailed the South Pacific aboard the *Tsukuba*, a voyage which had left him an enthusiastic advocate of southern expansion:

> Every year on the anniversary of the Emperor Jimmu's accession . . . [Shiga wrote in 1890] . . . and on the anniversary of his passing . . . we should ceremonially increase the territory of the Japanese empire, even if it only be in small measure. Our naval vessels on each of these days should sail to a still unclaimed island, occupy it, and hoist the Rising Sun. If there is no island, rocks and stones will do. Some will say that this is child's play; it is not. Not only would such a program have direct value as a practical experience to our navy, but it would excite an expeditionary spirit in the demoralized Japanese race.[8]

[7] Kenneth Pyle, *The New Generation of Meiji Japan: Problems of Cultural Identity, 1885-1895* (Stanford, Calif.: Stanford University Press, 1969), p. 158.

[8] *Ibid.*, p. 159.

Yet neither the government nor the navy encouraged such fanta-
sies, and on the few occasions when pretexts arose for staking a claim
to those islands whose titles as yet remained ambiguous, the opportunity was declined. In 1884, when the Marshall Islands still lay remote and unclaimed, the murder of Japanese fishermen at Lae atoll
in the Ralik chain moved the Japanese government, out of a sense of
amour propre, to send a mission to the islands to exact an apology
from local Micronesian chieftains. Yet the Foreign Ministry was quick
to disavow the flag-raising over the atoll by the mission's two official
Japanese representatives, Suzuki Keikun and Gotō Taketarō.[9]

In any event, the first Japanese presence in the South Pacific was
commercial, rather than naval or political. In small groups, Japanese
traders, lured by rumors of profit and dreams of adventure, began
sailing in tiny trading schooners out into the broad reaches of the
Pacific, first to the Bonins and then south into Micronesian waters,
largely Spanish in those times, to trade and to barter for copra and
coconut oil with the natives of the Marshalls and eastern Carolines.
Their voyages were made with great difficulty and greater risk, often
battling foul weather and heavy seas, the distrust of Spanish colonial
authorities, and the hostility of German traders. Their tiny trading
companies—*mini-shōsha* Yano Tōru has called them—first found root
in the eastern Carolines—on Ponape, Kusaie, and Truk—where the
Spanish were less suspicious and the commercial competition less
threatening.[10] On those islands they set up their few small stores and
warehouses and over the next three decades began to build networks
of trading stations and inter-island trade routes. Men like Mori Ko-
ben (1869-1945), whose checkered past and whose career of more
than fifty years on Truk as copra trader, merchant, planter, and sire
of numerous half-caste children were to make him a local legend,
established a small but permanent Japanese commercial presence in
Micronesia long before the arrival of the Japanese flag.[11]

Most of those Japanese who undertook to pioneer the trade lanes
of the South Pacific were unknowns—former samurai, fishermen, an
occasional farmer or two—whose names, like the tiny companies they
represented, are familiar to only the most avid researcher. Taguchi
Ukichi (1855-1905) is an exception. At thirty, Taguchi was not only

[9] Nagasawa Kazutoshi, *Nihonjin no bōken to tanken* [Adventures and Explorations of
Japanese] (Tokyo: Hakusui Sha, 1973), pp. 240-244.

[10] Yano, *Nihon no Nan'yō shikan*, pp. 66-68 and 119-120.

[11] For an interesting account of Mori's exploits see Kikuchi Masao, *Yakushin no
Nan'yō* [The Rapid Progress of the South Seas] (Tokyo: Tōa Kyōkai, 1937), pp. 44-
50.

deputy chairman of the Tokyo City Assembly, but had made a reputation as a politician, journalist, businessman, magazine editor and, as a vigorous and articulate advocate of free trade, when he took a gamble and agreed to head one of the first trading expeditions to Micronesia—to Yap, Palau, and Ponape—in 1889. His expedition to the South Pacific itself, embroiled in financial controversy even before his small schooner cleared Yokohama, and burdened with endless difficulties once at sea, is really less important in a commercial sense (for it accomplished little financially for Taguchi, his companions, or his backers) than for the information it generated for the general public about tropic lands and seas. Beginning with a brief essay on the commercial opportunities which awaited Japan in Micronesia, Taguchi's journal, the *Tokyo Keizai Zasshi*, published more than sixty articles on the South Pacific during the six months that he was at sea, all part of the first major campaign to stir popular interest in that part of the globe and in Japan's future in it.[12]

Taguchi's interest in the South Pacific passed quickly. By the turn of the century, as a Diet member and as an influential journalist, his attention turned to the continent and to the advance of Japanese armies there. Yet other Japanese, less well known, began to pick up the theme of Japanese opportunity in the South Pacific. Without influence in shaping government policy or even much personal success in establishing a Japanese presence in Micronesia, these writers for a brief time fired the Japanese popular imagination with visions of tropical utopias which could help to solve the nation's problems of land, population, and frustrated ambition.

As early as 1888 journalist and Peoples' Rights advocate Hattori Tōru, who had cruised the Marshalls, argued in his *Nihon no Nan'yō* (Japan in the South Seas) that Japan's destiny lay not on the Asian continent, but "in the vast reaches of the hazy ocean," where Japan could find the greatest scope for adventure and initiative. In a later work, *Nan'yō saku* (South Seas Policy), 1891, he spoke hopefully of an aggressive Japanese commercialism in the Pacific based on the discovery of as yet unclaimed islands, as well as upon the small commercial beginnings already planted in the Carolines and Marshalls. Shiga Shigetaka, in the various writings that I have already mentioned, had seen commerce as the spearhead of Japanese expansion into the South Pacific. About the same time his fellow publisher Su-

<hr>

[12] Yano, *Nihon no Nan'yō shikan*, pp. 31-35, and David Purcell, "Japanese Entrepreneurs in the Mariana, Marshall, and Caroline Islands," in *East Across the Pacific: Historical and Sociological Studies of Japanese Immigration and Assimilation*, Hilary Conroy and T. Scott Miyakawa, eds. (Santa Barbara, Calif.: ABC Clio Press), pp. 57-59.

giura Jūgo and the scholar-writers Suganuma Teifu (Sadakaze) and Fukumoto Nichinan (Makoto) in various novels and essays urged that Japan could fulfill its national destiny through a mission of commerce and colonization in the tropical Pacific, particularly the Philippines. In the first comprehensive treatment of Japanese expansionism, *Sekai ni okeru Nihonjin* (Japanese in the World), 1893, Watanabe Shūjirō concluded that expansion into the South Pacific would offer more reward and would be less costly than adventurism on the Korean peninsula.[13]

But arguments of many of these writers were often more fanciful than factual, founded more on speculation and distant promise than on the immediate realities of great power rivalry and on the problems of strategic security on nearby continental shores. Korea, China, and Manchuria, with increasing urgency, focused the attention of the nation's policy makers. Yet while the "South Seas fever" among the Japanese public subsided within a decade, a number of influential professionals in politics, business, and the military gave sober thought to the importance of Japanese expansion into the South Pacific, now increasingly seen as including Southeast Asia and its treasure house of natural resources. Their views, expounded on lecture platforms, in the national press, and in a steady flow of professional articles, collectively began to demarcate a gradually emerging debate as to the proper orientation for Japanese expansionist energies, a choice between an advance onto the continent in north Asia—*hokushin*—or an expansion southward—*nanshin*. Influential proponents like navy Commander Satō Tetsutarō and the journalist and Diet member Takekoshi Yosaburō (who figures in my chapter on Japanese colonial ideology elsewhere in this volume) grounded the *nanshin ron*—the concept of an advance of Japanese interest and influence south into equatorial lands—on the serious concerns of economic advantage, national security, and geopolitics. "Our future lies not in the north, but in the south, not on the continent, but on the ocean," insisted Takekoshi. Admonishing his countrymen to realize that "it is our great task as a people to turn the Pacific into a Japanese lake," he urged them to support an increase in the Japanese navy, an expansion of the merchant marine, an extension of trade routes, and unfettered emigration to tropic lands in the South Seas. To Takekoshi there was little doubt about the importance of the equatorial regions for the

[13] Iriye, pp. 38-39; Yano, *Nihon no Nan'yō shikan*, pp. 29-31; and Josefa Saniel, "Four Japanese: Their Plans for the Expansion of Japan to the Philippines," in *Journal of Southeast Asian History*, IV:2 (September 1963), pp. 1-12.

attainment of Japanese national ambitions: "Who controls the tropics controls the world," he declared.[14]

THE JAPANESE NAVY TAKES POSSESSION OF THE NAN'YŌ, 1914-1922

Because the concept of a southern advance essentially involved the prospects of maritime empire, it is not surprising that in the decade that followed the Russo-Japanese War the Japanese navy came to support its vague and somewhat inconsistent aspirations with enthusiasm. In doing so, the navy's priorities ran counter to the demands for continental expansion urged by the army. The *hokushin-nanshin* debate therefore must be seen within the context of competition between the two services for funds and national attention to support their large expansion/construction programs, claims which each service justified by the identification of a "hypothetical enemy" (the United States for the navy, Russia for the army) and by a geographic priority. In developing the concept of a "southern advance" the Japanese navy linked it with the need to protect Japanese commerce in the western Pacific and therefore with the necessity to establish naval hegemony in those waters against the advance of American naval power.

Yet by the beginning of the new century's second decade Japan had as yet no real foothold either in the South Pacific or in Southeast Asia, only vague aspirations in both areas. In what had become German Micronesia (since 1898) a few hundred Japanese traders and fishermen scattered from Palau to the Marshalls constituted the only Japanese presence in the South Seas. Nevertheless, by 1914, navy men on both sides of the Pacific could see that Micronesia had become a strategic area, for its component island groups stood athwart lines of communication west across the Pacific to Asia. For the United States, with its new responsibilities in the Philippines, that was a vexing, but not threatening, reality. Germany was not a maritime rival, the German presence in the Pacific was symbolic rather than strategic, and the largest German naval units were far north at Tsingtao on the Shantung peninsula. But in the staff rooms of the United States Naval War College it was readily appreciated how quickly the strategic value of the same islands would increase in the hands of a front-rank naval power in the Pacific whose interests and ambitions directly challenged those of the United States. Nor was this fact lost on the Japanese Naval General Staff in Tokyo. Given their interdictory position across the course of any American fleet steaming westward

---

[14] Cited in Yano, *Nihon no Nan'yō shikan*, p. 48.

across the Pacific, the islands of Micronesia inevitably figured in the strategic calculations of the Japanese Naval General Staff in the years immediately prior to World War I.

Japan's strategic interest in Micronesia as well as in the German leasehold on the Shantung peninsula thus impelled it to move quickly to absorb those territories into the empire when the opportunity presented itself in 1914. Recognizing that the cataclysmic events in Europe in August of that year would give it a free hand in China and in the West Pacific, Japan saw that it suited its plans to join the allies. Moving well beyond limited British requests for naval assistance (to search for and destroy the German Asiatic squadron which had escaped into the Pacific), Japan acted, with a haste which alarmed and vexed her treaty partner, to invoke the terms of the Anglo-Japanese naval alliance. Tokyo presented Berlin first with an ultimatum, then a declaration of war, and, within a few short weeks, directed swift military and naval offensives against Tsingtao and the German islands in the Pacific.[15] By early September two squadrons had been despatched into Micronesian waters north of the equator, while Australian warships moved against the German islands south of it. There was a curious furtiveness about this Japanese campaign, undoubtedly occasioned by fears of an alarmed and hostile American response. Though Japanese naval units occupied Ponape, Truk, Kusaie, Palau, and Angaur in the Carolines, and Saipan in the Marianas (almost without resistance) by October 1914, Japanese naval headquarters announced only the capture of tiny Jaluit atoll in the Marshalls, and for the rest of the war the Japanese navy excluded ships of even their British and Australian allies from Micronesian waters. Thus the Japanese occupation of Micronesia began with a secrecy which was to taint its administration of the islands and was to poison American attitudes toward the Japanese presence in the South Pacific.

Effectively withdrawing from hostilities after having advanced its territorial interests by force, Japan spent the next several years securing them by semi-secret diplomacy with its embattled European allies. Of Japan's intentions toward the post-war disposition of her wartime gains the United States was told practically nothing. While the Japanese Foreign Minister, at the navy's insistence, was informing Britain in December 1914 that his country deserved the former German islands as a reward for Japan's contribution to the war effort, no mention whatever was made to the United States of these intentions. It was not until September 1917, when America was at last a bellig-

---

[15] The diplomatic background to the opening of Japanese hostilities is covered in detail by Ian Nish in his *Alliance in Decline: A Study in Anglo-Japanese Relations, 1908-23* (London: University of London, The Athlone Press, 1972), pp. 115-131.

erent, that Viscount Ishii, Japan's urbane special envoy to Washington, remarked archly to Secretary of State Lansing that Japan must retain at least some of the South Pacific islands as "souvenirs" after the war for "sentimental reasons."[16] Until then, only the American navy brass had been much concerned about the drastically altered strategic situation in the South and West Pacific, but, as a peace settlement approached, Woodrow Wilson's attention at last focused on the strategic nature of Japan's new position in the Pacific and East Asia, causing him to denounce the diplomatic arrangements by which Japan had reinforced its claims to its wartime conquests.[17] While Wilson called down anathema on these secret covenants, Japan, calling in its diplomatic debts, asserted that the islands were hers by conquest and by prior agreement. In its insistence on right of possession over Micronesia, Japan was also indirectly supported by similar claims by Britain, Australia, and New Zealand to the former German territories in New Guinea and in the Pacific south of the equator.

At the peace table the clash of idealism and national self-interest in such territorial questions was resolved by creation of the mandate system, that mixture of hypocrisy, face-saving, and good intent, which was designed to transfer the former territories of defeated belligerents to the victors. While Japan may have wished to annex her Pacific conquests outright, the award of the mandate did enhance its international prestige by implicit recognition of Japan's position as an advanced nation which, by virtue of its resources, experience, and geographic position, was deemed capable of governing the primitive peoples entrusted to its care. More importantly, the "Class C" designation applied to Japan's Micronesian mandate amounted to territorial cession, for the terms of the mandate allowed Japan to govern the islands as if they were an integral portion of the empire, subject only to the limited obligations imposed on all mandatory powers by the League of Nations.

Seeing it impossible to prevent the Marianas, Carolines, and Marshalls from passing into Japanese control in one way or another, the Anglo-American maritime nations moved to withhold from Japan her right to turn these islands into strategic base areas. At the Washington Naval Conference Japan agreed to the insertion of a non-fortification clause which imposed a ban on the construction of fortifications on Japanese islands in the South Pacific in return for similar

[16] Yano, *Nihon no Nan'yō shikan*, pp. 112-113.

[17] William Braisted, *The United States Navy in the Pacific, 1909-1922* (Austin, Texas: University of Texas Press), pp. 444-445, and Earl S. Pomeroy, "American Policy Respecting the Marshalls, Carolines, and Marianas," in *Pacific Historical Review*, XVII:I (February 1948), pp. 44-47.

limitations on Anglo-American possessions in Southeast Asia and the West Pacific. This settled, American objections to Japanese jurisdiction over Micronesia came to focus exclusively on Yap in the Carolines, an island which served as a relay point for a number of trans-Pacific cables. The futility of the American position, the meager, concessions which were eventually extracted from Japan, and the fact that American interests in Yap soon became a dead letter, make the protracted and bitter negotiations over this flyspeck of land seem particularly pointless. But they mark the distrust with which the United States finally recognized the Japanese mandate, an attitude of suspicion which Japan, by its continuing policy of seclusion in Micronesia, did little to alleviate over the next two decades.[18]

From the outset of Japan's occupation of Micronesia there had been public demands and private pressures to annex the islands outright. In early September 1914, even before the navy's South Seas task force had left its ports, the director of one of the Japanese trading firms having business interests in the islands was distributing to newspapers, Diet members, and government bureaucrats a pamphlet on the former German territories, outlining the history of Japanese interest in the group and arguing for their acquisition on grounds of strategic necessity and economic advantage.[19] The press soon took up the cry and, once Japanese naval forces were in control of the islands, a number of commentators rejoiced that the occupation had broken the American stranglehold on the "natural" southward expansion of the Japanese race. A spate of articles and essays informed the Japanese public about the "new territories of the Pacific" and explained their strategic significance. Yamamoto Miono, noted economist at Kyoto University, struck the tone. Returning from a government-organized scientific tour of the islands, Yamamoto urged that Japan add Micronesia to its other colonial territories, not only because the islands might "serve as stepping stones in the event of a southward advance by the Japanese people," but also because, "in the event of a future crisis in the Pacific, the islands, situated as they are with Hawaii on the right and the Philippines on the left, could make a great deal of difference to Japan."[20]

[18] A somewhat more positive assessment of the 1922 American-Japanese Treaty concerning the mandated islands north of the equator, especially the island of Yap, is provided by Sumitra Rattan in "The Yap Controversy and its Significance," in *Journal of Pacific History*, VII (1972), pp. 124-136.

[19] David Purcell, Jr., "Japanese Expansion in the South Pacific," unpublished doctoral dissertation, University of Pennsylvania, 1967, pp. 152-153.

[20] Yamamoto Miono, "Nan'yō shinryōchi jijō" [Conditions in the New South Seas Territories], in *Taiyō*, XXI:12 (October 1914), p. 114.

But if some observers believed that Micronesia was strategically important to Japan in confronting the United States, others perceived that it was the United States which would oppose Japanese claims to the islands. Writing in April 1918, old South Seas hand Shiga Shigetaka expressed alarm that Wilson's widely proclaimed principles about territorial integrity and the self-determination of peoples might somehow be applied to Micronesia, thus depriving Japan of its wartime conquests. To prevent this, Shiga urged on the government a series of immediate measures in Micronesia, including the construction of permanent and impressively designed administrative buildings and an acceleration of programs to assimilate the native populations, in order that Japan's occupation of the islands become an accomplished and ineradicable fact by war's end.[21]

The government itself had not been slow in preparing for a permanent administration over the islands. In late December 1914, Tokyo had despatched a fact-finding mission of scholars and scientists (which had included Yamamoto Miono) to study every aspect of Micronesia, so that at the peace settlement Japanese representatives could not only submit evidence of international commitments supporting Japanese claims, but could buttress those arguments with an impressive understanding of Micronesia, as proof of Japan's ability to administer it wisely.[22]

The navy had not wasted time in putting together an effective administration over the islands. In December 1914, a South Sea Islands Defense Force (Nan'yo Guntō Bōbitai) commanded by a rear admiral (responsible to the Yokosuka Naval District) was established on Truk, with naval garrisons located on Saipan, Yap, Palau, Ponape, and Jaluit, each commanded by a senior lieutenant or lieutenant commander who held civil affairs authority over the islands within their jurisdiction. With zeal and efficiency the Japanese naval administration set about to establish a permanent Japanese presence. Officers from the Defense Force were assigned the task of setting up schools and Japanese language classes among the island populations, Japanese laws and regulations were promulgated to regulate civil affairs, and native chieftains and elders were invited on educational tours of the home islands to instill in them a respect for Japanese modernity and power. With varying degrees of success the navy encouraged private commercial and industrial entrepreneurs in Japan to

[21] Shiga's opinions were outlined in an article, "Nan'yō senryō shōtō no shōri" [Disposition of Japanese-Occupied Islands in the South Seas], which appeared in *Nippon Ichi*, April 1918. Relevant portions of the article are quoted in Yano, *Nihon no Nan'yō shikan*, pp. 209–210.

[22] Purcell, "Japanese Expansion," pp. 153–155.

participate in the economic development of the new Micronesian territory. Japanese steamship companies, heavily subsidized by the government, began the useful task of creating new South Pacific and inter-island trade routes. Commercial agents already on the islands rapidly expanded the scope of their activities, everywhere spreading their wares in return for copra, thus beginning the process of Japanizing the tastes and lifestyles of the native peoples.[23]

In July 1918, as civilian administrators were filtered into the civil affairs branches in Micronesia, the purely naval character of Japanese rule began to lessen. In July 1921, the Navy Ministry transferred all civil affairs in the islands to a civil administrator at Koror in the Palau group. With Japanese acceptance of both the League of Nations mandate and the naval restrictions which went with it, the naval garrisons were gradually withdrawn, and in March 1922 a purely civilian administration, the Nan'yō-chō—South Seas Bureau—was established under a governor charged with administering the new island territories and with fulfilling Japan's obligations under its mandate authority. Until 1929 this official was responsible in most matters to the Prime Minister's office. Thereafter, until the Pacific War, Nan'yō-chō governors reported directly to the Japanese Colonial Ministry (Takumushō).

But if the Imperial Japanese Navy no longer administered Micronesia, nor, except for a small liaison office at Nan'yō-chō headquarters at Koror, maintained a presence there, the South Pacific never slipped from the concerns of the Japanese naval high command. The navy had been the single most powerful voice in the councils of government urging that the islands be annexed. Like their American counterparts, the Japanese navy brass realized that control of the Nan'yō would always be a matter inextricably entwined with high naval strategy. Forced at the Washington conference to accept a position of global inferiority (in relation to the total tonnage of the American and British navies) and to abjure the transformation of Micronesia into an active base area, the navy never lost sight of the potential value of the islands in strengthening Japan's position as the predominant naval power in the West Pacific, and never lessened its insistence that they remain in Japanese hands.[24]

[23] Thomas J. McMahon, "Japanning the Marshall Islands," in *Sunset* (July 1919), pp. 31-33.

[24] In the immediate post-World War I years, the sizeable administrative expenses and annual subsidies for Japanese economic enterprises in the Nan'yō in conjunction with the initial failures of those ventures led a number of persons in the bureaucracy and in the Diet to call for the abandonment of Micronesia. The navy, quietly, firmly, and decisively, argued on strategic grounds for their retention. Hatanaka Sachiko,

JAPAN AS A MANDATORY POWER: AN EVALUATION

When Japan took possession of Micronesia under its League of Nations mandate, it was presented with a set of minimal obligations to the international community and to the indigenes and with a far greater range of opportunities to pursue national self-interest.[25] Under the terms of their charge by the League of Nations Mandates Commission, all nations holding mandates were obliged to "promote to the utmost the material and moral well-being and social progress" of the indigenous populations of their mandated territories: to control traffic in arms and ammunition; to ensure freedom of conscience and worship; to respect the rights of missionaries. In order to provide evidence that these obligations were being fulfilled, each mandatory nation was required each year to file with the Council of the League a report of its administration.[26] The collection of oversized volumes of Japan's annual reports on its South Sea Islands mandate, filled with masses of statistics on population, education, industry, navigation, and trade, and written in the blandest prose, attest to the methodical scrupulousness of the Japanese government in regularly meeting this bureaucratic responsibility. The real question, of course, is whether the Japanese government, specifically the Nan'yō-chō, lived up to the spirit, as well as to the letter, of its prime mandatory responsibilities. This essay can offer only a general assessment of the willingness and success of that government in meeting its principal obligation: the welfare and social advancement of the Micronesian indigenes.

As is so often the case when one contemplates the history of Japanese colonialism, the evidence on which such evaluation must be based tends to provide different impressions of the objectives and results of Japanese rule, depending on the decade from which it is drawn. If we are to take into account the comments of Western observers in the 1920's, the picture which emerges is one of typical Japanese energy, zeal, and efficiency, applied constructively to the material development of the islands and indirectly to the welfare of their native peoples. Commentaries by Western observers a decade later, taking note of the vast numbers of Japanese immigrants pouring into the islands, the failure of the native populations on the larger islands to hold their own numerically, the growing regimentation of

---

introduction to *A Bibliography of Micronesia Compiled from Japanese Publication* [sic] *1915-1945* (Tokyo: Research Institute for Oriental Cultures, Gakushuin University, 1979), p. 6.

[25] The conclusion of David Purcell in his "Japanese Expansion in the South Pacific," pp. 249-252.

[26] League of Nations, *Official Journal*, 2d year, Number one (Geneva, January-February, 1921), p. 87.

native life, and the obsessive secretiveness of Japanese officialdom, portray, a situation in which the interests of the Micronesian have been shunted aside.[27]

Despite the remote situation of Micronesia, the distance which separated its island groups, the hot, damp, enervating climate, and a native population with whom the Japanese shared little in the way of culture, ethos, or industry, Japanese policy toward Micronesia was from the beginning influenced by a sense of pride and purpose as a mandatory power and by a determination to exploit to the utmost its new position in the South Pacific. Where the Spanish had treated the islands with a neglect that was hardly benign and the Germans had seen them as little more than remote trading stations where the Pacific sun might shine on the Kaiser's flag, the new rulers of Micronesia set about administering their mandate with an intensity of attention, purpose, and industry unrivalled elsewhere in the tropical Pacific. As in all overseas Japanese territories, the administration was far larger than those of other colonial powers in East Asia or in the Pacific. From the broad verandas of the Nan'yō-chō headquarters building on Koror to the tidy little Jaluit district office standing behind its proud little stone gateposts, white-uniformed colonial bureaucrats, earnestly and diligently, collected their statistics, drew up laws and regulations, and presided over a host of public works and programs involving health and sanitation, harbor improvement, road construction, land surveys, and public education, which they could justly claim improved the conditions of the Micronesian populations in their charge and thus justified the trust which the international community had formally placed upon their nation.

Education was central to all that Japan hoped to achieve, both in fulfilling the terms of the mandate and in perpetuating its rule over the native population entrusted to its care. Before the arrival of the Japanese, most Micronesian education—what there was of it—came from the few mission schools on the islands. Under the Japanese, mission instruction was soon supplemented by public schools, run at first by uniformed Japanese naval officers, swords at their sides, although by 1918 these were largely replaced by civilian teachers. As

[27] Contrast, for example, the views of Junius B. Wood in "Japan's Mandate in the Pacific," in *Asia*, XXI:9 (Sept. 1921) and George H. Blakeslee in "The Mandates of The Pacific," in *Foreign Affairs*, I:1 (Sept. 1922) with Willard Price's *Japan's Islands of Mystery* (New York: John Day Co., 1944). Even in the 1930's, however, there were a number of foreign evaluations which were surprisingly laudatory of the Japanese regime. See, for example, Walter Harris "The South Sea Islands Under Japanese Mandate," in *Foreign Affairs*, July 1932, and Paul Clyde's *Japan's Pacific Mandate* (New York: MacMillan Co., 1935).

guaranteed by the terms of the mandate, the mission schools continued under Japanese rule, but gradually gave way to government institutions as public education began to make rapid strides. By 1935
attendance at government schools was made obligatory for Micronesian children within range of a school. For the Japanese colonial bureaucracy the primary school classroom was the place where the next
Micronesian generation could be bound closer to the ruling country,
while at the same time Japan could fulfill its obligations concerning
the material and moral well-being of their native charges. The heart
of their educational effort was therefore instruction in the Japanese
language and in Japanese ethics and history, all of which served to
mold the outlook of Micronesian youth and to instill in them a respect for Japan and its political and social institutions. This classroom
instruction was reinforced by other programs of social conditioning
to strengthen in native Micronesians a sense of identification with
Japan: the formation of young men's associations (seinendan) which
promoted moral education and group cooperation in a Japanese context, educational tours to Japan for potential leaders, and awards and
decorations for community service organized and supervised by the
Nan'yō-chō.[28]

If one can judge by the recollections of what is today the oldest
generation of Micronesians, these assimilative efforts seem to have
been quite successful. Educated in Japanese on the primary-school
level, they learned to revere Japanese symbols, to adopt Japanese customs, tastes, and values from the Japanese immigrants who settled in
increasing numbers around them, and to think of Japan as their nation.[29] Had they remained under civilian authority and had their islands remained at peace, this emotional link to Japan would probably
have remained unbroken. Certainly, their belief in the need for sacrifice to the Japanese state, demonstrated by the remarkable degree
of volunteering for military service at the outset of World War II,
attests to the considerable reservoir of loyalty and good will toward
Japan among the Micronesian population, though it was rapidly drained
by the insensitivity and brutality of the Japanese military once the
conflict reached Micronesian shores.

[28] Purcell, "Japanese Expansion," pp. 229-236.

[29] Hatanaka, 14-15; John Wesley Coulter, "The Japanese in Micronesia," in *Trade
Winds: Stories of the South Seas* (Milford, New Hampshire, 1969) pp. 38, 41, and 44;
Kitaoka Kazuyoshi, "Mikuronejia to Nihon o kangaeru" [Thinking about Micronesia
and Japan], *Asahi Jaanaru*, February 2, 1974, p. 39; and Felix Moos, "An Empire of
Islands," a paper presented at the Conference of the Japanese Colonial Empire, 1895-
1945, the Hoover Institution on War, Revolution, and Peace, Stanford University,
September 1979.

In the 1920's and 1930's, therefore, the Nan'yō-chō could assert with some satisfaction that it had indeed provided for the material and moral well-being of the Micronesians by directing them toward modernity. It would be considerably more difficult to argue that Japan's colonial government in the South Pacific did much to advance the "social progress" of the Micronesians, if that phrase is taken to mean an increased ability to compete with the Japanese for jobs and public position or to take charge of their own political affairs. In every respect, Micronesians, like their indigenous counterparts elsewhere in the empire, were second-class citizens in their own lands, and indeed were considered by the Japanese as considerably less worthy than Chinese and Koreans with whom the Japanese at least shared a common cultural heritage. The Nan'yō-chō itself made the distinction between Japanese and Micronesians very clear: the islanders (tōmin) were different in status and rights from Japanese imperial subjects (Nihon teikoku shimmin).[30] Their schools were separate from those of the Japanese and provided an inferior level of course work; vocational training was the only real education open to Micronesians after primary school; only a limited range of jobs were available to Micronesians; labor conditions and pay where Japanese and Micronesians did share employment were unequal; few Micronesians ever found employment in the civil government except for the lower ranks of the police; Micronesian land was subject to confiscation if not adequately documented, and there were no avenues for Micronesians representation or grievance. There was, in short, not the slightest effort by the Japanese colonial government to move the Micronesians toward economic or political autonomy, an obligation which was implied, however vaguely, in the mandate principle established by the League.

It was all the easier for the Nan'yō-chō to ignore this task because of the absence of any indigenous nationalism. Comprising a small population scattered through hundreds of widely separated islands, on some of which they were vastly outnumbered by growing throngs of Japanese, without any national consciousness of their own, without any educated elite or politically or intellectually sophisticated leadership to give voice to whatever resentments of a subject people must have inevitably arisen, and socially conditioned by Japanese language and other Japanese assimilative devices, the Micronesians, gentle, amiable, and unambitious, were not likely to offer an articulated criticism of Japanese rule.[31] Moreover, many islanders were only mini-

---

[30] Japanese Government, *Annual Report to the League of Nations on the Administration of the South Sea Islands under Japanese Mandate for the Year 1934*, p. 4.

[31] I make this statement in full knowledge of the existence of a non-violent nativist cult, *Modekngei*, which sprang up on Palau about 1918 and continued to gain adherents

mally influenced by Japanese rule or by a Japanese presence: in the remoter atolls of the Marshalls, for example, the islanders encountered only the single Japanese trader, the solitary policeman, a few Japanese fishermen, or the occasional trading schooner.

In sum, whatever noble task of advancing the interests of the indigenes may have been assigned to Japan by the League of Nations, it was Japanese interests—economic development, overseas emigration, and, by the 1930's, strategic security—which remained the paramount objectives of the Japanese administration.

ECONOMIC DEVELOPMENT IN THE NAN'YŌ

The economic development of the Nan'yō represents an interplay of private initiative and government capital, an approach which seemed at the time to offer the greatest chance of success and which would most likely support the greatest number of Japanese colonists. In practice, government policy in the Nan'yō encouraged monopolies, a situation which enabled private enterprises to overcome economic obstacles in the South Pacific—distance, small land area, and the limited scale of the Micronesian market—and undoubtedly made it easier for government to regulate commerce and industry in the region.

Commerce was the spearhead of Japanese economic penetration of the islands, of course. We have seen that, long before Micronesia fell under Japanese control, small groups of Japanese entrepreneurs had already established commercial ventures, starting with Truk, Ponape, and the Palaus. With determination, resilience, and skill these commercial pioneers, struggling under the most economically adverse conditions—isolation, lack of capital or any support from their home country, and placed under the suspicion and restrictions of the hostile German colonial government—came to exercise an economic influence out of proportion to their numbers. From their small trading stores and from the decks of their handful of schooners, dealing in sundries (and sometimes firearms) in return for copra and other native products, they came to control a significant portion of the trade of German Micronesia.

---

on the island for the remainder of the period of Japanese rule. The aims of the movement were directed toward a revitalization of Palauan culture and thus, by implication, a rejection of the assimilation efforts of the Japanese administration. But until the very last months of the Japanese presence on Palau the movement never effectively challenged the colonial order. More importantly, *Modekngei* never spread beyond Palauan shores to the other island groups. For an extended discussion of the *Modekngei* cult see Arthur Vidich, *The Political Impact of Colonial Administration* (New York: Arno Press), pp. 228-248.

By 1908 several of these struggling ventures had merged to form the Nan'yō Bōeki Kaisha (South Seas Trading Company)—"Nambō" for short—with a growing commercial network, including copra production, a chain of retail outlets, and a fleet of five vessels transporting inter-island freight, mail, and passengers. World War I, as it did for so much of Japanese commerce and industry, offered a windfall for the Nan'yō Bōeki. With the occupation of the German islands by the Japanese navy, the company was put under a lucrative navy contract to transport provisions and naval personnel within the islands and between Micronesia and the Japanese homeland. With heavy subsidies and preferential treatment by the government, its coffers bulging (with more than three million yen in assets by 1917), Nan'yō Bōeki was able to buy out several small competitive firms operating in the islands, and by 1920 it had attained a trading monopoly in the Nan'yō.[32]

The 1920's saw the firm expand into a variety of enterprises—general merchandise, fisheries, trade in fats and oils, and some construction—through its thirty-two branches spread throughout Micronesia. One of its principal ventures continued to be maritime transportation. Beginning in 1922, under arrangements with the Nan'yō-chō, the company maintained a regular inter-island service between the principal islands of the Mandate and some of the adjacent British islands.

But the majority of its merchants were single traders, under contract to the company, who managed those small trading stores which became a ubiquitous feature of the Japanese presence in the South Seas. It was from these far-flung commercial outlets, their corrugated tin roofs baking in the tropic sun, that the Nan'yō Bōeki was able to penetrate the village economies of Micronesia, introducing a range of Japanese goods and services which profoundly altered native tastes and life-styles.

The development of the Japanese industry in Micronesia was far more unsteady in the beginning. Indeed, the first industrial ventures represented a dismal picture of corporate greed, mismanagement, and callousness. Soon after Japanese naval forces took possession of Micronesia, the islands were quickly seen by Japanese business as an attractive area for speculation. Sugar seemed a particularly promising industry, given the hot, moist climate, the fertile soil of the Marianas, and Japanese success in sugar cultivation and refining in Taiwan. In order to take advantage of such an opportunity, several com-

---

[32] The best account of the formative years of the Nan'yō Bōeki is Gō Takashi's, *Nan'yō bōeki gojūnen shi* [History of fifty years trade in the South Seas] (Tokyo: Nan'yo Bōeki, K.K., 1942).

panies were formed, the Nishimura Takushoku and the Nan'yō Shokusan, by influential backers in Japan.

With little knowledge of either sugar cultivation or refining, and with inadequate investigation and planning, both companies in 1916 established themselves on Saipan, each bringing in Korean laborers, tenant farmers from the Bonins, and poor fishermen from Japan, to serve as a labor force. After several years of disastrous failure brought on by technical ignorance, corruption, and by a post-war world economic slump which caused the world price of sugar to plummet, the companies were on the verge of collapse. By 1919 they had both withdrawn from Micronesia, leaving a thousand or more Japanese laborers and farmers to their fate.[33] It was at the failure of these initial industrial ventures that voices were raised in the Japanese Diet and bureaucracy, advocating that Micronesia be abandoned altogether. As we have seen, the navy successfully argued otherwise.

It was not until the arrival of an entrepreneur possessed of determination, integrity, government backing, and technical skill in the sugar business that Japanese industry was to gain a solid base in the South Pacific. Matsue Haruji (Harutsuģu), trained at Louisiana State University, apprenticed with the Spreckles Company, and destined to be nicknamed the "Sugar King" of the South Pacific, had made his name and fortune in the sugar business in Taiwan. Just at the time when Matsue went to Saipan to investigate the potential of the Marianas for sugar cultivation and refining, the first governor of Nan'yō-chō was enlisting the aid of the Oriental Development Company (which figured so largely in the economic exploitation of Korea), for support of some sort of economic activity which would rescue those Japanese who had been abandoned on Saipan several years before. With capital from the Oriental Development Company and the approval of the government, Matsue was able to take over the assets of Nishimura Takushoku and the Nan'yō Shokusan. Thus, in 1921, was founded the Nan'yō Kōhatsu Kaisha (South Seas Development Company)—familiarly known as "Nankō"—with Matsue Haruji executive director. Employing the Japanese already on Saipan and bringing in more immigrants from Okinawa and the Tōhoku region, Matsue cleared the land, showed the immigrants how to cultivate and harvest the cane, and built his refineries.[34]

---

[33] The failure of the initial agricultural/industrial ventures of these Japanese firms is discussed in detail by Irie Toraji in "Remnants of a Defeated Dream: Pioneers of South Sea Island Development," in *Hōjin kaigai hattenshi* [History of the progress of overseas Japanese], Vol. II (Tokyo: Ida Shoten, 1942), pp. 234-256.

[34] The most interesting account of Matsue's pioneering efforts in the Marianas is his

His initial efforts (1922-1923) were ruinous: labor problems, delays in obtaining refining equipment from Germany, insect blight, carelessness in cultivating the sugarcane by tenant farmers with whom he had contracted to grow it, difficulties in constructing a narrow-gauge railway from the field to the refinery, the plummeting price of sugar, and the destruction of his first small shipment of sugar in a warehouse by the fire which swept Yokohama following the Great Kantō Earthquake of 1922, comprise a catalogue of discouragements and failures which brought Matsue's ventures to the brink of disaster and would have daunted a less determined entrepreneur. Yet, doggedly and resourcefully, Matsue undertook a series of measures to deal with these difficulties and by 1924 had begun to reverse his company's fortunes. By 1925 he had built an alcohol factory and ice plant on Saipan, had placed over three thousand hectares under field, had extended his operations to Saipan's neighboring islands, Tinian and Rota, and by the end of the decade had brought more than five thousand immigrants to the Marianas, where sugar had indeed become king, the main impetus behind the economic boom which followed.[35]

Reading Matsue Haruji's account of his triumph of hard work and determination over the most discouraging obstacles, one is struck by how much the old Meiji entrepreneurial spirit clings to him, in particular the idea of the concurrence between public service and private enrichment. Not content with mere economic success, Matsue viewed the growth of his sugar business in the far-off Pacific as a contribution not only to the prosperity of his nation but to its prestige as well. Similarly, he saw the award of the Nan'yō to Japan as a League of Nations mandate as a divine indication that the nation's future course (and his future profits?) pointed southward. The Nan'yō, in Matsue's view, was important not just in itself, but even more as a base for the economic penetration of the South Pacific and of Southeast Asia, and thus for the further pride and prestige of his country.[36]

To the student of Meiji industrialization, moreover, there is something very familiar about the whole process of economic development in the Nan'yō in the 1920's, for if Matsue was an echo of the Meiji entrepreneurial spirit, the mutual interest and support between Nankō and the Nan'yō-chō reflected arrangements typical of the interaction of private industry and government in mid-Meiji times.

Certainly Matsue's most heroic individual efforts would have been fruitless without major support from the colonial government, for

---

own, *Nanyō kaitaku jūnenshi* [History of Ten Years of Pioneering in the South Seas] (Tokyo: Nanyō Kōhatsu, K.K., 1932).

[35] Matsue, pp. 128-157.

[36] *Ibid.*, p. 53.

the rapid growth of the Nan'yō Kōhatsu was due in large part to the aid and favors that it received from the Nan'yō-chō: nearly rent-free use of land, subsidies to support the necessary ground-breaking, land-clearing, and planting efforts, a favorable tax policy, and a virtual monopoly on sugar production in the Nan'yō. Nourished by such favored treatment and propelled by Matsue's initiatives, the company became the dominant economic force not only in the Marianas but throughout Micronesia. With government backing, Nankō began moving out to the other Micronesian island groups and then ulti-mately to Melanesia and into the Dutch East Indies, diversifying its efforts into such enterprises as tapioca and coconut cultivation, ma-rine products, phosphates, and warehousing, as it went along. In return for its support, the Nan'yō-chō closely monitored Matsue's company and obliged it to cooperate in the development and admin-istration of the mandate. By the early 1930's Nankō's sugar-related industries accounted for more than sixty percent of the revenues of the Nan'yō-chō (largely through port clearance fees for its products leaving Micronesia), and by mid-decade the company was a substan-tial investor in the colonial government's own industrial enterprises.[37]

During the first decade of the mandate, in any event, the success of the two largest enterprises, the Nan'yō Bōeki and the Nan'yō Kōhatsu, aided by a friendly administration, had pulled along the fortunes of Japanese commerce, industry, and agriculture throughout the islands, which in turn opened the way for increased immigration. The Nan'yō not only became a self-sufficient territory, allowing the government to terminate its annual subsidy, but also contributed to the support of the empire as a whole, its small but growing surplus being transferred to the general account of the metropolitan govern-ment. Typically, Japanese efforts combining government backing and private initiative had turned an initial colonial liability into an asset.

JAPANESE IMMIGRATION INTO THE NAN'YŌ

What set this commercial industrial growth in the Nan'yō apart from that of most of the other colonies in the empire was the fact that it involved Micronesian labor to only a slight degree. By and large the

---

[37] The Nan'yō-chō was itself the third partner in the economic development of the Nan'yō. Its chief activity was the operation of the phosphate mines on Angaur in the Palau islands (an undertaking which represents one of the darker passages of the Jap-anese record in Micronesia, exploiting as it did forced indigenous labor in direct vio-lation of the League of Nations statutes for administration of the mandates). In 1936, the Nan'yō-chō turned over this and other industrial enterprises to a semi-govern-mental corporation, the Nan'yō Takushoku, K.K.

burden of Japanese economic growth in the Nan'yō was borne by a growing number of Japanese immigrants—laborers and farmers—whose presence in the Nan'yō and whose livelihood there depended on the success of the commercial and industrial ventures that I have just described.

There had seemed little reason at first to emigrate to Micronesia. At the outset of World War I there had been not more than a hundred Japanese in all the islands. The naval occupation had brought in a considerable number of naval personnel, government officials, and some additional merchants and traders. But while the new Japanese presence was enlarged in scale and activity, lacking any real influx of permanent settlers, it remained a colonial bureaucracy in all but name, and those Japanese who came to the Nan'yō were mostly men without families whose official tour or commercial interests were limited in time and expectation. Initial efforts by private capital to promote settlement in Micronesia during the first years of the Japanese occupation had proved a scandalous tragedy. The exhausting, sun-scorched experience of the first immigrant groups lured to the Marianas by the ill-considered schemes of Japanese speculators, and then marooned there when those financial ventures collapsed, had shown the terrible human cost of emigration to the tropics without proper planning or support from the home islands.

The formal award of the Nan'yō to Japan as a mandated territory and the subsequent creation of a sound economic base for Micronesia dramatically improved the prospects for permanent Japanese settlement there. The success by 1924 of Matsue Haruiji's efforts to establish a sugar industry in the Marianas, along with his recruitment of contract labor from the home islands, marked the beginning of an important change in the circumstances of the Nan'yō, a gradual shift from an occupation territory similar to most European colonies in the tropical Pacific, to settlement territory.

The Japanese government, once it had assumed official responsibility for Micronesia and had recognized the fact that a sound and growing economy for the islands would have to involve a Japanese rather than an indigenous labor force and consumer population, began to encourage emigration to the islands as a policy. Indeed, its support and assistance to the Nan'yō Kōhatsu was in part a recognition that the company's ventures offered the best prospects for Japanese immigration, not only by laborers employed in the sugar refineries, but even more by tenant farmers whom the company brought to the islands under contract to cultivate its lands.

Nankō rented land at reasonable terms, provided reasonable security and relatively generous economic support to immigrants who would clear the land and till the soil in return for tight company control over the use of the land and disposition of the sugar crop.[38] These conditions made the Nan'yō a more suitable area for the farmer under contract rather than for the independent cultivator (who usually faced considerable risks for small return), and thus it was the tenant farmer who began moving into the islands in increasing numbers in the late 1920's.

Matsue's initial recruiting efforts in the early 1920's were to shape immigration patterns in the Nan'yō for years to come. He selected farmers from Okinawa and from the other islands of the Ryūkyū group for a variety of reasons: of all the Japanese they were most used to a semi-tropical climate; they were familiar since childhood with the cultivation of sugarcane; and, of late, population pressures in their home islands had generated enthusiasm for emigration.[39] But immigrants from other parts of Japan also began arriving in the islands. From Fukushima, Yamagata, and Miyagi prefectures came poor farming families looking for a chance to better their hard-scrabble lives during a time of economic privation in the Tōhoku region. As recruiting efforts in Okinawa and Tōhoku continued and as word of mouth spread tales of opportunity and success in the South Pacific, those areas consistently furnished the greatest number of immigrants after 1920.[40]

The freshet of immigration naturally flowed first of all into the Marianas—Saipan, Tinian, and Rota—where the sugar industry drew them, then southwest into the Palaus. Drawn by reports of fertile soil and waters abundant with fish, other immigrants—largely from Okinawa, but now also from Hokkaido, Shizuoka, and even from Tokyo—began to move into the eastern Carolines, particularly Truk, Ponape, and Kusaie. Some worked in the Marianas and Carolines for a while until they saved enough money to move further east to the Marshalls, where, though the coral soil was too poor to nourish many crops, they could peddle their small stock of sundries—combs, fishhooks, hair oil, pots and pans—and eventually set up a tiny store on Jaluit or on one of the remoter atolls. On the heels of those who tilled the soil, fished the waters, or worked in the refineries and canneries, came the petty shopkeepers, restaurant, geisha house, and

[38] For a discussion of the conditions laid down by Nankō for tenant farming on its lands, see John A. Decker, *Labor Problems in the Pacific Mandates* (London: Oxford University Press, 1940), pp. 37-41.

[39] Matsue, p. 82.

[40] For discussion and appropriate tables relating to Okinawan emigration to the Nan'yō see Okinawa Ken, eds., *Okinawa Ken shi* [History of Okinawa prefecture], Vol. VII: *Imin* [Emigrants] (Tokyo: Iwanando Shoten, 1974), pp. 380-400.

brothel proprietors, as well as those in the other service trades. They were attracted to the South Seas for any number of reasons: the lure of easier living in a milder climate and an exotic environment, the desire to escape the grim statistics of unemployment and overcrowding, the wish to be free of military service, to flee difficult family or business situations, or to fulfill some dream of personal ambition or national destiny.[41] Their swelling numbers rapidly expanded the former German settlements into Japanese boom towns: Garapan and Charankanoa on Saipan, Sunharon on Tinian, Koror in the Palaus, Dublon on Truk, Colonia on Ponape, Jabor Town on Jaluit. In those towns the structures of modern civilization and administration—government buildings, hospitals, factories, radio stations, and newspaper offices—competed for space with private houses and shops which crowded along hot dusty streets with names like Ō-dori and Namiki-dori, where hand-cart peddlers, bicycles, and an occasional automobile shared the way with parasol-carrying housewives in white cotton, shopping for groceries and houseware items, fishermen and laborers on their way to and from work, postmen and policemen on their rounds.

By the mid-1930's Japanese immigration was spilling into Micronesia at a startling rate, producing a growth in the Japanese population from not quite twenty thousand in 1930 to more than fifty thousand in 1935. The American journalist Willard Price, who passed through the islands in 1935, called the influx of Japanese a "rip tide" movement.[42] Under this migratory onslaught, made heavier by a rising Japanese birthrate among the immigrants, the Micronesian population was rapidly imperilled, despite a gradually increasing birthrate of its own. In the Palaus, the Micronesians were outnumbered two to one and in the Marianas, where the greatest number of Japanese had settled, ten to one. On Tinian, Japanese immigrants comprised nearly the entire population of the island. Only in the eastern Carolines and Marshalls did the Micronesians remain a majority. Outnumbered, unable, or uninterested in competing economically with the Japanese, their language, customs, and cultural identity increasingly submerged beneath those of the dominant race, the indigenes in much of Micronesia might not have survived the century as an identifiable ethnic group had not the Pacific War dramatically obliterated the Japanese presence.

In the failure to stem the flow of immigration into Micronesia lies perhaps the single most important breach of the trust which had been

[41] Moos paper.

[42] Willard Price, *Pacific Adventure* (New York: Reynal and Hitchcock, 1936), pp. 161-173.

placed upon Japan by the League of Nations in 1922. Certainly, no one in the League's Permanent Mandates Commission had originally conceived of a situation in which the indigenous population, whose welfare the mandatory was supposed to guarantee, would be so completely overrun by immigrants from the metropolitan power. Indeed, viewing the positive encouragement given to limitless immigration by the Japanese government and by concurrent arrangements which provided a variety of economic assistance to Japanese but not to Micronesians, it is hard to escape the conclusion that Japanese policy in Micronesia was framed to suit the interests of its own nationals and not those of the native peoples who had been placed in its charge.

A Question of Bases: The Drift Toward Militarization of the Nan'yō

In the decade following the controversy over Yap, the Nan'yō rarely became a subject of international discussion. Year after year the Japanese government filed its annual reports on the mandate with the League of Nations whose Permanent Mandates Commission seldom probed beyond their colorless phraseology and clusters of statistics. Except for the occasional queries they raised as to Japanese immigration into Micronesia, the few in the international community who even cared that Japan had a mandate in the South Pacific saw no reason to doubt that Japan was fulfilling the terms of that charge.

The violent shift of events in East Asia provoked by Japan's sudden thrust into Manchuria in 1931 changed this international climate of aquiesence. By the next year all of Japan's overseas activities and policies were subjected to rigorous scrutiny by increasingly hostile powers. China, the United States, the Soviet Union, and the leading nations of Western Europe, all came to look askance at resurgent Japanese imperialism. Inevitably, suspicion touched upon the Japanese administration in the South Pacific. Rumors emanating from Geneva early in 1932 told of Japanese transgressions in the form of clandestine militarization of her South Pacific territories, though Japan's representative to the Permanent Mandates Commission asserted that his nation continued to adhere strictly to the non-fortification agreements that it had signed a decade earlier.[43]

The following year these suspicions merged with a new and unprecedented controversy over Japan's presence in the South Pacific. That May, Foreign Minister Matsuoka Yōsuke's abrupt and theatri-

[43] League of Nations, Permanent Mandates Commission, *Minutes*, 2d Session, "Report to the Council," p. 367.

cal walkout from the League of Nations signalled his nation's determination to resign from the body two years hence, an action which
immediately prompted a heated debate between scholars as well as
by statesmen over the legality of Japan's presence in Micronesia, once
Japan withdrew from the League. The official Japanese position made
it clear that Japan had no intention of relinquishing its mandate, yet
stopped short of asserting that the islands had now become Japanese
territory.[44] Japan held to this policy until the outbreak of World War
II, when the disappearance of the League made it possible to drop
the pretense that Japan remained in Micronesia to fulfill her obligations as a mandatory power.

Considering that Japan's departure from the League coincided with
an ominous increase in tension between Japan and the United States,
it is not surprising that Japanese intransigence on the mandate question was stiffened principally by the Japanese navy. Navy spokesmen
not only began to issue policy statements insisting on the Japanese
right to remain in Micronesia, but led a publicity campaign to con-
vince the Japanese public that the islands were vital as a "life-line"
(seimeisen) for Japanese security.[45] Once more there was vague but
urgent talk of the nation's destiny in the "South Seas," though that
term came increasingly to include Southeast Asian lands and waters.
Navy enthusiasts of a "southern advance" and the civilian publicists
who supported them now began to frame those geopolitical concepts
of self-sufficiency, Asian cooperation, and colonial liberation that were
to spring forth a decade later under the banner of "East Asian co-

[44] Hirota Kōki, Matsuoka Yōsuke's successor as Foreign Minister, explained the
rather curious Japanese stance in his response to questions put to him in the House of
Peers, February 22, 1934. According to Hirota, Japan's status as legal mandatory in
the South Pacific had nothing to do with her membership in the League for the following reasons: first, Japan had negotiated her occupation of the Micronesian Islands
with the principal Allied powers during World War I; second, though Japan had de-
ferred to current world trends after the war and had accepted the decision to place the
islands within the mandate system, the selection of Japan as a mandatory was the result
of negotiation with its principal war-time allies, not with the League as such. On the
other hand, while Japan administered Micronesia as if it were an integral part of the
empire, it did not in fact claim the islands as actual Japanese territory, but only insisted
upon the legality of its status as a mandatory power. For that reason the government
felt duty-bound to make annual reports to the Permanent Mandates Commission, just
as before. Kampō, gōgai [Official gazette, special issue], February 1, 1934, Kizoku-in
[House of Peers], Sokkiroku [Minutes], p. 407; February 22, 1934, p. 21, in Teikoku
gikaishi [Records of the Imperial Diet], 1st Series, Volume 17, Volume 18, 65th Diet
Session (1976 re-edition), Shakai Mondai Kenkyū Kai, eds. (Tokyo: Tōyō Bunka Sha,
1976).

[45] See, for example, Kaigunshō, Kaigun Gunji Fukyūbu, Umi no seimeisen [Our Ocean
Life Line] (Tokyo: Kaigunsho, Kaigun Gunji Fukyūbu, 1933).

prosperity." Indeed, by the early 1930's naval and civilian advocates of southern expansion saw Micronesia, now termed the "Inner Nan'yō" as a base for "advance" (the exact meaning of the word was usually left unclear) into Southeast Asia, now designated the "Outer Nan'yō."

Throughout the 1930's these attitudes, combined with the increasing reluctance of the Japanese government to open Micronesia to foreign observation, re-kindled the long-smouldering suspicions among the Anglo-American naval powers that Japan was engaged in clandestine militarization of its mandate in violation of its international pledge. Obsessive American anxiety concerning this dark possibility had dated from the early months of World War I and the establishment of a Japanese naval presence in Micronesia.[46] Immediately after the war, Colonel Earl Ellis of the United States Marine Corps had made his dramatic prediction that the inevitable war with Japan would require special strategy and tactics of an amphibious sort to drive that nation from the South Pacific. The fact that Ellis, the father of the Corps' amphibious warfare doctrines, died under apparently mysterious circumstances while on a clandestine intelligence mission in the Palaus heightened suspicions in the American navy that the Japanese did indeed have something to conceal in their Pacific territories.[47] By the late 1920's Tokyo was politely rejecting all requests for official visitation or international inspection of Micronesia, though a few unofficial Americans and Britons did manage to gain entry in the 1930's.[48] Then, in 1938, came the disappearance of Amelia Earhart, whose fatal course across the South Pacific ended in oblivion, stirring rumors in America that she had been forced down by the Japanese and imprisoned (or executed) for having seen first-hand aerial evidence of Japanese treachery (though, in fact, she never crossed Micronesian waters).

In the aftermath of the attack on Pearl Harbor, all these volatile suspicions were to fuse into the hardened conviction that Japan had constructed a vast network of naval bases, airfields, gun emplace-

[46] Early in the war the director of U.S. Navy's Office of Naval Intelligence, acting on missionary-inspired reports of Japanese fortifications on Truk and on Yap, proposed that a clandestine operation under cover of a civilian schooner be sent to the Carolines and Marshalls to verify these rumors, but the plan was promptly rejected by the Chief of Naval Operations. Jeffrey Dorwart, *The Office of Naval Intelligence: the Birth of America's First Intelligence Agency* (Annapolis, Maryland: U.S. Naval Institute Press, 1979), pp. 138-139.

[47] Jeter Isley and Philip Crowl, *The United States Marines & Amphibious Warfare* (Princeton, N.J.: Princeton University Press, 1951), pp. 25-27, and John J. Reber, "Pete Ellis: Amphibious Warfare Prophet," in *United States Naval Institute Proceedings*, Vol. 103: 11 (November 1977), pp. 53-64.

[48] Richard Dean Burns, "Inspection of the Mandates, 1919-1941," in *Pacific Historical Review*, XXXVII:4 (November 1968), pp. 445-462.

ments, and military camps in the South Pacific long years before the two nations were at war.

The evidence available before, during, and after the Pacific War does not support this belief. To begin with, the accounts of those few American and British visitors who were able to visit the Nan'yō as tourists in the 1930's either make no mention of the fact, or else categorically deny that the authors observed any sign of military construction in Micronesia.[49] During the course of the Pacific War, moreover, some of the greatest fortifications said to have been build by the Japanese, such as the vaunted naval base at Truk in the eastern Carolines, turned out to be the product of fevered American speculation. Finally, after the war it proved impossible to find evidence that the Japanese had set out from the earliest period of its mandate to break its written pledge to abjure the military and naval defense of the islands. The Allied International Military Tribunal for the Far East, convened in 1946 to try the wartime Japanese leadership, was unable to challenge a single witness whose testimony indicated that Japan, for the most part, had lived up to its international agreements as a mandatory power.[50]

Yet, given the fact that massive attacks on American possessions in the South Pacific and Southeast Asia were launched in the opening days of the Pacific War from Japanese islands in the South Pacific, it is obvious that by December 1941, at least, all three Micronesian island groups had been militarized to some extent. Where, then, is the truth of the question?

The facts, as historians and first-hand observers have been able to put them together from Japanese documents and testimony, are these: until it withdrew from the League of Nations in 1933, Japan appears to have been scrupulous in its pledge of non-fortification of the mandates.[51] From 1934 to 1939 the Nan'yō-chō, with some limited help

[49] See, for example, R.V.C. Bodley, *The Drama of the Pacific* (Tokyo: Hokuseido Press, 1934), pp. 105-107, and Paul H. Clyde, *Japan's Pacific Mandate* (New York: The MacMillan Company, 1935), pp. 202-224. Bodley, an Englishman, and Clyde, an American, toured the islands extensively in the mid-1930's. The American Willard Price, who visited Micronesia about the same time, changed his opinion radically over a decade on the basis of very little evidence. His *Pacific Adventure*, published in 1936 soon after his return, made little reference to possible Japanese violations of the terms of the mandate; his *Japan's Islands of Mystery* (New York: John Day Co., 1944), published during the war, makes it appear as if Japanese fortifications and treachery in Micronesia had been decades in the making.

[50] Masatake Okumiya, "For Sugar Boats or Submarines?" in *United States Naval Institute Proceedings*, XCIV:8 (August 1968), p. 73.

[51] My understanding of the timing and evolution of the Japanese militarization of its Micronesian mandate is largely based on Thomas Wilds's "How Japan Fortified the Mandated Islands," in *United States Naval Institute Proceedings*, LXXXI (April 1955),

from the navy, apparently undertook a modest construction program of harbor improvements, airfields, seaplane ramps, weather stations, communications centers, and petroleum dumps on Saipan, the Palaus, Truk, and later Ponape. While, obviously, all these improvements could easily be converted into military use if the Japanese so desired, it is arguable at least, as the Japanese then perceived it, that this construction amounted to upgrading the administrative and commercial services of an essentially civilian regime in Micronesia. It is also possible to understand how the Japanese government, fearful that foreign observers might be quick to place a less charitable interpretation on these material changes, concluded that it was prudent to keep the islands closed to any international inspection.

In 1939, in view of the moribund nature of both the League of Nations and of its mandate system, as well as the worsening global situation, the government decided to push ahead with a true military construction program which would strengthen the existing facilities, expand their number, and extend them to the Marshalls. Late in that year, the Japanese navy organized the Fourth Fleet with headquarters at Truk, charged with the protection of the Nan'yō. Yet this command existed mostly on paper throughout 1940. Provided with few combat vessels, its primary task was military construction, principally of naval air stations and fuel dumps throughout Micronesia, and particularly in the Marshalls.

This military buildup needs to be put in historical perspective. By late 1940, it is fair to say that the naval high commands in both Washington and Tokyo assumed that a collision between the United States and Japan was unavoidable within the next several years. Given these perspectives and the evaporation of any vestigial authority of the League, it seems unreasonable to charge that the Japanese fortification of a strategically critical forward area amounted to a long-planned and treacherous violation of international agreements. Certainly, American failure to strengthen its own possessions in the Western Pacific in the late 1930's appears to have had less to do with national scruples than it did with the unwillingness of a parsimonious Congress to allocate the funds for adequate defense.

In February 1941, in any event, the first combat units of the Fourth Fleet—four light cruisers, eight destroyers, an air flotilla, numerous auxiliary vessels, shore defense units, and construction battalions—began to take up positions on Truk, the Palaus, Saipan, and Kwajalein in the Marshalls. Yet, in the months immediately prior to the

pp. 401-407. As a research assistant engaged in a study of Japanese operations in the Pacific, 1941-1945, for the Office of the Chief of Military History, Department of the Army, Wilds based his account on Japanese documentary materials for the period.

outbreak of the Pacific War, much remained to make the Nan'yō a formidable base area. In January 1941 Vice-Admiral Inoue Shige-yoshi, Chief of Naval Aviation and one of the navy's most forward-looking officers, had urged accelerated progress in the construction of air and submarine bases in the South Pacific islands as part of a radically different approach to Japan's national defense requirements, but his recommendations and the brilliant plan which contained them were set aside by the Navy Ministry. That summer a staff officer based on Kwajalein touring the Marshalls returned with a furious denunciation of the lack of preparedness that he found there. His stinging memorandum to Tokyo was similarly ignored.[52] The truth about the "invulnerable fortress" myth of the Pacific War was that in fact Japan never completed the construction of the bases that it had begun less than two years prior to the Pearl Harbor attack, but was desparately pushing ahead to finish them when the American amphibious offensive overwhelmed the islands in the first half of 1944.

THE PACIFIC WAR: THE NAN'YŌ CONQUERED

Nevertheless, the key Japanese bases which did exist in the Nan'yō in December 1941 proved of great offensive value in the first few weeks of the war, since they not only protected Japan's eastern flank, but helped to support Japanese strikes against Pearl Harbor, the Philippines, Guam, Wake, the Gilberts, and British possessions in Melanesia. Japanese submarines which rendezvoused at Kwajalein were the first Japanese units to reach Hawaii for the Japanese attack there. Three of the six Japanese landings in the Philippines—at Legaspi, Davao, and the Jolo islands—in December 1941 were made by a Japanese task force and accompanying transports organized in the Palaus. Bombers from Saipan struck at Guam on December 8th and an invasion force from Truk landed the next day, quickly overcoming American resistance. The attack on Wake island began with aerial strikes launched from Kwajalein, and after an epic resistance by United States Marines the atoll was overwhelmed by a Japanese task force despatched from Fourth Fleet headquarters at Truk.

The first Allied counterblows against the Japanese colonial empire were struck early in 1942 by naval and air units of the United States Pacific Fleet against Kwajalein, Wotje, Taroa, and Jaluit atolls in the

[52] Sadao Asada, "The Japanese & the United States," in *Pearl Harbor as History: Japanese-American Relations, 1931-1941*, Dorothy Borg and Shumpei Okamoto, eds. (New York: Columbia University Press, 1973), p. 255; Sadao Seno, "A Chess Game with no Check Mate: Admiral Inoue & The Pacific War," in *Naval War College Review* (January-February 1944), pp. 26-39; and Okumiya, p. 71.

Marshalls. But these were light jabs along the periphery of the empire, more designed to lift sagging American morale than they were damaging blows to Japanese defenses. For the next several years, as the Allies first halted and then gathered their strength for a counteroffensive up through the South Pacific, the emperor's island territories remained inviolate.

With the beginning of the American offensives in the Solomon islands in the late summer of 1942, the Japanese base at Truk assumed increasing importance. While it never became the impregnable fortress that the United States Navy imagined it to be, it was greatly strengthened as an advance base for the Combined Fleet. Increasing numbers of naval shore personnel were stationed on its principal islands; heavy guns were placed on its mountain slopes (none, contrary to myth, from the captured British base at Singapore); and on the smaller, less rugged islands airfield runways were extended. To the splendid natural harbor formed by the vast ring of coral reefs around the islands came Admiral Yamamoto Isoroku and the greatest battleships that the world would ever see, the *Yamato* and later its sister, the *Musashi*, as well as an armada of lesser battleships, aircraft carriers, and heavy cruisers, shoals of destroyers, submarines, and fleet auxiliaries, scattered about the enormous lagoon.

Yet for all this mighty concentration of Japanese naval power, the sojourn of the Combined Fleet at Truk from the summer of 1942 to November of 1943 proved an exercise in futility. While Japanese battlefield commanders on Guadalcanal sent desperate pleas to the navy to despatch the *Yamato* with its sixteen-inch guns to pulverize the American enemy in the Solomons, the naval high command in Tokyo, still obsessed with the primacy of battleships and thus unwilling to risk them in anything but the long-awaited decisive encounter with their enemy counterparts, kept the main units of the Combined Fleet placidly at anchor at Truk. There Admiral Yamamoto, resplendent in his dress whites, presided over the fleet from the comfort and spendid isolation of his quarters aboard the "*Yamato* Hotel," as his flagship was known around the fleet, dispensing Scotch whiskey, English cigarettes, and examples of his calligraphy to his staff, while awaiting the opportunity, which never came, to strike a decisive blow at the enemy.[53] When at last, in early 1943, Yamamoto

---

[53] Interesting descriptions of life at Truk while Yamamoto and the Combined Fleet were there are found in Niina Masuo, "Rengō kantai no konkyō Torakku" [The Combined Fleet Base at Truk], in *Nihon shokuminchi shi* [Japanese Colonial History], Vol. 3: *Taiwan; Nan'yō guntō; Karafuto* (*Ichiokunin no Shōwa shi* [The History of One Hundred Million People During the Shōwa Period], Matsui Takanari, general editor, Tokyo: Mainichi Shimbun Sha, 1978), pp. 206-209, as well as in Hiroyuki Agawa *The*

determined to take an active hand in the combat being waged in the West Pacific, the decision cost the life of this, Japan's most famous naval commander. Alerted by a decoded Japanese radio message outlining the route of his inspection trip to the Shortland islands, American aircraft intercepted the bomber in which Yamamoto was a passenger and shot it out of the sky.

Yamamoto's successor as Combined Fleet commander, Admiral Koga Mineichi, suffered no better fate. With both the *Musashi* and the *Yamato* at his disposal, Koga kept the remainder of the fleet together at Truk for the realization of his "Z Plan," the annihilation of the United States Pacific Fleet in the decisive battleship encounter, which was an article of faith of Japanese naval high command. Twice Koga sortied to Eniwetok in the Marshalls, and each time the failure of the American fleet to materialize forced him to withdraw empty-handed. When Koga moved his aircraft and lighter surface units to Rabaul in late 1943 to threaten American beachheads in the Solomons, they were torn apart in savage aerial attacks on that port. Now shorn of sufficient protection, the Japanese super-battleships sat virtually immobilized at Truk lagoon. By this time, the enemy had begun to carry his aerial vengeance to the Marshalls, the most eastward territories of Japan's embattled empire, waging a war of attrition against Japanese airpower there and threatening Truk and the eastern Carolines. Forced to pull back his command to the Philippines, Admiral Koga perished with his aircraft when it went down in a Pacific storm during the withdrawal.

By February 1944 the advance of American amphibious power had reached the Marshalls. Majuro atoll was the first Japanese territory of the formal empire to be lost to the enemy, followed by Kwajalein, whose vast lagoon, larger even than that of Truk, provided a superb anchorage for the powerful American task forces bent upon the capture or neutralization of Japan's remaining bases in Micronesia. After a massive strike on Truk which sent over two hundred thousand tons of Japanese shipping to the floor of the lagoon in mid-February, the Fourth Fleet became an empty shell, its offensive capacities shattered, and its isolated garrisons on Truk and the remaining Japanese footholds in the eastern Carolines left desperately short of food and supplies as the tide of the American advance swept past them, heading northwest to the Marianas.

Until 1944 the Marianas had served principally as a supply and staging area for troops, ships, and aircraft committed to operations

Reluctant Admiral: Yamamoto and the Imperial Navy, John Bester, translator (Tokyo: Kodansha International, 1979), pp. 326-328 and 338-339.

far to the south and east. As a rear area their garrisons had been token-sized, but now, as the low atolls of the Marshalls fell one by one to the enemy, the Marianas, along with the western Carolines, became the front line of the empire's defenses. Forced to reorder its priorities, Imperial General Headquarters in Tokyo began pouring men, weapons, and aircraft into those island groups, a division and a brigade each for Saipan and the Palaus; an infantry regiment each for Tinian and Pelelieu, just south of Palau. By June 1944, the Japanese high command had despatched about forty-five thousand troops to the Marianas. Yet, well before the direct assault on Saipan by American surface ships and aircraft, American submarines had begun to play havoc with the Japanese effort to reinforce those islands. Scores of Japanese transports went to the bottom, carrying with them over thirty-five hundred troops and leaving another four or five thousand stranded without equipment on the shores of Saipan.

The Japanese on Saipan nevertheless had time to prepare formidable defenses, and the high command was determined that the island should serve as the bastion against which the American offensive in the West Pacific would shatter. Indeed, Japanese naval headquarters concluded that the defense of the Marianas and western Carolines had brought about the opportunity to defeat the United States Pacific Fleet in the long-sought, decisive encounter. Immediately upon receiving word of the American landings on Saipan, Admiral Ozawa Jisaburō was despatched from Philippine waters with the remainder of the Japanese battle fleet to attack American naval forces. But Ozawa's nine carriers and inexperienced pilots were no match for fifteen American carriers and their great number of veteran fliers. The Battle of the Philippine Sea, June 1944, or "The Great Marianas Turkey Shoot," as it was known at the time by jubilant American airmen and sailors, shattered Japanese naval and air power in the Southwest Pacific and obliterated all hope of any air support's reaching Saipan, now under attack by three American divisions.

On that island the Japanese defenders on the ground resisted from pill boxes and caves with frenzy and futility. Tragically, great numbers of the considerable Japanese civilian population on the island chose to perish with them, and the names "Suicide" and "Banzai" appended to the cliffs at the northern tip of the island mark the sites where hundreds, mostly women and children, leaped to their deaths on the rocks far below. The senior military commander on Saipan, the aging and infirm General Saitō Yoshitsugu, had called for one final counterattack by his men. His pledge, "I will leave my bones on Saipan as a bulwark of the Pacific," with which his last order concluded, is a stark epitaph to the futility of the Japanese military presence in Micronesia.[54] With his suicide and the exhaustion of the Japanese counterattack, all effective resistance on Saipan came to an end, and the island was secured by American forces in early July. The next month, Guam and Tinian fell in succession.

For those Japanese who had some understanding of the strategic issues involved in the Pacific War, the fall of Saipan pointed to the hopelessness of their nation's position. American capture of the Marianas breached Japan's inner line of defenses, enabling the enemy to cut communications with the western Carolines, as well as providing bases from which the Japanese home islands themselves could be aerially bombarded. It was from airfields on Tinian that B-29 bombers departed in August 1945 with their loads of awesome destruction for Hiroshima and Nagasaki.

In order to secure the eastern flank of the projected American drive to reconquer the Philippines, the Americans appeared off the Palau islands in September 1944 and on the fifteenth of that month landed on Angaur and Peleliu below their southern tip. These last of the Micronesian islands to be taken by storm, Angaur and Peleliu were the scene of merciless American attacks and terrible Japanese resistance. The fighting continued until November 1944, when the last of the defenders had been incinerated or blown to pieces in their caves and bunkers.

LIQUIDATION OF JAPAN'S NAN'YŌ

In this survey of Japan in Micronesia, it remains only to describe the miserable fate of those remnants of the Japanese empire in the South Pacific which had been bypassed as the American island offensive leap-frogged north to the Bonins and the Ryūkyūs. By autumn 1944 only four atolls in the Marshalls remained in Japanese hands: Jaluit, Mili, Wotje, and Maloelap; in the eastern Carolines the Rising Sun flag still flew over Kusaie, Ponape, and Truk; in the western Carolines, Yap and the northern Palaus; and in the Marianas, Rota and the ten smaller islands north of Saipan.

Cut off from any reinforcement by surface or air units from the home islands or other bases overseas by mid-1944 (except for occasional visits by supply submarines which surfaced at night), without any real defenses, let alone offensive air capability, periodically subjected to heavy surface and air bombardment, the remaining Japanese-held islands became useless bits of real estate whose inhabitants

---

[54] Quoted in Philip A. Crowl, *Campaign in the Marianas* (*United States Army in World War II: War in the Pacific*; Washington, D.C.: Office of the Chief of Military History, Department of the Army, 1960), p. 257.

struggled merely to stay alive for the rest of the war. Since most of their garrisons were supplied with provisions for approximately six months to a year, they suffered no privations for the first half of 1944, but, after that, forsaking all pretense at military activity, they turned their waning energies to fishing the lagoons, growing small truck gardens, and hunting what animal life existed.

This isolation and privation were sufficiently severe for the military and naval personnel on the islands, but the hardships suffered by the Japanese and Micronesian civilian populations were even more intense. In 1943, in face of the approaching American offensive, the administration of the Nan'yō had once more been turned over to the Japanese navy and the administrative center of the Nan'yō was once more located at Truk. This change not only disrupted the continuity of the administrative, economic, and educational programs of the Nan'yō-chō, but when the navy had no more planes or ships and when the district capitals of the various island groups lay in ruins after weeks of enemy bombardment, the navy and military personnel on the larger high islands took to the jungle, abandoning the Micronesians and the Japanese civilians to shift for themselves.[55] Without real shelter, deprived of supplies and medical aid, and desperately short of food, the island residents were reduced to grubbing for roots and leaves, and hunting for rats. On the by-passed low islands, life was even more grim. Of the forty-seven-hundred-man garrison on Mili atoll, about sixteen hundred died from disease, starvation, and eating poisonous fish, while another nine hundred died in American air raids.[56]

As the Japanese military situation grew more desperate, relations with the native islanders deteriorated. At the outset of the Pacific War the good will and loyalty of the native populations toward Japan had enabled the authorities to form a number of Micronesian volunteer units (teishintai),[57] but this good will soon evaporated with the great infusion of Japanese military and naval personnel, ignorant of native sensibilities and interested only in the Micronesians as a labor force for the construction of military facilities. Crowded into restricted

[55] Nan'yo Guntō Kyōkai (South Sea Islands Association), eds., Yashi no ki wa karezu: Naniyo guntō no genjitsu to omoide [The Palms Do Not Wither: Realities and Recollections of the South Sea Islands] (Tokyo: Sōshi Bunka, 1966), p. 109.

[56] Samuel Eliot Morison, Aleutians, Gilberts, & Marshalls, June 1942-April 1944 (United States Naval Operations in World War II) (Boston, Mass.: Little, Brown and Co., 1951), pp. 307-308.

[57] These native volunteer forces from the Palau islands generally suffered a dismal fate. Sent to Southeast Asia as construction units attached to the Japanese army, they were left stranded at war's end or were shipwrecked off the Palaus when the transports repatriating them were sunk by American Submarines. Kitaoka, p. 39.

areas, shipped from island to island as conscripted laborers, brutalized by Japanese soldiery, the Micronesians on those islands with large Japanese garrisons became sullen and hostile, although they apparently retained a degree of affection and respect for individual civilian officials and colonists. By and large, most Micronesians did not consider the war to be their affair and when the Americans landed many were only too glad to drop their Japanese loyalties.

For the Japanese, struggling, stranded, and abandoned on the southern rim of the empire, the end of the war came as a relief and an anti-climax. The surrender of all Japanese forces in the Nan'yō was taken August 30, 1945 in the wardroom of an American destroyer standing off the great fringing reef at Truk. Dazed from the shock of defeat and languid from long dietary privation, shaking from various fevers, the Japanese military staff on Truk laid bare the hollow shell of Japan's remaining defenses in the South Pacific and formally turned over to the United States Navy the vast section of the Pacific Ocean and its scattered fragments of land which for all practical purposes Japan had already lost.[58]

The end of Japanese rule in the South Pacific not only meant the liquidation of the Japanese administration and the withdrawal of the remaining Japanese garrisons, but the repatriation to their homeland of all Japanese civilians who remained in Micronesia. Throughout the autumn of 1945 the United States Navy completed the sad task of transporting these destitute remnants of a once-vigorous colonial society on the long voyage north to the hardships and uncertainties of a war-ravaged homeland. So ended the "southern destiny" of the Japanese colonial empire.

For the last decade two kinds of Japanese visitors have come to the island of Saipan. Each has visited the island for a different reason, and the difference perhaps symbolizes how greatly Micronesia has shifted in the Japanese perspective in the nearly forty years since the nation's defeat in the Pacific.

Each year since 1968 the Bereaved Families Association in Japan, in cooperation with the Ministry of Health and Welfare, has sent to Micronesia small parties of Japanese to comb the battle sites of the Pacific War for the remains of Japanese soldiers and civilians who died there. The battlefields of Saipan have naturally received the particularly devoted and careful attention of these "bone-recovery missions." Accompanied by Buddhist priests, the participants—usually

[58] The surrender is described by Charles S. Blackton, an eyewitness, in "The Surrender of the Fortress of Truk," in *Pacific Historical Review*, XV:4 (December 1946), pp. 400-408.

relatives of those whose remains they seek—search through the formidable tangantangan forests of northern Saipan, where Matsue Haruji's great sugarfields once stood, climb the slopes of Mt. Marpi, and probe the caves at Banzai and Suicide cliffs. As the bones are discovered, they are gently lifted from the soil and the rusting debris of war which surrounds them and placed with reverence in burlap bags. When the bags are full, their contents are placed on a pyre of branches nearby, the pyre doused with kerosene and then set afire, to the chanting of the priests, whose prayers confirm the faith of the Buddhist that the souls of these victims of wartime disaster are at last at rest.

It is but a short distance from Suicide cliff and the jungles of northern Saipan to the Saipan Inter-Continental and the Hyatt hotels, where a different kind of Japanese, the affluent young—tourists and honeymooners—come to sample the newly created comforts of the tropical Pacific. Just off the gleaming Japan Airlines 727s which fly in daily from Narita and Osaka, they fill the hotel lobbies, sun themselves at the poolsides, and choose from a wide variety of Japanese-made luxury items on display in the gift shops. These representatives of a new generation of Japanese, who see Micronesia as a vacationland for the work-weary rather than as a new homeland for the struggling immigrant, are but the most visible elements in a new and increasing Japanese presence in Micronesia. It is a presence partly based on the post-war Japanese leisure economy and in part on a resurgent and aggressive Japanese commercialism in the South Pacific. Throughout Micronesia Japanese goods, from Seiko watches to Toyota trucks, flood the islands; everywhere signs in their own language welcome Japanese tourists; and Micronesians, emerging after more than three decades of American trusteeship to try and find a national identity, worry about future Japanese economic dominance and exploitation. One can hardly doubt that Japan's southern advance, impelled now by the yen rather than by the farmer or the warship, is on the move once again.

PART II

Management of the Empire

CHAPTER 5

Police and Community Control Systems in the Empire

*Ching-chih Chen**

In Meiji Japan the government had imposed its reforms and carried these out through a newly created police force. The Meiji police system, formed in 1874 and patterned after the European police system, was under the Ministry of Home Affairs. All prefectural governors, except in Tokyo, supervised their police. Each local police system was comprised of a police station, and its chief with police substations in towns and large rural communities. Each police substation had from two to eight police officers responsible for law and order.

The Meiji police were expected to do more, however. They enforced the new government's programs related to public welfare, supervised druggists and public baths, controlled public rallies, managed food control and fire prevention, kept watch over people suspected of harboring "dangerous thoughts," and performed countless other tasks connected with the daily life of every Japanese.[1] For the average Japanese "political power was not personified by the remote and seldom-seen elite of the Diet, Cabinet, and higher civil service, but by the ubiquitous civil police."[2]

In the Japanese view, management of colonial peoples resembled management of society in early Meiji. Not surprisingly, then, the colonial police came to play a role in the colonies very similar to that played by the Japanese police at home. It was in Taiwan that the first colonial police apparatus was installed, and to Taiwan we must turn first to examine how the Japanese created a new police force and how that body carried out the tasks assigned to it.

* Research for this essay was made possible through support from the National Endowment for the Humanities (summer seminar, 1977, and summer stipend, 1981) and Southern Illinois University at Edwardsville.

[1] Robert M. Spaulding, Jr., "The Bureaucracy as a Political Force," in James William Morley, ed., *Dilemmas of Growth in Prewar Japan* (Princeton, 1971), pp. 36-37.

[2] *Ibid.*, p. 36.

THE COLONIAL POLICE IN TAIWAN

Occupying Taiwan in 1895 was easy for the Japanese; securing it for peaceful rule was another issue. Confronted with a superior military force, the Chinese turned to guerrilla tactics which taxed Japanese skills and imagination in suppressing them. At first the Japanese called upon the military to deal with these insurgents and entrusted the military police with handling general law and order matters.[3] Civil police officers from Japan were recruited and assigned to assist gendarmes. For the first three years this system remained intact. But the guerrilla resistant problem worsened. Governor-General Kodama Gentarō signaled a policy change in a speech delivered at a conference of high-ranking local officials in June 1898.[4]

> Bandits are political nuisances. . . . The important thing is to distinguish between them and deal with each group accordingly. If this is not done, errors will inevitably be committed. There are two institutions, the civil police and the military police, to cope with these bandits. Some people have argued that the military police are more qualified for such a task than the civil police. Having seen the actual conditions here, I am convinced that the civil police are better suited for civil administration than using military police.

Kodama formulated an entirely new policy for dealing with the Chinese guerrillas. He intended to use the civil police to handle all small affairs of violence and disorder and to rely only upon the military for incidents where guerrilla numerical superiority of force clearly exceeded that of the police. Kodama's policy, therefore, restricted the military forces to military activities, and he proceeded to cut back the number of troops and gendarmes to half. By setting up police branch offices with power over local community affairs,[5] Kodama then ordered the police to become an integral part of the local administrative system. The new guidelines were to deploy a large force to large towns and then to deploy many small police units to small towns and large villages. This spatial distribution of police permitted the Japanese to concentrate their forces in the island's few densely populated centers, yet to keep an eye over the bulk of smaller communities with a much smaller police force.

[3] For the wide-range functions of the military police, see *Taiwan sōtokufu keisatsu enkakushi* [A History of the Taiwan Government-General's Police, hereafter TSK], ed., Taiwan sōtokufu (Taipei, 1933-1941), I, 53-56; Taiwan kempeitai, ed., *Taiwan kempeitaishi* [A History of the Military Police in Taiwan] (Taipei, 1932), p. 19.

[4] The entirety of Kodama's speech is reproduced in Ide Kiwata, *Taiwan chiseki shi* [The Administrative Record in Taiwan] (Taipei, 1933), pp. 296-299, esp. p. 297.

[5] TSK, I, 474.

Looked at in retrospect, this policy ushered in a new era for the colonial police. In September 1895 there had been only seven police branch offices in Taipei and its environs, with the average contingent made up of 25 police officers. Other large towns came to have even larger size police units: Ilan had a force of 100 men, Chilung around 75, and Miaoli around 40. In 1898 the Japanese greatly increased the number of police substations. By 1901 the island had 930 police substations. Their number kept on increasing as the Japanese encroached into the aboriginal occupied areas of the island's interior. By the end of Japanese rule their number exceeded 1,000.[6]

By proliferating the countryside with many police substations the Japanese soon faced a shortage of well-trained policemen. Kodama's administration decided to enlist dependable local inhabitants as law-enforcement agents to assist the Japanese police. To be sure, the Japanese had already employed some Chinese as police officers (keiri), but their number really began to increase with the new Kodama police policy. The Japanese created a new position called assistant patrolmen (junsaho), who were subordinate to a Japanese policeman, and they proceeded to reduce the number of Japanese patrolmen (junsa) and to substitute more Chinese in their place.[7] As "the salary for a Japanese junsa was two to three times that of a Chinese junsaho," more Chinese could be recruited to assist the Japanese police.[8] In only two or three years a force of over 1,500 Chinese assistant patrolmen had been created to help to enforce law and order in the countryside. After 1903 their number stabilized around 1,300, but were increased to 5,000 around 1910.[9] About 3,000 of them later played an important role along the aboriginal zones in performing guard duty and were called keitei (police assistants).

Although a new police enforcement system had been established in the countryside, the Japanese were still faced with the problem of how to integrate that with local communities so as to control them effectively. The solution of this problem was achieved by Gotō Shimpei, Kodama's assistant, who believed that a centralized police was indispensable for controlling Taiwan.[10] Gotō saw the role of the police as first dealing with local bandits and guerrillas, then collecting

---

[6] TSK, I, 482; T'ai-wan-sheng wu-shih-i-nien-lai t'ung-chi t'i-yao [The Statistical Summary of the Province of Taiwan for the Past Fifty-one Years, hereafter TWT], comp., T'ai-wan-sheng hsing-cheng chang-kuan kung-shu t'ung-chi-shih (Taipei, 1946), Table 516 (pp. 1321-1323); Taiwan nichinichi shimpōsha, Taiwan ichiran [A Survey of Taiwan] (Taipei, 1912), p. 25.

[7] TSK, I, 491.

[8] "Keisatsu kaigichū no enjutsu" of October 1900 (TSK, VI, 57).

[9] TWT, Table 516, pp. 1321-1323.

[10] TSK, I, 98-102.

taxes and helping implement a range of reforms, and, finally, perhaps, most important of all, latching onto the Chinese system of self-policing—long used by the Chinese in the island—the *pao-chia* (*hokō* in Japanese) system.[11]

Historically, a number of households, usually ten, were grouped into a *chia*, and a number of *chia*, usually ten, were grouped into a *pao*, but their number varied according to the locality. Every *chia* and *pao* had their leaders, who were elected by household heads. Under Japanese rule, however, local police officers approved these elected leaders. Further, the Japanese applied the *pao-chia* regulations only to the Chinese, not to Koreans, foreigners, aborigines, or themselves. All *pao-chia* officers had to report periodically their number of residents and any arrivals and departures. Most important, however, the Japanese began using the *pao-chia* to enforce their public health programs, to combat epidemics and to prevent the spread of contagious diseases from one area to another. They also utilized the *pao-chia* to erradicate opium-smoking, widespread in Taiwan at that time, to repair roads and bridges, and to draft labor for large-scale works.

Each *pao* had an office in the local substation where a clerk, under strict police supervision, kept its accounts, rosters, and other documents. The county official and police actually supervised *pao-chia* activities. As early as 1895 in some areas of Taiwan young men between 17 and 40 had to accompany the police on patrol duty, and that practice continued even later. Just as in imperial Ch'ing times the *pao-chia* members covered their costs, so too did their officers under the Japanese work without pay, and households performed duties demanded of them without any compensation.

Another related community organization closely affiliated with the *pao-chia* which the Japanese organized and used was the local militia. The local police trained local militia leaders. Militia units played an important role during times of major natural calamities or if a notorious crime had occurred. The Kodama administration relied greatly upon local militia units, made of able-bodied male *pao-chia* members, in 1901 and 1902 to assist local police to combat guerrilla insurgents. By 1903 the Japanese had as many as over 130,000 militiamen assisting them to round up guerrilla bands. The Japanese disbanded most of these personnel in the next few years, but they were mobilized much later in the mid-1930s, when the colony was being put on a wartime footing.

By 1901 the police system throughout Taiwan had taken form and

[11] For a detailed study on the Japanese employment of the *pao-chia*, see my article, "The Japanese Adaptation of the *Pao-chia* System in Taiwan, 1895-1945," in *Journal of Asian Studies*, 34.2: 394-416 (February 1975).

would remain intact throughout the period of Japanese rule. At the very top, the police headquarters governed the system of two jurisdictional regions, one in the north and one in the south. Within each of those areas were ten districts, each with a police head charged with the duties of supervising all police officers. Under each of these district offices were many subdistrict offices, with an even larger number of police substations located in small towns and very large villages. The system certainly was not top-heavy but had achieved a spatial balance whereby all communities were brought under the watchful eyes of the police. Further, modern communications linked every substation to the echelon of police offices above, so that "by merely touching the electric bell with the tip of his little finger, the Chief of Police could at once collect all the police in the different districts."[12] All subdistrict police heads, some 90 in all, came from the rank of police inspectors and had considerable experience in their jobs.[13]

This structure, tied to the local *pao-chia* system in communities, worked hand in glove with colonial officials of all ranks. The police force served as a powerful, effective instrument for the administration to enforce its policies and to carry out sanctions when the Chinese refused to comply. As a part of the 1919 empire-wide colonial reform, the police headquarters was abolished in July 1919 and replaced by a new police bureau, making it on par with other bureaus within the government-general office. The following year, Den Kenjirō, the first civilian governor-general, cut back on police involvement in local administration and aimed at the "separation of the civil administration from the police."[14] He put an end to the practice of appointing police officers to head local administrative offices, especially those at the subdistrict level. Next, he deprived local government heads of any direct control over the police, making them totally responsible to the police administration. This meant separating the powers of even the mayors from jurisdiction over their police. In the end the police were detached from municipal government affairs. This separation did not occur at the county level, where police involvement in community affairs continued to be pervasive. For obvious reasons the Japanese refused to withdraw police management of general county affairs; they had too much at stake. The bulk of Taiwan's population resided in counties. Only at the county level could the rural popula-

---

[12] Yosaburō Takekoshi, *Japanese Rule in Formosa,* tr. from Japanese by George Braithwaite (London, 1907), p. 148.

[13] TSK, I, 521.

[14] *Den Kenjirō nikki* [The Diary of Den Kenjirō] in National Diet Library, Tokyo, March 6, 1920, April 23 and 26, 1921.

tion be carefully controlled. Certainly the fifth governor-general, Kawamura Takeji, recognized this. "If police affairs are to be separated from general county affairs, the county becomes meaningless. Adjudicating county affairs might not appear important, but without the police the county cannot be satisfactorily managed."[15] Not surprisingly, then, the reform of police administration never really affected the role of police in the county. Until 1945 the police system remained highly centralized and widely dispersed in the countryside, with awesome authority to manage and to intervene in the life of the Chinese.

Taiwan differed in one fundamental respect from Japan's other colonies: the existence of a large, separate ethnic minority—the aborigines. The problems posed by the aborigines for the Japanese were several. Until 1903 the Japanese had ignored them, allowing them to roam and live at will because they were entirely involved with pacifying the Chinese. Thereafter, however, the Japanese directed their forces to deal with the aborigines by a special, separate policy. Certain conditions dictated this new policy, which in turn required a different use of the police.

These new conditions arose from the past. The Chinese migrants to Taiwan had created their own organizations for dealing with hostile aboriginal tribes called the *ai-yung* (*aiyū* in Japanese) system.[16] Ad hoc as this system was, its general pattern was that of local elite employing a special force of able-bodied men to guard their estates and households. In the Taichung area, for example, wealthy landlords maintained small forces called *aiyū* for their self-protection from aboriginal attacks. During the summer of 1896 some of these private *aiyū* units even assisted the Japanese in suppressing Chinese resistance. The Japanese quickly realized the possibility of utilizing these small private armies as an auxiliary organ for their own police. Therefore, after 1902 the Japanese turned to these *aiyū* forces and integrated them with their police units.

This task, however, required some administration reorganization, and, to that end, the Japanese established an aboriginal affairs headquarters office (*banmu honsho*). The rationale for setting up this new bureaucratic appendage was the following. The Japanese had been trying to confine the aborigines to certain large tracts of land in the interior of the island. These efforts proved very expensive, sometimes exceeding two million yen a year, to construct some 500 miles of fences and guarded walls (*aiyūsen*). For supervising this huge area

[15] Kawamura Takeji, *Taiwan no ichinen* [A Year in Taiwan] (Tokyo, 1930), p. 48.
[16] Inō Yoshinori, *Taiwan bunka shi* [A Cultural History of Taiwan] (Tokyo, 1928), III, 720-722.

with its defense lines separating the aboriginal lands from those of the Chinese and Japanese, large numbers of special police (*banchi keisatsu*) were required. Rather than merge these special police forces responsible for all affairs related to the aborigines with the local police in Chinese communities, the Japanese decided to keep them separate and under the control of the special administrative wing, the aboriginal affairs headquarters.[17] These new police units, then, were assigned to guard and inspect the aboriginal districts. They, in turn, were assisted by the various private guard units, the *aiyū*, whose task was to help to protect villages adjacent to the aboriginal districts and the prime camphor forests which were often subject to aboriginal attacks.

Not eager to see private armies being developed in the interior, the Japanese first kept the numerical strength of these private *aiyū* to a limit of no more than 400 men.[18] Desperately in need of manpower assistance to guard the huge areas where the aborigines were to be confined, they finally in 1903 absorbed all private *aiyū* units as government-financed and directed units and also began to recruit more guards. At first the stretches of guarded boundaries were strictly watched only for defending the border districts and Chinese villages. The Japanese neither advanced nor extended these guarded boundaries. But later a more sophisticated boundary line was constructed and made into a defense line that truly encircled all aboriginal districts. The Japanese established this by cutting a path along the crest of the mountains which really became a guarded-road (*airō*), with guardhouses built at 120 yard intervals and connected by strong ramparts. The Japanese stationed two to four Chinese guards (*aiyū*) to each of these guardhouses, with a branch station at every fourth or fifth guardhouse where one or two Japanese patrolmen were stationed. Every four or five of these branch stations were placed under the control of a police inspector or his assistant. The Japanese even assigned doctors and additional Chinese manpower to these stations. All branch stations were connected with a system of alarms so that a disturbance at one point alerted all units up and down the line, and aid could be immediately summoned and concentrated at the endangered point. Finally, the Japanese established a circulating force of guards who moved up and down the line to provide back-up support.[19]

[17] TSK, I, 126-127.

[18] TSK, I, 379-383.

[19] Washizu Atsuya, *Taiwan keisatsu yonjūnen shiwa* [Forty-year Historical Anecdotes of the Taiwan Police] (Taipei, 1938), pp. 305-306; Government of Formosa, ed., *Report on the Control of the Aborigines in Formosa* (Taipei, 1911), pp. 14, 16-17; "Banchi

The Japanese, thus, had established a huge quard-line system comprised of strips up and down and across the interior to separate the Chinese from the forest regions where the aborigines lived. Neither aborigines nor anyone else could pass over this line without a special permit. From time to time large-scale disturbances erupted along this line. In 1915 the Japanese had to contain many of these. Thereafter, peace more or less prevailed, and the number of guards was reduced from some 5,000 in 1910 to less than 3,000 after 1915. At the same time, the Japanese began to move police officers, heretofore on guard duty beyond the guard border, into the aboriginal communities to man the police substations (*keisatsu chūzaisho*), which numbered around 500.[20]

THE POLICE SYSTEM IN JAPAN'S COLONIAL EMPIRE

Aside from the special police system designed to handle the aboriginal problem in Taiwan, the rest of the system became the model that the Japanese transferred and applied to their other colonies, with some minor exceptions. At first, as had been the case in Taiwan, a special gendarmerie or military police type force was used in the colonies at the outset of Japanese occupation and during the installation of a military and civil administration system. The length during which the military police were employed to handle matters of law and order, however, varied from colony to colony. In Karafuto (Southern Sakhalin) the gendarmerie, after only two years, were replaced by a civil police force in March 1907. The Japanese, however, did not end their use of gendarmerie in Korea, Kantō (Japan's leased territory and railway zones in southern Manchuria), and Nan'yō (the Japanese mandate in the western Pacific) until the summer of 1919. This was primarily because, while Karafuto had only about 2,000 indigenous people and was a settlement colony of Japanese,[21] natives accounted for over 95 percent of the total population of both Korea and Kantō and about 45 percent in Nan'yō.

In a sense, the gendarmerie's dominance over matters of general

---

keisatsu shokumu kitei" (issued on April 1, 1907), in *Taiwan Sōtokufu hō* [Bulletin of the Taiwan Government-General], ed., Taiwan sōtokufu, no. 2126; Takekoshi, pp. 214-215.

[20] TWT, Table 516; *Taiwan jijō* [Conditions of Taiwan], ed., Taiwan Sōtokufu (Taipei, 1916-1944).

[21] Japanese settlers accounted for about 92 percent of a total population of 26,268 in 1909 and 97 percent of 207,147 in 1926. Even the number of Koreans was twice that of Karafuto natives in 1926. Zenkoku Karafuto renmei, *Karafuto enkaku gyōseishi* [A History of the Development and Administration of Karafuto] (Tokyo, 1978), pp. 331-332.

law and order was unique. Let us briefly examine the development of the policing system in Korea. A modern-style police system began during the Russo-Japanese War (1904-1905), when Japanese police advisers were employed to enforce police reform. As Korea came increasingly under Japanese control, the Japanese military police were entrusted to be in charge of law and order. In June 1910, shortly before the annexation of Korea, Japan seized complete control of Korea's police affairs, merged the civil police, which was comprised of Koreans and Japanese, with the military police, and placed the combined forces under the direction of the newly created police headquarters in Seoul. The commander of the Japanese gendarmerie served concurrently as the chief of the merged policing force. In each province the captain of local gendarmerie became the head of the provincial police. Gendarmes and police were separately distributed in Korea. Police stations were set up in railway centers and "peaceful towns," while gendarme detachments policed strategic outlying districts.[22]

Scattered guerrilla resistance against the Japanese presence from 1907 to 1911 brought an increase in Japanese military police as well as in civil police. Along with the Japanese troops, the gendarmes brutally crushed the Korean resistance.[23] After 1911 relative peace and order was maintained, but the military police continued to control law and order. It was, according to Governor-General Terauchi Masatake, "easier to use the gendarmes than police to control a primitive people."[24] (As has been cited, Kodama held a completely different view—the civil police were more suitable in maintaining peace and order in Taiwan than the military police.)[25] With the assistance of Akashi Motojirō, the military police commander and chief of police, Terauchi and his successor transformed "the entire Korean peninsula into a

---

[22] *Chōsen sōtokufu shisei nempō* [Annual Report of the Administration of Korea], ed. Chōsen sōtokufu (Seoul, 1910-1945?), 1926, pp. 363-366.

[23] See *Chōsen no hogo oyobi heigō* [Protection and Annexation of Korea], ed., Chōsen sōtokufu (Seoul, 1917), pp. 243-256.

[24] Fukuda Tōsaku, *Kankoku heigō kinen shi* [A Memorial History of the Annexation of Korea] (Tokyo, 1911), p. 276. See also Gregory Henderson, *Korea, The Politics of Vortex* (Cambridge, Massachusetts, 1968), p. 79.

[25] See note 4. In Taiwan, Gotō Shimpei, Kodama's able civilian assistant, played "the key role in persuading the military in Taiwan to restrict itself to miliary affairs and permit the establishment of an administration of professional bureaucrats." This never occurred in Korea. "No civilian personality of Gotō's eminence ever appeared on the Japanese administrative scene in Korea, nor did any able civilian administrators acquired with their governors-general the unique relationship of Gotō with General Kodama in Taiwan, which provided the opening wedge of civilian hegemony." (Henderson, p. 402.)

military camp.''[26] The unwillingness on the part of the Japanese militarymen to switch from the gendarme-dominated policing system to a police system patterned after the Taiwan model accounted for the Japanese failure to prevent what was originally a localized demonstration from developing into a nation-wide, anti-Japanese movement in March 1919.

In August 1919, as a result of the internal and international pressures generated by the Independence Movement, the gendarmerie were abolished in Korea, and a civil police such as existed in Taiwan was installed as the sole policing force. Simultaneously, the Japanese also replaced the military police with the civil police in Kantō and Nan'yō. Thereafter, until Japan's surrender in August 1945, the police remained in charge of law and order in all of Japan's colonies except Kantō, which returned in the late 1920's to the system of military-and-civil police (keiken tōgōsei), a system copied from Korea and used in Kantō until 1919.[27]

Once established, the civil police system in each of Japan's other colonies shared several essential characteristics with that of Taiwan. The first characteristic was the centralized police hierarchy. In the smaller and less populated colonies, such as Kantō, Karafuto, and Nan'yō, the police hierarchy had three tiers—a police bureau at the top, a number of police stations at the county level, and an even larger number of substations at the township level. As a large colony, both in area and population, Korea, as was the case in Taiwan, had a four-tier police structure—a police department as the highest organ, 13 police bureaus at the provincial level, about 250 police stations at the county and municipality level, and more than 2,500 substations at the township level.[28] While the head of the police department con-

[26] Shakuo Shunjo, Chōsen heigō shi [A History of the Korean Annexation] (Tokyo, 1926), pp. 825-826. For Akashi's role, see Chong-sik Lee, The Politics of Korean Nationalism (Berkeley, 1965), p. 79.

[27] Kantōkyoku shisei sanjūnen shi [A History of Thirty-year's Administration of Kantō], ed., Kantōkyoku (Lushun, 1936), p. 769; Takahashi Yūhachi, Mantetsu chihō gyōsei shi [A History of the Local Administration of the Southern Manchurian Railway] (n.p., 1927), p. 465.

[28] For police system of Karafuto, see Karafuto enkaku gyōsei shi, pp. 1567-1657; Karafutochō shisei sanjūnen shi [A History of Thirty-year's Administration of Karafuto], ed., Karafutochō (Tokyo, 1936), pp. 763-904. For police system of Kantō, see Kantōkyoku shisei sanjūnen shi, pp. 763-906; Mantetsu chihō gyōseishi, pp. 462-481. For police system of Nan'yō, see Nan'yōchō shisei jūnenshi [A History of Ten-year's Administration of Nan'yō], ed., Nan'yōchō (Tokyo, 1932), pp. 173-212; Nan'yō guntō keisatsu gaiyō [A Survey of the Police in Nan'yō], ed., Nan'yōchō (Tokyo, 1937). For police system of Korea, see Chōsen keisatsu gaiyō [A Survey of the Police in Korea], ed., Chōsen sōtokufu keimukyoku (Seoul, 1922-?); Shisei sanjūnenshi [A History of Thirty-year's Admin-

tinued to supervise all police units in Korea, the control over local police was given to the provincial governors, thus enabling them to meet all local disturbances swiftly.

While highly centralized, the police force, which heretofore was held in concentration at various centers, was divided into very small parties and distributed throughout each of the colonies. The ultimate goal in the disposal of the police in Korea was "one substation for every township."[29] Within a few years after the 1919 police reform, the goal was reached; at least one two-to-eight-man police substation was set up in every township which covered an area of about four square ri (slightly less than ten square miles) and had an average of 800 households.[30] In Kantō and Nan'yō the same guideline of dispersing the police throughout each colony was followed. The majority of police substations in Nan'yō, for example, were of the small two-to-three-man detachment type.[31]

In order to form a network of police substations, it was necessary to maintain a numerically strong police force. Consequently, the size of colonial police in Korea, Kantō, and Nan'yō was significantly expanded immediately after the 1919 police reform. In Korea, for example, to augment the new police force, the colonial government hastily incorporated many Japanese gendarmes, converted all Korean gendarme assistants to patrolmen, and added a large number of new recruits, both Japanese and Koreans. This brought the total police force to 16,835 men, an increase of more than 2,000 in comparison with the pre-reform military-and-civil police.[32] More new recruits

---

istration], ed., Chōsen sōtokufu (Seoul, 1940), pp. 13-22, 141-146, 264-265, 292-295, 482-508.

[29] Chōsen sōtokufu shisei nempō, 1918-1920, p. 265; Chōsen tōchi hiwa [A Secret History of Japan's rule in Korea], ed., Chōsen gyōsei henshū sōkyoku (Tokyo, 1937), p. 108.

[30] Shisei sanjūnen shi, p. 421. Immediately after the annexation in 1910 there were about 4,300 townships (men in Japanese and myon in Korean). In 1914 administrative redistricting and consolidation reduced the number of men to about 2,400. The men was thus made an equivalent of mura in Japan proper. (Ibid.) Korea at the time had about 50,000 villages; a men would, therefore, consist of about twenty villages. For the number of Korean villages, see Bong-youn Choy, Korea, A History (Rutland, Vermont, 1971), 141.

[31] There were two major types of police substations, one headed by an assistant police inspector with several patrolmen and the other had only two patrolmen. In 1931, 17 of the 19 substations in Nan'yō were the small detachment type. (Nan'yōchō shisei jūnen shi, pp. 178, 181-182.)

[32] Chōsen sōtokufu shisei nempō, 1918-1920, pp. 264-265; Edward J. Baker, "The Role of Legal Reform in the Japanese Annexation and Rule of Korea," in eds. David R. McCann, John Middleton and Edward J. Shultz, Studies on Korea in Transition (Honolulu, 1979), p. 40.

joined the police force in the next few years. By 1926 there were 18,463 police officers, sufficient to man the 2,599 police substations; there was, therefore, at least one substation for each of the 2,504 townships in Korea.[33]

Again, as in Taiwan, the employment of indigenous peoples in all colonies—except Karafuto, where all police officers were Japanese—greatly strengthened the colonial police and expedited the establishment of a network of police substations in each colony. Security consideration, however, set a limit to the number of natives employed in the police. Between 1916 and 1922, Japanese patrolmen outnumbered Chinese assistants in Kantō by a ratio of three to one, and by four to one after 1922, when the number of Japanese patrolmen was raised until it reached 1,877 in 1925.[34] (A ratio of four Japanese patrolmen to one Chinese assistant patrolman was maintained in Taiwan in the 1910's.) In comparison, Nan'yō kept a ratio of a mere 1.2 Japanese patrolmen to one native assistant (junkei) in the 1920's and 1930's. The difference between Nan'yō and Kantō resulted from the fact that in Kantō the Japanese encountered the challenge of rising Chinese nationalism, the problem of bandits, and the potential threat of Russian interest in Manchuria, while their colleagues in Nan'yō had little problem with the "gentle and content" islanders who had never resisted the Japanese presence.[35]

Unlike Japan's other overseas territories that were obtained after Japanese military victories, Korea was annexed as a result of a treaty "agreement" between sovereigns. By treaty Japan was "obliged" to govern the Korean peninsula somewhat differently from its other colonies. Korean participation in the colonial administration of Korea, albeit limited, consequently was greater than, for example, Chinese involvement in the Taiwan colonial government.[36] All Korean police personnel were incorporated into the colonial police at the time of the annexation in 1910. Unlike other colonies, therefore, there were not only Koreans among the higher echelon of the police force but also a high percentage of Koreans in the pre-1919 policing force, military and civil. Indeed, between 1910 and 1919 Koreans constituted slightly more than 57 percent of the total policing force. After

[33] Chōsen sōtokufu shisei nempō, 1926, pp. 366-369.

[34] For the total strength of colonial police, see Nihon teikoku tōkei nenkan [Annual Statistical Report of the Japanese Empire] (Tokyo, 1882-1940).

[35] Nan'yō guntō keisatsu gaiyō, pp. 1-2, 46-47. See also, Yanaihara Tadao, Nan'yō guntō no kenkyū [A Study of the Nan'yō Islands] (Tokyo, 1935), pp. 416-417; Paul Clyde, Japan's Pacific Mandate (New York, 1936), pp. 70-71.

[36] For a comparison of administrative structure of Korea and Taiwan, see Edward I-te Chen, "Japanese Colonialism in Korea and Formosa," Harvard Journal of Asiatic Studies (1970), pp. 126-158.

the police reform, the percentage of Koreans in the police force dropped, but the Korean portion of the police force, proportionally as well as numerically, remained far greater than that of their Chinese counterparts in both Taiwan and Kantō; in 1930, for example, Korean police officers numbered 7,113 men or about 40 percent of a total force of 18,811.[37]

With the proliferation of both policemen and police substations in the colonies, particularly in Taiwan, Korea, and Kantō, the police directly managed and intervened in the life of the colonial subjects. A typical substation had three policemen, with one native assisting two Japanese.[38] It had jurisdiction over an average of twenty small villages or 800 households.[39] The policeman regularly foot-patrolled his assigned area. (Many of his counterparts in the cities, however, patrolled by bicycle.) He "knows every man in the village."[40] Communications between police substations, most of them equipped with telephones by mid-1930's, and between a substation and the police offices above it were well maintained.[41] Joint police actions, whenever necessary, could thus be taken swiftly to cope with major disturbances.

The Japanese further linked the already well-organized police to traditional self-policing or quasi-policing institutions of the colonies. As cited, the Japanese utilized the Chinese pao-chia as an auxiliary policing of the colonial police in Taiwan. Being a Chinese system, the pao-chia could be conveniently and profitably deployed only in a territory where the Chinese constituted an overwhelming majority of the population. Aside from Taiwan, therefore, Kantō was the only Japanese colony where the system was applied. In order to combat "bandits," the Japanese began in June 1909 to organize pao-chia units in Chinchou, the rural region of Kantō. All pao-chia units, as in the case of Taiwan, were placed under the direction of the local police

---

[37] Andrew J. Grajdanzev, Modern Korea (New York, 1944), p. 257.

[38] For example, see Kantōshū jijō [Conditions of Kantō], ed., Kantōchō rinji tochi chōsabu (n.p., 1923), I, 779-793.

[39] See note 30.

[40] These are the words of Inazō Nitobe, a former high-ranking official in Taiwan. Inazō Nitobe, "Japan as a Colonizer," in Journal of Race Development, II (April 1912), p. 355.

[41] As of the early 1930's Korea and Nan'yō were not as well supplied with police telephones as Taiwan was. In 1931 Taiwan had 3,739 police telephones, which outnumbered the number of police substations (1,510). Taiwan no keisatsu [Police of Taiwan], ed., Taiwan sōtokufu keisatsukyoku (Taipei, 1937), p. 131. In contrast, Korea had only 1892 police phones in 1937. Chōsen keisatsu gaiyō, 1938, appendices, p. 8. Nan'yō had only 12 phones in 1936. Nan'yō guntō keisatsu gaiyō, pp. 29-30.

substations.[42] As the Japanese invasion of China progressed in the 1930's, the *pao-chia* was extended into the occupied territories. In Manchuria, the Japanese organized *pao-chia* units to assist Japanese and Manchukuo troops and police forces in suppressing Chinese partisans.[43] Later on in Occupied China the *pao-chia* became an indispensable implement in the Japanese effort to maintain order in the countryside and to administer cities and towns, as well as villages.[44] It should be noted that in their use of the *pao-chia* for policing and administrative purposes, the Japanese were not as successful in Occupied China as in Taiwan.

In Korea, Nan'yō, and Karafuto the Japanese exploited the system of village elders, tribal chieftains, or neighborhood heads in assisting the police. In pre-Japanese Korea, there was in the village an informal structure designed to benefit the allied families. Certain family heads occupied a superior position as village elders and one of them as village leader. These persons were called upon "to arbitrate disputes, keep peace and order, stimulate public works, and act as liaison for higher political authority."[45] After the annexation, the Japanese continued the village system but imposed more rigid control on the village leaders than their predecessors, the Yi officials, did. The village leaders were part-time "officials," but worked without compensation.[46]

In Nan'yō, many tribal chieftains and some "qualified" natives were granted the title of village head (*sonchō*) and charged with the duty of performing tasks similar to those performed by Korean village leaders. Unlike Korean village leaders and Chinese *pao-chia* officials, however, the Nan'yō tribal chieftains were financially compensated for their work. But, since they were appointed as village heads they could be dismissed by their Japanese superior despite their hereditary

[42] *Kantōchō yōran* [A Survey of Kantō], ed., Kantō chōkan kambō bunshoka (Talien, 1925), p. 260; *Kantōshū jijō*, II, pp. 79-89; *Kantōkyoku shisei jūnenshi*, pp. 860-867.

[43] Ando Gentarō, *Mantetsu Nihon teikokushugi to Chūgoku* [Southern Manchurian Railway, Japanese Imperialism and China] (Tokyo, 1965), pp. 242-243, 251-256, 261; *Manshūkoku keisatsushi* [A History of the Manchukuo Police], ed., Manshūkoku chianbu keimukyoku (Matsuyama, 1976), pp. 252-259.

[44] Ramon H. Myers, *Agricultural Development in Hopei and Shantung, 1890-1949* (Cambridge, 1970), pp. 82-87, 92-107. It is interesting to note that the Nationalist Government also utilized the *pao-chia* system for local control, notably during its military campaigns against the Communists in South China in the late 1920's and the first half of 1930's. Hung-mao Tien, *Government and Politics in Kuomintang China, 1927-1937* (Stanford, 1972), pp. 94, 101-103, 110-112.

[45] George M. McCune, *Korea's Heritage, A Regional and Social Geography* (Rutland, Vermont, 1956), pp. 43, 45, 73.

[46] *Ibid.*

chieftainship.[47] In the settlement colony of Karafuto, the Japanese authorities used the neighborhood associations of the Japanese settlers as the auxiliary organization of the police. In short, be it in Korea or any other Japanese colony, the Japanese concentrated on reaching the people through the *pao-chia* officers, village leaders, tribal chieftains, or neighborhood heads. They tried to get control of these various local leaders and to control the people through them.

POLICE INVOLVEMENT IN GENERAL ADMINISTRATIVE AFFAIRS

The colonial police had a wide range of duties. First of all, as enforcers of law and defenders of colonial public order, the police officers censored publications, supervised public rallies, controlled firearms and explosives, rendered summary judgment in minor criminal cases, curbed illegal entry of laborers, kept domiciliary records, managed fire prevention, supervised pawn shops, bath-houses, hotels, restaurants, slaughter houses, licensed prostitution, administered sanitation matters, etc.[48] Furthermore, depending on the situation in a colony, the police took on additional duties. The enforcement of opium regulations, for example, was entrusted to the police of all Japanese colonies except Karafuto and Nan'yō, for neither of them had an opium problem. In Taiwan and Kantō, the police also supervised the *pao-chia* units. And the Taiwan police had the special task of controlling movements between the aboriginal areas and the rest of the island.

In additional to the numerous "normal" police functions, the colonial police regularly assisted local governments in their management of general administrative affairs such as information dissemination, tax collection, irrigation and water control, road building and maintaining, promotion of industries, and education. From the outset of Japanese rule, the completion of various reforms and programs required direct police involvement as well as police protection. Among the first major programs that the Japanese initiated in Taiwan were a population census and a land survey which were indispensable in the subsequent management of the colonial subjects and in the development of the island's resources. The population census was successfully completed in 1905, when none had yet been attempted even in Japan. Police assistance was crucial. First, the local police provided the all-important household registration records, which they had laboriously kept, as the basis of the census-taking. Then, they either directly participated in the process of census-taking or accompanied

[47] *Nan'yōchō shisei jūnenshi*, pp. 11-12, 56-64; Clyde, pp. 69-70; Yanaihara, *Nan'yō guntō no kenkyū*, pp. 421-427.

[48] *Chōsen keisatsu gaiyō*, 1929, pp. 67-125.

census-takers into hostile villages. Subsequent census-takings, which took place once every five years, continued to receive police assistance.[49] The police officers also played an important role in the gigantic land survey (1898-1903) which clarified land ownerships and uncovered heretofore untaxed lands. The Japanese succeeded where the Ch'ing Chinese officials failed in an earlier and more limited attempt. Widespread resistance was a major cause of the failure of the Ch'ing land survey. Strong police power, however, ensured the fairly smooth execution of the Japanese survey plan.[50]

In transforming Taiwan into a productive agricultural colony so that it supplied Japan with food and raw materials, the Japanese exerted considerable effort in promoting the cultivation of rice and production of sugar; both items became Taiwan's leading exports to Japan.[51] Special attention was given to the cultivation and processing of sugarcane. Sugar companies received preferential treatment from the government. Whenever their attempts at buying land from Chinese landowners encountered resistance, police officers always intervened to coerce the landowners to sell their lands. Local police were also known to have compelled villagers to switch from existing food crops to sugarcane.[52]

The use of higher-yielding sugarcane and rice seeds, application of chemical fertilizers, construction of irrigation projects, and popularization of some other new farming techniques have been identified as major factors contributing to increased rice and sugarcane production on the island of Taiwan. Police power, however, had to be employed to force new farming techniques onto rural communities resisting changes. One observer evaluated the role of the police in these terms: "In each district throughout the island the chief of police exercised the power to protect and change traditional behavior as well as introduce new customs and ideas; he also was dedicated to stimulate industry and increasing the wealth of his area and laying the ground for a new communication system."[53] Since the police penetrated every

[49] Ide, pp. 323-325; Mochiji Rokusaburō, Taiwan shokumin seisaku [Colonial Policy in Taiwan] (Tokyo, 1912), p. 82.

[50] A similar land survey in Korea had so greatly familiarized the Japanese police with the topography of Korea that they could easily determine where to station their police units. Asada Kyōji, Nihon teikokushugika no minzoku undō [Nationalist Movements under Japanese Imperialism] (Tokyo, 1973), p. 31.

[51] Samuel P. S. Ho, Economic Development of Taiwan (New Haven, 1978), p. 31.

[52] Ts'ai P'ei-huo, Nihon honkoumin ni atau [To the People of Japan] (Tokyo, ?), pp. 62-63. See also Yanaihara Tadao, Teikokushugika no Taiwan [Taiwan under Imperialism] (Tokyo, 1929), p. 36; Mochiji, p. 212.

[53] Cited in Ramon H. Myers and Adrienne Ching, "Agricultural Development in

village household through the *pao-chia*, it was relatively easy for them to insist on the adoption of new farming methods and to supervise their use in the early decades of this century.[54] Even after they had been removed from formal extension work after the Farmers' Association had been established on an island-wide basis by the early 1920's, police officers were occasionally called on to persuade reluctant farmers to adopt new agricultural techniques.[55] Mention has already been made of police assistance, through the *pao-chia* units, in constructing and maintaining roads, enforcing public health measures, collecting taxes, and combatting opium smoking. Police power was also used to spread the standardized measuring implements.[56]

The police involvement in aboriginal affairs in Taiwan was of paramount importance, in terms of both manpower committed to the aboriginal areas (slightly less than 50 percent of 11,166 patrolmen, including 3,252 *keitei*, formerly guards, in 1931) and of the crucial role that the police played in all administrative affairs in the aboriginal interior. Police officers were the only governmental representatives stationed in the remote aboriginal villages. In addition to controlling crime and maintaining order they taught the aborigines techniques of agricultural production, directed aboriginal laborers in building and maintaining roads, managed trading posts, administered and taught in educational stations for children (*kyōikujo*), and provided health care.

The promotion of industry was a major part of the Japanese concerted effort at guiding the aborigines "to switch from firearms to peaceful agricultural implements."[57] Under police direction, the aborigines tripled their rice yield and more than doubled their acreage in seven years, from 1924 to 1931. The number of domesticated animals such as water buffaloes and sheep also went up significantly.[58] At the trading posts, which numbered ninety-five in 1931, the police-managers, with the view of encouraging agricultural pursuits, paid more for agricultural products than for game brought in by the aborigines.

Taiwan under Japanese Colonial Rule," in *Journal of Asian Studies*, 23.4 (August 1964), p. 565.

[54] *Ibid.*

[55] Ho, p. 63.

[56] Chang Han-yu and Ramon H. Myers, "Japanese Colonial Development Policy, 1895-1906: A Case of Bureaucratic Enterpreneurship," in *Journal of Asian Studies*, 22.4 (August 1963), p. 441.

[57] By 1931 a total of 32,343 firearms had been confiscated from the aborigines. (*Taiwan no keisatsu*, p. 267.)

[58] *Ibid.*, pp. 271-272.

In their effort to introduce the Japanese value system and life style, particularly to the younger generation of the aborigines, the police managed and taught in some 180 special schools for children. According to a government study, in 1942, 207 patrolmen and 87 *keitei* assumed full-time education duties. The result of this effort was most impressive. The number of children attending the police-administered and -taught schools increased from 6,887 in 1931 to 10,355 in 1942, and the percentage of school-age children registered in all schools, including about 50 regular primary schools which had slightly more than 7,000 aboriginal pupils, rose from 60.23 percent to 86.35 percent.[59] The police also made considerable efforts to instill Japanese cultural values among adults. They organized and supervised various social groups; each of them was directed toward influential tribesmen, family heads, young men, adult females, or single girls. To popularize the Japanese language, policemen taught evening classes.[60] With considerable success at acculturalizing the aborigines, the Japanese claimed that the aborigines were more Japanized than were the Chinese.

In Korea the Japanese applied the general policy and many of the methods that they had developed in Taiwan.[61] To avoid repetition, mention will be made of only a few programs that were of special and of particular importance to Korea. As in Taiwan, a land survey (1910-1918) and a population census were undertaken in the initial stage of Japanese rule in Korea. At a time when Korean hostility toward the alien rule was intense, the power of military and civil police was used to ensure the successful completion of these two undertakings. Many Koreans were particularly bitter toward the land survey for depriving them of their traditional land rights. As a result of the survey the number of tenants rose to about seventy–five percent of the total farm population.[62] Confrontations between landlords, both Japanese and Koreans, and tenants increased as time went on. The police almost always intervened in favor of the landlords.[63]

As in Taiwan, the economic development of Korea was designed to complement and supplement that of Japan. The production of primary products was emphasized. Since the climate and soil of south-

[59] *Ibid.*, pp. 275-278; *Taiwan tōchi gaiyō* [A Survey of Japan's Rule in Taiwan], ed., Taiwan sōtokufu (Taipei, 1945), pp. 90-91.

[60] *Taiwan no keisatsu*, pp. 280-283.

[61] Palston Hayden, "Japan's New Policy in Korea and Formosa," in *Foreign Affairs*, 2.3 (March 1924), p. 479. See also Nitobe, p. 347; Yosaburo Takekoshi, "Japan's Colonial Policy," in *Oriental Review*, 3.2 (December 1912), p. 103.

[62] Lee, p. 94.

[63] Asada, pp. 149-324.

ern Korean were judged to be suitable for the cultivation of cotton, the Japanese decided early on to make Korea the supplier of cotton to Japan's textile industry. They gathered Korean farmers to local meetings held to induce Korean cooperation by offering "free new variety cotton seeds and chemical fertilizers . . . by subsidizing the transportation cost of farmers in remote and isolated areas . . . and by honoring productive farmers."[64] A former Japanese official, however, recalled the use of coercion by the police to make many farmers switch from food crops to cotton.[65]

Still much larger acreage was committed to rice cultivation in Korea. As was the case in Taiwan, the Korean peninsula was destined to become a major rice supplier for Japan. Here again the police were expected to assist in the introduction of high-yield rice seeds, chemical fertilizers, and other new farming methods, and to supervise their use.[66] Zealous police intervention was the main cause for many of the March Independence demonstrators' complaints, such as "The encouragement of industry is mostly against the will of the people, and methods used are coercive."[67] Police assistance in agricultural matters continued after 1919. The task of promoting the so-called "Village Rejuvenation Movement" initiated by Governor-General Ugaki, for instance, was assigned to local police, townships officials, and schoolteachers.[68]

In the other colonies of Japan, police involvement in local administrative matters was even more pervasive, primarily because lower-level administrative organizations were either underdeveloped (in Kantō) or non-existent (in Nan'yō).[69] As was the case in both Taiwan and Korea, the police of Kantō and Nan'yō were involved in the promotion of industry, improvement of animal husbandry, expansion and maintenance of roads, popularization of the Japanese language, care and cure of patients, etc.[70] One of the special tasks of the Kantō deserves a comment. The bulk of Manchukuo's farm workers came from two Chinese provinces, Shantung and Hopei. Every year

[64] *Chōsen tōchi sannenkan seiseki* [Results of Three-years' Administration of Korea], ed., Chōsen Sōtokufu (Seoul, 1914), appendices, pp. 51-53.

[65] Yamabe Kentarō, *Nihon tōchika no Chōsen* [Korea Under Japanese Rule] (Tokyo, 1971), pp. 22, 111-112.

[66] *Ibid.*, pp. 107-111; Watanabe Manabu, ed., *Chōsen kindai shi* [History of Modern Korea] (Tokyo, 1968), pp. 210-214.

[67] This was one of many complaints of Korean Independence demonstrators of 1919. (Cited in Lee, pp. 95-96.)

[68] Yamabe, pp. 156-166; Watanabe, pp. 240-243.

[69] *Kantōchō yōran*, p. 722; *Kantōshū jijō*, I, group 2, pp. 1-48.

[70] *Kantōkyoku shisei sanjūnenshi*, p. 772; *Mantetsu chihō gyōsei shi*, p. 467; *Nan'yō guntō keisatsu gaiyō*, p. 22.

in the 1930's the number of Chinese farm laborers who entered Manchuria ranged from half a million to over a million. Since most of them migrated to Manchukuo by way of Talien, a major port city of Kantō, the Manchukuo authorities requested Japanese assistance in regulating the flow of Chinese farm workers.[71] The control of the movement of the Chinese was entrusted to the colonial police of Kantō.

In the 1920's some efforts were made, particularly in Taiwan and Korea, to separate the colonial police from general administration. Although the attempt was not a complete success, the role of the police in assisting the management of general administrative matters did become more limited.[72] As soon as Japan brought the colonies into the ever-expanding war in the late 1930's, the colonial police, particularly those of Korea, Taiwan, and Kantō, once more played an active role in general administration. After the outbreak of the China War in July 1937, Japan needed not only material resources but also manpower from its colonies. First, an increasing number of colonial laborers were needed by the military to work in the Japanese arsenals, to build airfields, and to construct roads and bridges. Township officials as well as police officers enforced the labor service regulations.[73] According to a Japanese official report, from 1939 to 1944 a total of 422,262 Korean laborers were sent to Japan, and 22,044 went to Karafuto and Nan'yō.[74] Taiwan, on the other hand, had supplied (by the end of 1943) about 150,000 men for military labor service.[75] In addition to those sent abroad, there was an even greater number of people doing labor service at home. By the end of the war, claimed one author, a total of 2,616,900 Koreans had performed forced labor service at home.[76]

Aside from labor service, able-bodied natives were also expected to serve in the military. In February 1938 Japan initiated the "Army's Special Volunteer Systems" in Korea. The system was applied to Taiwan in 1942. In the same year a similar system for the Japanese navy was developed simultaneously in Korea and Taiwan. Admin-

[71] *Kantōkyoku shisei sanjūnenshi*, pp. 832-833.

[72] *Taiwan no Keisatsu*, p. 109.

[73] "Dai hachijūgo kai teikoku gikai setsumei shiryō" [Explanatory Materials for the 85th Imperial Diet, hereafter cited as Setsumei shiryō], in Kōndō Ken'ichi, ed., *Taiheiyō senka shūmatsuki Chōsen no chisei* [Administration of Korea at the End of the Pacific War] (Tokyo, 1961), p. 85.

[74] *Ibid.*, pp. 153-155.

[75] Kōndō Ken'ichi, ed., *Taiheiyō senka no Chōsen oyobi Taiwan* [Korea and Taiwan during the Pacific War] (Tokyo, 1961), pp. 39-40.

[76] Woo-keun Han, *The History of Korea* (Honolulu, 1971), p. 496.

istration of these programs was entrusted to the colonial police.[77] "Since more volunteers from a jurisdiction meant a better record to show to their superior, police officials exerted pressures to bring in as many recruits as possible."[78] During a five-year period from 1938 to 1943, 802,047 Koreans "volunteered" to serve in the Japanese army, while in just two years, 1942-1943, Taiwanese "volunteers" numbered 1,360,423. The number of volunteers taken into the army, however, was much smaller—17,664 Koreans and 3,505 Chinese.[79] When the war had become world-wide, full-scale conscription was put into effect, first in Korea (August 1943), and then in Taiwan (January 1945), and the volunteer system was abandoned.

From the end of 1937 on, all the economic life of the empire was frozen, and materials, funds, prices, as well as labor, were placed under government control. The economic police enforced the wartime economic regulations. Wartime rationing of food and other essential necessities, for example, required the assistance of the police, particularly since confrontations between rationing officials and the people increased as the hardships suffered by the latter intensified.[80]

To indoctrinate the colonial subjects after the China Incident, local police were charged with the new duty of organizing local residents into numerous "current [political and military] situation discussion groups (jikyoku zadankai)" and holding group meetings regularly. Japanese officials in Korea credited these groups with helping to cut down rumors, giving parties honoring Koreans who had volunteered for military service, aiding defense fund-raising drives, converting people harboring "dangerous thought," and persuading Korean Christians to visit Shinto shrines.[81] To intensify their anti-Communist campaign, the Japanese in 1938 formed the "Anti-Communist Association." There was an allied branch in every province, with local branches at police stations.

In an effort to secure total support for the war, the Japanese government initiated the "Patriotic Spiritual Mobilization Movement." This was begun in Japan in September 1937 and transplanted to the colonies within the following year. "Patriotic groups" were formed throughout each colony, each group consisting of several households. Under the supervision of the police, the network of patriotic

[77] *Shisei sanjūnenshi*, pp. 483, 500; *Taiwan tōchi gaiyō*, pp. 71-72; Kōndō, *Taiheiyō senka no Chōsen to Taiwan*, pp. 33-35.

[78] Lee, p. 266.

[79] Kōndō, *Taiheiyō senka no Chōsen oyobi Taiwan*, pp. 32-34.

[80] "Setsumei shiryō," pp. 84-86; Lee, 263; *Taiwan tōchi gaiyō*, pp. 109-115.

[81] *Shisei sanjūnenshi*, pp. 489-490; Takashi Hatada, *A History of Korea* (Santa Barbara, 1969), p. 125.

groups "served both as a controlling mechanism over the people and a rapid, sure system of communication."[82] Under the pressures of war the Japanese created new control mechanisms to add to the existing ones. While the various control groups inevitably overlapped, they were, nevertheless, all directed by the local police at the police substations. The local police coordinated the efforts of these groups to enforce various wartime programs, such as the "name change (*kaiseimei*)." In order to accelerate the assimilation process, the Japanese "permitted" prominent Chinese and Koreans in the colonies to change their monosyllabic surnames to multi-syllabic Japanese forms. The police enforced the program, and in some cases the food ration was cut off or children were barred from schools if families failed to comply within a given time.[83]

The decisive role that the police played in assisting the government in its management of various administrative matters is unmistakable. A large amount of the police working hours or manpower was devoted to that end. According to an official police study, in Taiwan (1931) patrolmen spent a total of 459,962 hours, or 57,494 work days, in managing general administrative affairs. This meant that 191 men (or 4 percent) out of a total number of about 4,800 patrolmen, not including those assigned to aboriginal areas for special duty since aboriginal affairs were classified officially as police matters, worked full-time in non-police matters.[84] By comparison, the Nan'yō police spent a far greater proportion of their time in managing general administrative affairs. In 1936, an equivalent of 13.2 percent of the manpower of the 102-man patrolman force was used for this purpose.[85] Because in Nan'yō the local administrative organization was less developed than that in Taiwan, Nan'yō police had to employ a greater proportion of their manpower in helping out with general local affairs than did their Taiwan counterparts. One can also surmise that in Taiwan the police manpower employed for assisting the management of local administrative affairs before 1919 and after 1937 must have been considerably larger than the 191 men (or 4 percent of total patrolman force) needed in 1931, when in the period between 1919 and 1937 the police were restrained from playing an active role in non-police matters.

In 1931, the six major categories of general administrative (or non-police) affairs that the Taiwan police were involved in were: land matters, production, government monopolies, education, transpor-

---

[82] Lee, p. 261; *Taiwan tōchi gaiyō*, pp. 78–80.
[83] Lee, p. 265.
[84] *Taiwan no keisatsu*, pp. 109–115.
[85] *Nan'yō guntō keisatsu gaiyō*, pp. 23–25.

tation and communication, and military related matters. The first two together consumed 58 percent of the total hours that patrolmen spent in taking care of non-police matters. More specifically, the non-police activities that demanded police manpower were; road building (29 percent of total time spent by patrolmen in general administrative affairs), camphor industry (17 percent), agriculture, particularly Farmer's Association (11.6 percent), irrigation and water control (5.7 percent), popularization of Japanese language (3.5 percent), land survey (3.2 percent), postal service (2.7 percent), and labor supply (2.1 percent).[86] As in Taiwan, the activity that claimed the greatest share of police time in Nan'yō in 1936 was road building (20.1 percent of total time spent in non-police matters). The other activities, however, were significantly different from those of Taiwan. These activities and the percentage of total time required for each of them were as follows: taxation (10.4 percent), harbor survey (5.1 percent), animal husbandry (4.9 percent), training and supervision of the youth corps (4.4 percent), forestry (3.9 percent), labor supply (3.8 percent), and agricultural matters (3.7 percent).[87]

RECRUITMENT, TRAINING, and DISCIPLINE OF THE COLONIAL POLICE

In order to prepare newly recruited policemen for service in the colonies, the Japanese early on established a patrolman training station (*junsa kyōshūjo*) in each colony, except in Nan'yō, which had the smallest police force (about 170 men in 1937) in the empire, since the natives had presented the government with no serious problem of control.[88] In their early years of existence, however, none of these training stations was adequately manned and equipped to train a sufficient number of patrolmen for colonial service. It took some years for most of these patrolman training stations to develop into full-fledged police officer-training schools (*keisatsukan renshūjo*), which trained senior police officers as well as patrolmen. In the meantime, the Japanese colonial authorities in each colony had to be content with many "old or incompetent" patrolmen transferred from Japan.[89]

In both Taiwan and Korea the expanded police officer-training

---

[86] *Taiwan no keisatsu*, pp. 109–117.

[87] *Nan'yō guntō keisatsu gaiyō*, pp. 23–25.

[88] *Ibid.*, pp. 9–10.

[89] Both Japanese and Chinese residents in Taiwan, according to an American observer, reported that "he [the policeman in Taiwan] was of a distinctly lower type than the police in Japan proper." (Hayden, p. 476.) A high-ranking police officer in Korea at the time of the 1919 police reform later recalled that many of the roughly fifteen hundred policemen transferred from Japan were "either old or incompetent." (*Chōsen tōchi hiwa*, p. 113.)

schools were supplemented by a number of provincial stations that were for training native recruits only. In the 1920's entrance examinations were regularly administered to Japanese aspirants at each police training school. The shortage of qualified Japanese candidates in the colonies compelled the colonial governments to send recruiters to Japan. Natives were recruited separately at the provincial level. From the mid-1920's to 1937 there was for Korea such a great number of Japanese and Korean applicants that for every patrolman position reserved for Japanese there were four to ten Japanese candidates, and for every Korean patrolman position ten to twenty Koreans.[90] This was also true for the other colonies of Japan. Encouraged by the tremendous response, the editor of a Taiwan police report exclaimed, "Recently, applicants thronged to every [recruiting] place. We, consequently, not only have no problem in getting the number of men needed but also are able to freely select the well-qualified ones."[91]

The keen competition for entrance to the police force resulted in upgrading the educational level of Japanese and native patrolmen. In 1928, only 27 out of a total of 9,381 Japanese patrolmen in Korea did not have a primary education, while the number for Korean patrolmen was 382 out of 6,787 (or 6 percent). Ten years later (in 1937) the number of Japanese patrolmen without a primary education dropped to 15 out of a total of 9,979, and that of Koreans to 257 out of 7,346 (or 3.5 percent).[92] The situation was just as positive in the other colonies.[93] Since virtually all Chinese patrolmen in Taiwan and Korean patrolmen had received their primary education in Japanese schools, they were, in the opinion of Japanese officials, "very skillful" in the Japanese language. In 1928 only one Korean patrolman was reported to have some problem in spoken Japanese.[94]

To gain admission, all candidates had to pass physical examinations, background checks, as well as academic tests. Japanese and natives were given separate and different academic tests. The academic tests for Japanese consisted of composition, dictation, and arithmetic, while those for Taiwanese had questions on Japanese language, composition, history, geography as well as arithmetic.[95] In

[90] *Chōsen keisatsu gaiyō*, 1929, appendices, pp. 21-22, and 1938, appendices, pp. 30-31.

[91] *Taiwan no keisatsu*, p. 116.

[92] *Chōsen keisatsu gaiyō*, 1929, appendices, pp. 26-27, and 1938, appendices, p. 30.

[93] In 1931 only 16 Japanese patrolmen and 142 Taiwanese did not have primary education. *Taiwan no keisatsu*, p. 61. In 1938 all of the 108 Japanese patrolmen in Nan'yō had at least a primary education. *Nan'yō guntō keisatsu gaiyō*, pp. 13-14.

[94] *Chōsen keisatsu gaiyō*, 1929, p. 28.

[95] *Taiwan junsa shiken mondai oyobi tōanshū* [Collection of Taiwan Patrolman Examination Questions and Answers] (Taipei, 1928).

Nan'yō the academic test was waived for a native candidate if he had a primary education.[96]

Once admitted, the newly recruited Japanese underwent rigorous training for four months. The training course for native recruits was shorter; it lasted for three months in Korea, two in Taiwan, and one in Kantō. The subjects required of the new recruits varied somewhat from colony to colony and from one ethnic group to another. In Korea, Japanese were taught a good number of subjects, such as ethics, law, police administration, criminology, sanitation, fire prevention, background information on Korea, Korean language, martial art, and military drill. New Japanese recruits in Taiwan were required to learn all of the above, except, of course, Korean language and information on Korea; Chinese language and background information on Taiwan were added. In addition, they had lessons on the *pao-chia* system and aboriginal police matters. The patrolman training for the Chinese residents of Taiwan and Koreans was almost as vigorous as that for the Japanese. In Kantō the Chinese recruits were not as well prepared educationally before joining the colonial police as were the Taiwanese Chinese and Koreans. They were, therefore, required to take courses in the Japanese language. In addition, they received a more military-like training than did native recruits in other colonies.[97] The Nan'yō native recruits were the least educated of all. Nor did they undergo a formal training course. As soon as they were recruited, they were assigned separately to police units to begin their police work. During the first three months with the police force, the native recruits received on-job training; they spent an average of two hours every day learning from their Japanese police chief such subjects as the Japanese language, law, police regulations, ethics, manners, and the use of a police rope.[98]

The great majority of the patrolmen were in their late twenties and early thirties; in Taiwan the average age of the patrolmen was thirty-two. Native patrolmen were younger than their Japanese counterparts.[99] Most of the patrolmen had many years of experience in the police force. In 1931, 57 percent of the patrolmen in Taiwan had been with the island's police for at least five years. For Korea, it was 55 percent in 1936. Even the newest of Japan's colonies, Nan'yō, had 31

[96] *Nan'yōchō shisei jūnenshi*, p. 185.

[97] *Kantōkyoku shisei sanjūnenshi*, p. 782; *Mantetsu chihō gyōseishi*, p. 466.

[98] *Nan'yō guntō keisatsu gaiyō*, p. 28.

[99] *Taiwan no keisatsu*, pp. 49-55; *Chōsen keisatsu gaiyō*, 1937, appendices, pp. 20-21. Thirty-nine of the fifty-one Nan'yō native assistants were under 30. *Nan'yō guntō keisatsu gaiyō*, pp. 12-13.

patrolmen (or 30 percent of a total of 108) with more than five years of service.[100]

In the early years of Japanese administration, the rate of turn-over in the police force exceeded 20 percent of the total force every year.[101] The turn-over rate, however, dropped steadily in the following years. In Korea, an average of 10 percent of the police personnel left the service every year (as shown earlier, there was little problem in filling the openings) in the late 1920's. This dropped to around 7 percent by the mid-1930's. In a typical year, say 1935, 1,361 men (or 7 percent of the total police manpower) became disassociated with the police force for various reasons. Of these, 59 percent failed to rejoin the police because of illness, 18.9 percent family reasons, 6.8 percent death, 6.7 percent retirement or transfer, 5.6 percent dismissal, 3 percent other reasons.[102]

Swift and stern disciplinary actions were taken against policemen for "failure to abide by their written vows or to observe official discipline," for "conduct damaging police honor and public confidence in the police," for neglect of duty, etc.[103] In the four years immediately following the 1919 police reorganization in Korea, the annual number of patrolmen who were disciplined exceeded 2,000. The peak year was 1921, when 2,892 patrolmen (about 15 percent of the total force) received disciplinary penalties. They included 1,217 men dismissed, 1,340 fined, and 355 censured. The number of Korean patrolmen disciplined accounted for 56 percent of the total.[104] The great number of patrolmen disciplined in the early 1920's reflected the poor quality of Korea's police, a result of the hasty upward adjustment of the numerical strength of the force made in late 1919 and early 1920. It also showed the eagerness of the Japanese in upgrading the quality of their police force by resorting to stern disciplinary actions and by bringing better qualified new recruits into the service. After 1925 the

[100] *Taiwan no keisatsu*, pp. 68-69; *Chōsen keisatsu gaiyō*, 1937, appendices, p. 25. The Nan'yō native assistants were not experienced in police work; in 1936 77 percent of them had been with the police force for less than two years. *Nan'yō guntō keisatsu gaiyō*, pp. 13-14.

[101] Ide, p. 314.

[102] *Chōsen keisatsu gaiyō*, various issues.

[103] *Ibid.*, 1929, pp. 30-31. For an example of the Japanese instructions to the police stressing moral and other desirable conducts, see Terauchi's "Instruction to Commanders of Gendarmerie Corps and Chiefs of Provincial Police Departments" (given on July 5, 1911), in *Results of Three Years' Administration of Chōsen since Annexation*, ed., Government-General of Chōsen (Seoul, 1914), appendices, pp. 50-54.

[104] *Chōsen keisatsu gaiyō*, 1929, p. 161.

number of patrolmen who were disciplined decreased greatly; by the 1930's it was about 400 yearly.[105]

Japan's colonial police, particularly those of Taiwan and Korea during the period between 1925 and 1937, were adequately educated, vigorously trained, experienced, closely supervised, and extremely well organized. The Japanese generally were satisfied with the performance of their colonial police. The police were not only instrumental in ensuring public order but also essential in general administration in the colonies. The Japanese considered the police apparatus "the root and trunk of the government-general system."[106] They called the police officers "the hands and feet of the governor-general in direct contact with the people."[107] Gotō and other Japanese colonial officials of the early twentieth century referred to Taiwan under Japanese rule as a "police state" because the police were so deeply involved in the administration of the island.[108]

[105] *Ibid.*, various issues.

[106] Baker, p. 14.

[107] Tsurumi Yūsuke, *Gotō Shimpei den* [Biography of Gotō Shimpei] (Tokyo, 1937-1938), II, 151.

[108] Gotō Shimpei, "Taiwan keisatsu no sanjūnen kaiko" [Recollection on Thirty Years' of the Taiwan Police], in *Taiwan keisatsu kyōkai zasshi* (November 1929); Mochiji, pp. 67-68.

CHAPTER 6

The Attempt To Integrate the Empire: Legal Perspectives

Edward I-te Chen

In general, Western colonial powers in the nineteenth century pursued two contrasting alternatives in regulating their legal relations with their overseas territories. France, for example, adopted "Systeme de Rattachment," whereby Algeria was regarded as an integral part of metropolitan France, giving the African colony equal legal status with all the departments (provinces) of the mother country. The system even allowed the application of the French constitution without modification and permitted Algeria to elect its representatives to the Senate and to the Chamber of Deputies at Paris.[1] Britain, on the other hand, viewed most of her overseas possessions in Asia as colonies, granting colonial governors broad powers to rule them. The home government did not tax the colonies, and the parliament made no effort to repeal, amend, or enact colonial laws. Where colonial peoples were permitted to participate in elections, they did so only in the election of local legislative councils.[2]

When Japan acquired her first colony, Taiwan, in 1895, she was confronted with the question of which of the two systems of government she should use to determine her relations with the new territory. The Bureau of Taiwan Affairs (Taiwan Jimukyoku) was hastily organized under the personal supervision of Premier Itō Hirobumi to study the legal implications of the alternatives. The British system of regarding the island as a colony would preclude the application of the provisions of the Meiji Constitution to the new territory. The colonial government of Taiwan would then be free from all constitutional limitations, able to make its own decisions, enact its own laws, and develop its own legal system. Such an arrangement had the obvious advantage of giving the colonial government considerable power and flexibility to manage its affairs as it saw fit. Under

[1] Takekoshi Yosaburō, *Japanese Rule in Formosa*, trans. by George Brathwaite (London: Longmans, Green, and Co., 1907), pp. 29-30. Also, Crocker, W. R., *On Governing Colonies* (London, 1947), p. 59.

[2] *Ibid.*, p. 27.

this system Taiwan would be a legally separate entity from metropolitan Japan, an idea clearly incompatible with the norm of "one nation under one emperor."

The other alternative, of making the island legally a part of metropolitan Japan, like French Algeria, would immediately bind all political and legal institutions of the colony with those of Japan. Thus, the central government and the Imperial Diet would, respectively, make decisions and enact laws, and the colonial government would be reduced to a mere prefectural administration of Japan. Such an arrangement, however, would necessitate immediate implementation of the constitution in Taiwan, extending to the indigenous population all the civil liberties guaranteed in it, a step that the Japanese government was not willing to take. The Bureau of Taiwan Affairs was unable to make any final choice between these two alternatives, though it strongly preferred the second of the two.

In the twenty years following the annexation of Taiwan, Japan acquired four additional territories: Korea, Karafuto (the southern half of Sakhalin Island), Kantōshū (comprising the leased territory on the Kwantung peninsula and the South Manchuria Railway and its narrow right-of-way), and the Nan'yō (the mandated islands of Micronesia). Meanwhile, through trial and error, Japan developed a complex legal compromise between the British and French systems regarding relationships between the metropole and overseas territories. The heart of the compromise was the decision by the government that metropolitan Japan consisted of the territories already under the control of Japan when the Meiji Constitution was promulgated (1899). All other territories annexed afterward were regarded as colonies or *shokuminchi*, where the laws enacted by the Imperial Diet and the executive orders of the central government were not, as a rule, enforced. In the colonies, instead, they were governed by the special ordinances of the colonial governments. As for the constitution itself, the Japanese government maintained that it was applicable only to sovereign colonies (Taiwan, Korea, and Karafuto) but not to non-sovereign colonies (Kantōshū and the Nan'yō). Even in the sovereign colonies, not all portions of the constitution were enforced. Precluded were those provisions related to the political rights of the people, especially the right to elect members of the House of Representatives.

In an effort to clarify some of the confusion and to demonstrate that the ultimate goal was the integration of all sovereign colonies with metropolitan Japan, two contrasting terms were introduced in the late 1930's in the official vocabulary of the Japanese colonist administration: *gaichi*, referring to all colonies, and *naichi*, meaning metropolitan Japan. *Gaichi* literally meant areas *outside* the jurisdiction of laws and regulations enforced in the *naichi*. It implied that the special ordinances issued by the colonial governors of all *gaichi* were temporary in nature, to be replaced gradually by the laws and regulations of the *naichi*. From the legal point of view, integration would be considered as completed when all the territories within the empire were brought under the uniform jurisdiction of the Meiji Constitution and Japanese law.

It must be emphasized that legal integration was not the same thing as the cultural integration of indigenous societies. The first was aimed at legal and institutional uniformity, to be achieved by issuing laws and decrees; the other, assimilation of the indigenous peoples, depended upon education and other non-legal programs. Logically, the assimilation of indigenous peoples should precede legal integration; but, in its eagerness to create the appearance of uniformity, the Japanese government often put the cart before the horse, leaving a considerable gap between the theoretical structure of a colony and the shadow-like acceptance of Japanese culture by the indigenous population.[3]

LEGAL STATUS OF THE COLONIES

The Japanese government possessed exclusive sovereignty over Taiwan, Korea, and Karafuto. In contrast, in the Kantōshu, a leased territory (*soshakuchi*), and the Nan'yō, a mandated territory (*inintōjichi*) of the League of Nations, the Japanese government held only limited sovereignty and exercised it according to those international agreements which governed their annexation. This difference of authority implied three other distinctions of equal legal importance.

First, Taiwan, Korea, and Karafuto were regarded as under the jurisdiction of the Meiji Constitution from the time of their annexation, a judgment which implied that the legislation of colonial laws by the colonial governments would be unconstitutional without the authorization of the Imperial Diet. It was the official view of the Japanese government, on the other hand, that the supreme law of the land was not applicable to Kantōshū and the Nan'yō, a view with which the Japanese government justified governing those two colonies by imperial ordinances without seeking the consent of the Im-

---

[3] In 1942 only 20 and 62 percent, respectively, of the indigenous populations of Korea and Taiwan were able to comprehend the Japanese language. See Kondō Ken'ichi, ed., *Taiheiyō senka no Chōsen oyobi Taiwan* [Korea and Taiwan During the Pacific War] (Tokyo: 1961), p. 20.

perial Diet.[4] Secondly, while the peoples of Taiwan, Korea, and Karafuto were regarded as Japanese nationals by virtue of the annexation of their homelands, the populations of the Kantōshū (mostly Chinese) and the Nan'yō (mostly Micronesian) remained aliens unless they fulfilled legal requirements for naturalization. Thirdly, in 1942, when Japan was at the height of her territorial expansion, the Ministry of Colonial Affairs was abolished, and the five colonies which had been under its jurisdiction were reassigned to two different ministries: Taiwan, Korea, and Karafuto to the Ministry of Home Affairs, and the Kantōshū and the Nan'yō to the newly established Ministry of Greater East Asia Affairs, together with Japan's other occupied areas in China and Southeast Asia. The strategic position of the latter two colonies as key links in Japan's outer defense line was undoubtedly an element which influenced this administrative reorganization. The fact that the former three colonies were sovereign territories, whereas the latter two were not, was an equally important reason for making this distinction. Inasmuch as these distinctions were based on the different legal status of the colonies, we must examine the international treaties which determined that status.

Under Article 2 of the terms of the Treaty of Shimonoseki, concluded at the end of the war with China in 1895, Japan acquired sovereignty over the Kantōshū, but was forced to retrocede it to China as a result of the so-called Triple Intervention, and a few years later Russia obtained from China a twenty-five year lease over the peninsula. In 1905, Japan was victorious over Russia, and the lease was transferred to Japan with the consent of the Chinese government under the terms of the Treaty of Portsmouth (Articles 5 and 6). Also transferred under the same treaty was the right to control the Russian-built South Manchuria Railway and the lands adjacent on both sides of the railroad. In 1915 in the celebrated Twenty-One Demands, Japan forced China to extend the lease of the Kantōshū to ninety-nine years. China was to retain the residual sovereignty until the lease terminated in 1998.

The German islands in the South Pacific were seized in 1914 and were governed as a zone of naval occupation during and several years after World War 1. Under the terms of the Treaty of Versailles (Article 119) the sovereignty of all German territories in the Pacific were transferred to the League of Nations. In turn, the League awarded to Japan the nearly fourteen hundred Micronesian islands scattered to the north of the equator as a Class C mandate. Japan was allowed to

[4] Minobe Tatsukichi, *Kempō teiyō* [A Summary of the Constitution] (Tokyo: Yūhikaku, 1932), pp. 137-138 and 140. Also, Yamazaki Tansho, *Gaichi tōjikikō no kenkyū* [A Study of Japanese Colonial Institutions] (Tokyo: Takayama Shoin, 1943), p. 6.

regard the islands as "an integral portion of the Empire" and to apply to them "the laws of the Empire of Japan" (Article 22 of the League Covenant). The authority of Japan over Micronesia, however, was restricted by conditions imposed by a resolution approved by the Security Council of the League of Nations in 1920, including non-fortification of the islands, promotion of material and moral well-being of the indigenous population, guarantee of the free exercise of all forms of worship and freedom of missionaries to preach, travel and reside in the islands; submission of an annual report to the Security Council; and agreement to submit to the International Court of Justice for solution of all disputes arising from the interpretation of regulations regarding the mandate of the Japanese government.[5] In 1933, when Japan withdrew from the world organization, the Japanese government simply decided to retain the mandate, arguing that it was awarded to her not because she was a member of the League, but because she was a principal member of the Allied Powers to which Germany surrendered all of her colonies.[6] The League made no move to terminate the Japanese mandate and appeared to have acquiesced to the Japanese contention.

Taiwan and Karafuto were both annexed as a result of military conquest, Karafuto having been conquered before the conclusion of the peace treaty and Taiwan several months afterward—a distinction which gave the people of Taiwan a choice to stay on or leave the island. Such a choice was guaranteed in the treaty, making the legal status of the resident Taiwanese more explicit than that of the residents of any other colony. Under provision of the Treaty of Shimonoseki (Article 2), China ceded permanently to Japan the sovereignty of Taiwan and the Bōko Rettō (Pescadores Islands), together with "all fortifications, arms factories, and other public properties thereon." In 1905, in conformity with the Treaty of Portsmouth (Article 9), Russia ceded "in perpetuity" to Japan "the complete sovereignty" of Karafuto, described as "the portion of the Sakhalin Islands south of the 50th parallel."

Unlike the two treaties in which the vanquished transferred Taiwan and Karafuto of the victorious, the Treaty of Annexation, which

---

[5] Nan'yōchō chōkan kambō [The Office of the Governor of the South Sea Islands], *Nan'yōchō shisei jūnenshi* [The Ten-Year History of the Administration of the Government of the South Sea Islands] (Tokyo, 1932), pp. 68-70.

[6] Takumu-shō [Japan, Ministry of Colonial Affairs], *Takumu yōran* [A Handbook of Colonial Affairs], Annual (Tokyo, 1935), p. 29. Also, Yanaihara Tadao, "Nan'yō Inintōji-ron" [A Study on the Mandate Rule of the South Sea Islands], in *Yanaihara Tadao zenshū* [The Complete Collection of the Writings of Yanaihara Tadao] (Tokyo: Iwanami Shoten, Vol. 5, 1963), pp. 138-139.

reduced Korea to a Japanese colony, was a treaty between two theoretically equal sovereigns, though it was almost entirely the result of military coercion. In 1910, after five years under a Japanese "protectorate," the Emperor of Korea offered and the Emperor of Japan accepted, the "complete and permanent cession of all rights and sovereignty over the whole of Korea" (Articles 1 and 2). Thus, despite the different circumstances involved in the annexations, Japan's claim to sovereignty over all three colonies was solidly based on legal documents that transferred their control to Japan.

Though not an international treaty, special mention needs to be made of the Imperial rescript issued on the occasion of the annexation of Korea. The rescript declared that the new colony would be governed by a governor-general *on the personal behalf* of the Meiji Emperor. It was issued to recognize, in part, the extraordinary nature of the annexation and, in part, the political and military importance of Korea to Japan arising from the historic ties and geographic proximity of the two countries. No similar rescript was ever issued after the annexation of other colonies. The governor-general of Korea was thus given enormous power and prestige to advance his views in the central government. This made it difficult for the civil authorities of the central government to bring the governor-general of Korea under civil supervision.

A special mention needs to be made in regard to the legal status of the people of Taiwan, which was significantly different from those accorded to the peoples of other colonies, especially Korea. In the Treaty of Shimonoseki (Article 5) the Japanese government agreed to permit those who were unwilling to remain under Japanese rule to dispose of their properties and emigrate to China within two years after ratifications of the treaty were exchanged. According to the treaty they had to leave by May 8, 1897, after which the Japanese government might regard those remaining on the island as Japanese nationals.[7] At the time when the treaty was concluded, the Japanese had not yet occupied Taiwan. The purpose of the provision to permit the unwilling Taiwanese to leave for China was to minimize the Taiwanese resistance to the Japanese occupation of their home island. In 1899 the Nationality Law was implemented in Taiwan, and in March 1906, by a special decree of the governor-general, all people in Taiwan were declared to be Japanese nationals retroactive to May 8,

[7] By May 8, 1897, only about 5,460 persons of an estimated total population of 2.8 million had moved to the Chinese mainland. See: Taiwan Shiryō Hozonkai (The Society to Preserve Historical Materials Related to Taiwan), ed., *Nihon tōjika no minzoku undō* [Nationalist Movements in Taiwan Under Japanese Rule], Vol. 1: *Buryoku teikō-hen* (Armed Resistance) (Tokyo, 1969), p. 668.

1897.[8] In contrast, neither the Treaty of Portsmouth nor the treaty of annexation of Korea made any mention of the legal status of the indigenous populations. This was unimportant in the case of Karafuto, since the tiny indigenous population (Ainu—less than 1,300 in 1906) was soon vastly outnumbered by Japanese settlers.[9] The large population of Korea, however, was left in a legally ambiguous state. Such a legal ambiguity was compounded by the fact that the Nationality Law, a Japanese law, was never implemented in Korea and that the governor-general of Korea regulated the legal status of Koreans by the Census Registration Act, an ordinance of his own. Nevertheless, while Korea was under Japanese rule, no problem arose from such ambiguity. After 1945, however, the legal status of Koreans became a matter of controversy. During the peace treaty negotiations in the early 1960's the South Korean government insisted that Koreans never had Japanese nationality (*kokuseki*), only the census registry (*koseki*).[10]

The Japanese government regarded the indigenous populations of Taiwan, Korea, and Karafuto as Japanese nationals by virtue of annexation and not because of the application of the Japanese Nationality Law. The fact that the Nationality Law was never enforced in Korea did not mean that the governor-general of Korea intended to deny Japanese nationality to Koreans, nor did it suggest that Koreans were treated less favorably than Taiwanese. Rather, it meant that the Nationality Law could not be applied to Korea without modification. In order to avoid the cumbersome procedural requirements needed to amend the Japanese Nationality Law, the governor-general enacted his own regulation, the Census Registration Act. Such fine distinctions did not affect the right of Koreans or Taiwanese to free emigration to Japan. Aside from this, however, Japanese nationality meant very little to both of them in terms of civil liberties and racial equality which nationality was supposed to guarantee.

APPLICATION OF THE CONSTITUTION

The decision to apply the constitution to Taiwan, Korea, and Karafuto was a lengthy process. It was the result not of a legal interpre-

[8] *Nihon tōjika no minzoku undō*, Vol. 1, p. 653.

[9] According to the census record the population of Karafuto at the end of 1906 was 12,361, of which 10,800 were Japanese settlers. See, Karafuto Government, ed., *Karafuto-chō shisei sanjūnenshi* [The Thirty-Year History of the Administration of Karafuto] (published originally in 1936, reprinted by Tokyo: Hara Shobō in 1973), Vol. 1, pp. 86-87.

[10] Hagihara Hikozō, *Nihon tōjika ni okeru Chōsen no hōsei* [The Legal System of Korea Under Japanese Rule] (Tokyo: Yūhō kyōkai, 1969), pp. 11-13.

tation of the constitution, but the consequence of several political compromises after many years of controversy between the colonial government of Taiwan and the Imperial Diet. At the heart of the controversy was the question of whether it was the Imperial Diet or the colonial government that should have the right to legislate colonial laws. Article 5 of the constitution clearly designated the Imperial Diet as the only institution to give its consent to the Emperor when he exercised his legislative power. The Imperial Diet, then, had the exclusive power to legislate colonial laws. But such a position was completely unacceptable to the colonial authorities in Taiwan, who believed the responsible officials in Taiwan, not in Tokyo, should have the power to enact laws for the colony.

They based their belief on both legal and practical grounds. Taiwanese colonial authorities maintained that none of the provisions of the constitution should be applicable to Taiwan unless explicitly decreed by an imperial ordinance because the constitution contained no provision for its extension over newly acquired territory. They reminded their critics in Tokyo of the fact that the constitution itself was implemented in Japan by means of an imperial ordinance. The absence of an imperial ordinance, extending the constitution over newly acquired territory, meant that Taiwan was outside the jurisdiction of the Imperial Diet. From the practical point of view, the officials in Taiwan believed that they needed to exercise a broad legislative power to govern effectively the nearly three million Taiwanese whose customs and traditions were vastly different from the Japanese, and whose loyalty to Japan was very uncertain. In their view, the Imperial Diet was not familiar enough with the conditions on Taiwan to legislate appropriate laws, nor was the Imperial Diet capable of speedy passage of emergency legislation in time of crisis.[11]

The strong opposition to the constitution from Taiwanese colonial officials put the Tokyo government in a quandary. To permit the colonial government to legislate its own laws without the consent of the Imperial Diet would be unconstitutional, unless the island was declared to be outside the jurisdiction of the Meiji Constitution. Yet, to say that the constitution was not applicable to Taiwan would be denying that the emperor of Japan was the ruler of the island; for the constitution explicitly stated that the emperor, as head of the Empire, "exercises the rights of sovereignty in accordance with the provisions

[11] Governor-General Nogi Maresuke's statement to Premier Matsukata Masayoshi: "The Opinion of the Governor-General on the Implementation of the Constitution in Taiwan," in *Gotō Shimpei monjō* (Microfilm) [Documents Related to Gotō Shimpei], Reel 23, 7-5. Nogi urged that the jurisdiction of the constitution be confined to the boundary of 1889 through an imperial ordinance or a constitutional amendment.

of the present constitution" (Article 4). Moreover, to hold that the constitution was inapplicable in Taiwan would directly contradict the goal of integration cherished by the Tokyo government. The Taiwan authorities might be permitted to develop their own legal system, but they should be directed to do so within the framework of the supreme law of Japan.

The upshot of this controversy was a compromise, reached in 1896, whereby the Imperial Diet passed the "Law concerning Laws and Regulations to be enforced in Taiwan" (hereafter abbreviated as LLR of Taiwan). The law granted legislative power to the governor-general for a duration of three years, under certain restrictions. The Imperial Diet thus delegated, for a limited period, its constitutional prerogative of legislating for Taiwan to the chief executive officer of the Taiwan administration. This compromise, known as (*inin rippō*) "delegated legislation," satisfied both the Imperial Diet, whose ultimate goal was uniform legislation for Japan and Taiwan, and the Taiwan administration, which favored flexibility in achieving the gradual integration of the Taiwanese legal system with that of Japan. The LLR of Taiwan, which became known as Law 63, was promulgated in 1896 and was repeatedly renewed until 1921, when the law was drastically altered and made perpetual.

When Karafuto and Korea were annexed, the Imperial Diet enacted, without constitutional dispute, laws corresponding to the LLR of Taiwan: Law 25 for Karafuto, promulgated in 1907, and Law 30 for Korea, promulgated in 1911. Each colony had its own reason for not precipitating a constitutional controversy. The population of Karafuto was ninety percent Japanese, and the colonial government did not feel it necessary to have its own legislative power. It preferred to have Japanese laws extended to Karafuto. Consequently, the LLR of Karafuto, consisting of only one article, merely stipulated that the laws of Japan could be extended by imperial ordinance, and that if changes were needed to adapt them to local conditions they could be modified by imperial ordinance. In the case of Korea, the LLR was readily accepted by the Imperial Diet largely because of the precedent established in Taiwan, which had convinced many diet members that colonial governors needed extensive legislative power.

Since Taiwan set the pattern for the other colonies, it is important to investigate in greater detail how the Japanese government determined the applicability of the constitution to Taiwan at the time of its annexation.

The question of whether the jurisdiction of the Meiji Constitution should be extended to the territories added to the empire after its promulgation in 1889, first arose in 1895, shortly after the conclusion of the Treaty of Shimonoseki. The problem arose when Japan was preparing to govern Taiwan, which China had ceded to Japan as part of the conditions for peace. Totally without experience in colonial administration and unable to find a clear-cut answer in the provisions of the constitution, the Japanese government consulted two foreign advisors in the Ministry of Justice. Michel Lubon, a French adviser, recommended that Taiwan be regarded as "a prefecture of Japan in the future, if not now," and that those sections in the Japanese constitution that related to the people's rights and liberties, and criminal law be implemented at once in the new territory. He suggested the creation of several local courts and a high court in Taiwan under direct control of the Supreme Court of Japan. In short, Lubon asked the Japanese government to follow the example of French relations with Algeria and predicted that the people of Taiwan could be made to "resemble" the Japanese in every aspect.[12]

A different view was submitted by Montague Kirkwood, a British adviser. He made clear that it would be to the advantage of both Japan and the people of Taiwan to regard the island as a *colony*, legally, politically, culturally, and financially separate from Japan, in the same way that the British colonies of India and Hong Kong were separate from Great Britain. He recommended that the Japanese government create a legislative council in Taiwan, appointed by the governor-general, with himself as ex-officio president, to enact necessary colonial laws. He also urged the appointment of several Taiwanese as its members. He also suggested the appointment of as many Taiwanese as possible as local administrators and judges.[13] Kirkwood argued that the jurisdiction of the constitution should be limited to the lands already under Japanese control at the time of its promulgation: the four main islands, Okinawa, and the Ogasawara Islands. He supported his contention by citing the examples of the Dutch Constitution of 1815 and the Spanish Constitution of 1876, both of which restricted the jurisdiction of the supreme law of the land to their respective territories in Europe, but reserved the right of the central government to enforce any portion of it through special legislation. He advised the Japanee government that the blanket application of the constitution in the colonies would mean extending to their indigenous majorities the right to elect representatives to the

[12] Contained in Itō Hirobumi, ed., *Hisho ruisan* [Classified Collection of the Private Documents of Itō Hirobumi Relating to Meiji Development], Volume on *Taiwan shiryō* [Sources Related to Taiwan] (Tokyo, 1936), pp. 399-409.

[13] For Montague Kirkwood's recommendation, dated April 30, 1895, under the title, "Shokuminchi seido" (Colonial System), see: Hisho ruisan, Volume on *Taiwan shiryō*, pp. 108-148.

Imperial Diet, a step Kirkwood believed Japan was not ready to take. It would also mean the imposition of Japanese taxes on the Taiwanese population. Kirkwood feared that such an attempt might adversely affect the Japanese administration in Taiwan, as when Parliament, in the reign of King George III, tried to impose British taxes on his North American colonies. He suggested that if Japan wished to extend the constitution to Taiwan, she should follow the examples of the Dutch and Spanish constitutions, but conceded that it would require amendments to the present constitution.[14]

On June 14, 1895, the hastily organized Taiwan Affairs Bureau met and discussed the conflicting proposals of the two foreign advisers.[15] In the ensuing debate the French proposal found an articulate supporter in the person of Hara Takashi, who represented the Ministry of Foreign Affairs in the Bureau. In a written opinion, "Two Views on Taiwan," Hara rejected the British proposal and urged his government to regard Taiwan as an integral part of Japan in the same fashion as Alsace and Lorraine were parts of Germany and Algeria a part of France.[16] He expressed his belief that, as far as possible, Taiwan should adopt a legal system similar to that of Japan, with the understanding that all dissimilarities be eliminated. He proposed to enforce in Taiwan all Japanese laws deemed feasible under Taiwanese conditions and to regulate by imperial ordinances only such matters which could not be regulated by existing Japanese laws. Hara's optimism for the integration of Taiwan stemmed from what he regarded as the relative proximity of the island of Japan and the ethnic and cultural similarity between Taiwanese and Japanese.[17]

[14] Contained in *Hisho ruisan*, Volume on *Taiwan shiryō*, pp. 78-107. In particular, see, pp. 83-84, 85-86, 88, 105-106.

[15] The Taiwan Affairs Bureau was empowered to oversee all military and civil affairs related to Taiwan. The governor-general was allowed to communicate with the central government only through the medium of the Bureau, and various ministries and agencies within the central government were required to present any communication to Taiwan to the Bureau for prior approval. (See Articles 2, 3, and 4 of the Organic Regulation of the Taiwan Affairs Bureau, June 14, 1895.) The nine members who comprised the Bureau were selected from various ministries and agencies in the central government. They included: Itō Hirobumi (Premier), Kawakami Sōroku (Vice-Chief of Staff), Itō Miyoji (Chief Cabinet Clerk), Hara Takashi (Foreign Affairs), Kodama Gentarō (Army), Yamamoto Gon'nohyo'e (Navy), Suematsu Kenchō (Justice), Tajiri Inajirō (Finance) and Den Kenjirō (Communications). The Taiwan Affairs Bureau was intended to be a "little cabinet" to oversee the Taiwan administration.

[16] Hara's proposal, "Taiwan mondai ni an" [Two Views on Taiwan] is included in its entirety in *Hisho ruisan*, Volume on *Taiwan shiryō*, pp. 32-34.

[17] Actually, Hara gave three reasons to support his position for an integrated Taiwan: (1) that the island was not as distant from Japan as many European colonies were from their mother countries, and the distance would be "shortened" even more with

To judge from the policy pursued in Taiwan during the first three years of Japanese rule, it would appear that Hara's view governed the conduct of the Taiwan Affairs Bureau. For most of the members of the bureau, including Premier Itō, the British view of "colony" carried an unfavorable connotation of white people exploiting the black and yellow peoples in the remote lands of Africa and Asia. They felt that the aims of Japanese rule in Taiwan should be, first and foremost, to incorporate the island into the Japanese empire and then to assimilate its inhabitants into the Japanese nation. They were convinced that the extension of the constitution and the maximum application of Japanese laws were two preliminary steps necessary to achieve the goal of cultural and political integration. Uniformity, not flexibility, appeared to be the main concern of the Japanese leaders in determining the goal of the Japanese administration in the new colony.

In Taiwan, the unexpectedly fierce resistance of the indigenous population to the Japanese rule showed that consideration of extension of the constitution was unrealistic when internal peace could not be maintained. In addition to the problem of pacification, there were many problems of a more practical and pressing nature which could be handled much more effectively if the Taiwan administration were given a greater amount of flexibility, including the power to legislate the colonial law. Thus the controversy in the Taiwan Affairs Bureau quickly abated, and the Bureau itself was disbanded in April 1896. A different mood prevailed, however, in the Imperial Diet.

There the controversy began on March 17, 1896, when the Ninth Session of the House of Representatives received a bill from the governor-general of Taiwan, with the support of the cabinet of Premier Itō. It sought authorization for the governor-general to issue executive ordinances "having the same effect as the law of Japan." The state of "rebellion" in Taiwan, the remoteness from Tokyo, and the difference in the customs and traditions of the Taiwanese people were cited as reasons for requesting such an extraordinary measure.[18]

---

the completion of submarine cables (then under construction) and the development of the shipping industry; (2) that, unlike European colonies, where the whites ruled the natives, the Japanese and the Taiwanese belonged to the same race and used the same script; and (3) that for the Japanese government not to rule the island as an integral part of Japan would create an administrative contradiction between her domestic and foreign relations, and the United States to extend the existing treaties to all ports in Taiwan. See *Hisho ruisan*, Volume on *Taiwan shiryō*, pp. 32-33.

[18] These reasons were given orally on the floor of the House of Representatives by the civil administrator of Taiwan. See: Gaimushō (Japan, Ministry of Foreign Affairs), ed., *Taiwan ni shikō subeki hōrei ni kansuru hōritsu no gijiroku* [The Diet Record on the

The controversy revolved around the constitutionality of giving such sweeping legislative power to a single colonial executive, but it was resolved when both sides accepted the formula known as "delegated legislation," as explained earlier. The bill became law on March 30, 1896, with the stipulation that it would expire on March 30, 1899.

When Korea was annexed in August 1910, the Imperial Diet was not in session. Invoking the constitutional prerogative of the emperor, the Japanese government promulgated the LLR of Korea in the form of an emergency imperial ordinance, its contents virtually identical to the LLR of Taiwan. In the following year the imperial ordinance was laid before the twenty-seventh session of the Imperial Diet, which gave its ready consent to an imperial fait accompli. As a result, not only was the colonial government of Korea spared a constitutional controversy, such as that which embroiled the colonial government of Taiwan, but it gained a significant advantage not enjoyed by its counterpart in Taiwan: the LLR of Korea was not limited to any specific duration. The prestige of Premier Katsura Tarō, who had benefitted from the sweeping legislative powers granted to him by the LLR of Taiwan during his brief tenure as governor-general of that colony and that of Governor-General Terauchi Masatake, who held the concurrent position of the Minister of War in Tokyo, were no doubt additional reasons for the absence of opposition in the Diet to the LLR for Korea. More importantly, many members of the Diet were convinced of the need, amply demonstrated in Taiwan, for broad legislative powers to be exercised by the governor-general of new colonies.

The difference in the time limitations between the Taiwan LLR and that of Korea had important consequences for both colonies. The Taiwan administration was compelled to seek renewal each time the law expired, opening the way for amendment of the law itself and the possibility of a new constitutional controversy. In fact, the law was renewed in 1899, 1902, 1905, and 1907. In the 1907 renewal, the Taiwan administration succeeded in extending its duration for five years, after which it was renewed twice again for a total of ten years. Finally, in 1921 the Imperial Diet did away with the time limit when the Taiwan administration agreed to limit the use of its legislative power to those circumstances under which "no appropriate Japanese law was available, or the enforcement of a Japanese law is difficult in the light of the prevailing conditions in Taiwan."

Meanwhile, a new constitutional controversy began to develop as

Law Concerning Laws and Regulations to be Enforced in Taiwan] (Tokyo, 1966), p. 3.

the legislative power of the governor-general became the paramount feature of the colonial government of Taiwan. The dispute centered on the contention that, if the legislative power of the governor-general of Taiwan had been given to him by the Imperial Diet, then it must be assumed that the constitution had been extended to the colony. If so, one could argue that the portion of the constitution dealing with the political rights of the people should also be extended to the people of Taiwan, so that, through elections, they could participate in the process of legislation. Such a view was supported by a number of liberal members of the Imperial Diet.[19] Fueling the controversy was the formation, in 1921, of a Taiwanese political organization called the League for the Establishment of a Taiwan Congress (*Taiwan Gikai Kisei Dōmei*). The League lobbied the Imperial Diet fifteen years for the passage of a bill authorizing the establishment of a popularly elected congress in Taiwan to serve as a legislative balance to the power of the governor-general.[20]

Although the movement was not successful, it did bring into the open the constitutional dilemma that faced both the Japanese government and the Taiwan administration: how to extend the constitution to Taiwan while preserving a separate legal system. Against the charge of inconsistency from its critics in the Imperial Diet and from Taiwanese intellectuals, the colonial government of Taiwan defended itself, arguing that it would never agree to the creation of a legislative institution in Taiwan separate from the national legislative body in Tokyo, but that it would agree, at some future point, to enforce the Election Law for the House of Representatives, so that the Taiwanese people could be represented in the lower house of the Imperial Diet. It insisted, however, that progress in the assimilation of the Taiwanese to Japanese culture would determine how soon such an election could be held in Taiwan.

From a comparative viewpoint, the significance of this controversy is that it arose only in regard to Taiwan, and not in regard to Korea. That the Koreans were far more interested in independence than in home rule was no doubt an important reason. Equally important was the permanent nature of the legislative power of the governor-general

---

[19] Perhaps the earliest Japanese to support the concept of allowing the Taiwanese to participate in the process of legislation was Izawa Shūji, who, in 1899, aired such a view on the floor of the House of Peers, of which he was an appointed member. For details about his view see: *Taiwan ni shikō subeki hōrei ni kansuru hōritsu no gijiroku*, p. 60. Later supporters included Tagawa Daikichirō, Kiyose Ichirō, and Kanda Masao, all members of the House of Representatives in the 1920's.

[20] Edward I-te Chen, "Formosan Political Movements Under Japanese Colonial Rule, 1914-1937," in *Journal of Asian Studies*, Vol. 31, No. 3 (May 1972), pp. 483-489.

of Korea which made it unnecessary for him to appeal to the Imperial Diet for renewal of his legislative power, thus preventing him from being entangled in a similar controversy. Sharpening the contrast was the fact that the LLR of Karafuto was abolished in 1943, and the colony itself was declared a part of metropolitan Japan. While all those changes were taking place, the LLR of Korea alone remained intact (except for minor technical changes) until the end of Japanese rule.

JAPANESE LAWS AND COLONIAL LAWS

Depending on their place of origin, all laws and regulations enforced in the five colonies could be classified into two categories: those promulgated in Japan and those enacted in the colonies.[21] The first category included laws legislated by the Imperial Diet, imperial ordinances, decrees of the prime minister, and decrees of cabinet ministers. The second category consisted of ordinances of colonial governors and executive orders of district and subdistrict governors. Each group, moreover, was divided into several sub-groups. As if this was not confusing enough, the Japanese government adopted no uniform rule regarding how those bewildering number of laws and regulations were to be applied to each of the five colonies. For instance, a matter regulated in a colony by a Japanese law could be regulated in another colony by an ordinance of the colonial governor; likewise, the bulk of the laws and regulations enforced in one colony could be the ordinances of the colonial governor, yet imperial ordinances could constitute the majority of laws and regulations in another colony.

One thing is clear, however: the greater the number of laws and regulations originating in Japan and enforced in a particular colony, the more that colony could be said to have attained a high degree of legal integration. Conversely, the greater number of locally enacted laws would indicate a lesser degree of legal integration.

DIET-ENACTED LAWS

As a rule, a Diet-enacted law (*hōritsu*, sometimes simply called Japanese law) was not enforced in the colonies. There were, however, three exceptions to this rule. A Diet-enacted law was considered automatically extended to all the colonies if its universal enforcement

---

[21] Laws usually referred to Diet-enacted laws, whereas regulations were decrees or ordinances of executive officers. The Japanese term *hōrei*, meaning laws and regulations, is a combined word of *hōritsu* and *meirei* (executive decree).

throughout the Japanese empire was clearly the intended aim of such a law; e.g., the National Security Law (1941), the Aviation Law, Shipping Protection Law, and so forth. Enactment of a law with the explicit aim of enforcing it in a certain colony or colonies was another exception. The LLRs of Taiwan, Karafuto, and Korea were good examples of this. Also, the laws regulating the Bank of Taiwan, the Bank of Korea, and other government-controlled commercial institutions (such as the Taiwan Colonization Company) fell in this category of laws. It is important to note, however, that the Imperial Diet never enacted a law for exclusive enforcement in the Kantōshū or the Nan'yō, on the ground that they were not sovereign territories.

Thirdly, an existing Japanese law could be extended to Taiwan, Korea, and/or Karafuto by imperial ordinance. Normally this meant that a colonial government which desired the extension of a certain Japanese law would secure, through the prime minister or an appropriate minister an imperial ordinance ordering the extension of such law. Again, no Japanese law was ever extended in this fashion to the Kantōshū or the Nan'yō.

In extending the Diet-enacted laws to the three colonies mentioned above, modification was frequently necessary to fit such laws to the different legal system of each colony. For example, the title of "Prosecutor-General" referred to in a Japanese law would have to be amended to read "the Chief Prosecutor of Korea" if the law were to be extended to Korea; likewise, the phrase "the approval of the Home Minister" in a Japanese law would have to be replaced by the new phrase "the approval of the governor of Karafuto" before its enforcement in that colony. The difficulty (or ease) with which such modifications could be attained affected the volume of the Diet-enacted laws to be extended and, hence, the legal integration of the colonies themselves. For instance, in 1945 when Japanese rule came to an end, Karafuto had the greatest number of this type of laws. Taiwan was second and Korea had the least number of laws that were enacted by the Imperial Diet.[22]

The reason for such discrepancy can be found in the respective LLRs of Karafuto, Taiwan, and Korea. The LLR of Karafuto con-

---

[22] In 1945, 275 Japanese laws were enforced in Taiwan but only 120 were enacted by the governor-general. In the same year Korea had about 130 Japanese laws, while there were 270 ordinances issued by the governor-general. For Taiwan see: Okurashō (Japan, Ministry of Finance), *Nihonjin no kaigai katsudō ni kansuru rekishiteki chōsa* [Historical Investigation Regarding the Overseas Activities of Japanese People] (Tokyo, 1947), Vol. 17; *Taiwan tōji gaiyō* (A Summary of Japanese Rule in Taiwan), p. 3. For Korea see Hagihara, *Nihon tōjika ni okeru chōsen no hōsei*, pp. 4 and 5.

tained—but those of Taiwan and Korea did not—a provision allowing the modification of the Diet-enacted laws to be effected by imperial ordinances, a mere formality because the extension of the laws
had already been decided. In 1943, even such formality was abolished
when the LLR of Karafuto was replaced by a new law (Law 85),
which made automatic the extension of all *future* laws to be enacted
by the Imperial Diet. This change was accompanied by an official
announcement, with much fanfare, that Karafuto would henceforth
be removed from the category of *gaichi* and be regarded as part of
the *naichi*. Needless to say, the fact that Karafuto was essentially a
settlement colony played a crucial role in bringing about such a change.

Because of the lack of equivalent provision of the LLRs of Taiwan
and Korea, the colonial governments were forced to seek, every time
a certain Japanese law was to be extended, a new law from the Imperial Diet setting forth, item by item, modifications to be effected
in such a Japanese law. The enactment of a special law by the Diet
regarding modifications of the Customs Law at the time it was extended to Korea in 1920, is a case in point. Such a cumbersome procedure tended to discourage the governors-general of the two colonies from seeking extension of Japanese laws and to encourage them
to rely on their own legislative power.

In 1921 a significant change was introduced in the LLR of Taiwan,
as a part of a massive reform program instigated by the island's first
civilian governor-general, Den Kenjirō. The amended LLR of Taiwan (Law 3 of 1921) not only allowed the modification to be made
by imperial ordinance, it went a step further by requiring the governor-
general to exercise his legislative power only when no appropriate
Japanese law was available or when the enforcement of a Japanese
law was difficult in the light of existing local conditions. In other
words, after 1921 the application of the Diet-enacted laws to Taiwan
became a principle rather than an exception.

While Karafuto and Taiwan were inching steadily toward the goal
of legal integration, the LLR of Korea (and its entire legal system)
remained unchanged from its inception in 1911 to the end of Japanese
rule in 1945, with the result that far fewer Japanese laws were enforced in Korea. The fact that the LLR of Korea did not undergo a
single major amendment was never officially explained. It appears,
however, that the principal reasons for this state of affairs was the
traditional hostility of the governors-general of Korea to any attempt
by the institutions of the central government in Japan (especially the
Imperial Diet) to dictate the affairs of the peninsula, their unwillingness to subordinate themselves to anyone in the central government
except the prime minister and the emperor, and the reluctance of the

central government to force the politically prominent colonial chief of Korea to come in line with less prominent heads of other colonies.

IMPERIAL ORDINANCES

There were three categories of imperial ordinances (*chokurei*): emergency ordinances promulgated while the Imperial Diet was not in session, ordinances used to cause the extension of Japanese laws to the colonies, and ordinances, the issuance of which was the constitutional prerogative of the emperor, subject to no restriction by any Diet-enacted law. The first category of imperial ordinances needed to be approved by the Imperial Diet at the following session in order to remain in force in the future. Such ordinances were rarely seen in the colonies except, perhaps, for Imperial Ordinance 324 of 1910, which became the LLR of Korea when the Imperial Diet gave its approval in the following year. The second category of imperial ordinances was found in large number in Taiwan, Korea, and Karafuto. They were merely used as catalysts for the extension of Japanese laws and, therefore, did not contribute substantively to the legal systems of the three colonies. The imperial ordinances which exerted the most influence on the legal systems of the colonies belonged to the third category, which could be further divided into two groups: ordinances "necessary for the maintenance of public peace and order and for the promotion of the welfare of his [Emperor's] subjects" (Article 9 of the constitution), and ordinances issued to "determine the organization of the different branches of the administration" (Article 10).

The first type of ordinance was especially important for the Kantōshū and the Nan'yō, where the Diet-enacted laws were not enforced at all, and where all matters which in Japan would normally require laws to regulate were regulated by imperial ordinances. In terms of flexibility and freedom from the control of the Imperial Diet, this was an advantage for the two colonies. In Karafuto an imperial ordinance of this type was also an important source for its legal system, for unlike the governors-general of Taiwan and Korea, the governor of Karafuto did not have his own legislative power and had to rely on imperial ordinances to regulate such matters, as Japanese laws were unable to do because of differences in local conditions. In Taiwan and Korea imperial ordinances were not usually used substantively because the governors-general of those colonies had the option of legislating their own laws. Instead, the imperial ordinances were used to supplement the Diet-enacted laws, or to provide detailed guidelines regarding the enforcement of such laws. For example, when the Anti-Air Raid Law (a Diet-enacted law) was enforced in 1942, an imperial ordinance was issued separately for Taiwan, Korea, and Karafuto, setting forth the manner by which the law should be implemented in the respective colonies (Imperial Ordinance 643 for Taiwan, 645 for Karafuto, and 661 for Korea).

The second type of ordinance which was used to determine the functions and organizations of various colonial institutions was of utmost importance to the legal and administrative systems of all five colonies. An imperial ordinance of this type, known as *kansei* or organic regulations, covered a wide range of institutions from the Ministry of Colonial Affairs in Japan to all levels of government in the colonies (save the lowest level of local governments). Even public educational institutions were regulated by this type of imperial ordinance. Perhaps, however, the most important *kansei* of all were the organic regulations of the five colonial governments. They are listed below and will be compared in the next section dealing with the relationship between the central government and colonial governments.

1. Taiwan Sōtokufu kansei or Organic Regulations of the Government-General of Taiwan (ORGG of Taiwan), Imperial Ordinance 362, 1897.
2. Chōsen Sōtokufu kansei or Organic Regulations of the Government-General of Korea (ORGG of Korea), Imperial Ordinance 354, 1910.
3. Kantō Totokufu kansei or Organic Regulations of the Government-General of Kantōshū (ORGG of Kantōshū), Imperial Ordinance 196, 1906.
4. Karafutochō kansei or Organic Regulations of the Government of Karafuto (ORG of Karafuto), Imperial Ordinance 33, 1907.
5. Nan'yōchō kansei or Organic Regulations of the Government of the South Sea Islands (ORG of the South Sea Islands), Imperial Ordinance 107, 1922.

CABINET DECREES

Cabinet decrees, like imperial ordinances, were executive orders of the central government, but with one distinction: the enforcement of imperial ordinances in the colonies was very frequent, while the enforcement of the cabinet decrees, except in Karafuto, was not. Usually the cabinet decrees, including the prime minister's decrees, called *kakurei*, and other ministerial decrees, called *shōrei*, were used to set forth guidelines for the enforcement of certain Japanese laws of a technical nature. For instance, when the Patent Law was enacted, the

Ministry of Commerce issued guidelines regarding its enforcement. Likewise, the Pension Law was accompanied by a set of instructions issued by the prime minister's office. When both the Patent Law and the Pension Law were extended to the colonies, all accompanying cabinet decrees were also extended. There were a number of military-related laws enforced in the colonies, such as the Law regarding the Fortified Zones and the Law regarding Naval Ports. All instructions of the Ministers of Army and Navy about their implementation were considered automatically extended to the colonies.

Special mention needs to be made regarding Karafuto, where the judicial system was an integral part of the Japanese system. As a result, Karafuto saw a large number of decrees by the Ministry of Justice enforced within its boundaries. Moreover, because of the much narrower scope of power given to the governor of Karafuto than that of his counterpart in the other colonies, a far greater number of decrees by the Ministry of Colonial Affairs were implemented in Karafuto.

ORDINANCES OF COLONIAL GOVERNORS

By virtue of the authorization stipulated in the organic regulations of their respective colonial governments (*kansei*), all five governors had the power to issue executive ordinances and to penalize the violator of such ordinances with a fine and/or a penal servitude. They were known as *furei* in Taiwan, Korea, and Kantōshu (*kyokurei* after 1934 which were issued by the ambassador to Manchukuo) and *chōrei* in Karafuto and the Nan'yo.[23]

Far more important than these ordinances, however, were the ordinances issued by the governors-general of Taiwan and Korea known respectively as *ritsurei* and *seirei*. Unlike *furei* or *chōrei*, ordinances of this type derived their legal authority from the special legislation of the Imperial Diet (i.e., the LLRs of Taiwan and Korea). They were regarded as "having the same effect as laws of Japan." It is for this reason that the two governors-general were said to have the power to write their own laws.

[23] With the exception of *chōrei* issued by the governor of Karafuto, all other ordinances carried a maximum penalty of one-year imprisonment and/or a fine of up to 200 yen against any violator (Article 5, ORGG of Taiwan; Article 4, ORGG of Korea; Article 7, ORGG of the Kantōshū; and Article 4, ORG of the Nan'yō). In the case of *chōrei* of Karafuto, the maximum penalty was a three-month imprisonment and/or a fine of no more than one hundred yen. (The governor of Karafuto was dealing primarily with Japanese settlers.)

In issuing *ritsurei* and *seirei* the two governors-general were required to observe a set of rules. It was necessary for them to obtain, through the prime minister or an appropriate minister, prior imperial sanction. Although they were permitted to issue such ordinances without imperial sanction in an emergency, subsequent imperial approval was needed for the ordinances to remain in force. Failure to obtain the needed sanction would require them to announce at once that the ordinances would cease to be effective in the future (Articles 1, 2, 3, and 4 of the LLR of Taiwan and Articles 1, 2, and 3 of the LLR of Korea). Also, no *ritsurei* or *seirei* could come into conflict with Japanese laws or imperial ordinances already in force in Taiwan or Korea (Article 5 of the LLR of Taiwan, as amended in 1906 and Article 5 of the LLR of Korea).

Additional restrictions were imposed on the governor-general of Taiwan. Before he could request imperial sanction for his *ritsurei*, he was required to submit a draft to a special council called the *Hyōgikai* for its approval (Article 2, LLR of Taiwan). In Korea, too, there existed an institution, called the *Chūsuin*, consisting of former high-ranking officials of the pre-annexation government of Korea and given the function of advising the governor-general regarding the customs and traditions of the Korean people. The LLR of Korea, however, did not require the governor-general to seek the consent of *Chūsuin* in issuing *seirei*.

This distinction between Taiwan and Korea in seeking imperial sanction for colonial ordinances was a meaningless formality, however. In the first place, the *Hyōgikai* of Taiwan was created *within* the government-general and was presided over by the governor-general himself. All heads of bureaus and departments and other high-ranking officials of the colonial government were ex-officio members of the council. Secondly, if the governor-general should disapprove of any decision reached by the *Hyōgikai*, he could explain the reason for his disapproval and order its reconsideration. Thus, the council was nothing more than a conference of subordinates, designed to provide the formality of giving consent to the governor-general in meeting a requirement stipulated in the LLR of Taiwan. So meaningless, in fact, had it become that it was convened only for a few years and eventually became completely inactive. When the LLR was amended in 1906, the consent of the council was dropped as a requirement.

The real difference came about in 1921, when the LLR of Taiwan underwent the second major overhaul. The amended LLR instructed the governor-general of Taiwan to enforce as many Japanese laws as local conditions would permit and allowed him to resort to his *ritsurei* only when he could find no appropriate Japanese law or when local conditions would not warrant the enforcement of a Japanese law. Beginning in 1923, a large number of Japanese laws, including the civil code and commercial law, were extended to Taiwan. This made it even more difficult for the governor-general to find an area to which he could apply his *ritsurei* without infringing upon the Japanese laws "already in force in the colony" (Article 5, LLR of Taiwan, as amended in 1921).

This is not to say, however, that the *ritsurei* of Taiwan was less useful a tool in controlling the indigenous population than the *seirei* of Korea. In fact, without the *ritsurei*, it would have been difficult, if not impossible, for the government-general of Taiwan to restore and maintain peace and order quickly and effectively in the early years of Japanese rule. For example, in the first three years after the enactment of the LLR of 1896, the governor-general of the island issued in rapid succession more than forty *ritsurei*. One of these, *Ritsurei* No. 2, 1896, the *Rinji hōin jōrei* (Ordinance Regarding ad hoc Law Courts), authorized the establishment of ad hoc law courts at the place of rebellion and permitted judges to sentence the captured "rebels" to death or hand down some other severe penalty. Another was *Ritsurei* No. 24, 1898, known as *Hito keibatsurei* (Bandit Punishment Ordinance), which made the death sentence mandatory for those who acted as a group whose activities caused the death of a person or persons and/ or the destruction of public property. The famous *Ho kō jōrei* was also a *ritsurei* (No. 21, 1898), which penalized an entire group of people if they should fail to report a crime committed by any one among them. None of those ordinances would likely have been approved had they been submitted to the Imperial Diet, because of their excessive severity.

It is estimated that, in the fifty years of Japanese rule in Taiwan, some 275 *ritsurei* were issued by nineteen governors-general, of which about 120 were still in force in 1945.[24] In glaring contrast, 676 *seirei* were promulgated in the 35 years of Japanese rule by nine governors-general of Korea. Some 270 were still in force when Japanese rule came to an end.[25] As late as 1943, *ritsurei* were used in Taiwan to regulate law courts, local autonomy systems (such as municipal and prefectural councils), government monopolies (such as camphor law, opium law, etc.), and customs and taxation. In Korea, in contrast, not only those areas mentioned above but also additional areas of importance to the daily life of an average Korean were regulated by *seirei*. For example, such fundamental laws as the Criminal Code,

---

[24] Okurashō, *Nihonjin no kaigai katsudō*, Vol. 17, p. 3. (For full citation see Note 30.)
[25] Hagihara, *Nihon tōjika ni okeru chōsen no hōsei*, p. 5.

Criminal Procedure, Civil Code, Civil Procedure, Commercial Law, Maritime Law, Law regarding Real Estate, Census Registration Act, were all *seirei*.

CENTRAL GOVERNMENT AND COLONIAL GOVERNMENTS

The extent to which a colonial government was required to subordinate itself to the authority of the central government is an important yardstick in measuring the degree of legal integration. The extent of the supervision of the central government, in turn, was determined by the scope of power granted to the colonial government: the more extensive the power of the colonial government, the less effective was the control of the central government. The extensiveness of the power of colonial government (vis-à-vis the prestige and political status of the colonial governor) was, in turn, determined by the size and importance of the colony it governed. To put it in a different way, the larger and the more important a colony was, the more prestige and higher status were accorded to its chief executive. He wielded a greater amount of power and enjoyed a greater degree of independence from the central government. Conversely, to the extent that the power of a colonial governor was reduced, the scope of the power of the central government to control a colonial governor was enlarged; and it could be said that the central government was that much closer to the goal of legal integration. Thus, the comparison of the different status enjoyed by the five colonial governors vis-à-vis their relations with the central government as represented, for example, by the five sets of organic regulations listed on page 258, should reveal the difference in the degree of legal integration achieved in each colony.

The governor-general of Korea enjoyed the highest status and wielded the greatest amount of power among the five colonial governors. Before 1919, the only person with a clear legal mandate to supervise the governor-general of Korea was the Emperor. An official of *shin'nin* rank, the highest in the Japanese bureaucracy, he had to be a general or an admiral on active duty at the time of his appointment so that he could be appointed concurrently the commander-in-chief of the colonial garrison. To reflect the spirit of the famous Imperial rescript (see page 245, the ORGG of Korea stipulated that he was to be placed under the direct supervision of the Emperor (*Ten'nō ni chokurei*), but he was required to "address the throne and receive imperial sanction through the office of the prime minister." Whether he should accept the supervision of the prime minister (let alone other cabinet ministers) was not even mentioned in the organic law. In Taiwan, the governor-general was also an official of *shin'nin* rank. While he, too, assumed the concurrent position of commander-in-chief of the colonial garrison, he could be a lieutenant general or a vice-admiral, but was required by the ORGG of Taiwan in no uncertain terms to accept the supervision of the prime minister. He was also required to be directed by the army and navy ministers and the two chiefs-of-staff in matters related to the defense and mobilization of the island. In the case of the Kwantung leased territory, the foreign minister was the chief supervisory officer of the governor-general in the central government. Like the governor-general of Taiwan, the governor-general of the Kantōshū held the rank of *shin'nin*, was a general or a lieutenant general on active duty, and held the post of commander-in-chief of the colonial garrison. Additionally, he was charged by the ORGG of the colony with the responsibility for protecting and supervising the Railway Zone and the Manchuria Railway Company. Like the governor-general of Taiwan he, too, was placed under the supervision of the army minister and the army chief-of-staff in reaching decisions regarding military personnel changes, defense, and mobilization.

It is important to note that the governors-general of Taiwan, Korea, and the Kantōshū were chosen in almost the same fashion as the prime minister. Their selection was made only after close consultation with *genrō* and the army. The emperor, acting on the recommendation of the prime minister, made the appointment amidst pomp and ceremony reserved only for the officials of the *shin'nin* rank.

In contrast, the governor of Karafuto, who held only the rank of *chokunin*, second highest, was not required to be a military officer, although the commanding officer of the garrison could be appointed as the governor. The supervisory power of the central government over the governor of Karafuto was considerably more extensive and was stipulated in stronger terms than in any other colony. He was required to accept the direction and supervision (*shiki kantoku*) of the home minister for the overall administration of the colony. In addition, he was instructed to obey the orders of the communications, and finance ministers in matters related to postal, communications, banking, and customs affairs (Article 9). Also, unlike any other colonial governor, the governor of Karafuto did not have supervisory power over judicial affairs which were controlled directly by the justice minister in Tokyo. As for the Nan'yō, where civil administration was not established until 1922, following several years of military rule, the governor was an official of *chokunin* rank and did not need to be a military officer, though he could request the use of force from the commanding officer of the naval force in the colony. He was under supervision of the prime minister but was instructed also to accept orders from other cabinet ministers for such matters as postal and telegraphic affairs (communications), currency, banking and customs affairs (finance), and weights and measures (commerce).

Between 1919 and 1942 a number of important changes were introduced to the organic regulations of several colonial governments, all of which were designed to decrease the power of colonial governors and to increase correspondingly the supervisory power of the central government. In 1919 under Premier Hara Takashi, an ardent believer in the creation of a totally integrated empire, the ORGGs of Korea, Taiwan, and Kantōshū were ordered amended so as to make civilians eligible for the position of governor-general. Thus, from 1919 until the late 1930's, when the rule of a military governor was resumed in Taiwan as a result of Japan's deepening involvement in the war in China, civilian rule theoretically prevailed in all five colonies. This fact, combined with the elimination from the ORGG of Korea of the clause stating that the governor-general was "under the direct supervision of the Emperor," appears to suggest that the supervisory power of the central government over the colonial government of Korea increased significantly. In reality, however, this was not true. Despite the reform, the post of the governor-general of Korea continued to be occupied by generals in mufti. While he was no longer considered "under direct supervision of the emperor," his many powerful friends in the Privy Council were able to prevent the amended ORGG from stating unequivocally the subordination of the governor-general in Korea to the prime minister. Thus, the prime minister's control over the governor-general of Korea remained de facto even after 1919 and continued to remain so until 1942.

In 1929 a cabinet-level Ministry of Colonial Affairs was created for the first time, charged with the power to oversee the management of the five colonial governments, including the government-general of Korea. The organic regulations of all colonial governments were ordered amended again to conform to this change. The attempt to centralize the control of the colonies, however, ran into strong resistance from Korea when General Yamanashi Hanzō, then the governor-general of Korea, threatened to resign if he were forced to accept the supervision of the minister of colonial affairs and ordered his administration to ignore all communications from Tokyo signed by the minister. The result of this crisis was that the ORGG of Korea was allowed to remain unchanged, thanks again to the supporters of the governor-general of Korea in the Privy Council. Thus, between 1929 and 1942 there existed a legal discrepancy between the organic law of the Ministry of Colonial Affairs, which recognized the power of the minister to supervise the governor-general of Korea, and the ORGG of Korea, which mentioned nothing about the subordination of the governor-general to either the prime minister or the minister of colonial affairs.

In 1934, in connection with the establishment of Manchukuo, sweeping changes were introduced to the ORGG of the Kantōshū, drastically reducing the power of its governor-general. His power to control the Railway Zone and the Manchuria Railway Company was transferred to the ambassador in Mukden, and he was reduced to a mere chief civil administrator of Kantō peninsula under the supervision of the ambassador. His rank was reduced from *shin'nin* to *chokunin*, and he was demoted to a lower rank, *chōkan* or governor, the same title as that of the governors of Karafuto and the Nan'yō. In Tokyo a special subcabinet-level Bureau of Manchurian Affairs (Taiman Jimukyoku) was created to direct the affairs of both Manchukuo and the Kantōshū.

The efforts of the Japanese government to achieve the legal integration of the colonies were completed, at least in appearance, in 1942 when the Ministry of Colonial Affairs and the Bureau of Manchurian Affairs were abolished and their functions dispersed to the Ministry of Home Affairs and the newly-created Ministry of Greater East Asian Affairs. The change placed the governors of the Kantōshū and the Nan'yō under the supervision of the minister of Greater East Asian affairs and brought the governors-general of Korea and Taiwan and the governor of Karafuto under the control of the Minister of Home Affairs. In 1943, it was announced that Karafuto was to be considered legally as a part of the *naichi*.

To insure the obedience of the governors-general of Korea and Taiwan, the central government secured at the time of the reorganization an imperial ordinance ordering the two colonial chiefs to accept the "direction and supervision" of the home minister in the overall management of their respective administrations. Also listed in the same ordinance as their superior officers were six cabinet ministers whose supervision they were required to accept in dealing with matters directly related to the function of the respective ministers: finance, education, agriculture, commerce and industry, communications, and transportation.

If actually implemented, these changes would have created a substantially integrated colonial empire, with Tokyo dictating virtually every aspect of colonial policy. They would have reduced the governors-general of Korea and Taiwan to a position not dissimilar to any prefectural governor in Japan. The fact was, however, that these changes were less than real, being designed to achieve psychological unity between the colonial governments and the home government in time of war. There is no evidence that the operation of the colonial government of the two colonies was interfered with by the ministers mentioned in the remaining three years of Japanese rule, nor is there any evidence to indicate that changes in the legal and administrative systems were contemplated inside Korea and Taiwan to conform to the changes which took place in Tokyo. It is more likely that the war, which contributed to the isolation of the colonies from Japan, increased the opportunities for the two colonial governors to exercise their independent authority and forced the central government to tolerate that autonomy. In short, the legal systems of the two colonies continued to remain separate from that of Japan, reorganization of 1942 notwithstanding.

Colonial Judiciary and Its Relations with Japanese Courts

Judicially Karafuto was a part of metropolitan Japan. As early as 1907 (the same year the ORG of Karafuto was promulgated) the Organic Law of the Japanese Law Courts (Saibanshō kōseihō) was extended to that colony, making its judicial system an integral part of the Japanese judiciary. Thus, a decision of the single local court in Karafuto could be appealed to the Court of Appeals in Sapporo, Hokkaido, whose judgment could be appealed further to the Supreme Court of Japan, a feature duplicated in no other colony. In the Karafuto court Japanese laws were used except for cases involving only the indigenes, in which case special regulation (imperial ordinances, justice minister's decrees or governor's executive ordinances) or native custom could be applied. All judges appointed by the Ministry of Justice were protected by the constitution against dismissal without due cause. Moreover, when the Imperial Diet enacted in 1918 the *kyotsūhō* or the Coordination Law to provide a number of guidelines for the application of various laws to civil and criminal cases involving the jurisdiction of more than one colony, Karafuto was singled out to be regarded judicially as a part of the *naichi*.

In the Kantōshū and the Nan'yō the constitution was not applicable, and judicature was considered a part of the executive functions of the colonial governors. Accordingly, judges in both colonies were appointed and could be dismissed at will by the colonial governors. (In the Kantōshū this power was transferred to the Japanese ambassador to Manchukuo after 1934.) Both colonies adopted the bi-level court system, with emphasis on speed and efficiency, namely, one high court (*kōtō hōin*) and several local courts (*chihō hōin*), the judgment of the high court being final. In the Kantōshū after 1924, however, two divisions were created in the high court—*fukushinbu* and *jōkokubu* (both are translated as division of appeal)—with the latter, *jōkokubu*, functioning as the colonial supreme court for appeals of very limited nature. The former, *fukushinbu*, had jurisdiction over appeals against judgments of the local courts and Japanese consuls in Manchukuo, where Japanese enjoyed extraterritoriality rights until 1937.[26]

The judicature in Taiwan and Korea, too, was exercised by the colonial governors as a part of their executive function. It was they, not the central government, who wrote the organic regulations of their respective law courts, through *ritsurei* in Taiwan and *seirei* in Korea. It was they, not the Minister of Justice or the Supreme Court of Japan, who had the ultimate control over the judicial affairs within the boundary of their respective colonies. Nevertheless, unlike the judicial system of the Kantōshū and the Nan'yō, the court systems of Taiwan and Korea were more elaborate, resembled more the court system of Japan, and contained measures of assurance for judicial independence. In both colonies, for example, a judge was protected from arbitrary dismissal by the colonial governor unless he was convicted of a crime or disciplined by a board of judges comprised of his own peers preselected by the governor-general.

As for the organization of courts, Korea followed the example of Japan, adopting the tri-level court system of local courts, courts of appeal, and the high court. Local courts were divided into one-judge courts and three-judge courts, the latter having jurisdiction over such civil cases as litigation involving an object valued at more than 1,000 yen or criminal cases involving a penalty of more than one-year imprisonment. In Taiwan the bi-level system was adopted: local courts and the high court. A local court, consisting of a one-judge court and a three-judge court, had jurisdiction virtually identical to that of its Korean counterpart, except that the three-judge court in Taiwan had jurisdiction over civil litigation involving an object valued in excess of 2,000 yen. The high court of Taiwan, like the high court of Kantōshu, was divided into *fukushinbu* and *jōkokubu* (both translated as division of appeal). The judgment of *fukushinbu* was normally considered final, but under highly restricted circumstances an appeal against its judgment could be made to *jōkokubu*.[27] *Jōkokubu* was given

---

[26] Kantōchō (Government-General of the Kantōshū), ed. *Kantōchō shisei nijūnenshi* [The Twenty-Year History of Japanese Rule in the Kantōshū] (Tokyo: Hara Shobō, 1974) (reprint of the original published in 1926), p. 239.

[27] The *jōkokubu* of the Taiwan High Court would accept only the appeals against an order or decision of *fukushinin* or local courts on the ground of technicality, but would not accept appeals against the substance of the sentence.

additional jurisdiction over such extraordinary criminal cases as rebellion and attempts on the life of the imperial family or high-ranking government officials. No appeal was allowed against judgment rendered on those cases.

To compare the organization of the courts in Korea and Taiwan: justice was probably better served in Korea than in Taiwan, where speedy and efficient intimidation of the indigenous population seemed to be the overriding concern of the Japanese rulers. In Korea even before the annexation, Japan's dominant position in the peninsula enabled it to remodel the court system after the pattern of Japanese courts (the Organic Regulation of the Law Courts of Korea was promulgated in 1909).[28]

By the Treaty of Annexation, moreover, Japan was committed to "employ in the public service of Japan in Korea" as many Koreans as "circumstances permit," and by a *seirei* of the governor-general issued in 1910, Koreans who had completed three years of legal education at an imperial university or a college designated by the governor-general were eligible for appointment as judges in Korean courts. No corresponding treatment was ever accorded to Taiwanese, and no more than three Taiwanese ever served on the bench of courts in Taiwan.

SUMMARY AND CONCLUSION

Except for a brief initial period of vacillation after the annexation of Taiwan, its first colony, the Japanese government during its fifty years as a colonial power was committed to achieving the legal integration of its empire. The goal of Japanese colonial policy was to create a tightly welded, centrally controlled empire within the legal framework of the Meiji Constitution. All colonies eventually were to be governed by laws and regulations originating from Tokyo. At no time were self-governing colonies, similar to the British Dominions, the goal of the Japanese government.

On the other hand, the Japanese government recogized the need to allow each colony to develop its own legal system, tailored to meet the need of local conditions. Thus, each colonial government was given power and responsibility far more extensive than any of the prefectural governments of Japan. In certain colonies the governors were even permitted to enact laws independent of the Imperial Diet.

---

[28] In 1935, 39 Korean judges and 7 Korean prosecutors were employed as opposed to 163 and 86 respectively for Japanese. The figures for Koreans in the earlier years were not available, but it must be assumed that they were considerably larger. See Ōkurashō, *Nihonjin no kaigai katsudō*, Vol 3, p. 141.

In all but one colony the judicial system was independent, and the Supreme Court of Japan had no jurisdiction over colonial courts. While these arrangements appear to undercut the ultimate goal of the legal and administrative integration of the empire, the Japanese government always regarded local colonial laws as an interim structure, to be replaced gradually by the laws and regulations of Japan. The ultimate design of the Japanese government was to replace all colonial laws by Japanese laws and to end the distinction between Japanese and colonial legal systems. All *gaichi* would thereby become part of the *naichi*.

Yet it is clear that Japan did not achieve this goal. For example, those provisions of the constitution related to the political rights of the people were never extended to the colonial populations. Nor did the Japanese government enforce in any colony the Election Law of the House of Representatives of the Japanese Diet, the most visible symbol of total legal integration. Even in those colonies where Japanese settlers outnumbered the indigenous population, certain special features inconsistent with the ultimate goal of integration were retained in their legal and administrative systems. What follows is a balance sheet showing the factors, both pro and con, which affected legal integration of the five colonies at the conclusion of World War II.

Karafuto was by far the most integrated colony. It was officially incorporated into the *naichi* in 1943 and had a Japanese population representing over 93 percent of its total population.[29] There was little doubt that in the near future the Election Law of the House of Representatives would have been implemented in Karafuto in the same fashion as Hokkaido was merged into metropolitan Japan in 1886, followed by the extension of the Election Law several years later. Nevertheless, in 1945 Karafuto had not yet achieved complete legal integration. Only those Japanese laws enacted after 1943 were enforced in Karafuto without going through the special process of extension by imperial ordinance. All modifications and exceptions of Japanese laws already in force in the colony remained intact, and formed a final hurdle that had to be removed before Karafuto could be completely integrated into the Japanese legal system.

After Karafuto the Nan'yō offered the greatest possibilities for legal integration with the *naichi*, much in the same manner that the Bonin (Ogasawara) Islands became part of metropolitan Tokyo. Two factors worked in favor of integration. The Nan'yō had a Japanese

[29] In 1943 the population of Karafuto was 399,697, of which 373,223 (93.38 percent) were Japanese and only 413 (1.03 percent) were natives. There were 25,765 Korean laborers. Ōkurashō, *Nihonjin no kaigai katsudō*, Vol. 18, p. 161.

population which after 1935 was more numerous than the indigenous inhabitants.[30] Also, the Japanese government exercised a high degree of administrative control over the Nan'yō-chō, reducing the power of the colonial governor nearly to the level of prefectural governors of Japan. On the other hand, the major obstacle to integration was the non-enforcement of Japanese laws, including the constitution. Since it was a non-sovereign colony, most affairs of the Nan'yō were regulated by imperial ordinances. Therefore, the normal legislative process required by the constitution did not apply to this territory. This, however, was a political pretension designed to circumvent the constitutional requirement that the Imperial Diet enact all needed colonial legislation. Although the Nan'yō was, in theory, a mandated territory of the League of Nations, Japan as the mandatory power was authorized to regard her Micronesian territories as "an integral portion of the empire" and apply to them "the laws of the empire of Japan." The Nan'yō could easily have become a part of the *naichi*, if the Japanese government had abandoned its pretension of not extending the constitution and allowed the Imperial Diet to legislate the colonial law.

The Kwantung Leased Territory, another non-sovereign territory, was unique in that the Japanese government never intended to integrate it. It was governed by the ambassador to Manchukuo, who also controlled the Manchuria Railway Company and the Railway Zone (until its transfer to Manchukuo in 1937). All indigenes (Manchurian Chinese)[31] were legally classified as aliens and no efforts were made to assimilate them culturally.[32] Although the Japanese population showed rapid increase,[33] it was highly unlikely that the Japanese population could ever surpass the indigenous population as happened in Karafuto and the Nan'yō.

[30] In 1940 approximately 81,000 out of the total population of more than 132,000 were Japanese. While the native population had maintained a steady level of 50,000 throughout the 30 years of Japanese rule, the Japanese population increased from a mere 220 in 1915 to nearly 20,000 in 1930; 51,000 in 1935; and 81,000 in 1940. *Takumu yōran*, 1940 edition, p. 31.

[31] In 1943 the population of the Kantōshu was 1,681,872, of which 1,442,841 or 86 percent were Manchurian Chinese. Ōkurashō, *Nihonjin no kaigai katsudō*, Vol. 25, p. 154.

[32] The aim of education in the Kantōshū, for example, was declared to be the promotion of understanding between Japanese and Manchurian Chinese of their respective cultures and the development of awareness that Manchuria was an area where Japanese and Manchurian Chinese should coexist and coprosper in friendship. See: Kantōchō, ed. *Kantōchō shisei nijūnenshi*, Vol. 1, p. 191. (For full citation, see note 26.)

[33] In 1905 there were some 5,000 Japanese in Kantōshū. The number rose to 100,000 in 1928; 200,000 in 1940, and 230,000. See Ōkurashō, *Nihonjin no kaigai katsudō*, Vol. 25, p. 6.

With no large Japanese population to hasten the process of integration[34] or any legal restriction which would prevent the application of Japanese laws, Taiwan and Korea are better examples by which to measure the degree of success in legal integration of the empire. The most visible signs of success were the application of the constitution (except for those provisions related to the political rights of the people) and the extension of a significant number of Japanese laws. Another important evidence of integration was that the two colonies after 1942 were brought under the jurisdiction of the Ministry of Home Affairs, and the two governors-general were placed under the supervision of several cabinet ministers in the central government. On the minus side was the system of "delegated legislation" which authorized the two governors-general to enact their own laws. While the original intention of such a system was to give the colonial government the flexibility to cope with local unrest, in 1945 their power to legislate colonial laws was the greatest barrier separating the colonial legal systems from the Japanese legal system.

In Korea, Japan faced an additional disadvantage. The political prominence of the governor-general, as recognized in the imperial rescript of 1910, which enabled him to spurn successfully, until 1942, the efforts of the Japanese government to bring him under full control. In contrast, the Japanese government was able to expand steadily its supervisory power over the colonial government of Taiwan. After the installation of a civilian governor-general, it even succeeded in limiting his legislative power so that he could exercise it only when no comparable Japanese laws were available. The upshot was that a far greater number of Japanese laws were enforced in Taiwan than Korea, making Taiwan the more legally integrated colony. Yet this was only a difference of degree. For both colonies the complete integration which would make them parts of the *naichi* was still a remote goal.

To sum up, none of the colonies except for Karafuto came even close to achieving the goal of complete legal integration. What prevented the Japanese government from achieving it? Why, in particular, was it so reluctant to extend to the colonies *all* portions of the constitution and the Election Law of the House of Representatives, two essential steps toward complete legal integration? The answer lies in its inability to assimilate culturally the indigenous population

[34] In 1942 the population of Taiwan was 6,427,932 and that of Korea, 26,361,401. Of these, Japanese residents in Taiwan numbered 384,847 and in Korea, 752,823, representing 6 and 2.9 percent, respectively, of their total populations. Kondō Ken'ichi, ed., *Taiheiyō senka no Chōsen oyobi Taiwan* [Korea and Taiwan During the Pacific War] (Tokyo, 1961), p. 2.

of the colonies. What the Japanese government had accomplished in its fifty years of colonial experience was the integration of *systems* and *institutions*. Behind the appearance of an integrated empire, the indigenous populations, especially those of Taiwan and Korea, remained adamant in refusing to accept the Japanese culture as their own. Without their support and loyalty, the extension of all portions of the constitution and the Election Law of the House of Representatives would have been a disaster for Japan. To extend to Taiwanese and Koreans, for example, the right to the freedom of speech and assembly would have been tantamount to giving sanctions to their criticism of Japanese rule and encouraging the growth of their nationalistic aspirations. To allow the Koreans and Taiwanese (numbering nearly 33 million in 1942) to elect members to the Japanese House of Representatives would have placed in the Diet a large number of persons whose loyalty to Japan was an unknown factor. Their combined votes could adversely influence the legislative process of the entire empire.[35]

When the Meiji leaders followed the counsel of the French adviser and adopted integration as Japan's ultimate goal in Taiwan, they assumed that the Taiwanese could easily be assimilated because they "belong to the same race and use the same script." They believed that, unlike Western colonialism, which they characterized as the rule of the white race over non-whites, the "ethnic similarity" in Taiwan should help to promote integration. When Korea was annexed, a similar goal was proclaimed, based on the even stronger assumption that there had been frequent mixing of blood between Japanese and Koreans in their distant past. What the Japanese failed to realize was that the ethnic similarity had little, if any, effect on the assimilation of Taiwanese or Koreans. In both colonies the Japanese were always regarded as aliens, and assimilation was a means of destroying and replacing indigenous cultures and traditions. Confronted by intense resistance, the Japanese government could only make slow and small progress in acculturation. On the other hand, the legal and administrative integration of the empire was speeded up following Japan's military intervention in China in the 1930's. The resultant gap created by the appearance of integration unaccompanied by a commensu-

[35] Similar arguments were used by Taiwanese nationalists to persuade the Japanese government to abandon the idea of electing representatives from Taiwan to the Diet. They wanted the Japanese government to support the creation of a colonial congress on the island, to be popularly elected by both Taiwanese and Japanese residents. See, Sai Bai Ka (Tsai-Pei-huo) *Nihon hongokumin ni atau* [An Appeal to the Japanese People in Japan] (Tokyo, 1928).

rating degree of cultural assimilation had detrimental effects on the relationship between indigenous populations and Japanese residents.[36]

Though grossly outnumbered by the indigenes, there was a sizable number of Japanese residents in Taiwan and Korea. Holding virtual monopoly of higher positions in the colonial government and managerial and skilled positions in colonial finance and industry, they opposed integration, fearing that it would eventually wipe out the political and economic advantages they enjoyed. To protect their interests, they turned to the colonial government, a move which often resorted to such measures that could only be construed as a thinly disguised form of racial discrimination. For example, when the election of local councils was finally introduced in Korea (1930) and Taiwan (1935), it was announced with much fanfare that Koreans and Taiwanese were about to receive the same privilege of home rule as enjoyed by the Japanese in Japan. By means of *seirei* and *ritsurei*, however, the governors-general of the two colonies decreed that the suffrage in the election was contingent upon the payment of a certain amount of taxes (thus effectively eliminating the vast majority of potential native voters), and that elections be held in the cities and selected districts where there were large concentrations of Japanese residents. To further insure the Japanese dominance, it was decided that only a portion of the members of each council would be elective, the remainder would be appointed by the governors-general or local governors. Likewise, when the Educational Ordinance of Korea was amended in 1938 and that of Taiwan in 1941, it was declared that the purpose of the change was to abolish the segregated elementary education of Japanese and indigenous children and to make the educational system of the two colonies "identical" with that of Japan. The two colonial governments, however, were allowed to establish two curriculums, one for schools educating those children who spoke Japanese habitually and the other for schools teaching those who did not. Japanese residents who feared the lowering of the quality of their children's education if indigenous children were admitted to the previously all-Japanese schools succeeded in thwarting the intent of educational integration.

These are just two of the many examples of how integration actually worked to alienate the people whose support and loyalty the

---

[36] The gap between the appearance of integration and the reality of large unassimilated indigenous populations is vividly demonstrated by the fact that in the very same year (1942) when the Japanese government placed Taiwan and Korea under the jurisdiction of the Ministry of Home Affairs, only about 62 percent of Taiwanese and 20 percent of Koreans were recorded as being able to comprehend the Japanese language. See: Kondō, *op.cit.*, p. 20.

Japanese government sought to gain. The actions of the colonial governments only convinced Taiwanese and Koreans that integration was nothing but a scheme to make them accept the role of permanent colonial subordination. Integration intensified, rather than diminished, their resolve not to submit to the pressure of acculturation.

Japan, of course, had a better alternative, one that would enable her to control her colonial empire just as effectively without needing to assimilate its millions of indigenous population. As Montague Kirkwood suggested in 1895, the Japanese government could have treated all colonies legally and culturally separate from Japan. It could have allowed each colony to have its own legislative council, with power to enact its own laws and approve the budget of the colonial administration. These already existed in Taiwan, the *Hyōgikai*, and in Korea, the *Chūsūin*, both of which could have been transformed into legislative councils by simply allowing Taiwanese and Koreans to elect the members of those institutions. The Japanese government could still have retained firm control over these two colonies by exercising veto power over any colonial legislation that was deemed incompatible with the interest of the whole empire. Given the enthusiasm generated by the League for the Establishment of a Taiwan Congress, the creation of a popularly elected legislative council in Taiwan would have attracted widespread support among the Taiwanese. It is less certain that the same policy would have generated similar support in Korea. Yet even in the hostile environment of that colony, it would have had far greater popular appeal in competing with Korean aspiration for outright independence than trying to integrate the colony by representation in the Imperial Diet.

Naive confidence in their ability to transform the Taiwanese and Koreans into "loyal subjects of the emperor" caused the Meiji leaders to reject the British system of colonial administration. As Japan grew in size in the first two decades of the twentieth century, creation of one empire under one emperor, run from the center, Tokyo, became a national passion. Following the Japanese invasions of China in the 1930's, integration was no longer just a passion but a strategic and economic necessity upon which the fate of the entire empire rested. Japan's scheme for integration came to an abrupt end only with her defeat in World War II.

CHAPTER 7

Colonial Education in Korea and Taiwan

E. Patricia Tsurumi

MEIJI EDUCATION, NATION-BUILDING, AND IMPERIALIST EXPANSION

Travelling in North America and in Europe at the beginning of the
Meiji era, Japan's new leaders decided that widespread education was
a crucial contributor to the strength of the Western societies they
observed. They concluded that massive educational offensives would
be necessary in their own country, to provide skills and attitudes
required by life in a great power and to produce an elite possessing
technological and managerial abilities needed to direct the policy and
economy. Their pre-Meiji experience with education also encouraged
them to think this way: by the end of the Tokugawa period (1600-
1867) not only samurai but many commoners too regarded schooling
and learning as forces for material as well as spiritual betterment.[1]

The first Meiji establishment for training an elite clearly indicate
that this elite was expected to come overwhelmingly from the former
samurai class, which, as almost ten percent of the population, was
not short of likely candidates. Yet, unlike their counterparts in the
West, Meiji rulers were never afraid to educate the lower orders.
Nothing in their Tokugawa encounters with commoner education
suggested that a literate farmer or artisan was less obedient than his
or her illiterate cousins. On the contrary, orders could be transmitted
more efficiently to the educated. Education might provide an exper-
tise-hungry state with talent that, if left untapped and unrewarded,
might provide intelligent leadership for the discontented.[2] But schooling
could also serve as a vehicle for reminding the less talented ninety
percent of the population of its proper sphere in life.

Quickly the Meiji leaders began spending generously to establish
public educational facilities which would accomplish these two different objectives. Meanwhile, Christian missionaries and their native
converts, Western-influenced intellectuals, traditionalists, and various

[1] The definitive work on Tokugawa education remains Ronald P. Dore, *Education
in Tokugawa Japan* (Berkeley: University of California Press, 1965).

[2] See Kuno Osamu and Tsurumi Shunsuke, *Gendai Nihon no shisō* [Modern Japanese
Thoughts] (Tokyo: Iwanami, 1956), especially pp. 126-137.

varieties of patriotic mavericks began offering alternative schooling. Until the end of the century the government tolerated this, both because it took three decades to create abundant government schools and because there was reluctance to provoke the Western missionaries, influential under that instrument of gunboat diplomacy known as the unequal treaty system.[3] By 1899, the year that Britain gave up extraterritoriality in Japan, public-school facilities were no longer scarce. That year the Private School Rescript obliged all private schools to confine their activities to government-style education, and henceforth the major difference between public and private schooling was financial: only the former continued to receive government funds.[4] Thus all schools were brought within the educational planners' two-track system, aptly depicted by Ivan Hall as a " 'dumbbell' configuration: a small corp of highly, even liberally, educated scholars, technicians, and bureaucrats on one end; on the other, an entire population trained to basic literacy and economic usefulness and political obedience, up through the primary level; and very little in between."[5]

The heaviest educational outlays went into the government's first priority, production of the elite corp, which by 1899 was being trained in Western-style academies, colleges, and the first two of a series of national universities. Despite the lavish investment of the people's monies that this entailed, the first blueprints of the Meiji planners simultaneously assumed strong government financial initiative in basic schooling for the entire population. This double thrust may, through the lens of hindsight, appear hopelessly idealistic and ambitious. But it does demonstrate the extraordinary faith that the Meiji government placed in education.

The very success of the burgeoning elementary school system, however, had soon put intolerable strains upon governmental resolution to finance the base as well as the apex. By the end of the 1870's, national treasury subsidies to primary schools were being cut back sharply; in 1880, as part of the famous retrenchment and deflation policies of Finance Minister Matsukata Masayoshi, they were

[3] In a memorandum probably written before he became Education Minister in 1893, Inoue Kowashi reminded his colleagues that the powerful Western nations with whom Japan was trying to improve treaty relations demanded freedom of religious activity for Christians in Japan, Kaigo Tokiomi, ed. *Inoue Kowashi no kyōiku seisaku* [Inoue Kowashi's Education Policy] (Tokyo: Tokyo Daigaku Shuppankai, 1968), pp. 984-986.

[4] *Ibid.*, pp. 969-987; Nakajima Tarō, *Kindai Nihon kyōiku seidoshi* [A History of the Education System in Modern Japan] (Tokyo: Yamasaki Shoten, 1966), pp. 557-564.

[5] Ivan P. Hall, *Mori Arinori* (Cambridge, Mass.: Harvard University Press, 1973), p. 411.

discontinued altogether.[6] Suffering on all fronts from deflation and retrenchment, poor families—a resource that Meiji Japan was always rich in—had to withdraw youngsters from school, temporarily setting back the campaign to spread elementary schooling. In response to declining numbers of children in school, the central government tried to decrease the schools' dependency upon tuition fees, which by 1889 provided one-quarter of all public primary school revenues. General cost-cutting was combined with moves to increase the local administrations' financial obligations to elementary schooling.[7] By 1899, local governments' contributions had risen to seventy percent of the funds spent on public elementary schooling. Although achieved only at the price of considerable hardship to individual communities, elementary education had by then firmly become a financial burden of local consumers rather than of the central government.[8]

Education had been immediately perceived as a key to nation-statehood; it took the Meiji leaders slightly longer to conclude that a great power held overseas possessions. Seventeenth-century Tokugawa rulers had withdrawn Japanese energies from the international arena, and later the expanding Western presence in South, Southeast, and East Asia had been viewed with apprehension. That Western presence was a part of the tangle of responsibilities that the Meiji leaders took from the failing Tokugawa government in 1868. And by the 1880's, some of the country's new leaders were beginning to wonder if colonial conquest was not an essential part of the nationhood, which, dissolving Japan's own semi-colonial treaties with the Western imperialists, would ensure that Japan would never be in such a humiliating situation again. Foreign Minister Inoue Kaoru expressed this increasingly popular line of thought in 1887: ". . . we have to establish a new, European-style empire on the edge of Asia."[9] When in 1895 Japan

[6] Government subsidies to primary schools, begun in 1873, climbed from 240,000 yen to 600,000 yen in just three years. Kaigo, p. 120.

[7] Such "luxuries" as school hats and athletic meets were discontinued, and school buildings were occupied in turn by different shifts of pupils. Right down through the 1890's prefectural governments urged hard-pressed communities to seek new ways to raise school funds. Projects like tree planting, poultry husbandry, ferry and bridge tolls, special imposts on salaries, household possessions, marriages, births (presumably a death tax would have been too hard to collect) were all tried with some success and considerable hardship to individual communities.

[8] Naka Arata, *Nihon kindai kyōiku seido* [A History of Modern Education in Japan] (Tokyo: Kodansha, 1973), pp. 1-165; Ebihara Haruyoshi, *Gendai Nihon kyōiku seido* [Education Policy in Modern Japan] 2 vols. (Tokyo: Sanichi Shobō, 1965-1967), I, 154-155; Kaigo, pp. 97-163; Mombushō [Ministry of Education], *Gakusei hyakunenshi* [A Hundred-Year History of the Education System], 2 vols. (Tokyo, 1972), I, 292. The subsidies were partially restored in 1896.

[9] Cited in Marius B. Jansen, "The Meiji State: 1868-1912," in James B. Crowley,

acquired Taiwan, along with other booty from the Sino-Japanese War of 1894-1895, the first step toward formation of such an empire was begun. During the next two decades new colonies were acquired—Karafuto (1905), Kantōshū (1905), Korea (1910), Nan'yō (1915). All but the last addition to Japan's "European-style empire" were "on the edge of Asia."

Even by 1895 schooling in Japan had weakened regional loyalties, introduced new skills and attitudes, and selected an able few for higher training. It was not unreasonable to assume that education could perform similar services overseas. The model could not be applied without alteration to the non-Japanese peoples in territories governed under varying circumstances. As the colonial empire expanded, the pattern grew clearer: the peoples ethnically closest to the Japanese, dwelling in lands most firmly attached to Japan, were the targets of the heaviest educational attack. Everywhere in the empire Japanization was desirable, but in these areas it was essential. Karafuto, with a small aborigine population, was mainly a colony of Japanese settlers. Educational efforts there meant providing Japanese children with the school facilities that less remote parts of the home islands enjoyed.[10] In Kantōshū, a leasehold with residual sovereignty remaining in Chinese hands, Japanese administrators encouraged Chinese residents to send their youngsters to Japanese public schools, but these, unlike Japanese schools for indigenous peoples in other parts of the empire, emphasized Chinese language studies almost as much as Japanese language studies.[11] In the mandated trust colony in the South Seas, educational assimilation trod a golden mean: Japanese language schools were built for Nan'yō islanders, but the standards of these were lower than their counterparts in Kantōshū, Taiwan, or Korea and their numbers were limited.[12]

---

ed., *Modern East Asia: Essays in Interpretation* (New York: Harcourt, Brace and World, 1970), p. 114.

[10] See Takada Ginjirō, *Karafuto kyōiku hattatsushi* [A History of Educational Progress in Karafuto] (Tokyo: Karafuto Kyōikukai, 1936).

[11] The *kōgakudō* of Kantōshū were four-year elementary schools which taught Chinese children twenty-eight weekly hours of basics. Ten of these hours were spent on Japanese, and another eight were devoted to Chinese. See Mombushō, *Meiji ikō kyōiku seido hattatsushi* [A History of the Development of the Education System After Meiji), 12 vols. (Tokyo: 1938), XIII, 41-122. In supposedly independent Manchuria, the Japanese actually supported schooling in the Chinese language. Hirano Ken'ichirō, "Manshū ni okeru Nihon no kyōiku seisaku, 1906-1931" [Japanese Educational Policy in Manchuria, 1906-1931], *Ajiya kenkyū* [Asian Research], 15.3 (October 1968), pp. 24-52.

[12] Regarding the products of these three-year schools Yanaihara Tadao reported in 1934 that "the education they received at present enables them to read Japanese *hiragana* characters with facility at the end of their public school course." Yanaihara Tadao,

Taiwan and Korea were not held in trust, not leased lands, not outlying Japanese settlements. Their major populations were not South Sea islanders but fellow East Asians, not quite Japanese but perhaps capable of becoming Japanese. In both Taiwan and Korea, education was made a central pillar of colonial development. It was given all but one of the tasks that the Meiji rulers first assigned to it in Japan— all but one because it was a rare mind among the Japanese colonial rulers that dreamed of Taiwanese or Korean recruitment into the Tokyo-based elite.

MAKING SEA BREAM OUT OF FLOUNDERS: TAIWAN, 1895-1945

In 1895 there was one Japanese mind that dared to dream thus. A senior education officer with a distinguished career in teaching and school administration already behind him by the 1880's, Izawa Shūji hopelessly opposed the central government's cutbacks to local elementary schools. He felt strongly that all education should be financed by the state. During the 1890's he even left the Education Ministry to campaign publicly for restoration of the subsidies to local primary schools. In 1895, viewing Taiwan as a last hope for his ideas about state education, he persuaded the colony's first governor-general, Rear Admiral Kabayama Sukenori, to put him in charge of the colony's educational affairs. In Taiwan he hoped to duplicate *all* the functions of education that the home islands were now familiar with.[13]

For two years, while Japanese troops battled Taiwanese★ irregulars and aborigine headhunters unhappy about the takeover, Izawa Shūji opened tuition-free Japanese language schools to which he invited islanders of all classes, ages, and both sexes. He also enlisted Japanese normal-school graduates to teach in these schools, subjecting them to intensive training in Taiwan's Chinese dialects before they took

Pacific Islands Under Japanese Mandate (London: Oxford University Press, 1940), p. 246. This is a translation of *Nan'yō Gunto no kenkyū* (Tokyo: 1935). See also *Meiji ikō kyōiku seido hattatsushi*, XIII, 824-931 and Nan'yō Guntō kyōiku kai [Education Society of the Pacific Islands], *Nan'yō Guntō kyōikushi* [A History of Education in the Pacific Islands] (Tokyo: 1938).

[13] For biographical data on this interesting Meiji educator see Heibonsha, *Dai jimmei jiten* [Great Biographical Dictionary] 10 vols. (Tokyo, 1935-1955), I, 171-172, and Kaminuma Hachirō, *Izawa Shūji* (Tokyo: Yoshikawa Kōbunkan, 1962).

★ Native islanders of Chinese ancestry who had crossed the Taiwan Strait and settled on the island largely between the seventeenth and the nineteenth centuries, but in some cases even earlier. They had opened up farm land, hunted deer, fished in the coastal waters, and engaged in trade with the Chinese mainland and with other parts of the world. From 1624 to 1662 they were ruled by the Dutch East Indian Company, from 1662-1683 by the Cheng Ch'eng-kung family, from 1683-1895 by the Chi'ing dynasty.

up their posts. In memoranda for the governor-general he mapped out long-range plans to give the emperor's newest subjects all that was available in the schools and colleges of Japan. As a start toward post-elementary schooling he founded the Japanese Language School, where, he hoped, Taiwanese would master the Japanese language and begin higher academic training, while Japanese would study the languages and culture of Taiwan, in two separate, parallel courses equal in academic standard and status.[14] Also at the post-elementary level he established three normal schools to train Taiwanese to teach in his Japanese-language elementary schools.

Once again Izawa was defeated by financial constraints: by 1897 the colony's deficit-ridden budget could no longer be hidden in military funds appropriated to finish off remnants of the Sino-Japanese War, and when government-general monies were cut, Izawa's education estimates were among the first to go. By 1898, when the fourth governor-general, Kodama Gentarō, and his chief civil administrator, Gotō Shimpei, arrived, a bitter Izawa had given up his dream of state-financed public universal elementary education for all Taiwanese and advanced training for the most able among them. Even Izawa Shūji, it seems, gave little serious thought to the education of Taiwan's aborigine population. Although this population numbered about 150,000 compared to more than two million Chinese settlers at the time of the takeover, systematic extermination campaigns by Japanese forces soon reduced this population to less than two percent of the colony's total residents. Aborigine education was neglected until the 1920's, and even during the last half of the island's Japanese colonial period, its development remained primitive and under the jurisdiction of the colonial police.[15] Kodama's administration, famous both for ending the guerrilla resistance and for firmly laying the foundations of all future colonial rule, shifted the costs of schools directly onto the backs of local consumers and discarded Izawa's plans for elite educational opportunities for Taiwanese. But it organized

---

[14] Kaminuma puts great emphasis upon Izawa's desire to treat Taiwanese and Japanese equally. Izawa's educational memoranda tend to support this contention. In 1899, probably before anyone else, Izawa, in a speech in the House of Peers, publicly supported Taiwanese participation in the Japanese legislative process. Gaimushō [Foreign Ministry], *Taiwan ni shikō subeki hōrei ni kansuru hōrei no gijiroku* [Diet Record of the Law for Laws and Regulations Enforced in Taiwan] (Tokyo: 1966).

[15] Regarding the aborigines and their sad plight see Taiwan sōtokufu [Government-General of Taiwan], *Taiwan banjin jijō* [Conditions of Taiwan Aborigines] (Taihoku: 1900); Government of Formosa, *Report on the Control of Aborigines in Formosa* (Taihoku: 1911); Taiwan Sōtokufu, *Riban shikō* [Aborigines of Taiwan] (Taihoku: 1941); Janet B. M. McGovern, *Among the Head-Hunters of Formosa* (London: T. Fisher Unwin, 1922).

his elementary schools into a system of common schools (kōgakkō) in content and organization stamped with Izawa's mark.

Between 1898 and 1906 the Kodama administration halted Izawa's aspiration for all-out efforts toward universal elementary education. Instead, Kodama and Gotō concentrated upon common schools for the children of those Taiwanese wealthy enough to finance these institutions. Although Izawa had reached out to children and adults of various backgrounds, he had also made special overtures to the local gentry—or to what was left of them, since some of them chose to return to Ch'ing China rather than to suffer Japanese rule. Izawa told them that China's loss of Taiwan demonstrated that the Ch'ing emperor had lost the mandate of heaven and thus they would be well advised to send their children to the schools of the Japanese emperor, whose dynasty had ruled from time immemorial.[16] Kodama and Gotō followed this up with their own appeals to the gentry class, which they honored in a host of small ways. Like Izawa, they tried to make their schools attractive to gentry parents. This meant that the schools taught classical Chinese as well as a core of Japanese language, arithmetic, and some basic science, leavened with a sprinkling of singing and gymnastics to win the children.

In education as in all other areas within the colony, Gotō Shimpei, a colonial engineer on a par with Cecil Rhodes or Stamford Raffles—how he would have cherished such comparisons!—was the mastermind. Although he approved of a moderate version of Izawa's elementary school program, he had no intention of permitting Taiwanese to be prepared for attractive and remunerative employment that would not be made available to them. Native teachers would be needed, but even these would be limited. Gotō closed two of Izawa's normal schools for natives and carefully regulated the numbers admitted to the remaining teachers' training course for Taiwanese. Liberal education for Taiwanese in the Japanese Language School was stopped, and the parallel course in Taiwanese culture and language for Japanese was allowed to peter out. The most able and ambitious Taiwanese youths were urged to seek a career in modern medicine. When Gotō had arrived in Taihoku, he had found a small medical training center functioning within the Japanese hospital there. With budgetary aid from the Japanese Diet in 1899, he turned this into a medical school to train Taiwanese doctors. This institution's standards were lower than those of medical colleges (igaku senmon gakkō) in Japan, but it was fairly well equipped and designed to turn out

[16] Kaminuma, Izawa Shūji, pp. 215-217.

about fifty graduates a year.[17] From the beginning it concentrated upon medical problems relevant to the island, and its graduates played important roles in the public health and hygiene facilities that the colonial government initiated.[18] Few opportunities in fields other than teaching and medicine were available to graduates of the common schools. A handful of islanders were accepted as trainees at experimental stations set up to encourage improvements in sugar and other agricultural products, but such openings were rare.

Education of the children of Japanese nationals in the colony was not neglected. The primary schools (shōgakkō) erected for Japanese elementary school-aged children were made as grand as possible; great care was taken regarding their staffing and equipment. As secondary schools for boys, middle schools, and secondary schools for girls, higher girls' schools began to be established, these too were made as fine as resources permitted. Gotō considered it absolutely necessary that life for the Japanese community in Taiwan be made attractive enough to give those who had crossed the sea a vested influence in the colony, and he wanted to attract first-class men into the colonial service. But he also meant to remind native islanders of the superiority of their new rulers.[19] Thus the primary school belonged to a world different from that of the common school, and the secondary-school facilities for Japanese little resembled the humble institution that trained Taiwanese teachers. The Kodama administration did continue Izawa's interest in training Japanese to teach in the schools for Taiwanese. The administration's aim was colonial self-sufficiency and, although teachers from the ruling country were always welcome, they were not always available.

Despite limited post-elementary education in selected areas and special care for schools for Japanese nationals, after Izawa Shūji's departure it was the lower level of the Meiji educational system that Japanese colonial education in Taiwan sought to duplicate. The model was the track which had been designed to enlighten, discipline, and indoctrinate the Japanese masses. In Taiwan the main vehicle of that

[17] Mochiji Rokusaburō, Taiwan shokumin seisaku [The Colonial Policy of Taiwan] (Tokyo: Fuzanbō, 1912), p. 309.

[18] In 1907 the medical school took responsibility for training traditional native doctors. These practitioners of Chinese medicine were allowed to practice their healing arts, but the government-general kept track of them and hoped to replace them eventually with physicians trained by the medical school.

[19] Gotō admired the way that the British, as colonial rulers, instilled in natives a sense of awe for the British presence. See Mochiji, pp. 282-293, and Ide Kiwata, Taiwan chiseki shi [The Administrative Record in Taiwan] (Taihoku: Taiwan Nichi Nichi Shimpōsha, 1933), pp. 330-331.

track was the common school. Its first task was to enroll the children of wealthy and educated Taiwanese.

Unlike the ninety-five percent of the Taiwanese population made up of illiterate farmers, fisher-folk, and other humble laborers, such children did not dwell in an educational vacuum. Taiwan had been a Ch'ing frontier, integrated into the empire only in 1683 and not raised to provincial status until 1887. Yet, even in this remote outpost, prefectural and district academies as well as community schools (*i-hsüeh*) had been maintained, and countless private schools and tutors prepared young hopefuls to sit for the imperial examinations and to try for literati rank.[20] With the Japanese takeover and the exodus of Ch'ing officialdom, the Ch'ing government schools closed their doors, and the community schools were absorbed into the various types of private schools that the Japanese lumped together under the classification *shobō* (*shu-fang*, private school). Dislocation and disruption during the takeover affected the schools that continued. Perhaps this helps to explain the Japanese scorn for many of them; and it is possible that these traditional, one-teacher establishments reminded the Japanese of the commoner schools of their own not-so-distant "backward" Tokugawa past. Yet continue these schools did: in 1899 the *shobō* claimed approximately thirty thousand pupils.[21] It was these pupils rather than children who did not go to any school that the common schools were first designed to attract.

Later the Japanese in Taiwan would claim that classical Chinese had been made an important subject in the early common school curriculum in order to enable Japanese and Taiwanese to communicate.[22] In reality it was included to woo gentry parents. During their first four years in common school, children worked their way from the *Three Character Classic* primer up to the *Analects of Confucius* under the eagle eye of a native scholar. Only in the fifth and sixth grades did they learn to read these texts in tortured Japanese "upside-down" fashion.[23] Most attention was given to written and spoken Japanese, but Confucian ethics were inculcated with the Japanese written syllabary and pronounciation system. Confucian ethics were presented as Japanese ideals or universal principles shared by but not unique to

[20] By 1887 over two thousand individuals were reportedly studying for the imperial examinations, Inō Yoshinori, *Taiwan bunkashi* [Taiwan's Cultural History), 3 vols. (Tokyo: Tokō Shoin, 1928], II, 139.

[21] Taiwan kyōiku kai [Taiwan Education Society], *Taiwan kyōiku enkakushi* [A Record of the Development of Education in Taiwan; henceforth TKES] (Taihoku: 1939), p. 984.

[22] Ide, p. 331.

[23] TKES, pp. 232-233.

the Chinese people. Still, many gentry parents were probably not unhappy to know that their youngsters were being urged to behave in a filial fashion during daily Japanese language drill and the weekly ethics lesson as well as during the Chinese class, when a Chinese teacher taught the *Classic of Filial Piety*. The common school also tried to impart practical skills that could be appreciated by parents. In arithmetic classes, for example, pupils mastered the romanized letters of a local Taiwan dialect which were printed on bags of sugar produced in Taiwan. In schools with pupils from merchant families, lessons were given in the letter-writing styles employed in trade with the Chinese mainland.[24]

At the same time, gentry leaders were lectured about the pressing need for "modern" as well as traditional education. In March 1900, for instance, the government-general hosted a gala affair in Taihoku to which all ranking gentry were invited. Those who accepted—and approximately half of the island's top gentry did so—were wined and dined, shown over the colonial government's physical facilities, and given sermons in praise of the administration's schools.[25] In two separate addresses Gotō Shimpei stressed new pedagogical needs. He asked his audience to stop patronizing the Chinese private schools and to support the common schools and to send their brightest youths to the medical school. Japan's new education system, he claimed, had done much to enable Japan to meet the Western nations on their own ground, and Taiwan's future would similarly depend upon an ability to become a land of modern, educated people. Although the literati would continue to be respected for their Confucian learning and morality, they would have to become heavily involved in the new learning if they wished to retain their positions of social and intellectual eminence.[26]

On a third front, the government-general quietly worked to make *shobō* unattractive to gentry parents and children and more difficult for teachers to operate. The measures taken to accomplish this were similar to the Meiji governmental policies regarding private schooling. In November 1898 the island's regional administrations were ordered to closely supervise *shobō* affairs: hours of instruction were to be fixed, only government-approved textbooks were to be used, *shobō* instructors were to attend summer schools set up for them by the administration, Japanese language and arithmetic were gradually

[24] Kaminuma, *Izawa Shūji*, pp. 244-245.

[25] Ide, pp. 351-355; Harry J. Lamley, "The Taiwan Literati and Early Japanese Rule, 1895-1915" (Ph.D. Diss., University of Washington, 1964), pp. 354-369.

[26] Ide, pp. 352-355.

to be made required subjects.[27] The regional administrations were far too busy at this time to be able to closely observe a thousand or more *shobō*, but they did sometimes use their powers to suspend or dissolve Chinese schools thought to have "unsuitable facilities" or to be propagating anti-Japanese ideas.[28] And official interference in organization, hours, and curricula in some schools may have made these less convenient to Taiwanese parents. They remained a formidable rival to the common schools throughout the Kodama administration, but as the common school system expanded, *shobō* often came to supplement a Japanese language education rather than to serve as an alternative to it. In 1915 an observer noted, "After common school classes are dismissed many pupils go to a *shobō* to master Chinese learning."[29] By 1906 the number of *shobō* pupils had dropped to about twenty thousand, but from then until about 1918 these institutions more or less held their own.[30]

While Japanizing the *shobō* curricula and stealing their students, Japanese officials did not ignore the handful of Christian mission schools on the island at the time of the takeover. When Taiwan was ceded to Japan, Dominicans ran a school for girls near Takao, and a Canadian Presbyterian mission in the north at Tamsui and a British mission in the south at Tainan both operated Christian mission schools for young islanders of both sexes. In 1905 the Japanese promulgated private-school regulations to control these, but no clashes occurred between colonial officials and missionaries associated with these institutions. They were required to teach Japanese, but religious instruction—extremely difficult to teach in private schools in the ruling country after the private school regulations of 1899—was permitted. The pupils in these schools were so few that the colonial government could afford to be less strict than was the Ministry of Education in Japan, and thus court the good will of the Western missionaries. Smaller and less well-established Christian schools attached to local congregations were sometimes disbanded and their pupils invited to attend common schools. The missionaries seem to have regarded this interference as more than compensated for by the satisfaction of witness-

[27] TKES, pp. 974-975.

[28] Among the Taiwanese scholars who rejected invitations to teach Chinese in the common schools were patriots who not only kept alive the literary traditions of Chinese learning but reminded their pupils that "China in the future would rise again to its former glories." "The Taiwan Literati," p. 438.

[29] Takeuchi Sadayoshi, *Taiwan kanshū* [Customs of Taiwan] (Taihoku: Taiwan Nichi Nichi Shimpōsha, 1915), p. 635.

[30] E. Patricia Tsurumi, *Japanese Colonial Education in Taiwan* (Cambridge, Mass.: Harvard University Press, 1977), p. 246.

ing modern education advance at the expense of the "pagan" Chinese schooling that most of them abhorred.[31]

During the decade that followed, both *shobō* and missionary schools were targets of steadily intensifying pressure. Although not always enforced, the 1905 private school regulations spelled out prohibitions akin to those in Japan's private school regulations of 1899.[32] Colonial administrators tolerated the outstanding mission schools which predated Japanese rule, but they made it very difficult for anyone, including Japanese nationals, to open new private schools. *Shobō* were allowed to exist, but they were not encouraged.

Western missionaries had been educating a few girls and women for church work, but if gentry families taught any of their daughters to read they usually did so at home. In 1899, out of a total of 29,941 *shobō* pupils only 65 were female.[33] Everything thought possible was done to welcome girls to the common schools, but during the early decades they stayed away in droves. Taiwanese women with dress-making skills were employed in the schools to teach girls how to sew Chinese-style clothing. Nevertheless, Taiwanese who were willing to send their sons to school often kept their daughters at home. The problem was not new to Japanese educators: the primary-school attendance of girls had lagged far behind that of their brothers during the first two decades of the Meiji period. Patiently the colonial government turned a girls' school started by Izawa Shūji into a teachers' training school to prepare young Taiwanese women to teach domestic science and handicrafts in the common schools. Although most well-to-do Taiwanese families had to be persuaded that post-elementary education was desirable for daughters, this school steadily drew increasing numbers of would-be teachers. By 1918 its enrollment exceeded 200, and it had become fashionable as a finishing school for the daughters of some upper-class Taiwanese families.[34]

Careful educational planning gradually began to reap dividends. By 1905 individual literati were conspicuous patrons of Japanese education; several of their number initiated movements to open common schools in areas where schools had always been scarce or had never existed.[35] By 1920 twenty-five percent of the Taiwanese school-

---

[31] Although the extraordinary Canadian missionary, George Leslie MacKay, showed great respect for Confucian education, most missionaries saw anything to do with Confucianism as an enemy.

[32] TKES, pp. 991-992.

[33] TKES, p. 984.

[34] Yoshino Hidekimi, *Taiwan kyōikushi* [A History of Education in Taiwan] (Taihoku: Taiwan Nichi Nichi Shimpōsha, 1927), p. 332; Julean H. Arnold, *Education in Formosa* (Washington, D.C.: U.S. Bureau of Education, 1908), p. 44.

[35] "The Taiwan Literati," p. 432.

aged population was in common school: thirty-nine percent of the boys and nine percent of the girls.[36] By this year *shobō* influence was on the wane, and most of the 7,639 pupils still enrolled in them were probably also going to Japanese schools.[37] Despite objections from Taiwanese parents, some common schools had begun to drop Chinese language studies. Other schools put less and less emphasis on Chinese, which became an optional subject in 1922. Thereafter it was given little attention, although it was not officially discontinued until fifteen years later—about the time that the *shobō* became extinct.

This relatively positive Taiwanese response to Japanese education challenged the colonial government's determination to prevent islanders from being educated above their stations in life. Taiwanese leaders began to demand the kind of secondary-school facilities that they saw Japanese in the colony enjoying. Those who could afford to do so began to send their children to Japan, where they were free to enter schools of their choice, provided they could pass the required entrance examinations. Administrators ignored Taiwanese petitions for higher academic training for several years. Then an abortive assimilation movement led by veteran Japanese politico Itagaki Taisuke and enthusiastically supported by Japanese-educated Taiwanese made officials change their minds. The assimilation movement was quickly crushed in 1915 as soon as Itagaki returned to Tokyo, but policy makers decided it was safer to expand secondary schooling for Taiwanese within the colony rather than to witness an accelerated exodus of students to Japan, where they might become involved with "misguided" Japanese like Itagaki. Thus in 1915 the government-general reluctantly allowed the colony's first middle school for Taiwanese boys to be built at Taichū, largely with donations from wealthy Taiwanese. The Taichū middle school's standards were lower than that of a Japanese middle school, but there was no shortage of able applicants. It is some sort of tribute to the prestige of Japanese education by 1915 that Taiwanese leaders lobbied for a public middle school, teaching the academic subjects studied by Japanese middle-school students, rather than for a second medical school or a specialized vocational institution.[38]

Three years later the seventh governor-general, Akashi Motojirō, recognized not only Taiwanese pressures for post-elementary academic schooling, but the labor-power needs of the colony's expanding industries as well. He upgraded and expanded academic secondary schooling, founded secondary vocational schools and even

[36] TKES, pp. 408-410.
[37] TKES, pp. 985-986.
[38] E. P. Tsurumi, *Japanese Colonial Education in Taiwan*, pp. 66-71.

specialized colleges to produce Taiwanese trained in agricultural, forestry, commercial, and engineering professions and trades. He also raised the standards of the medical school and the teachers' training programs for Taiwanese and added a broad layer of two-year vocational schools between the common schools and the advanced tiers of the colony's educational facilities for native islanders. For the first time, all of the colony's public schools for Taiwanese became part of a single, coordinated system. This system offered educational opportunities inferior to what schools for Japanese provided in the home islands and in Taiwan, and all Taiwanese continued to be denied access to the Japanese nationals' facilities in the colony. Still, qualitatively and quantitatively, Governor-General Akashi improved Taiwanese post-elementary schooling substantially, and his education rescript of 1919 was warmly received by Taiwanese leaders.

Old Taiwan hands among his subordinates reacted differently. They vehemently opposed the expansion. Some of them had been in the administration since the days when Gotō Shimpei had laid out the gradual assimilation policy, with its emphasis on a slow growth of elementary school facilities and its careful containment of higher schooling. They recalled how well Gotō had understood the difficulties and dangers of trying to alter the Taiwanese too rapidly. As he had bluntly put it twenty years earlier, "You do not turn a flounder into a sea bream overnight."[39] Subordinates who had for years been carrying out gradualist policies in the name of successive governors-general thought that they, rather than a new governor-general from Tokyo, knew best what was possible and practical in Taiwan. But Lieutenant-General Akashi was an officer used to obedience from his troops, and characteristically he overruled the strong objections of his staff.[40] Undoubtedly he was aided in this not only by Taiwanese pressure for more and better higher education but also by tacit support from the Japanese managers in public and private industry who, because of an upsurge in demands for skilled labor in the ruling country, were finding fewer and fewer skilled Japanese workers available to colonial industries.[41]

[39] Tsurumi Yūsuke, Gotō Shimpei den [A Biography of Gotō Shimpei], 4 vols. (Tokyo: Gotō Shimpei Denki Hensankai, 1937-1938), II, 25-26.

[40] Komori Tokuji, Akashi Motojirō (Taihoku: Taiwan Nichi Nichi Shimpōsha, 1928), I, pp. 50-59.

[41] The First World War, which stimulated the Japanese economy remarkably, created a strong demand for skilled workers in industries in Japan. Thus there were fewer of these available for employment in the colonial economy, which also surged ahead during the war. Yanaihara Tadao, "Teikokushugika no Taiwan" [Taiwan under Im-

The ink was barely dry on Akashi's education rescript before it was apparent that an even greater overhaul was in store for education in Taiwan. Akashi's death in October 1919 gave Prime Minister Hara Kei the opportunity to make the kind of reforms in the governing structures of Taiwan and Korea that he had long favored.[42] To carry out his reform program in Taiwan he appointed Den Kenjirō as the colony's first civilian governor-general. Reform meant a policy switch from gradual to accelerated assimilation of the colonized people under civilian instead of military governors-general. Educational change was a key part of the reform package.

In 1922 Den replaced Akashi's education rescript with his own— loudly hailed by the Japanese as an edict of integration and equal treatment. Under it, the prestigious primary schools, previously the preserve of the children of Japanese colonials, were made available to Taiwanese children with fluency in the Japanese language. The rest of the Taiwanese elementary school pupils would continue to attend common school. There is some evidence that Den would have liked to integrate all elementary schools.[43] Certainly the results of extensive testing of both Taiwanese and Japanese schoolchildren done by education experts for Den's administration demonstrated that the twenty-eight percent of the Taiwanese school-age population in common school could more than hold its own with the ninety-seven percent of the Japanese colonists' school-age population attending primary school.[44] But thorough integration would have forced Japanese children in primary schools to share their superior facilities and better-qualified teachers with large numbers of Taiwanese youngsters and to give up their favorable teacher-pupil rations. Yet to admit that Japanese children could not be asked to make sacrifices would be embarrassing for an administration proclaiming a policy of assimilation and equal treatment. Thus "Japanese language backwardness" provided a convenient excuse for restricting Taiwanese admission to the better-equipped schools. At the same time, the common school curriculum was brought closer to that of the primary school, and during Den's tenure from 1919 to 1923 common schools increased

perialism], in *Yanaihara Tadao zenshū* [Collected Works of Yanaihara Tadao], 29 vols. (Tokyo: Iwanami, 1963-1965), II, p. 344.

[42] E. P. Tsurumi, *Japanese Colonial Education in Taiwan*, p. 91.

[43] See, for example, Den's first major policy speech, in Kuroda Kōshirō, *Den Kenjirō den* [A Biography of Den Kenjirō] (Tokyo: Den Kenjirō Denki Hensankai, 1932), pp. 390-404.

[44] Taiwan sōtokufu, *Taiwan ni okeru gakkō jidō ni kan suru kenkyū* [A Study of School-Children in Taiwan] (Taihoku: 1923). This work was meant for circulation within the government-general only. It was clearly marked "not for sale."

from 438 to 715 and the numbers of children attending them almost doubled.[45]

The new rescript integrated all post-elementary facilities. Theoretically all secondary and higher schools became equally open to Japanese and Taiwanese alike. In actual practice, however, officials were far from blind to the ethnic origins of applicants to the most prestigious schools. The rescript raised the standards of the formerly all-Taiwanese facilities and provided for university preparatory training and university education. When Taihoku Imperial University opened its gates in 1928, the colony was declared to have all the educational tiers of Japan's own education system. On paper and in the pious speeches of officials, Taiwanese educational opportunities took giant steps forward, but the Japanese who controlled school admissions did not abandon their long-standing habit of putting the interests of the rapidly growing Japanese community first. Japanese soon swamped the best of the formerly all-Taiwanese schools—even the medical school, long a Taiwanese stronghold—while only a few native islanders were able to enter the formerly Japanese elite institutions. It was still easier for Taiwanese to get into famous schools in Japan than to gain admittance to the "integrated" ones in the colony.[46]

Taiwanese critics were not slow to point out that this was so. Loudly mocking the government-general's self-congratulatory declarations, they denounced their rulers as rank hypocrites. They began to state their educational grievances in a new fashion: by means of an anti-colonial movement which, until it was completely suppressed in the middle of the 1930's, articulated widespread discontent with many aspects of Japanese rule. The anti-colonial movement had a heroic left wing, which, although it had gained impressive support by the late 1920's, was always under heavy attack from the colonial police. The conservative wing, because it took a mild reformist approach and pressed its demands legalistically through constitutional means—especially through a petition movement for home rule—was tolerated for a decade and a half, even though the colonial government tried hard to discourage it. At the core of the conservatives' demands, which were enthusiastically supported by upper- and middle-class Taiwanese, were desires for more and better-quality Japanese-style education. They called on the regime to introduce compulsory elementary schooling for all children in Taiwan, as well as to stop protecting the monopoly of higher educational facilities enjoyed by Japanese colonials. The conservative anti-colonialists and their followers

[45] TKES, p. 409.
[46] E. P. Tsurumi, *Japanese Colonial Education in Taiwan*, pp. 102-103.

were almost all Japanese-educated themselves, and for their children they sought the best Japanese education possible. Although some of them also campaigned for Taiwanese vernaculars to be taught in the schools and for more encouragement to be given to Chinese and Taiwanese culture, none of them questioned the necessity or desirability of Japanese education—as more radical anti-Japanese critics did. Some analysts have regarded the reformist approach as purely tactical, employed to prevent their organizations from being smashed as the radicals' were.[47] Yet the business and other connections of the conservatives, leaders and followers alike, and their attitude toward Japanese education suggests that, although they wanted a better place in the world than their conquerors had created, they did not necessarily reject that world itself. They lashed out at the niggardly provisions for their children's education in comparison with those of colonial Japanese and at the fact that they were financing the schooling of both ethnic groups. They did not attack the education system itself.[48]

Despite protests from Taiwanese political activists, Den Kenjirō's rescript of 1922 was the last major educational reform in Taiwan. Thereafter common schools continued to become gradually more and more like primary schools. They did not, however, cease to be shortchanged in teacher-pupil ratios, physical facilities, and trained teachers. In the wartime atmosphere of 1942 common schools and primary schools were given similar names, but little else changed. The following year, with more than sixty-five percent of Taiwanese children in school—including more than half of the female school-age population—the administration inaugurated compulsory elementary education, which managed to get more than seventy percent of Taiwanese children into school before defeat in the Pacific War ended Japanese rule in 1945.

Post-elementary schools continued to be dominated by Japanese, but their numbers increased, so both ethnic groups gained new educational opportunities. The only post-elementary institution to escape Japanese dominance was the lowest level vocational school, offering two- or three-year courses. Most of these were agricultural schools; but some taught commercial, engineering, or fishery skills,

[47] See Ts'ai P'ei-huo et al., *T'ai-wan min-tsu yün-tung shih* [A History of the Taiwanese Nationalist Movement] (Taipei: Tsu-li wan-pao ts'ung-shu pien-chi wei-yuan-hui, 1971); Ching-chih Chen, "Japanese Socio-Political Control in Taiwan, 1895-1945" (Ph.D. Diss., Harvard University, 1973); Edward I-te Chen, "Formosan Political Movements under Japanese Colonial Rule, 1914-1937," in *Journal of Asian Studies*, 31.3 (May 1972), pp. 477-497.

[48] See E. P. Tsurumi, *Japanese Colonial Education in Taiwan*, pp. 177-211.

one was a women's technical institute, and by 1940 at least twenty were schools of home economics for women.[49]

Taihoku Imperial University, the seventh of Japan's imperial universities to be established, began with a faculty of literature and politics and a faculty of science and agriculture; in 1936 a medical faculty was fashioned out of part of the medical school; and in 1943 agriculture and science split into separate faculties. Taihoku was organized primarily for research focusing on Taiwan, South China, and the South Seas, and thus, although it had admirably low student-faculty ratios, the number of students it trained was relatively few. Taiwanese difficulties in gaining entrance were compounded by the practice of favoring Japanese over Taiwanese applicants.[50]

The flow of students to Japan continued unabated. In 1922 the government-general put the Taiwanese student population in Japan at about 2,400; these estimates were up to 7,000 by 1942.[51] Since transportation between the colony and ports in Japan was available and Taiwanese needed no visas or passports to make the journey, there may have been many more—perhaps thousands more—who made it to Japan before 1945, but were never included in official statistics. Of the more than 7,000 listed for 1942, about 750 were female.[52] Girls, in lesser but increasing numbers, were studying in Japan, and like their brothers often heading for medical college. The importance of these pioneers, who provided female role models which never before existed, far exceeded their number. By the end of the colonial period Taiwanese women had been trained both in the colony and in Japan for careers in medicine, midwifery, dentistry, pedagogy, commerce, home economics, esthetics, economics, and science.[53]

Between 1922 and 1945 private schools continued to play a marginal role in Taiwan's education system. Those which existed were mainly middle schools or higher girls' schools. However, none of these received official recognition from the colonial government before 1938, and therefore before that date none of their graduates was entitled to sit for examinations to higher institutions. Even during

[49] Taiwan sōtokufu, *Taiwan sōtokufu daiyonjūichi tōkeisho* [Taiwan Government-General Statistical Yearbook Number Forty-one] (Taihoku: 1940), pp. 84-85.

[50] T'ai-wan-sheng hsing-cheng chang-kuan-shu t'ung-chi-shih, ed., *T'ai-wan-sheng wu-shih-i-nien-lai t'ung-chi t'i-yao* [A Statistical Summary of the Province of Taiwan for the Past Fifty-one Years; henceforth TWT] (Taipei: 1946), pp. 1214-1215.

[51] Taiwan tsūshinsha, *Taiwan nenkan 1944* [Taiwan Yearbook 1944] (Taihoku: 1944), p. 505.

[52] *Ibid.*

[53] Chang Tzu-hui, ed., *T'ai-wan shih jen chih* [A Who's Who of Taiwan] (Taipei: Kuo-kang Ch'u-pan Shē, 1946), pp. 219, 223.

the early 1940's, when about a half a dozen private secondary schools had received accreditation, very few of their graduates went on to higher schooling.[54] Since the education provided by a higher girls' school—public or private—was usually terminal, private schools for girls were better able to satisfy Taiwanese demands than could private middle schools. The former were always inundated with student applications.[55]

By 1922 there were less than 100 *shobō* teaching a few thousand pupils compulsory lessons in Japanese language, ethics, and mathematics as well as Chinese language and literature; in 1940 there were only 17 left with fewer than 1,000 students.[56] When compulsory education was introduced in 1943 they were banned, but by that time there were few doors to close and few pupils to send home. Although they had been forced to add the common school's core subjects to their curricula, *shobō* did not have the latter's alluring music exercises nor the much appreciated physical education program.

The sports and games which Japanese public schooling introduced to Taiwan had helped to bring about the *shobō's* demise. When the parents of the first Taiwanese students at Izawa's Japanese Language School saw their children performing gymnastic drills, they were horrified. They were sure that their offspring were being trained to serve as soldiers. Chinese schooling had never been associated with physical exercise. Indeed, traditional Confucian values opposed participation in athletics because "The body, hair, and skin are received from parents, [and thus] none should dare to injure or ruin them."[57] Track and field meets, competitive league games, and physical culture displays soon altered this perception. The genuine pleasure that boys and girls took in playing and watching games was communicated to their elders. Beginning in 1912 Taiwanese adults began to organize local athletic meets, and in the countryside whole villages eventually turned out for radio calisthenics. Baseball became especially popular: leagues were organized for amateur players of various ages. Visits to Taiwan by famous Japanese baseball teams—islanders watched the Waseda University team play in 1916—helped to boost the game's already extraordinary popularity. By the end of the Japanese period, Taiwanese of all classes had become enthusiasts for the

[54] Lin Ching-ming, *Shirarezaru Taiwan: Taiwan kokuritsu undōka no sakeki* (The Taiwan Yet To Be Known: The Cry of Taiwanese Independence Activists) (Tokyo: Sanshōdō, 1970), p. 74.

[55] *Taiwan nenkan 1942*, p. 240; *Taiwan nenkan 1944*, p. 507.

[56] E. P. Tsurumi, *Japanese Colonial Education in Taiwan*, p. 246.

[57] Chiu-sam Tsang, *Nationalism in School Education in China* (Hongkong: Progressive Publishers, 1933) p. 82.

sports and games introduced along with Japanese education; athletics appear to have created substantial Taiwanese good will toward their rulers.

To Be Educated Was To Be Anti-Japanese: Korea, 1905-1945

Although Korea was not annexed until 1910, Japanese educational policies began to be enforced in the peninsula at least from the beginning of the protectorate. In Korea, Japanese educational aims, approaches, and structures were similar to those in Taiwan. Like the natives of the older colony, Koreans were to be transformed gradually into loyal Japanese subjects equipped for modern but humble life and work. In Korea too the Japanese tried to concentrate upon slow but steady expansion of basic elementary education and to discourage "unnecessary" higher education; but, as in Taiwan, they ended up as reluctant architects of a reproduction—albeit an inferior "colonial" reproduction—of the ruling country's entire education system. During the early days especially, traditional Chinese-style private schools were accommodated and overtures were made to Confucian scholars. Educational affairs had a similar status in both governments-general, and educational affairs staff were assigned similar duties.[58] The curriculum of the ordinary school (*futsu gakkō*) in Korea was almost identical to that of the common school of Taiwan, and public secondary and higher facilities in the two colonies were very similar too. In Korea, as well as in Taiwan, the education system was revamped in 1922 by a rescript proclaiming integration and assimilation. In fact, from pre-protectorate days, the Japanese in Korea looked to Taiwan for educational models for Korea: Japanese "advisors" to the hard-pressed Yi government called in Gotō Shimpei as an educational consultant in 1903.[59] Nevertheless, it became rapidly apparent that education in Korea was not going to be quite like education in Taiwan.

For one thing, the situation that existed before the protectorate was proclaimed was far more complex. In addition to the Korean equivalent of Taiwan's pre-1895 Chinese schools, there existed a variety of educational institutions. Korea's traditional Chinese schools were of two types: in each county the royal government sponsored a *hyanggyo*, a provincial school run by the local county administration; and everywhere in the land could be found *sŏdang* (shōdō) private schools patronized by the *yangban*, Korea's aristocrat class, and by

[58] *Meiji iko kyōiku seido hattatsushi*, X, 577-578; *ibid.*, XI, 1045.

[59] For Gotō's address to Korean officials in Seoul see Ōno Ken'ichi, *Chōsen kyōiku mondai kanaken* [Views on the Problems of Education in Korea] (Keijō: Chōsen Kyōiku Kai, 1936), pp. 19-28.

others who desired the Chinese classical education customarily acquired by upper-class Koreans. As in Taiwan, Western missionaries had been active in the peninsula from about the 1880's, but in even greater numbers, and the number of Korean converts had grown more rapidly. Although the missionaries began with an evangelical rather than an educational emphasis, they soon found that in order to convert they had to teach. They also found that it was extremely difficult and perhaps not wholly desirable to limit mission education to Christian Koreans only.[60] By the turn of the century they had not only established numerous elementary schools offering basic literacy in simple Korean, but were rapidly founding secondary schools and even colleges for both young men and young women.[61] In the 1890's, a reforming Yi government laid the groundwork for what was intended to be a modern education system: Western-style elementary schools, middle schools, foreign-language schools, vocational schools, a normal school, and a medical school were opened.[62] About the same time, public-spirited Koreans began to found private schools which also taught Western-style subjects and employed the *onmun*, the Korean vernacular script which was beginning to be used in newspapers, another sign that times were changing.[63] By 1905 a country-wide movement of "education for the nation" was underway, and as a result of this burst of patriotic energy, night schools, laborers' schools, and short-term training centers were opened in urban areas. The movement also brought changes in curricula of some *sŏdang*, and everywhere books and periodicals discussing education found eager readers.[64]

Japanese advisors to the Korean government, like Shidehara Hiroshi, who had been sent to Seoul in 1904 to increase Japanese educational influence there, were alarmed by the "education for the nation" movement. As soon as Korea was made a protectorate in 1905,

[60] James Earnest Fischer, *Democracy and Mission Education in Korea* (New York: Bureau of Publications, Teachers' College, Columbia University, 1928), pp. 19-28.

[61] Americans were especially active. In 1903 the U.S. Northern Presbyterian Mission founded a medical and pharmaecological college; three years later Union Christian College was organized along the lines of an American denominational college; in 1910 Mrs. M. F. Scranton founded Ewha College for women.

[62] For details of the Yi government schools, see Pak Kyŏng-sik, *Nihon teikokushugi no Chōsen shihai* [Rule of Korea under Japanese Imperialism], 2 vols. (Tokyo: Aoki Shoten, 1973), I, 145; Han Ki-ŏn, *Kankoku kyōikushi* [A History of Korean Education], trs. by Han Ki-ŏn, and Inoue Yoshimi (Kashiwa-shi, Chiba: Kashiwa-shi, 1960), p. 243.

[63] Chong-sik Lee, *The Politics of Korean Nationalism* (Berkeley: University of California Press, 1963), p. 90.

[64] Pak, *Nihon teikokushugi no Chōsen shihai*, I, 145.

the Japanese moved against this surge of Korean consciousness. The residency-general took over the most promising of the Yi government's Western-style schools, but it shut the doors of many private schools—on the grounds that they were strongholds of actual or potential anti-Japanese sentiment. Schools with clearly identifiable nationalistic tendencies were outlawed at once, but no private schools other than the *sŏdang* escaped hostile scrutiny. Schools organized by Christians or by other religious groups were not above suspicion. All private schools were required to obtain approval of the residency-general for continued operation, but by the end of 1909 only 820 out of 1,995 requests from private schools for permission to conduct classes had been granted.[65]

After annexation of Korea the government-general came down even harder upon "education for the nation." The colony's first governor-general, Terauchi Masatake, immediately made his position clear in a policy speech expressing Japanese fears regarding the connection between Korean private education and national consciousness.

Among the private schools, there are schools that teach songs and use other materials which encourage independence and incite rebellion against the Japanese empire. This is forbidden, and utmost care must be exercised to ensure that the prohibition of these activities is enforced. Koreans themselves should deeply reflect upon the consequences of fostering this type of thought. For instance, the cry for independence will eventually lead Koreans to rebel against Japan. Will this promote the happiness of Koreans? Japan will just suppress such rebellion with force. This will not hurt Japan; only Koreans will suffer.[66]

The authorities found "the number of private schools with 'Independence to Great Korea' and 'Restoration of the State' printed on posters or written on their school walls to be countless."[67] Since such schools were deemed to be "teaching nationalistic philosophy, language, and economics," they were very quickly put out of business.

Officials also had some doubts about the "loyalty" of Christian schools, some of which were run directly by foreigners. As in Japan

[65] Pak, *Nihon teikokushugi no Chōsen shihai*, I, 147.

[66] Ōno, *Chōsen kyōiku mondai kanken*, p. 31.

[67] Kang Tŏk-sang, "Kempei seijika no Chōsen" [Korea Under Military Police Government], in *Rekishigaku kenkyū* [Historical Studies], No. 321, quoted in Park, I, 158. See also Yuge Kotarŏ, *Chōsen no kyōiku* [Education in Korea] (Tokyo: Jiyū Tokyūsha, 1923), pp. 73-80; and Yagi Hobuo, *Gakusei kaikaku to gimu kyōiku* [Reform of the Education System and Compulsory Education] (Keijō: Ryokki Renmei, 1940), pp. 47-48.

before the turn of the century, however, Western missionaries were protected by their treaty privileges and, at any rate, the Japanese could not afford to provoke powerful Western governments.[68] There were also some genuine respect for some of the missionaries' educational work. Japanese authorities were much more willing to acknowledge that the Christian missionaries had been pioneers of modern, scientific education in Korea than they were to give any credit to the Yi educational innovations of the 1890's.[69] They also praised the missionaries for their pedagogical efforts on behalf of women and girls, who in traditional Korea had neither been sent to school nor encouraged to become scholars.[70] On the other hand, missionaries were sometimes suspected of being "too close" to their Korean converts, who like the rest of their compatriots did not welcome Japanese rule. Their very presence was sometimes an annoyance: witnesses to the harshness of Japanese rule, they were in the habit of reporting on events from their own point of view rather than from that of the government-general.[71]

Administrators viewed Confucian scholars and the private schools which trained them much more favorably. For centuries both Koreans and Japanese had shared in the Chinese cultural tradition, which emphasized written Chinese, the teachings of the Chinese sages, and a range of values: benevolent rule, loyalty, hierarchical status relations, and family morality. When the Japanese honored this tradition, they made it clear that they were respecting their own past as well as that of upper-class Koreans. They founded a new Confucian academy to promote study of the Confucian classics and to hold religious services for the Chinese sages.[72] As in Taiwan, they hired native scholars to teach Chinese studies in Japanese public school; but their

[68] In his outline of educational policy, Terauchi mentioned that private schools run by foreign missionaries must be handled very carefully because "although supervisory authority belongs fundamentally to the government, historically under the name of extraterritoriality these schools have been left alone." However he stressed that "religion and politics must not be mixed." Ōno, Chōsen kyōiku mondai kanken, p. 32.

[69] Shibata Yoshisaburō, "Bunka seiji to gakusei kaikaku" [Civil politics and revision of the education system], in Chōsen shimbunsha ed., Chōsen tōchi no hihan [Recollections and Criticism of the Administration in Korea] (Keijō: 1936), p. 215, and Yuge, pp. 77-80.

[70] Ōno, Chōsen kyōiku mondai kanken, p. 12.

[71] See Fischer. For an excellent sketch of the Western missionaries in Korea see Frank Baldwin, "Missionaries and the March First Movement: Can Moral Men be Neutral? in Andrew C. Nahm, ed., Korea Under Japanese Colonial Rule (Kalamazoo: Center for Korean Studies, Institute of International and Area Studies, Western Michigan University, 1973).

[72] Chōsen Sōtokufu, Chōsen kyōiku yōran [A Survey of Education in Korea] (Keijō: 1919), pp. 108-109.

accommodation policy in this instant went even further, as native teachers in the ordinary schools (*futsu gakkō*)—counterparts of the common schools—were permitted to teach Korean language along with Chinese. As in Taiwan the government-general undertook restoration of the damage done to Confucius' temple during the takeover, so the administration of Terauchi Masatake sought to maintain the *hyanggyo* and its adjoining temple in each county.[73] And the more than sixteen thousand *sŏdang* that were scattered throughout the peninsula received more toleration than did the *shobō* of Taiwan.

Regulations governing *sŏdang* were not promulgated until 1918, and it was 1929 before serious measures became compulsory. The 1918 regulations, which made allowances for regional conditions in a country geographically diverse, declared that Japanese language and arithmetic were to be added to *sŏdang* curricula where possible and practical, that *sŏdang* teachers were to be encouraged to take instruction from the staff in public elementary schools, and that instead of "unsuitable textbooks" Japanese-edited editions of the Chinese classics should be used in the *sŏdang*.[74] The 1929 reform required that government-general textbooks for Japanese, Korean, and arithmetic classes be used and that pupils be taught Japanese ethics, including loyalty to the emperor.[75]

This toleration was not only a function of reconciliation and respect toward Confucian scholarship and its *yangban* patrons, and of Korea's rugged geography, with its as yet primitive transportation and communication in an area six times as large as Taiwan's. In Meiji Japan the government had supported some private schools as second-best makeshift substitutes for government schools, which would replace them as soon as practical. Until a public school could be built, a local community was encouraged to seek private education. As soon as a public school was operating all official aid and encouragement to private institutions were withdrawn.[76] This pattern was reproduced in the *sŏdang* policies of Japanese administrators in Korea. The *sŏdang* were viewed as makeshift substitutes—to be maintained at private Korean expense—until the administration's ordinary schools could be built. When an ordinary school was opened, the *sŏdang* pu-

---

[73] Kaminuma, pp. 243-244 and Wi Jo Kang, "Japanese Rule and Korean Confucianism," in Nakm, p. 68.

[74] *Chōsen kyōiku yōran*, pp. 90-91.

[75] Ōno, p. 246, and Wi Jo Kang, p. 70.

[76] *Meiji ikō kyōiku seido hattatsushi*, II, 151-154; Mombushō, *Gakusei kyūjūnenshi* [A Ninety-Year History of the Education System] (Tokyo: 1964), p. 18; Kaigo, pp. 984-986.

pils in the district were legally required to attend it.[77] In districts which lacked public schools the administration encouraged *sŏdang* education "for the time being."

The Ordinary School Rescript was promulgated in 1906, but authorities had to resort to extreme measures to get youngsters into the ordinary schools. It was commonplace enough for Japanese public schools to entice pupils by providing them with textbooks, school supplies, and lunches free of charge, or to send the *myŏn* (district) chief and the police to pressure families to send their children to school. Sometimes pupil-hungry officials went so far as to hold parents in detention and release them only on condition that their children attend school.[78] The segment of the urban population that was already patronizing modern educational facilities by 1905 was appalled at the indiscriminate suppression of "education for the nation" and the high-handed attitude toward all Korean private schools. It is no wonder that Terauchi's administration and that of Governor-General Hasegawa Yoshimichi from 1916 to 1919 sought to win the *yangban* class by tolerating their traditional academies. The *yangban* were far more willing to pay for *sŏdang*, even *sŏdang* in which Japanese language and arithmetic were being gradually added, than they would have been to finance large numbers of modern Japanese schools. And as in Japan and Taiwan, local communities were being made to pay for local education.

Gradually the ordinary schools managed both to enroll and to keep pupils. By 1918 there were 464 ordinary schools with nearly 88,000 pupils of whom one in 7 was female.[79] At the same time there were 26 private ordinary schools serving 2,830 pupils, including 555 girls.[80] The combined private and public ordinary school populations amounted to about four percent of the Korean elementary school-aged population.[81] By 1918 the Ordinary School Rescript was twelve years old, and this four percent was close to the achievement of the common schools in Taiwan: between five and six percent of Taiwanese children in school by 1910, twelve years after the Common School Regulations had been introduced. In 1918, over 24,000 *sŏdang* claimed enrollments totalling 1,148,516.[82]

---

[77] Han Ki-ŏn, *Kankoku kyōikushi*, pp. 264–265.

[78] Ebihara, I, 244–245; C. I. Eugene Kim, "Japanese Colonial Education and Korea's Nation Building," in C. I. Eugene Kim, ed., *A Pattern of Political Development: Korea* (Korea Research and Publication, 1964), pp. 7–8; Chung Tai-shi, " 'Yesterday' of Korean Education," *Korea Journal*, 3.4 (April 1, 1963), p. 18.

[79] *Chōsen kyōiku yōran*, pp. 44–46.

[80] *Ibid.*, p. 48.

[81] Ōno, *Chōsen kyōiku mondai kanken*, p. 397.

[82] *Chōsen kyōiku yōran*, p. 92

The ordinary school's course was two years shorter than that of Taiwan's six-year common school; and, as mentioned above, Korean language was taught along with Chinese classics. In most other respects, however, the two types of school were very similar. In both, the largest amount of time was devoted to Japanese language; arithmetic ranked second in importance; Korean and Chinese lessons in ordinary school received the same attention that Chinese did in the common school until 1918; other subjects included music, physical education, vocational studies, and sewing and handicrafts for girls. Formal ethics lessons were given only once or twice a week, but teachers in both colonies were urged to inculcate "the Japanese spirit" with everything that they taught.

The Terauchi administration took over what were considered the most promising of the Yi government schools, in some of which Japanese "advisors" had been involved with before 1905. It would have been wasteful and impolitic to close the doors of the best equipped of the private secondary and tertiary facilities, especially those run by foreign missionaries. Hence, government-general planners were faced with the formidable task of welding various kinds of post-elementary educational institutions into orderly levels of secondary and college schooling. Their post-elementary-school inheritance included both public and private insitutions offering academic and vocational training in a wide range of fields. Many of the secondary vocational institutes taught agriculture and forestry, but there were also commercial and engineering schools and, at the college level, religion, liberal arts, pharmacological, and medical studies. A proper status and function had to be assigned to each government-general institution; private schools and colleges had to be supervised and made as Japanese as possible. Those assigned to attack these problems may well have longed for a transfer to the much simpler scene in Taiwan.

Pre-Japanese educational developments in Korea, then, forced the government-general into a commitment to secondary and tertiary education for Koreans that its counterpart in Taiwan did not have to make. The Japanese in Korea were no more willing to see the colonized rise above their proper stations in life than were Japanese colonial rulers anywhere else. They made sure that the post-elementary institutions for Koreans were lower in standard than for their counterparts in Japan and that public facilities served as models for the private schools and colleges. But it was a constant struggle to keep private education, always in demand, in its proper place on the periphery of post-elementary education in Korea. Because of the strength of private education—in terms of both its prestige and the numbers it served—the colonial government had to make some concessions.

Graduates of private schools could not be completely barred from entrance to public higher education, nor could their professional credentials be completely ignored by Japanese employers.[83]

Although the Yi government schools included a normal school and although teachers' training had been given a great deal of attention by the earliest administrators in Taiwan, Terauchi and Hasegawa do not seem to have worried much about formal training for Korean teachers of ordinary schools. From the beginning more than twice as many Koreans as Japanese taught in the ordinary school[84] but no great care seems to have been taken regarding their training. No normal school rescript appeared among the 1910 school rescripts to govern almost every other kind of school, and the ordinance covering all schools issued the following year simply noted that a one-year course to train teachers was to be set up in *Kōtō futsu gakkō*, secondary academic schools for young men, and in *joshi kōtō futsu gakkō*, the equivalent for young women. Realization of the need to train Koreans appears to have been an afterthought: in 1913 a temporary teachers' training center attached to Keijo Kōtō Futsu Gakkō was split into two sections, one to produce Korean teachers for ordinary schools and the other to prepare Japanese to teach in the same institutions.[85] Normal schools designed to train Koreans for this occupation came only after 1919.

The year 1919 was even more important for Japanese education in Korea than was the case in Taiwan. The vivid and tragic events of that year finally convinced even the Japanese of what everyone else in the peninsula already knew: acceptance of Japanese schooling did not mean docile loyalty to Japan. What began on March 1, 1919, the day set for the Korean king's funeral, as a peaceful procession to petition the government-general to answer Korean grievances against Japanese rule, soon turned into a peaceful but militant demonstration joined by Koreans in all walks of life in all parts of the country, calling for independence from Japanese rule. Labeling peaceful demonstrators as rioting rebels, government-general armies ruthlessly suppressed protestors all over the colony. Despite the uneven contest—soldiers with modern firearms who did not hesitate to shoot unarmed, passive civilians—it took the Japanese two months, ap-

[83] Abe Munemitsu and Abe Hiroshi, eds., *Kankoku to Taiwan no kyōiku kaihatsu* [The Development of Education in Korea and Taiwan] (Tokyo: Ajiya Keizai Kenkyūjo, 1973), pp. 25-34.

[84] *Chosen kyoiku yōran*, p. 46.

[85] Chōsen Sōtokufu, *Chōsen sōtokufu shisei sanjūnenshi* [Thirty Years of Government-General Administration in Korea] (Keijō: 1940), p. 76.

proximately 2,000 Korean deaths, and almost 20,000 Korean arrests to silence the stubborn cries for independence.[86]

Viciously and unhesitantly the Japanese stamped out the rebellion, but they could not help noticing that public as well as private school students took a very active part in it. And, historically appearing in significant numbers in the public arena for the first time, female students could be seen demonstrating side by side with male students.

> In the early stages of the movement, only the students of middle school level and higher were involved, but pupils in elementary schools participated later. Japanese government statistics indicate that out of a student population of 133,557 there were 11,113 who took part, mostly from the middle schools and above. Immediately after the movement began, most schools closed for several weeks. Those in Seoul were not reopened until June. The school closings, caused either by student or teacher strikes, contributed to what might be called, from the Japanese viewpoint, a subversive atmosphere.[87]

Acceptance of Japanese colonial education, then, did not necessarily result in acceptance of Japanese culture and values, inculcation of which was the main purpose of that education. As the best scholarship on Japanese rule has repeatedly pointed out, Japanese efforts at assimilation through education in Korea played a central role in the formation of a modern Korean nationalist consciousness which was bitterly anti-Japanese.[88] Contemporary Japanese of all political persuasions had to agree. Japanese liberals like Yoshino Sakuzō and Yanaihara Tadao were horrified by the systematic terror in the government-general's response to the rebellion.[89] Other Japanese felt that both Koreans and Japanese had been in the wrong. And even colonial governmental officials and their lackeys—most of the Japanese residents in Korea—who believed that Japanese behavior during the suppression had been blameless, felt that something had gone wrong with the schools.

A typical example of the latter line of thought was forcefully articulated in Shin Chōsen (New Korea), a book published in Keijō (Seoul) in 1925. Its author, Aoyagi Tsunatarō (whose ideas regarding the

---

[86] For information on those arrested see Kondō Ken'ichi, Banzai sōjō jiken [The Independence Disturbance Affair] (Tokyo: Yūhō Kyokai, 1964), pp. 179-182.

[87] Lee, The Politics of Korean Nationalism, p. 120.

[88] See Lee; Kondō; Yamabe Kentarō, Nihon tōchika no Chōsen [Korea under Japanese Rule] (Tokyo: Iwanami, 1971).

[89] See Mark R. Peattie, "Japanese Attitudes Towards Colonialism, 1895-1945" in this volume for a discussion of the views of Yoshino Sakuzō and Yanaihara Tadao.

"moral degeneracy" of Korea are discussed in Mark Peattie's essay in this volume), spoke for many of his fellow Japanese in the colony as he uneasily discussed the post-rebellion challenge. Sadly he reported that nearly all educated Koreans, even those who were fluent in Japanese—even those who had studied in Japan—rejected Japanese rule. This was true among Confucianists, he sighed, as it was among the modern educated. The "independence problem" existed in the countryside as well as among the over-educated who lived in urban areas. The schools had definitely failed to do the job assigned to them.

In Aoyagi's view, the integration policy introduced by Prime Minister Hara Kei was a sound approach to the problem. He approved of the "civilian politics" being brought in by Admiral Saitō Makoto, whom Hara appointed as governor-general.[90] The educational policy emphasis definitely had to be changed; that of Terauchi at the time of the takeover had been a mistake. The earlier policy had tried to prevent Koreans from studying their own past because such knowledge might give them dangerous nationalistic inclinations. Thus not being allowed to find out the truth, Koreans had erroneously come to suppose that their country possessed a great and glorious past. Koreans were fond of saying that "Japan annexed Korea, but Japan cannot annex Korea's history." In reality, argued Aoyagi, Korea did have a four-thousand-year-old history, but certainly not as an independent country. And the Yi dynasty at the end of that history was, according to him, the worst Korean government ever. It had been a mistake not to teach Koreans the history of their country as it really existed as a mere appendage of the Chinese empire which had endured centuries of mediocre, faction-ridden Korean politics.

Aoyagi supported the post-rebellion decision to add Korean history and geography to the ordinary school's curriculum as well as the general overhaul of the school system in 1922, duplicating the educational changes in Taiwan during the same year. He thought integration of all post-elementary institutions to make them accessible to Japanese and Koreans alike was a good step. He also supported extending ordinary school courses two years and making the curricula of these schools more like those of primary schools. Yet he warned that such changes, along with projects to write Korean history textbooks for the schools, would not be enough to quiet rebellious sentiments. Koreans in the cities as well as in the countryside still led

[90] Hara wanted to replace the military governors-general in both colonies with civilians, but static from powerful military figures prevented him from getting his way in Korea. Thus Admiral Satō Makoto was appointed to initiate civilian rule in that territory.

lives of grinding poverty. To improve their lot, industry and vocational education were urgent necessities.[91]

Korea's Education Rescript of 1922 was, of course, very much a part of the reform package of accelerated assimilation being instituted in both of Japan's major colonies. The March First Movement had enabled Prime Minister Hara to initiate reform in both territories, and it was largely in response to this uprising—rather than as an answer to future troubles that something like Taiwanese pressures for higher education might bring—that the reform was viewed by the Japanese in Korea.

As in the older colony, up until 1922 the Japanese in Korea had their own segregated, superior school facilities, emphasizing the elitist position of the ruling ethnic group. Under the 1922 rescript all the post-elementary facilities of both ethnic groups were combined into one education system, in theory equally accessible to Koreans and Japanese. But since in Korea there were recognized private alternatives to government-general secondary schools and specialized colleges, even on paper this measure was less of a gain than it had been in Taiwan. And in Korea too, Japanese students tended to dominate the best of the formerly all-Korean facilities.[92] Japanese-speaking Korean children became eligible to enter the generously endowed primary schools for the children of Japanese colonials. But, as in Taiwan, the numbers of those actually admitted were carefully controlled so as not to endanger the superior education that these schools gave Japanese children.[93] Such selective admissions would never spread Japanese language and thought quickly enough: the next step was an all-out campaign to quantitatively and qualitatively improve public elementary schooling.

Curriculum concessions to win Korean hearts with history and geography lessons have already been mentioned. Korean and Chinese studies continued to be a compulsory subject in ordinary school; the hours of this subject were not reduced. The rest of the ordinary school course, now six years in length, like a common school or a Japanese primary school, became very like what was taught in the elementary schools of Taiwan and Japan.[94]

Saitō Makoto and his successors carried out a serious program of

[91] Aoyagi Tsunatarō, *Shin Chōsen* [New Korea] (Keijō: Chōsen Kenkyūkai, 1925), pp. 126-150.

[92] Chōsen sōtokufu gakumukyoku [The Educational Affairs Bureau of the Korean Government-General], *Chōsen shōgakkō ichiran* [A Survey of Korea's Various Schools] (Keijō: 1939), pp. 109-218.

[93] *Ibid.*, pp. 5-80.

[94] *Meiji ikō kyōiku seido hattatsushi*, X, 117-118.

rapid ordinary school expansion. During the 1920's the slogan was "one school for every three districts" and from 1929 the aim was "a school in every district." During the first part of this two-phase campaign especially, the necessity which had forced toleration on the *sŏdang* remained a virtue. In districts which still lacked ordinary schools *sŏdang* maintained at private expense helped to stretch the colony's educational budgets. By the late 1920's, however, many *sŏdang* had been pushed into teaching Japanese subjects, and some of them had been transformed into short-term Japanese language centers.[95] By 1929, preparing for the second stage of the ordinary school campaign, the colonial government felt confident enough to bring in *sŏdang* regulations making compulsory the use of government-general textbooks and instruction in arithmetic and Japanese language.

Administrators found the results of the ordinary school expansion program heartening: by 1933 twenty percent of the elementary school-aged population was in more than two thousand ordinary schools.[96] Hidden in this colony-wide estimate of twenty percent were wide discrepancies between school attendance rates in the cities and in remote country districts and between male and female attendance rates. This twenty percent contained about seventy-three percent of the school-age males and slightly less than forty percent of the school-age females in developed urban areas; it embraced almost thirty-one percent of the school-age males and about seven and a half percent of the school-age females in country districts.[97] The educational gaps between city and country, boy and girl, were narrowing, but universal elementary education still seemed a long way off. Administrators continued to open new schools and to expand older ones, so that, despite the budgetary constraints of wartime, by 1940 half of all Korean school-age children were attending elementary school.[98] Colonial government projections estimated that this would rise to seventy percent by 1946 and began planning to introduce compulsory schooling during that year.[99] This accomplishment slightly bettered Taiwan's record of forty-three years of Japanese rule to get fifty percent of the Taiwanese population in school.[100]

At the post-elementary level, Koreans stuck to their preference for private schools run by their compatriots or by Western missionaries.

---

[95] Abe and Abe, p. 57.

[96] Ōno, *Chōsen kyōiku mondai kanken*, p. 400.

[97] Ōno, *Chōsen kyōiku mondai kanken*, p. 402.

[98] Chōsen sōtokufu, *Chōsen jijō 1944* [Korean Affairs 1944], p. 200.

[99] *Ibid.*

[100] Taiwan sōtokufu, *Taiwan no gakkō kyōiku* [School Education in Taiwan] (Taihoku: 1940), p. 119.

Private secondary schools and colleges educated large numbers of young people. Not all of these had pre-annexation roots either: for example, Chōsun Christian College (the present Yonsei University) was not founded until 1915; it received specialized college (*senmon gakkō*) status in 1917. By 1942 there were nine public specialized colleges with a total of 313 Korean and 377 Japanese students and eleven private specialized colleges with nearly 4,000 Korean students and over 2,700 Japanese students.[101]

Life was not easy for Koreans or for foreigners who operated colleges or indeed any Korean private schools, but the demand for a private education remained strong. Western missionaries claimed that governmental pressure jeopardized continuance of Christian schools because they lacked funds to meet government standards for buildings and equipment. They complained that they could not meet the demands of their students for fashionable athletic uniforms or for school excursions enjoyed by students in public schools.[102] They pointed out that their graduates were systematically excluded from the best higher educational opportunities and had less chance of attractive employment. The government-general's curriculum requirements—that Japanese language, history, and ethics be taught—missionaries found particularly burdensome. After the rebellion, Governor-General Saitō relaxed the most hated prohibition of all, the ban on religious instruction at school; but the missionaries and what they taught continued to be carefully watched by a wary government-general. Missionaries had not taken part in the March First Movement, but many of their Korean colleagues had done so.[103]

The events of the 1920's and the 1930's suggest that during the last decades of Japanese rule in Korea many Koreans accepted Japanese schooling in order to acquire the material advantages that such schooling sometimes afforded one, but the intensified efforts to win Korean hearts and minds through educational means did not succeed. The united cry for independence had been silenced, but Koreans found other ways to express their growing nationalist spirit. One of these was through a growing Korean language press and publishing industry (discussed in detail in Michael Robinson's essay in this volume); another was private educational endeavor.

It was the latter which brought about the hurried organization of an imperial university for the colony. Keijō Imperial University was opened in 1926 to undercut Korean nationalists who were collecting

[101] *Chōsen jijō 1944*, pp. 304-305.

[102] Fischer, *Democracy and Mission Education in Korea*, pp. 5-10, 65-93.

[103] Kondō, pp. 186-189. See also Henry Chung, *The Case of Korea* (New York: Fleming H. Revell, 1921).

funds for a private "people's university" to consist of a medical school, an engineering school, and a liberal arts college.[104] Keijō began with a faculty of medicine and a faculty of law and literature; in 1942 a faculty of science and engineering was added. The colonial government hoped that Keijō would help to stem the tide of thousands of Koreans going to Japan for a higher education—Korean students were even more likely to imbibe "dangerous thoughts" in the ruling country than were Taiwanese students.[105] This of course did not happen. Japanese students were always in a majority in the colonial university, and as a result there were relatively few places available to Koreans.[106]

The missionary teacher's lament about the popularity of public school athletic uniforms notwithstanding, games and sports associated with public schooling did little to soften Korean perceptions of their rulers. Certainly Japanese athletic programs did not lead Koreans to reject the *sŏdang*: there were 3,504 of them left, with 1,183,929 pupils, as late as May, 1942.[107] Missionaries felt that the public connected mission education with sports, and perhaps this was so.[108] Koreans rejoiced in the summer of 1936 when two of their compatriots won first and third places in the marathon of the eleventh Olympic Games. Yet although the two heroes were members of the Japanese Olympic team, the jubilant celebration of their victory by the Korean public and newspapers had strong anti-Japanese overtones.

Student anti-Japanese activity by no means ceased completely once the rebellion was crushed. During the summer vacation students traveled throughout rural Korea, ostensibly in aid of general educational betterment and anti-literacy campaigns. But what the students taught was often highly nationalistic in tone.[109] Student strikes flared up from time to time in the public schools. Such strikes reached a peak in late 1929 and early 1930 when an incident between Korean and Japanese students in Kwangju set off a rash of strikes all over Korea. About 54,000 students from 194 schools public and private eventually took part in these strikes. The main thrust of their protests appear to have been against the attitudes of superiority displayed by Japanese teachers and students.[110] In Taiwan student demonstrations

[104] Lee, pp. 240-241 and Ōno, p. 141.

[105] Taiwan sōtokufu, *Taiwan sōtokufu keisatsu enkakushi* [A History of the Taiwan Government-General Police] (Taihoku: 1933-1941), III, 23-24.

[106] *Chōsen jijō 1944*, p. 206.

[107] *Chōsen gakkō ichiran* (1942), p. 211.

[108] Fischer, *Democracy and Mission Education in Korea*, p. 95.

[109] Lee, p. 242 and Chung Tae-shi, p. 19.

[110] Lee, p. 253. Chung Tae-shi, p. 19.

against favoritism toward Japanese classmates had also surfaced from time to time, but although serious incidents occurred in individual schools, these never became a stepping stone to city-wide student protest, and anti-Japanese defiance in Taiwan never knew the country-wide solidarity shown by Korean students.[111]

CONCLUSION

The goal of Japanese educational policy in Taiwan and Korea, then, was to fashion the lower track of the two-track Meiji education system. It had worked so well in Japan—education had brought about psychological unity, had engendered loyalty to the modernizing state, had replaced old patterns of life and work with new skills, habits, and disciplines. Why should it not also work in the two most important colonies populated by peoples who also shared the East Asian cultural heritage?

Despite the cultural sharing of the quickly receding past, Koreans and Taiwanese were not as "progressive" peoples as were their conquerors. Thus for a very long time to come—as far ahead as anyone could see—their proper places would be at the bottom of the new order that Japan was creating. Some sort of safety valve—had not education in Japan effectively cut off potential leadership to the malcontents?—might be needed to accommodate the very ambitious and able, but the bottom of the ladder was where most Taiwanese and Koreans belonged. This conviction was shaken somewhat by the shocking events of 1919, after which many a gradualist among the ranks of colonial administrators changed his mind. Colonial officials who did not change their minds had to go along with the decisions of their superiors: accelerated assimilation and Japanization were now in vogue. This meant that educational safety valves were to be enlarged, or at least were to seem to have been enlarged. It also meant that colonial governments had to spend more energy and money on the base; and an all-out effort to get Koreans and Taiwanese into elementary school was made during the last two and a half decades of Japanese colonial rule.

The Japanese were educational initiators, but the Koreans and Taiwanese were forced to finance Japanese colonial educational policies. This was, of course, similar to what was happening in Japan—there local consumers had to finance local education. But in the colonies

---

[111] See Yamakawa Hitoshi, "Shokumin seisakuka no Taiwan" [Taiwan Under Colonial Policies], in *Yamakawa Hitoshi zenshū* [Collected works of Yamakawa Hitoshi], 20 vols. (Tokyo: Purebuso Shuppansha, 1966), VII, 287-288 for a vivid account of the Taihoku Normal School strike. See also TSK, III, 173-174.

there were two important differences. In the first place, neither Tai-wanese nor Koreans had initially demanded Japanese education but had it foisted upon them, regardless of their own preferences. In the Korean cases many preferences had been outlawed. In the second place, the Taiwanese and Koreans also paid for the segregated, elite educational facilities of colonial Japanese, which until 1919 were completely off limits to all Taiwanese and Koreans and only partially, grudgingly, made available to some of them afterward. The superior education provided for all Japanese children in the colonies—not just for a select few Japanese, as in Japan—was a galling reminder of policy priorities in all spheres of colonial life: Japanese first, Koreans or Taiwanese get the leftovers.

Korean and Taiwanese responses to this unhappy reminder dif-fered, as did their responses to Japanese education generally. By the end of the colonial period, the Japanese-educated Taiwanese of the island's native middle and upper classes had absorbed a whole spec-trum of Japanese tastes and attitudes. In Korea these same classes were seething with militant nationalism; 1919 had taught costly les-sons about the futility of open rebellion, but the psychological gap between ruler and ruled remained enormous. Why was the influence of Japanese education upon the Taiwanese and the Koreans so dissim-ilar?

There were some differences in the way that educational policies were introduced and pursued in the two territories. One is struck by the careful planning and control exercised in Taiwan from the days of Kodama Gentarō and Gotō Shimpei onward. Great pains were taken to train native teachers, and although in remuneration teaching ranked behind medicine as a profession for Taiwanese it was a very honorable calling which the Japanese treated with great respect. Be-cause of the proliferation of modern-style schools before 1905 in Ko-rea, Japanese administrators there were not as free to plan and to build from scratch. They could outlaw what they considered the most pernicious of private schools, but they could not, for example, take a hard line toward Christian education. What they considered to be "the wrong sort of teacher" colonial officials treated very badly; and no special energy went into training native teachers until quite late in the period. Material conditions were worse for Koreans under Japa-nese rule than for Taiwanese. In Taiwan, land policies and agricul-tural technology brought a good deal of prosperity to the rural elite and some benefits to other segments of the agrarian population. Al-most all the Korean farming population suffered enormously from the land registration policies and the switch, which came after annex-ation, from a barter-based to a monetary-based economy. A few Ko-reans did become rich landowners, but the rise of Japanese landlords was more obvious. By many other indices, agricultural and industrial policies brought more hardships to Koreans than to Taiwanese. Wage differentials between Japanese and natives performing the same jobs differed: these were much greater in Korea than in Taiwan. But differences in maneuverability and thoughtfulness on the part of early administrators and differences in economic conditions are probably only a part of the story.

In 1895 Japan acquired an outpost of the Ch'ing empire, populated mainly by Chinese who were there because they, their parents, or grandparents, or greatgrandparents had found it difficult to eke out a living on the mainland. Since the Japanese government provided a two-year period of grace during which Chinese who wished to do so could return to China, members of the gentry who stayed behind more or less chose to do so. In 1905 Japan acquired an entire country with its own proud royal traditions and ancient civilization. Governing from the former royal capital and keeping the Korean royal family in docile captivity, the Japanese kept alive memories of the days when Koreans ruled Koreans. The gentry of Taiwan knew from their study of Chinese history that rule by a foreign invader was nothing new or particularly shameful. Legally and socially treating all Taiwanese as one class and all Japanese as another was nothing new either. And many well-to-do Taiwanese were merchants who could appreciate the Japanese interest in trade and commerce. But in highly stratified Yi-dynasty Korea the privileged position of the *yangban*, whose only profession was government employment, was a function of traditional class distinctions. Thus, when the Japanese espoused equality among all Koreans, they made enemies of the entire aristocratic class.

Japan annexed Korea just after the seeds of a modern nationalist movement had begun to sprout. The colonial government made every effort to cultivate "the Japanese spirit" in Korean soil, but, like the garden variety of noxious weed, nationalist thoughts were hard to root out. They were nourished by the educational expansion in which the colonial government played such an important role but was never able to control completely. As Michael E. Robinson reminds us elsewhere in this volume, increasing availability of Japanese education was accompanied by rising literacy in the Korean language. Until the end, government-general schools remained one alternative among others. Japanese educational policies could not stamp out the growing Korean consciousness; what they did was to give this consciousness and its grievances a focus. Schools established before 1905 reminded Koreans that Japanese education was not the only road to modernization. The continuing presence of Christian missionaries from the

West prevented the Japanese from claiming to be the only foreign innovators in the country. Indeed, it was the missionaries, not the Japanese, whom Koreans praised for introducing sports and for efforts to advance the status of women. Taiwanese usually responded to the inadequacies and discrimination in colonial schools by demanding a better version of the model from which the colonial school system had been fashioned. Koreans, on the other hand, always wanted independence—immediately.

CHAPTER 8

Colonial Publication Policy and the Korean Nationalist Movement

Michael E. Robinson

Control of the written word, an important aspect of Japanese colonial policy, was used to limit the spread of radical ideas within the empire and to curb criticism of Japanese colonial administration. Colonial bureaucrats were especially concerned with controlling publications in the colonies because of serious nationalist challenge to their rule. Publication controls were most highly developed in Korea, but in Taiwan, where similar legal forms and administrative techniques prevailed, these were not as highly developed because other forms of control proved more suitable and a serious nationalist challenge never existed.[1]

Previous writing on Japanese press controls and censorship in Korea has emphasized its repressive aspects. Indeed, the Japanese severely limited both the numbers and content of Korean publications. Yet closer examination of Japanese publication policy reveals that its success did not stem from that kind of brute repression. Instead, the flexibility of Japanese censorship control enabled them to shape the content of Korean publications to their satisfaction.

Publication controls in Korea and Taiwan naturally were based on laws and administrative procedures developed in Japan since the early Meiji period.[2] As in Japan proper, administrative authorities enjoyed broad powers with respect to publications. Although the Meiji Constitution guaranteed in principle the rights of freedom of speech, press, writing, assembly, and association (Chapter Two, Article 29) "within

---

[1] Ching-chih Chen, "Community Control Systems and the Police in Japanese Colonies," *Workshop on Japanese Colonial Empire*, August 1979, Passim.

[2] The development of Japanese press controls has been described by Peter Figdar, "Newspapers and their Regulation in Early Meiji Japan," in *Harvard University East Asia Research Center Papers on Japan*, 1972. See also: Okudaira Yasuhiro, "Political Censorship in Japan from 1931-1945," unpublished paper, Institute of Legal Research, University of Pennsylvania, 1962. For an excellent discussion in Japanese see: Okudaira, "Ken'etsu seido" [The Inspection System], *Kōza Nihon kindaihō hattatsushi* [Lecture Series on the History of Developing Modern Law in Japan] (Tokyo: Keisō Shobō, 1967), 11, pp. 3-73.

the limits of the statutes," in reality these freedoms were limited considerably by the force of administrative and legal precedent and by the cabinet's using its emergency powers.[3] As Edward Chen has pointed out in this volume, colonial subjects did not enjoy such constitutional rights, although some groups in both Korea and Taiwan pressed for these rather than for independence.[4] The government-general of Korea freely enacted laws and imposed penalties on writers and publishers without judicial or legislative constraints. It took a great interest in controlling the press because of security considerations and it refined the legal framework for the press, patterned on that of Japan's, into a finely woven net of regulations backed by its broad administrative powers.

Korean resentment toward Japanese rule exploded into massive and sustained demonstrations in the spring of 1919. This popular upheaval, in part a response to the harsh nature of the first ten years of Japanese administration under Governor-Generals Terauchi and Hasegawa, stimulated a serious Japanese reappraisal of its colonial policy. The "cultural policy," *bunka seiji*, implemented by Saitō Makoto attempted to defuse Korean resentment by removing the more repellent aspects of Japanese rule in Korea, and it was parallelled by a similar, if less comprehensive, reassessment of policy in Taiwan.[5]

The Saitō reforms represented a fundamental policy shift from coercion to manipulation.[6] Some relaxation of colonial authority was accompanied by more emphasis on efficiency and flexibility. In short, rule by brute force gave way to administrative finesse. This shift from repression to manipulation was reflected in publication controls, manifested by a change in administrative application of the law, while the legal framework remained intact. In fact, the publication law for Taiwan was actually strengthened in 1921.[7]

In Korea, the Japanese hoped to reduce tension by allowing more cultural freedom. They did not, however, intend to allow a vital and vociferous Korean press the freedom to criticize Japanese rule or to foment insurrection. Moving carefully, the colonial government opened

[3] Okudaira Yasuhiro, "Ken'etsu seido," p. 19.

[4] Edward Chen, "Formosan Political Movements Under Japanese Colonial Rule, 1914-1937," in *Journal of Asian Studies*, 31, 3 (May 1972), pp. 477-497.

[5] *Ibid.*, p. 481. See also: E. Patricia Tsurumi, *Japanese Colonial Education in Taiwan, 1895-1945* (Cambridge: Harvard University Press), 1977, Chapters 4 and 5.

[6] Frank Baldwin, "The March First Movement; Korean Challenge and Japanese Response," unpublished Ph.D. Dissertation, Columbia University, 1969, p. 189. Baldwin has published a more recent article: "Participatory Anti-Imperialism: The 1919 Independence Movement," in *Journal of Korean Studies*, 1 (1979), pp. 123-163.

[7] Naikaku kampō kirokuka, *Hōrei shūran* [Compilation of Laws] (Tokyo, 1929), p. 218.

the door to Korean publications, but at the same time moved to weed out dangerous thought and blatantly anti-Japanese publications. Increased Korean publishing opportunities helped to stimulate nationalist activity. Having abandoned total repression, the Japanese dealt with increased nationalist activity by suppressing, selectively, the most dangerous and radical elements within the nationalist movement and tolerating the more moderate wing. In no other aspect of colonial governance can the manipulative Japanese approach toward control be seen more clearly than in the conduct of publication policy.[8]

Indeed, as a case study, publication policy mirrors the zigs and zags, the freeze and thaw, of colonial policy in Korea: first a modulating publication controls after the repression of 1910-1919, to the comparatively relaxed period between 1920-1928, and then ending with renewed restrictions after 1929. Furthermore, this ebb and flow of Japanese colonial policy ran parallel with the changing social and political situation in Japan proper, as well as with new controls imposed to squelch social unrest in the metropole.

The policy and administrative techniques used in Korea between 1910 and 1930 foreshadowed developments in Japan during the militarist era of the mid and late 1930's. The government-general of Korea, from its beginning, possessed summary powers and an autonomy that were the hallmark of Japanese governance in that decade.[9] The censorship and publication policies developed in Korea before 1919 and the era of home party government seemed to foreshadow the thought control and censorship used in Japan after 1925.

Much has been written about the effect of this state of affairs on the development of authoritarianism and "fascism" in prewar Japan. Dominated by prominent military men with close connections to the upper echelons of the Japanese government, the governor-general of Korea was never hampered by demands of Japanese political elites and the new pressure groups that emerged in the twentieth century. This situation must have been enviable to British viceroys of India, who were continually hampered by the demands and obstructive tactics of opposition leaders in the British parliament.[10] Responsible only to the emperor and not to the civilian government under the prime minister, the government-general of Korea clearly reflected Meiji au-

<hr>

[8] Michael Robinson, "The Origins and Development of Korean Nationalist Ideology, 1920-1927: Culture, Identity, National Development, and Political Schism," unpublished Ph.D. Dissertation, University of Washington, 1979, Chapters 4 and 5.

[9] Edward Chen, "Legal Systems of the Colonies," in *Workshop on Japanese Colonial Empire*, August 1979, pp. 2, 9.

[10] N. Gerald Barrier, *Banned: Controversial Literature and Political Control in British India, 1907-1947* (Columbia: University of Missouri Press), 1974, p. 13.

thoritarianism. In this perspective, Japanese colonial policy in Korea is more than an exercise in analyzing the Japanese colonial experience; it is also a study of Japanese political development.

Finally, Japanese publication policy directly affected the development of the Korean nationalist movement. The Japanese attempted to control ideas in Korea, basing their policies not only on their reading of the colonial political situation but also on their experience in Japan with the expansion of radical thought in the Taishō period. Publication policy was important to them because they sought to control the avenues of ideological debate and inquiry. The Japanese had to control dissent in Korea without creating a unifying focus for nationalist demands through increased oppression. Their publication policy eventually encouraged benign ideological trends and chastised radical movements. As we shall see below, this manipulative policy toward Korean publications produced just that effect.

COLONIAL PUBLICATION POLICY: THE LEGAL-ADMINISTRATIVE FRAMEWORK AND CENSORSHIP STANDARD IN KOREA AND TAIWAN

The legal foundation of the Japanese publication policy in Korea was laid with the promulgation of the Newspaper Law (*Shimbunshi hō*, 1907) and the Publication Law (*Shuppan hō*, 1909) during the protectorate.[11] Formally, these laws were issued in the name of the Korean government, but they were in fact a creation of Japanese advisors. The immediate impetus for these two laws was the apprehension of the resident-general concerning widespread criticism of Japanese activity in Korea and the increasingly strident nature of press support for violent demonstrations against the Japanese after the disbanding of the Korean army in 1907. The principal target of the Japanese newspaper law was the *Korea Daily News (Taehan maeil sinbo)*. Like the *Hwangsŏng sinmun* before it, the *Korea Daily News* was the main anti-Japanese newspaper in Korea between 1905 and 1910.[12] The *Korea Daily News* continued publication while other papers ceased because it was owned and edited by a foreigner, E. T. Bethell. The Publication Law previous to the 1907 and 1909 laws did not provide the Japanese with a means for pre-publication examination of for-

[11] For a full text of the 1907 Newspaper Law (Shimbunshi hō), the 1908 Newspaper Regulations (Shimbunshi kisoku), and the 1909 Publication Law (Shuppan hō) see: Chōsen Sōtokufu, *Chōsen hōrei shūran* [Compilation of Laws in Korea] (Keijō: Chōsen sōtokufu, 1915), pp. 15-23.

[12] Chŏng Chin-sŏk, *Han'guk ŏllon t'ujaengsa* [The Struggle of the Korean Press] (Seoul: Chongum mungo, 1975), pp. 30-34.

eign-owned publication.[13] The Newspaper Regulations and Publication Law brought the system of publication control in Korea in line with practices in Japan, but the power of the government over the press was even greater.

The 1907 Newspaper Law of fifty-one articles established many of the same requirements for publications previously developed in Japan. By law, newspapers had to obtain a general news permit, *jiji kyoka*, more difficult to obtain than more specialized permits because it allowed reporting of current events and political editorials. In addition to permits, the law required, as in Japan, security deposits (300 yen) for newspapers.[14] They also detailed the procedural matters on submission of specimen copies for pre-publication inspection. The Japanese also included provisions for suspending and abolishing newspapers which persisted in publishing material harmful to the general peace and order.[15]

Although similar to Japanese law, the 1907 Newspaper Law differed in one significant respect. The inspection system for censorship relied upon the pre-publication examination of newpaper galleys. As in Japan, the Publication Law of 1909 provided for pre-publication inspection of book and magazine manuscripts, an arrangement easily put into operation in Korea, where the number of publications was small. Under this system each newspaper composed the daily galleys, sent several copies to the local censoring office, proceeded to set type and to prepare for the daily run. Normally the manuscript, newspaper, or magazine received permission for printing. In the case of serious problems, however, the Japanese authorities would demand deletion of offending articles, or inflamatory or otherwise unacceptable passages.[16] At this point, the newspaper could freely publish the existing edition, with blank spaces substituted for deletions. In some cases, an entire edition would be suppressed and confiscated by the authorities. The newspapers were then allowed to publish an extraordinary edition (*gaihō*) that excluded any material from the confiscated edition.[17]

The Publication Law promulgated in 1909 applied to magazines and books. Publication permits were more easily obtained under the Publication Law than under the Newspaper Law. Reasoning that

[13] C. I. Eugene Kim and Han-kyo Kim, *Korea and the Politics of Imperialism, 1876-1910* (Berkeley: University of California, 1967), p. 189.

[14] Chōsen Sōtokufu, "Shimbunshi hō, Article 12," in *Chōsen hōrei shūran*, p. 21.

[15] *Ibid.*, p. 21.

[16] Chŏng Chin-sŏk, "Nōhon ken'etsu" [Manuscript Censorship] in *Ajia Kōron*, 3.10 (October 1974), p. 1.

[17] *Ibid.*, p. 2.

magazines and books usually dealt with more specialized matters and were of limited circulation, the Japanese granted more permits for books and specialized magazines than for newspapers.[18] The Japanese applied the same system of pre-publication inspection to books and magazines as to newspapers.

The distinction between the general news permit for newspapers and specialized permits for technical, religious, and educational books and magazines influenced the type of Korean magazines published between 1910 and 1919. Thus, intellectual journals and political magazines were non-existent in name, yet so-called youth and religious magazines carried subject matter hardly limited to their specialties, a fact not missed by the Japanese.[19]

Publication controls on Taiwan were based on statutes similar to those in Korea. The Taiwan Newspaper Law (*Taiwan shimbun hō*, 1907) and Taiwan Publication Regulations (*Taiwan shuppan kisoku*, 1901) separated newspapers and other periodicals and books for purposes of control.[20] One important distinction remained, however: newspapers in Taiwan were not subject to pre-publication censorship.[21] This was due to the fact that almost all newspapers in Taiwan were published in Japanese.[22] Another difference between the regulations in Taiwan and Korea was the requirement in Taiwan for maintaining a legally designated import agent for incoming magazines, newspapers, and books.[23] The agent requirement helped Japanese authorities to monitor imported materials, which constituted a large portion of publications in Taiwan.[24] In general, Taiwan, as a smaller colony, proved to be easier to control with regard to publications. For this reason, even though Japanese authority and legal structures were almost identical to those in Korea, the Japanese found it easier to manage the Taiwan publishing industry.

[18] Chōsen Sōtokufu keimukyoku, *Chōsen ni okeru shuppanbutsu gaiyō* [Survey of Publications in Korea] (Keijō: Keimukyoku, 1930), p. 51, 64, 138 (hereafter, *Shuppan gaiyō*, 1930).

[19] *Sonyŏn* was suspended for three months in August of 1910 and continued until closed down in May of 1913. *Ch'ŏngch'un* published for fifteen issues from October 1914 until September 1918. See Pack Sun-jae, "Chapchi rŭl to'onghae ilche sidae ŭi kŭndaehwa undong" [Modernization Movements Seen Through Korean Magazines], *Sindonga*, 18 (January 1966), pp. 396-398.

[20] For the full text of the Taiwan Shimbun hō (1908) and the Taiwan Shuppan kisoku (1901), see *Hōrei shūran* [Compilation of Laws] (Tokyo: 1929), pp. 213-219.

[21] *Ibid.*, p. 217.

[22] Taiwan Sōtokufu, *Taiwan kōji gaiyō* [Survey of the Later Taiwan Colonial Administration] (Taihoku: 1945), p. 67.

[23] *Hōrei shūran*, p. 218.

[24] Taiwan Sōtokufu, Keimukyoku, *Taiwan no keisatsu* [The Taiwan Police] (Taihoku: 1935), p. 144.

In addition to the pre-publication censorship distinction for Korean publications, there was a second peculiarity in the control system used in Korea. Contrary to the practice in Taiwan, there were two separate sets of laws which distinguished Korean from Japanese publications. Throughout the protectorate and the later colonial period, Japanese materials were subject to post-publication censorship (as in Japan), and these were not limited by the distinction between general and specialized permits. After 1910 Japanese publications were administered under domestic publication laws by order of the governor-general of Korea.[25] Therefore, although Japanese publications remained bound by censorship standards and publication procedures existing in Japan, Japanese publishers had considerably freer access to permits and were unburdened by the red tape and uncertainty of pre-publication censorship.

Publication control laws in Korea also made a distinction between Japanese and Korean materials with regard to confiscation and subscription procedures. When the police seized Korean materials, they became the property of the colonial authorities. When Japanese materials were confiscated, they were often returned to the publisher after a waiting period.[26] In both cases seizure involved financial hardship for the publisher, but in the Japanese case there remained the possibility of selling the material at a later date. Publication laws also discriminated against Korean publishers in the matter of subscriptions. Koreans were not allowed to sell magazines on a subscription basis, while Japanese publishers could.

In vain, Korean publishers complained to the authorities about the inequity and disadvantage inherent in this discriminatory treatment. Finally, in 1932, in keeping with the general desire to further the legal integration of the empire, the Japanese abolished the system of dual laws in favor of a unified publication code for both Japanese and Korean publications in the colony.[27]

By 1910, the Japanese system of publication controls in Korea was in full operation and remained substantially unchanged until the end of Japanese rule. Through the power invested in the government-general rule of Korea, the colonial police had almost total power over publication in Korea. Since the pronouncements of the governor-general had the power of law (through directives from the governor-general called *seirei*), there was no recourse to the Diet or the courts. In Japan the Home Ministry gradually built its authority over pub-

[25] Chōsen Sōtokfu Keimukyoku, *Shuppan gaiyō*, 1930, p. 33.

[26] Chŏng Chin-sŏk, "Nōhon ken'etsu," p. 2.

[27] Chōsen Sōtokufu, Toshoka, *Chōsen shuppan keisatsu gaiyō* [Korean Publication Police Survey] (Keijō: Toshoka, 1940).

lications in the face of some resistance on the part of the Diet, which, in theory, held the only power to limit freedom of speech granted in the Meiji Constitution.[28] The government-general of Korea was under no such constraint. The colonial Publication Police (*Shuppan keisatsu*) held the power to issue permits and enforced the rules governing all prepublications.[29] For any violations, the police decided upon deletions, erasures, and seizure of materials, as well as suspensions (*teishi*), both temporary and permanent, of publication.

The Newspaper Law and Publication Law gave colonial authorities the power to censor publications in the colonies. Censorship in Korea developed before the formal enactment of the colonial publication laws during the Russo-Japanese War. For security reasons, the Japanese assumed control of the Korean telegraph, telephone, and mail in July of 1904; they also prohibited news concerning all matters relating to the course of the war.[30]

The censorship standard (*ken'etsu hyōjun*), a guideline rather than a legal device, expanded, in Korea as in Japan, to include a wide range of topics. In the 1905-1910 period the Japanese extended the scope of censorship to include all matters relating to Korean-Japanese relations. The Japanese authorities were anxious to control public order as they prepared annexation.[31] The Newspaper and Publication Laws (1907, 1909) provided definitive powers of censorship and expanded the range of proscribed topics.[32] These laws also established specific punishments for criminal breach of the standards.[33]

In the second half of the colonial period the censorship standards continued to expand. By 1939 detailed lists of proscribed topics had been distributed by the Publication Police. Certain categories were given special attention: defamation of the emperor or imperial institution, military matters, radical ideology, Korean-Japanese relations,

[28] Okudaira Yasahirō, "Ken'etsu seido," pp. 16-18.

[29] During the early part of the colonial period (1910-1920) censorship was the responsibility of the Book Section (*toshoka*) of the colonial police. During the 1920's and the reorganization of the police, the Publication Police (*shuppan keisatsu*) were created as a unit within the High Police (*Kōtō keisatsu*) and charged with the responsibility for censorship.

[30] Ch'oe Ch'un, "Kyop'o sinmun kwa ilbon ŭi ch'imnak chŏngch'aek" [Korean Newspapers and Japanese Suppression Policy], *Chungang taehak pŏpchŏng nonjip*, 15 (no date), p. 17.

[31] *Ibid.*, pp. 27-28.

[32] For a text of Article 21 of the Newpaper Law and Article 11 of the Newspaper Regulation see: *Chōsen hōrei shūran* [Compilation of Laws in Korea] (Keijo: Chōsen sōtokufu, 1915), pp. 15-23.

[33] *Ibid.*, p. 20.

and Korean nationalism.[34] This standard was virtually identical to the standards applied in Japan and Taiwan, except for the additional proscription of publications relating to independence movements in the colonies and statements construed to be against the government-general.[35]

As far as the actual censorship standard was concerned, Korean publishers were only slightly more restricted than their Japanese counterparts. The reality of the censorship system lay in the way in which censors applied the standard, since it was applied with varying degrees of rigor, depending on overall policy considerations and political circumstances. The standard itself was applied subjectively, and as a result Korean publications were almost never given the benefit of the doubt in ambiguous cases. Nevertheless, the brunt of discrimination in publication policy lay in its implementation as a whole. In Korea, the ultimate source of discrimination was the application of a dual set of publication laws which favored Japanese publishers over their Korean counterparts.

The colonial authorities flexibly applied the instruments of censorship in Korea. In implementing publication control, the Japanese manipulated the issue of permits, exercised a sophisticated pre-publication warning system to avoid problems before the fact, and ultimately used their power to delete passages or articles, ban entire editions of newspapers and magazines, and suspend publications.

The power to issue permits for publication was absolute. In the 1910-1919 period the Japanese choked off Korean publication by simply issuing no permits for Korean language newspapers outside the government-general's Korean language newspaper, the *Daily News (Maeil sinbo)*. Though books continued to be published during this period, magazines were not given general news permits, and this limited Korean publications to specialized academic, youth, and religious periodicals. The issue of permits was relaxed after 1920, and some magazines even obtained general news permits. After 1930, the number of permits issued under the Publication Law stabilized at levels above the yearly increases in the previous decade.[36]

Another device to control the Korean press was a pre-publication

---

[34] For a complete text of the censorship standard for Korea see: Chōsen Sōtokufu, Keimukyoku, Toshoka, *Chōsen shuppan keisatsu gaiyō* [Korean Publication Policy Survey] (Keijō: keimukyoku, Toshoka, 1940), pp. 68-73.

[35] The Korean standard can be compared with a standard used in Japan, which Okudaira traces back to 1928, see: Naimushō keihokyoku, *Shōwa jūnen chū ni okeru shuppan keisatsu gaikan* [A Conspectus of Police Publications in 1935] (Tokyo: Naimushō, 1935). In Okudaira, "Ken'etsu seido," p. 30.

[36] Please refer to table on page 325.

warning system that was almost identical to the system in Japan, where censorship officials wanted to prevent publication problems before they arose. There were four levels of warnings: "consultation" (*kondan*), "caution" (*chūi*), "warning" (*keikoku*), and "ban" (*kinshi*). At each of these levels of warning, the authorities expressed their concern over sensitive topics so that publishers might exercise discretion and avoid censorship voluntarily. *Kinshi* was the most serious level of warning, and that label put all publishers on notice that material concerning the banned topic would be automatically censored.

For earlier levels, the warnings were simply cautioning publishers of potentially sensitive material, so that they would use circumspection in dealing with these matters. A list of formal warnings issued between 1920 and 1930 in the *Survey of Publications in Korea* (1930) shows that the Japanese were most often concerned with matters relating to public disorder, radical thought, and defamation of the imperial household.[37]

In addition to formal warnings issued by the colonial police, Japanese officials publicized policy regarding censorship in the Korean press through interviews and public announcements. In the aftermath of the closure of the socialist magazines *Sinsaenghwal* and *Sinch'ŏnji* in late 1922, Maruyama Tsurukichi, the head of the colonial police, granted interviews to the *Tong's ilbo* in order to clarify Japanese policy. In one interview on January 10, 1923, Maruyama warned Korean publishers that the actions taken against *Sinsaenghwal* and *Sinch'ŏnji* were not isolated incidents but a demonstration of Japanese commitment to oppose the radical trend in Korean publications, especially with regard to socialist and social revolutionary thought.[38]

In spite of their warning system, the Japanese could not rely on the tractability of the Korean press after 1920. When publishers ignored those signals, they turned to their ultimate weapon, suppression and doctoring of the publications themselves, as well as prosecution of publishers and writers.

Actual censorship also involved a gradation of steps equivalent to the perceived severity of the offense. Censors had the power to order erasure of parts of articles or books. Deletion (*sakujo*) applied during pre-publication inspection in time for inclusion in the final printing.[39] Deletion became the most common form of censorship in Korea, and between 1930 and 1939 the Publication Police recorded 3,847 such cases.[40] Although no records for all deletion cases seem to exist for

---

[37] Chōsen sōtokufu, *Shuppan gaiyō*, 1930, pp. 212-213.

[38] *Tonga ilbo*, "Sinsaenghwal sagŏn" [The Sinsaenghwal Incident], January 10, 1923.

[39] Chŏng, *Han'guk ŏllon t'ugaengsa*, p. 56.

[40] Chōsen sōtokufu, *Shuppan keisatsu gaiyō*, 1940, p. 65.

the 1920's, the total number was probably equivalent, if not greater, considering the higher level of conflict during the decade.

A second technique available to the censors was seizure of offending materials. As provided by law, the censors could seize an entire issue of a newspaper or magazine as well as books when they determined that such materials would be detrimental to the maintenance of peace and order. For the four major Korean newspapers published between 1920 and 1939, the incidence of seizure was considerable (see table on page 327).[41] Although records on the actual numbers of newspapers seized are incomplete for the period, they do indicate that in the period between 1927-1939 Japanese seizures amounted to nearly five million copies.[42]

Suspension of publication was the strongest action taken against publishers. Suspension was either temporary (teishi) or permanent (hakkō kinshi). In the case of suspension, authorities would negotiate with the magazine or newspaper in order to assure themselves of future compliance with censorship standards before revoking the suspension. Magazines considered too dangerous or incorrigibly intransigent were suspended permanently. The ultimate weapon of permanent suspension was reserved for the most serious cases. In all cases, magazines suspended permanently were those that continued to propagate social revolutionary thought.[43] During the colonial period only three magazines were suspended permanently: Sinsaenghwal, November 1922; Sinch'ŏnji, November 1922; Kaebyŏk, July 1926.

Having committed themselves, after 1920, to allow publication of several Korean language newspapers, the Japanese were usually reluctant to invoke permanent suspension, in spite of continued difficulties. Temporary suspension, however, proved to be an effective weapon against the Korean newspapers.[44] Since it was in the Korean newspaper's interest to resume publication for both financial and ideological reasons, the Japanese could effectively bargain for revisions in editorial policy during the suspension period. This bargaining even extended to demanding changes in editorial personnel and reporters.[45]

The censorship system in Korea, as in Japan, was thus extremely subjective. Administrative authorities enjoyed wide summary powers

[41] See table on page 327. Chŏng, "Nōhon ken'etsu," p. 4.

[42] Ibid., p. 42.

[43] Chosen Sōtokufu, Shuppan keisatsu gaiyō, 1940.

[44] Chŏng, "Nōhon ken'etsu," p. 6.

[45] Chŏng, Han'guk ŏllon t'ujaengsa, p. 86. During the fourth suspension of the Chosŏn ilbo the Japanese were very concerned about the fact that the senior editors were members of the newly formed Korean mass organization, the Singanhoe.

and were free of both legislative and judicial interference. The Japanese censors could pick from a wide range of controls which varied in severity. This allowed them to apply different punishments according to their interests. The ultimate weapon of permanent suspension was applied to socialist or otherwise radically oriented publications, while "less serious" cases were dealt with more circumspectly. This censorship system kept politics out of the Korean press by rewarding the more tractable, non-politically oriented, publications and punishing those which were critical. In this effort Japanese policy was successful, shaping the publication climate in Korea toward a more commercially oriented press and a reduced level of political dialogue after 1930.

JAPANESE PUBLICATION POLICY AND THE GROWTH OF THE KOREAN PRESS

The history of Japanese publication policy can be divided into four periods. Between 1905-1910 the Japanese constructed the administrative and legal basis for censorship in Korea. In the second period, between 1910 and 1919, the Japanese tightly controlled permits, and there were no Korean-managed newspapers. At that time the Japanese suppressed all Korean publications. Many Korean historians refer to that phase as the "dark period" (*amhŭkki*) of publication, and most treatments of Japanese repression of free speech in Korea are based on the Korean experience during this period.

In some ways Korea was more fortunate than Taiwan in this respect. During the fifty-year rule of Taiwan there was only one newspaper owned and operated by Taiwanese (*Taiwan Minpō*). Begun as *Taiwan* and renamed *Taiwan Minpō* in 1923, this paper was the only one to include sections written in Chinese (as much as three-fourths by 1932). By 1937, however, this newspaper again became an exclusively Japanese publication.[46]

The dramatic rise in the number of publications in both Taiwan and Korea was in part due to high literacy rates fostered by Japanese colonial policies. In Taiwan the Japanese educational system complimented the traditional Taiwanese *shobō*, and with a fifteen-year headstart on Korea, literacy in Japanese as well as Chinese was climbing rapidly in Taiwan by the time the Japanese occupied Korea.[47] Korea also had an extensive network of traditional village schools (*sŏdang*)

---

[46] Taiwan Sōtokufu, *Taiwan kōji gaiyō*, p. 67. See also Wang Ching-te, *Taiwan kumon suru sono rekishi* [Taiwan's Bitter History] (Tokyo: 1964), p. 102.

[47] For a discussion of the traditional Taiwanese shobō, see Tsurumi, *Japanese Colonial Education in Taiwan*, pp. 20, 30-31.

which taught basic skills in reading and writing Chinese.[48] Although Korea lagged behind Taiwan in the proportion of literates in the population, the vernacular movement made great progress after 1900.[49] Education and literacy were valued highly in both traditional Taiwanese and Korean societies, and Japan's successful implementation of mass education in both colonies served to strengthen this value, laying the basis for the expansion of the publishing industry in the 1920's.

Although the first ten years of Japanese rule were particularly harsh in Korea, there was a steady, if not modest, rise in the number of Korean publications. In fact, between 1910 and 1919 the publication of books on all subjects increased, and a total of thirty-three Korean language magazines received permits.[50] Although the Japanese granted no general permits for magazines, after 1931 they did allow a number of specialized permits for religious and youth magazines, the so-called "enlightenment" journals.[51] The Ch'ŏndogyo Monthly (Ch'ŏndogyo wŏlbo, 1910-1913), Boys (Sonyŏn, 1908-1911), Youth (Ch'ŏngch'un, 1914-1918) were three prominent magazines published with specialized permits, by which they were obligated to restrict their subject matter to non-political topics. Nevertheless, they became a public forum for the growing nationalist movement in Korea and came to encounter censorship problems. The decision in 1913 to permit a certain number of specialized magazines was in response to foreign criticism of the oppressive nature of Japanese rule. While the Japanese had allowed more publications after 1913 in order to mollify public opinion, they continued to guard against the rise of a strong nationalist press.

In the third period of Japanese publication policy, 1919 and 1929, the Japanese granted more publication permits for general magazines and permitted three Korean language newspapers to circulate. This change in policy came after the spring and summer riots of 1919. Although the post-1919 publication climate was more relaxed compared to the years before, the Japanese had only partially opened the floodgates to Korean publication, since they wanted to create an atmosphere of liberalization without losing control of society alto-

[48] Andrew Grjdanzev, Modern Korea (New York: The John Day Co.), 1944, pp. 261-270.

[49] Michael Robinson, "Ch'oe Hyŏn-bae and Korean Nationalism: Language, Culture and National Development," Occasional Papers on Korea, No. 3 (Summer 1975), passim.

[50] Paek Sun-jae, "Chapchi rŭl t'onghae pon ilche sidae, ŭi kŭndaehwa undong" [The Modernization Movement During the Colonial Period as Seen Through Magazines], Sindonga, No. 22 (May 1966), p. 400.

[51] Ch'oe Ch'un,"Han'guk ŭi ch'ulp'an yŏn'gu: 1910 ŭrobut'ŏ 1923 kkaji" [Studies on Korean Publishing: 1910-1923], in Sŏuldae sinmun yŏn'gu hakbo, 1 (1964), p. 14.

gether. Actually, the Japanese granted the coveted general permit to only six magazines and allowed fifty-four applications for similar permits to languish.[52]

Although the Japanese firmly controlled how many general news permits could be issued, their number under the Publication Law expanded dramatically. Regular permits pertained to specialized magazines and books of all types. I have compiled the number of regular permits granted under the Publication Law between 1920 and 1939 to show how rapidly these expanded after 1920:[53]

Korean Language Publication Permits Granted
(Under Pub. Law)

1920	409	1930	1,556
1921	627	1931	1,663
1922	854	1932	2,050
1923	884	1933	2,044
1924	1,116	1934	2,101
1925	1,240	1935	2,154
1926	1,466	1936	2,272
1927	1,328	1937	2,383
1928	1,425	1938	2,054
1929	1,425	1939	2,749

Another development corresponding to this shift in publication policy came in the early 1920's, when twelve of the twenty Korean newspapers which appeared between 1892 and 1935 greatly expanded between 1920 and 1927.[54] In Taiwan, the number of all publications expanded in a similar fashion, doubling between 1927-1935.[55]

The Japanese created more difficulties for their censorship system in Korea by expanding the issuance of permits. Not only did censors have to inspect daily three major Korean newspapers after 1920, but they also had to cope with a flood of magazines and books which created a backlog in the inspection department, just as the tremendous growth in newsaper circulation created problems in case of seizure.

Growing from almost a zero base, Korean language newspaper

[52] Chŏng, *Han'guk ŏllon t'ujaengsa*, p. 101.

[53] For figures for 1920-1929 see: *Keimu ihó* [Police Report] (April 1930), pp. 73-74. The 1930-1939 figures are taken from the *Chōsen shuppan keisatsu gaiyō*, pp. 61-63.

[54] Chŏng Chin-sŏk, "Illcheha Han'guk ŭi ŏllon ch'ulp'an yŏn'gu" [Studies on Korean Media and Publishing Under the Japanese], in *Sinmun yŏn'gu* (Spring 1978), p. 245.

[55] Taiwan sōtokufu, *Taiwan no keisatsu*, p. 145.

circulation expanded during the 1920's to a daily total circulation of 103,027 in 1929, with four major dailies having the following shares.[56]

Chosŏn ilbo	24,286
Tonga ilbo	37,802
Chungoe ilbo	14,267
Maeil sinbo	23,015
(GGK Organ)	

In spite of the demise of the *Chungoe ilbo*, circulation in 1939 had increased to 163,134:[57]

Tonga ilbo	55,977
Chosŏn ilbo	95,939
Kidokkyo sinmun	5,128
Chungmin sinbo	2,972

Japanese publication policy entered a fourth phase after 1926. Although we find no public statement of a formal shift in policy, the pattern of seizure and suspension seems to indicate a renewed tightening of Japanese policy after 1926. From 1920 to 1925 confrontation between the nationalist press and the Japanese censors continued. The demise of *Sinsaenghwal* and *Shinch'ŏnji* newspapers and continued Japanese surveillance over radical thought and irresponsible criticism of Japanese policy indicated their anxiety about the ideological trends of the early 1920's. The Japanese suspended both the *Tonga ilbo* (once) and the *Chosŏn ilbo* (twice) in 1920, for a total of 177 days.[58] After 1925, however, the Japanese evoked more frequent suspensions to an elicit Korean compliance to censorship standards.[59] We can observe this trend in Table 1.

Of the twelve incidents of suspension (temporary and permanent) between 1920 and 1939, six fell between 1925 and 1930. In terms of number of days suspended, over half of the total suspension time occurred in these five years.[60] The same pattern is evident for seizure. The incidence of seizure rose after 1924 and peaked in 1930. In Taiwan, however, the incidence of seizure rose in direct correlation to

[56] Chōsen Sōtokufu, *Shuppanbutsu gaiyō*, 1930, pp. 19-34.

[57] Chōsen Sōtokufu, *Shuppan keisatsu gaiyō*, 1940, pp. 26-30.

[58] Chŏng, "Nōhon ken'etsu," p. 6.

[59] *Ibid.*, p. 4. This table, quoted from Chŏng, is a combination of statistics from both the *Chōsen ni okeru shuppanbutsu gaiyō* (1930) and the *Chōsen shuppan keisatsu gaiyō* (1940).

[60] *Ibid.*, p. 6.

TABLE 1
Number of Newspaper Seizures between 1920–1939 by Name

Source	Year	Tonga ilbo	Chosŏn ilbo	Chungoe ilbo	Maeil ilbo	Total
x	1920	16	24			40[a]
x	1921	15	23			38[a]
x	1922	15	23			38[a]
x	1923	14	20			27[a]
x	1924	56	48	49		153[a]
x	1925	57	56	26		151[a]
y	1926	33	53	26	3	115[b]
y	1927	44	54	38	3	139[b]
y	1928	26	21	25	3	76[b]
y	1929	28	21	24	4	78[b]
y	1930	21	16	21	1	61[b]
x	1931	17	9	6	6	38[a]
x	1932	7	8	5	4	24[a]
y	1933	6	9	6	1	22[b]
y	1934	12	4	4	1	21[b]
y	1935	2	3	3	5	13[b]
y	1936	9	13	8	6	36[c]
z	1937	2	8	ceased pub.	8	18[c]
z	1938	5	7		5	17[c]
z	1939	8	5		3	16[c]
	1940	Korean newspapers abolished				
Totals:		393	414	257	53	1,117

Sources: [a] Ommon shimbun o sashioseru kiji shūroku
[b] Chōsen ni okeru shuppanbutsu gaiyō (1930)
[c] Chōsen shuppan keisatsu gaiyō (1940)

Japanese military involvement on mainland China, peaking in the 1931-1937 period.[61]

In Korea, therefore, the publishing atmosphere of the 1930's was less antagonistic than that of the previous decade. The incidence of seizure and suspension dropped during this period, and the number of regular publication permits rose, indicating that the Japanese had screened out radical publications and dampened the will of publishers to fight the system. The dual Japanese policy of repressing radical publications while tolerating more apolitical materials took effect gradually, and the increasingly commercial nature of the Korean media confirmed this trend.

[61] Taiwan Sōtokufu, Taiwan no keisatsu, pp. 149-150.

In the 1920's the Japanese authorities created a dual standard by which to regulate the burgeoning Korean press. In the Japanese view, the advantage of allowing more publication freedom was lost if the new newspapers, magazines, and books served to spread radical ideology and to act as a forum for criticism of Japanese governance. The Japanese, therefore, moved swiftly to check the growth of socialist thought and magazines, while allowing, on the other hand, freer reign to publications that followed censorship guidelines. The actions against *Sinch'ŏnji* and *Sinsaenghwal* relatively early in the Saitō administration (1922-1923) served to set limits to Japanese tolerance toward freedom of the press. Although Korean newspapers continued publication, the first suspensions all dealt with continued publication of socialist and otherwise radical articles. Clearly, the Japanese "safety valve"—relaxing their issue of permits and allowing a "nationalist" press—did not mean that they tolerated the spread of radical nationalist or revolutionary thought.

The Japanese analysis of the post-1919 situation in Korea became more sophisticated. Having relaxed their repressive measures of the previous ten years, they now attempted to remove the immediate causes of widespread discontent in Korea without stimulating further nationalist demands. In a published speech given in April of 1922, the head of the Japanese police, Maruyama Tsurukichi, outlined Japanese views toward nationalist movements in Korea and their potential disruptive effect on colonial rule. Maruyama observed that the situation in Korea was at that time outwardly calm but that serious problems remained. The key problem, observed Maruyama, was whether or not the statistics that indicated decreasing violence and crime actually reflected real pacification in Korea.[62] Maruyama believed that the decrease in open hostility only reflected shift in tactics by Korean nationalists:[63]

> Another reason [for the decrease in violence] is the disillusionment with violence after the 1919 movement and a growing awareness that independence will not be easy. The diplomatic efforts at the Washington Conference and Versailles have failed. That failure was a result of a growing awareness in the United States of the true situation in Korea. . . . All diplomatic and foreign aid efforts have failed, and the realization of this has now sunk deeply into the Korean psyche.

[62] Maruyama Tsurukichi, *Chōsen chian no genjō oyobi shōrai* [Public Peace and Order in Korea, Present, and Future] (Keijō: Chōsen Sōtokufu, Jimukan, 1922), pp. 4-5.

[63] *Ibid.*, pp. 4-5.

Although the realization by Koreans that foreign help was not possible pleased Maruyama, he urged his government to watch carefully the rising trend of nationalist activity in Korea.

Maruyama divided the nationalist movement into two camps. One camp was made up of "cultural nationalists":[64]

> They [the cultural nationalists] advocate independence through their own means and methods. They realize that they can only depend on their own devices and have no real military power to gain independence now. Thus, they advocate self-strengthening for the future. There is a clear trend since 1919, that is, to work for independence for their grandchildren and reject dependence on great powers. The culture movement is essentially this type of independence movement; they hide their demands in cultural activities.

Maruyama took a cautiously optimistic attitude toward the cultural nationalists because of their program of non-violence. But behind their peaceful means lurked a dangerous tendency:[65]

> Speaking of national consciousness and cultural nationalists' psychology. . . . These new nationalist demands simply reflect the new times. Since World War I there has been a spread of the idea of nationalism and also democracy, liberalism and of self-determination. The cultural nationalists are most concerned about fair and impartial government. Because things are quieter now, they feel they must stimulate national consciousness.

Maruyama's second camp was made up of social revolutionaries. He argued that the leftist movement was rapidly gaining strength in Korea. Noting the proliferation of labor groups and radical youth groups which espoused the principles of class struggle and social revolution, Maruyama concluded that although these movements were as yet small and weak, they posed a very dangerous trend which was "here to stay and must be carefully handled."[66]

The new liberalization after the Terauchi repression (1910-1919) was a direct response to rising nationalist demands in Korea. This new policy tried to co-opt the nationalist movement by including more Koreans in the colonial government, and by allowing greater freedom to publish and organize, thus liberalizing Korean cultural life. Maruyama believed that this policy placed the Japanese in a di-

[64] *Ibid.*, p. 6.
[65] *Ibid.*, p. 10.
[66] *Ibid.*, p. 13.

lemma. Speaking of the future of Japanese policy and its relation to Korean nationalism, Maruyama declared:[67]

> Koreans will probably realize a larger role in the governing of Chōsen. But how fast and in what manner this transformation occurs is a serious problem and we must procede with caution. In the face of this trend toward more self-government our policy of fair government and soft treatment of the Koreans is risky because it will only provide further stimulus to the trend of increasing nationalist demands. So we are caught in a dilemma, as Koreans everywhere are beginning to realize their common nationality. It will be difficult to slow this trend or maybe even impossible to stop it.

Here, Maruyama struck upon the basic Japanese problem in Korea: how to continue control without inciting further Korean demands for self-rule. By giving in to some nationalist claims the Japanese were only laying the basis for future demands, and to allow publication of Korean newspapers was exactly the type of reform which would provoke this probability.

Maruyama continued his analysis with reference to India and Egypt and to British handling of the independence movements in those colonies. He concluded that the British had failed to realize that continued repression merely stimulated further nationalist demands. As a case in point he referred to the incarceration of Gandhi and the impetus that it gave to more mass demonstrations during the recent visit of the Crown Prince to India. Maruyama also worried that the passive resistance and massive boycott movements in India might become tactics used by nationalist groups in other colonies. The lesson of British bungling in India was clear to Maruyama:[68]

> But when we compare our rule to the British in India and Egypt we can see that we have done a better job in a much shorter time. We have achieved higher literacy rates in Korea than the British have in India or Egypt. The English are just trifling with reforms to curry favor with world opinion. . . . Theirs is still a cruel and unjust rule. Not to mention cultural and spiritual matters, our rule in Korea has been entirely different from the British and others who rule by various means such as "divide and conquer" (*bunbu shugi*). The fact remains, however, that nationalist demands and the trend for realizing nationalist demands will continue to grow

[67] *Ibid.*, p. 13.
[68] *Ibid.*, p. 19.

and we must be prepared to use all means and policies available to weaken the growth of the Korean nationalist spirit if we are to continue our rule.

Maruyama was urging Japanese policy makers not to fall into the trap in which the British found themselves in India while attempting to control the nationalist movement. Having adopted a policy of allowing limited Indian participation in colonial administration, the British had reduced the effectiveness of administrative attempts to control dissent.[69] The Indian nationalists had appealed to world opinion as well as to sympathetic political groups in England. Although the legal and administrative apparatus for restraining opposition in India had been in place and consistent after 1910, its implementation varied widely.[70] Indian nationalists played on British ambivalence and inconsistency; Maruyama was convinced that such a policy in Korea would bring increased chaos, especially by inviting public criticism of Japanese rule in the press.

Japanese awareness of the dilemma posed by a "soft" policy toward nationalist sentiment colored later colonial policy. The *bunka seiji* tact was their response to this problem: to loosen authority without abandoning objective controls. It is clear that the Japanese based their publication policy on this principle. Believing that the nationalist coloration of the new Korean press after 1920 was unfortunate but unavoidable, the Japanese wielded the censor's pen selectively by repressing social revolutionary thought as a first priority and then attempting to control by indirect means the nationalist tone of more moderate publications which represented a less immediate threat to Japanese interests. Maruyama's analysis of the political climate in Korea in the early 1920's further supports my contention that Japanese policy shifted from repression to manipulation during this period. Increased Korean participation in local governance and bringing more Koreans into the colonial bureaucracy after 1920 are examples of a deliberate Japanese strategy to confer more self-government in order to co-opt nationalist interests away from demanding total independence.[71]

But even after committing themselves to a policy of partial auton-

[69] Barrier, *Banned: Controversial Literature and Political Control in British India*, p. 155.
[70] *Ibid.*, p. 157.
[71] For a discussion of Japanese policy with regard to Korean participation in local government see Baldwin, "The March First Movement: Korean Challenge and Japanese Response," p. 211. See also Dong Wonmo, "Japanese Colonial Policy and Practice in Korea," unpublished Ph.D. Dissertation, Georgetown University, 1965, pp. 350-368.

omy in cultural matters and limited Korean participation in local government, the Japanese still encountered nationalist demands. By relaxing publication controls the Japanese still created new problems for themselves in their attempt to control the flood of materials produced after 1920. The Korean response to these relaxed controls clearly illustrated their desire to capitalize on new opportunities, both political and commercial, created by the new publication policy of 1920.

THE KOREAN RESPONSE TO COLONIAL PUBLICATION CONTROLS

In viewing the actual Korean response to Japanese publication restraints in the 1920's we find a picture of a defiant Korean press willing to take chances in order to stimulate national consciousness and anti-Japanese activity. This picture is in contrast to the conventional view of an intimidated press languishing helplessly under total colonial repression. In fact, the decade of the 1920's witnessed the resurgence of Korean publishing, and it was during this period that Korean publishers most aggressively challenged the Japanese censor.

The system of publication control established by the Japanese in Korea was by no means foolproof. The system itself provided numerous loopholes and logistical problems for the Japanese censors, and Korean publishers exploited the ambiguities in the law and administrative procedures to their advantage.

To begin with, the colonial censorship, based on the principle of pre-publication restraints, created a fundamental weakness for itself in dealing with daily newspapers. The law required each Korean newspaper to present a copy of the daily edition in exact form intended for printing before each press run. However, because of the logistical demands in publishing a daily, the Japanese permitted the setting of print to continue while presenting the specimen manuscript. The entire system was based on "trust between publisher and the police," according to one Japanese official experienced with censorship matters.[72] But what happened when "trust" broke down and the newspaper continued to print in the face of the censor's demand for revisions or delections? In such a case, the authorities issued a seizure order and attempted to recover newspapers previously printed. But in many cases the paper had already been distributed, necessitating the arduous job of collecting copies from the newsstands and the mails. After-the-fact seizure of newspapers was a time-consuming and difficult process. There are no figures for recovery rates of cen-

---

[72] Kōryoku (Pseud.), "Chōsen ni okeru shuppanbutsu no kōsatsu" [An Analysis of Publications in Korea], *Keimu ihō*, 296 (December 1930), p. 39.

sored newspapers in Korea, but in the case of Japan the police were never very successful, and one can assume that the Japanese encountered similar problems in Korea.[73] The difficulties inherent in recovering materials previously printed and distributed was the main reason for the predominance of pre-publication measures, both formal and informal.

Another problem in Korea was that a censorship order focused attention on a particular newspaper item or magazine article. In many cases, a seizure order or erasure stimulated increased curiousity and interest in a publication, as a result of which copies eluding the censor received wider circulation than would have been the case without a seizure order.[74] For this very reason, the Japanese used a cancellation order (kaijo) revoking various warnings and ban orders. Such an order was issued in the fall of 1929, rescinding the ban on reporting the Kwangju riots and related disturbances. The Japanese decided that the original news ban on the Kwangju riots created an atmosphere of rumor and innuendo worse than open reporting of the incident itself.[75]

Yet another problem in the censorship system was the fact that it dealt with a foreign language—namely, Korean materials. The police examined an increasing number of publications during the 1920's and were responsible for the three major Korean dailies. This required the hiring of language experts and a staff of Koreans to handle the increasing volume of material. The Korean staff did the initial screening, but a Japanese official was responsible for the final decisions on erasure, deletion, or banning of a particular piece.[76] The censors appear to have been less than thorough. Article after article in the nationalist press contained erasures and wholesale deletions; yet where the censor deleted the four Chinese characters for Korean independence (Han'guk tongnip) or class struggle (kyegŭp t'ujaeng), he often overlooked the identical phrases in the pure Korean alphabet (han'gŭl). Thus, Japanese unfamiliarity with the Korean language provided another chink in the armor of censorship.

Finally, the complicated nature of the censorship law in Korea provided loopholes for publication unintended by the system's creators. The dual system of laws, one for newspapers and one for magazines

---

[73] Okudaira gives the following recovery rates for censored newspapers in Japan: Newspapers, 15%; Political magazines, 20-30%; Books, 30-70%. Okudaira, "Political Censorship in Japan from 1931-45," pp. 50-51.

[74] Kōryoku, "Chōsen ni okeru shuppanbutsu no kōsatsu," p. 41.

[75] Chŏng, Han'guk ŏllon t'ujaengsa, p. 51.

[76] Kim Tong-in, "Chinan shijŏl ŭi ch'ulp'anmul kŏmyŏl" [Past Censorship of Published Materials] in Tongin chŏnjip (Seoul: Saja ch'ulp'ansa, 1964), p. 323.

and books, with different permit regulations (stricter for newspapers and less severe for books), created a loophole for Korean publishers to exploit. Having been denied a permit for a general magazine, a permit that would allow political criticism and discussion, a Korean publisher could and did apply for a book permit and publish his magazine as a series of books.[77] One source, writing for the Korean Police Report (*Keisatsu ihō*), cited eighty-two different violations of permit regulations using this gambit. The offending "magazine" published as many as three issues as "books" before running afoul of the censor.[78]

In addition to the permit loophole, there was confusion over the definition of a newspaper as opposed to a magazine, and therefore difficulties arose in determining which permit system to apply. In many cases the final decision was up to the Japanese official, who could employ his own subjective judgment. Some political publications gained permits because of this confusion.[79] Duality of laws was not limited to the type of publication, that is, the distinction between newspapers and magazines-books. The two sets of laws, one for Japanese publications and the other for Korean materials, provided additional problems for the censors. Korean publishers could publish in Japan and send these materials to Korea, thereby avoiding the stricter censorship in the colony.

Korean publishers exploited the loopholes and ambiguities in the censorship system with varying results throughout the colonial period. During the protectorate, when the Japanese were still establishing their control over publications as well as over other areas of governance in Korea, Korean publishers used figurehead foreign editors to avoid censorship. The most prominent case of this tactic was the editorship of E. T. Bethell of the *Korea Daily News*, previously discussed.[80]

In 1908 the Japanese promulgated amendments to the 1907 law, bringing foreign newspapers published in Korea under the existing censorship regulations. Simultaneously, the Japanese appealed to the British consul general to remove Bethell, a Briton, from Korea and eventually, successfully pressed charges against Bethell in the Consular Court in Shanghai in the spring of 1908.[81] Although the 1908 regulations placed foreign-owned publications under identical restric-

---

[77] Kōryoku, "Chōsen ni okeru shuppanbutsu no kōsatsu," *Keimu ihō*, 298 (February 1931), p. 16.

[78] *Ibid.*, p. 16.

[79] *Ibid.*, pp. 19-20.

[80] Chŏng, *Han'guk ŏllon t'ujaengsa*, pp. 33-35.

[81] Kim and Kim, *Korea and Politics of Imperialism*, pp. 185-188.

tions as Korean, publishers continued to exploit the dual nature of the law. Between 1910 and 1919, the most repressive period for publications, Korean publishers continued to use dummy and figurehead editors and authors, often sympathetic Japanese.[82] In addition, Koreans published under the less restrictive Japanese law in Japan and then imported these materials into the colony.[83]

Korean publishers also exploited Japanese unfamiliarity with the Korean language. Many writers and editors, aware of the censorship standards, exercised artful self-censorship by deleting words and phrases which, while obviously against the standards, could still be implied through context.[84] The judicious use of x marks (fuseji) gave rise to what were referred to as "brickwall" newspapers (pyŏkdol sinmun). By using the same x marks as the censor but including them before submission of the manuscript for the censor's inspection, writers were able to construct essays and articles in such a manner as to clearly telegraph their message without running afoul of the censor. This was also a common technique in Japan, where censorship officials were finally obliged to issue a warning about the inclusion of too many x marks in manuscripts.[85]

Perhaps the most effective method of avoiding the censor was also one of the boldest. This method involved rushing to press an issue of a newspaper or magazine that the editors were certain would not pass the censor. With careful timing and the new high-speed printing presses, many copies could be printed and distributed before the formal order to hold the edition or delete a certain article was received from the censor. A vivid account of this tactic was described in the Chōsen keisatsu ihō, where an anonymous censor described the rush to press gambit as follows:[86]

> There are ways to get around the system by using secrecy. High-speed presses make it possible to print many copies of a paper at the rate of 30,000 pages or 15,000 newspapers an hour. The Koreans start the presses as soon as the sample copy is sent to the censor. They then keep the presses rolling until they get an order to stop, distributing the papers as quickly as possible.

[82] Yi Myŏng-jae, "Ilche ŭi kŏmyŏl i sinmunhak e kichin yŏnghyang" [The Effects of Censorship on Modern Korean Literature], Ŏmun yŏn'gu, Vol. 3, Nos. 1 and 2 (May 1975), p. 2.

[83] Ibid., p. 264.

[84] Ibid., p. 258.

[85] Okudaira, "Political Censorship in Japan from 1930-1945," p. 12.

[86] Kōryoku, "Chōsen ni okeru shuppanbutsu no kōsatsu," Keimu ihō, 296 (December 1930), p. 40.

Considering the difficulty of recovering newspapers once distributed, it is obvious that this particular trick was effective. The Japanese official reports on publishing controls in Korea were noticeably silent about this particular problem.

Finally, the separation of laws, one for Koreans and another for Japanese, caused continued problems for the Japanese censors. The *Japanese Publication Police Survey* noted that:[87]

> There are at least ten newspapers published in Japan but intended for distribution in Korea. Because of different laws these papers are able to publish in Japan with just a report (no pre-publication inspection), but in Korea they might not be allowed to publish in the first place. It has been difficult to determine what law to apply to these newspapers.

The dilemma for the authorities was solved by a Japanese High Court (*Kōtō-hōin*) decision of May 1926, which stated that if most newspapers of a particular publication were sent to Korea, they had to abide by Korean regulations.[88] The Japanese concern for imported materials is understandable, considering the increased volume of such imports during the colonial period. The total imports of newspapers and magazines into Korea (the majority coming from Japan) increased from nearly 1,200 in 1927 to over 550,000 by 1939.[89]

Japanese authorities in Taiwan were also concerned about the rising number of imports. Although they had always strictly monitored incoming publications, the government-general of Taiwan further strengthened the system by creating a government-general of Taiwan inspection office in Tokyo in 1930.[90] All Japanese publications bound for Taiwan had to first pass inspection in Japan.

The above chronicle of "abuses" and "weaknesses" in the system aptly demonstrates why the Japanese were interested in solving censorship problems before they arose. Indeed, as we have seen, the system was predicated on the desire to avoid problems through pre-publication warnings, the threat of financial loss due to seizure, and, finally, formal legal charges and imprisonment of offenders. Indeed, one aspect of the system is never adequately discussed, that is, the personal relationships between Korean publishers and Japanese police. As mentioned before, the system was based to a great extent on "trust" and cooperation between publishers and police. The Japanese

[87] Chōsen Sōtokufu, *Shuppanbutsu gaiyō*, 1930, pp. 175-176.

[88] *Ibid.*, p. 176.

[89] Chōsen Sōtokufu, *Shuppan keisatsu gaiyō*, 1940, p. 126. Well over 95 percent of imported materials came from Japan.

[90] Taiwan Sōtokufu, *Taiwan no keisatsu*, p. 149.

hoped that Korean publishers would follow the guidelines, thereby avoiding nasty confrontations. This would allow a Korean press to publish without the Japanese having to worry about the media's fomenting criticism and, worse yet, insurrection in Korea. But Koreans, angered by the discriminatory publishing laws and infused with nationalist enthusiasm after 1920, refused to "cooperate" in the manner of Japanese publishers in Korea.[91]

The extensive pre-publication warning system and the use of consultation and discussion to ward off problems before they arose indicate that the Japanese relied greatly upon informal controls. The informality of this system is impressive. The friendly discussion (*kondan*) used by the censor to persuade recalcitrant publishers into modifying or changing an editorial line was based on an appeal to the interests of both the editor and censor. If problems could be avoided, the editor could continue without financial loss or court action, and the censor could control the disruptive social consequences of "dangerous" thought or irresponsible criticism.

Because of the informal nature of the system, it is difficult to determine how effective consultation and compromise were in shaping the tone of the colonial press. This also raises important questions about Korean resistance. The 1920's were characterized by significant conflict between Korean publishers and the censor and a growing Japanese repression in the latter part of the decade. But a glance at the statistics for seizures, bans, and suspensions in the 1930's shows a decrease in such actions. Had Koreans given up the struggle or otherwise moderated their tone to fit the censor? Or did Japanese repression effectively choke off more militant publications which, ceasing to exist, can no longer appear as statistics?

The answer to these questions is complex. To begin with, the Japanese singled out radical publications from the very beginning. Even after the relaxation of publication controls in 1920, the first publications to be banned were socialist and otherwise radical magazines. But what of the more moderate publications and the Korean newspapers? Although suspended repeatedly in the 1920's and otherwise harassed by the Japanese authorities, they continued publication until the opening of the Pacific War. In addition, the 1930's witnessed a decrease in the number of censorship actions against the newspapers. The answer to why this trend emerged lies in the changing nature of the Korean press.

While the 1920's marked the emergence of the nationalist press and its confrontation with Japanese authority, the 1930's were less com-

[91] Chōsen Sōtokufu, *Shuppanbutsu gaiyō*, 1930, p. 84.

bative. Paek Sun-jae has described the 1930's as a period that marked the advent of general, well-financed, and mass-circulation magazines (*chonghap chapchi*), a significant contrast to the smaller but more politically daring magazines of the earlier decade.[92] A process of financial attrition and Japanese oppression had slowly eliminated smaller organ magazines and politically oriented journals during the 1920's. The decline of the smaller and more politically oriented magazines (*tonginji*) coincided with a growing commercialization of the press in Korea. New commercial *chonghap chapchi* such as *New Asia* (*Sindonga*, published by the *Tonga ilbo*), *Korean Light* (*Chogwang*, published by the *Chosŏn ilbo*), *Korea* (*Samch'-ŏnji*) and *Eastern Light* (*Tonggwang*) had sound financial backing, were printed for a mass audience, and were no longer platforms for political debates.[93] The advent of the *chonghap chapchi* was accompanied by the rise of large circulation women's magazines and other special audience publications, often related to the large *chonghap chapchi* published by the major Korean newspapers.

Indeed, publishing in the 1930's had become big business. The successful publications were products of major publishing groups and were well financed and slickly produced for mass tastes. The growing commercial trend in the Korean press of the 1930's diverted newspapers and magazines from their earlier anti-Japanese efforts. Certainly, as major Korean publications, they continued to view themselves as the main organs of Korean public opinion, but the strident nationalism of the 1920's had been replaced by less political themes.[94] Censorship and confrontation, after all, meant a larger financial gamble in terms of mass publishing, and seizure or suspension could involve tremendous losses.

As early as 1925, criticism appeared, attacking the growing commercial trend in the press. An anonymous author, writing in the December 1925 issue of *Kaebyŏk*, raised some important issues concerning the role of the press and its position in colonial society. After describing the power of the media and their vital role in shaping public opinion, the author continued by criticizing the loss of political commitment in favor of profit:[95]

[92] Paek, "Chapchi rŭl t'onghae pon ilche sidae ŭi kŭndaehwa undong," in *Sindonga*, 22 (May 1966), p. 362.

[93] *Ibid.*, p. 365.

[94] *Ibid.*, p. 366.

[95] XY Saeng (Pseud.), "Hyŏnha sinmun chapchi e taehan pip'an" [A Critique of Contemporary Newspapers and Magazines], in *Kaebyŏk*, Vol. 6, No. 10 (December 1925), p. 47.

In their day-by-day struggle, the leadership of the media seem only concerned about money. Money translates itself into editorial strength. It is most common to have a group invest money to start a paper, but they only expect a return on their investment. They fight for their money to the detriment of the paper, and the managers [editors] do not oppose this.

Contrasting this new commercial emphasis with earlier newspapers, the author continued, betraying his political predilections by criticizing commercialism in the press:[96]

Early newspapers and magazines had ideals and aspirations for society and thus a constructive educational value. Yet in a capitalist system newspapers are now only concerned with selling goods and print anything to gain a readership. They consider themselves the clarion of society, but in reality they only support the class structure . . . money and power.

The article concluded by positing questions on the future role of newspapers in society and their relationship with the colonial government:[97]

Each paper does not maintain a consistent position toward government policy. They search for the good in the government-general policy even when they wish to criticize it, calculating their advantage even in confrontation. In the end, they fall into line with the *Maeil sinbo* (GGK Organ). There is no consistent position but only a wandering pursuit of the business at hand. The question remains, is this a compromise or is it not? Political debate is possible only within the approved limits of the colonial order. Will the media go out to meet the challenge or will their position remain vague and dream-like? The decision will be interesting to watch.

The decision was made in favor of commercial interests instead of political confrontation as in the 1930's. The above criticism reflected the views of only one author, but these observations came at a critical period in colonial publication history. After 1926, the new Peace Preservation Law was applied to Korea by government-general order, and there was increased confrontation with the press in Korea. The highest rates of deletion and seizure came in the 1927-1930 period, after which the statistics reflect a drop in censorship actions.[98] It seemed the Japanese were weeding out all political and radical pub-

[96] *Ibid.*, p. 50.
[97] *Ibid.*, p. 56.
[98] See table on page 327.

lications which had emerged in the late 1920's in accordance with their generally more severe line toward radical thought in metropolitan Japan. Thus the publishing world in the 1930's, comprised of those newspapers and magazines which managed to continue and even thrive, was characterized by a more pliable Korean stance toward Japanese rule. Opposition and criticism continued, but it was overshadowed by the growth of large, more commercially oriented enterprises. This phenomenon was a product of Japanese repression, which provided a financial incentive for cooperation, but suspension, seizure, or prison for publishers who attempted to continue the nationalist struggle.

CENSORSHIP, INTELLECTUAL CLIMATE, AND THE DEVELOPMENT OF KOREAN NATIONALISM

Colonial censorship directly affected the development of the nationalist movement by setting the limits of public political discussion. Publishing and public debate were vital to the development of nationalist ideology. After the turn of the century, publishing became synonymous with nationalist activity. Newspapers, enlightenment magazines, and books on Western political thought and systems became the nationalist intelligentsia's vehicle for creating a new national identity, as well as a means of communicating the nationalist message to the Korean masses. Japanese publication controls skewed the development of the Korean media in general, but in particular it shaped the context of the nationalist media and the way that it was disseminated within Korean society.

A dual standard in censorship policy affected the development of nationalist ideology by totally suppressing radical and social revolutionary thought, yet tolerating, to a point, more moderate nationalist writing. Even during the relatively relaxed period between 1920-1925, social revolutionary thought and radical nationalist ideology bore the brunt of Japanese censorship. The closure of the two principal socialist publications in 1922-1923 was a clear indication of the limits of Japanese tolerance, even after they had made a commitment to allow more Korean publications after 1920. While the Japanese could and did tolerate certain nationalist themes in the Korean newspapers and other major intellectual journals, any avowedly revolutionary magazine was suppressed. The Japanese risked the public uproar that accompanied the closure of Kaebyŏk (Creation), the most prestigious colonial intellectual journal, in 1926 because they could no longer ignore its radical editorial line. Kaebyŏk was suspended only after lesser measures had failed to change its tone.

The suppression of radical thought removed the discussion of socialism and other radical ideas from the Korean press. In doing so, the Japanese greatly hampered the more radical wing of the Korean nationalist movement in its ideological struggle with the moderate cultural nationalists. Although the harassment of leftist journals and articles, combined with the successive arrests of nascent Korean communist organizations, glorified leftists as intransigently anti-Japanese patriots, it also removed them from public view in the ongoing ideological debate over the form and future of the Korean nation.[99]

Cultural nationalists and other moderates continued their publishing efforts in the main Korean newspapers and journals. Their moderate posture of non-confrontation was thus rewarded by the Japanese censor in two further respects. By more closely following the censorship standard, the moderate Korean press became, by default, the leader of public opinion and perhaps the most important force shaping national identity among the growing literate population of the colony. Secondly, Japanese toleration of the more moderate elements in the Korean press rewarded these publishers financially.

The growing commercialization of the press in Korea during the 1930's was evidence of a new consideration in the minds of Korean publishers beyond politics. The 1920's had been a period of growth for the nationalist press, a press infused with idealism and a sense of mission. Much of the initial enthusiasm of the nationalist press to confront the Japanese and to champion Korean nationalism in the early 1920's seemed lost to Korean publishers in the next decade. By the 1930's, media was big business, and political confrontation with the Japanese was bad for business. All Korean newspapers continued to advocate Korean nationalism, but the strident tone and willingness to take losses and chances were replaced with financial caution. Both the *Chosŏn ilbo* and the *Tonga ilbo* became the nucleus of large financial conglomerates. As commercial concerns they developed new interests beyond politics, and one might speculate that the Japanese were gratified by the growing commercialization of the Korean press, at least in so far as it reduced the level of ideological turmoil in the colony.

Although the Korean press seemed more tractable politically in the 1930's, its increased sophistication and expanding circulation offered new problems for the Japanese authorities. The theoretical basis of Japanese colonial policy was a political, economic, and cultural as-

[99] The main arrests of Korean Communists occurred in Nov. 1925 (First KCP Incident), June 1926 (Second KCP Incident), February 1928 (Third KCP Incident), and August 1928 (Fourth KCP Incident). See Chongsik Lee and R. Scalapino, *Korean Communism*, Vol. I (Berkeley: University of California Press, 1972), Chapter 2.

similation of Korea with Japan. The expansion of the Korean language press worked directly counter to this ideal. Korean language publications undermined linguistic assimilation by spreading the use of the Korean language and providing the main vehicle for its transformation into a modern vernacular. In addition, the growth of a Korean press stimulated Korean national identity and provided a basis for the development of a modern Korean literature. Although the Japanese were very successful in transmitting the use of the Japanese language in the colony through the school system, the gains in Japanese literacy were offset by the expanding use of Korean.[100]

In contrast, liberalization of colonial policy after 1919 did not correspond to an expansion of cultural freedom in Taiwan. In fact, the policy of gradual assimilation was dropped, and changes were made to further reduce the cultural distance between Taiwan and the mother country.[101] The Japanese never relaxed their control over the press in Taiwan. Although there was a movement after 1921 to promote Taiwanese identity—the Taiwan Cultural Association—the absence of a vernacular press inhibited the growth of a strong nationalist identity in Taiwan. Indeed, most established nationalist groups in Taiwan limited their demands to autonomy within the empire.[102]

Faced with the prospect of continued discontent in Korea after 1919, the Japanese loosened restrictions on cultural autonomy in order to moderate resentment of Japanese rule. At the same time, this policy demanded a heightened vigilance over the new force represented by the Korean vernacular press. Aware of the potential of the press for stimulating nationalist consciousness, the Japanese chose to monitor publications flexibly. Conceding that the very presence of an expanding nationalist press countered the long-term goal of assimilation, they made the relative political tone of each publication the principal determinant of censorship. The censor in Korea tolerated moderate publications and vigorously suppressed any publication which immediately menaced the public order.

This flexible policy profoundly effected the Korean nationalist movement. The Japanese tacitly supported more moderate elements in the nationalist camp in their struggle with the radical wing by curbing all leftist publications. Yet, even though the moderate nationalists had found a way to remain relatively active during the colonial period, their very success in getting by in colonial society com-

[100] Dong Wonmo, "Assimilation and Social Mobilization in Korea: A Study of Japanese Policy and Political Integration Effects," in A. Nahm, ed., Korea Under Japanese Colonial Rule, pp. 146-184.

[101] Tsurumi, Japanese Colonial Education in Taiwan, pp. 79-80.

[102] Chen, "Formosan Political Movements Under Japanese Colonial Rule," passim.

promised their legitmacy as nationalist leaders after the demise of Japanese rule. Because the persecution of the left strengthened the nationalist credentials of the radical wing in the struggle for control of the movement after 1945, the stage was set for a bitter confrontation with the moderates in the post-colonial era. Although moderate nationalists believed that their involvement with the commercial press in the 1930's was patriotic work, radicals who had languished in Japanese prisons saw this same activity as self-serving collaboration. In the immediate post-colonial era, the issue of collaboration was a constant thorn in the side of moderates who had survived during the colonial era by avoiding open confrontation with the Japanese administration in Korea.

The Japanese publication policy continued to affect the Korean experience after 1945. The establishment of a republic did not eliminate the idea of governmental control over publication. In fact, the Japanese publication laws remained on the books in South Korea until 1953.[103] The experience of Korean publishers since liberation has not been a happy one. Except for brief periods of relaxed government supervision, publishing in Korea, and Taiwan for that matter, remains a tightly regulated activity. The Korean Constitution, much as the old Meiji Constitution, provides for the right of free speech, except where limited by statute. Intimidation of Korean newspapers and endless red tape for magazine publishers in both halves of the country, as well as in the Republic of China, is reminiscent of the pre-publication warning system of the colonial period, though now it is indigenous officials who monitor the work of indigenous writers and publishers. The press policies of those countries continue to be based on governmental interest and pervasive distrust of a free media, a legacy of their Japanese colonial heritage.

[103] Chŏng, *Han'guk ŏllon t'ujaengsa*, p. 30.

PART III

The Economic Dynamics of the Empire

CHAPTER 9

Colonialism and Development: Korea, Taiwan, and Kwantung

Samuel Pao-San Ho

This essay measures and analyzes economic growth in three colonies within the broad context of Japanese imperialism.[1] The essay first discusses Japan's needs and how they determined the economic role played by her colonies. It then examines Japanese policy in its colonies, the economic programs, and how the Japanese financed those programs. Next, I analyze the pattern of colonial development, particularly growth and structural changes in the major economic sectors and in trade. In treating these themes, I show how Japanese administrators and Japanese colonists controlled their colonial economies and captured an economic surplus. This discussion is followed by an analysis of how colonial development improved the economic conditions of the native populations. The essay concludes by comparing my findings to the conventional wisdom on Japanese colonial development.

JAPANESE NEEDS AND COLONIAL DEVELOPMENT

Like the European colonial powers, Japan managed its colonies for its own interest. Japan looked to its colonies to supply goods and raw materials scarce at home. As Japan developed and its economic structure altered in the early 1900's, developing colonies were viewed by many as a way to resolve Japan's balance-of-payments difficulties. As Japan became more urbanized and industrialized, the colonies were viewed for their agricultural products. As Japan's modern sector expanded, its colonies also became important as a source of fuels and industrial raw materials for its industries and a secure market for its manufactured goods (e.g., textiles). Finally, in the 1930's, prepara-

[1] Japan's three colonies had a total land area of 260,693 sq. km., distributed as follows: Korea, 220,974 sq. km.; Kwantung (including the SMR zone), 3,760 sq. km.; and Taiwan, 35,959 sq. km. In 1930, Korea's total population was 20.4 million; Kwantung's (including the SMR zone), 1.5 million and Taiwan's 4.6 million.

tion for war played an increasingly important role in determining the pattern of development in the colonies.

A Source of tropical imports

Despite rapid agricultural export growth during the early Meiji period (made possible by a significant rise in the growth rate of agricultural production), Japan's total exports were unable to keep pace with the import demands of rapid industrialization. Like so many of today's developing countries, Japan faced serious balance-of-payments difficulties throughout the early years of its economic development. In twenty-two of the first twenty-eight years of the Meiji era, Japan imported more goods and services than it exported.[2] When Japan acquired Taiwan in 1895, it had a modest modern sector but still depended primarily on its traditional agricultural and craft sector for its exports. With the modern sector as yet unable to contribute its share of export earnings to help to finance the still growing imports, one of Japan's most urgent needs was to find ways to ease its balance-of-payments difficulties.

Annexing Taiwan gave Japan its first large area climatically suited to sugarcane cultivation. Between 1896 and 1904, Japan annually used an average of ¥22 million of its foreign exchange earnings to finance its sugar imports, an amount that accounted for more than 50 percent of its trade deficit during this period.[3] Not surprisingly, considering Japan's foreign exchange needs and Taiwan's natural endowment, Japan adopted the import substitution policy of imposing high import duties on foreign sugar while promoting cane cultivation in Taiwan. Under this protectionist policy, sugar production in Taiwan rapidly increased, and Taiwanese sugar helped to ease Japan's balance-of-payments problem.

The Colonies as agricultural appendages

During the Meiji period Japanese agriculture supported industrial growth by supplying labor. Even though population density was high in rural Meiji Japan, the marginal product of labor was not zero, so that, other things being equal, labor could not be shifted from agriculture to the modern sector without agricultural output being re-

[2] Kazushi Ohkawa, Nobukiyo Takamatsu and Yūzō Yamamoto, *Estimates of Long-Term Economic Statistics of Japan Since 1868, 1, National Income* (Tokyo: Tōyō Keizai Shimpōsha, 1974), table 7.

[3] Calculated from *Hundred Year Statistics of the Japanese Economy* (Tokyo: Bank of Japan, 1966), pp. 278-279 and 282-289.

duced and prematurely ending the development process. When Japan first began to modernize, it was able to increase agricultural productivity by exploiting internal growth potentials, thereby facilitating the transfer of resources from agriculture to the modern sector. These internal sources of agricultural progress were improvements in traditional farming methods and the transfer of better techniques (superior seeds, intensive use of fertilizer, and better farming methods) to backward areas of western and eastern Japan.

By the 1910's these "indigenous" sources of growth were exhausted, and output growth in agriculture slowed, declining from an average annual rate of 2.38 percent between 1897 and 1901, to 1.91 percent from 1901 to 1917, to only 0.44 percent between 1917 and 1931. Even though Japan's modern sector was now quite large, and the country was no longer as dependent upon agriculture as before, this slower agricultural growth presented Japan with a serious problem.

Population growth and rising per capita income reinforced the strong demand for agricultural goods, while farm production lagged. The immediate consequence was a shortage of rice and a sharp increase in agricultural prices that ultimately led to riots in major Japanese cities in 1918. The long-term consequence was that labor could not leave agriculture for industry without causing the terms of trade between agriculture and industry to shift adversely for the modern sector. Wages in the modern sector would therefore rise even though underemployment continued to exist in agriculture. A rise in real wages threatened to reduce industrial profits and cut back on industrial investments. If investment in the modern sector fell, fewer laborers could leave agriculture for the modern sector, thus slowing up the pace of modernization. These gloomy consequences posed a serious problem for Japan's rapid industrialization.

The problem could be resolved in one of several ways. Japan could try to increase food production at home by supplying new inputs to agriculture. Or the country could import food from abroad to keep agricultural prices in line. Finally, Japan could import rice from its colonies, Korea and Taiwan. Understandably, Japan rejected the first two alternatives. New farming inputs would have required substantial investments in research, and the uncertain rate of return on these investments made that action unattractive. In any event, large investments in agriculture would have taken resources away from the modern sector, and Japanese policy makers were reluctant to do that. To import food from outside the empire was equally unacceptable because Japan would have had to reduce its import of capital goods and industrial supplies.

The third alternative was more attractive. Because farming techniques were more advanced in Japan than in the colonies, agricultural productivity within the empire could be raised significantly by transferring superior Japanese farming techniques to the colonies. While this transfer of technology was not without its difficulties, it appeared less risky and less costly than the other options—less risky because Korea and Taiwan were already important rice producers, and the rice technology involved was familiar to the Japanese; less costly because the resources needed to develop agriculture in the colonies could be supplied largely by the colonies themselves, without interrupting the pace of Japan's industrialization by taking resources away from its modern sector.

By selecting this third option, the Japanese determined Korea's and Taiwan's economic position in the empire: they became agricultural appendages of Japan. They were to supply inexpensive rice to prevent Japan's industrial wages from rapidly rising. These colonies also served as markets for Japanese manufactures. This decision had far-reaching implications for all parties concerned.[4]

Unlike the situation in Korea and Taiwan, Japan's primary interest in Kwantung was not in its agriculture, which had little potential to produce rice, but in its commercial and strategic importance. The occupation of Kwantung (and the South Manchuria Railway, SMR, zone) gave Japan a foothold in Manchuria and the operational base to extend its control over Manchuria's natural resources and market. Consequently, Kwantung was administered and developed with two primary aims: (1) to help Japanese businesses to capture the Manchurian market and (2) to facilitate the development and extraction of Manchuria's natural resources for Japan's benefit.

Sources of industrial raw materials

After 1930 a new phase in colonial development took place. Again, the impetus for change came from Japan. The 1930's were marked by Japanese military adventure and imperial expansion in Manchuria, growing protectionism in the West against Japanese products, rising militarism and increased emphasis on war preparations in Japan. The new political and economic environment helped to create in Japan a strong desire for self-sufficiency and an increase in military power, developments that moved Japan to diversify its economy and to ex-

---

[4] The consequences of this policy on Japan are analyzed in Yujirō Hayami and Vernon W. Ruttan, "Korean Rice, Taiwan Rice and Japanese Agricultural Stagnation: An Economic Consequence of Colonialism," in *Quarterly Journal of Economics*, LXXXIV (November 1970), pp. 562-589.

pand its strategic heavy industries. Accordingly, Japan's colonial policy was again modified to support this new industrialization drive.

The new colonial policy called for a tighter integration of the colonies with Japan. In strategic terms Taiwan was the natural base from which Japan could extend its influence in South China and Southeast Asia. Taiwan already served as the main naval base for Japanese operations in the South Seas. Korea and Kwantung became even more important after Japan annexed Manchuria and displayed an interest in North China. To be self-sufficient within the empire, Japan had to develop the industrial resources in her colonies and to rearrange the division of labor between her industries at home and those in the colonies.

Although Japan continued to manufacture for the empire, industries in the colonies were now encouraged to develop, partly to provide raw materials and industrial supplies for Japan's heavy industry and partly to relieve Japan's hard-pressed manufacturing sector. But the Japanese took pains to select only certain industries that complemented and supported the industrial development program in Japan. In order to release more resources to develop heavy industry at home, the Japanese also tried to move some labor-intensive light manufacturing industries, such as textiles, to Taiwan, but World War II ended this program before it could bear fruit.

JAPANESE COLONIAL DEVELOPMENT POLICIES

Not surprisingly, the Japanese tried to develop Korea, Kwantung, and Taiwan as they had developed their economy in the late nineteenth century. Many economic programs initiated in the colonies had their origin in policies drafted in the Meiji era. In early Meiji the government played a key role in mobilizing resources for development and provided entrepreneurial leadership to new economic enterprises. Active government participation in the economy was repeated in the colonies, and it proved to be more extensive than in Japan. Colonial economic growth was initiated and sustained through powerful government efforts to expand the economic infrastructure, to increase investment in human capital through health and education, and to raise productivity.

The Economic infrastructure

After Japan gained control of Korea, Kwantung, and Taiwan, colonial officials began investing heavily in railroads, harbors, roads, warehousing, banking, etc., and these investments continued at a high level throughout the colonial period.[5] Transportation and communication projects consistently absorbed the largest share of the colonial governments' investments.[6] From the Japanese viewpoint, an inexpensive and efficient transport and communication system was indispensable to control and to manage properly the colonies as well as to promote closer economic ties between the colonies and Japan. Since these infrastructure projects were too risky and costly for private entrepreneurs to finance, the government led the way.

Expanding the economic infrastructure lowered transportation and transaction costs, barriers that had kept communities in the colonies isolated from one another, and transformed fragmented economies into integrated market systems. At the same time an expanded economic infrastructure increased the profitability of private investments in agriculture, commerce, and industry. In Kwantung, developing transportation and communication also advanced Japan's strategic and commercial interests in Manchuria.

Health and education

That health, education, and labor skills improved and that colonial officials brought this about can be readily documented. The sharp drop in death rates dramatizes the healthier environment created in the colonies. In Taiwan the death rate declined from 33 to 19 deaths per 1,000 between 1906 and 1940, and in Korea it declined from 35 to 23 deaths per 1,000 between 1910 and 1935-1940.[7] Better diet, increased availability of modern medical services, and a general improvement in the public health environment reduced mortality.[8]

[5] In 1900 Taiwan had few roads or railroads, but in 1920, it had 637 km. of public railways, 3,553 km. of roads, and considerable harbor facilities at Keelung and Kaohsiung. Similar rapid transport and harbor development occurred in Korea and the Liaotung.

[6] Toshiyuki Mizoguchi, *Taiwan Chōsen no keizai seichō* [The Economic Growth of Taiwan and Korea] (Tokyo: Iwanami Shoten, 1975); and Samuel P.-S. Ho, "The Development Policy of the Japanese Colonial Government in Taiwan, 1895-1945," in Gustav Ranis, ed., *Government and Economic Development* (New Haven and London: Yale University Press, 1971).

[7] Samuel P.-S. Ho, *Economic Development of Taiwan 1860-1970* (New Haven and London: Yale University Press, 1978), Table A. 11. Reliable death rates cannot be computed directly from Korea's household registration data. I have used Tai-hwan Kwon's estimates in Tai-hwan Kwon et al., *The Population of Korea* (Seoul: The Population and Development Studies Center, Seoul National University, 1975), Table 11.4. These are similar to estimates in Yunshik Chang, *Population in Early Modernization: Korea*, Ph.D. diss., Princeton University, 1966, p. 268.

[8] In Korea, per capita calorie intake did not increase, so improved diet did not account for the decline in Korea's death rate.

The colonial governments' annual expenditure on health and medical services was small, e.g., in Taiwan it was usually below ¥0.5 million, about 1–1.5 percent of total government expenditure. Not surprisingly, access to modern medical facilities and services in the colonies was limited and improved only gradually. Further, the distribution of modern medical services favored the urban areas, where most of the Japanese colonists lived. Yet the Japanese created a healthier environment in the colonies by relying heavily on administrative measures and direct control. They controlled infectious diseases and improved sanitary conditions by enforcing quarantine regulations, compulsory testing for and treatment of malaria, vaccination campaigns, supervised collection of human waste, and regular public health inspections. Significantly, the police department carried out these assignments in addition to maintaining law and order.

Impressive advances were also made in the field of formal education. The educational institution with the greatest impact was the publicly financed elementary school. A broad spectrum of Chinese, Korean, and Taiwanese youth received their education in these schools. In Kwantung and the SMR zone, the enrollment in Japanese-style primary schools increased from about 1,000 students in 1906 to 36,000 in 1920 and nearly 93,000 in 1935. Even though one-half of these students were Japanese, in 1935 some 19 percent of the school age (6–15) Chinese population in Kwantung and the SMR zone were enrolled in Japanese-style elementary schools.[9] Enrollment of Korean students in primary schools similarly increased, rising from 20,000 in 1910, to 90,000 in 1920, and 901,000 in 1937, but the last figure represented only about 17 percent of the total school age (5–14) children in Korea.[10] Primary education was most fully extended in colonial Taiwan, where about one-third of the school age (6–14) children were in schools in 1930–1931, and this share eventually climbed to 71 percent in 1943–1944.[11]

As in other countries, elementary education in the Japanese colonies was financed by the local governments, but the government-general office continued to draft education policy. Before 1920 the government did little to expand elementary education. In Taiwan,

[9] About 30 percent of the total population in the age group 6–20 in Kwantung and the SMR zone were enrolled in schools. See Kantōkyoku tōkeisho [Kwantung Administration Statistics Book], No. 30 (Darien, 1936), 303–304.

[10] Andrew J. Grajdanzev, Modern Korea (New York: Institute of Pacific Relations, 1944), p. 261. In 1935, the population between the ages of 5 and 14 was 5.4 million.

[11] T'ai-wan-sheng hsing-cheng chang-kuan kung-che t'ung-chi shih [Statistical Bureau of the Taiwan Provincial Government], T'ai-wan shen wu-shih-i nien-lai t'ung-chi t'i-yao [Taiwan Province: Statistical Summary of the Past Fifty-one Years] (Taipei, 1946), pp. 1241–1242.

the annual combined expenditure on education by all levels of government before 1920 seldom exceeded ¥1.5 million, and not all of this went to elementary education. This policy changed in the 1930's, when the colonial governments began to Japanize the colonial populations and made primary education the chief instrument to do that. Local governments in Taiwan and Korea allocated one-third and one-fourth of their annual outlays respectively to education.

An economy functions poorly with an illiterate, unskilled, and unhealthy population. The Japanese realized that, and their investments in human capital through public-health measures lowered death rates, improved the health of their colonial populations, and raised labor productivity by reducing absenteeism from sickness and enhancing the quantity and quality of work that people could do. Declines in mortality increased life expectancy and produced higher rates of return from investments in human capital. This process probably encouraged colonizer and subjects to make additional investments in human capital, thereby enlarging the colonies' stock of human capital.

While spending on formal education represents another form of human capital investment, the contribution of formal schooling to the development of the Japanese colonies should not be over-exaggerated. First, the expansion of elementary education in the colonies, measured either by government expenditures or by enrollment, largely occurred in the 1930's. Because such investments have long gestation periods, labor productivity was not significantly affected until well after the colonial period. Indeed, investments in elementary education during the late 1920's and the 1930's may have had a greater impact on post-colonial development than on economic growth during the colonial period.

Secondly, the colonial education system was devised and administered to discriminate against the colonial populations, and this effectively reduced the positive effects of schooling on the productivity of the colonial populations. Finally, formal education enlarges the human capital stock because it transmits knowledge and skills to people. But knowledge can be transferred and skills acquired through learning-by-doing and on-the-job training. Even though the average farmer or worker in the colonies in the 1930's probably had higher skills and greater knowledge than his counterpart at the beginning of the colonial period, this improvement was chiefly acquired through extension services and on-the-job training and not through the formal school system.

Production

A distinctive feature of Japanese colonialism was that its colonial governments, in addition to providing essential services such as law and order, health, education, modern transportation and communication, also actively promoted selected industries, introduced new technology, and funded economic undertakings. The Japanese planned their development programs with considerable care, paying unusual attention to research. They systematically surveyed and investigated economic resources and local customs and planned their economic programs on the basis of these studies.

Official concerns first centered on agriculture in Korea and Taiwan, and less so in Kwantung. Drawing on the lessons learned from Japan's agricultural development, agricultural programs were devised for the colonies, and their aim was to improve the economic and technical environment within which farmers operated.

Among the first actions that officials took was to clarify and legitimize private property rights. They initiated expensive cadastral surveys and investigations of traditional institutions to gather information and then to reorganize the land tenure system in the colonies.[12] By simplifying the land tenure system and eliminating certain traditional landownership claims, colonial governments collected more land tax and yet created new incentives for farmers. By eliminating claims of parties on the periphery of agriculture (e.g., the *ta-tsu-hu* in Taiwan and some of the *Yangban* elites in Korea), the Japanese redistributed income from those who were neither involved nor interested in agriculture to those who had a direct stake in agriculture and would use their resources productively and respond to economic opportunities. The clarification of property rights also encouraged large, long-term investments in land. Colonial officials also successfully reformed the land-tax system to generate more tax revenue than ever before.

Contributing even more directly to agricultural production were government programs that developed and distributed new technology and modern inputs (e.g., chemical fertilizer and new seeds) to farmers. Government effort to develop agriculture was least evident in Kwantung. The Kwantung government (central and local) budget

[12] Yunshik Chang, "Colonization as Planned Change: The Korea Case," in *Modern Asian Studies*, 5 (1971), 165-169, Ho, *Economic Development of Taiwan*, pp. 10-13, and 42-45, and Santarō Okamatsu, *Provisional Report on Investigation of Laws and Customs in the Island of Formosa* (English ed., Kyoto: Provisional Commission for Research on Customs in Formosa, 1903), pp. 26-75.

shows only a few expenditure items directly related to agricultural development. In the early years officials allocated small sums to agricultural experimentation, sericulture, and forestry.[13] However, these programs not only did not expand, but in the 1930's some were terminated. On the other hand, the Taiwan government-general consistently allocated about 10 percent of its current expenditures to agricultural research, extension, and subsidies. In both Korea and Taiwan the government spent about ¥5-6 million annually on agricultural development programs (excluding irrigation and water-control projects) in the 1930s. The major achievement of these efforts was the successful development of high yield, fertilizer-sensitive seeds (rice in Korea and rice and sugarcane in Taiwan) suitable to local conditions. In addition to agricultural research and extension, the governments also promoted irrigation through loans, capital grants, and direct investments, and supported rural institutions (e.g., farmers' associations) that served agriculture. In effect, the Japanese colonial governments had created the necessary conditions for a seed-fertilizer revolution.

The colonial governments also promoted the lion's share of industrial development in the colonies. Of course, they developed only mining and certain manufacturing industries that did not compete with but rather complemented the industries in Japan. Indeed, these colonial governments discouraged general industrial development by giving preferential treatment to industrial ownership by Japanese businessmen and therefore placed obstacles in the way of indigenous entrepreneurs.[14] The industrial programs were designed to attract Japanese businesses, especially the zaibatsu, and cooperating with zaibatsu was crucial because its members possessed the technical know-how and investment funds that colonial officials lacked.

To entice Japanese businesses to invest in the colonies, colonial officials offered the following incentives: infrastructure, favorable regulations, low taxes, guaranteed dividends in selected industries, subsidies, and, most importantly, a cordial and cooperative officialdom. These incentives attracted Japanese businesses to invest in sugar and other light industries. The colonial government often joined with private Japanese businesses to form semi-official companies in mining

[13] *Kantōkyoku tōkeisho* [Kwantung Administration Statistics Book], No. 14 (Darien, 1921), Table 275.

[14] The Corporation Law enacted in Korea in 1911, "Severely restricted investments in non-agricultural sectors, and discouraged private Japanese capital inflow into these sectors in order to prevent the establishment of new industries that might compete with industries in Japan." (Sang-chul Suh, *Growth and Structural Changes in the Korean Economy* [Cambridge: Harvard University Press, 1978], pp. 9-10.)

and processing of minerals. One such company, the South Manchuria Railways, planned and directed the industrialization of Kwantung and the SMR zone. The drive to bring heavy industries to Taiwan in the 1930's was spearheaded by two such semi-official companies: the Taiwan Electric Power Company and the Taiwan Development Company. In Korea, companies such as the Oriental Development Company and Nihon Iron (Chōsen) played a similar role.[15]

Financing government programs

The colonial governments' ability to initiate and implement its economic programs depended on the productivity of its fiscal system. At first the colonial governments received Japanese government subsidies, but that transfer proved so burdensome to Japan that opposition soon ended it, thus forcing the colonies to mobilize their own resources. Thus, the speed by which colonial government developed their fiscal systems and became financially independent determined the success of their economic policies.

The sources of revenue were the same in all three colonies. The cadastral surveys made the land tax an important source of income for the governments-general in the early years.[16] The other main sources of government income were indirect taxes (most importantly, the excise taxes on alcohol and sugar), monopoly profits (from camphor, opium, salt, and tobacco in Taiwan and from ginseng, opium, salt, and tobacco in Korea), and the net income from government enterprises (railways and communications). From an official perspective, among the merits of excise taxes, monopoly profits, and enterprise net income were that they could be directly controlled and easily administered. These revenues grew, and by the mid-1930's they accounted for about two-thirds of the total revenues (including borrowings and grants from Japan, but excluding transfers from preceding years) received by the governments-general in Korea and Taiwan.

Government revenues depend not only on the government's ability to divert resources from the private sector but also on the size and growth of the tax base. In the Japanese colonies most of the resources

[15] Suzuki Masabumi, Chōsen keizai no gendankai [The Current Stage of the Korean Economy] (Seoul, 1938), pp. 256-261.

[16] About 20 percent of the Taiwan Government-Generals current receipts in 1905-1919 was from the land tax. Samuel P.-S. Ho, "The Economic Development of Colonial Taiwan: Evidence and Interpretation," in Journal of Asian Studies, 34 (February 1975), Table 6. In Korea, the land tax in the 1920's accounted for about one-third of the total tax revenues (Suzuki, p. 892).

mobilized by the governments were used to stimulate economic growth, and this in turn broadened the tax base and produced a steady growth in government revenue. Increased revenue permitted greater government activities and greater government influence on the economy. In Taiwan, government expenditure on goods and services, measured in constant prices, increased more than seven-fold between 1903 and 1938, and in Korea it increased six-fold between 1911 and 1938.

A shortage of government revenue never restricted Taiwan government activities as it did in the other colonial governments. Taiwan quickly developed a productive fiscal system. Japan terminated its subsidies to Taiwan in 1904 (five years earlier than anticipated). In contrast, Japan annually granted ¥4 million to Korea and ¥4 million to Kwantung until the end of the colonial period. The Taiwan government-general also depended less on borrowing than did the other colonial governments. Except for the early years, the annual net borrowing of the Taiwan government-general seldom exceeded ¥4-5 million or 3-4 percent of its total annual receipts (excluding transfers from preceding years). In the 1920's and the 1930's debt servicing in the Taiwan budget absorbed only 7-8 percent of its total annual expenditures. The Korean experience was very different. In the 1920's and the 1930's net borrowing accounted for 15 to 30 percent or more of the Korean government-general's total annual receipts, and upwards to 20 percent of its total annual expenditures was earmarked for debt servicing.

THE PACE AND PATTERN OF COLONIAL DEVELOPMENT

Aggregate growth

The economic records achieved in Korea, Kwantung, and Taiwan during the colonial period are summarized in Table 1 in the form of selected economic growth indicators. These indicators are based on data of differing quality and are not equally reliable. While a detailed analysis of the statistics used in constructing these indicators is not appropriate here, it can be said that the production data are fairly reliable and complete. However, because many of the statistics for estimating total product were non-existent or only infrequently gathered, the estimated figure, of total product in Table 1 are preliminary and crude.

Table 1 shows that the colonies experienced considerable growth. We have no estimate of aggregate production for Kwantung, but there exist two measures of aggregate output for Korea and two for

Taiwan. Suh's estimates of commodity product for Korea and Lee's estimates of Net Domestic Product (NDP) for Taiwan were both constructed by the value-added approach, while Mizoguchi's estimates of Gross Domestic Product (GDP) for Korea and Taiwan were calculated by the expenditure approach. The two approaches produce estimates that are unfortunately very different, both in their magnitude and year-to-year movements. Because the value-added measures consistently follow the individual production indexes, I shall refer to them.

Over the three decades (1910-1914 to 1935-1939) for which there are fairly reliable data, total product in constant prices more than doubled in Korea and nearly tripled in Taiwan. Between 1912 and 1937, Korea's total commodity product increased at an annual compound rate of 3.06 percent and Taiwan's NDP at 4.08 percent. However, the growth of aggregate output was not steady: Taiwan's NDP grew much more rapidly in the 1920's and the first half of the 1930's, and Korea's commodity product increased more rapidly in the 1910's and the 1930's. Output growth was accompanied by a dramatic rise in population, caused primarily by a declining death rate. Between 1910 and 1940 population increased by 78 percent (from about 3.3 million to 5.9 million) in Taiwan, and by 59 percent (from about 14.8 million to 23.3 million) in Korea. In other words, for the period 1910-1940, population grew at an annual compound rate of 1.6 percent in Korea and 2.0 percent in Taiwan. Therefore, the rate of growth of per-capita output was about 1.5 percent per year in Korea and slightly above 2 percent per year in Taiwan. For economies in their early stage of economic transition, these are respectable rates of development and represent a break from the traditional pattern of development in Korea and Taiwan.

The Pattern of agricultural development

The sectoral growth patterns reveal more clearly the intent and consequences of Japan's colonial policy, and therefore they are more interesting for our purposes than the aggregate output trend. Because Japan's colonial policy was to develop Korea and Taiwan as a major supplier of sugar and rice, agriculture became responsible for much of their economic growth and contributed greatly to export expansion.

The fundamental features of agricultural development in Korea, Kwantung, and Taiwan are now fairly well understood.[17] Estimates

[17] Sang-hwan Ban, "The Long-Run Productivity Growth in Korean Agricultural Development, 1910-1968," Ph.D. diss., University of Minnesota, 1971; Samuel P.-S. Ho, "Agricultural Transformation Under Colonialism: The Case of Taiwan," in *Jour-*

of agricultural value-added and of agricultural production in Table 1 show that while agricultural growth occurred in all colonies, growth was more consistent and more rapid in Taiwan. Only in Taiwan did agricultural productivity increase steadily and continuously throughout the colonial period. In Kwantung, agricultural growth increased even more rapidly than in Taiwan, but its pace declined dramatically in the 1930's. The annual compound growth rate of agricultural production in Kwantung was 4.93 percent during 1912-1927 but only 2.14 percent during 1927-1937. In fact, agricultural production stagnated in the mid-1930's and then declined steadily for the rest of the colonial period. The rate of agricultural growth was slowest in Korea, and the growth rate of its agricultural value-added, unlike Taiwan's, declined after 1927, falling from an annual compound rate of 1.85 percent in 1912-1927 to 1.3 percent in 1927-1937.

Agricultural growth in the colonies was the result of the interaction between changing demand and supply conditions. On the demand side, the opening of the Japanese market to agricultural products from the colonies stimulated their exports. Improvements in transportation and communication reduced transport costs for both exportables and goods for the internal market, and falling transport costs, made it more profitable for farmers to produce for the market. However, for agriculture to expand, it must also have the productive capacity to respond positively to the demand stimulus. In the Japanese colonies this capacity existed, and agricultural production increased, but the source of the increase was different in each case.

Around 1900, land was relatively plentiful in Kwantung, so agricultural production could be increased by simply tilling more land. After 1905, increased foreign and local demand for agricultural products speeded up land settlement. Kwantung's land statistics are less reliable before 1924, when all land was finally surveyed. After adjusting for under-reported land before 1924, Myers and Ulie esti-

nal of Economic History, XXVIII (September 1968), pp. 315-40; Yhi-min Ho, Agricultural Development of Taiwan, 1903-1960 (Nashville: Vanderbilt University Press, 1966); T. H. Lee, Intersectoral Capital Flows in the Economic Development of Taiwan, 1895-1960 (Ithaca: Cornell University Press, 1971); Ramon H. Myers and Adrienne Ching, "Agricultural Development in Taiwan under Japanese Colonial Rule," in Journal of Asian Studies, 23 (August 1964), 555-570; James I. Nakamura, "Incentives, Productivity Gaps, and Agricultural Growth Rates in Prewar Japan, Taiwan, and Korea," in Bernard S. Silberman and H. D. Harootunian, eds., Japan in Crisis (Princeton: Princeton University Press, 1974); and Sang-chul Suh, Growth and Structural Changes in the Korean Economy, Chapters 1, 2, and 5; and Ramon H. Myers and Thomas R. Ulie, "Foreign Influence and Agricultural Development in Northeast China: A Case Study of the Liaotung Peninsula, 1906-42," in Journal of Asian Studies, 31 (February 1972), pp. 329-350.

mated that cultivated area in Kwantung doubled between 1910-1914 and 1930-1934. Perhaps as much as two-thirds of the increase in Kwantung's agricultural production during the colonial period resulted directly from the increase in land.

Yields also improved, partly by farmers' switching to the more profitable and productive commercial crops (e.g., beans, peanuts, and vegetables) and partly by the more intensive use of traditional and commercial fertilizers (e.g., bean cakes). But new inputs were not systematically developed and disseminated. True, in 1906, the Kwantung government established an agricultural experiment station in Dairen, but this was a limited operation, and at the height of its activity in the early 1920's its total budget was less than ¥30,000.[18] Thereafter, the government reduced its expenditure for developing agriculture. Responding to Japan's needs, much of the government's efforts in agriculture went to develop and to distribute improved rice seeds. But conditions in Kwantung were not favorable for rice cultivation, and rice occupied less than 1 percent of the total agricultural area. With so little land growing rice, the government's agricultural program was not a major influence in Kwantung. In the early 1930's land became scarce, so that further agricultural growth in Kwantung could be produced only through a new technology (modern inputs and improved seeds) and investments in fixed capital. When these did not appear, agriculture stagnated. Agriculture's position deteriorated further in the late 1930's, when rapid industrialization moved labor from agriculture to the non-agricultural sector, and both yield and production plummetted as a consequence.

Table 2 presents a different process of agricultural growth in Korea and Taiwan. After 1920, cultivated area remained nearly constant in Korea and increased only slightly in Taiwan, so that the cultivation of new land was not a major source of agricultural growth. A more important factor was the systematic introduction and widespread dissemination of new technology. At the beginning of the twentieth century, agricultural yield per unit area in Japan was substantially higher than in Korea and Taiwan. The rice yield in Japan was more than twice that in Korea and Taiwan. Japanese colonial policy tried to narrow this yield gap by transferring to Korea and Taiwan superior techniques and new inputs (high-yield seeds, better water control, improved rural infrastructure, and better use of commercial fertilizers), mainly from Japan but also from outside the empire. Technological transfer was supported by the colonial governments and guided by agricultural specialists from Japan, who drew heavily

---

[18] *Kantōkyoku tōkeisho*, No. 14 (Darien, 1921), Table 275.

on Japan's agricultural development experience. This process required time and resources. Not surprisingly yield had hardly increased by the mid-1920's (Table 2), but, thereafter, yield rose rapidly.

Why, under similar policies, was the pace of agricultural development in Taiwan more rapid than in Korea (Tables 1 and 2)? The answer, I believe, is that factor proportions greatly differed in these colonies. The mix of modern agricultural inputs used in Korea was different from that used in Taiwan. Specifically, irrigation facilities developed much more slowly in Korea. As late as 1935-1939, only 28 percent of Korea's cultivated area was irrigated (Table 2), a rate reached some three decades earlier in Taiwan.

Because improved seeds, fertilizer, and water interact so dependently with each other, the lack of one input—in the Korean case, water—significantly reduces the effectiveness of the others. Because of lack of water and improper water-control facilities in Korea, the first Japanese rice varieties introduced into Korea were not the fertilizer-responsive, high-yield strains.[19] Fertilizer-responsive rice varieties were introduced into Korea only in the 1930's, after irrigation had expanded somewhat. Even though a much lower fertilizer-rice price ratio prevailed in Korea than in Taiwan, Korean farmers used less fertilizer than did Taiwanese farmers. Thus, the slow pace of irrigation development in Korea retarded the introduction of fertilizer-responsive rice seeds, the spread of multiple-cropping, and the greater use of fertilizers.

Without irrigation, farm output expanded at a much slower rate than inputs, so that the growth rate of agricultural value-added in the 1930's was not only well below that of gross output, but it was also lower than it had been in the 1920's (see Table 1). This meant that the index of total factor productivity (the index of agricultural output divided by an aggregated index of all quantifiable inputs to agriculture) declined after the early 1920's.[20]

Taiwan agriculture had a much better mixture of modern inputs in the late 1920's and the 1930's. To promote sugarcane production, the colonial government began to encourage irrigation construction shortly after 1900. A good water-supply system and superior seeds

[19] Yujirō Hayami and Vernon W. Ruttan, *Agricultural Development: An International Perspective* (Baltimore: Johns Hopkins Press, 1971), p. 209.

[20] Suh's calculations show the index of total factor productivity (1915-1919 = 100) to be 103 in 1920-1924, 86 in 1925-1929, 90 in 1930-1934, and 93 in 1935-1940. See his *Growth and Structural Changes in the Korean Economy*, Table 35. Ban's estimates of total factor productivity show a similar trend; see his "The Long-Run Productivity Growth in Korean Agricultural Development," Table 24.

(developed in the early 1920's) made fertilizers highly profitable to use after the mid-1920's. From the mid-1920's to the end of the 1930's, gross agricultural output increased rapidly (Table 1), as did agricultural value-added and total factor productivity.[21]

After the rice riots in 1918, Japan looked to Korea and Taiwan to solve its food problem. The two colonies responded with similiar programs, but Taiwan was in a better position to implement its program. By 1920 Japan already had ruled Taiwan for a quarter of a century, and the colonial government had developed the agricultural sector and created a broad revenue base. These two conditions made it possible for Taiwan's rice production program to be quickly and effectively implemented. In the 1920's irrigation construction surged, and nearly every area was adopting superior seeds and using fertilizers.

Korea's program also relied on an extension of controlled irrigation facilities. The "Program to Increase Rice Production," launched in 1920, called for reclaiming and improving 800,000 hectares of paddy land in thirty years.[22] Korea had neither a sound economic base nor a productive revenue system to finance such an ambitious program. Financial shortages and low rice prices in the early 1920's forced the government to discontinue that program in 1925. A year later, the government revised that program with larger subsidies and low interest loans. At first, progress under the revised program was fairly rapid, but after 1930 it slackened.[23]

During the 1930's Japan's priorities changed. Japan's rulers called for greater self-sufficiency within the empire and for a build-up of heavy industry, which meant shifting resources from agriculture to other industries. Meanwhile, the import of inexpensive rice from the colonies was threatening the livelihood of Japanese farmers and causing considerable discontent in rural Japan. By the early 1930's, farmer interest groups were exerting pressure on the government to impose a duty on rice imports from Korea and Taiwan. The government declined, paying heed to commercial and industrial groups in Japan, who argued that such restrictions would significantly raise rice prices

[21] Ho, *Economic Development of Taiwan*, Table 4.3.

[22] Chang, "Colonization as Planned Change: The Korean Case," pp. 171-175; Bruce F. Johnston, *Japanese Food Management in World War II* (Stanford: Stanford University Press, 1953), pp. 52-56; Hoon K. Lee, *Land Utilization and Rural Economy in Korea* (Chicago: University of Chicago Press, 1936), pp. 122-131, and Government-General of Chōsen, *Annual Report on Reforms and Progress in Chōsen, 1920-21*, and *Annual Report on Administration of Chōsen*, various issues after 1921.

[23] By 1933, a total of 165,000 hectares of land had been improved under the various "rice-increase" programs. Shigeru Ishikawa, *Economic Development in Asian Perspective* (Tokyo: Kinokuniya, 1967), p. 105.

and industrial wages. The government compromised by agreeing to abandon programs for increasing rice production in the colonies, in the hope that a slower agricultural growth would help to improve conditions in rural Japan.

In Taiwan, this new colonial policy exerted only a minor impact. Rural infrastructure and irrigation facilities were already in place and could not be removed. The government could only encourage the Taiwanese farmers to produce crops other than rice. While this move did increase the production of fiber crops (cotton, jute, and ramie) in the 1930's, it did not significantly shift resources from rice to the other crops, and rice production continued to expand steadily.

In Korea the new policy had more success. In 1934, the colonial government terminated the "rice-increase program," thus ending its support of irrigation development. This had far-reaching consequences for Korea. With irrigation development discontinued, fertilization became less effective, and agricultural growth declined. Meanwhile, Korean farmers still had to compete in the Japanese imperial market against the more productive Taiwanese farmers.

The Pattern of industrialization

The 1930's constitutes a watershed for colonial industrial policy. Table 3 shows that from 1913 to 1927 manufacturing production increased at an annual compound rate of about 6 percent in Korea and Taiwan and 11 percent in Kwantung. In this same period, the growth rate of mining production was about 8 percent in Korea, 5 percent in Taiwan, and 10 percent in Kwantung (Table 1). As expected, mining industries in mineral-abundant Korea and Kwantung grew more rapidly than in mineral-poor Taiwan. In addition to natural endowment, the pattern of development in manufacturing in this period was also influenced by (1) Japan's desire to reserve the colonial markets for its manufacturing industries at home, and (2) the stimulative effects of World War I.

The Japanese moved cautiously in formulating their industrial programs. They encouraged agricultural processing, the two most important being sugar and vegetable (soybean) oil, while textiles, likely to compete with the home industry, were not generally promoted. Sugar production in Taiwan increased rapidly, encouraged by subsidies and protection from world competition. Output rose from an annual level of 82,000 MT in the 1900's, to 251,000 MT in the 1910's, 498,000 MT in the 1920's, and 948,000 MT in the 1930's.[24] Vegetable

[24] Ho, *Economic Development of Taiwan*, Table A43.

oil production, the most important industry in Kwantung, also flourished because of the marketing network and improved transportation. Demand for soybeans rose when the South Manchuria Railway Co. developed new uses for soybean oil. Ceramics was another industry that developed because of government (SMR) research and expanded construction activities in the colonies. More than anything else, the pace of industrialization in the colonies before 1930 was set by the growth of agriculture-related industries. In the 1920's food and vegetable oil accounted for over 50 percent of the gross value produced by manufacturing industries in Korea and about 70 percent in Taiwan and Kwantung.

The stimulative effects of World War I proved even more important. When the Western powers went to war, Japan responded to the decline in Western exports to Asia by expanding its industrial exports to China and to other Asian countries. Consequently, for the war's duration, Japan exported less to its colonies, and a shortage of manufactured goods encouraged more local manufacturing establishments to appear in the colonies. All the production indexes cited in Table 3 reflect this growth and the subsequent contraction of industrial activities after the war's end, when Japanese manufactured goods again flowed into the colonies in large quantities. In Korea the industrial production index increased by 150 percent from 1914 to 1918, but declined until the early 1920's. In Taiwan the index of manufacturing production (1937 = 100) was 19 in 1913, 47 in 1917, 40 in 1918, 36 in 1919, and 30 in 1920.[25] In Kwantung industrial production increased by nearly five-fold between 1914 and 1919 and then declined sharply in 1920.[26] This early spurt in colonial industrial growth was largely an indigenous response to profit opportunities that appeared suddenly in the colonial markets, but few large modern enterprises emerged in this period.

In the 1930's the Japanese conceived of industrial development in the colonies and Japan as complementing each other rather than competing. The colonial governments began to join forces with big business in Japan to launch new mining and large-scale manufacturing undertakings in the colonies, activities that influenced the pace and pattern of industrial growth.

From 1927 to 1937, the real value-added from Korea's mining sector increased at an annual compound rate of 19 percent, more than four times the growth rate achieved before 1927 (Table 1). The real

[25] Ho, *Economic Development of Taiwan*, Table A49.

[26] Kungtu C. Sun, assisted by Ralph W. Huenemann, *The Economic Development of Manchuria in the First Half of the Twentieth Century* (Cambridge: East Asian Research Center, Harvard University, 1969), Tables 20 and 22.

growth rate of Korea's manufacturing production and value-added also averaged over 10 percent per year during the 1930's. Mining and manufacturing accounted for nearly 80 percent of the overall growth in Korea's net commodity product between the five-year periods of 1928–1933 and 1934–1939. At the aggregate level, achievements in Kwantung and Taiwan appeared less impressive. From 1927 to 1937 Taiwan's mining production increased at an annual compound rate of only 3.5 percent, and its manufacturing production at less than 6 percent. In both sectors, the growth rate was lower after 1927 than it was before. In Kwantung, where data are available only through 1936, real value-added in mining and that in manufacturing increased annually at 2.2 percent and 7.4 percent respectively between the three-year periods of 1926–1928 and 1934–1936.

One reason that industrial growth in the 1930's was so rapid in Korea was that it began from a relatively small initial base. But the high growth rate also reflected Korea's abundant energy resources and its proximity to North Manchuria, then under Japanese control and rapidly industrializing. In the early 1930's industrial output in Kwantung (coal and vegetable oil) and that in Taiwan (sugar) were already sizeable, so that rapid rates of growth were more difficult to attain. Industrial growth in Kwantung also had been adversely affected by the world depression, which dampened demand for its agricultural processed goods, and by the political disruptions caused by the Mukden Incident and the subsequent formation of the puppet state of Manchukuo. In Taiwan meager mineral resources more than any other factor kept mining production from rising rapidly. Between 1930–1934 and 1935–1939, after considerable Japanese investments and an 81 percent rise in mining employment, mining output in Taiwan still increased only by 31 percent.[27]

The industrial growth rates presented for Kwantung in Tables 1 and 3 probably understate by a considerable margin the extent of industrialization that actually occurred in the 1930's. First, much of Kwantung's industrial growth came in the late 1930's and the early 1940's, after the period covered by the production indexes that underlie the growth rates in Tables 1 and 3. More importantly, by the 1930's the whole of Manchuria was under Japanese control. Therefore, industrial growth in Kwantung and the SMR zone became closely linked to developments in Manchuria. When statistical coverage is extended to all parts of Manchuria, Sun's estimates show that industrial (mining and manufacturing) production more than doubled between 1929–1931 and 1939–1941. Recently, Eckstein, Chao, and Chang

[27] Ho, *Economic Development of Taiwan*, Table 5.2.

published national product estimates for Manchuria for selected years between 1924 and 1941, and their calculations showed that its industrial sector experienced an average annual growth rate of 4.4 percent from 1924 to 1936 and 9.9 percent from 1936 to 1941.[28] The pace of industrialization definitely accelerated in the second half of the 1930's.

From the disaggregated data in Table 3, the type of industrialization that the Japanese attempted to bring to the colonies, and its success, can be more clearly perceived. Unlike the industrial growth of the early years that was primarily based on agriculture, the industrialization in the 1930's was based upon energy, mineral resources, and hydro-electric power.[29] New electric power capacity was used to provide energy for the metallurgical and chemical industries. From 1927 to 1939, chemical production expanded at an annual compound rate of over 17 percent in Korea, and metal production increased at an annual compound rate of about 10 percent in both Korea and Taiwan. In Kwantung, between 1927 and 1935, metal production increased at an annual compound rate of 22 percent.

This growth changed the output composition in the manufacturing sector of the colonies (Table 3). In Korea, energy-intensive heavy industries (chemicals, metals, and machinery) accounted for 44 percent of the total value of manufacturing output produced between 1938 and 1940, as compared to only 26 percent during 1926 and 1929. In Kwantung, the relative position of its metal industry also improved, climbing from 5 percent of the real gross value of manufacturing in 1926-1928 to 15 percent in 1934-1936. But, in the 1930's, with little growth in vegetable-oil production, the relative importance of Kwantung's chemical industry in total manufacturing declined, even though the output of industrial chemicals increased rapidly. Table 3 also shows that between 1926-1928 and 1938-1940 the output composition of Taiwan's manufacturing sector changed only slightly. But Japan's effort to establish a metal industry in Taiwan did not bear fruit until the early 1940's. After sugar, aluminum was the most important industry developed by the Japanese in Taiwan, and it absorbed nearly all the increase in Taiwan's electric power in the 1930's.

[28] Alexander Eckstein, Kang Chao, and John Chang, "The Economic Development of Manchuria: The Rise of a Frontier Economy," in *Journal of Economic History*, XXXIV (March 1974), Table 5.

[29] In 1929, Korea's electric power capacity was slightly below 48,000 KW, and 72 percent of that was accounted for by thermal plants. By 1938, its electric power capacity reached 868,000 KW, of which 83 percent was hydroelectric. In Taiwan, total electric power generation increased from 167 million KWH in 1930 to a peak of 1,195 million KWH in 1943 (when total installed electric power capacity was 308 thousand KW, of which 82 percent came from hydro stations).

Industrialization in the colonies was not broadly based. Growth was selective, occurring only in the government-promoted industries, so that the industrial sector became dominated by a small number of large, government-sponsored companies. Of the industrial (manufacturing and electric power) and mining corporations in Taiwan, only 31 had authorized capital of more than ¥1 million in 1932, 37 in 1936, and 49 in 1941.[30] Yet, in these years, this handful of firms controlled approximately 90 percent of the paid-up corporate capital in Taiwan's mining and manufacturing sectors. In 1939, large factories (those with 200 or more workers) in Korea accounted for a little more than 1 percent of the total number of factories, but produced nearly two-third of the output by value.[31] In the same year, large factories in Korea accounted for 88 percent of the output produced in the metal industry and 76 percent of that in the chemical industry.

These large companies were surrounded by a large number of tiny manufacturing establishments. Unlike the large enterprises, which used modern technology and were heavily capitalized, the small establishments used traditional technology and were under-capitalized. Because of the numerous small establishments, the average sizes of manufacturing factories in the colonies were quite modest.[32] In short, the colonial industrial sector took on distinctly dualistic characteristics. A handful of large, modern, heavily capitalized enterprises, producing goods that were predominantly exported to Japan, existed side by side with a large number of very small traditional establishments producing for the domestic market. However, it was the large companies that dominated manufacturing and accounted for most of the industrial growth.

Industrial development in the colonies complemented and supported Japan's industrial growth, particularly in the 1930's. The metal and the chemical industries developed in the 1930's were mere extensions of Japan's heavy industry, located in the colonies to tap their energy and mineral resources, but always were outside the colonial economic system. By world standards the Japanese colonies were not low-cost producers of metal or of industrial chemicals. These industries survived only because they received substantial government

[30] Taiwan Sōtokufu, *Taiwan shōkō tōkei* [Taiwan Commercial and Industrial Statistics], 1932, pp. 84–85; 1936, pp. 122–123; and 1941, pp. 6–7.

[31] This and the following figures are from Suh, p. 109. The original source is Kawai Akitake, *Chōsen kōgyō no gendaikai* [The Current State of Korean Manufacturing] (Seoul, 1943), pp. 252–253.

[32] For example, in 1940, the average manufacturing factory in Taiwan employed only 14 workers, and "factory" is defined here to exclude establishments with fewer than five workers and which do not use power. See *T'ai-wan-sheng wu-shih-i nien-lai t'ung-chi t'i-yao*, p. 763.

subsidies and protection. In fact, Taiwan's sugar industry would not have expanded as rapidly as it did if it had to compete with other sugar producers on the world market without government subsidies and protection. The colonial industrial sectors had developed not according to their comparative advantages but rather to meet specific Japanese needs.

External trade

As output increased in the colonies, trade expanded at an even faster pace (Table 4). Between the period 1906-1910 and 1936-1938, Taiwan's export volume, in real terms, increased more than sixfold, and import volume quadrupled. In Korea, from 1911-1915 to 1936-1938, real exports grew from a relatively small initial base nearly seventeen times, and real imports more than five times. Because the Kwantung trade also included goods that were either from or destined for Manchuria, it is necessary to consider Kwantung and Manchuria statistically as a single unit. Since what interests us is the total trade impact, the combined measure may, in any case, be more appropriate. Between 1907 and 1929, real exports from all parts of Manchuria increased ten-fold, and real imports nearly five-fold.[33] Trade expansion slowed down considerably in the 1930's, partly because of the world depression and partly because the rate of agricultural growth in Manchuria declined. In the mid-1930's, as industrial development gained momentum in Manchuria, imports surged ahead of exports, with the growing trade deficits financed by capital imports from Japan. In the 1930's, total trade (exports plus imports) as a share of GDP was about 25 percent in Manchuria, 50 percent in Korea, and over 60 percent in Taiwan. Clearly, trade was a prominent part of the colonial economies.

The colonial exports were dominated by agricultural products and industrial raw materials (mainly minerals, but increasingly in the 1930's also intermediate goods). During the entire colonial period, food (rice and sugar) and industrial raw materials accounted for between 80 to 90 percent of the exports from both Korea and Taiwan. Korea's mineral resources made possible larger exports of industrial raw materials, and their share of total exports grew rapidly. Manchuria's principal exports around 1900 were soybean and derivatives that made up 80 percent of its total exports. As Manchurian agricultural growth slackened, and minerals and metal industries developed, the impor-

---

[33] Eckstein, Chao, and Chang, "The Economic Development of Manchuria: The Rise of a Frontier Economy," *Journal of Economic History*, Table 3.

tance of soybean declined and that of industrial raw materials in export increased. By 1929-1931, the share of soybean products in Manchuria's exports had declined to about 60 percent, while that of coal, iron, and steel had risen to 15 percent.[34]

The colonies imported mostly industrial goods (Table 4).[35] Manufactured consumer goods (most importantly, textile products) accounted for a large share of the industrial imports, but imports of producer goods were also important, particularly in the mid- and late-1930's, when Japan intensified her efforts to industrialize the colonies. Interestingly, both Korea and Taiwan imported large amounts of food, even though both were food-surplus countries. Why? Colonial food imports catered to Japanese needs. Some food and drinks were imported from Japan to satisfy the special demand of the half million Japanese who made Korea and Taiwan their home. But, above all, Taiwan imported rice and Korea imported barley, millet, and wheat so that a larger quantity of the Japonica rice grown in Korea and Taiwan, a variety befitting Japanese tastes, could be exported to Japan.

Japan, of course, dominated the colonial trade. Her dominance over Korea's external trade dates from the beginning of this century, when Korea first came under its sphere of influence. Formal annexation in 1910 made these trade ties even more secure, and throughout the entire colonial period 80-90 percent of Korea's trade was with Japan (Table 4). Before it was a Japanese colony, Taiwan traded with the Chinese mainland, and only 1 percent of its imports and 10 percent of its exports were with Japan.[36] This trade pattern quickly altered after 1895 when, in 1910, 70 percent of Taiwan's trade was with Japan, later to rise to 90 percent. Before 1932, 39 percent of Manchuria's exports went to Japan, and 41 percent of its imports came from Japan. By 1939, Japan received nearly two-thirds of Manchuria's exports and accounted for 85 percent of its imports.

That the colonial trade was important to Japan and the colonies is simple to demonstrate. Over 90 percent of Taiwan's sugar was exported, and, in the 1920's and 1930's, between one-quarter and one-half of the rice produced in Korea and Taiwan was also exported to Japan. In the interwar period, one-quarter of Japan's total imports consisted of food (including beverages and tobacco), the largest com-

[34] *Manshū kaihatsu yonjūnenshi* [A History of Forty Years of the Development of Manchuria] (Tokyo, 1964), II, 795 and 805.

[35] For Manchuria, see *Manshū kaihatsu,* II, 805.

[36] *Shina kakuminato bōeki nemhyō Taiwan no bu* [Annual Trade Tables for Various chinese Ports] (Taiwan), 29v.

ponent being rice and then sugar. In the late 1930's, Korea and Taiwan supplied over 90 percent of the sugar and 98 percent of the rice imported by Japan. In effect, the development of colonial agriculture enabled Japan to achieve self-sufficiency in food.

OWNERSHIP AND ECONOMIC CONTROL

Japan's need to control the economic surplus produced in the colonies further required that she protect the vested interests of Japanese colonists and keep economic power out of the hands of the indigenous populations. She achieved this by dominant control over economic assets and limiting native access to economic opportunities.

Land ownership and control of agriculture

Land ownership was the most important determinant of economic power and of rural income distribution. Japanese acquisition of farmland produced considerable hostility among the natives, and the colonial governments naturally were reluctant to make public land ownership data by nationality. However, there is sufficient evidence to estimate roughly the size of Japanese holdings of farmland in Korea and Taiwan.

In Taiwan government land policy helped Japanese and large Japanese corporations to gain control of much land. The cadastral survey conducted between 1898 and 1904 and other subsequent surveys uncovered large amounts of untitled land, which then became government property. Most of that land was later sold to Japanese firms engaged in agricultural or forestry activities, and small land grants were made to Japanese settlers and to colonial officials. The government also pressured "owners of private lands in areas suitable for cane growing . . . to sell their lands to sugar corporations, an action that created resentment."[37] As sugar companies reinvested part of their profits in land, they eventually became the most important landowners in Taiwan. In 1946 the Chinese government took possession of over 176,000 hectares of farmland owned by Japanese nationals, of which approximately two-thirds were owned by the sugar companies.[38] This figure suggests that Japanese land holdings prob-

[37] Edgar Wickberg, "The Tenancy System in Taiwan, 1900-1939," University Seminar on Modern East Asia: China, Columbia University, March 12, 1969, p. 7.

[38] Ho, *Economic Development of Taiwan*, p. 161. In 1945, the sugar companies owned over 111,000 hectares of farmland.

ably accounted for between 20 and 25 percent of the total cultivated area in Taiwan before World War II.

Japanese acquisition of farmland in Korea followed a similar pattern.[39] Land without properly documented titles uncovered by the cadastral survey of 1906-1915 was taken over by the colonial government, and in this manner many Koreans lost their land. Most of the Crown land also became government property, and much of this government land was sold to large Japanese land-management companies, including the semi-official Oriental Development Company, involved in buying and managing agricultural land in Korea. The Oriental Development Company also made low-interest loans to Japanese immigrants who wished to settle and buy land in rural Korea.[40] Although it failed to attract many Japanese settlers to rural Korea, the Oriental Development Company eventually became the most important landowner in Korea.

Government statistics show that Japanese holdings of farmland in Korea increased by 43 percent in the 1920's, rising from 240,000 hectares in 1921 to 343,000 hectares in 1927. This means that, in the 1920's, Japanese holdings accounted for about 6 percent of all farmland. However, the data are misleading since "all land belonging to corporations with a Korean charter [which was considerable] is classed as Korean in ownership, though the ownership of the concern may be Japanese."[41] Professor Brunner, who investigated rural conditions in Korea in 1926, reported that "various careful estimates of fair-minded non-government Japanese and Koreans place the proportion of land owned . . . by the Japanese at a point between 12 and 20 percent."[42]

The evidence further suggests that in the 1920's and 1930's the government land-improvement schemes that accompanied the rice-promotion program worked to increase Japanese land holdings in Korea. The colonial government had provided generous subsidies to help to cover the cost of irrigation improvements that involved more than 10 *cho* (about 9.9 hectares) of land. By Korean standards, 10 *cho*

[39] For Japan's land policy in Korea see Chang, "Colonization as Planned Change: The Korean Case," pp. 165-169; Hoon K. Lee, Chapter IV; and Kyōji Asada, *Nihon teikokushugi to kyū shokuminchi jinushisei* [Japanese Imperialism and the Colonial Land-ownership System] (Tokyo: Ochanomizu Shobō, 1968), Chapter 3.

[40] See Hoon K. Lee, *Land Utilization and Rural Economy in Korea*, ch. XII, and Hyun-kil Kim, *Land Use Policy in Korea: With Special Reference to the Oriental Development Company*, Ph.D. diss., Univ. of Washington, 1971.

[41] E. de S. Brunner, *Rural Korea* (International Missionary Council, 1928), p. 126 and quoted by Grajdanzev, p. 106.

[42] Grajdanzev, *Modern Korea*, p. 106.

was a very large holding,[43] so that any subsidy scheme benefitted primarily the large landowners and those with access to capital who could organize and finance such large projects. Because the Japanese comprised a disproportionate share of both of these groups, the irrigation subsidy scheme encouraged Japanese to acquire more farmland. In 1931 more than one-third of the land that belonged to irrigation association founded with the help of government subsidy was owned by Japanese. In light of this evidence, a conservative estimate is that in the 1920's and 1930's Japanese holdings probably accounted for 20 percent or more of the total arable land in Korea.

These ownership figures show that the main bulk of the farmland remained in native hands. But Japanese ownership, because of its other characteristics, was much more important than the numerical figures suggest. First, only a very small proportion of the Japanese who owned farmland actually worked it, so that most of the Japanese-owned farmland was leased to native peasants. Even the sugar companies in Taiwan directly managed only a small portion of the land that they owned.[44] Thus a very large share of the land cultivated by tenants in Korea and Taiwan, perhaps in the order of 35 to 40 percent, was owned by Japanese. A preponderant share of the large landowners were also Japanese.[45] In both colonies Japanese holdings concentrated land ownership in fewer hands and increased the number of absentee landlords. Their considerable landholdings, when combined with the support that they received from the colonial government, gave Japanese landowners tremendous economic and political leverage over individual Korean and Taiwanese peasants, and they undoubtedly used this leverage to maximize their rent and to gain a larger share of agricultural income than would otherwise have been the case.

Japanese-owned land was also better-quality farmland. In Korea, tax records indicate that Japanese owned more than 50 percent of the farmland in some southern counties, where land was particularly productive. In both Korea and Taiwan the Japanese owned mostly paddy fields, which were more productive than dry fields. With rent payments between 40 and 60 percent of total harvest, the Japanese

---

[43] In 1927, only 1.4 percent of the landowners in Korea possessed ten *cho* or more of farmland.

[44] In 1938-1939, less than 17 percent of the total area under sugarcane was directly managed by the sugar companies.

[45] Hoon K. Lee, Tables 61 and 62. In 1942, of the 1,133 owners in Korea with holdings in excess of 100 *cho* (99.2 hectares), 586 were Japanese (Chosŏn Eunhaeng Chōsabu, *Chosŏn kyŏngche yŏnbo* [Annual Economic Review of Korea, 1948], p. I-30).

controlled a huge share of the agricultural surplus produced in the colonies. About 60 percent of the rice exported from Korea was supplied through Japanese landowners.

Control of the modern sector

Through direct ownership and through using their licensing and regulatory power in the industrial sector, the colonial governments successfully kept economic power from the native populations. The colonial government owned and operated the modern transport and communication sector. The Japanese owned and managed nearly all modern industrial enterprises. Statistics for 1929 show that Japanese owned more than three-quarters of the capital in Taiwan organized as joint-stock companies, limited partnerships, or unlimited companies. In mining and industry (manufacturing and power), Japanese share of capital was 72 and 91 percent, respectively. In 1939, 96 percent of the paid-up capital and 80 percent of the production in Kwantung's factory sector were accounted for by Japanese-owned enterprises. The predominance of Japanese ownership in the non-agricultural sector was also evident in Korea, where 91 percent of the total capital reported by factories (enterprises with 5 or more workers) was owned by Japanese. Japanese control of the modern sector enabled them to capture a preponderant share of the non-wage income produced outside of agriculture.

The Japanese also held overwhelming economic power in the markets connecting peasant agriculture to the export sector. Sugar production in colonial Taiwan was concentrated among a small number of Japanese corporations. Monopsony power was granted to these companies by a 1905 government regulation that divided the sugarcane-growing areas into supply regions, with each region assigned to a specified refinery. Without government permission, cane produced in one supply region could not be transported outside the region or be used other than for sugar manufacturing. Sugar refineries became legal monopsonistic buyers of sugarcane, and their market power helped to keep the price of sugarcane low and their profits high.[46] The rice price acted as the price floor to which sugarcane prices could fall before peasants shifted from cane into rice production. Not surprisingly, sugar companies tied the price of cane to that of rice.[47]

[46] In the 1930's, profits were 20 to 45 percent of paid-up capital.

[47] The correlation coefficient of the price of rice and the price of cane was 0.92, and that of the price of cane and the price of sugar was 0.53. See R. J. Yu, "T'ai-wan mi-

The market structure of paddy rice differed only in degree from that of sugarcane. In the 1930's four Japanese commercial firms controlled 90 percent of the rice export market in Taiwan. Because 40 to 50 percent of Taiwan's rice harvest was exported, these four firms enjoyed substantial market power and used it to influence prices in their favor. In Korea rice exports were concentrated in a few large Japanese-owned trading companies, and rice milling was done by a few large plants. This market structure allowed the Japanese-owned mills and trading companies to capture much of the benefits from the expanding rice export trade. The profits from exporting rice were immense. When the colonial government in Taiwan monopolized the rice export trade in 1939, it made a profit of ¥37.4 million in the subsequent five years, nearly equal to the land tax collected in these same years (¥41.6 million).

The colonial governments' power to raise revenue was another way of transferring resources from the native populations into Japanese hands. In the colonies nearly all current government receipts came from the land tax, excise taxes, and net income from government monopolies in tobacco, liquor, camphor, opium, and ginseng. Most of the tax burden fell on peasant agriculture, over which the Japanese did not have complete and direct control. The tax system clearly favored the Japanese-dominated commercial-industrial corporate sector. Although the corporate sector was the most obvious source of government revenue, it was never effectively tapped. Direct tax on the corporate sector was insignificant, and, with its monopolistic power, it probably was able to shift forward to the consumers, mostly native peasants, most of the excise taxes on the goods that it produced. By taxing consumption, the government shifted resources from consumption to other uses.

Access to opportunities

Another means of keeping economic power from the natives was to limit their access to opportunities. In no area was this more apparent than in education, where the colonial governments' policy was to restrict the indigenous populations to certain quality, types, and levels of education. Although the colonial education system changed over the years, it remained basically a two-track system—one for the Japanese colonists and another for the natives. Because the Japanese

t'ang pi-chia chih yen-chiu" [Research on the Relative Price of Rice and Sugar in Taiwan], in *T'ai-wan yin-hang chi-kan* [Bank of Taiwan Quarterly], V (March 1953), p. 50.

considered an educated native population a threat to their control of the colonies, educational opportunities for the natives beyond the primary grades were kept extremely limited. Furthermore, the education which the natives received was significantly inferior to that provided to the Japanese colonists. In the 1930's, even in Taiwan, where education for natives was funded more generously than in the other colonies, expenditure per student in schools primarily for Japanese children was twice that of schools for Taiwanese children. Indeed, the bulk of the government-general's education budget was used to support the senior-middle schools and institutes of higher education, all of which served the colonial Japanese almost exclusively. Education for the natives was seen not so much as a ladder to success as a way of teaching the natives to remain in their "proper place." In school, native children were taught to follow their parents' occupations and not to aspire for change or improvement. In short, the Japanese saw the colonial education system as a useful way to instill in the natives a proper code of conduct and to assimilate the natives at the bottom of the Japanese social order.

The Japanese could afford to restrict natives from acquiring higher education and from entering skilled occupations because skilled workers, technicians, and professionals could always be obtained from Japan. There always was a steady migration of Japanese to the colonies. In 1935 more than one million Japanese lived in Korea, Kwantung (including the SMR zone), and Taiwan. The colonial governments had encouraged this migration for two reasons. First, they believed that a growing Japanese population would give greater stability and security to the colonies. Second, they correctly realized that this migration eased the problem of staffing both the political and corporate establishments in the colonies without diluting Japanese control of the colonies. Favorable treatment was accorded to the Japanese by both the colonial government and Japanese enterprises in the colonies. Not only were the more coveted positions reserved for Japanese, but even for similar work Japanese workers were usually paid a wage that was twice that given to their native counterparts.[48] Even the relatively unskilled Japanese found it to their advantage to migrate to the colonies, where they enjoyed a standard of living and social status not easily achieved at home. Japanese colonists used their position and power to maintain their privileged status and to protect their interests, largely at the expense of the native populations.

[48] Wage data for Taiwan are in *T'ai-wan-sheng wu-shi-i nien-lai t'ung-chi t'i-yao*, Tables 301 and 302, and those for Korea are reported in Chōsen Sōtokufu, *Chōsen tōkei nempō* (Statistical Yearbook of Korea).

Japanese migration to the colonies and discrimination against natives prevented many natives from participating in the changes that accompany economic development. Until the 1930's, economic development in Korea and Taiwan had not noticeably changed the industrial distribution of native workers. Agriculture consistently absorbed 70 percent of the occupied Taiwanese and about 80 percent of the occupied Koreans.[49] Only in the 1930's, when the colonial Japanese population could not supply the new demand for mining and industrial workers, can we discern a change in the employment structure. More striking was occupational distribution. After 45 years of occupation, Taiwanese accounted for only 31 percent of the technicians and 27 percent of the government employees in Taiwan.[50] Because more than a third of the Taiwanese technicians were physicians and pharmacists, the extent of Taiwanese involvement in running and managing the country was even more limited than these aggregate data indicate. Taiwanese accounted for only 6.6 percent of the technicians in transport and communications, 20.3 percent in mining and manufacturing, and 36.7 percent in agriculture, forestry, and fisheries. The native population continued to perform the unskilled and menial tasks.

Part of the resources that the Japanese controlled flowed out of the colonies as profits, but a considerable share was reinvested there. Government and Japanese capitalists' savings were the most important sources of investment funds. By controlling savings and investments, the Japanese increased their ownership of economic assets in the colonies. These investments were an important source of economic growth, and although the gains from growth may not have been shared equitably, they brought economic benefits to both the Japanese and the natives, a topic I now turn to examine.

[49] Ho, *Economic Development of Taiwan*, Table 5.4, and Yunshik Chang, "Planned Economic Transformation and Population change," in C. I, Eugene Kim, and Dorothea Mortimore, eds., *Korea's Response to Japan: The Colonial Period 1910-1945* (Kalamazoo: The Center of Korean Studies, Western Michigan University, 1977), Table 10.

[50] George W. Barclay, *A Report on Taiwan's Population to the Joint Commission on Rural Reconstruction* (Princeton: Office of Population Research, Princeton University, 1954), Tables 19 and 20. The Korean data also show a high proportion of technicians and managers to be Japanese. See Chōsen Sōtokufu, *Shōwa jūkunen gogatsu ichijitsu jinkō chōsa kekka hōkoku* [Report of the Results of the 1944 Population Survey], 1945, v. 2, Tables 2 and 3. In 1935, Japanese comprised less than three percent of the population in Korea and about five percent of the population in Taiwan. In earlier years, its share of the population was even smaller.

COLONIAL DEVELOPMENT AND THE
ECONOMIC CONDITIONS OF SUBJECTS

How economic growth under Japanese colonialism benefitted the indigenous populations is a matter of income distribution. We know
very little about income distribution by nationality, so we must rely
on less satisfactory statistics related to per capita consumption. Table
5 presents several of these statistics for Korea and for Taiwan. Except
for one, the index of real wages for male Taiwanese workers in manufacturing, the others are per capita consumption measures for the
entire colonial population, both natives and Japanese. However, because the Japanese accounted for only a very small part of the colonial
population, these per capita consumption measures are still useful
indicators of economic conditions for Koreans and of Taiwanese.

Taking first per capita consumption of food, the dominant consumption item in the Korean and the Taiwanese family budgets, Columns 1 and 4 in Table 5 present calorie estimates of daily per capita
food availability in Korea and Taiwan. The estimates for Korea have
been adjusted for the suspected under-reporting of rice output in the
1920's and the 1930's. These estimates show that during the colonial
period the daily per capita calorie consumption in both Korea and
Taiwan fluctuated around the 2,000 calorie level,[51] close to the daily
minimum caloric requirement.[52] But the population figures used in
the calculations were not standardized for age and sex, so these per
capita measures probably understate food availability. During the
colonial period, population increased rapidly and altered the age
structure of the population, making it more "youthful." With more
children in the population, presumably fewer calories are required
per person. Therefore, the recorded constant per capita food availability implied some improvements in food intake on a per adult male
basis.

Given that income elasticity of food in colonial Korea and Taiwan

[51] The evidence that James Nakamura cites in support of his view that the calorie
consumption figures for Taiwan in Table 5 are much too low is Han-yu Chang's
finding that the daily calorie consumption in Taiwan was about 3,600 in the 1930's
(see Han-yu Chang, "A Study of the Living Conditions of Farmers in Taiwan, 1931-
1950," *The Developing Economies*, VII [March 1969], Table 17). However, Chang's
estimates and those in Table 5 measure different things: Chang measures the daily
calorie consumption *per adult farmer* while the estimate in Table 5 measure the daily
calorie consumption *per capita*.

[52] Ralph Gleason, using the United Nations Formula, calculated the average daily
per capita calorie requirements to be 2,030 for Taiwan. See his *Taiwan Food Balances,
1935-1954* (Taipei: JCRR, 1956).

was probably just below one,[53] the fact that per capita food consumption did not rise or rose only slightly even as real per capita total income expanded, suggests that the average real incomes of Koreans and Taiwanese increased only modestly. The available data on consumption pattern appear to support this conclusion. Theoretical considerations suggest that when income rises, household consumption pattern changes in important ways; most importantly, food expenditure declines as a share of total outlay. Small sample surveys of rice-farming families in Taiwan show little change in their consumption pattern from 1931 to 1941. The share of food in total household expenditure was 51 percent in 1931 and 1936 and 50 percent in 1941. This suggests that in the 1930's rural income in Taiwan did not change significantly.

Food availability in the colonies did not rise, despite rising per capita agricultural output, because of the large food exports to Japan. Between the years 1911-1912 and 1937-1938 Taiwan's average annual rice exports to Japan increased from below 100,000 MT to nearly 750,000 MT, and Korea's average annual rice exports to Japan increased from 37,000 MT to over 1.5 million MT. The export of rice from the colonies to Japan had reduced the annual per capita availability of rice from about 100 kg to 75 kg in Korea, and from about 130 kg to 100 kg in Taiwan. These exports also enabled Japan to maintain its annual per capita availability of rice at about 160 kg.[54] The Koreans and the Taiwanese maintained their caloric consumption by substituting inferior grain (sweet potato in Taiwan; barley and millet in Korea) for the preferred rice.

These findings are supported by the other four measures in Table 5. Three are real wage measurements, since Mizoguchi used real wage indexes to estimate per capita consumption measures for both Korea and Taiwan (Columns 3 and 5, Table 5). Mizoguchi's estimates of real per capita consumption and my estimate of real industrial wage (Column 6, Table 5) behave very similarly—they all show that real wages in Korea and Taiwan increased during the early 1920's, a period when nominal prices declined by more than nominal wages, after both had risen rapidly during World War I. Except for this early

---

[53] Empirical evidence suggests that the income elasticity of food is high when per capita income is low. See U.S. Department of Agriculture, *Elasticity of Food Consumption Associated with Changes in Income in Developing Countries*, Foreign Agricultural Economic Report no. 23, Chapter IV. Considering Korea's and Taiwan's very low per capita income in the colonial period, I conjecture that the income elasticity of food was probably 0.8 or 0.9.

[54] Ho, *Economic Development of Taiwan*, Table 6.2, and Suh, Table 40. Measures in *suk (Koku)* are converted to kg on the assumption that 1 *suk* of brown rice equals 150 kg.

period, however, real wages remained fairly constant and in fact declined after the mid-1930's. Suh also has estimated the per capita availability of consumer goods in Korea during the colonial period, and his estimates (Column 2, Table 5) show little change from the end of World War I to the late 1930's, when availability increased dramatically. But the increase in the late 1930's may have been largely statistical rather than real. Suh points out that the statistical coverage of manufacturing products improved over the years and that he could not adjust for the rapid build-up of inventories that began in Korea in the mid-1930's, when Japan began to prepare for war.

The colonial populations did benefit from a steadily expanding flow of publicly financed services, of which public health and education were most important. Government expenditures on education and health were treated earlier as investments in human capital. But those expenditures also have welfare effects that are not already reflected in personal consumption measures. Better public health improved the quality of life, and life expectancy among natives increased. From 1906 to 1936-1940 the mean life expectancy of Taiwanese males at birth increased by 13.4 years to 41.1, and that of Taiwanese females by 16.7 years to 45.7.[55] Similar advances were made in Korea, where life expectancy at birth reached 40.4 for males and 41.7 for females in 1935-1940.[56] The gains from education, other than its effects on earnings and therefore personal consumption, cannot be easily measured, but they were certainly not negligible. But these intangible benefits were not distributed equally among the native populations. The quality and availability of education favored urban rather than rural areas and Taiwan rather than other colonies.

AN ASSESSMENT OF ECONOMIC DEVELOPMENT UNDER JAPANESE COLONIALISM

The economic development of Japan's colonies can be analyzed by a well-known model of colonial development.[57] This model, based upon

[55] George Barclay, *Colonial Development and Population in Taiwan* (Princeton: Princeton University Press, 1954), p. 154.

[56] Tai-hwan Kwon et al., *The Population of Korea*, Table II.4.

[57] See examples in Paul A. Baran, *The Political Economy of Growth* (New York: Monthly Review Press, 1957); Andre Gunder Frank, *Capitalism and Underdevelopment in Latin America* (New York: Monthly Review Press 1969); Douglas A. Paauw and John C. H. Fei, *The Transition in Open Dualistic Economies* (New Haven: Yale University Press, 1973); Kenneth E. Boulding and Tapan Mukerjee, eds., *Economic Imperialism* (Ann Arbor: The University of Michigan Press, 1972); Robert I. Rhodes, ed., *Imperialism and Underdevelopment* (New York: Monthly Review Press, 1970); and Charles

the European colonial experiences in Asia and Africa, also identifies some of the major differences and similarities between economic development under Japanese colonialism and under European colonialism. In the model, the colonial economy is perceived to be open; however, its external relations, whether they be via trade or investments, are confined primarily to the colonizing country, so that bilateralism may be a more appropriate description than openness.

This model of a colonial economy specifies a "triangular mode of operation" represented graphically in Figure 1.[58] In one corner, X and H, there is a primary sector, with agriculture its main economic activity; another corner, N, denotes a small, emerging non-agricultural sector of services (trade, financial services, transportation and communication) with some manufacturing. A colonial government decides to promote a small number of resource-based industries in the primary sector after assessing the colony's endowment and the needs and objectives of the colonizing country. These industries, collectively shown as X, become commercialized and closely integrated with the non-agricultural sector, N, and the foreign trade sector, F to form a "triangular" relationship.

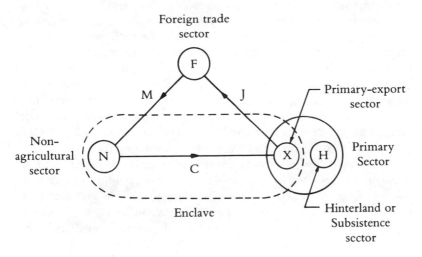

Figure 1

K. Wilber, *The Political Economy of Development and Underdevelopment*, 2nd. ed. (New York: Random House, 1979).

[58] Figure 1 is borrowed, with some minor modifications, from Paauw and Fei, p. 4.

Real resource flows between these sectors are as follows. Primary exports, J, flow from X to F; manufactured imports, M flow from F to N, and to complete the flow, N supplies X with manufactured goods and commercial services, C. When properly working, these activities produce what Paauw and Fei call an "export surplus," which is defined as "the surplus from exports over and above imports required to maintain the existing level of production."[59] For colonists and the colonial government, the main aim is to produce and to control that surplus.

The model also specifies the colonial economy as made up of two sectors, physically contiguous but economically separated. Sectors N and X form an enclave, highly commercialized and closely tied through trade and investments to the colonizing country. The colonists own and operate this enclave. Because the colonists and their colonial government have little interest in developing the hinterland, H, that sector remains undeveloped and uncommercialized. The enclave requires labor only from the hinterland, and native workers receive a wage determined by the income that they can earn in the subsistence sector. The colonial government has no interest or need to develop the hinterland (indeed, its interest is to keep it undeveloped). Because productivity and income in the subsistence sector is low, wages in the enclave are also kept low. This allows the colonists to retain as profits and property income the preponderant share of the surplus generated in the enclave. Very little inter-industry or commercial linkages take place between the enclave and the hinterland, so the economic growth experienced by the enclave is never transmitted to the hinterland, where most of the native population reside. This model sees economic development under colonialism as primarily enclave growth, with little development for the native population.

How closely did economic development in the Japanese colonies conform to this model? In many respects the Japanese colonies developed in the manner suggested by the model. The colonies were closely tied to Japan to create the "bilateralism" so conspicuous of colonialism. The Japanese colonies merely supplied primary products (food, minerals, and energy-intensive intermediate goods) to Japan and served as markets for Japan's manufactures. Japan also created the triangular flows of resources in its colonies to generate an "export surplus." Creating this surplus was apparently a prime Japanese objective, one that she achieved with considerable success.

However, the precise magnitude of the surplus is unknown. We can calculate the trade balance (exports minus imports), but the trade

[59] Paauw and Fei, *The Transition in Open Dualistic Economies*, p. 5.

balance and the export surplus are two very different concepts. Depending on how the surplus is used, a positive export surplus may be associated with either a positive or a negative trade balance. How the surplus is used is determined by the stage of development of the colony and the needs of the empire. When the colony is first developed, and when the empire's demand for the colony's exports is vigorous and expanding, much of the surplus is likely to be reinvested in the colony. In other times, the bulk of the surplus is repatriated to the colonizing country. While the repatriation of export surplus increases the trade balance, the import of producer goods for increasing the colony's productive capacity reduces the trade balance.

Except for the early years, when imports exceeded exports, Taiwan's trade balance was not only consistently positive but grew rapidly; after 1915 it became huge, never falling below 20 percent, and often nearing or even exceeding 30 percent of total exports.[60] This pattern also characterized Kwantung-Manchuria[61]—a negative trade balance in the early years of the colonial period and a large, growing trade surplus from 1930 to 1933. Thereafter Kwantung-Manchuria consistently imported more than they exported. The trade balance in Korea was persistently negative, with the import surplus particularly large in the early years and at the end of its colonial period.

But what about the "export surplus" in the Japanese colonies? First, a positive trade balance is prima facie evidence of an "export surplus." We can say that huge amounts of export surplus were generated in Taiwan after 1915 and in Kwantung-Manchuria in the 1920's. As Kwantung-Manchuria and Taiwan imported substantial amounts of producer goods throughout the colonial period, the size of their export surplus generated was undoubtedly much larger than their trade balance. Secondly, the negative trade balance in the early years for Taiwan and in Kwantung-Manchuria suggests that to generate an export surplus, resources first had to flow into the colonies.

Finally, because a trade deficit may occur even when an export surplus is produced, the persistent negative trade balance in Korea and the large trade deficits in Kwantung-Manchuria in the 1930's reflect not their inability to generate an export surplus but their need to import large amounts of producer goods in the 1930's. For devel-

[60] Trade balance data for Korea, Manchuria, and Taiwan are from Wontack Hong, *Statistical Data on Trade and Subsidy Policy in Korea* (Seoul: Korea Development Institute, 1977), Table B.4; *T'ai-wan-sheng wu-shih-i nien-lai t'ung-chi t'i-yao*, Table 321; and Eckstein, Chao, and Chang, Appendix Table I.

[61] Here and elsewhere I use Kwantung-Manchuria to remind the reader that, while my focus is on Kwantung, the data used (and the relevant concepts discussed) extend beyond Kwantung to include all parts of Manchuria.

oping agriculture in Korea in the 1920's and heavy industries in Kwantung–Manchuria and Korea in the 1930's, Japan reinvested much of the export surplus that it controlled in the two colonies. Even so, Korea produced less export surplus than the other two colonies, and this explains its persistent trade deficits. Korea was climatically less suited for agriculture than Taiwan, and in 1910 its agricultural infrastructure may have been even more backward than in Taiwan at that time. With little unsettled land, Korea also had less potential than Kwantung–Manchuria to expand agricultural production. Secondly, unlike Taiwan, where a government had consistently encouraged agricultural development, the government in Korea abandoned its promotion of agriculture after only a decade. Consequently, agricultural development in Korea never gained the momentum that it did in Taiwan. Finally, with rice production rising rapidly in the empire, the price of rice sharply declined in the 1920's. This affected Korea's export earnings much more than it did Taiwan's; whereas Taiwan had two major export crops, Korea had only rice.

The development experiences of the Japanese colonies did not conform in all respects to our model. Most importantly, economic development in the Japanese colonies was not restricted primarily in the Japanese-dominated enclave while the subsistence sector languished. Why? Dualistic growth is the result of three conditions: first, a colonial power has little interest in developing the subsistence sector. Second, the subsistence sector does not have sources of economic growth that are independent of colonial control. Third, the spread effects of growth are weak, so that growth in the enclave is not transmitted to the hinterland. In each Japanese colony one or more of these conditions did not hold.

Perhaps Kwantung deviated the least from these conditions, particularly if we view Kwantung as the enclave and the rest of Manchuria as the hinterland. The Japanese developed only mining and other non-agricultural activities in Kwantung (including the SMR zone), but increased economic activities in the enclave did facilitate agricultural commercialization throughout the economy. Still, Kwantung–Manchuria was a frontier economy and not a full Japanese colony until 1932. Because of its unsettled land, Kwantung–Manchuria had independent sources of growth that did not exist in the other Japanese colonies. When these sources of growth disappeared in the 1930's, agriculture stagnated, and development in Kwantung–Manchuria became less balanced and more dualistic.

In Korea and Taiwan their export sectors included not only the extractive and the energy-intensive industries but also peasant agriculture. Agriculture was both the export sector and the mainstay of the economy. When the Japanese promoted rice, a crop widely grown in both colonies for subsistence as well as for cash, agricultural development in Korea and Taiwan was extended to the subsistence sector, and nearly the entire agricultural population in Korea and Taiwan were drawn into the development process. More than anything else, the development of peasant agriculture improved the economic conditions for Koreans and Taiwanese and prevented the two economies from becoming as strictly compartmentalized as our model predicts.

Two other factors also contributed to the more balanced and broadly based development pattern in the Japanese colonies. First, the Japanese were unusually development-oriented. As noted earlier, both the colonial governments and Japanese capitalists reinvested in their colonies a substantial share of the surplus that they controlled. Although these investments served their interests, the huge growth of the infrastructure spread benefits throughout the economy. Secondly, Japan never introduced the plantation system to its colonies, so that natives participated in agricultural development as capitalists and entrepreneurs and received greater income benefits. Why was the plantation system never introduced? Some plausible reasons are: (1) export crops (sugarcane and rice) were already widely grown, so that a new institution to transfer resources from traditional subsistence crops to export cash crops was not needed. (2) The Japanese colonists were comfortable with the landlord-tenant system that existed in the colonies because it was similar to the system in Japan. (3) With property rights already firmly established in both Korea and Taiwan, the introduction of a plantation system would have required a radical redistribution of rural assets, a change that might be too disruptive and counter-productive. (4) Perhaps most importantly, the Japanese realized that developing peasant agriculture under the plantation system would have involved enormous supervision costs. It was easier and less costly to use market incentives to induce peasants to increase production.

From Japan's viewpoint, its colonial record was reasonably successful. The material resources in the colonies were systematically developed for Japan's benefit. Because the colonial governments and the Japanese colonists owned and operated much of the modern sector, owned considerable land, possessed great market power, and firmly controlled agriculture, they could capture most of the economic benefits of development. By doing so, they effectively controlled the surplus produced in the colonies and diverted it for their own uses.

Japan's success was facilitated by the fact that Japanese colonists planned their development programs and projects with considerable care, paying an unusual amount of attention to detail. Colonial administrators were pragmatists, and to solve problems in their colonies they followed a consistent pattern of study, planning, enactment, further study, further planning, and revision. Planning alone does not ensure the successful execution of programs. Competent and careful supervision is also needed. Unlike other colonial powers that relied heavily on native administrators, the colonial governments and Japanese corporations imported large amounts of human capital from Japan—competent and loyal personnel to place in high and lower echelons of the colonial establishment, to manage both the government and the economy.

From the natives' viewpoint, the colonial record proved to be a mixed one. The development of peasant agriculture involved nearly the entire agricultural population in the development process, and the benefits of development were also widely shared, so that the Japanese colonies escaped the worst aspects of dualistic growth. But the Japanese, with their considerable economic and political power, did capture a large share of the gains from development, and the native populations had to be satisfied with a slower pace of improvement in their material welfare than would otherwise have been the case. The natives also had to accept the prospect of very limited opportunities to rise from their subordinate position in society. Sudden shifts in colonial policy to accomodate Japan's changing needs were detrimental to the colonies' long term interests. Finally, colonialism burdened the native populations with many intangible costs that we have so far neglected: the humiliation of being second class citizens, the loss of political and often personal freedom, and the lost opportunity to develop their own type of society. These intangibles cannot be measured, and if a general assessment of the colonial period is to be made, they must somehow be taken into account.

TABLE 1
Selected Indexes of Production, Korea, Taiwan, and Kwantung
(1925-1929 = 100)

KOREA

Period	Aggregate Measures		Agriculture		Mining		Manufacturing	
	GDP[b]	Commodity product[c]	Value-added[d]	Production[e]	Value-added[f]	Production[g]	Value-added[f]	Production[g]
1910-14	48.12[1]	67.07	75.90	73.68	54.76	26.86[2]	18.66	31.25[2]
1915-19	60.25	83.27	91.88	87.72	91.67	61.35	42.63	66.71
1920-24	96.07	90.93	97.51	96.49	55.95	76.24	55.65	70.91
1925-29	100.00	100.00	100.00	100.00	100.00	100.00	100.00	100.00
1930-34	100.99	122.91	117.42	113.16	203.57	160.52	123.97	126.36
1935-39	122.46[3]	142.49	113.79	127.19	572.62	467.28[4]	244.34	269.19
			Annual Compound Rates of Growth[a]					
1912-27	5.32	2.70	1.85	2.06	4.11	7.46[5]	11.84	5.69[5]
1927-37	2.39	3.60	1.30	2.43	19.07	18.70[6]	9.34	10.41
1912-37	4.15	3.06	1.63	2.21	9.84	11.82[7]	10.83	7.81[3]

TABLE 1 (cont.)

Period	Domestic Product		TAIWAN Agriculture		Mining Production		Manufacturing Production	
	Lee[h]	Mizoguchi[i]	Value-added[j]	Production[k]	Ho[l]	Shinohara[m]	Ho[l]	Shinohara[m]
1905–09	—	41.57	—	57.18	—	—	—	—
1910–14	55.24[1]	49.74	69.25[1]	61.13	50.95[9]	51.66[9]	38.26[9]	33.73[9]
1915–19	61.85	58.66	56.77	71.83	59.82	53.66	65.56	59.43
1920–24	68.52	85.61	64.32	77.46	66.60	73.58	64.98	60.80
1925–29	100.00	100.00	100.00	100.00	100.00	100.00	100.00	100.00
1930–34	125.45	111.23	108.57	120.56	107.58	131.20	124.19	117.43
1935–39	152.48	119.61[10]	135.22	144.51	140.94	177.28[4]	177.59	166.29
Annual Compound Rates of Growth[a]								
1905–27	—	4.18	—	2.96	—	—	—	—
1905–37	—	3.32	—	3.20	—	—	—	—
1912–27	3.93	4.77	2.07	3.33	4.92	4.85[11]	6.61[11]	6.53[11]
1927–37	4.31	1.47	3.05	3.75	3.50	6.70[6]	5.91	5.22
1912–37	4.08	3.44	2.47	3.49	4.32	5.50[12]	6.33[13]	6.00[13]

TABLE 1 (cont.)

KWANTUNG

Period	Aggregate Measures	Agricultural Production[m]	Mining		Manufacturing	
			Value-added[b]	Production[p]	Value-added[b]	Production[p]
1905-09	—	31.26[14]	—	—	—	—
1910-14	—	48.55	23.23	23.25	18.75	20.06
1915-19	—	50.40	34.39	34.42	59.99	63.92
1920-24	—	67.80	60.29	60.38	74.71	86.81
1925-29	—	100.00	100.00	100.00	100.00	100.00
1930-34	—	142.56	103.52	103.72	121.96	114.34
1935-39	—	123.56[15]	123.44[15]	123.54[15]	193.02[15]	160.93[15]
Annual Compound Rates of Growth[a]						
1912-27	—	4.93	10.22	10.21	11.80	11.30
1927-37	—	2.14	2.27[16]	2.29[16]	7.44[16]	5.22[16]
1912-37	—	3.81	7.39[17]	7.39[17]	10.27[17]	9.15

TABLE 1 (*cont.*)

[1] 1911-14   [2] 1914   [3] 1935-38   [4] 1935-36   [5] 1915-27   [6] 1927-35   [7] 1915-35   [8] 1915-37   [9] 1912-14   [10] 1935-38   [11] 1913-27   [12] 1913-35   [13] 1913-37   [14] 1906-09   [15] 1935-36   [16] 1927-35   [17] 1912-35

[a] Based on 5-year averages centered around the initial and terminal years of each period. When 5-year averages are not available, 3-year averages are used.

[b] Gross Domestic Product in 1934-36 average prices estimated by the expenditure approach. The estimates are from Toshiyuki Mizoguchi, *Taiwan Chōsen no keizai seichō* [The Economic Growth of Taiwan and Korea], Tokyo: Iwanami Shoten, 1975, Table 5.3.

[c] Sum of value-added in 1936 prices originating from agriculture, fishery, forestry, mining, and manufacturing. The estimates are from Sang-chul Suh, *Growth and Structural Changes in the Korean Economy 1910-1940*, Cambridge: Harvard University Press, 1978, Table A12.

[d] Suh, Table A12.

[e] Suh, Tables 35 and A10. This is an output index of rice, barley, beans, other grains, and cotton. Sung-hwan Ban has also constructed a production index that includes more commodities (for his estimates see his "The Long-run Productivity Growth in Korean Agricultural Development 1910-1968," Ph.D. dissertation, Department of Agricultural Economics, University of Minnesota, 1971, Table 2). I use Suh's estimate here because he adjusted for the very serious underreporting of rice during 1924-1935. For the reasons why underreporting is suspected and Suh's adjustments, see his *Growth and Structural Changes in The Korean Economy*, pp. 16-20.

[f] Suh, Table A12.

[g] Mizoguchi, Table 3.7.

[h] Net Domestic Product in 1937 prices estimated by the value-added approach. The estimates are from T. H. Lee, "Inter-sectoral Capital Flows in the Economic Development of Taiwan, 1895-1960," Ph.D. dissertation, Cornell University, 1968, Appendix Table 6.

[i] Gross Domestic Product in 1934-36 average prices estimated by the expenditure approach. The estimates are from Mizoguchi, Table 5.3.

[j] The value-added in 1937 prices produced by the primary sector (agriculture, forestry, and fisheries). The estimates are from T. H. Lee, "Inter-sectoral Capital Flows in the Economic Development of Taiwan, 1895-1910," Appendix Table 6.

[k] Based on an index of agricultural production composed of 79 commodities. The estimates are from Samuel P.-S. Ho, *Economic Development of Taiwan 1860-1970*, New Haven: Yale University Press, 1978, Table A33.

[l] Based on an index of production. The estimates are from Ho, *Economic Development of Taiwan*, Table A49.

[m] The value of production in 1934-36 prices. The estimates are from Miyohei Shinohara and Shigeru Ishikawa, *Taiwan no keizai seichō* [Taiwan's Economic Growth], Tokyo: Ajiya Keizai Kenkyūjo, 1972, Table 15.

[n] This is an index of 41 agricultural commodities with 1935-37 average prices as weights. Ramon H. Myers and Thomas R. Ulie, "Foreign Influence and Agricultural Development in Northeast China: A Case Study of the Liaotung Peninsula, 1906-42," *Journal of Asian Studies*, 31 (February 1972), Table II.

[p] Production is the gross value of industrial output in 1926 prices. The value-added estimates for each industry group are obtained by applying the ratio of value-added to gross value found for 1936, 1938, and 1940 to the annual gross value estimates in 1926 prices. The data are from Kungtu C. Sun (assisted by Ralph W. Huenemann), *The Economic Development of Manchuria in The First Half of The Twentieth Century*, Cambridge: East Asian Research Center, Harvard University, 1969, Tables 20 and 22.

TABLE 2
Measures of Agricultural Output and Inputs, Korea and Taiwan

Period	(1) Crop output index	(2) Cultivated area index	(3) Crop area index	(4) Labor input index	(5) Fertilizer input index	(6) Percentage of cultivated area irrigated	(7) Percentage of paddy land using improved seeds	(8) Yield (kg/ha) rice	(9) Yield (kg/ha) Sugar cane
KOREA									
1915–19	100	100	100	100	100	NA[b]	39	1384	—
1920–24	110	113	107	101	168	17%	64	1407	—
1925–29	114	115	112	106	457	22%	73	1553	—
1930–34	129	116	116	101	736	26%	77	1823	—
1935–39[a]	145	116	118	97	1129	28%	85	2084	—
TAIWAN									
1910–14	85	95	92	98	59	33%	NA[b]	1330	25,390
1915–19	100	100	100	100	100	37%	NA[b]	1413	30,873
1920–24	108	104	103	97	123	42%	2[c]	1468	30,842
1925–29	139	110	112	100	167	48%	18	1642	49,919
1930–34	170	113	121	102	218	55%	29	1808	66,945
1935–39	202	118	130	111	315	59%	46	2052	70,332

[a] Because of an extremely poor rice harvest in 1939, figures for 1940 are substituted for those for 1939.
[b] NA, data not available. Irrigation facilities deteriorated badly during the Yi Dynasty. In 1910, perhaps only 20 percent of Korea's paddy fields (or 7 percent of total cultivated area) was irrigated. For crude estimates of irrigated area in this early period, see Shigera Ishikawa, *Economic Development in Asian Perspective* (Tokyo: Kinokuniya, 1967), Table 2.6.
[c] 1922–24.

[1] For Korea, this is a weighted output index of rice, barley, beans, other grains, and cotton. Rice output figures have been adjusted upwards to correct for suspected underreporting during 1924-35. The data are from Sang-chul Suh, *Growth and Structural Changes in The Korean Economy, 1910-1940*, Cambridge: Harvard University Press, 1978, Table 35. For Taiwan, this is an output index of 70 crops. Weighting is by 1935-37 average value of production. The data are from Samuel P.-S. Ho, *Economic Development of Taiwan, 1860-1970*, New Haven: Yale University Press, 1978, Table A33.

[2] For both Korea and Taiwan this is an index of paddy field and dryland. The Korean data are from Sung-hwan Ban, "The Long-run Productivity Growth in Korean Agricultural Development 1910-1968," Ph.D. dissertation, University of Minnesota, 1971, Table A6.11. The Taiwan data are from Taiwan Sotokufu, *Taiwan nōgyō nempō* [Taiwan Agricultural Yearbook], various issues.

[3] Total crop area. The Taiwan figures exclude green-manure crops and are adjusted for areas under temporary crops with growing periods longer than one year (e.g., sugar cane). The Korean data are from Ban, Table A6.12. The Taiwan data are from Samuel P.-S. Ho, "Taiwan Statistical Appendix," Yale Economic Growth Center, mimeo, Table V-18.

[4] Labor input is the gainfully occupied persons in agriculture in male equivalent. The Korean data are from Suh, Table 34. The Taiwan data are from Yhi-min Ho, *Agricultural Development of Taiwan, 1903-1960*, Nashville: Vanderbilt University Press, 1966, pp. 43-44.

[5] Weighted average of organic and commercial fertilizers. The Korean data are from Suh, Table 34. The Taiwan data are from Ho, *Economic Development of Taiwan*, Table 4.2.

[6] The figures for Korea represent irrigated paddy field as a percent of total cultivated area and are for the years 1925, 1930, 1935, and 1940. The Korean data are from Ban, Table 11 and the Taiwan data are from Ho, "Taiwan Statistical Appendix," Table V-12.

[7] The figures for Taiwan represent the area under *ponlai* rice as a percentage of total rice land. The Korean data are from Suh, Table 34, and the Taiwan data are from Ho, "Taiwan Statistical Appendix," Table V-20-B.

[8] and [9] The Korean yield figures are based on Suh's adjusted rice production data for 1925-36. For the other years, Korea's rice production data are from Wontack Hong, *Statistical Data on Trade and Subsidy Policy in Korea*, Seoul: Korea Development Institute, 1977, Table B9. Korea's crop area figures are those in Ban, Table A6.12. The Taiwan figures are from Ho, "Taiwan Statistical Appendix," Tables V-20-A and V-22.

TABLE 3
Growth and Composition of Manufacturing, Korea, Taiwan, and Kwantung

Period	Total	Food	Textile	Wood and Wood Products	Chemicals (inc. veg. oil)	Non-metallic Mineral Products	Metals	Machinery	Others
KOREA									
Production growth rates[a]									
1913-27	5.99	6.68	5.92	14.23	7.82	15.15	5.08	6.49	1.18
1927-39	10.29	7.87	10.04	1.95	17.38	10.79	8.66	10.49	2.40
1913-39	8.12	7.27	7.96	7.91	12.50	12.95	6.85	8.47	1.79
Production composition[b]									
1914-16	100%	35	13	1	12	3	16	2	18
1926-28	100%	43	14	3	16	3	7	3	10
1936-40	100%	27	18	2	30	3	11	3	6
TAIWAN									
Production growth rates[a]									
1913-27	5.95	4.96	6.25	11.78	1.06	11.13	11.63	19.46	7.49
1927-39	5.92	7.18	7.03	6.23	5.41	5.92	10.03	6.95	5.24
1913-39	5.94	6.06	6.64	8.97	3.21	8.49	10.82	13.03	6.36
Production composition[c]									
1914-16	100%	70	1	1	20	1	2	1	3
1926-28	100%	71	2	2	13	2	4	2	4
1938-40	100%	73	2	2	11	2	5	2	3

KWANTUNG

Production growth rates[a]

1913-27	11.33	10.75	—		10.30	12.85	13.76[e]	6.35	—
1927-35	4.63	6.93	11.24	5.90	-.13	6.93	21.94	4.95	—
1913-35	8.85	9.35	—		6.39	10.66	17.13[f]	5.84	—

Production composition[d]

1914-16	100%	13	g	g	71	3	2	11	—
1926-28	100%	11	7	3	61	5	5	7	—
1934-36	100%	13	12	3	42	7	15	7	—

[a] Annual compound rates of growth of real output based on 3-year averages centered around the initial and terminating years of each period.
[b] The average percentage distribution of gross output in current value.
[c] The average percentage distribution of gross output in 1934-36 prices.
[d] The average percentage distribution of gross output in 1926 prices.
[e] 1916-27.   [f] 1916-35.   [g] less than 0.5%.

Sources: Based on data in Mizoguchi Toshiyuki, *Taiwan Chōsen no keizai seichō* [The economic growth of Taiwan and Korea], Tokyo: Iwanami Shoten, 1975, Tables 3.6 and 3.7; Shinohara Miyohei and Ishikawa Shigeru, *Taiwan no keizai seichō* [Taiwan's economic growth], Tokyo: Ajiya Keizai Kenkyūjo, 1972, Tables 15 and 18, and Kungtu C. Sun (assisted by Ralph W. Huenemann), *The Economic Development of Manchuria in the First Half of the Twentieth Century*, Cambridge: East Asian Research Center, Harvard University, 1969, Table 20.

TABLE 4
Growth and Structure of the Colonial Trade: Korea and Taiwan
(Annual Averages)

Period	Index of export volume		Export to Japan as % of total export	Export Structure (% of total)			
				Foodstuffs[a]	Manufactures		Industri raw materia
					Consumer goods[b]	Producer goods[c]	
				KOREA			
1911–15	100		78	72	5	1	22
1916–20	456		83	68	5	1	26
1921–25	640		92	68	4	2	26
1926–29	735		91	67	6	2	25
1930–35	956		90	61	8	2	29
1936–38	1,688		84	49	15	3	32
				TAIWAN			
	A	B					
1906–10	66	74	66	80	15	e	5
1911–15	100	100	75	77	13	e	10
1916–20	176	148	73	78	8	1	13
1921–25	199	189	77	83	7	2	8
1926–29	292	284	78	85	7	2	7
1930–35	348	381	87	87	5	1	7
1936–38	421	526[f]	90	89	5	1	5

Period	Index of import volume		Import from Japan as % of total import	Import Structure (% of total)			
				Foodstuffs[a]	Manufactures		Indus rau mater
					Consumer goods[b]	Producer goods[c]	
				KOREA			
1911–15	100		62	19	47	13	21
1916–20	114		67	18	44	13	25
1921–25	215		66	22	41	13	24
1926–29	334		72	25	37	12	26
1930–35	433		83	17	40	13	30
1936–38	556		86	15	39	18	28
				TAIWAN			
	A	B					
1906–10	69	69	60	23	36	22	19
1911–15	100	100	71	30	29	17	24
1916–20	105	102	68	30	24	16	30
1921–25	121	138	68	32	27	14	27
1926–29	201	223	68	28	29	15	28
1930–35	244	275	81	22	30	16	32
1936–38	305	334[f]	87	24	29	20	27

a food and raw materials for processed food.

b clothing, apparels, consumer durables, printed matters, charcoal, and miscellaneous goods.

c timber, metals, glass, cement and stone products, machinery and equipments, and transport equip-
ents.

d fiber, leather, rubber, chemical products (including fertilizers), oil (excluding edible oil), coal, and
inerals.

e less than 0.5 percent of total.

f the average of 1936 and 1939.

Notes and Sources: The volume indexes of imports and exports for Korea and set A of the index for
aiwan are constructed by deflating the values of imports and exports by, respectively, price indexes
˙ imports and exports. The price indexes are those constructed by Toshiyuki Mizoguchi and can be
und in his "Foreign Trade in Taiwan and Korea under Japanese Rule," *Hitotsubashi Journal of Econom-*
, 14 (February 1974), Table 4. Set B of the volume indexes for Taiwan are from Samuel P.-S. Ho,
:onomic Development of Taiwan 1860-1970, New Haven: Yale University Press, 1978, Table A49. These
e Laspeyres indexes with 1925 value weights. For details of how these indexes were constructed see
e notes following Table A49. The share of exports to Japan and imports from Japan are calculated
ɔm current price data in Wontack Hong, "Statistical Data on Trade and Subsidy Policy in Korea,"
ɔrea Development Institute, 1977, mimeo, Table B. 4 and in T'ai-wan sheng hsing-cheng chang-kuan
ɪng-che t'ung-chi-shih [Statistical Bureau of the Taiwan Provincial Government], *T'ai-wan-sheng wu-
ih-i nien-lai t'ung-chi t'i-yao* (Taiwan Province: Statistical Summary of the Past Fifty-one Years), Taipei,
▪46, Table 321. The export and imports structures are also based on current price data and are from
ɔshiyuki Mizoguchi, "Foreign Trade in Taiwan and Korea under Japanese Rule," Table 3.

TABLE 5
Economic Conditions of Koreans and Taiwanese (Annual averages)

| | KOREA | | | TAIWAN | | |
| | Daily per capita food availability in calories | Per capita consumer goods available (Yen in 1936 prices) | Per capita consumption (Yen in 1934-36 prices) | Daily per capita food availability in calories | Per capita consumption (Yen in 1934-36 prices) | Index of real industrial wage 1910-4 = 100 |
Period	(1)	(2)	(3)	(4)	(5)	(6)
1910–14	2,133[a]	n.a.	61	2,011	111	100
1915–19	2,206	42[b]	61	2,023	111	100
1920–24	2,033	43	92	2,158	159	138
1925–29	1,924	42	88	2,208	160	145
1930–34	1,812	49	83	2,057	155	161
1935–39	2,033	57	87[c]	1,865	135[c]	152[c]

[a] The figures in this column are for the following periods: 1912-15, 1916-20, 1921-25, 1926-30, 1931-35, and 1936-40.
[b] The figures in this column are for the following periods: 1919-21, 1924-26, 1929-31, 1934-36, and 1939-40.
[c] 1935-38

Sources by column:

(1) Sang-chul Suh, Growth and Structural Changes in the Korean Economy, 1910-1940, Cambridge: Harvard University Press, 1978, Table 41. These estimates assume that calories from rice, barley, and wheat made up 70 percent of the total. (2) Sang-chul Suh, Growth and Structural Changes in the Korean Economy, 1910-1940, Table 29. These were estimated from production and trade statistics. (3 and 5) Toshiyuki Mizoguchi, Taiwan Chōsen no keizan seichō [The Economic Growth of Taiwan and Korea], Tokyo: Iwanami Shoten, 1975, Tables 5.3 and 5.4. These figures are based on an index of real wage. (4) Samuel P.-S. Ho, Economic Development of Taiwan, 1860-1970, New Haven: Yale University Press, 1978, Table 6.2. These estimates, except for 1935-39, assume that calories from rice and sweet potatoes made up 70 percent of the total. (6) Samuel P.-S. Ho, Economic Development of Taiwan, 1860-1970, Table 6.1. This is the index of real wage of male Taiwanese workers in manufacturing.

CHAPTER 10

Capital Formation in Taiwan and Korea

Mizoguchi Toshiyuki and Yamamoto Yūzō

This essay examines capital formation in Taiwan and Korea before World War II in terms of its structure and impact on those two economies within the context of their general economic growth. The general economic activities of any economy can be measured either by Gross Domestic Product (GDP) or Gross Domestic Expenditures (GDE). For estimating the trend of general economic activities for Taiwan and Korea, there are reliable data on production for the primary and secondary industries, but very little data for the tertiary or service industry. Gross domestic expenditures are derived from private consumption, government consumption, capital formation, exports and imports. Although there are some difficulties in estimating private consumption and capital formation, we will mainly rely on our GDE indicator to show the trend of economic growth in both colonies.[1]

First, several comments on our use of the gross domestic expenditures measurement. In Table 1 we have compared GDE measures for both colonies with the preceding GDP estimates, and the differences and similarities between them should be noted.[2] Our GDE estimate in absolute terms is higher than the GDP estimate for Taiwan. This difference is probably explained by the upward bias for private consumption expenditures in GDE, a bias originating from the family budget we used, which reflects higher-income households. Fur-

[1] Mizoguchi Toshiyuki, *Taiwan Chōsen no keizai seichō* [Economic Growth of Taiwan and Chōsen] (Tokyo: Iwanami Shoten, 1975). Yūzō Yamamoto, "Shokuminchika Chōsen Taiwan no ikigai shūshi" [Balance of Payments Estimates of Colonial Chōsen and Taiwan], Jimbungakuhō, No. 35 and 40 (1972 and 1975). On the national income data for Japan proper, we rely on the estimates by the Ohkawa project. Kazushi Ohkawa et al., eds., *Estimates of Long-Term Economic Statistics of Japan since 1868* (Tokyo: Keizai Shinpōsha, 1965-).

[2] For Taiwan, two kinds of GDP estimates have been done by T. H. Lee and M. H. Hsing. See the review by Samuel Pao-San Ho, *Economic Development of Taiwan, 1860-1970* (New Haven: Yale University Press, 1978). The pioneer work of Korean GDP estimate is Y. H. Lee's in Y. K. Lee et al., eds., *History of People's Living of Korea under Japanese Occupation* (Seoul: Minjung Seokwan, 1971).

ther, the GDP estimate appears to understate the true value of production because of insufficient coverage of basic data.[3] The growth rate figures for GDE and GDP are nearly the same for the long-term period. However, the growth rates differ when this period is subdivided into short time phases, and the different price deflator index used for both series probably explains this difference.

For Korean figures, there is little difference in absolute value between GDP and GDE. However, the growth rate in the period of 1926-1935 is only 0.71 percent in our GDE estimate, in contrast to 4.8 percent in Lee's GDP. In addition to the different deflators used in each estimate, the growth rate of nominal agricultural production in Lee's estimate seems to be too high when we compare it with other estimates of agricultural production.

ECONOMIC GROWTH IN TAIWAN AND KOREA

We now compare the long-term changes in economic activities for both colonies and compare them with Japan.[4] In Figure 1 and Table 1 the reader will observe that the growth rates for Taiwan and Korea were higher than for Japan. Prior to 1917, the growth rate for Japan and Taiwan was low, but growth accelerated between 1913 and 1922. Korea's economic growth was also very high in that decade, but during the 1920's growth slowed in both Korea and Japan, whereas Taiwan's economy continued to expand rapidly.

Turning now to the components of GDE in Table 2, we note that while private consumption made up the largest share of GDE, its contribution was small because private consumption grew so slowly. We estimated private consumption expenditures by selecting a benchmark year when family budget survey data were available and then extrapolated by an index from that year with an estimated wage-rate index. Returning to our GDE measures, we find that exports played an important role in economic growth for all three countries. Although the Taiwan export growth was lower than in Korea, its contribution to Taiwan's GDE's expansion was considerable because its share was so large.

Our GDE measurements can be compared with various produc-

---

[3] Official statistics for the Japanese colonies omitted coverage of many economic activities in the early years, and their quality and coverage gradually improved as administrators learned how to govern their areas.

[4] For the economic growth of Taiwan and Korea, see Toshiyuki Mizoguchi, "Economic Growth of Korea under the Japanese Occupation: Background of Industrialization of Korea," *Hitotsubashi Journal of Economics*, Vol. 20, No. 1 (1979).

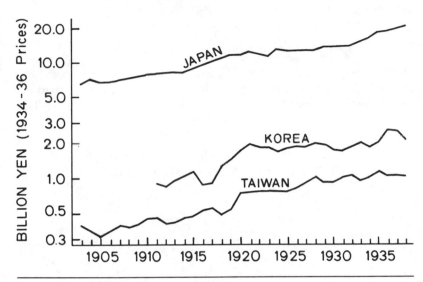

GNE AND GDE INDICATORS FOR
JAPAN, KOREA, AND TAIWAN (1903-1937)

FIGURE 1
Source: Ohkawa et al. (1965-) and Mizoguchi (1975)

tion time series, which we have presented in Table 3.[5] The reader will observe that agricultural production grew more slowly in Japan and Korea, particularly between 1918-1927, but Taiwan agricultural output grew rapidly over the entire period. The expansion of manufacturing was also rapid in all three, especially in Korea between 1928-1937. The reason for this striking difference was that Korea

[5] On the production index, we have two types of estimates: "gross production" index and "value-added" index. For Taiwan, we have value-added data by T. H. Lee. For Korea, there is Y. K. Lee's estimate and the value-added data on commodity production by S. C. Suh, Sang-chul Suh, *Growth and Structural Change in the Korean Economy, 1910-1940* (Harvard: Harvard University Press, 1978). The value-added data would be preferable in some respects, but we cannot neglect the high-quality data for gross production estimated by Japanese scholars from their examination of the government-general statistics. Shinohara estimated gross production for manufacturing and mining in Taiwan, and Mizoguchi compiled the corresponding figures for Korea. Ishikawa is now estimating agricultural production for Taiwan and Korea. Miyohei Shinohara and Shigeru Ishikawa, eds., *Taiwan no keizai seichō* [Economic Growth of Taiwan] (Tokyo: Ajiya Keizai Kenkyūjo, 1975); Mizoguchi (1975); unpublished worksheets by Ishikawa.

industrialization originated from mining and industries that processed minerals, while in Taiwan manufacturing depended chiefly upon food processing.[6]

THE PATTERN OF INVESTMENT IN TAIWAN AND KOREA

Having presented the context of general economic growth for these two colonies, let us now turn to investment for capital formation. Our investment analyses are based upon three sources of data. The

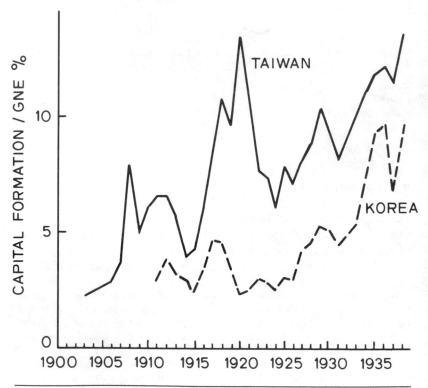

THE CAPITAL FORMATION/GDE RATIO FOR TAIWAN AND KOREA (1903-1937)

FIGURE 2
Source: Mizoguchi (1975)

[6] See Mizoguchi, "Economic Growth of Korea" (1979), especially Figure 3.

first originates from our GDE series, the second is derived from colonial government budget data, and the third comes from data showing the financial flows between Japan and her colonies.

In Figure 2 we present the long-term change in ratio of capital

CAPITAL FORMATION IN JAPAN, TAIWAN, AND KOREA (1896 - 1937)

(A) CONSTRUCTION

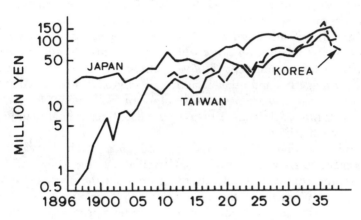

(B) EQUIPMENT

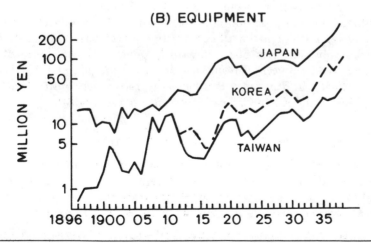

FIGURE 3
Source: Mizoguchi (1975)

formation to GDE for both colonies. We observe that both ratios project an upward trend similar to the "trend acceleration" in capital formation for Japan already mentioned by Kazushi Ohkawa.[7] We also note that the ratio was higher in Taiwan than in Korea, and a large upsurge occurred in Taiwan during the late teens.

We have presented the structure of capital formation in Table 4. The expansion of capital formation was much more rapid in Taiwan and Korea than in Japan, a phenomenon due to the very small capital stock in the colonies when Japan acquired them. A large part of the investment went to constructing buildings and other structures, and oddly the value of construction investment was the same for both colonies for the period 1910-1938. We conjecture that because Korea's economy size was roughly four times larger than that of Taiwan's, Taiwan had roughly four times the construction investment than Korea. Our data do not enable us to identify the specific kind of construction investment, but we believe that most construction went for irrigation and other facilities directly related to agriculture. For investment in machinery and equipment, the amount for Korea was twice that of Taiwan. Korea accumulated her capital mainly in the teens and 1930's.

Turning to Figure 3, we have plotted on a graph the value of investment to show cycles of capital formation. Investment of machinery and equipment violently fluctuated, but the over-all pattern after World War I for all three countries is very similar. This pattern suggests that change in equipment investment probably depended upon Japan's business cycle behavior. Two upsurges in Taiwanese equipment investment around 1901 and 1910 correspond to the investment on transportation and the building of sugar factories, respectively. The fluctuation of construction investment is rather stable and less obvious. But one noteworthy point is the existence of a reverse trend between Taiwan and Korea for the period 1915-1920. The upswing in Taiwan in this period is due to the construction of irrigation facilities like Chianan Reservoir in Tainan district.

THE ROLE OF GOVERNMENT IN CAPITAL FORMATION

We have used budget reports of the government-general offices in Taiwan and Korea to estimate the government sector's capital formation.[8] Figure 4 shows the long-term trend for government investment in real terms. We observe an increase in government invest-

---

[7] Kazushi Ohkawa and Henry Rosovsky, *Japanese Economic Growth* (Stanford: Stanford University Press, 1973).

[8] Mizoguchi, *Taiwan Chōsen no keizai seichō* (1975).

ment in Korea, but not for Taiwan. In Table 5 we have calculated the share of government capital formation. Very possibly these ratios contain an upward bias, because some government spending went for purchasing land and old equipment. We still believe that the statistical findings reliably show some major differences in the role of government in both colonies. While government share of capital formation in Taiwan was very high during the early period of Japanese rule, it declined sharply thereafter. In contrast, the government share

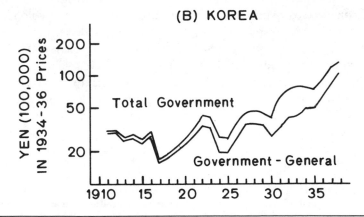

COLONIAL GOVERNMENT
CAPITAL FORMATION
IN TAIWAN AND KOREA

(A) TAIWAN

(B) KOREA

FIGURE 4
Source: Mizoguchi (1975)

of capital formation in Korea was continuously high and became more than half of total investment during the 1930's. We will show later that the Taiwan economy enjoyed an annual surplus in trade, and the private sector in Taiwan contributed considerably to capital formation. The financial conditions in Korea were the opposite, because the colonial government assumed the lion's share of financial responsibility for capital formation.[9]

What is the composition of government investment by economic use? In Table 6 we have excluded local government spending and calculated two types of government investment spending: (1) direct investment, which includes budgeted sums for specific capital investment projects; (2) direct investment and indirect investment by government, which includes total subsidies for other sectors and spending by public enterprises (estimated by taking 10 percent of their current expenditures for investment).[10]

Table 6 shows that the investment category for transportation and communications in both colonies was the largest of capital formation. This is not surprising. The Japanese placed enormous emphasis upon infrastructure for promoting production and developing the market. Investment in agriculture was also very considerable in Taiwan, and government subsidies played an important role in stimulating private investors to develop industries like sugar manufacturing. Even though government spending in agriculture for Korea grew in the 1920's, its share of government investment spending remained small over the period. It is very interesting to point out that in Korea government investment spending for the category "others," which was for general administration, proved to be very large. The Japanese had a very difficult task of maintaining law and order in this huge colony, so that general administration costs ran much higher there.

Identifying these different patterns of capital formation and origins of investment spending as we have just done also explains why economic growth in the two colonies differed. Capital formation in Taiwan proved very effective to raise agricultural productivity and give Taiwan's agricultural performance very high marks. Agricultural investment in Korea, being much smaller, obviously did not help to contribute to a very dramatic farm production performance in that colony. To be sure, the Korean colonial government had conceived

[9] Toshiyuki Mizoguchi, "Nihon tōchi-ka ni okeru Taiwan Chōsen no sōtokufu zaisei shishitsu no hikaku" [An Examination of Budgets of Government General of Korea and Taiwan], *Discussion Paper No. 9*, Hitotsubashi University (Tokyo, 1978).

[10] Samuel Pao-San Ho, "The Developing Policy of the Japanese Colonial Government in Taiwan, 1895-1945," in Gustav Ranis, ed., *Government and Economic Development* (New Haven: Yale University Press, 1971).

of a rice-development plan in the early 1920's, but soon discontinued it. If that plan had borne fruit, Korea's agricultural performance might have been very different. The delay in making investment expenditures in Korean agriculture, and the stop-and-go character of agricultural policy in that colony, undeniably was a major reason why Korea's agricultural development was inferior to that of Taiwan.

Investment spending for manufacturing and mining in Korea was very large, and the Japanese created an impressive industrial base that depended greatly upon cheap and abundant labor. Industrialization came very late in Taiwan, as reflected in the pattern of government investment spending. But a curious anomaly appears when we relate the employment structure in both colonies to the patterns of industrialization and capital formation.

In Table 7 the reader will note that the employment composition in Taiwan was tilted slightly more toward an industrial gainfully employed economy than in Korea, even though the growth of industry was more rapid and capital formation more concentrated in mining and manufacturing in Korea than in Taiwan. Further, there was a larger number of workers employed in services in Taiwan than in Korea.

In order to gain some picture of the unemployment conditions in both colonies, we have produced a dependency ratio derived by dividing the number of no-jobs by the total population. This ratio was higher in Korea and Taiwan than in Japan, as might be expected.

FINANCING CAPITAL FORMATION AND JAPAN'S CONTRIBUTION

How did Taiwan finance the expansion of capital stock more effectively than did Korea? The government-general offices in both colonies concentrated on initiating institutional and administrative reforms to promote economic growth. But in Taiwan officials selected economic activities that would rapidly stimulate economic development and produce a quick, high pay off. Their success in doing this produced huge tax revenues in the early years, which enabled officials to pursue other programs. S. P.-S. Ho shows in his essay that expenditures for Taiwan's development projects alone accounted for over 40 percent of the total expenditures of the colonial government.[11]

Private savings and investment in Taiwan also made a major con-

[11] The extensive discussion on the balance-of-payments of Taiwan and Korea is found in Yūzō Yamamoto, "Nihon tōchi-ka ni okeru Taiwan Chōsen no kokusai shūshi" [Balance of Payments of Taiwan and Korea under the Japanese Rule] in Mataji Umemura et al., eds., *Nihon keizai no hatten* [Development of Japanese Economy] (Tokyo: Nihon Keizai Shinbunsha, 1976).

tribution to capital formation, which was not the case in Korea. Taiwan landlords who benefited from the land-tax reform continued to save and to invest in commercialized agricultural enterprises such as sugar and rice processing. The Yangban landlords in Korea continued to collect their rents, but they displayed less entrepreneurial enterprise.

Turning to the relationship of colonial trade balance and financial capabilities for capital formation, we already noted in Table 2 that export growth proved to be a major factor contributing to the economic development of both colonies. Yet the balance of trade was very different in both cases. The Taiwan trade balance remained in deficit in the early years but turned into a surplus after 1910. The surplus in trade balance continued to grow and exceeded one billion yen by the mid-1930's. The Korean trade balance remained in deficit throughout the entire period, and a deficit of one billion yen eventually accumulated. This comparative performance of current account of visible trade would not differ even if we included transactions of services and specie flow. We present the accumulating surpluses or deficits of trade in Figure 5, below, which sets the stage for an examination of capital flows to the colonies.[12]

In Figure 6 we have presented long-term capital flow from Japan to Taiwan and Korea. These series include portfolio and direct-investment from Japan and net transfers from Japan to the two colonies. Between 1896 and 1904 Japan's subsidy to Taiwan helped to balance the colonial government's annual budget. If we include the transfer of the sugar consumption tax with these subsidies, the total transfer amount comes to 90 million yen for the period 1896 to 1914, which nearly equalled the total spending of the government-general of Taiwan.[13] Further, Taiwan issued 80 million yen worth of bonds to Japanese buyers. But, as time passed, public revenue from various sources rapidly grew, so that the colonial office was able to finance all of its activities from current revenue alone. Therefore, any inflow of long-term capital other than for government bonds was extra for the economy before 1930. Then in Taiwan there remained a huge amount of surplus in the basic balance, because this surplus was accumulated as short-term credit to Japan.

From the point of view of external financing, there were two channels through which short-term capital flowed from Taiwan to Japan. First, Taiwan's central bank, the Bank of Taiwan, loaned surplus

[12] These subsidies ended in 1904, but the central government continued its financial support by remitting the sugar consumption tax until 1914.

[13] Some of these loans should be considered long-term capital transactions, but Yamamoto excludes them from his estimate of long-term capital flows.

TAIWAN'S NET SURPLUS
AND KOREA'S NET DEFICIT

(A) TAIWAN'S NET SURPLUS

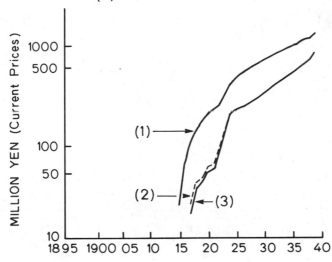

(B) KOREA'S NET DEFICIT

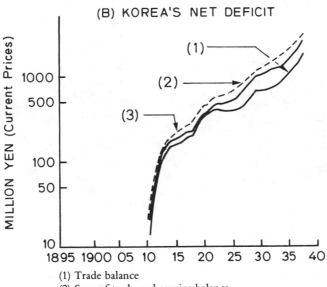

(1) Trade balance
(2) Sum of trade and service balance
(3) Sum of trade, service, and specie balance

FIGURE 5
Source: Yamamoto (1976)

THE NET INFLOW
OF LONG-TERM CAPITAL
INTO TAIWAN AND KOREA

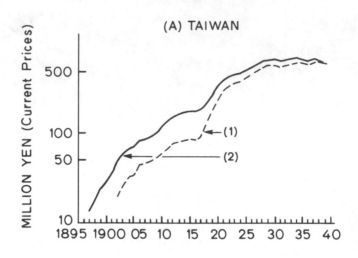

(A) TAIWAN

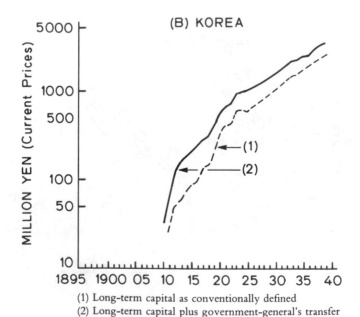

(B) KOREA

(1) Long-term capital as conventionally defined
(2) Long-term capital plus government-general's transfer

FIGURE 6
Source: Yamamoto (1976)

FIGURE 6
Source: Yamamoto (1976)

funds to firms in Japan such as Suzuki Shōten. Second, the Taiwan government-general sent its reserve funds to Japan. Taiwan became a net creditor to Japan, although she had earlier borrowed some long-term capital. This means that the Taiwanese economy already had achieved a high rate of savings because of its favorable balance-of-payments, and an investment fund could be financed easily from its domestic market.

In sharp contrast to Taiwan, Korea's deficit on current account was huge. This deficit had to be covered by either long-term or short-term capital from Japan. Yamamoto has estimated that long-term capital and subsidy from Japan offset this deficit. For this reason short-term capital inflows to Korea were nil. In Table 8 we observe that the subsidy funds and revenues from bond sales were large enough to finance all colonial government spending for capital formation if we exclude the years 1935-1938. This suggests that Korean capital formation was financed mainly by government spending, which came from Japan. The Korean colonial government's great reliance upon capital inflows and subsidies from Japan to finance capital formation clearly shows the inability of the Japanese to mobilize savings from the Korean private sector. Colonial government investment in agriculture during the 1920's also failed to induce Koreans to increase their investment sufficiently to generate a large flow of tax revenue.

In the private sector Korea received four times the amount of long-term capital from Japan than Taiwan did. Japanese capital investment proved crucial for the rapid spurt of industrialization which took place in the 1930's in Korea. This investment consisted of corporate investment through loans, stocks and bond issues, and subsidiaries under the tight control of Japanese capital. The participation of Japanese business enterprise in Korean industrialization can also be observed from the angle of factory ownership. In Table 9 we present data showing the share of Japanese factory ownership for both colonies. The Japanese share of ownership of factories in Taiwan was rather low except for machine-tool production, although the very large factories were indeed owned by Japanese. For Korea, the share of Japanese ownership was much higher except for factories producing ceramics, paper, metals, and food processing—activities which belong to the traditional sector.

CONCLUSION

Reviewing our findings briefly, we find that our comparative study of capital formation in Taiwan and Korea under Japanese rule shows that Taiwan's economy grew rapidly and steadily over the period, based upon the healthy improvement of agriculture. Taiwan exported agricultural products and produced a huge trade surplus on its current account in balance-of-payments. The Korean economy grew more slowly because agriculture never was modernized very extensively. Only in the 1930's did an industrialization spurt take place, not based upon agricultural development, but induced and sustained by a very large capital investment from Japan. Spending for capital formation, then, proved to be agriculture-oriented in Taiwan from the very outset, but capital spending for agriculture in Korea was never achieved on a large enough scale to transform and to modernize agriculture. For that reason, Japanese capital investment was necessary to promote industrialization in Korea in the 1930's.

Yet, in both colonies, the colonial governments played the leading role in making investment spending and relating that to economic development. Colonial officials planned for and spent from their budgets for infrastructure development: railroads, harbors, warehouses, and communications. These structures and buildings, along with their necessary equipment and machinery, proved to be indispensable for producing the economic growth which both colonies experienced.

TABLE 1
Growth Rate of Real GNE, GDP and GDE Indicator (percent)

Estimator	GNE Japan Ohkawa	GDE Indicator Korea Mizoguchi	GDE Indicator Taiwan Mizoguchi	GDP Taiwan Lee
1903–1938	3.24		3.21	
1911–1938	3.36	3.57	3.80	
1903–1912	2.27		2.73	
1908–1917	3.09		3.16	
1913–1922	5.21	8.74	6.67	2.03
1918–1927	1.50	2.73	5.09	5.91
1923–1932	2.35	0.70	3.55	5.93
1928–1937	4.70	2.98	1.21	4.07

Source: Ohkawa et al. (1965–), Mizoguchi (1975), and Ho (1978).

TABLE 2
Growth Rate of GDE Components and Their Shares in GDE Indicator
(Growth rate: 1911-38, Shares: 1935)

	Growth Rates Japan	Growth Rates Taiwan	Growth Rates Korea	Shares Japan	Shares Taiwan	Shares Korea
Private consumption	2.8	3.2	3.1	64.5	64.1	85.7
Government consumption	5.1	4.1	6.5	15.7	5.6	7.3
Capital formation Construction	3.1	6.7	5.8⎫	19.1	9.3	6.4
Producer's durables	2.8	6.4	9.0⎭		2.1	2.8
Export	6.7	6.5	10.6	25.3	40.5	22.5
Import	5.8	4.9	8.4	−24.2	−22.0	−24.7
GDE Indicator	3.3	3.8	3.6	100.0	100.0	100.0

Source: Mizoguchi (1975) and Ohkawa et al. (1965–).

TABLE 3
Growth Rate of Production Indices (percent)

		Agricultural or Primary Industry			
Estimator	Japan Ohkawa	Taiwan Ishikawa	Taiwan Lee	Korea Ishikawa	Korea Suh
1903–12	0.9	1.5			
1908–17	2.7	2.0			
1913–22	0.4	1.8	0.3	2.4	1.6
1918–27	−0.0	4.4	6.0	−0.9	0.7
1923–32	1.2	4.2	5.0	1.4	2.9
1928–37	0.7	3.5	3.4	3.7	1.6
1911–38	0.6	3.4		1.9	

		Manufacturing or Secondary Industry			
Estimator	Japan Ohkawa	Taiwan Shinohara	Taiwan Lee	Korea Mizoguchi	Korea Suh
1913–22	5.4	4.2	2.3	6.1	10.6
1918–27	3.1	6.9	2.8	6.2	9.1
1923–32	7.1	7.0	5.3	4.4	6.5
1928–37	2.8	4.6	6.6	12.2	10.9
1914–38	5.6	5.3		6.7	

Source: Ohkawa et al. (1965-), Mizoguchi (1975), Shinohara-Ishikawa (1975), Ho (1978), and Suh (1978).

TABLE 4
Capital Formation in Japan Empire
(1934–36 Prices)

	Construction			Equipment		
	Japan	Taiwan	Korea	Japan	Taiwan	Korea
Growth Rate (%)						
1903–12	6.9	14.5		11.0	23.2	
1908–17	3.6	2.8		9.6	−17.2	
1913–22	6.1	11.3	2.3	12.0	15.2	14.4
1918–27	4.9	4.9	3.4	−13.9	5.3	1.8
1923–32	1.2	7.5	11.3	−0.4	9.0	6.0
1928–37	3.5	7.4	7.6	12.1	6.3	11.6
1911–38	3.1	6.6	5.7	2.8	6.4	8.9
Total amounts of investments (milion yen)						
1911–38	18,515	1,451	1,567	18,370	323	699
Per capita investments (Yen/Year)						
1911–38	11.01	12.08	3.00	10.89	2.30	1.34

Source: Mizoguchi (1975).

TABLE 5
Share of Government Capital Formation in Total Capital
Formation (percent)

	1903-12	1913-22	1923-33	1933-38
Taiwan	74.1	37.0	27.9	30.0
Korea		60.3	57.1	59.1

Source: Mizoguchi (1975).

TABLE 6

Composition of Capital Formation of Government General by Economic Use
(percent)

	Transportation and Communication	Road and Harbors	Non-agricultural Industries	Agricultural Industry and River control	Other Activities
	Direct Investments				
	Taiwan				
1901–05	66.05	11.86	1.54	6.04	14.51
1906–10	32.49	22.84	2.81	20.54	21.33
1911–15	15.20	20.09	0.90	36.86	26.95
1916–20	32.22	18.67	1.14	28.14	19.82
1921–25	41.33	25.26	0.32	19.29	13.81
1926–30	24.06	27.01	1.09	30.40	17.44
1931–35	22.19	30.69	0.61	34.52	12.00
1936–38	32.96	29.30	4.00	20.99	12.75
	Korea				
1906–10	4.04	14.35	6.01	1.00	74.08
1911–15	56.69	21.76	0.74	4.35	16.46
1916–20	53.48	14.89	3.51	3.67	24.47
1921–25	48.94	12.34	1.09	13.76	23.87
1926–30	48.23	10.95	0.78	21.41	18.62
1931–35	53.50	10.97	0.34	24.72	10.69
1936–38	66.99	9.89	2.27	12.81	8.04
	Direct and Indirect Investments				
	Taiwan				
1901–05	50.43	6.82	1.37	4.42	36.96
1906–10	35.75	17.22	3.53	9.48	34.01
1911–15	22.46	14.21	2.82	19.82	40.63
1916–20	35.61	14.25	4.87	18.07	27.20
1921–25	38.04	15.99	2.57	15.90	27.50
1926–30	28.15	19.08	2.49	22.52	27.74
1931–35	28.29	19.75	2.77	22.37	26.82
1936–38	31.42	18.70	6.56	15.57	27.75
	Korea				
1906–10	1.44	5.10	5.03	0.58	87.85
1911–15	42.45	14.52	3.40	4.48	35.15
1916–20	37.64	9.03	5.43	7.79	40.11
1921–25	33.81	6.32	2.93	13.47	43.47
1926–30	33.89	4.68	4.24	15.50	41.73
1931–35	31.82	4.01	3.29	14.81	46.06
1936–38	41.88	5.04	3.68	11.74	37.66

Source: Mizoguchi (1978).

TABLE 7
Dependency Rates and Employment Structure in
Japan Proper, Korea and Taiwan (percent)

		Dependency Rate	Employment Structure		
			Agriculture	Manufacturing	Other
Korea	1930	53.6	79.7	6.4	14.2
	1940	62.1	77.4	7.2	15.4
	1944	59.5	71.1	23.2	5.7
Taiwan	1930	61.0	66.9	9.7	23.4
	1940	61.8	63.9	11.8	24.3
Japan	1930	54.1	48.5	20.4	31.3
	1940	53.3	43.3	26.3	30.4

Source: Figures for 1930 and 1940 are taken from the Population Census and data for 1944 comes from the Special Labor Survey for Korea.

(1) Trade balance.
(2) Sum of trade and service balance.
(3) Sum of trade, service, and specie balance.

(1) Long-term capital as conventionally defined.
(2) Government-general. Long-term capital plus governor-general's transfer.
Source: Yamamoto (1976).

TABLE 8
Sources of Capital Formation: (Million Yen in Current Prices)

	1901-05	1906-10	1911-15	1916-20	1921-25	1926-30	1931-35	1936-38*
Taiwan								
Total Gov. Investments	28.8	45.7	67.8	84.8	110.7	121.7	143.2	234.6
Transfer Receipts of Gov. General***	13.3	23.9	29.0	0.0	0.0	0.0	−17.1	−64.8
Issues of Bonds by Gov. General	31.9	0.4	−6.8	15.6	47.7	23.2	14.1	− 5.8
Korea								
Total Gov. Investments			81.7	117.5	214.1	240.5	339.3	718.5
Transfer Receipts of Gov. General***			92.6	89.1	169.8	178.0	157.0	208.5
Issues of Bonds by Gov. General			52.5	78.3	106.7	86.2	123.6	272.3
Taiwan								
Total Capital Formation	25.3	70.8	112.5	340.5	353.8	972.0	383.2	733.0
Long–Term Capital Imports**	40.1	50.4	54.6	173.0	186.3	153.3	14.0	−18.1
Korea								
Total Capital Formation			101.8	237.0	314.2	494.0	589.3	1126.5
Long–Term Capital Imports**			108.2	340.6	434.8	581.5	891.5	1289.3

Note * multiplied by 5/3. ** including the net transfer receipts from the central governments.
*** the net transfer receipts from the central governments.
Source: Mizoguchi (1975) and Yamamoto (1972), (1975) and (1976).

TABLE 9

Distribution of Number of Factories by Industry, Size of Factory, and Factory Owners

(Percentages of factories owned by Japanese)

	Taiwan		Korea	
	1929	*1939*	*1934*	*1939*
Textile	25.0	19.6	62.8	41.5
Metal	26.5	14.1	39.3	38.2
Machinery	45.9	39.7	76.9	64.6
Ceramics	12.2	4.2	35.7	36.2
Papers and Chemical	8.4	18.2	23.0	23.7
Wood	21.0	23.1	78.5	67.1
Printing	—	33.3	68.3	27.8
Rice Mill	5.8	7.0	11.0	54.0
Food	26.5	18.1	52.2	56.7
Others	28.1	20.5	77.4	69.0
5- 49 Employees	14.4	15.1	39.1	39.1
50- 99 Employees	42.4	46.0	69.4	57.6
100-199 Employees	83.0	61.8	66.7	77.2
200- Employees	85.2	96.5	87.2	92.0
Total	18.2	18.4	41.1	41.6

Note: Chemical includes fishery fertilizer.

Source: Government General of Korea and Taiwan, *Name List of Factories*.

CHAPTER 11

Agricultural Development in the Empire

Ramon H. Myers and Yamada Saburō

By the late nineteenth century the villages of Japan, Korea, and Taiwan represented the prototype agrarian system of East Asia. To be
sure, distinctive variations of land use and farming organizations existed throughout these countries, yet agriculture remained the backbone of the economy and generated most of the taxes for the public
sector or state.

This agrarian system had achieved a remarkably high level of productivity, considering that these societies had not yet developed a
modern farming technology. Further, all three had achieved considerable regional economic integration, but they differed greatly in this
respect, and foreign trade, at least before the 1870's, remained min-
uscule. As yet the state only lightly extruded into the market town-
village world, so that rural communities possessed an autonomy that
they would begin to lose only in the early twentieth century.

This system was dramatically transformed by what we will refer
to as the Meiji state agrarian strategy. In brief, this strategy called for
transferring as few resources to agriculture as possible—simply because the state had little to transfer—and extracting as much tax revenue and marketed surplus from agriculture as conditions permitted.
The state achieved this resource outflow from agriculture by redis-
tributing property rights so that property owners were induced to
increase output, sell more for the market, and pay an annual land
tax. By conferring new property rights to the agriculturalists, the
state also created the new machinery by which to extract more tax
revenues from cultivators. Consequently, the state extracted more
and more revenue, while production increased and the marketable
surplus rose. In turn, the state began spending more to create new
organizations by which to transfer a modern agricultural technology
to farmers and their tenants. In this fashion the state initiated a modern agricultural revolution, first in Meiji Japan between 1873 and
1900 and later in its two major colonies of Taiwan (1895-1910) and
Korea (1910-1930).

While this strategy worked successfully in all three countries, the pattern of agricultural development it produced in each country differed. Part of the reason for this difference had to do with the timing and manner in which this strategy was actually implemented. Yet other considerations influenced those different development patterns, and these related to the complex socio-economic organizations, institutions, and customs of market town-village society and to the quality of human and physical resources found in each country.

In spite of such complexity and variation in all three countries, the Meiji state agrarian strategy produced an agricultural revolution in all three which contributed greatly to the successes of Japan's formal colonial empire. At the same time, the different pattern of industrial and agricultural development in all three produced serious problems of low rural income, income inequality, and a high proportion of rural households without property and wealth. We will describe and analyze these developments by first reviewing the traditional agrarian system of East Asia on the eve of reform, discuss the Meiji state agrarian policy in action, examine the patterns of agricultural development that flowed from that policy, and finally evaluate those different development patterns within the context of Japan's colonial empire development.

THE EAST ASIAN AGRARIAN SYSTEM

The East Asian agrarian system depended upon rice, although by the twentieth century more and more rural people substituted inferior grains for their rice consumption and marketed rice because of its higher price. In late-nineteenth-century Japan rice made up about 64 percent of the total farm crop value, and farms allocated 60 percent of their land to its production. In Korea rice accounted for about 55 percent of farm output value, and farmers allocated around 55 percent of their land to its production. In Taiwan, rice made up around 50 percent of farm output value, with around 70 percent of the land use for its production.

In Japan, even though farmers rarely planted two crops of rice during the year, in southern Japan farmers planted a second crop, barley or wheat, during the fall-winter months. For this reason around one-third of the land was cropped more than once during the year. But in Korea only 14 percent of the cultivated land was farmed more than once during the year, whereas in Taiwan nearly one-half of the land was double-cropped. A warm climate, adequate rainfall, more irrigation, and a longer growing season favored Taiwan but not Japan and Korea.

Yet all three rice-farming areas had similar characteristics. First, farmers used many different seeds selected from each year's harvest, so that many strains of the Indica variety were grown in the same district. Crop diseases failed to destroy a rice crop because so many kinds of disease-resistant seeds existed. Second, farmers had learned over the centuries how to rotate their crops on the same unit of land so as to restore nitrogen to the soil, and to this end they applied large quantities of man-made fertilizer or compost to the fields.[1] Therefore, rice yields were very high in East Asia on the eve of modernization.

In Table 1 we note that Japanese farmers produced 2 m.t./ha., while Korean and Taiwan farmers produced 1.4 m.t./ha. Although the average yield was high, yield variation within and between districts was enormous because of differences in soil fertility and farming practices. But Japan's average yield was 43 percent higher than that of Korea and Taiwan yields. Until we learn more about the pattern of yield differences in all three countries, we can only say that there was a great potential for raising crop yields in Korea and Taiwan if the proper agricultural policy could be introduced and carried out.[2]

Aside from rice, farmers planted many coarse grains throughout Japan and Korea, especially in the north. Taiwan's sub-tropical climate permitted farmers to cultivate special crops like sugarcane and various fruits and vegetables. Legume crops also played an important role in the crop rotations of this agrarian system.

To make this land productive required the labor of around three-quarters to 80 percent of the workforce (Table 1). As a result of so many people participating in farming, agriculture contributed to between one-third to nearly one-half of the national income produced in these countries. While urbanization had advanced furthest in Japan,

[1] For comments on fertilizing of soil practices in Japan and Korea see F. H. King, *Farmers of Forth Centuries* (Emmaus, Pennsylvania: Rodale Press, Inc., 1911), pp. 368-370 for Korea and pp. 378-380 for Japan.

[2] This issue is analyzed by James I. Nakamura, "Incentives, Productivity Gaps, and Agricultural Growth Rates in Prewar Japan, Taiwan, and Korea" in Bernard S. Silberman and H. D. Harootunian, eds., *Japan in Crisis: Essays on Taishō Democracy* (Princeton, N.J.: Princeton University Press, 1974), pp. 329-373. Nakamura contends that in the Tokugawa period the Japanese applied more labor and fertilizers to their land, irrigated more land, and invested more in human capital through education and population control. He further argues that Japanese institutions did not stifle incentives to work and innovation as they did in Taiwan and Korea. This provocative argument certainly will not be the last word on the subject, and the issues are so complex as to deserve a book-length study. Our intention instead is to show general uniform patterns in the East Asian rural order and focus upon those policies that transform that order in the late nineteenth century and early twentieth century.

the majority of people still lived in villages ranging in size from as few households as 50 to as many as 500 or more. These villages clustered around market towns of varying size, where rural laborers congregated to find employment and farmers sold their crops and purchased luxuries and necessities.

In Japan, villages had become increasingly crowded, and the land-labor ratio was only half that of the villages in Taiwan and Korea (Table 1). Hokkaido had not yet been settled, and land was becoming scarce on the three main islands. The typical farm producing tea or silk in the 1870's was only around a half acre in size.[3] By the early 1890's around 40 percent of the land was farmed by tenants.[4] Even in Korea many households did not own their land. In 1912 rural data reveal that around 41 percent of all rural households were tenant households, renting and farming plots as small as a tenth of a hectare to as large as 3 ha.[5] Another 32 percent of rural families owned and rented part of the land that they farmed, and only 23 percent owned all of the land that they farmed (3 percent were landlords). In Taiwan tenancy was lower in the south than in the north, and around 40 percent of the rural households were tenants.[6] In all three countries population had increased during the seventeenth and eighteenth centuries, villages had become larger, and all of the fertile land was under cultivation. By the end of the nineteenth century the process of more families becoming bonafide family farms by first renting and then buying land had slowed, and more households had to seek non-farming activities to earn a living.

In all three societies there also were landlords who probably made up around 10 percent or less of the households in any village. Many of these landlords belonged to a privileged class because they paid no taxes, did not perform corvée labor for the state, wore special dress, and held high social status. They also managed the market towns and large administrative villages. Whether they were the privileged daimyo or samurai in Japan, the *yangban* in Korea, or the *shen-shih* in Taiwan, they received rent from the land they leased to villagers and performed no farm work. Not all landlords remained powerful and

[3] Nōgyō hattatsushi chōsakai (comp.), *Nihon nōgyō hattatsushi* [A History of the Development of Agriculture] (Tokyo: Chūō kōronsha, 1954), vol. 3, p. 227. Henceforth *NNH* with volume number.

[4] Kondō Tetsuo, *Chiso kaisei no kenkyū* [Studies of the Land Tax Reform] (Tokyo: Miraisha, 1967), p. 155.

[5] Chōsen Sōtokufu, *Chōsen no kosaku kanshū* [The Customs of Tenancy in Korea] (Keijō: Kōsei gakkai insatsujo, 1929), p. 28.

[6] Ramon H. Myers, "Taiwan's Agrarian Economy Under Japanese Rule," *Journal of the Institute of the Chinese University of Hong Kong* 7:2 (1974), p. 470.

TABLE 1

Agriculture Conditions in the Empire on the Eve of Agrarian Reform[a]

Agrarian characteristics	Japan (1880)	Taiwan (1915)	Korea (1920)
(1) Rural labor force (%)	75.0[b]	71.0	84.3
(2) Share of national income (%)	34.6	39.6	—
(3) Net value of farm products[c] (%)	64.2	55.0[c]	86.2
(4) Cultivated land area (1,000 ha.)	4,735	704	4,337
(5) Number of agricultural workers (1,000)	15,588	1,155	7,243
(6) Cultivated land area per worker (ha.)	0.30	0.61	0.60
(7) Agricultural output[c] (mil. yen)	1,332	165	834
(8) Production of brown rice (1,000 m.t.)	5,293	718[e]	2,054[d]
(9) Agricultural output per hectare (yen)	281	234	192
(10) Rice yield (m.t./ha. of planted rice)	2.00	1.47	1.43
(11) Agricultural output per worker (yen)	86	143	115

Sources: Data for Japan proper from Saburō Yamada and Yūjirō Hayami, "Agricultural Growth in Japan, 1880-1970" in Agricultural Growth in Japan, Taiwan, Korea and the Philippines, eds. Yūjirō Hayami, Vernon W. Ruttan, and Herman Southworth, Honolulu: University of Hawaii Press, 1979, except for the items (1), (2), and (3); (1) from Yūjirō Hayami in association with Masakatsu Akino, Masahiko Shintani and Saburō Yamada, A Century of Agricultural Growth in Japan, Tokyo: University of Tokyo Press, 1975, p. 6; and (2) and (3) from Kazushi Ohkawa, Miyohei Shinohara, and Mataji Umemura, eds., Chōki keizai tōkei (Estimates of Longterm Economic Statistics of Japan since 1868), Vol. 1, Tokyo: Tōyō keizai shinpōsha, 1974, pp. 202 and 204. Data for Taiwan from Teng-hui Lee and Yueh-eh Chen, "Agricultural Growth in Taiwan, 1911-1972," in Agricultural Growth in Japan, Taiwan, Korea and the Philippines, except for the items (1), (2), (3), (8) and (10); (1) and (2) from Samuel P.-S. Ho, Economic Development of Taiwan, 1860-1970, New Haven: Yale University Press, 1978, p. 82 and p. 284; (3) George W. Barclay, Colonial Development and Population in Taiwan, Princeton: Princeton University Press, 1954, p. 38; (8) and (10) from Tables 5 and 16 in this study. Data for Korea from Sung Hwan Ban, "Appendix to Growth Rates of Korean Agriculture, 1918-1968" paper presented to the Conference on Agricultural Growth in Japan, Korea, Taiwan and the Philippines held in Honolulu in February 1973, except for the items (1), (3), (5), (8) and (10); (1) and (5) from the Government-General of Korea, Chōsen sōtokufu tōkei nempō (Statistical Yearbook of the Government-General of Korea), 1925, pp. 52 and 54; (3) from Chul Won Kang, "An Analysis of Japanese Policy and Economic Change in Korea," in Korea under Japanese Colonial Rule, Andrew C. Nahm, ed., Michigan: Western Michigan: Western Michigan University, 1973, p. 87; and (8) and (10) from Tables 5 and 16, respectively.

[a] Data are five-year averages for years when the earliest reliable statistical data became available.

[b] Includes forestry and fishery.

[c] Share of farm products of total net value production, which includes primary, mining, and manufacturing products.

[d] Real output at 1934-36 prices.

[e] 1915-19 average.

influential from one generation to another. Many samurai households declined in wealth and status, and the same was true for the Korean *yangban* and Chinese *shen-shih* households.

While taking note of this small, powerful, privileged class living amid the bonafide family farms, tenant families, and day-laboring households, we must also consider how family farms behaved in the context of two types of markets: product and factor markets.

Households sold their goods and services, whether exchanging their products for cash or other goods, in market towns or within large villages. The proportion of field crops harvested and then marketed each year seems to have ranged between a third to as much as half of the crop. As villages developed around small or large towns, their households marketed farm products according to the marketing schedule of the lunar calendar. While the largest share marketed usually occurred at the harvest, farmers and landlords still stored much of their food grains and special crops over the year and marketed only when prices were high. Many tenants, however, sold most of their crops after the harvest, when prices were depressed, because they urgently needed cash to repay debts and to buy commodities during the winter months. In spring and summer they again incurred debts (grain prices were then at their zenith), to buy seed and food to cover the planting and growing season until harvest time. These rural markets seem to have been very competitive, because buyers or sellers did not corner the market and fix price. Farm prices also fluctuated enormously from year to year, partly because weather influenced the harvest, but sometimes because new trade outlets had been opened by merchants and demand had suddenly increased. Farmers responded to rising or falling price trends by substituting more profitable crops for those producing less profit while trying to make themselves self-sufficient by planting food crops. Individual household response to price change varied, depending upon the amount of land and labor available to each family.

Families passed through their life cycles by first enlarging and then subdividing after the transfer of property to a married son or to all sons. These life-cycle patterns varied in the three societies because of different marriage and inheritance customs. These variations need not concern us, but we must note the imbalance of household land to labor that inevitably occurred during the household life cycle. Households that had just inherited land and had began their life cycle usually had neither enough land nor enough labor to farm. Therefore they bid for these resources from other households, either renting land or hiring labor services. Such exchanges were informal and conformed to the customary law of the area. Households sometimes drew up written contracts of tenancy or of hiring labor on a long-term basis, but households usually concluded these agreements by word of mouth because they were of the same lineage or neighbors. As families passed through their life cycles, some formed lineages and became wealthy; others declined and disappeared from view. Everywhere, families bid for land, labor, and capital (cash or equipment) and paid for their services with cash or kind as rent, wages, or interest. These household contractual relationships made it possible for families to balance their resource mix and produce for the market.

Amid the exchanges in product and factor markets, family farms decided which techniques to use in production. The supply of household capital stock consisted of man-made fertilizers, wells and other irrigation networks, seeds, tools, carts, labor-animals, and structure. The supply of this capital expanded with the labor force, so that the labor-capital ratio remained relatively constant, and the quality of this capital improved only very slowly over long periods. Farmers either selected their seeds from the harvest or purchased them in markets. They used trial-and-error methods to perfect irrigation, produce fertilizers, and control voracious insects and plant diseases. Sometimes they applied a new farming technology learned from another area. While the transfer of new technology did occur, often promoted by local officials, it was usually limited only to areas of thriving commerce and agriculture. Meanwhile, farming remained extremely labor-intensive, and households made every effort to conserve scarce resources, such as land, and relied upon cheaper labor to grow their crops and harvest them.

The public sector, manned by samurai officials in feudal Japan and Confucian bureaucrats in Korea and Taiwan, controlled the private sector of villages and towns. The state collected taxes, regulated farming through sumptuary laws governing consumption and daily behavior, and managed commerce. In Tokugawa Japan, the daimyo-samurai class tightly controlled the villages and taxed them heavily, perhaps extracting as much as one-fifth of their output. They mobilized village labor for local projects and for the building of castle towns. In Korea and Taiwan state officials collected taxes, dispensed the law, and managed schools, temples, and charity organizations. Korean and Taiwan villages did not pay such high taxes as in Tokugawa Japan, and they had more independence to manage their own affairs. In all three countries the state provided famine relief when harvests failed and tried to maintain the stability of the rural order.

In the cellular, semi-isolated villages of East Asia, handicraft, farming, and commerce were integrally joined in the tens of thousands of village-market town networks through contractual relations and labor-intensive methods of production and transportation. Although general similarities persisted for all three societies, they differed from each other. Japan already had reached a very high level of population density and rural overcrowding. As much as one-third of its land was cropped more than once a year, and farmers produced very high yields through labor intensive methods. Land productivity was high, but labor productivity very low. Taiwan, favored with fertile land, was still a frontier area, and its land and labor were more productive then in Korea. Korea ranked lowest of the three in agricultural productivity, but had considerable idle land which could be cultivated and improved. In all three countries yield variation was enormous, and the best and most current farming practices remained confined to only a few advanced areas, rather than being smoothly transferred to backward areas.

THE MEIJI STATE AGRARIAN POLICY

The new Meiji leaders were determined to modernize Japan's military and economy, and to that end they made the consolidation of their power and introduction of reforms to increase production and collect taxes the order of the day. In 1871, the state had abolished the system of feudal *han* and eliminated the property rights of the old daimyo. In July, the state began issuing new land deeds, and by 1872 landowners could freely buy and sell land or transfer it to other parties.[7]

In that same year, the state legalized the hiring of labor for farmers. These reforms redistributed property and income and liberated family farmers from the myriad of feudal restrictions that had made the management of their land difficult and costly. While making it easier and more profitable for farmers to manage their land, the state searched for the means to tax it more efficiently and fairly. Recognizing the importance of the harvest tax, the Meiji bureaucrat Matsukata Masayoshi in 1871 proposed a plan to build upon the old tax system.[8]

> If we consider the 1762 land survey as based on the old land measure of the *tan*, and then we add to that estimated amount the land for which taxes were not paid, the new cultivated land since that time, and other land not included in that survey, we can refer to this new estimate as the land currently being utilized. If we then

[7] *NNH*, vol. 3, p. 220.

[8] Tokutomi Iichirō, *Kōshaku Matsukata Masayoshi Den* [The Biography of Count Matsukata Masayoshi] (Tokyo: Kōshaku Matsukata Masayoshi denki hakkō-jo, 1935), pp. 560-561.

calculate the market value of rice from that land, we can determine that land's value. From that land value we can decide where to lower and raise the new land tax.

What Matsukata proposed was a new land survey which would identify and measure all land and then determine land values upon which a new, standardized land tax would be imposed. The state adopted this idea, and in early 1872 officials launched a pilot project to measure and value land in the Tokyo area and to confer property deeds to all owners of land. This scheme provided the basis for initiating a national land survey in 1873, which was not completed until 1881, however, because of delays brought about by rural insurrection and by unrest, culminating in the great Satsuma samurai uprising of 1877. By completing this land survey, however, the state was able to tax more land and to ensure itself of a stable, annual land tax revenue. The survey revealed the farming area to be 4,841,571 ha. instead of only 3,256,653 ha., as indicated by the Tokugawa Land Tax records.[9]

This same phase of Meiji agrarian policy was carried out in Taiwan in 1898 and completed around 1903; it was launched in Korea in 1910 and completed around 1918. In both colonies the Japanese surveyed all land, classified its use, identified ownership, valued the land by capitalizing future estimated net income with the current rate of investment return, and then assessed a new land tax. In Taiwan, the taxable area increased from roughly 361,000 ha. to 777,000 ha., and the land tax revenue from 920,000 yen to 2.9 million yen.[10] Between 1910 and 1918 the cultivated area in Korea increased from 2.4 million ha. to nearly 4.5 million ha., and some of that increase was due to the land survey, which found concealed land.[11] The land tax came to 6.6 million yen in 1910 but steadily rose to 9.8 million yen by 1918.[12]

This reform in Taiwan cost the Japanese government around 3 million yen, and in Korea it cost more than six times that figure, around 20 million yen. The Japanese state benefited enormously from this reform. First, it now had accurate records of all land and could tabulate all future transactions any households made regarding their land. Second, as had been the result in Japan, the state could depend

[9] *Kondō Tetsuo*, p. 110 for a comparison of old and new land to be taxed and on p. 113 we have referred to the land area as ha. instead of chō because 1 chō = .992 ha.

[10] Ramon H. Myers, "Taiwan's Agrarian Economy Under Japanese Rule," in *Journal of Chinese Studies of the Chinese University of Hong Kong* 7:2 (1974), p. 456.

[11] Kobayakawa Kurō (comp.), *Chōsen nōgyō hattatsushi* [The History of Korean Agricultural Development] (Tokyo: Yūhō kyōkai, 1955), vol. 1, p. 91.

[12] Chōsen Sōtokufu, *Chōsen Sōtokufu tōkeisho, 1918* [Annual Statistical Abstract for Korea, 1918], p. 954. For 1910 see same series, p. 221.

upon a stable source of land tax each year. Even when the harvest was poor, landowners still had to pay their land tax. Because of this dependable source of revenue, the state could now plan its expenditures for economic development. In both colonies the landholders also received titles to their land, which were also recorded and matched with the new land cadastral maps produced by the recent land survey and housed in new land-tax offices. Landowners also could buy and sell land freely and transfer land to other parties, as long as they recorded these transactions and paid the annual land tax.

More important, this land tax reform represented an important redistribution of property rights and income in all three societies. In Japan, other reforms accompanied the land tax, in which the old daimyo lords and samurai households gave up their former privileged rights for long-term bonds as compensation. The farmers who had farmed their land as tenants became the new title holders. In Taiwan, the land survey uncovered nearly 40,000 ta-tsu households who once had developed large tracts of land and then leased them to tenants on a life-time basis, collected rents, and paid the land tax to the state. The Japanese gave those ta-tsu households long-term bonds in exchange for their tenants, who numbered around a quarter of a million households. In Korea, the survey identified all of the land which belonged to the Yi royal family, Yi government officials, schools, and temples.[13] That land reverted to the Japanese government, which then sold much of it to Japanese land development companies.

The standard view of how the land-tax reform influenced the distribution of property rights is as follows. First, the land survey made it possible for Japanese companies like the Oriental Development Company to appropriate very large tracts of land. Second, many Korean property owners lost their claims to land, went into debt, and "were forced to seek a new tenantship with landlords—a majority of which were Japanese nationals."[14] This interpretation has gained wide acceptance, but it has recently been criticized as erroneous and misleading. Several American scholars who have researched the land and household registration records for a number of Korean rural communities compiled and kept by the Japanese colonial administra-

[13] For the various types of non-taxed, state owned land of which a large part in fact was privately owned by Korea's privileged upper classes see Wada Ichirō, *Chōsen tochi chiso seido chōsa hōkokusho* [An Investigation Report of the Land Tax System in Korea] (Tokyo: Sōkō shobō, 1967), p. 118. This work was first published in 1920 and reprinted in 1967, and it provides a useful sketch of the pre-1910 land-tax systems and the land-tax reform carried out by the Japanese.

[14] Young-Iob Chung, "Japanese Investment in Korea 1904-1905," in Andrew C. Nahm (editor), *Korea Under Japanese Colonial Rule* (Kalamazoo, Michigan: Western Michigan University, 1973), p. 101.

tion found that very few Korean households lost their land as a result of this survey.[15] Much more research needs to be done to measure the possible redistributive costs and benefits as related to farmers' incentives.

The former *yangban* households did receive formal title to their land, but in exchange they now had to develop that land to pay the new land tax. The land-tax reform, then, at least forced those land-owners to make their land produce wealth, and in case they could not, to sell it to other parties who would. It also redistributed income from those who formerly received privileged rents to a new class of landowners who instead paid the land tax, but often at a rate below their former rental rate. The reform also forced more households to rely on the market more than in the past, because the land tax had to be paid in cash, and therefore landowners and their tenants had to convert part of their harvest to cash. Therefore, the reform encouraged much more commercialization, monetized economic transactions, and directed resources toward activities producing higher income returns. While providing the state with a large, dependable annual tax revenue, this reform also increased resource productivity, production, and the marketed surplus. How?

We now describe how land and labor productivity increased within that agrarian structure of small family farms managing their fragmented parcels scarcely larger than a half acre. Let us consider the farming activities of households involved in two different processes that influenced production and income.

In the first instance, farming technology did not change. Instead, transportation improved and a widening of the market took place. Villagers began to note that they could market a larger quantity of their crop while still buying other goods at the same price or even cheaper. Farmers responded by allocating more land and labor to produce the more profitable crops for the market. This increased crop specialization was associated in the short run with increased returns to scale. In other words, when farmers allocated more resources to the same crop on the farm, the scale of production for that crop activity was enlarged. Land and labor in that crop activity became more productive, and output per unit of resource input also rose. Even if the terms of trade in the market place remained unchanged, farmers gained more proceeds because specialization increased output and a higher proportion of that output was marketed.

We believe that this process of increased specialization and ex-

[15] See papers by Edward J. Baker and Edwin H. Gragert presented at a Conference on the Colonial Period in Korea, January 2-4, 1981, sponsored by the Social Science Research Council of the United States.

change with increased returns to scale began taking place throughout Japanese agriculture during the inflationary 1870's when transportation improved, barriers blocking exchange collapsed, and the export trade expanded. "Both landlords and farmers gained alike from these favorable conditions in the market place."[16] As a result, the pattern of land use began to change, with some areas specializing in rice and others in silk or tea; meanwhile, markets efficiently distributed the imports of cotton, indigo, and grain to farmers and to city people alike. Villages also began specializing in fruit and vegetables. A study of three villages outside Tokyo, located on ordinary rain-fed land, revealed that their land for rice production had steadily declined during the late nineteenth and twentieth centuries, and vegetable cultivation had replaced rice.[17] While part of the reason for this land-use change came about because new rice seeds and fertilizers enabled those farmers to produce higher rice yields and thus the same rice output on less land, improved transportation and new market demand had also encouraged greater specialization in vegetable farming. The increase in resource productivity and farm output attributed to increasing returns from scale naturally did not last very long, because once specialization ceased and farmers applied even more labor to the land, productivity peaked and declined.

Along with specialization and increased returns to scale, farmers also gradually began to acquire a new farming technology with new capital such as high-yield, disease-resistant rice seeds, fertilizers, farm implements, and means for eradicating pests. In the 1870's, this technological diffusion throughout the countryside was very slow, but by the 1890's it had speeded up, so that by the early 1900's evidence of new farming practices could be observed everywhere. New rice seeds like *aikoku* and *shinriki* were being used throughout the country; the application of soya-bean waste for fertilizer was widely practiced.[18] What organizations made these new developments possible?

The networks for producing and promoting a new farming technology were numerous. In 1878 the government established Farmer Discussion Societies (*nōdankai*) of landlords, ex-samurai turned farmers, and wealthy farmers—in other words, the local rural elite—who assembled their tenants and arranged for veteran farmers (*rōnō*) to instruct them in the best farming practices of the day.[19] In 1881, The

---

[16] *NNH*, vol. 3, p. 222.

[17] Kawada Shin'ichirō, "Kinkō nōgyō gijutsu ni kansuru ichi kōsatsu" [A Survey of Suburban Agricultural Technology] in *Nōgyō keizai kenkyū* 18:4 (April 1943), pp. 44-71. See p. 54 for changes in land use.

[18] *NNH*, vol. 10, pp. 10-11.

[19] *NNH*, vol. 3, pp. 262-263.

Greater Japan Farmers' Association (*Dai Nihon Nōkai*) was created and organized with similar purposes, except that its members paid dues and met periodically with veteran farmers, who again gave their lectures.[20] By 1888 there were around 5,000 such members throughout the country. Then in 1895, all *nōdankai* and *nōkai* were integrated into a single national farmers' association.[21]

Meanwhile, the first provisional agricultural experimental station had been set up in 1893 in Nishigahara, a suburb of Tokyo, for the purpose of developing upland and paddy rice cultivation.[22] In 1893, this unit became the first permanent agricultural station, and its activities were expanded to develop high-quality mulberry trees and silk cocoons. By 1900 there were six more of these agricultural experimental stations operating in other prefectures, concentrating mainly upon developing standard, high-yield rice varieties. By 1900 the national farmers' association had been linked to these agricultural stations. These stations began transferring their new seeds and methods for their use through the national farmer's association, which then instructed its members how to use them. To that end the national farmers' association also established its experimental plots, where new seeds were used for display and instruction.

More specialization and exchange and the adoption of improved seeds and new fertilizers by farmers combined to increase agricultural output in Taiwan and Korea during the first decade of Japanese rule. In Taiwan, the Japanese completed the trans-island railroad from Taipei to Kaohsiung by 1906. They restored law and order throughout the island by 1902, standardized market weights and measures, and created a new monetary standard pegged to Japan's monetary unit, the yen. All these measures greatly improved markets and encouraged an increase in the marketed surplus, as indicated by expanded exports. Taiwan's exports had increased most rapidly between 1868 and 1880, when the island had been opened to foreign trade as a consequence of the unequal treaties signed between Imperial China and various foreign powers. Even so, exports rose only four-fold during that period, whereas between 1897 and 1905 exports to Japan in-

[20] See also Dai Nihon Nōkai, Dai Nihon Sanrinkai, and Dai Nihon Suisankai, *Seiritsunana jūgo-nen kinen* [A 75 Years' Memorial Commemorating the Establishment of Farmers' Associations] (Tokyo: Anshin insatsu kōgyō kabushiki kaisha, 1955), which gives detailed activities of this association each year since its founding on March 5, 1881.

[21] *NNH*, vol. 5, p. 324.

[22] *NNH*, vol. 5, p. 678.

creased over six-fold.[23] This comparison suggests that specialization and exchange, primarily for the export market, provided a powerful inducement for farmers to increase their marketed surplus. Meanwhile, the Japanese rapidly began building the infrastructure to introduce a new technology to Taiwan's farmers.

In 1898 they established the first agricultural experimental station outside Taipei, and by 1906 a half dozen more such stations operated in various districts throughout the island.[24] In September 1900, the first farmers' association appeared outside Taipei, and by 1910 farmers' associations could be found in every district. In June 1902, the Provisional Taiwan Sugar Affairs Bureau began operations to improve sugarcane production and distributed new cane seeds to farmers, especially the Rose Bamboo and Lahaina varieties from the Hawaiian Islands. By 1910, the Taipei agricultural experimental station had selected 300 Indica rice varieties from 1,679 varieties alleged to have been grown throughout the island.[25]

Between 1905 and 1910, when Japan governed Korea as a protectorate, the Seoul-Pusan railway was completed and reforms initiated to standardize market weights and measures. By 1920, a new monetary system had long been intact and pegged to the monetary standard in Japan. Between 1910 and 1920, Korea's exports to Japan rose from 25.3 to 143.1 million yen, and of that amount of value agricultural products in current prices amounted to 10.7 million yen and 110.3 million yen, respectively.[26]

We can identify two phases of infrastructural development for the promotion of modern agricultural technology in Korea. The first lasted from 1905 to 1910, and the second covered the next decade of formal Japanese rule. In 1906 the Japanese set up the first agricultural experimental station, and in 1907 the Korean government created a 13 ha. horticultural experimental station east of Seoul.[27] Both governments agreed in 1906 to set up a cotton cultivation cooperative society,

[23] See data contained in Yamazawa Ippei and Yamamoto Yūzō, *Bōeki to kokusai shūshi* [Foreign Trade and Balance of Payments] (Tokyo: Tōyō keizai shimpōsha, 1979), vol. 14, p. 210, for Taiwan's exports to Japan, and Samuel P.-S. Ho, *Economic Development of Taiwan, 1860-1970* (New Haven and London: Yale University Press, 1978), p. 14, for Taiwan's exports in the late nineteenth century.

[24] See Ramon H. Myers, "Taiwan's Agrarian Economy Under Japanese Rule," pp. 459-460.

[25] Teng-hui Lee, *Intersectoral Capital Flows in the Economic Development of Taiwan, 1895-1960* (Ithaca and London: Cornell University Press, 1971), p. 40.

[26] See Yamazawa Ippei and Yamamoto Yūzō, p. 205 and p. 204.

[27] Kobayakawa Kurō (comp.), *Chōsen nōgyō hattatsushi* [The History of Korean Agricultural Development] (Tokyo: Yūhō kyōkai, 1959), vol. 2, pp. 54-55.

which then received 100,000 yen over the next three years to promote the use of American cotton seeds in ten selected areas of Cholla Pukto and Cholla Namdo provinces. In March 1908 two seedling experimental stations were established in Kyongsan Namdo and Ch'ungch'ŏng Namdo provinces, and by 1910 there were five more seedling experimental stations in other provinces. In November 1906 the Korean-Japan Agricultural Society established the Korea Central Agricultural Association, which soon formed branches in various cities and which was the precursor of the Korean Farmers' Association which began flourishing in the teens. The Pusan Agricultural Association, for example, began studying how to adopt Japanese vegetable-growing methods and after mastering some of these introduced them to landlords in nearby locales.[28]

Upon obtaining unlimited control over Korea in 1910, the Japanese began an even more vigorous effort to develop agriculture. They created special technical offices for soil improvement in 1912 and sent special technologists on agriculture to Taegu and P'yongyang. Perhaps the most important step occurred in March of 1912 with the publication of rules for setting up an Agricultural Technology Bureau (Nōgyō Gijutsukan) in every province to plan the development of animal husbandry, silk, cotton, and rice production. These bureaus were also responsible for creating special stations to promote new rice-seed varieties in experimental plots and then to distribute their seeds to farmer associations, landlords, other agricultural societies and finally to the superior farmers, ordinary farmers, and tenant farmers.[29] By January 1917 the Suwon agricultural experimental station, just south of Seoul, began publishing monthly reports on its ongoing work of diseases that affected cotton, rice, and fruit (particularly the apple), throughout Korea.[30]

This second phase of Meiji state agrarian policy, the creation of a new infrastructure of state sponsored organizations to produce a new farming technology for the East Asian agrarian system, depended greatly upon the active participation of local elites—village landlords

[28] Ibid., p. 123.

[29] Ibid., pp. 193-198, for a discussion of how these organizations functioned to transmit new rice varieties to farmers.

[30] See Chōsen Sōtōkufu kangyō mohanjō, Kangyō mohanjō kenkyū hōkoku, dai ichi [Research Report of the Agricultural Experimental Station for the Promotion of Agriculture] (No. 1, January 1917). This issue was devoted entirely to the study of the cotton disease Glomerella Gossypii and its control. This bacteria, apparently widespread in Korea, infested soy beans, cotton, onion, spinach, and the kidney bean. The issue contained findings reporting cotton yields from plants effectively controlled for this disease as opposed to those having the disease; see pp. 63-72.

and veteran farmers. Their activities made possible the transmission of the new farming technology to ordinary farmers and tenants. How successful was this transmission?

We have compiled the following table which identified two important elements of this modern farming technology transmission: new rice-seed varieties that germinated earlier than traditional varieties, resisted disease, and responded to fertilizers of a high nitrogen content, and improved fertilizers of the green-manure crop, soy-bean waste, or chemical types that contained a high nitrogen content. Table 2 shows trends in rice-paddy land use of new varieties as well as in the quantity of improved fertilizer per unit of land allotted to growing rice. These trends can be compared to the average rice yield and to the ratio of fertilizer to rice price in the same table.

By 1915 around 40 percent of paddy land in Japan was using the newest Japonica standardized varieties. The data for Taiwan pertain only to the new *p'eng-lai* rice variety developed in the late teens in the Hsinchu and Taipei experimental stations and to the Taichung No. 65 variety developed in the Taichung experimental station. By 1935 farms in Taiwan used these two rice seeds on nearly half of the island's paddy land, although it is not known to what extent these seeds were used for both the first and second crops on this paddy land. In Korea, there was a remarkable spread of new rice-seed varieties, from about one-fifth to more than four-fifths of the paddy land in only fifteen years.

In Japan the fertilizer applied for rice cultivation increased more than three-fold between 1895 and 1915. Accurate data for fertilizer consumption became available only at a later date for Taiwan and Korea. Even so, there was an impressive expansion of new fertilizers to rice land between 1920 and 1935. Farmers in Japan were encouraged to apply more fertilizer to their rice land because fertilizer prices declined as the rice price rose. This price incentive operated more weakly in the two colonies, because the fertilizer-rice price ratio remained fairly constant between 1920 and 1935. Even so, by producing and marketing more rice, farmers still increased their farm income.

This biological revolution in rice production was reflected by the rising rice yield per unit of land. In Table 2 we note that the rice yield slowly increased in Japan except during the 1920's. Why the stagnation of yields during that decade? One reason is that new rice varieties were transmitted to farmers only prior to World War I, and, during the teens, experimental stations failed to develop new varieties for the farmers' associations. New varieties were later developed in

TABLE 2

Seed Improvement, Fertilizer Input per Hectare, Fertilizer-Rice Price Ratio, and Rice Yield per Hectare in Japan, Taiwan, and Korea

Year[a]	Seed improvement[b]			Fertilizer input per ha.[c]			Fertilizer-rice price ratio[d]			Rice yield per ha.[e]		
	Japan (1)	Taiwan (2)	Korea (3)	Japan (4)	Taiwan (5)	Korea (6)	Japan (7)	Taiwan (8)	Korea (9)	Japan (10)	Taiwan (11)	Korea (12)
1895	0.04			13			7.0			2.06		
1905	0.30			24			5.2			2.46		
1915	0.40			49			4.4			2.79	1.47	
1920	0.42		0.22	63	12	1.3	3.5		3.3	2.91	1.47	1.43
1925	0.42	0.13	0.57	79	20	3.4	3.0	4.5	3.0	2.84	1.63	1.50
1930	0.56	0.23	0.72	96	33	12	3.0	4.5	3.5	2.89	1.75	1.48
1935	0.56	0.46	0.84	104	55	28	2.2	4.2	2.5	3.04	1.97	1.82

[a] Five-year averages centering on the years shown.
[b] Ratio of area planted in improved varieties to total paddy area planted in rice.
[c] Kg. of $N + P_2O_5 + K_2O$.
[d] Metric tons of brown rice purchasable with a ton of $N + P_2O_5 + K_2O$.
[e] Metric tons of brown rice.

Source: Yujirō Hayami and Vernon W. Ruttan, *Agricultural Development, An International Perspective*, Baltimore and London: The Johns Hopkins Press, 1971, p. 202.

the 1920's, but these could be transmitted to farmers only in the 1930's.

In Taiwan and Korea, the rice yield steadily rose, rising more rapidly in Taiwan than Korea. Two impressive achievements were associated with this increase in rice yield. First, rice yields for double-cropped land steadily rose, a singular achievement because the second rice crop was always poorer than the first. More important, rice yield variation within the same district and between districts steadily declined in all three countries. This development was not just a function of the biological revolution taking place. It related more directly to the impressive increase in irrigated land, and the stabilizing effect that water control had upon land once dependent upon erratic rainfall.

In Table 3 we have compiled information to show the expansion of rice paddy and sugarcane land and of irrigated and double-cropped land within Taiwan and Korea. In Japan, most of the irrigation development had taken place before 1900 and, thereafter, less land became irrigated. The largest increase of rice paddy and sugarcane land in Taiwan occurred between 1915-1920 and 1930-1935, whereas in Korea it was between 1915-1920. The sugarcane-cultivated area had greatly expanded in Taiwan between 1900-1910 and continued to grow during the teens, but then it declined because more and more sugarcane land was being allocated to grow rice. Because new sugarcane seeds produced high yields, less land needed to be allotted to sugarcane, for it still produced a higher total output.

More important, however, was the large expansion of irrigated land in Taiwan which occurred between 1920-1930, after the great Chia-i reservoir and its network of canals had been constructed. Irrigation development already had taken place as early as 1900 but on a more modest scale.[31] In Korea the great development in irrigation did not come until afer 1925. This new thrust was associated with the second rice production expansion plan launched in 1926, which called for the irrigation of 350,000 ha. of rice land.[32] This project was discontinued by the authorities in 1934 because of political pressure from Japanese farmers, who argued that Korean cheap rice exports to Japan were undercutting their rice prices.

Although we cannot be certain what proportion of rice paddy land and sugarcane fields were irrigated through man-made means, it is

[31] Kawano Shigetō, *Taiwan beikoku keizairon* [A Study of the Taiwan Rice Economy] (Tokyo: Yūhikaku, 1936), p. 43, shows that irrigated area between 1900 and 1912 increased from roughly 150,000 to around 200,000 ha.

[32] See Hishimoto Chōji, *Chōsen mai no kenkyū* [Studies of Korean Rice] (Tokyo: Chisō shobō, 1938), pp. 53-62, for the role that irrigation was to play in this plan.

TABLE 3

Irrigation and Double-Cropping on Paddy Land for Korea and Taiwan (1,000 ha.)

	Paddy area		Sugarcane area	Irrigated area		Double-cropping paddy area		Percentage ratio of irrigated area		Percentage ratio of double-cropping	
	Taiwan	Korea	Taiwan	Taiwan	Korea	Taiwan	Korea	Taiwan	Korea	Taiwan	Korea
Year[a]	(1)	(2)	(3)	(4)	(5)	(6)	(7)	$(8) = \frac{(4)}{(1)+(3)}$	$(9) = \frac{(5)}{(2)}$	$(10) = \frac{(6)}{(1)}$	$(11) = \frac{(7)}{(2)}$
1915	343	1,168	83	239			160	56			14
	(1.4)[b]	(5.6)	(4.8)	(2.3)			(8.4)				
1920	367	1,531	105	268		246	240	57		67	16
	(0.4)	(0.3)	(3.9)	(5.5)		(1.6)	(2.1)				
1925	374	1,551	127	350	758	266	266	70	49	71	17
	(1.1)	(0.7)	(−3.6)	(4.8)	(4.7)	(1.9)	(5.8)				
1930	396	1,605	106	442	953	292	353	88	59	74	22
	(3.9)	(0.8)	(2.2)	(1.1)	(3.9)	(1.4)	(4.0)				
1935	479	1,668	118	466	1,152	313	429	78	69	65	26

[a] Five-year averages centering on the years shown.

[b] Figures in parentheses are annual compound rate of growth between the subsequent five-year averages.

Source: Yujirō Hayami and Vernon W. Ruttan, Agricultural Development, 1971, p. 208.

clear that even in Taiwan by 1915 slightly more than half of the rice paddy and sugarcane land had been irrigated, and by 1935 nearly four-fifths of that land was under irrigation. Not only had yield variation within and between districts declined because of the stabilizing effect irrigation had upon rice yields, but the annual rice output variation was much more mild in Taiwan than in Japan or in Korea.[33]

In Korea about half of the rice paddy land already had become irrigated by 1925, but the great surge in construction in the next decade irrigated more than two-thirds of rice paddy land as cultivated paddy land expanded by nearly 10 percent. Taiwan's irrigation construction and semi-tropical climate made it possible for Chinese farmers to plant two consecutive crops on more than two-thirds of their land in a year. Korean farmers could only use a quarter of their rice paddy land more than twice a year.

Taiwan's agriculture had become more productive because of greater capital investment in agriculture, that is, capital that improved markets and represented organizations producing a modern agricultural technology and transmitting it to farmers. Although the same agricultural policy had been launched in all three countries, the Japanese colonial government in Taiwan invested far more in agriculture than it did in Korea. For example, in Taiwan between one-fifth to one-third of the government-created capital formation went for agriculture between 1900 and 1938, but in Korea that level was not reached until 1928.[34] Part of the reason for this difference was that very early in the colonial period the authorities in Korea had to allocate nearly three-quarters of government financing for administration and control, whereas in Taiwan that amount was only one-fifth. Although, in both colonies, these budget shares for administration and control converged and declined to around 10 percent by 1930, the Japanese made greater capital investment for agriculture in Taiwan than in Korea.

[33] Op.cit., Taiwan beikoku keizairon, p. 109, for a comparison of the annual standard deviation of rice production for all three countries between 1918 and 1937. See also Chang Han-Yu, "Development of Irrigation Infrastructures and Management in Taiwan, 1900-1940: Its Implication for Asian Irrigation Development," Economic Essays (The Graduate Institute of Economics, National Taiwan University), 9:1 (May, 1980) pp. 133-157. Also see p. 150 for the decline in Tsai-lai (Indica Rice) yield fluctuation from the standard deviation of 9.5 percent (1902-1914) to 8.8 percent (1915-1925) to 6.4 percent (1926-1938).

[34] See Mizoguchi Toshiyuki, Nihon tōjika ni okeru Taiwan-Chōsen no sōtokufu zaisei shishitsu no hikaku [An Examination of the Budget for the Governal-General Offices of Taiwan and Korea] (Tokyo: Institute of Economic Research, Hitotsubashi University, 1978), p. 13.

THE PATTERN OF AGRICULTURAL DEVELOPMENT

What kind of agricultural development took place in these three countries? Was the pattern similar in all three, or were there distinct differences? If the growth patterns differed, what factors accounted for that?

To put this development story into a proper perspective, we first should understand the contribution of each country to the agricultural output of all three. In 1935 the total value of agricultural output of Japan, Taiwan, and Korea amounted to around 4.5 billion yen, of which Korea and Taiwan's share came to 30 percent.[35] In 1920 these two colonies contributed only 27 percent, and while we do not have accurate information for earlier years, it is conceivable that between 1900-1905 their share was as low as 20 percent or less. As agricultural development rapidly advanced in these two large colonies, their contribution to the empire's total production definitely rose. What were the major crops making up this output?

In Japan around 1880 rice production alone constituted 58 percent of the value of total agricultural production, and while the importance of rice would remain supreme until World War II, its share declined to around 50 percent in the 1920's and 1930's.[36] Rice ranked first in Taiwan and Korea, being around 46 percent and 50 percent, respectively, of total output in the 1930's. A variety of coarse food-grains and fiber crops also bulked large in the farm output of all three, but in Taiwan sugarcane, tea, and tobacco were especially important, as was livestock (pigs and poultry), to account for around 20 and 15 percent respectively of the value of agricultural production. In Japan special products related to sericulture accounted for a little over 10 percent. Korea never produced any special farm products of high value for export except rice. Korea's comparative advantage lay primarily with rice, whereas Japanese farmers also earned income from sericulture, and Taiwan farmers from sugarcane, tea, and live-

---

[35] We define agricultural output as the total value of agricultural production minus intermediate products such as seeds and feeds. These percentages and value of agricultural output, in 1934-1936 prices, were obtained from Saburō Yamada and Yujirō Hayami, "Agricultural Growth in Japan, 1880-1970," and Teng-hui Lee and Yueh-eh Chen, "Agricultural Growth in Taiwan, 1911-1972," both in Hayami and others, eds., *Agricultural Growth in Japan*, Taiwan, Korea, and the Philippines (Honolulu: The University Press of Hawaii, 1979); and from Sung Hwan Ban, "Appendix to Growth Rates of Korean Agriculture," paper presented at the Conference on Agricultural Growth in Japan, Korea, Taiwan, and the Philippines held in Honolulu in February 1973. The base years were 1935-1937 for Taiwan and 1934 for Korea respectively.

[36] Our data for principal crops comes from the same sources cited in the last footnote and from Kazushi Ohkawa and others, ed., *Chōki keizai tōkei*, vol. 9, 1965, pp. 146-147.

stock. Agriculture was most diversified in Taiwan, and farmers planted their crops throughout the entire year, alternating between different crops as market prices changed. Japanese farmers specialized in both rice and mulberry-silk cocoon production. Korean farmers had to depend solely upon rice as their main source of cash income, and they planted coarse grains and vegetables for subsistence.

Turning now to the growth of agricultural production in all three countries, we have calculated the five-year coverage compound growth rates for farm output in all three and then classified these growth rates according to four principal phases we defined as initial growth, acceleration, stagnation and decline. These results appear in Table 4.

For Japan, we defined the period 1870 to 1890 as a phase of initial growth because the annual growth rates, when averaged for five-year periods, reflected a growth rate slightly over one percent. During the next two decades production grew even faster, but between 1920-1940 production definitely slowed, expanding even more slowly than population did over this same period. During the war years, farm production declined because manpower was diverted for the war effort and chemical fertilizer became very scarce.

In Taiwan, farm production gradually increased during the first quarter century of Japanese rule, and then spurted upward even more rapidly during the next fifteen years as large irrigation projects were completed and standardized rice and sugarcane seed varieties were being used throughout the island. After 1935 production began to slow up and then declined after 1940. In the mid-1930's the Japanese made an unprecedented effort to industrialize the island and mobilized resources for that purpose, but after 1940 more and more labor were brought in from the countryside to support the war effort.

In Korea, we observe a similar growth pattern as in Taiwan, except that the growth rates were lower. Production slowly began to grow in the first two decades of Japanese rule, but much slower than in Taiwan. Farm output then spurted ahead rapidly in the early 1930's after large irrigation projects were completed, but neither achieved the high rate that Taiwan had nor sustained it as long. After 1935 production even fell and continued to decline through the war years.

These countries shared a similar pattern of agricultural development: gradual expansion of production, acceleration of growth, a slowing up or stagnation, and then decline. Although these growth phases differed in each country, we can still conclude that prior to World War I the Meiji state agrarian strategy had successfully mobilized resources to speed up farm production in all three countries.

Probing more deeply into the sources of that growth, later stagnation and decline, we examine the trends for cultivated land and

TABLE 4
Growth Rates[a] of Agricultural Output for Different Development Phases
in Japan, Taiwan and Korea (percent)

| | Japan | | Taiwan | | Korea | |
Phase	Period (1)	Growth rate (2)	Period (3)	Growth rate (4)	Period (5)	Growth rate (6)
I. Initial growth:	1880–1900:	1.6	1915–1920:	1.5	1920–1930:	0.8
II. Acceleration:	1900–1920:	2.0	1920–1935:	4.1	1930–1935:	3.1
III. Stagnation:	1920–1940:	0.7	1935–1940:	0.8	1935–1940:	−0.1
IV. Decline:	1940–1945:	−3.7	1940–1945:	−7.3	1940–1945:	−2.3

[a] Annual compound rate of growth between five-year averages centering on the years shown.
Source: See footnote 35.

rural labor supply. By focusing upon land and labor, we can learn whether these factors of production became more productive, and if so how rapidly their productivity grew. For this purpose, we have measured the expansion of cultivated land and labor supply, and then measured the productivity of each factor by dividing the annual output by the amount of land and labor; finally, we estimated the compound rate of growth for the growth of land and labor and their productivity trends. We present our findings in Table 5.

In Japan, cultivated land increased very slowly before 1900 and only slightly faster during the next two decades; farm land scarcely expanded at all before World War II and then rapidly declined. By the late nineteenth century the Japanese already farmed most of their arable land, and only by reclaiming upland areas and draining swamps and lowlands did farmers expand tillage. After 1900 the growth of cities and transport networks devoured some of the most fertile farm land.

The rapid growth of the modern sector attracted rural transients who eventually took up permanent residence in cities, so that the farm labor force scarcely grew; in fact it even declined slightly between 1900 and 1940. After 1940, the government ordered city people to evacuate to the countryside to farm and to escape the dangers of aerial bombardment. Because of the large migration of rural people to cities and the high cost of reclaiming more farm land, the number of rural households scarcely increased but continued to farm nearly the same amount of land as in the early Meiji period. Under these circumstances, the growth of farm production on the long-term basis of around 1.5 to 1.7 percent per year could have been achieved only by the rapid expansion of land and labor productivity, but after 1920 farm production grew more slowly, as did land and labor productivity.

The story was very different in Taiwan and Korea. In Taiwan, farmers and officials heavily invested to clear more land for farming so that cultivated land grew rapidly in the early period only to expand more slowly during the 1920's and 1930's. The rural work force declined slightly during the late teens because of a sudden rise in mortality caused by an outbreak of malaria and influenza. But as mortality declined after 1920, the population growth surged to nearly 2 percent per annum so that the rural labor force naturally grew rapidly until the war years. The colonial administration made no plans for Taiwan's modern industrial-urban development until Japan went to war with China in 1937. The huge migration of rural labor to the cities that characterized Japan during this same period never occurred in Taiwan nor in Korea. Even though more labor was confined to

TABLE 5

Growth Rates[a] of Cultivated Land Area, Number of Agricultural Workers, and Land and Labor Productivity in Different Phases in Japan, Taiwan and Korea (percent)

Area	Item	Initial growth (1)	Acceleration (2)	Stagnation (3)	Decline (4)
Japan	Period	1880-1900	1900-1920	1920-1940	1940-1945
	Cultivated land area	0.5	0.7	0.1	-0.8
	No. of agri. workers	0.1	-0.6	-0.2	0.8
	Output per hectare	1.2	1.3	0.6	-2.8
	Output per worker	1.6	2.6	0.9	-4.5
Taiwan	Period	1915-1920	1920-1935	1935-1940	1940-1945
	Cultivated land area	1.1	0.8	0.5	-0.7
	No. of agri. workers	-0.7	1.1	0.5	-2.6
	Output per hectare	0.4	3.3	0.3	-6.6
	Output per worker	2.1	3.0	0.4	-4.8
Korea	Period	1920-1930	1930-1935	1935-1940	
	Cultivated land area	0.2	0.2	0.0	
	No. of agri. workers	0.5	-0.8	0.5	
	Output per hectare	0.6	2.9	-0.2	
	Output per worker	0.3	3.9	-0.6	

[a] Compound rate of growth between five-year averages centering on the years shown.

Sources: Data obtained from source cited in foot note 35 and Chōsen sōtokufu (Office of Government General of Korea), Chōsen Sōtokufu tōkei nempō [Annual Statistical Abstract for Korea], various issues.

the land, labor productivity still grew rapidly because Taiwan's agricultural growth was so rapid. Labor could work all year round in farming except in the north, where transient rural labor moved into Taipei city during the winter months, seeking work. The rate of growth of land productivity was also very impressive, again attesting to the successful biological revolution in rice, sugarcane, and tea.

The case of Korea was somewhat different. Farm land gradually increased, but never at the high rate achieved in Taiwan where the marginal lands chiefly were developed so rapidly for farming. In Korea, the Japanese invested for irrigation construction, to develop horticulture, cotton, and rice, but little else. Therefore, they allocated few resources to reclaim new farm lands. They left that task to Korean farmers, so that the expansion of cultivated land advanced more slowly than in Japan or Taiwan. The rural workforce steadily expanded because there were few opportunities outside of agriculture to find permanent employment until the late 1930's, and then mainly in north Korea, where the Japanese promoted mining and processing of ores. Even so, land and labor productivity also expanded, but more slowly. How can we measure those changes in factor productivity?

A well-known procedure now used to identify the chief sources of agricultural output growth is to construct an index of farm inputs by summing the indices of land, labor, fixed capital and non-farm capital, according to their weights for each factor's contribution to farm production.[37] By dividing the index of agricultural output by the index of all farm inputs, we can obtain a measure of the productivity of all four inputs. If output grows more rapidly than farm inputs, then one or more of the component inputs is becoming more productive, and input productivity increasingly accounts for the growth of agricultural production. By relating the contribution of only input growth to output growth, we can measure very roughly the contribution of these inputs to the growth of output. By making the same comparison between output growth and the productivity of inputs, we can show how productivity contributed to output growth.

Our Table 6 sets forth the growth rates for agricultural output and

[37] The input index is most sensitive to the choice of factor share weights. To make allowance for that, we have adopted the following chain-linked index

$$I_t = (\Sigma \omega_{i0} \frac{q_{i1}}{q_{i0}}) \cdot (\Sigma \omega_{i1} \frac{q_{i2}}{q_{i1}}) \ldots \ldots (\Sigma_i \omega_i \, t - 1 \frac{q_i \, t}{q_i \, t - 1})$$

where I_t is the total input index at period t; q_{it} is the quantity of i-th input at period t; and ωit is the share of i-th input in the total cost of production in current prices at period t. The index of total productivity shows the ratio of the total output index to the total input index. The index of total output, of course, represents agricultural output as defined earlier.

the composite farming input index as defined above. From these output and input indices we then estimated total input productivity. We then measured the relative contribution of input growth and input productivity to output growth for all countries. These findings show some very interesting trends.

We note that in Japan the growth of input productivity was very great between 1880 and 1920, but in the next two decades it slowed and then disappeared after 1940. Prior to 1920, land, labor and capital became more productive in farming and accounted for about three-quarters of the growth rate of output that took place. Thereafter, the growth of inputs increased in importance to account for around two-fifths of the growth rate of output.

In Taiwan the mobilization of farm inputs prior to 1920 proved crucial for making possible the rapid growth of output. Between 1920 and 1940 those inputs became increasingly productive so their productivity accounted for nearly a third of the growth of output. The same pattern can be observed in Korea.

In all three countries input productivity eventually played an important role in promoting both rapid but sustained agricultural growth. Yet this kind of development came only after the state had vigorously mobilized farm inputs and increased their supply sufficiently to promote a higher growth of farm production than under the ancien regime. We cannot ignore this first development phase because the state had little to invest in agriculture at that time. Only by expanding market opportunities and income rewards to farmers was the state able to encourage greater mobilization of land and labor for agricultural production.

It is commonly believed that input growth in traditional times had been very slow and merely approximated the slow growth rate of farm output; probably at growth rates of only 0.2 to 0.5 percent per year. After this initial development phase, however, input productivity began to play a larger contribution to the expansion of output. This new development phase signals the beginning of a transfer of modern farming technology to the small family farms that traditionally had used labor-intensive practices. As a modern agricultural revolution began to take place, first in Japan and then spreading to Taiwan and Korea, we can say this was the first example of modern agricultural development in Asia.

The Dysfunctions of Modern Agricultural Development

Enough has already been said as to why agricultural development was more successful in Taiwan than in Korea: an earlier head start to

TABLE 6

Growth Rates[a] of Total Agricultural Output, Input and Productivity, and Relative Contributions of Input and Productivity to Output Growth in Japan, Taiwan and Korea

| Area | Phase[b] | Period | Growth rates | | | Relative contribution | |
			Output (1)	Input (2)	Productivity (3)	Input (4) = (2)/(1)	Productivity (5) = (3)/(1)
Japan proper:	I.	1880–1900	1.6	0.4	1.2	25.0	75.0
	II.	1900–1920	2.0	0.5	1.5	25.0	75.0
	III.	1920–1940	0.7	0.3	0.4	42.9	57.1
	IV.	1940–1945	−3.7	−1.5	−2.2	40.5	59.5
Taiwan:	I.	1915–1920	1.5	2.5	−1.0	166.7	−66.7
	II.	1920–1935	4.1	2.7	1.4	65.9	34.1
	III.	1935–1940	0.8	0.6	0.2	75.0	25.0
	IV.	1940–1945	−7.3	−4.1	−3.2	56.2	43.8
Korea:[c]	I.	1920–1930	0.8	1.0	−0.2	125.0	−25.0
	II.	1930–1935	3.1	1.9	1.2	61.3	38.7
	III.	1935–1940	−0.1	0.2	−0.3	−200.0	300.0

[a] Compound rates of growth between five-year averages centering on the years shown.

[b] Phases I, II, III, and IV stand for phases of initiate, acceleration, stagnation, and decline respectively.

[c] Estimated by Saburō Yamada as follows: First, he constructed indices of land, labor, fixed capital and current inputs. The index of fixed capital was estimated by applying capital-output ratios for South Korea found in Sung Hwan Ban, "Growth Rates of Korean Agriculture, 1918–1971," in *Agricultural Growth in Japan, Taiwan, Korea and the Philippines*, to Korea's output data. The index for current inputs was estimated by using fertilizer data for Korea and the ratio of fertilizer to current inputs for South Korea, found in Sung Hwan Ban, "Appendix to Growth Rates . . . ," 1973. Those indices were aggregated into a single index of total input by the factor-share weights for each five-year average period. Finally, a chain-linked index was constructed by using the indices for the five-year periods.

Source: See footnote 35.

adopt the Meiji agrarian strategy, larger investments in agriculture, a more diversified farming system favored by year-round good climate, more trade with Japan, and greater market exchange within the colony.

By emphasizing the successful Meiji agricultural policy for Japan and her two colonies, we should not ignore several serious dysfunctions which occurred as agricultural production became modernized. Two dysfunctions, economic in character, affected all areas of rural life. The first we will refer to as the unequal distribution of wealth and income in the countryside, which reflected the very unequal distribution of property rights to land. The second we will refer to as the low income and purchasing power of the rural population. Their living standards increasingly fell behind those of city people. These two dysfunctions later set off powerful social and political forces within Japan, but limited space prevents us from considering that issue here. How did these two dysfunctions arise in all three societies, and why were they similar in character?

We have already pointed out that before the Meiji Restoration and Japan's administration of Taiwan and Korea, the East Asian agrarian order had been comprised of small family farms, of which a high proportion were tenant families farming the lands of elite classes who possessed special economic and social privileges. Other tenant households also farmed the lands of rich farmers. The proportion of both groups varied in our three countries, but when lumped together were perhaps as high as four out of ten in Japan and five out of ten in Taiwan and Korea. These tenant households depended upon wage income and the net income from renting the land of the privileged and wealthy farmers, but a proportion of these tenant households in fact farmed on a perpetual lease basis and could transfer that lease right to their progeny.

In Japan, the Meiji leaders expanded the number of households with property rights, and their reforms in Taiwan produced the same results. In Korea, the consequence of these reforms was more controversial, and future research will have to determine whether property rights were extended or reduced. After the 1870's there still remained as many as three out of ten rural households in Japan which farmed as tenants for various landowners, and after the 1890's and 1910's about four out of ten rural households in Taiwan and Korea, respectively, also were tenant households.

In Japan, the Matsukata deflation of the early 1880's forced many farmers to sell some of their land and become tenants so that the share of tenants slightly increased. The Meiji government, concerned with other political and economic issues during the 1870's and 1880's, had reacted to the rural distress caused by the Matsukata deflation by lowering the land-tax rate from three to two and a half percent. But the government failed to consider any further steps to enact laws and initiate policies to expand property rights to tenant households until the late 1920's.[38] Perhaps the reason for this oversight was that after the early 1880's economic development, particularly agricultural progress, advanced sufficiently to make the plight of the tenant less conspicuous and more easily ignored. Not until the 1920's, when agriculture was beset by a series of new problems, did the tenant question appear serious to the Japanese government and society as a whole.

Between 1910 and 1926, while the percentage of owner-cultivator declined from 33 to 31 percent, the share of tenant households remained constant at 27 percent, and the number of owner-tenant farmsteads rose slightly from 39 to 41 percent.[39] From 1914 to 1923 around 100,000 farmers lost some or all of their land, and there was "a marked increase in the proportionate and absolute number of those dependent entirely, and those dependent partially, upon rented land."[40] In 1926 tenants farmed 46 percent of the cultivated land. Given the fact that two-thirds of the nation still lived and worked in the countryside, resources were poorly distributed among the near 5.5 million households engaged in agriculture.

The outbreak of tenant disputes, the emergence of tenant unions, and the response of the newly formed landowners associations in the mid-1920s created such turmoil and violence that radical political groups began to form and to manipulate grievances and disputes to their advantage. In 1927 the Ministry of Agriculture tried to solve the property rights problem by introducing into the Diet a bill which would provide for the government to spend roughly 2.8 billion yen

[38] The original civil code of 1890 mentioned the desirability of extending property rights to tenants, but neither the government nor private parties ever took action in the 1890's and early 1900's to amend the code or enact policy to that end. See Ogura Takekazu, *Agrarian Problems and Land Reform in Japan* (Tokyo: Agricultural Policy Research Center, 1977), pp. 7-8.

[39] Dorothy J. Orchard, "Agrarian Problems of Modern Japan," in *The Journal of Political Economy* 37:2 (April 1929), p. 139. Net income of tenants was also extremely low and amounted to a little over one-third of the value of crop yields (see p. 140 of the same article); For another excellent source on tenant farmer income in the early 1920's, see J. W. Robertson Scott, *The Foundations of Japan* (London: John Murray, 1922), pp. 33, 187, 194-195, 301-302.

[40] Daniel H. Buchanan, "The Rural Economy of Japan," in *The Quarterly Journal of Economics* 37:4 (August 1923), p. 549.

($1.4 billion) to buy 1,960,000 acres of land from landlords and to convert that into small plots for tenant holders.[41] The bill called for the government to pay the landlords bonds bearing 5 percent and tenants to pay annual installments to the government over a 36-year period. This scheme was heatedly debated and criticized by both the landlord- and tenant-backed political factions and eventually shelved, but it demonstrates that the government at least was receptive to the kind of major land reform program undertaken two decades later by American Occupation authorities.

Just as the gap between rural and urban incomes widened in Japan, and more and more rural households failed to acquire land or to keep their property, Taiwan, too, experienced similar tendencies, but in a different way. In 1921, an island land survey of landownership distribution found that 64 percent of the rural households owned only 14 percent of the land, whereas 11 percent owned as much as 62 percent.[42] Taiwan's land ownership distribution was very unequal, but other evidence strongly indicates that this situation did not worsen, as in Japan, but that more rural households of tenant status did acquire land because of rapidly rising rural income. For example, between 1910 and 1939 the number of rural households increased 38 percent, or a 1.2 percent growth per annum. As rural households proliferated during this quarter century, the percentage share of tenant households declined from 42 to 36 percent, and the share of part-tenant, owner households rose from 24 to 33 percent.[43] At the same time, the share of owner cultivator families fell from 34 to 31 percent. In spite of the very unequal distribution of resources among rural households, the share of tenant households fell and those of owner-tenants greatly increased. While this modest expansion of property rights to tenant families took place, some owner cultivator families did lose some land and had to rent land, but they still managed to retain some claims to land property.

In the early 1920's Taiwan also experienced conflicts between tenants and landlords, but these disputes centered on demands by the tenants to formalize lease agreements in writing, whereby rents were fixed for certain periods irrespective of food grain price change. Landlords resisted these demands, and the Japanese officials were soon confronted with the spread of rural violence. In the late 1920's, the administration initiated a program to organize tenant-landlord asso-

[41] See part 2 of the Dorothy J. Orchard essay in *The Journal of Political Economy* 37:3 (June 1929), pp. 308-309.

[42] See Ramon H. Myers, "Taiwan's Agrarian Economy Under Japanese Rule," p. 470.

[43] *Ibid.*, p. 470.

ciations by which to settle such disputes and to establish the practice of formalizing contracts and making them long term. By 1935 the administration had spent 300,000 yen to establish 166 of these associations, and this program thereafter became the vehicle by which the Japanese hoped to broaden property rights by fixing the terms of lease and rentals so that tenants could improve their lot and eventually buy some land.[44]

Meanwhile, rural wages in Taiwan rose more slowly than urban wages, so that the gap in living standard between countryside and town widened. This gap was perceived during the 1920's by many Taiwan intellectuals and by the urban middle class, which had started to press for greater participation of Taiwanese in local governance. By the mid-1930's the Japanese began making greater investments for industrial development, encouraging private capital from Japan to move to Taiwan and allocating a larger share of the Taiwan budget for promoting that capital transfer. As the economy moved toward a war-time footing, the income gap stabilized, but reappeared after the war, when inflation worsened.

In Korea, the number of rural households increased from 2.5 million in 1913 to 3.0 million in 1936, a 20 percent increase over twenty-three years or a growth rate of .8 percent per year.[45] Within the context of this gradual rural population growth, the share of tenant households increased from 41 to 51 percent, while the share of owner and part-tenant owner households declined from 22 to 17 percent and from 32 to 25 percent, respectively. The trend for property rights in Korea was very different from that in Taiwan. Tenancy definitely increased, and the distribution of property rights appears to have become increasingly unequal. The average farm size, around 1 ha. in 1912, gradually increased to around 1.5 ha. in 1940, but around 63 percent of all family farms still operated plots less than a ha. in the aggregate, with another 30 percent farming between 1 and 3 ha.[46] In spite of the slightly larger farm size in Korea, the huge size of the rural population, the absence of diversified farming, and the lower proportion of marketed surplus made it very difficult for family farms to increase their income very rapidly, even though a biological rev-

[44] *Ibid.*, p. 472.

[45] *Kobayakawa Kurō*, vol. 3, Table 3, p. 93. Consult this same table for land tenure data. The percentage of tenant-farmed land over this same period rose from 52 to 57 percent, whereas that for owner-cultivator land fell from 48 to 43 percent. See Table 9, p. 99, in the same volume.

[46] Hisama Ken'ichi, *Chōsen nōgyō keiei chitai no kenkyū* [A Study of Regional Farm Management in Korea] (Tokyo: Shibundo, 1946), pp. 5 and 7. This work is the best farm-management study of Korean agriculture during the period of colonial rule.

olution gradually worked to increase output and yields. Furthermore, less than 10 percent of rural household labor worked outside of agriculture to earn income in Korea, irrespective of the region.[47] Finally, rural wages rose only very slightly in the 1920's, whereas urban wages rose must faster. Therefore, the dysfunctions in Korean agriculture appear to have been more severe than in either Japan or Taiwan.[48]

We close our analysis with some general conclusions about agricultural development in the Japanese colonial empire. While the Japanese government through its Meiji-style agrarian policy had eliminated elite class privileges, extended property rights to farmers, improved rural markets, and created new organizations for transferring a modern agricultural technology to the countryside of Japan, Taiwan, and Korea, the government failed to extend property rights to tenant households. While it successfully had launched a modern agricultural revolution by increasing the productivity of farming, land, labor, and capital so that sustained output growth took place, rural incomes lagged far behind urban incomes. Japan's industrial sector advanced furthest, so that cities absorbed most of the growth of rural population that occurred after the 1870's. Therefore, the rural–urban income gap or rural–urban dualism in Japan was smaller than in Taiwan and in Korea. In Taiwan and Korea, Japanese colonial administrations had paid for less attention to industrial development until the 1930's, at which time the growth of rural population merely had prevented per capita rural income from rising very rapidly. This situation was more serious in Korea than in Taiwan, where agriculture had more of the attributes of a mono-cultural farming system.

By 1946, all three countries had inherited an agrarian structure which included modern production features, but the resources of which were very unequally distributed and in which resource owners earned very low incomes. In the postwar period these problems were resolved in part by land reform, whereby all three countries extended property rights to tenant households, and in part by agricultural policies which invested more resources with modern technology for the agriculturalists. As these latter policies differed in all three, their impact was also very different, so that agricultural development in East Asia still continues to reveal different patterns and new problems.

[47] Ibid., p. 37.

[48] From village surveys carried out by the Japanese we cannot find any evidence of villages being influenced by modernity. See Chōsen Sōtokufu, Chōsen buraku chōsa tokubetsu hōkoku [A Special Report on Surveys of Korean Villages] (Tokyo: Chōsen sōtokufu, 1924), vol. 1. Also Chōsen Sōtokufu, Chōsen buraku chōsa shisatsu hōkoku [A Report of Surveys of Korean Villages] (Tokyo: Chōsen sōtokufu, 1923), vol. 1.

PART IV

The Japanese Empire in Historical and Global Perspective

CHAPTER 12

Post World War II Japanese Historiography of Japan's Formal Colonial Empire

Ramon H. Myers

Japanese scholars did not begin to study and to appraise Japan's modern colonial history until the 1960's. The study of Japanese imperialism, however, resumed right after World War II and has flourished ever since. Why the delay in examining Japan's modern colonial history? Perhaps the reasons have to do with the bitter memories, guilt, and shame associated with Japan's aggression and defeat. As for the rekindling of an interest in colonial history, it was the curiosity of Asians who had lived under Japanese colonial rule that seemed to stimulate and to encourage Japanese scholars to view again their modern history from some very different perspectives.

By the 1960's many Koreans and Chinese who had spent their early childhood in a primary school learning Japanese were studying in Japanese universities and beginning to write doctoral theses on topics related to Japan's colonial rule. Frustrated by the failure of Korean and Taiwanese national liberation movements immediately after World War II to establish democratic governments, many of these scholars began to examine how Japan had established such firm control over its colonial territories and why the nationalist movements protesting Japanese rule never achieved very great success. Others explored capitalist development and modernization of these colonies.

Any review of the post World War II historiography of Japan's formal colonial empire must take into account both the writings by Japanese and by the nationals from the old colonies. I have selected various monographs and journal articles written in Japanese which I believe best represent the post World War II historiography about Japan's formal colonial empire.[1] Rather than summarize them in se-

---

[1] How large is the post August 1945 historiography in Japanese that treats only the themes of imperialism and Japan's formal colonial empire? I have tried to count the number of journal articles, books, and compendium of materials where some detailed mention of these two themes is discussed. I used the following method. I examined an extensive bibliography listing 636 items pertaining only to Taiwan, published be-

rial fashion, I have grouped them around the principal themes treated in this volume. In doing so I briefly compare the principal arguments and findings of these works with those of this study, to illustrate both the differences and the similarities of interpretation, emphasis, and coverage.[2] The reader, therefore, is given some guidance about new directions in the scholarship pertaining to Japanese colonialism written in Japanese.

THE ORIGINS OF JAPANESE COLONIALISM

This volume contains only two essays on the topic of why Japan acquired colonies. We have ignored the complex issue of the origins of Japanese imperialism, preferring instead to offer the following broad view of the process by which Japan acquired colonies. Looking out upon a world rapidly being carved up by powerful western states, Japan's leaders had responded in the 1870's and 1880's to Western imperial aggression by gradually rearming Japan and establishing new institutions to modernize the country. As Japan began to probe the peripheral areas of north China, Korea, and Taiwan to take advantage of nearby targets of opportunity, Japanese businessmen also eyed the potential profit that such territories might provide. The new, emerging coalition between state and private enterprise which would extend Japanese imperial influence into this periphery was prompted as much by the example of Western imperialism as by the anticipation of private and strategic gains. Because of the serious foreign

tween August 1945 and December 1979, that appeared in a new journal called *Taiwan kingendaishi kenkyū* [Historical Studies of Taiwan in Modern Times], No. 3, 1980. I identified about 80 items which focused entirely upon Taiwan under the topic of Japanese imperialism. If we double this figure to include the materials written about Korea for the same period (many items of the above bibliography also related to colonial Korea), and then add another 40 items as a rough estimate for the materials written about other Japanese colonies within the formal Japanese empire, we arrive at a total figure of around 200 items, an estimate probably on the high side. The materials discussed in this essay, therefore, represent a sample of around 20 percent of the post World War II historiography written in Japanese on the subject of Japanese colonialism and imperialism. I also want to emphasize that most of the items in the sample cited in this essay were published by distinguished commercial or university presses or appeared in outstanding Japanese scholarly journals.

[2] In 1979 Asada Kyōji reviewed Japanese scholarship on imperialism and colonialism, and he adopted a five-issue classification scheme which included all of the categories which the essays of this study were grouped. These were: (1) the origins and evolution of Japanese imperialism in East Asia; (2) the establishment of Japanese occupation during the 1937-1945 war years; (3) a comparison of Japan's colonial empire with the Western colonial empires of roughly the same period; (4) imperial Japan's colonial management; (5) the impact or influence of Japanese colonialism upon the colonial peoples. (Asada Kyōji, 1979, pp. 50-51.)

threats to Japan's security in the 1890's and the fact that businessmen were hoping to find new markets and sources of raw materials abroad, the profit motive and an ebullient nationalism soon coalesced to embroil Japan in war, thereby to acquire several colonies.

Some Japanese scholars have agreed with this general explanation. As early as 1963, Yamabe Kentarō had pointed out that Japan's acquisition of colonies was really based upon policy decisions to deal with threats to her security. For Japan to be secure, she needed guarantees that Korea would be stable and friendly. For Korea to be secure, the continental hinterland of Manchuria and Mongolia had to be brought under Japan's influence (Yamabe, 208-209). Finally, the Japanese occupation of the German South Sea islands in 1918 also bore no real relationship to the actual economic resources of that region; it was undertaken strictly for military and strategic purposes (Yamabe, 205-206).

Most Japanese scholars have preferred to discuss the take-over of colonies within the context of imperialism (teikokushugi), a phenomenon of enormous complexity about which much Japanese ink has been spilled (Fujimura Michio, 1965). Japanese scholars have examined imperialism in several ways. Some have explained it principally in terms of domestic development, either concentrating exclusively upon economic development patterns and characteristics or emphasizing the military and political forces at work. Others have located the reasons for Japan's war with Ch'ing China and Imperial Russia as a response to international crises. Both approaches have naturally been concerned with identifying a periodization sequence as to when Japan really became an imperialistic country. Scholars have generally argued that the critical turning point period when Japan became an imperial power was sometime between 1894-1895 and 1904-1905.

In 1959 Ono Yoshihiko argued that Japanese imperialism could best be explained in terms of the Leninist thesis, with an analysis of the economic substructure (keizaiteki kabu kōzō) (Ono Yoshihiko, 1959). In 1961 Satō Noboru tried to clarify and to support Ono's point of view by advancing a new criteria to identify when Japanese capitalism had really become imperialistic (Satō, 1961). This criteria included such economic characteristics as large-scale enterprises using a lot of fixed capital, widespread monopolistic enterprise behavior, the export of finance capital, and the activities of large international cartels. Satō did not regard the role of the superstructure (state policies, leadership styles, and ideology) as having any casual connection with imperialism.

Such a one-sided analytical approach was bound to be criticized sooner or later, and in 1963 Matsukuma Norihito pointed out that the power relationships in Japan's polity and society could not be ignored because these were important forces determining how and when a country like Japan had become an imperial power (Matsukuma, 1963). These two opposing analytical approaches merely represented a continuation of pre-war scholarly debates on imperialism. As early as the 1920's and 1930's Takahashi Kamekichi, Noro Eitarō, Inomata Tsunao, and Yanaihara Tadao were arguing the importance of whether domestic or international factors were more crucial for shaping the emergence and for influencing the timing of Japanese imperialism.

By the late 1960's and 1970's Japanese monographs began treating imperialism in a much more sophisticated, scholarly way. In 1968 Inoue Kiyoshi stated that the turn of the century had marked Japanese imperialism's entry upon the international stage. According to Inoue, by 1900 Japan had acquired Taiwan and begun to draw Korea into its sphere of influence; she had participated with other imperial powers to carve out zones of influence in China; she now competed with these same imperial powers to extend her economic and political influence abroad (Inoue, 34). Inoue points out that, while these imperialistic attributes had become full-blown, Japan still lacked any of the significant characteristics of monopoly capitalism which Germany, France, and England already possessed. At the same time, Japan differed from these same states in still another fundamental way: her system of governance depended upon a powerful military establishment and a corps of bureaucrats very closely connected to that establishment (Inoue, 37). This militaristic-feudal ruling elite, as Inoue called it, had governed Japan with the assistance of the institution of the imperial household (*tennōsei*) and responded in very limited ways to popular demands for greater political participation. This same elite also took a tough stand when it came to international crises by mobilizing popular support to beef up the military services and to wage a war when necessary. For Inoue, several wars really had strengthened the power of this ruling circle whose members, meanwhile, also had become inextricably linked with powerful business interests.

In 1974 Nasu Hiroshi elaborated still further on Inoue's thesis by arguing that the wars in the 1890's and early 1900's had produced larger budget outlays for the militaristic establishment, a sum amounting to around 295 million yen that exceeded all other categories of the state budget (Nasu, p. 120). These expenditures could be made only by deficit spending, which in turn had rewarded a number of capitalistic businessmen and involved them in overseas business ventures (Nasu, p. 104). Other scholars also made the same assertion by pointing out that the passage of the January 1896 ten-year plan to extend Japan's military forces from 6 to 12 divisions had bestowed great profits to many manufacturers (Fujii Shōichi, 124). The support for this legislation could be mobilized only from land-lords and urban businessmen who had investments in the new state-managed shipping companies, state-owned railway companies, and state-sponsored banks with overseas-colonial business interests (Mae-jima Shōzō, 243-252).

It was within this new state and society relationship of the mid-Meiji that the events leading to the annexation of Korea should be viewed, argued Harada Katsumi (Harada Katsumi, pp. 204-219). According to Harada, a series of complex decisions made at home in response to crises developing in the periphery, namely Korea, put Japan on the inexorable road to imperialism. On November 18, 1905 Japan had assumed the responsibility of overseeing Korea's political system. From the outset, high officials like Itō Hirobumi had pressed the Koreans to allow more Japanese to enter Korea to develop mines, railroad, harbors, and postal services. Even though Japan was supposed to allow these same advantages to foreign investors, it cleverly tried to exclude foreign capital while advancing the investments of its nationals. Whether such actions were part of a grand design to take over Korea, Japanese scholars still disagree. But in February 1906 some Koreans expressed their outrage at Japanese duplicity and staged several anti-Japanese demonstrations which the Japanese quickly suppressed. This retaliation prompted some Koreans to assassinate several important Japanese officials, and regional rioting quickly erupted. These civil disturbances quickly reduced tax revenues for the Japanese, who could not receive financial help from Tokyo because of serious budget problems at home. To resolve the problems of weakening Japanese civil control and the evaporation of tax revenues, the Japanese took matters into their own hands and annexed Korea on August 28, 1910. Having now full control to carry out their fiscal reforms, the Japanese intended to make Korea pay for its own development because the home treasury lacked the means to do so.

To this end, the new Japanese colonial government in Korea introduced fiscal reforms like those launched in Taiwan by Kodama Gen-tarō and Gotō Shimpei. As a result, the annual subsidies from the Tokyo Imperial Treasury gradually declined in 1913 and ended by 1919. A retrenchment policy by Governor-Generals Terauchi and Hasegawa brought about an unavoidable decline in the level of investment in railroad construction and other projects, as well as the dismissal of some 1,000 Korean high officials from government services. (Hori Kazuo in Kang Chae-ŏn and Iinuma Jirō, 1982, 200-202.)

Although the studies cited above have explored more deeply the connection between imperialism and the acquisition of colonies than the essays of this volume, many of these authors have exaggerated the economic linkage between the private and public sector as a force behind Japan's military expansion, both at home and abroad. Studies of imperialism and the events leading up to acquiring colonies surely should not omit any reference to the cultural ethos of the time. Furthermore, by failing to mention the public views, widely held by individuals and groups, that society should patriotically serve Japan to find her true place in East Asia, Japanese scholarly works still provide an incomplete historical understanding of the critical decisions and events that made Japan become an imperialistic power.

MANAGEMENT OF THE COLONIAL EMPIRE

Some of the essays in this volume have focused upon how the Japanese carried out a Meiji development strategy at home in the 1870's and 1880's and then applied it to their colonies in the 1890's and early 1900's. The Japanese knew how to create an effective police system to maintain law and order in the colonies, because they had successfully done this at home. They also recognized the importance of making a heavy investment in education to upgrade human skills. But the legal-cultural policies pursued by the Japanese for the assimilation of non-Japanese Asians into their empire were always rooted in a profound ambivalence as to how far to go and as to whether their colonial servants could ever really become Japanese citizens.

The reason for this ambivalence originates in large part from the separate laws and political independence that Japan's leaders granted their colonial officials. This volume has pointed out that, upon acquiring colonies, the Japanese government decided to transfer considerable power to the colonial administrators so that they could create special laws and institutions that they regarded as necessary for managing colonial affairs. This finding also has been supported by Haruyama Meitetsu, who has argued that Itō Hirobumi was the chief official responsible for permitting Taiwan and Korea to be governed separately [bunken teki ni] from the laws and institutions that applied to Japan (Haruyama Meitetsu and Wakabayashi Masahiro, 74).

After World War I, when political demonstrations for independence erupted in the colonies, the cabinet under Premier Hara Kei began to adopt a new guideline that urged colonial officials gradually to modify the laws related to public assembly and publication of printed materials so that all colonial subjects might ultimately acquire the same legal rights as Japanese. This new doctrine of colonial management, which Haruyama Meitetsu has called *naichi enchōshugi* (the principle of gradually extending Japanese laws to apply to colonial subjects) could be reversed at any time if Japan's leaders perceived that their empire was being threatened by developments from without or from within. Yet *naichi enchōshugi* continued to prevail, and officials both in the colonies and at home practiced this in a flexible way.

Much of the post World War II scholarship on colonial management, however, greatly differs in thematic treatment from the findings offered in this volume. Asada Kyōji, for example, has focused largely upon the specific instruments of Japanese colonial control and how these instigated popular movements for national liberation. Asada cited three instruments which gave the Japanese considerable control over their colonies: their control and ownership of land; their regulation of the money supply and taxation; and their management of railroads (Asada Kyōji, Dec. 1975, pp. 64-69). After expropriating considerable private land in Taiwan and Korea, and even in Manchuria after 1932, the Japanese formed private companies to manage that land strictly on a commercial basis for Japanese nationals. By also carrying out a land tax reform and centralizing the collection of the land tax with many new commodity taxes, the Japanese quickly earned revenue to spend on projects such as new roads, railroads, and harbors. By establishing a modern infrastructure, the Japanese colonial bureaucracy could also impose new taxes upon commerce and agriculture, which at the same time had benefited from an expanding local market and more foreign trade. Asada refers to landlords as being parasitic because they collected rent from their tenants and reinvested in financial and urban business enterprises. The landlords in the colonies behaved just like landlords in Japan. The emerging banking and transport structure also looked very much like the government-regulated banks and railroads at home. By opening up the colonial markets to Japanese exports, Japanese businessmen expanded their activities and contributed to the rapid industrialization at home. For Asada, colonial control meant Japanese economic control over land, financial instruments and transportation (Asada Kyōji, April 1975, pp. 179-186). Political and social instruments of control seem to be far less important or, rather, were made possible by economic control.

Asada also contended that the Japanese colonial landlord system had its unique structure. Large Japanese companies and numerous Japanese nationals had amassed private land for commercial and industrial purposes. By 1939 Japanese privately owned land amounted to 13 percent of the cultivated land in Taiwan, whereas in Korea in

1934 that amount came to nearly 16 percent and included holdings larger than fifteen hectares. These lands, irrigated and fertile, produced a disproportionately large amount of farm output. Impressive as these figures are, Asada perhaps exaggerates when he argues that this colonial landlord system had been mobilized to preserve the well-intrenched interests of landlords at home (Asada Kyōji, 253). Although similarities in the distribution of property rights do exist between these different systems, Asada provides little evidence to connect the two landlord systems.

How important was the landlord system within the colonies as a means of political, social, and economic control over colonial subjects? The Japanese had carried out a land survey and institutionalized property rights for those who managed their land, while eliminating property rights for certain households which never farmed their land. Even this reform still left nearly four or five out of every ten households in the colonies without land and having to rent or labor for those who owned land. The Japanese certainly recognized how unequal property rights distribution had become by the 1920's, but the high economic costs to redistribute property rights more equally while trying to maintain social stability probably made further land reform out of the question. In Taiwan during the 1930's, the Japanese tried to protect tenant rights by encouraging landlords and tenants to formalize their contracts in writing with appropriate guarantees for tenants. But did the landlord-tenant system make Japanese colonial control easier? Studies by Asada and others never examine the social and political power of local elites, nor try to determine whether landlords always constituted the mainstay of local elites. In other words, we are likely to be misled by economic statistics that merely describe land tenancy and land-rent systems without a clear picture of how Japanese colonial control linked up with local elite power.

The Japanese ruled their colonies by a centralized bureaucracy formalized within the colonial governments general. Scholars have not yet examined this institution in sufficient detail to show how this office actually governed, how policies were formed, how officials were recruited, and whether the power of the government-general increased or declined throughout the colonial period. The Taiwanese scholar Ng Yuzin Chiautong provides an all-too brief picture of how these institutions in Taiwan and Korea compared (Ng, 208-210). It was not until 1942, for example, that the procedures became the same for designating the governor-general to head this office in both Korea and Taiwan. Until that year, the selection in Korea had been an imperial appointment, whereas in Taiwan it had been a cabinet appointment.

Although Japanese control over the colonies remained extremely tight, popular resistance to colonial authority continued throughout the period. The Taiwanese scholar Kō Se-kai, who graduated from Tokyo University's Faculty of Law, has produced the most detailed and revealing account of Taiwanese resistance to Japanese rule (Kō Se-kai, 1972). His account is based upon an extensive historical record to show how the Japanese suppressed early Taiwanese movements for independence and later demands for some participation in actual governance. Kō's description of the first seven years of Japanese efforts to establish their rule is an excellent account of the long struggle by Japanese police and gendarmerie to crush island-wide Taiwanese guerrilla resistance. Kō describes the different strategies which were tried and then abandoned by the first three governor-generals. It was not until Governor-General Kodama combined police with militia to isolate guerrilla bands and offered rewards to guerrilla chiefs as well as amnesty to their men that resistance ceased.

By the teens and early 1920's, many Taiwanese had adopted a different strategy to deal with Japanese rule rather than the use of force and direct confrontation. New leaders from the urban professional classes tried to get politicians in Japan to support their demands for greater participation in home rule. But these Taiwanese activists soon split into factions—some moderate and others radical—and engaged in public demonstration and labor strikes. On the basis of a thorough examination of police records for this period, Kō explains how the Japanese, by penetrating the cells of the Communist party leadership in some of these resistance efforts, were able to eradicate them by the early 1930's (Kō, 358-374).

Taiwanese resistance and Japanese response seems to have conformed to cycles of alternating Taiwanese popular protest and government suppression. When the Japanese perceived that some Taiwanese had begun to mount greater opposition to their rule than was tolerable, they mobilized their police to crush the opposition. By the 1930's the vanguard of Taiwanese opposition had come to consist of physicians and lawyers, many trained in Japan. Their high social status and leadership skills earned them popular respect and support, and their family connections in local communities also permitted them to draw a large following. Having received much of their education in Japan, and learning how to interact with the Japanese both socially and politically, these leaders developed moderate tactics to press for home rule. Further supportive of these actions were the modern values and ideas that were broadcast through the new vernacular literature which the Japanese allowed to circulate in journals and books.

Yet Japanese scholars like Asada Kyōji have argued that Japanese colonial control was based upon indigenous class relations that were shaped and determined by those groups owning the means of production and other groups paid to work with those facilities. Because the colonies depended largely upon agriculture, in Asada's view class exploitation became crucial for shaping the system of colonial control. Naturally, the Japanese colonial governments made certain from the outset that property rights were carefully defined and taxes collected. At the same time, their surveys of forests and upland resources enabled state organizations to have more land under their control than by villages, as in the past (Asada Kyōji, 1973, 35-39).

Yet, scholars like Asada mistakenly see colonial control rooted only in a proprietary occupation of land and resources by private parties, whether Japanese or local elite. By ignoring the bureaucratic systems of law, security, and education outside the private sector, they confuse the operation of the colonial administration with that of the private sector and the various private and public groups which have claims to land and resources. Landlords, farmers, and part-tenants worked and produced for the market, and, while some campaigned at times for reforms to redress the unequal flow of income from property rights, their social and economic control of property seems to have had little relationship to the interest groups or factions within the colonial bureaucracy trying to influence colonial policy.

Sometimes, local elite groups eager to have funding did enlist the state's support to alter local property rights or even to extend public property rights where none had previously existed, as in the case of new irrigation construction. When the Chia-nan irrigation project commenced in 1917, local farmers and tenants resisted public encroachment upon their land and complained about the high water usage charges. But this example merely shows that local elite groups could split on the perceived benefits of state programs for large-scale irrigation works. Asada records this popular protest movement as yet another example of popular uprisings under a particular socioeconomic system of Japanese and local elite control (Asada Kyōji, 139-147). He fails to differentiate among local elite groups, or to note why some elites supported and others opposed such an irrigation system.

Japanese scholars also argue that in Korea a very unequal distribution of land ownership made it possible for Japanese officials to control the countryside through a small landlord elite. The percentage of tenant households steadily rose in the 1920's and 1930's and the share of part-tenant and owner-farmer households declined. By the late 1930's, when the percentages for all three groups had stabilized, at least five out of every ten rural households were tenants.

The Japanese land-survey and land-tax reform completed in 1918 supposedly never extended land-ownership rights to very many new households. Even though a green revolution slowly spread in the 1920's, when new rice seeds became available and massive irrigation schemes became operational, the land-ownership distribution pattern had worsened by the late 1930s.

In describing the Japanese efforts to develop tenant, irrigation, and farmer associations for extending this green revolution, Asada Kyōji argues that land-tenure conditions worsened with the proliferation of new landlord-farmer organizations. He believes that these two developments greatly increased the number of tenancy disputes in the 1930's (Asada Kyōji, 1973, 200-201). For example, Asada's data show that between 1935 and 1939 more annual disputes occurred than at any previous time. Paradoxically, as the annual number of disputes more than trebled after 1934, rural conditions began to improve compared to the preceding years, when world depression had depressed farm prices. Asada never explains why tenant-landlord disputes increased as prices and wages gradually rose, nor does he say that the authorities had encouraged tenants to seek legal action for resolving contractual disputes with their landlords. Both at home and in the colonies in the 1930's Japanese officials began urging tenants to formalize their contracts with landlords. Under these circumstances, we would normally expect that more disputes of this kind might occur, and very likely this is the explanation for Asada's figures for rising tenancy disputes after 1934, when rural economic conditions improved. Asada finds considerable regional variation for these tenancy disputes during the 1930's, with north and south Cholla provinces having the highest number of disputes (Asada Kyōji, 1973, 243).

A number of Japanese scholars have tried to explain the management of Japan's colonies in terms of class ownership of land rather than in terms of bureaucratic policies and institutions. The essays in this volume have minimized the importance of socio-economic class relations, but it is important to give at least passing attention to these elements and to assay their importance in the development of Japanese colonial management.

Economic Dynamics in Japan's Colonies

The economic essays of this volume have presented quantitive measurements of colonial agricultural and industrial performance, Japanese investment flows to the colonies, colonial public expenditures, and colonial foreign trade with Japan, which together convey a picture of rapid colonial economic development and partial economic structural change made possible by large public investments and expanding exports to Japan.

In this view, Japanese officials transferred the Meiji economic development strategy to their colonies by taxing agriculture and commerce. These revenues then became the source for public-sector spending for the creation of a modern infrastructure, investment in education and public health, and the distribution of seeds, fertilizer, and irrigation to develop agriculture. Decades later, all colonial administrations imported capital and technology from Japan to the colonies in order to establish the industries necessary for producing energy and for processing metals for military use. As a rapid industrial spurt took place in Taiwan, Korea, and the Liaotung Peninsula, the regulatory procedures for organizations managed by the bureaucracy became cumbersome and restrictive. Industrial production became more inefficient as firms failed to acquire sufficient labor and raw materials. Meanwhile, Japan paid a high price by transferring so many scarce resources to its colonies.

The economic perspectives of the literature of post-war Japanese scholarship on the colonial empire are very different and focus upon other themes: the obstacles created in the economic processes within the colonies, which distorted economic development; the exploitative characteristics of colonial economic development; the specific reforms and instruments used by the Japanese to initiate colonial economic development. Because these approaches vary from those contained in this volume, I have treated them in different categories, while still identifying by method and conclusions.

Chinese and Korean scholars, rather than Japanese, have produced the most detailed and thorough economic studies of colonial Taiwan and Korea. Tō Sho-en's (T'u Chao-yen) huge work, containing 220 tables and graphs, reviews Taiwan's colonial economic history in the context of the commercialized agricultural development of the Ch'ing period. Tō's intent is to show the "dependent" (jūzokuteki) and "malformed" (kikeiteki) characteristics of the Taiwan economy as it evolved under Japanese colonial rule. These descriptions imply that Taiwan's economic development until 1895 had been normal, but thereafter Taiwan's economy became increasingly dependent upon Japan, and a Chinese capitalist class never had the opportunity to evolve because Japanese capitalism and state power controlled the Taiwan domestic market.

How did such economic dependency arise, and why did the economy become deformed. According to Tō, Japanese bureaucrats had made substantial investments to develop sugar- and rice-processing industries, and the export of these products to Japan made these industries entirely dependent upon the Japanese home market. Only after 1935 did this situation change because the colonial government created new industries to support the Japanese war machine and asked the sugar and rice companies to lend a helping hand. Because Japanese capital had been encouraged and protected by the state to develop the sugar industry, these new enterprises earned considerable monopoly profits which their owners then reinvested in the service sector or in other colonies. Meanwhile, Tō argues that Chinese businessmen with their capital funds found it very difficult to compete with the Japanese on an equal footing. Admittedly, Chinese firms were more labor-intensive, smaller in scale, and earned less profits, yet Tō compares only the superficial attributes of Chinese and Japanese enterprises, and never examines the motivations and attitudes of Chinese businessmen, which would provide another view of the economic obstacles that Chinese capitalists perceived they had to overcome. He does not consider, moreover, whether the disadvantaged circumstances of Chinese firms actually originated from the monopoly advantages possessed by Japanese businessmen.

Meanwhile, Chinese landlords continued to manage their local business affairs as they always had done, and, with few notable exceptions, they did not try to develop new urban enterprises. Tō does not inform his readers about the economic cultural orientations of local landlords or of how their management of assets differed, if at all, from those few Chinese capitalists who began establishing modern enterprises in the teens and twenties which he has described in considerable detail (Tō, 412-433). Certainly, much of the ground covered by Tō is already well known, and his basic findings pretty well conform to what we know about colonial economic development in other parts of the world. While giving notable credit to Japanese entrepreneurial bureaucrats to open up Taiwan's economy to foreign trade and modern technology, Tō never fails to remind us that the great power of Japanese monopoly-capitalists limited the prospects for Chinese entrepreneurs to develop on an equal footing. While this indeed might be true, and the facts do suggest that Chinese capitalists lagged woefully behind their Japanese counterparts in modern management procedures and technology, the obstacles which Chinese entrepreneurs conceived as thwarting their development are neither fully explored nor made clear.

Lim Byon-yun's study of Korean agricultural development under colonial rule also highlights certain economic contradictions which colonial economic policies allegedly produced. According to Lim, these economic contradictions moved Korea's economy away from a pattern of indigenous capitalist development toward a trend of small-scale rural commercialization in Korea and excessive Japanese capital export to Korea to initiate rapid industrialization (Lim Preface, 1971). Lim links the commercial-agricultural development under colonialism to pre-1910 conditions, to show that a sharp change in rural socio-economic relations took place after Japanese bureaucrats began charting Korea's economic destiny.

How did economic development, then, became derailed in Korea? Lim argues that the late nineteenth-century Korean economy still had little specialization and exchange. Land was unequally distributed between the privileged Yangban class and commoners. Very little technological improvements had occurred in agriculture and handicraft in previous centuries. Against this background, the sudden burst of foreign trade in the 1890's and after rapidly encouraged a taste for luxury goods and stimulated new commodity specialization and exchange, but with considerable price inflation. In the early years of Japanese rule, the monetization of the economy accelerated even more rapidly, but in the countryside the number of tenants rapidly increased as more land became concentrated in fewer hands (Lim, Chapter 2).

Meanwhile, according to Lim, the shortage of food grains in Japanese cities had sparked wide-spread disturbances, forcing home officials to import more food grains from the colonies. Toward that end, officials in Korea began spending for programs to introduce new rice seeds and to irrigate fertile land to raise rice yields. Lim argues that these large-scale capital projects diverted considerable resources from developing urban industry, and, because urban industry did not expand rapidly and attract more rural people to the cities to find work, villages had to accommodate the population growth that took place. As a result, the land tenure situation worsened, with more and more households sinking to tenant status. But Lim cannot have it both ways. The population growth spurt already underway certainly would have made income and wealth distribution more unequal in the short run anyway, whether the Japanese had fostered urban industrial expansion or had concentrated on agricultural development through a green revolution. The long-term distribution effects, however, might have been very different. Suppose the Japanese had pushed for the development of capital-intensive industries in the cities. Land ownership distribution still would have worsened! The real question that Lim should have asked is why the Japanese did not redistribute property rights in order to reduce tenancy when they tried to increase rice production in the 1920s.

By the 1930's the mono-cultural characteristics of agriculture already were self-evident (Lim, Chapter 5). As rice production rapidly grew, the percentage of rice exported to Japan rose more rapidly than ever before. As farmeres and tenants earned higher income from their rice sales, more households began consuming inferior food in order to sell more rice. Consequently, rice consumption per capita declined. As more households tried to farm rice, the buying and selling of land increased, and tenancy rose under these new circumstances. Rice farming required far more labor than for cultivating other crops, so that more women began to work in the fields (Lim, 268). The gap between poor and rich households also began to widen. In spite of the logic of Lim's argument, it is not clear from his evidence that the economic conditions of the poor declined in absolute income terms. In fact, the incomes of all households might have risen, but that of landlords and farmers rose more rapidly, to increase the inequality of income distribution. Furthermore, most rural households began to supplement their farm income in the 1930's with more off-farm earnings because of expanding employment opportunities in the cities, factories, and mines.

In the same vein, Kobayashi Hideo describes how a new industrial structure arose in Taiwan after the decision was made on September 9, 1938 to build power plants and metal-processing mills in the colony. The financial resources of both the colonial governor-general's office and of private capital in Japan were mobilized to establish new, large corporate holding companies to channel capital into the construction of new plant and machinery (Kobayashi Hideo, 1973). These actions diverted considerable labor and raw materials from Taiwan's traditional industries, so that a very lopsided economy began to emerge in the early 1940's. At the same time, the technology and management of this new economic sector remained very independent upon corporate links with capitalist enterprises in Japan. According to Kobayashi, financial subordination to Japan and a deformed economic structure became inter-related and made Taiwan extremely vulnerable to economic collapse when the war ended.

Turning to the theme of exploitation, which is widely stressed in these works, we find it paradoxical that while Japanese scholars have admitted that an agricultural revolution took place in colonies like Korea, they deny that this revolution provided any favorable benefits for the colonial peoples. Their logic for this argument is based upon the fact that economic policies originated from the metropolitan country and that colonial subjects had no voice in the matter. Moreover, these economic policies were designed to favor Japanese interests, and therefore their colonial subjects did not share the fruits of economic development. This argument differs from the findings of this volume, which show that colonial economic development produced mixed results for colonial subjects.

A specialist on modern Korean socio-economic history, Iinuma Jirō, has correctly defined an agricultural revolution as a rapid increase in output originating from technical improvements that raise the productivity of factor imputs. Yet, Iinuma sees that process in Korea as being associated with the penetration of Japanese capital, which supposedly produced the same destructive effects upon the local economy as English capitalism did upon nineteenth-century India (Kang Chae-ŏn and Iinuma Jirō, 1982, 95). Further, Iinuma contends that the Japanese decided to increase Korean rice production during the 1920's only to supply cheap grain for Japanese consumers. Therefore, this program did not really benefit Korean farmers. Why?

In order to attract private investment to this program, Iinuma points out that the governor-general's office lavishly provided local officals with public funds for promoting a green revolution. Although Korean landlords did take the lead to introduce new seeds and fertilizers and supervise irrigation and road improvements, Iinuma contends that their tenants bore the primary costs and received few benefits because their rent payments ran between 50 to 60 percent of rice production (Iinuma Jirō, 1892, 98). Iinuma never examines whether landlords extracted rent from other field crops, nor does he explain whether the same rent share applied for the first or second rice crop, or both. Although his study presents much evidence of the technical improvements taking place in Korean agriculture after 1910, he somehow concludes that Korean tenants and tenant-farmers did not really derive any benefit from this agricultural revolution because of the exploitative land tenure system that existed (Iinuma Jirō, 1981, pp. 183–197).

This same theme of exploitation is cited in other works, especially those dealing with Japanese wartime colonial policies, which mobilized human and material resources to support the military. A study of Japanese rural labor policies in Korea states that in May 1938 new laws were passed to mobilize women and old people for farming to replace the young men who had left for the mines and factories (Kang Sung-ŏn, 25-26). By these policies, the Japanese successfully maintained almost the same amount of land in cultivation between 1939 and 1942, and while rice output between 1942-1944 declined compared to the 1937-1941 years, it stabilized at around 3 million metric tons.

Where power becomes concentrated in the state and officials have both the law and security forces to justify their policies and can compel society to comply, some parties will naturally be able to exploit others and to gain an upper hand in contractual relationships. But the argument that these exploitative relations are primarily responsible for producing these state policies in the first place puts the cart before the horse. This kind of analysis is neither confirmed nor substantiated by sufficiently convincing evidence. Not all Japanese studies, however, have concluded that state policies, public and private organizations, and private socio-economic relations can be structured and linked only to economic relations. Preferring to clarify how a specific policy or institution actually worked rather than to envision a colonial system built solely upon exploitative private relationships, some scholars have produced findings more likely to be of value because of the new evidence sifted from archives about how colonial institutions and policies really evolved.

For example, Chiang Pin-kung's discussion of how the Japanese carried out their land-survey and land-tax reform in Taiwan between 1898 and 1902 is a model of clarity and exposition (Chiang, 1974). His conclusions conform to those already fairly well known. The land-tax reform greatly increased land tax revenue and made it possible for the Japanese to establish a new fiscal system based upon a reliable collection of assorted taxes. Second, this reform readjusted private property rights and institutionalized private land holdings. The Japanese recorded land deeds so that private transactions in land could be regularized and enforced with less risk and lower cost. Finally, this reform gave the state the capability of supervising the private property ownership system of land and reassessing land values to increase the land tax. Readers will be impressed by what a huge and difficult undertaking this proved to be for the Japanese and how this reform made it possible for private enterprise, both Japanese and Chinese, to develop rapidly thereafter.

Takashima Masaaki's description of how the branch of the Dai-ichi Bank of Tokyo and the Eighteenth National Bank functioned in Korea to finance railroads, experimental research stations, and enterprises distributing Japanese textile products provides another illuminating study of early Japanese national finance in Korea. The Eighteenth National Bank proved to be a very effective financial instrument for supplying working capital to Japanese foreign traders doing business in Korea, as well as for permitting them to build up large capital reserves (Takashima Masaaki, 1978, 261-305). Murakami Katsuhiko documents the same lending activities of the Dai-ichi Bank's branch in Seoul (Murakami Katsuhiko, 1973). Ko Sung-je narrates the activities of different banks in Korea between 1940 and 1945 and how they contributed to both Japanese and Korean economic development

(Ko Sung-je, 1972). Kobayashi Hideo provides a detailed account of how the Japanese Nitrogenous Fertilizer Corporation was established in Korea and greatly increased its capacity to produce fertilizer in that colony by 1942. We learn, for example, that the fertilizer produced from those plants located in North Korea sold at prices even below those in Japan (Kobayashi Hideo, 1973). Hirokazu Hirai has recently shown how the fiscal budgets for all five colonies were gradually consolidated into Japan's annual budget process in the 1920's. By 1938 all colonies were spending more from their budgets to support the national war effort (Hirokazu Hirai, 1982).

NEW ORIENTATIONS IN POST-WAR JAPANESE COLONIAL STUDIES

Although post-war Japanese scholarship about Japanese colonialism is of varying quality, a number of important works have broken new ground and raised some important questions about Japanese colonialism which have been neglected by the essays of this volume. The two most important of these new themes treated in these studies are the national liberation movements in the colonies and the social and cultural conditions of the Japanese who managed their colonies.

Documenting and interpreting the many protest movements of colonial subjects against their Japanese masters is a difficult task because the historical materials that shed light on how leaders organized anti-Japanese activities are scarce and not easy to use. The Taiwanese scholar Ng Yuzin Chiautong has produced so far the most informed and useful account of the short-lived Republic of Formosa, which was created just after the Ch'ing Court ceded Taiwan to Imperial Japan (Ng Yuzin Chiautong, 1970). This work shows how a handful of Taiwanese gentry from various parts of the island tried to cooperate and to resist the Japanese under the most adverse circumstances. A major reason for their failure was that these leaders did not have enough time and sufficient means to build a strong base for popular support of the new republic.

Other scholars have examined the role of women in various resistance movements in Korea and the influence of important scholars and patriots who wrote to encourage their middle-class professionals and activists to organize criticism and to resist Japanese policies (Kang Chae-ŏn and Iinuma Jirō, 1981, 1982). And to this same genre of literature we should also refer to the important chapters in Asada Kyōji's impressive 1973 account of popular resistance struggles in Taiwan, Korea, and Manchuria to Japanese rule.

The social conditions and intellectual trends as reflected in newspaper articles and editorials and the popular literature of the day are themes which Japanese scholars have just begun to examine but only superficially.[3] For example, the Mainichi Newspaper Syndicate in 1978 published three beautiful volumes of photographs about the life and social conditions in the colonies including Manchuria after 1932 (Mainichi Shimbunsha, 1978, 3 volumes). What is fascinating about these photos is how much they reveal of the small, privileged enclave of the Japanese colonial masters, who lived so apart from their colonial subjects, and the relatively untouched landscape of those subjects where they can be seen working and playing. Many photographs were obviously lifted from travel brochures of the 1920's and 1930's which had begun to circulate in Japanese cities to enchant and to entice the more wealthy to consider a relaxing and amusing vacation to a spa or hotel in one of the quiet colonies. But the photographs of South Sea Islanders, Koreans, and Chinese in their natural working and living conditions speak much for how life went on as usual, with little concern about who the new rulers really were.

What was it like for a young Japanese boy or girl to be raised and educated in the colonies? What was the cultural values of the colonial bureaucrats and their families? What scandals and moral outrages shocked the staid community of Japanese officials who busily went about their duties, trying to impress upon their subjects the importance of keeping to their proper place but still remaining friendly and intimate? The many photographs of young Koreans and Chinese studying in school or engaged in professional work attests to a large, emerging urban middle class. This new social class must have held ambivalent attitudes and opinions of their relationship with the Japanese, yet none of the social aspects of Japanese colonialism which I would call popular culture have yet been explored and examined. The materials exist. The questions have not yet been posed. These three Mainichi volumes vividly evoke a colonial past and suggest an agenda of social and cultural issues for future research.

[3] In 1978 a group of Japanese scholars, many of Chinese origin born in Taiwan, organized the Taiwan Kingendaishi Kenkyūkai [The Society for the Study of Taiwan's Modern History], which published the annual study titled *Taiwan kingendaishi kenkyū* [Historical Studies of Taiwan in Modern Times]. So far this annual study has appeared in 1978 (No. 1), 1979 (No. 2), and 1980 (No. 3). Its articles include studies of prominent Japanese like Tōgō Minoru and Mochiji Rokusaburō, of colonial protective policy for developing the Taiwan sugar industry, of Japanese control of the aboriginal mountain regions, and of important Taiwan writers and cultural-literary associations.

Bibliography for Chapter 12

I want to thank Mark Peattie, Peter Duus, Wonmo Dong, and Michiko Kiyohara for reading the initial drafts of this essay and providing critical remarks.

Asada, Kyōji. *Nihon teikokushugi to kyūshokuminchi jinushisei* [The Old Colonial Landlord System and Japanese Imperialism] (Tokyo: Ochanomizu Shobō, 1968).

Asada, Kyōji. *Nihon teikokushugika no minzoku kakumei undō* [National Revolutionary Movements under Japanese Imperialism] (Tokyo: Miraisha, 1973).

Asada, Kyōji. "Nihon shokuminshi kenkyū no genjō to mondaiten" [The Current Status and Issues of Research on the History of Japanese Colonialism], *Rekishi hyōron* [The Historical Review] 300 (April 1975), pp. 178-198.

Asada, Kyōji. "Nihon shokuminshi kenkyū no kadai to hohō" [Themes and Methods of Research in Japanese Colonial History], in *Rekishi hyōron* [The Historical Review] 308 (December 1975), pp. 63-86.

Asada, Kyōji. "Saikin ni okeru Nihon shokuminshi kenkyū no mondai ten" [Some Issues in Recent Japanese Colonial Historical Studies], in *Shakai keizai shigaku* [The Journal of Social-Economic History] 42:3 (1976), pp. 89-95.

Asada, Kyōji. "Nihon shokuminshi kenkyū no seika to kadai" [Achievements and Issues in Studies of Japanese Colonial History], pp. 50-57, in Chihōshu Kenkyū Kyōgikai (edit.), *Nihonshi bunken nenkan* [Yearbook of Written Materials on Japanese History] (Kashiwa Shobō, 1979).

Chiang Pin-kung. *Taiwan chisō kaisei no kenkyū* [A Study of the Taiwan Land Tax Reform] (Tokyo: Tōkyō Daigaku Shuppankai, 1974).

Fujii, Shōichi. "Nichi-Rō sensō" [The Japanese-Russian War], in *Iwanami Kōza, Nihon rekishi: gendai* [Japanese History: The Modern Period], Vol. 18 (Tokyo: Iwanami Shoten, 1963), pp. 111-152.

Fujimura, Michio. "Nihon Teikokushugi no seiritsu" [The Establishment of Japanese Imperialism], in Nihon Rekishigakkai (comp.),

Nihonshi no mondaiten [Issues in Japanese History] (Tokyo: Yoshikawa Kōbunkan, 1965), pp. 332-349.

Harada, Katsumasa. "Chōsen heigō to shoki no shokuminchi keiei" [The Annexation of Korea], in *Iwanami Kōza, Nihon rekishi: gendai,* Vol. 18 (Tokyo: Iwanami Shoten, 1963), pp. 197-244.

Haruyama Meitetsu and Wakabayashi Masahiro, *Nihon shokuminshugi no seijiteki tenkai: 1895-1934* [The Political Development of Japanese Colonialism: 1895-1934] (Tokyo: Ajiya Seikei Gakkai, 1980) p. 230.

Hirai, Hirokazu. "Nihon shokuminchi zaisei no tenkai to kōzō" [The Evolution and Structure of Financial Policies in Japan's Colonies], *Shakai keiza shigaku* [The Journal of Social-Economic History] 47:6, 1982, 48-70.

Inoue, Kiyoshi. *Nihon teikokushugi no keisei* [The Formation of Japanese Imperialism] (Tokyo: Iwanami Shoten, 1968).

Kang Chae-ŏn and Iinuma, Jirō (editors). *Kindai Chōsen no shakai to shisō* [Society and Thought in Modern Korea] (Tokyo: Miraisha, 1981).

Kang Chae-ŏn and Iinuma, Jirō (editors). *Shokuminchiki Chōsen no shakai to teikō* [Society and Resistance in Korea under Japanese Colonial Rule] (Tokyo: Miraisha, 1982).

Kang Sung-ŭn. "Senjika Nihon teikokushugi no Chōsen nōson rōdōryoku shūdatsu seisaku" [The Policy of Expropriating Korean Village Labor Power under Japanese Imperialism in World War II), in *Rekishi hyōron* [The Historical Review] 355 (Nov. 1979), pp. 24-42.

Ko Sung-je. *Shokuminchi kin'yū seisaku no shiteki bunseki* [An Historical Analysis of Colonial Financial Policies] (Tokyo: Ochanomizu Shobo, 1972).

Kobayashi, Hideo. "1930-nendai kōhanki irai no Taiwan kōgyōka seisaku ni tsuite" [Industrialization of Taiwan in the Late 1930's], in *Tochi seido shigaku* [The Journal of Agrarian History] 16:1, October 1973, 21-42.

Kobayashi, Hideo. "1930-nendai Nihon Chisso Hiryō Kabushiki Kaisha no Chōsen e shinshutsu ni tsuite" [The Japanese Nigrogenous Fertilizer Company's Penetration of Korea in the 1930's], in Yamada Hideo (editor), *Shokuminchi keizaishi no shomondai* [Issues in Colonial Economic History] (Tokyo: Ajiya Keizai Kenkyūjo, 1973), pp. 139-189.

Kō Se-kai. *Nihon tōchika no Taiwan* [Formosa under Japanese Rule] (Tokyo: Tōkyō Daigaku Shuppankai, 1972).

Lim Byon-yun. *Shokuminchi ni okeru shōgyōteki nōgyō no tenkai* [Evolution of Commercialized Agriculture in a Colony] (Tokyo: Tō-kyō Daigaku Shuppan Kai, 1971).

Maejima, Shōzō. *Nihon teikokushugi to gikai* [The Diet and Japanese Imperialism] (Tokyo: Mineruba Shobō, 1976).

Mainichi Shimbunsha. *Bessatsu ichiokunin no Shōwashi: Nihon shoku-minshi*; Vol. I, *Chōsen*; Vol. II, *Manshū*; Vol. III, *Taiwan, Nan'yō, Karafuto* [Special Edition of Shōwa History for 100 Million People: Japan's Colonial Territories: Vol. I, Korea; II, Manchuria; III, Taiwan, South Sea Island, Karafuto] (Tokyo: Mainichi Shimbunsha, 1978).

Matsukuma, Norihito. "Teikokushugi fukkatsu no gainen ni tsuite" [The Concept of the Revival of Imperialism], in *Seiji kenkyū* [Political Studies] 10:11 (March 1963).

Murakami, Katsuhiko. "Dai Ichi Ginkō Chōsen shiten to shokumin-chi kin'yū" [The Korean Branch of the Dai-ichi Bank and Colonial Finance], in *Tochi seido shigaku* [The Journal of Agrarian History] 16:1 (October 1973), pp. 43-56.

Nasu, Hiroshi. *Teikokushugi seiritsuki no tennōsei: Meiji kōki seijishi* [The Emperor System in the Period of the Formation of Imperialism: Political History in the Latter Half of the Meiji Period] (Nagoya: Fūbaisha, 1974).

Ng Yuzin Chiautong. *Taiwan minshukoku no kenkyū* [A Study of the Republic of Formosa] (Tokyo: Tōkyō Daigaku Shuppankai, 1970).

Ng, Yuzin Chiautong. *Taiwan Sōtokufu* [The Taiwan Governor-General Office] (Tokyo: Kyoikusha, 1981).

Ono, Yoshihiko. "Nihon teikokushugi fukkatsu no gendankai" [The Current Stage of Revival of Japanese Imperialism], in *Gendai Nihon no keizai to seiji* [The Economy and Polity of Modern Japan], vol. 4 (Tokyo: Ōtsuki Shoten, 1957).

Satō, Noboru. *Gendai teikokushugi no kōzō kaikaku* [The Structural Reform of Modern Japanese Imperialism] (Tokyo: Aoki Shoten, 1961).

Shiga, Yoshio. *Nihon Teikokushugi ni tsuite* [Japanese Imperialism] (Tōkyō: San'ichi Shobō, 1972).

Taiwan Kingendaishi Kenkyūkai (edit.). *Taiwan kingendaishi kenkyū* [Historical Studies of Taiwan in Modern Times], No. 1 (1978), No. 2 (1979), No. 3 (1980).

Takashima, Masaaki. *Chōsen ni okeru shokuminchi kin'yūshi no kenkyū* [Studies of the History of Colonial Finance in Korea] (Tokyo: Ōhara Shinseisha, 1978).

Tanaka, Shin'ichi. "Kankoku zaisei seiri ni okeru chōzei taichō seibi ni tsuite" [Adjustment of the Tax Collection Account Book When

Japan Supervised Korea's Public Finances], *Tochi seido shigaku* [The Journal of Agrarian History] 16:3 (Spring 1974), pp. 1-20.

To Shōgen (T'u Chao-yen). *Nihon teikokushugika no Taiwan* [Taiwan under Japanese Imperialism] (Tokyo: Tōkyō Daigaku Shuppankai, 1975).

Yamabe, Kentarō. "Nihon teikokushugi to shokuminchi" [Japanese Imperialism and Colonialism], in *Iwanami Kōza, Nihon rekishi* [Japanese History], Vol. 19, pp. 205-245 (Tokyo: Iwanami Shoten, 1963).

CHAPTER 13

The Legacy of Japanese Colonialism in Korea

Bruce Cumings

From time to time an American journalist will find a way to travel to North Korea and, amid the usual humorous asides about a country that strikes Americans as a weird never-never land, the journalist will write that North Koreans have this amazing national myth about resistance to the Japanese. Of course, they talk about resisting the Yankees as well, but throughout the country one finds monument after monument to the anti-Japanese struggle, thirty-five years after the Japanese quit Korea. Kim Il Sung, it is said, commanded this movement; all military and political life is patterned after the resistance. Clearly, this is the North Korean version of a myth of national foundation.

Americans have much more access to South Korea, but there one will not hear much talk about the Japanese period. When asked, Koreans will say the Japanese were terrible, made Koreans speak their language, took away their names. But one does not hear much about a resistance movement. The end of the colonial period and the foundation of the Republic of Korea, with a three-year break for an American Occupation, also seem to get passed over fairly quickly, for it is a murky period. After a while one might get around to speaking Japanese with Koreans in the South, and find that they warm quickly to this sort of exchange, some of them preferring to speak Japanese rather than their native Korean. Or, one can note the bustle in areas where Japanese publications are sold, and in the 1970's the quickly rising popularity of Japanese language study. An older and more knowledgeable traveler will observe that Korean schoolboys bear a strange resemblance to Japanese students of an earlier era, with their black uniforms and shaved heads. A truly sophisticated observer might note that the capitol building in Seoul is not simply in the style of colonial architecture the world over, but when seen from the air is shaped like the first of the two characters that we translate as "Japan."

Our same American might fret about the apparent lack of American influence in either Korea. After all, the period of heavy American involvement in Korea now matches the entire tenure of Japanese colonialism (36 years). Of course, there is the flotsam and jetsam of cultural influence: bell-bottom pants, pop music, lots of English loan words. But our most cherished models—let us say, free elections, liberal democracy, basic human and political rights—seem not to have taken hold. No, it was Japan's impact that lasted and that in a variety of ways has structured both halves of postwar Korea.

In politics we observe that in the North, Kim Il Sung has ruled since 1946 and that the core of the leadership continues to come almost exclusively from the ranks of Kim's few hundred allies from the days of the resistance in Manchuria.[1] In the South, it is only in 1980 that a leader (Chon Doo Hwan) has emerged who is not associated with the Japanese era. Syngman Rhee, first President of the Republic of Korea, was an anti-Japanese patriot who presided over a bureaucracy and a military that had been trained almost entirely by the Japanese. Chang Myŏn, who ruled briefly in 1960-1961, had elite status and took a Japanese name during the latter years of colonial rule,[2] and Park Chung Hee had been an officer in the Japanese Kwantung Army. The influence of the colonial period, of course, runs much deeper than these individual leaders.

From 1945 to 1980 the leading officers of the South Korean military came largely from those individuals who, in the 1940's, were trained in Manchurian and Japanese military academies.[3] The big central bureaucracy in Seoul was not only carried over virtually intact after 1945, but American Occupation authorities usually required that Koreans have experience in the colonial apparatus before employing them.[4] Such agencies as the Oriental Development Company simply had their names changed (in this case to the New Korea Company), and Americans found that they had to use Japanese systems of recruitment to staff the bureaucracy. Even such a quintessentially American institution as free elections had to be conducted, in the first instance in 1946, according to colonial rules and procedures. Whether

---

[1] See Dae-Sook Suh, "Communist Party Leadership," in Dae-Sook Suh and Chae-Jin Lee, *Political Leadership in Korea* (Seattle: University of Washington Press, 1976), pp. 159-191.

[2] See biography section, Keijō Nippōsha, *Chōsen nenkan 1945* [Korean Yearbook, 1945] (Seoul, 1945), p. 393.

[3] Chŏnsa p'yŏnch'an wiwŏnhoe, Han'guk chŏnjaeng-sa [History of the Korean War], V. 1, *Haebang kwa kŏn'gun* [Liberation and the Establishment of the Army] (Seoul, Kukpang-bu, 1967), pp. 247-303.

[4] Bruce Cumings, *The Origins of the Korean War*, I (Princeton: Princeton University Press, 1981), ch. 5.

it was in the military, the bureaucracy, or the polity, Americans during the Occupation found themselves playing midwife to a Japanese gestation, rather than bringing forth their own Korean progeny.

Both Korean states have had strong bureaucracies at the center and relatively weak political impulses flowing up from the periphery. In the North there is a peculiar mixture of a highly organized top-down politics, with a Maoist-style "mass line" from the bottom up; in the South the strong leaders like Park stilled participation at the lower reaches (community councils, etc.) very quickly. Both Korean states (the North since 1945, the South since 1961) have utilized this strong state to foster economic development, a pattern first instituted by the Japanese. Both states have relied on nationally organized and centrally responsive police and intelligence structures as instruments of rule. The Japanese in both Korea and Taiwan, as Professor Chen's paper shows, relied on the national police as the key element of their ruling apparatus.

It might even be said that the Japanese period structured the postwar political spectrum, and particularly the opposition. In the North there has been no opposition since 1946, although factional conflicts that developed in the 1950's had cleavage lines structured by the region of Northeast Asia in which the factions resisted the Japanese: that is, the Yenan, Soviet, Kapsan, and "domestic" factions.[5] In the South the opposition from 1945 to 1960, and from 1961 to 1980, traced its origin to notables like Kim Sŏng-su and Yun Po-sŏn, who formed the Korean Democratic Party in September 1945. The key elements in this party came from the Chŏlla provinces, a rich rice-producing region and, during the colonial period, the home of a new group of so-called landlord-entrepreneurs who became active in the 1920's in cultural, educational, and political activities.[6] (These are the "cultural nationalists" that Dr. Robinson discusses.) Finally, there was another sort of opposition that also had a Japanese gestation. During the period 1945-1950 widespread disorders dotted South Korea: massive worker and peasant uprisings in several provinces in the autumn of 1946; major rebellions leading to guerrilla movements on Cheju Island and in the Chŏlla and Kyŏngsang Provinces in the period 1948-1950. As I have argued elsewhere, such disorders were led by Koreans who had achieved different social and political status during the latter years of colonial rule. As the Japanese mobilized Koreans for the war effort or for industrialization, millions of Koreans

[5] Robert Scalapino and Chong-sik Lee, *Communism in Korea*, I (Berkeley: University of California Press, 1972), ch. 7.

[6] Cho Ki-jun, *Han'guk kiŏpga-sa* [History of Korean Entrepreneurs] (Seoul: Pag'yong-sa, 1973).

went to work in Manchuria, Japan, or northern Korean industry. In 1945, when the colonial edifice abruptly shattered, they all came home. But they were no longer the same people. Peasants before, worker-peasants or peasant-soldiers now, they had changed and adapted imperfectly to what they found upon their return. Some sought revenge against those who had aided the Japanese; many more sought alternative political and social institutions. This, too, was a Japanese legacy and played a role in the origins of the Korean War.[7]

Today both Koreas have been remarkably successful in economic development based upon two entirely different models. The socialist North has always had growth rates among the highest in the communist world; it has one of the few dynamic collective agricultures; and its cities impress foreign travelers as being on a par with urban life in Eastern Europe. The capitalist South has been *the* model of export-led development and rapidly rising GNP in a Third World setting. Between 1965 to 1978 the South had the lowest capital-to-output ratio in the world (2.2),[8] which also shows extraordinary high productivity. Few analysts, however, date the origins of such development before 1960. But the colonial period played an undeniable role in placing Korea above most Third World nations by 1945. Looking back over Korea's development in this century, one can see rapid spurts in the first two decades, the third decade, and the sixth and seventh decades. The depression and two wars (the Pacific and the Korean) account for much of the backsliding in between. This is not to say that Koreans owe the Japanese anything for developing or modernizing their country. It is more correct to emphasize that Korea's capitalist revolution began—and got a long running start—during the colonial period, and, like capitalism everywhere, it moved forward in waves of creation and destruction that transformed old Korea.

This brief summary of some aspects of Korea's colonial legacy represents an outsider's judgments. Nothing about the colonial period makes easy reading for Koreans, and this analysis is undoubtedly no exception. This collective revulsion at the memory of the colonial experience explains why there is so little serious research by Koreans on the period, and why one Korea indulges in a myth that everyone

[7] Bruce Cumings, "Political Participation in Liberated Korea: Mobilization and Revolt in the Kyŏngsang Provinces, 1945-1950," in *Journal of Korean Studies*, v. 1 (1979), pp. 163-203; see also John Merrill, "The Cheju-do Rebellion," in *Journal of Korean Studies*, v. 2 (1980).

[8] U.S. Central Intelligence Agency, "Korea: The Economic Race Between the North and the South," in ER78-10008 (January 1978), p. 2; see also various articles on North Korea by Henry Scott-Stokes, *The New York Times*, July, 1980.

resisted and the other in a myth that no one collaborated. This is why one encounters the curious pattern of surface rejection *in toto* of everything that the Japanese did, combined with *de facto* adoption of many Japanese practices. Korea's march to modernity coincided with imperial aggression and colonial exploitation: this is hard enough for any people to take. But aggression and exploitation also coincided with fairly remarkable development and a learning-by-doing experience of how education, military, polity, and economy can be modernized. Thus the Japanese set up a love-hate conflict that has gnawed at the Korean national identity ever since.

Professor Etō remarks that Japan's vices were no different than those of European colonists. This may be true, but its virtues were quite different. There was no legitimizing myth that the Japanese could make stick. They were not good tutors to teach their subjects how to achieve the goal of independence, as at least some Filipinos thought was true of American colonialism. They were not good exemplars of liberal democracy, as at least some thought that the British were in India. The virtues that the Japanese shared were hard to justify philosophically, but easy to adopt practically: military success, the uses of a strong state, rapid economic development, modern industrial structure. Thus Koreans greeted liberation in 1945 with a profound rejection of Japanese colonialism, yet have never been able to rid themselves of its Janus-faced influence.

Some Reflections on Japanese Imperialsim

Japan's imperial experience was different from that of the West in several fundamental respects: it was *late* in world time; it involved the colonization of *contiguous* territory; it involved the location of industry and an infrastructure of communications and transportation *in* the colonies, bringing industry to the labor and raw materials, rather than vice-versa; finally, it was accomplished by a country that always saw itself as *dis*advantaged and *threatened* by more advanced countries. Japan was "weak and puny," Professor Etō says, and this Japanese self-perception affected their colonial enterprise throughout. All of these characteristics made themselves felt most strongly in Korea, the closest and perhaps strategically the most important of Japan's possessions.

Japan entered upon colonization late in world colonial development, in the context of a globe with hundreds of years of colonial experience and where, as King Leopold said three years before the Meiji Restoration, "the world has been pretty well pillaged already." With most of the good colonial territories already spoken for, and with Western powers knocking at her door, Japan had little space for maneuver. Furthermore, for several decades Japan faced the possibility of becoming a dependency, perhaps even a colony, of one of the Western powers. With imperial attention mostly focused on China and its market of supposedly vast dimensions, however, Japan got what E. H. Norman called a "breathing space" within which to mobilize its resources and to resist the West. Her success was manifest in victories over China and Russia within the decade 1895 to 1905, but that should not blind us to Japan's perception of her position as poised between autonomy and dependence in a highly competitive world system, nor to the very real threats posed by the West. While the British and the Americans marveled at Japanese industrial and military prowess at the turn of the century, the Kaiser sent his famous "yellow peril" mural to the Tsar, and the French worried about Japanese skills being tied to a vast pool of Chinese labor, posing a dire threat to the West.[9] In such circumstances the Japanese were hardly prone to worry about the sensitivities of Taiwanese or Koreans, but rather saw them as resources to be deployed in a global struggle; and, of course, Japan never lacked for Westerners (including socialists like Sydney and Beatrice Webb, and hardy Americans like Theodore Roosevelt)[10] who were quick to justify Japanese aggression.

The relative lateness of this endeavor imparted several characteristics to it: first, a post-haste, anticipatory quality to colonial planning; second, an extraordinary interest in and mimicking of previous colonial experience; third, a rather quick anachronism to the whole enterprise; and, last, the simple fact that Japan had little choice but to colonize its contiguous neighbors.

Many have spoken of Japan's defensive reform and industrialization after 1868, and so it was with Japan's imperial expansion: aggressive to Taiwanese and Koreans, it looked defensive to Japanese planners in a predatory world. And, like reform at home, the colonial effort included an aspect which was anticipatory, preconceived and planned. The characteristic figure in this architectonic endeavor was therefore not an adventurous Cecil Rhodes type, but an administrator

[9] Jean-Pierre Lehmann, *The Image of Japan: From Feudal Isolation to World Power, 1850-1905* (London: George Allen & Unwin, 1978), p. 178.

[10] On a 1911 trip to the Orient, Beatrice found Koreans to be "a horrid race," but lauded Japan as a model for the coming socialist state (!). J. M. Winter, "The Webbs and the Non-White: A Case of Socialist Racialism," in *Journal of Contemporary History*, 9:1 (January 1974), pp. 181-192. Theodore Roosevelt's views on Japan and Korea were influenced by George Kennan, elder cousin to our George Kennan, a man who thought that the Japanese would play a civilizing role in Korea.

and planner like Gotō Shimpei. Ever watchful of the previous behavior of the West, colonial planners would both mimic the West and seek to avoid its errors (as Robinson's paper demonstrates). When one has a real model to follow, one can both copy and anticipate future developments. Thus, Japanese bureaucrats intervened at home with social schemes designed to nip in the bud the agitation of a newborn working class,[11] and intervened abroad to steam off pressure in the colonies by giving certain moderates a voice (while always mindful not to go too far as, in Japanese eyes, the British had in India). Thus, whether it was Itō Hirobumi discovering the secret of the German state, a colonial administrator studying French policies of assimilation, or an architect designing a railroad station in the classic style for Seoul or Harbin, Japanese behavior mirrored the European experience.

There was also something anachronistic about Japanese imperialism, perhaps not in the seizure of Taiwan, but certainly by 1910 in the annexation of Korea and *a fortiori* in 1931 with the invasion of Manchuria. Japan since the 1880's has always seemed in some vague way to be about twenty years behind European and American developments, and therefore to be persisting in the lathered pursuit of things of which the West was tiring. By 1910 strong anti-imperialist movements had developed in England and America, and shortly thereafter Woodrow Wilson not only called for self-determination in the colonies but pursued an American neo-imperialism that envisioned organizing great spaces in the world for free trade and competition, thereby branding the unilateral possession of colonial territory as outmoded or immoral, or both.[12] The enlightened powers, Wilson thought, should follow the League of Nations mandate system, holding colonies in trust. For this reason, some at the time, like Syngman Rhee, urged that Korea become a mandate under the United States.

Another great power, Russia, emerged from World War I with an equally potent idea: self-determination and national revolution for colonial peoples. Whether it was Lenin or Wilson, both had the effect of changing the rules of the game for latecomers like Japan. The swashbuckling, sword-carrying colonist suddenly looked to the West like an artifact in a museum. Within Japan pressure from liberals and socialists was also manifest, and in Korea socialist and communist

[11] Kenneth B. Pyle, "Advantages of Followership: German Economics and Japanese Bureaucrats, 1890-1925," in *Journal of Japanese Studies*, v. 1. no. 1 (Autumn 1974), 127-164.

[12] Gordon Levin, Jr., *Woodrow Wilson and World Politics* (London: Oxford University Press, 1968), pp. 1-9, 236-251.

groups soon emerged after the 1919 independence uprisings. For Japan this unanticipated anti-imperialism was a nasty shock. Just as it marched out to join the "progressive" nations with its newly acquired accoutrement of colonies, the established colonial powers changed the rules and condemned Japan for pursuing the backward ideas of the nineteenth century. These and other pressures combined to produce under Hara Kei a reform movement in the colonies, but also, and more importantly, I think, a dogged determination to hold onto the Japanese sphere, irrespective of events in the West.

In order to acquire colonies in the first place, Japan had to maximize its comparative advantages by seeking territory close to home. The West, always stretched a bit in East Asia, could be thwarted in the near reaches of Japan. Thus, unlike virtually any other colonial power, Japan colonized countries that nearly touched its borders (the Nan'yō was clearly the exception, of course). This then made feasible a tight, integral linking of the colonial territories to the metropole. Contiguity could also facilitate the settling of colonial migrants, especially an insular, homogenous people who abhor distance from the homeland. It also made possible extraordinarily rapid exchange-time in market relations. Japan wasted no time in enhancing this possibility through laying railroads, opening ports, and making heavy investments in communications sectors. Contiguity maximized control close to home, so that anti-colonial resisters had to flee abroad; what guerrillas existed (or subsisted) within the Japanese sphere by the 1930's did so in remote regions, such as the wild Sino-Korean border areas. The rest fled into central China, to the Soviet Union, or gave up the struggle entirely. The difference with, say, France in Vietnam, is obvious. Japan's lateral expansion also meant that the military, in the form of a land army resident in the colony, was the preferable coercive force—not a navy or a tiny cadre of colonial ministers à la England. Edward Chen documents the uses of this military force in Taiwan and Korea, and Mark Peattie notes the appropriateness of Hannah Arendt's continental expansion formulation for the case of Japan. One of Arendt's points, additionally, was that empires that expand by using armies to annex contiguous territory and to control foreign populations tend to be more repressive.

Unfortunately for Japan, her nearby territories were not like those in Africa, thinly populated by tribes and possessing little or no claim to recognized nation-state territorial status. Places like Taiwan were heavily populated, and places like Korea were both heavily populated *and* well recognized for having a unitary state stretching back more than a milennium. Japan could not claim that it had carved a new nation out of the wilderness; instead it had to destroy the Yi Dynasty, which had stood for five hundred years, and put an end to an ancient nation rather than begin to forge a new one. Thus Japan's attempt at legitimating the colonial enterprise in Korea always struck Koreans as absurd. Koreans had nothing for which to thank them and the liquidation of Korean sovereignty for which to hate them, along with their Korean collaborators. Japan's colonization of Korea therefore is much more comparable to, say, the historical relationship between England and Ireland,[13] or Germany and Poland, than it is to European colonization in Africa or Southeast Asia. Korea's political, economic, and social level was not so far from Japan's as to justify a civilizing colonial mission. Japan colonized a state, not a people, *substituting* for a state that had long considered itself superior (in the Confucian way of looking at things) to the "island barbarians" from Japan.

A political force that lacks in authority and legitimacy uses coercion, and Japan was no different. Yet in Korea the colonial power emphasized not only military and police forms of control, but also the development of the peninsula under strong state auspices. This was particularly true after the depression, when Japan utilized a "mighty trio" of state organization, central banks, and *zaibatsu* conglomerates to industrialize Korea and parts of manchuria.[14] The colonial state in Korea bulked much larger in the economy than in Taiwan, as shown by figures on government capital formation in the Mizoguchi and Yamamoto article; much like its role in the decades after Meiji, the state substituted for an absent or at most incipient entrepreneurial class. David Landes writes that, in Japan,

> It was the State that conceived modernization as a goal and industrialization as a means, that gave birth to the new economy in haste and pushed it unrelentingly as an ambitious mother her child prodigy. And though the child grew and developed its own resources, it never overcame the deformity imposed by this forced nurture.[15]

The deformations were even more marked when such a role for the state was imposed on Korea, a state that stood above and apart from a society that had not yet reached Japan's level of social, political, and economic development. Thus a highly articulated, disciplined,

---

[13] See for comparison Michael Hechter, *Internal Colonialism: The Celtic Fringe in British National Development, 1536-1966* (Berkeley: University of California Press, 1975).

[14] E. B. Schumpeter, ed., *The Industrialization of Japan and Manchukuo, 1930-1940* (New York: The MacMillan Co., 1940).

[15] David Landes, "Japan and Europe: Contrasts in Industrialization," in William W. Lockwood, ed., *The State and Economic Enterprise in Japan* (Princeton: Princeton University Press, 1965), p. 182.

penetrating colonial bureaucracy substituted both for the traditional Yi Dynasty and for indigenous groups and classes that under "normal" conditions would have accomplished Korean development themselves. When a foreign bureaucracy replaces an indigenous one, or when foreign entrepreneurs run roughshod over indigenous enterprise, or when colonial education replaces Confucian teaching, the act of substitution rather than creation makes colonization that much more difficult to justify in the eyes of the colonized.

The colonial state replaced an old weak state, held society at bay, so to speak. This experience goes a long way toward explaining the subsequent (post 1945) pronounced centralization of both North and South Korea, and it has certainly provided a model for state-directed development in the South since 1961.

COLONIAL INDUSTRIALIZATION

Japan is the only colonial power to have located various heavy industries—steel, chemicals, hydro-electric power—in its colonies, a remarkable fact when considered comparatively. They were built during the second grand phase of Japanese industrialization and probably accounted for about a quarter of Japan's industrial base by 1945.[16] Even today China's industry remains skewed toward the northeast, and since 1945 North Korea has always been the most industrialized socialist state in Asia, imparting an urban and industrial aspect to Korean socialism that accounts for many of the differences between it and the more rural socialist China.

The concern for industry and the contiguity of Korea led Japan to lay an extensive network of railways in the colony, so that by 1945 Korea had the most developed rail system in Asia outside of Japan. In the early 1940's Korean rails carried almost fifty percent as much traffic as in all of China.[17] By 1945 only the remote central portion of the east coast and the wild regions along the Sino-Korean border were untouched by rails. Along with the development of roads and ports, this infrastructure put Korea substantially ahead of other developing countries in 1945 (something almost always forgotten in discussing economic development in North and South Korea in the post-Korean War era). The extensive transportation infrastructure also facilitated Japanese, and subsequently Korean, political control. The strength of the southern infrastructure, including the strong central state, helps to explain why southern Korea (unlike southern Vietnam)

[16] Schumpeter, *op.cit.*

[17] Cumings, *Origins of the Korean War* (Princeton: Princeton University Press, 1981), ch. one. See Note No. 27 for full citation.

developed no strongly rooted insurgency in the late 1940's. Railroad and road length per square mile was much higher in Korea than in Vietnam or China.

The Mizoguchi and Yamamoto essay documents the extraordinary expenditure levels for infrastructure in Korea as compared to Taiwan: sixty to eighty percent of state capital formation in Korea, compared to about fifty percent on the average in Taiwan. Further, Peter Duus's concern with infrastructure does indeed add weight to an economic interpretation of Japanese imperialism. The colonial state provided Japanese entrepreneurs with facilities that they could never imagine funding themselves: not simply railroads, which greatly cheapened transport costs, but also stable currency, credit and banking facilities, uniform weights and measures, and perhaps above all the rule of law, which along with physical structures like the railways provided a basis for commercial and industrial activity that enabled a stable and predictable investment environment.

All this was not a matter of capitalists dictating to the state, as Duus points out; it also involved more than simply the "context of economic thinking" in Japan. The development of colonial infra-structure was part and parcel of Japan's competition with more ad-vanced powers in the world economy. Lacking large spaces to or-ganize, Japan concentrated on her contiguous territory and sought to carve out its own sphere. This was much more pronounced in the 1930's, when almost all nations repudiated free trade and erected pro-tectionist barriers to the flow of commerce. One can mark the change in Japan's position in the world economy by comparing its free trade position in, say, 1929, with the autarkic rationale advocated by the *Asahi Shimbun* for colonial industrialization in the mid-1930's:[18]

> The chief object of a planned economy is successful competition in world markets through a complete industrialization of the country . . . in the execution of (the) standardization of national life which is quite economic in nature, some limitation may be placed upon the laissez faire policy, but that is a world-wide tendency, and even the U.S. of America has not been free from the influence. . . . This is not to be taken as the harbinger of a fascist regime.

Therefore, industrialization of the colonies provided—or so it seemed until 1945—a way out for Japan in the sharp economic competition that began with and followed upon the depression. Thus, while Peat-tie is certainly correct in seeing the period 1931-1945 as one in which Japan rejected the European colonial pattern, it was also a time when

---

[18] Asahi Shimbun, *Present-Day Nippon* (Tokyo, 1936), p. 23.

the increasing world trend toward economic blocs made abandonment of the old colonial forms by Japan a not unreasonable change.
When Japan pursued free trade policies abroad and liberalism at home
in the 1920's, an atmosphere of greater accommodation to the interests of colonial peoples was possible in Korea. But when protectionism stalked the world in the 1930's, Japan went authoritarian at home
and subjected Korea to an intense, regimented, forced-draft colonialism. This fact reinforces the point that Japanese colonialism had peculiar characteristics because of Japan's inferior position in the world
system and because it saw colonies as adjuncts of competition with
the rest of the world. In any case, we can appreciate how global
disturbances for Japan quickly reverberated throughout its colonies.

Quite apart from its rationale for industrializing Korea and Manchukuo, we can acknowledge how different were Japan's relations to
its colonies from the usual relationship between metropolitan and
underdeveloped nations. Most developmental theory holds that colonies are in some way *de*-developed (in Andre Gunder Frank's phrase,
the development of underdevelopment).[19] Although there was much
distortion of the infrastructure to serve metropolitan needs, the fact
remains that there is something hard and enduring about factories
and railroads, leading, in Korea, to what we might call *overdevelop-
ment*. That is, the infrastructure in 1945 bore little relationship to
Korean society. During the 1930's and early 1940's Korean groups
and classes were largely excluded from all of the modernizing activity, except as laborers or low-level technicians and bureaucrats. Paid-
up capital in the big enterprises was always ninety percent or more
Japanese. Developed in the interests of the core, the structure was
located in a peripheral society that had not changed or developed at
the same rate. Once the structure was wrenched from Japan, both
North and South Korea had to invest much time and effort in developing the appropriate human resources to use that structure to
their own ends.

The period from 1935 to 1945 was when Korea's industrial revolution began and it produced the usual characteristics: uprooting of
peasants from the land, the emergence of a working class, widespread
population mobility and urbanization. Because the Japanese accomplished industrialization from above, the social change accompanying
this revolution was greatest in the lower reaches of society. In other
words, Korean labor was what was needed, and the Japanese got it
mostly in Korea's southern, rice-producing, populous provinces. Very

[19] Andre Gunder Frank, *Capitalism and Underdevelopment in Latin America* (New York:
Monthly Review Press, 1969), pp. 1-13.

large population movements occurred within and without Korea in this period. Irene Taeuber estimated that by 1945 as much as 11.6 percent of the Korean population was outside Korea, most of it in Japan and Manchukuo, and that fully 20 percent of all Koreans were residing abroad or in a province other than their native one. This massive redeployment of population produced severe dislocations of Korean society because population mobility had historically been very low. In this period Korean peasants first became uprooted from their villages and entered industry or urban life, or both, in Japan, Manchukuo, and northern Korea. As mentioned earlier, much of this uprooted population returned to their native homes after liberation to participate in the politics of postwar Korea.

SOCIAL DYNAMICS OF THE COLONIAL REGIME

We also should remember that the Japanese and Korean societies which confronted each other after 1905 were very different. Put simply, Japan emerged out of a feudal past, whereas Korea, unlike Japan but like China, had an agrarian-bureaucratic past. Unlike Japan, Korea did not develop an extensive commercialization of agriculture before the nineteenth century, and had an even stronger landed gentry than China. Unlike Japan, Korea did not benefit from competition among feudal domains (there were none), nor did a flourishing commerce develop in the cities, as it did in places like Osaka and Edo. Korea had a centralized and ostensibly strong bureaucracy, but the Yi was in fact a relatively weak state which competed with the aristocracy for surplus resources and often lost out.[20] Like the Chinese bureaucracy, this state was weak at the periphery so that peasant rebellions occurred periodically. The landed class exercised an hegemony of very long-standing in the nineteenth century. Relying on the bureaucracy, tradition, and coercion to maintain its dominance, this class so inhibited commercialization that it was only incipient in the eighteenth century and had largely disappeared by the time Japan arrived.[21]

Once they had established colonial rule, the Japanese found it advantageous to use Korean landlords to extract rice and to keep the countryside stable, while providing most of the modernizing inno-

[20] James Palais, *Politics and Policy in Traditional Korea* (Cambridge: Harvard University Press, 1975), pp. 16-18.

[21] Susan Shin, "Some Aspects of Landlord-Tenant Relations in Yi Dynasty Korea," *Occasional Papers on Korea*, no. 3 (Seattle, 1975), pp. 49-88; also Martina Deuchler, *Confucian Gentlemen and Barbarian Envoys: The Opening of Korea, 1875-1885* (Seattle: University of Washington Press, 1977), pp. 8, 224-225.

vations and technologies themselves. Landlords were given few incentives to invest in industry or in commerce, and every incentive to
remain on the land. The Korean scholar Sang Chul Suh has estimated
that in the 1930's the annual return on investments in land for Koreans was about eight percent and that on common stocks about six
percent.[22] Industrial and commercial returns were less. Institutions to
mobilize Korean capital were weak, and the Japanese wanted to keep
the landlords in the countryside to control their communities and to
market their agricultural products. Most of the Korean economic elite
by 1945 were landlords or landlord–entrepreneurs who had not really
cut their ties to the land. Those few who had prospered in commerce
and industry did so in league with the Japanese, and they were viewed
by most Koreans as *parvenu* servitors of foreign influence whose fortunes were not due to entrepreneurial talent but to colonial connections.

Japanese colonial policies toward landed classes help to explain some
of the divergence in Taiwanese and Korean agricultural development
noted in several essays in this volume. Neither landlords nor peasants
were given incentives to diversify, produce, be enterprising, respond
to innovation, and so on. Landlords were encouraged to stay on the
land, reaping their surpluses, but having few other avenues for investment. Peasants were not provided incentives to produce more
from which they could gain. Nor were peasants much involved in
marketing; most Korean peasants remained subsistence–oriented
throughout the colonial era, while their product was generally marketed by others: grain merchants, landlord agents, shippers, warehouse operators, colonial bureaucrats. The Japanese, moreover, spent
much more in Korea on infrastructures for control than they did in
Taiwan, leaving more funds available for investment in agriculture
on that island, a fact demonstrated in the statistical tables provided
in the essay by Mizoguchi and Yamamoto. There is also, I might
add, a rather gross underestimation of Korean agrarian change prior
to 1910 in some of the papers. Many of the best Korean historians
working today, such as Kim Yŏng-sŏp,[23] have written extensively of
certain shifts in the agricultural economy toward more commercialization and the rise of managerial peasants and new tenancy arrangements, demonstrating that change did indeed occur and that the conventional picture of a stagnant economy is a false one.

---

[22] Sang Chul Suh, *Growth and Structural Changes in the Korean Economy, 1910-1945*
(Cambridge: Harvard University Press, 1978), p. 85.

[23] Kim Yŏng-sŏp, "Yang'an ŭi yŏn'gu: Chosŏn hugi ui nonka kyŏngje" [A Study
of the Land Registers: the Economy of Peasant Households in the Late Yi Dynasty],
parts 1 and 2, *Sahak yŏn'gu* (Seoul: May and November 1960).

The Japanese found it to their advantage to ally with the non-entrepreneurial landed class in Korea which resided in every village, and they encouraged that class to govern the countryside for them. Not surprisingly, Korean landlords who had long relied on Confucian bureaucrats during the Yi Dynasty period continued to depend upon their new overlords—the Japanese—in very much the same way. Therefore, these landlords had no reason to respond to market forces and to organize resources in different ways. Yet they responded well to the coercion imposed upon them by the Japanese, just as they too used coercive methods to maintain order in their communities.[24] The Japanese could not have it both ways in Korea. While they could control the countryside through a passive and parasitic landlord class, they were continually thwarted in their efforts to force that same class to behave as entrepreneurs and modernize agriculture.

In 1945 the Korean landed class was still intact and powerful. Their values and behavior naturally did not change overnight. The 1945-1960 period became stagnant and one of artificial underdevelopment, even when discounting for the horrors of the Korean War. After that war, stagflation set in, and even though some economic improvements occurred under those conditions, development remained retarded. Those conditions might not have occurred after 1945 had the rural social structure undergone rapid change like the economic structure. Glancing at that period, we can assess it as one of aging landlords and a small commercial and industrial urban class fighting over revenue shares in a contracting economy. These socioeconomic conditions accounted for much of the reactionary politics of that era.

To return to the 1920's: as Michael Robinson has pointed out, the landed classes were encouraged to diversify their livelihoods through entry into publishing and educational activities. This period of reformism and relative tolerance came about because of the 1919 uprisings, the emergence of radical nationalist groups and parties, and because, as we noted earlier, liberal trends in Taishō Japan were felt in Korea and in the other territories in the empire. Japanese policy in Korea of this period seems to provide an excellent example of what Herbert Marcuse called "repressive tolerance,"[25] although he used the term in a much different context. It was tolerant, because the Japanese allowed moderate nationalists to organize, to study their native

---

[24] Jeffrey Paige, *Agrarian Revolution* (New York: The Free Press, 1975), pp. 17-25; also Samuel Popkin, *The Rational Peasant* (Berkeley: University of California Press, 1979), pp. 33-34.

[25] Herbert Marcuse, "Repressive Tolerance," in Robert Paul Woolf, Barrington Moore, Jr., and Herbert Marcuse, *A Critique of Pure Tolerance* (Boston: Beacon Press, 1965), pp. 81-117.

language, and to publish in a press which was often freer than in North and South Korea today. It was repressive, because the price of breathing space for Korean moderates was exile, imprisonment, or worse for Korean revolutionaries and radicals. It is not mere co-incidence that it was during this period that most of the political leadership of post-war Korea got its start. Kim Sŏng-su, Song Chin-u, Chang Tŏk-su, Cho Pyŏng-ok, and other moderates established rep-utations both as nationalists and as publicists and entrepreneurs. In September 1945 they and a handful of other moderate nationalists formed the core of the Korean Democratic Party,[26] which then be-came the progenitor of much of the postwar South Korean opposi-tion.

In contrast, more radical nationalists like Yŏ Un-hyŏng, Hŏ Hŏn, and Yi Kang-guk ran afoul of the police or went into exile, although they also enjoyed short-lived activity within Korea. Communists like Pak Hŏn-yŏng and Yi Yŏng started the first Korean Communist Party and became active in organizing labor. Such people structured the left side of the political spectrum after liberation, with Yŏ and Hŏ Hŏn emerging as leaders of the Korean People's Republic in Sep-tember 1945, and Pak and Yi fighting over who should lead the Ko-rean Communist Party.[27] Abroad, exiles like Syngman Rhee, Kim Ku, Kim Kyu-sik, Kim Wŏn-bong, and Yi Ch'ŏng-ch'ŏn organized to influence politics back home and in Japan with little success. The political activity of the 1920's became dormant in the 1930's, how-ever, and this reversal deeply affected post-war politics.

When Japan launched its conquest of Manchuria in 1931, it faced a strong anti-Japanese resistance in this new semi-colonial sphere, ne-cessitating harsh counter-insurgency measures, including the incin-eration of villages, the creation of "collective hamlets" designed to separate people from the insurgents, and a large commitment of mil-itary force.[28] Koreans served as many of these insurgents and bore the brunt of Japanese repression, and it was in such struggles that Koreans like Kim Il Sung and his allies turned to violent resistance. Japanese repression was felt in Korea as well, and thousands of com-munists were jailed, many of them imprisoned until August 15, 1945. As Japan's war in China deepened in the late 1930's the period of

[26] Han T'ae-su, Han'guk chŏngdang-sa [History of Korean Political Parties] (Seoul: Sin t'aeyang-sa, 1961).

[27] Cumings, The Origins of the Korean War I: Liberation and the Emergence of Separate Regimes, 1945-1947 (Princeton: Princeton University Press, 1981), ch. three.

[28] Chong-sik Lee, Counterinsurgency in Manchuria: The Japanese Experience, 1931-1940 (Santa Monica, Ca.: The Rand Corporation, 1967).

relaxation ended, and Korea entered its last phase of intense colonial mobilization. Colonial police broke up moderate nationalist groups, closed their newspapers, and enforced a harsh Japanization on most Koreans. Radical intellectuals had their thoughts examined and reformed through the intense measures that we have come to associate with Chinese Communism. They were then marched before the Korean people as exemplars of right thinking.

The 1930's also witnessed, however, a prolonged economic boom from the industrialization of Korea and Manchukuo. As the Japanese empire became enlarged and its military, economic, and political commitments became more extensive, a labor shortage developed throughout Korea. For peasants and workers, this simply meant their being mobilized for far-flung work details, but for educated Koreans more opportunities than ever before were opened. There began in the colonial administrative apparatus an upward movement of Korean talent. This Japanese colony had both the economic elasticity and the bureaucratic space to accommodate those Koreans willing to serve the war effort. When such opportunity combined with harsh pressures on resisters, many Koreans quite naturally took the path of least resistance. Many turned from being nationalists into being collaborators, and they became sharply differentiated from those Korean resisters who remained at home and from those who were in exile. These cleavages played upon the postwar polity for many years after colonial rule ended.

In Korean society Japanese policies in this last decade ended the previous junction of ethnicity and privileged position and differentiated Korean social classes still further. While in the 1920's the colonial regime had presented itself to Koreans mostly in the person of a Japanese official or gendarme, now a Korean was as likely to be an official in the middle and lower ranks as a Japanese, and, of course, the Japanese liked to use Koreans in the more disagreeable tasks such as mobilizing laborers. A minority of Koreans did very well at the precise time when the majority was doing very poorly. The result was a Janus-like quality to the undeniable "modernization" which occurred in this period: as Koreans moved into responsible bureaucratic and technical positions, they were forced to pay the price for their collaboration at a time when the Japanese colonial presence was most repressive.

This dilemma was particularly poignant for the cultural nationalists, who saw their efforts in the 1920's come to naught. Because many of them had become accustomed to gradualism and lacked the steely determination of more radical resisters, a number of them became collaborators. The great nationalist writer Yi Kwang-su, the

early modernizer Yun Ch'i-ho, and the nationalist activist and ideologue Ch'oe Nam-sŏn come to mind as typical of this group. Had
things developed as they had hoped, such people might in the 1950's
and 1960's have been the self-confident, legitimate leaders of a post-
colonial Korea. But in the last decade of colonial rule the upper stratum of a whole generation was turned into a collaborationist elite.
Many moderate nationalists who were not forced into open collaboration still profited from the economic boom, tainting their nationalist credentials in the eyes of many Koreans. Cho Pyŏng-ok ran the
Poin Mining Company, Chang Tŏk-su operated a bank, and Song
Chin-u and Kim Sŏng-su funnelled the assets of the *Tong-a ilbo* (a
newspaper suppressed in 1940) into a real-estate company until 1945.[29]
This subject is so painful for South Koreans today that most cannot
or will not discuss it, and I have met a number of college-educated
young Koreans who have never been told that this happened. The
history of this period is obscure for most Koreans, and it is made
more so in the willful erasure and burying of facts. Many county
histories, for example, will not name those Koreans who served as
county magistrates in the period 1937-1945; there are simply blanks
where their names should be.

The colonial period ended with a paroxysm of activity in which
virtually all Koreans were enrolled in or confronted by the repression
of the era. Their apparent collaboration with the colonial oppressor
stripped legitimacy from Korean elites who had remained in the
country, and it encouraged those Koreans who resisted (or subsisted)
in exile to think that no one who remained inside Korea could have
resisted without succumbing to Japanese pressures. From this perspective they were convinced that leadership of post-war Korea would
have to come from elements who had remained abroad and whose
reputations had not been besmirched through accommodation with
the colonial regime. Those who continued to resist inside the country, like Yŏ Un-hyŏng and Pak Hŏn-yŏng, thought of course that
their stubborn recalcitrance deserved more reward than did the activities of those who were comparatively safe in exile. Thus, when liberation came, the conflict between the exiled Kim Il Sung and the
resident Pak Hŏn-yŏng dominated Communist politics. One of the
first acts of the nationalist Kim Ku upon his return to Korea was to
order the assassination of former gradualist Song Chin-u (in late December 1945).[30]

---

[29] Cumings, *The Origins of the Korean War, I: Liberation and the Emergence of Separate Regimes, 1945-1947* (Princeton: Princeton University Press, 1981), ch. three.
[30] *Ibid.*, ch. six.

Looking back over the thirty-five-year span of Japanese domination of Korea, we must surely conclude that one of the practical
Japanese accomplishments was their manipulation of Korean internal
cleavages, from the beginning of their occupation and its encouragement of the pro-Japanese *Ilchinhoe* to its end by the extraordinary
stimulation of intra-elite conflict in the last decade. Colonial rule left
Korea with no single indigenous leader or leadership legitimized by
popular support, but rather an assortment of political aspirants whose
origins, ideas, and ambitions were so varied that cooperation among
them to establish a strong, unified, independent Korean state would
never have been possible. As the now-tainted moderate nationalists
and numerous collaborators consolidated their position in South Korea in the late 1940's, an older generation of leftists and Communists
resisted their rule. In the North, there emerged an entirely new and
much younger leadership, hardened by resistance in Manchuria, by
years of exile in China or the Soviet Union. An aging and tainted
leadership in the South met a young and vigorous leadership in the
North, and the result, in part, was civil war. Such was the divisive
political legacy which Japanese colonialism bequeathed to the Korean
peninsula.

CHAPTER 14

Western and Japanese Colonialism: Some Preliminary Comparisons

Lewis H. Gann

The breakdown of Western dominion in Asia and Africa has occasioned a tidal wave of print. Over the last two decades, presses have run off more histories, surveys, handbooks, and journalistic accounts on the subject than during the entire heyday of European rule overseas. The history of Japanese colonialism and of its demise is much less well known in the West. Works of synthesis relating the Japanese to Western experience are rarer still. On the face of it, the scarcity of such studies might seem a matter of surprise at a time when terms like "interdisciplinary approach" and "comparative dimension" have become words of praise in book reviews, project outlines, and applications for foundation grants. There are good reasons for the scarcity of such studies. Few historians and few political scientists can master several languages equally well; fewer still can read Japanese.

Specialization is part of the scholarly tradition. The historian learns his craft as a doctoral student by detailed investigation of minute problems; he is apt to be better at describing a particular tree rather than a whole forest. Hence only a handful of scholars today are equally familiar with the problems that beset Portugal, Great Britain, Belgium, and France in even a relatively restricted area such as sub-Saharan Africa, not to speak of the Third World as a whole. Scholars, moreover, must cope with an extraordinary diversity of colonial practice under the same flag. The Kaiser's colonies in Africa alone, though not comparable in extent, wealth, or population with the former British and French possessions, were so variegated that a historian can speak—quite legitimately—not of one but of several quite dissimilar German empires in Africa. The style of Japanese colonial governance in countries as far afield as Korea, Taiwan, Manchuria, or the South Pacific islands was just as full of diversity and incongruity.

MODES AND MOTIVES OF COLONIALISM

Political theory of the classical kind lists several categories of colonization. From the mid-Victorian's standpoint, the ideal dependency was a "settlement colony" such as Canada, Australia, or New Zealand—dependencies that would rid the motherland of surplus manpower, that would pay for themselves, govern themselves and, if well treated, would develop into independent British states tied to the metropolis by ties of amity and commerce. Apart from the Dutch in South Africa and the French in Quebec, none of Britain's competitors—continental European or Japanese—managed to create overseas a new nation in its own image as the British had done. The Japanese settled Hokkaido. Later they sent substantial numbers of colonists to Karafuto and to a few islands in Micronesia. But Japanese—like German—colonization did not solve any of the motherland's demographic problems. The *Volk ohne Raum*, whatever the theorists might say, preferred to stay in Japan or Germany, respectively, rather than to settle overseas under their respective imperial flags.

When the Japanese turned to colonization, they no longer had the opportunity of settling in such great semi-empty spaces as Australia or Canada. Even had they been able to do so, Japan's centralizing tradition would have prevented the emergence of Japanese "daughter nations" comparable to those that grew up in the British dominions. A sizable body of Japanese emigrants did make new homes for themselves in Korea and Manchuria. They varied widely in their social origins—ne'er-do-wells, semi-skilled workers, technicians, specialists, farmers. In some sense they resembled the *pieds noirs* in Algeria, but the Japanese settlers never remotely attained the political importance achieved by the French in Algeria, not to speak of the whites in Rhodesia.

In addition, Victorians differentiated between plantation colonies—territories like Malaya or Kenya, where immigrant estate owners built up an export economy by pioneering the commercial cultivation of tropical crops such as rubber, sisal, or coffee. There were Japanese plantations in a number of South Sea islands. There were Japanese agricultural companies in Taiwan, but, as Saburō Yamada shows, the bulk of Taiwan's rice, its main export, came from the fields of Taiwanese cultivators whose labor productivity by World War II had become greater even than Japan's own.

The strategic colonies formed a third category. These included naval bases like Malta and Gibraltar or islands like Cyprus, acquired for their real or assumed military and naval value. The strategic element played even a greater role in Japanese empire building than in the experience of a European naval power such as Great Britain. As Mark Peattie indicates in his essay, Japanese colonizers were greatly concerned with their country's immediate strategic interests. The Japanese surrounded their island home with concentric chains of naval bases designed to protect not merely trade routes, but the heartland of empire itself.

The typology of colonialism is linked to the question of its origin. The most influential explanation of imperialism today derives from the pen of Lenin. Its central themes are well known, and have now become part of an established orthodoxy that academicians in the Socialist third of the world must accept at the risk of their lives, livelihood, or liberty. Lenin linked modern imperialism to the export of capital from developed to backward countries. But contrary to his fundamental assumption, there was in fact little correspondence between the pattern of Western capital investment abroad and the "new imperialism" that supposedly formed the political superstructure of monopoly capitalism in the backward regions of the world. By 1911, a generation after the "scramble for Africa" had started, the largest percentage by far of British capital was invested not in Africa but in the United States and in the "white" dominions. The newly acquired colonies in tropical Africa took but a negligible share. French colonies remained the neglected stepchildren of the Paris Bourse. Only an insignificant share of German capital went to the German colonies. The Western nations likewise conducted but a small proportion of their trade with their newly acquired colonies. (By the outbreak of World War I German commerce with the Grand Duchy of Luxemburg was greater than that with the whole of the Kaiser's *Kolonialreich*.)

Lenin's explanation for colonial expansion is even less convincing when applied to Japan's historical experience than to the experiences of Italy or Germany. Between 1895 and 1919 Japan acquired an impressive empire. The dates of its acquisition and its extent may be summarized as follows (see p. 500).

Financial motives played little part in the creation of this empire. No Japanese banker before or during World War I ever had to worry about an excessive supply of savings that could most profitably be invested only abroad, under colonial auspices. On the contrary, one of Japan's main economic problems was an extreme shortage of capital. What funds existed were mainly put to use at home. Neither did the Japanese conquer Korea nor Taiwan primarily in order to protect their commerce. Korea and Taiwan accounted for a very minor por-

Territory	Means and Year of Acquisition	Land Area (sq. km.)
Japan proper (Naichi)		382,561
Taiwan	Sino-Japanese War, 1895	35,961
South Sakhalin (Minami Karafuto)	Russo-Japanese War, 1905	36,090
Kwantung Leased Territory (Kantō-shū)	Russo-Japanese War, 1905	3,462
Korea (Chosen)	Annexed, 1910	220,788
Pacific Mandated Islands	World War I, 1919	2,149

Nar-yo

Source: Shinkichi Etō, "Asianism and the Duality of Japanese Colonialism, 1879-1945," in H. L. Wesseling, ed., History and Underdevelopment, Leiden, Centre for the History of European Expansion, 1980, p. 114.

tion of Japan's foreign trade. (Japan's best customer before the outbreak of World War I was the United States. By 1912 Japanese exports to Taiwan amounted to less than 19 million yen, as compared to Japan's total exports of 680 million yen, of which 184 million went to the United States.) Foreign conquest, of course, had its economic dimensions. Planting the flag overseas would forestall foreigners as well as profitable special interest groups. The conquering power, in its own estimation, might acquire real estate that, however valueless at the time, might appreciate in the future. But, in a direct sense, the charges that colonialism derived from the intrigues of bankers and merchants able to force their will on the government make no sense when applied to Japan, France, or Germany.

A more sophisticated socioeconomic interpretation sees colonialism as a device to quiet the poor at home by winning glory abroad. According to Hans-Ulrich Wehler, a modern German scholar, Bismarck, among others, used colonialism as a tool of social manipulation.[1] The Wehler school claims that the German establishment, resting on an unstable alliance between the great industrialists and the landed aristocracy, the barons of iron and grain, resolved to exclude the lower orders from effective political power at home. This exclusion became increasingly hard to sustain during the economic depression that struck the Reich from the 1870's onward. Colonial expansion therefore served as a means of tightening social bonds, protecting trade, and diverting the German workers' attention from Social

[1] See, especially, Hans-Ulrich Wehler, Bismarck und der Imperialismus (Cologne: Kiepenheuer und Wietsch, 1969).

Democratic subversion to foreign glory. But in fact there was no link between Bismarck's colonial ventures and working-class discontent; by the time Bismarck passed his *Sozialistengesetz* to suppress the Social Democrats, he had lost all interest in the colonies.

In Japan the revolutionary danger was equally slight. Admittedly, Japan had social tensions of its own. Contrary to legend, Japan was far from being the world's most deferential society. After the Meiji revolution (1868), many of the former samurai were profoundly dissatisfied with their declining social status and looked for glory abroad. (The Satsuma rebellion of 1877-1879 was occasioned in part by the government's failure to launch an expedition against Korea.) But Japan had no need for colonization as a prophylactic against rebellion from the poor. The small Social Democratic Party, formed in 1901, was immediately banned and, unlike the Social Democratic Party in Germany, failed to gain any real importance.

Yet another socioeconomic model, elaborated by "revisionist" scholars such as Immanuel Wallerstein, seeks to explain modern colonialism in terms of international "dependency." World capitalism supposedly developed as a unified system that exploited the rural periphery of the imperialist powers through colonization, the extraction of super-profits, and the deliberate destruction of existing social organization in the Third World. But the concept of unified world capitalism in the nineteenth century is even more shadowy than the notion of a unified world communism in the twentieth. The model does not make allowance for the diversity of the imperial states nor for their regional distinctions. (Each of the capitalist states during the age of the new imperialism also had a backward rural periphery at home—Sicily, Pomerania or Mecklenburg, Corsica, or Britain's "Celtic fringe.") The dependency model greatly exaggerates the role of colonial trade during the Industrial Revolution, at the time when the European powers carried on most of their commerce with each other, not with the so-called Third World. Most important of all, the dependency theory is Eurocentric. It does not explain how a peripheral Third World state like Japan was able to transform itself, as did South Africa, from a relatively rural country to a modern industrial state.

Japanese colonialism was, of course, linked to industrialization. Without modern steel mills, docks, and shipbuilding yards Japan could not have become a great seapower. But when Japan began to build its empire at the end of the last century and in the first decade of the present one, the country still mainly relied on farming for its income—unlike Great Britain or Germany. Even as late as 1941, when the island empire entered World War II, more than 40 percent of the

Japanese people were employed in agriculture, which continued to be the country's most important industry.

The Japanese bourgeoisie lacked the self-confidence of its British or French equivalent. Nor did the Japanese middle class possess any kind of missionary spirit; Japanese colonialism, unlike its British counterpart, had no evangelical inspiration. British missionaries played an important part in securing British overlordship in Uganda; French Protestant missionaries helped to secure British influence in Barotse-land (in what is now Zambia). British missionary work was closely linked to social reform at home. From converting and "improving" the pagan proletariat in the slums of Birmingham and Glasgow it was but a short step to evangelical and social work among unbelievers in the African bush. A considerable proportion of British colonial administrators were born in an Anglican parsonage or, less often, in a Calvinist manse. Colonialism was, in a certain sense, an "overspill" of domestic reformism. But Japan was not a Christian country. Japan participated neither in the slave trade nor in the battle for its abolition. Colonialism of the missionary kind, though not unknown in Japan, was not a great imperial driving force as it was in Victorian Britain.

In a way, Japanese colonialism was a matter of prestige. At the end of the nineteenth century and going on to the first third of the twentieth, nationalists regarded colonies as a status symbol. Colonization was—among other things—a form of conspicuous consumption on a national scale. Great powers were expected to show their prowess by foreign conquests, past or present. The bishop of Ely fawningly suggested to his liege lord in Shakespeare's *Henry V*:

> Your brother kings and monarchs of the earth
> Do all expect that you should rouse yourself,
> As did the former lions of your blood.

The Japanese were impressed by the prestige of European colonialism and even more so by the splendor of the ancient Chinese empire, from which Japan had inherited so much of its historic culture. The new Japan, united for the first time in an economic sense by a modern system of railways, took great pride in its own achievement and in its future. Colonialism also went with modernization and Japanese notions of self-defense. Ever since Commodore Perry's expeditions, Japanese thinkers and statesmen had become convinced that the potential or actual threat from the Western powers could be met only by making Japan strong in a military, industrial, and political sense. To preserve its independence, Japan must become a great power. A great power required colonies. This element of national pride—strong also in Wilhelminian Germany—should not, however, be exaggerated in the case of Japan. In Tokyo there was no great popular party calling for conquests abroad. There was not much colonial romanticism. Japan produced no Kipling, not even a Karl May. Mark Peattie points out that colonial matters rarely became a subject of public debate; the Japanese public was little moved by colonial events.

When the Japanese established their overseas empire, they imitated the external of imperial glory valued by their Western European competitors. The faded snapshots that survive from Japan's imperial era at the beginning of the present century look surprisingly like the photographs found in the albums of retired British officers—the same stiff group pictures, the same stern-faced officials wearing pith sun helmets and riding breeches, the same formalized gubernatorial buildings that remind visitors of grand hotels, the same clubs, complete with bars and tennis courts. Yet Japanese colonialism, unlike that of the British, was overwhelmingly military in character. When the Japanese took Taiwan, and later Korea and Manchuria, they were not unmindful of the economic potential—including the agricultural and mining wealth—of their new possessions. But the Japanese acquired these regions on grounds similar to those for which the Prussian General Staff in 1871 insisted on the annexation of Alsace-Lorraine: on grounds of assumed strategic necessity. (The administration of Taiwan was patterned, in the first place, on the governance of Alsace-Lorraine as a German *Reichsland*. The most admired foreigner in Japan at the beginning of the twentieth century was Bismarck.) Military security, as Japanese planners envisaged it, necessitated the creation of vast defensive networks thrust ever farther outward. This policy resulted in ever-new campaigns. Moderate objectives turned into immoderate objectives. The soldiers marched from Korea to Manchuria, from Manchuria deep into China, from the inner island defenses to the "Greater Asian Co-Prosperity Sphere." The pursuit of total security ultimately ended in total insecurity.

Soldiers and sailors both tended to favor imperial expansion, but they were by no means agreed on how the new empire ought to be shaped. The navy, enjoying considerable support from merchants and manufacturers of liberal inclination, was apt to look southward. The army was more apt to look for imperial glory on the Asian mainland, though the division was by no means clear-cut. Japan, though an island power, gave precedence to the army over the navy.

The role of the military in Japan was greater than in any European country save Germany in World War I. Japanese military theoreticians, unlike their British counterparts, particularly emphasized the role of the fleet as an instrument for transporting troops, safeguarding their seaborne supplies, and warding off enemy counterblows. Colonial planning on the whole centered more on the needs of the army than on those of the naval forces.

The motives of military planners were mixed. They looked for strategic security; they hoped to provide Japan and its industries with secure supplies of raw materials. They also looked to foreign dependencies for a dependable source of food, an important consideration for Japan—a densely populated country which, before World War I, was still primarily dependent on farming, fishing, forestry, and other primary industries. In addition, the army had a taste for glory. The desire for military prestige was, of course, not limited to the Japanese and the Germans. French soldiers in North Africa thirsted for action; French campaigns in the Sudan in the latter part of the last century were often provoked by the men on the spot, who sought the consent of Paris only after victory had been won. But the French colonial general at his most arrogant was no match for his Japanese colleague in the ability to force his will upon civilian leaders. In Japan, unlike in Victorian Britain or in the France of the Third Republic, the military element was predominant.

Japan in this respect resembled Wilhelminian Germany, which, in some ways, Japan tried to copy. Max Weber has pointed out that the Prussian Junker during the nineteenth century had long ceased to be a truly feudal lord, if ever he had been one. The Junker was rather an agricultural entrepreneur, frugal, hard-fisted; his spirit of work, discipline, dedication to duty, and *Haltung* (a peculiar form of stiff-backed stoicism) provided an ethos well suited to the needs of entrepreneurs and administrators in a capitalist society, as well as to the needs of soldiers. The Japanese samurai provided Japanese entrepreneurs with a similar ethos—a subject to which I shall return. In a certain sense, Junker and samurai understood one another extremely well.

The Japanese owned an equally substantial debt to German scholarship. During the latter part of the nineteenth century, for instance, Ludwig Riess—one of Ranke's youthful disciples—introduced to Japanese savants his master's concepts concerning historical research. Riess and his students also disseminated from Japanese universities Ranke's notions with regard to the dominant role of the state in history, and Ranke's doctrine concerning the *Primat der Aussenpolitik* designed to prove Ranke's belief that the dictates of foreign policy determine a country's domestic policy, a doctrine most convenient to empire builders. At the same time, German officers took a leading part in training Japan's army. They included men of distinction like General Klemens Meckel, one of the most brilliant tacticians in the Wilhelminian army, who placed special emphasis on the employment of riflemen and on tactics of envelopment in which Japanese soldiers came to excel. Throughout the heyday of Japan's military power its military organization was fashioned essentially on the organization of the Kaiser's armies before World War I. The parallel between the two countries was not lost on Japan's German tutors. When Karl Haushofer, the foremost theoretician of *Geopolitik*, published his great study *Dai Nihon: Betrachtungen über Gross Japans Wehrkraft, Weltstellung und Zukunft* (Berlin: E. S. Mittler, 1913), he thus deliberately chose a title that would emphasize the analogy between Greater German and Greater Japanese ambitions.

Japanese planning in general was of the collegiate kind, akin to the managerial approach of the German General Staff, with its emphasis on anonymity. Japanese empire building had no Bonapartist element, owing nothing to military *caudillos*. Japanese planning was even further removed from the civilian approach, with its flair for money-making and for the manipulation of public opinion, even of humanitarian public opinion, that characterized the work of British colonial magnates like Sir George Goldie, Sir William Mackinnon, and—above all—Cecil John Rhodes. British expansion into Zambia (formerly Northern Rhodesia) and Zimbabwe (formerly Southern Rhodesia) derived primarily from the personal initiative of Rhodes, architect of the British South Africa Company, which sought unsuccessfully to combine imperial splendor with profits for Rhodes's shareholders. The Congo Free State similarly was the personal creation of Leopold II. But for the monarch's own enterprise, his speculative drive, his financial diplomacy, his thirst for dividends, there would have been no Belgian empire in Central Africa. There was no Japanese Rhodes, however; there was no Japanese equivalent to the Coburg king.

THE COLONIAL ÉLITES: MILITARY AND CIVILIAN

Japan's early colonial expansion was indeed linked to economic motives, especially in Korea. But in the partnership between businessmen, soldiers, and bureaucrats, the generals and the senior civilian administrators occupied the positions of command. Military expansion, in fact, helped to create new economic interests. From the start of Japan's modernization period, army and naval chiefs resolved to use the technical know-how and commercial skills of selected entrepreneurs to build arms factories, chemical and engineering works, steel mills, and similar ventures. Military expansion benefitted the arms industry; the arms industry in turn looked with favor on military ambitions. The growth of the Japanese empire increasingly turned Japanese industry toward protected colonial markets.

Japanese conquests in World War II likewise had economic motives, but, again, strategic considerations predominated. The Japanese did not go to war in order to protect foreign investments; neither did they simply take up arms in order to maximize profits for their industrial concerns. By controlling Southeast Asia and a great ring of Pacific islands, the Japanese meant to make themselves independent of foreign good will for their supply of vital strategic imports like rubber and oil. Militarily, Japan would become invulnerable against foreign attack. From a logistic standpoint, Japanese colonialism depended on seapower. But in a wider sense—the point bears repetition—the structure of Japan's empire resembled more that of great European power blocs on the continent than the tropical empires created by France and Great Britain in Africa. Germany's drive for *Mitteleuropa* forms a closer parallel to Japanese empire building than Rhodes's dream for an all-British route from Cape to Cairo.

The character of the different colonial systems was reflected in the armies used to conquer the new empires. The new imperialism that had led to the partition of Africa at the end of the last century was peripheral to the economies of Western Europe. The peripheral element of Western European colonialism was mirrored—in some measure—in the field of military organization. For instance, the French *Armée coloniale* in Africa was a separate administrative entity; so was the Indian army that secured British predominance over the subcontinent; so was the *Force Publique* in the Belgian Congo. Even the German *Schutztruppe*, strange as it may appear in an empire where the soldiers seemed supreme, was administered through the *Kolonialabteilung* (later the *Reichskolonialamt*), a civilian body.

Japanese forces at home and abroad enjoyed a much greater degree of integration than their opposite numbers who served respectively under the Union Jack, the French *Tricolore*, or Germany's Imperial Eagle. The Japanese armies that served abroad were much more fully integrated with the home army than were the European colonial forces. This does not mean that the Japanese army was a wholly homogeneous body. The Japanese forces in Manchuria, for instance, developed a spirit of their own, with their own drives and their own ambitions. But they were not a separate body as was the old Indian army. In peacetime, the main force was concentrated in the four main islands of Japan. (By the 1920's, after the original empire had been consolidated and before the war against China had begun, of seventeen infantry divisions, fourteen were kept in Japan, two divisions and some independent units were stationed in Korea, one division and six independent battalions were in South Manchuria, two infantry regiments and three specialist battalions were deployed in Taiwan. The overseas units were periodically relieved by homeland units, normally after two years.)

Japanese and the European military forces differed in the structure of their respective prestige. Karl Marx found that the military mind, exemplified by Napoleon III, worshipped only one trinity: infantry, cavalry, artillery. But the three components of this deity were by no means equal in social standing. The Western European cavalrymen, legatees of the knight in armor, came first; the infantry came second; the engineer and the commissariat officer, middle-class people with a technical training, came last. (In the United States the position was almost reversed; the cavalryman, a cowboy in uniform, stood at the bottom; the engineer, a highly trained specialist with a skill highly paid in civilian life, stood at the top.)

In Western Europe, there were also striking differences of prestige within the same arm. A guard officer was always superior to a line officer. But even line regiments were not always of equal standing. In England, a unit's prestige corresponded, roughly speaking, to the distance of its regimental depot from London, reflecting the socioeconomic predominance of London and the Home Counties within the kingdom at large. There were similar differences between the colonial and the metropolitan forces; an officer in the Indian army was apt to be patronized by colleagues of equal rank within the British army proper. The highest commands did not normally go to Indian army officers. In Belgium, the *Force Publique* occupied an even more lowly place within the structure of military prestige; up to the outbreak of World War I its commander could expect no more than a colonelcy, though the colonial forces were the only ones that had done any fighting. The French *infanterie de marine* was notorious among the *bien pensants* for its anti-clericalism, its addiction to Free Masonry, its militantly Republican sympathies, and the petty bourgeois background of its officers. No one accused the German *Schutztruppe* officers of similar failings. The *Schutztruppe* contained a high proportion of noble-born officers, tired of garrison duty in Hinter-Kottwitz or Klein-Britznow, with its never-ending drill parades, its kit inspections, regimental dances, its petty intrigues, and the interminable need for being polite to the colonel's lady. Pay was high; there was a chance of making one's name in action. But, tough as they might be, the *Schutztruppe* officers ranked lower in social esteem than the smartly turned out *Marineininfanterie*, the Kaiser's favorites, not to speak of a Prussian Guards regiment with battle honors dating back to Fehrbellin and Leuthen.

The Japanese officer corps, on the other hand, was more homogeneous in a social sense than its British or even its German equivalent. According to Haushofer's findings, the Japanese armies that surprised the world by shattering czarist might in the Far East drew its main strength from the countryside. The best soldiers came from the farms and from small towns. Above all, Japan owed a tremendous debt to the 400,000 or so samurai families who had played a major part in shaping the new Japan. The samurai were not feudal landowners in the European sense; even before the Meiji revolution, they were but a sword-bearing service nobility, mostly men of modest circumstances. There were no *latifundia* in Japan. By 1911 three-fifths of Japan's arable land were farmed by peasant proprietors, the remainder by tenant farmers. There was no cult of the aristocratic horseman; Japan, with its emphasis on rice farming, consistently experienced difficulties in putting good cavalrymen into the field. The samurai, like the Prussian Junkers, were bred to a life of hard work, obedience, courage, and honesty. Their outlook provided Japan with an equivalent of the so-called Protestant ethos, an ideology well adjusted to the task of starting the country on its career as a modern military, industrial, and commercial power. The average Japanese army officer was the son of a soldier or perhaps the son of a teacher, a professor, or a civil servant—not the scion of a great landowner.

In a social sense, the Japanese army in certain respects was comparable before World War I to the Belgian army, one of the most bourgeois forces in Western Europe. Belgian officers before World War I widely complained at their lack of social prestige at home and looked for glory to the Belgian Congo. Japanese officers in the 1920's likewise felt that their country did not accord them the honor that they deserved, and they turned abroad for prestige. The Belgian army before World War I, like the Japanese army, was a relatively new force. Belgium had become independent only in 1830; its army was fashioned in the wake of the Belgian revolution within the confines of a state shaped in the image of the Francophone bourgeois. The Japanese, like the Belgians, prized education, especially technical education. The Japanese, unlike their tutors in Wilhelminian Germany, made some provision for advancing qualified noncommissioned officers into the commissioned ranks.[2] For all their pride in the samurai

---

[2] Before World War II, Japanese middle-school graduates with adequate training could apply for admission to the military preparatory school (*Yōnen Gakkō*). Subsequently they entered the officers' training school (*Shikan Gakkō*). Some places were

tradition, the Japanese army was essentially a middle-class—even a lower-middle-class—institution. Its officers were expected to work hard and to study hard, a system appropriate to a country that, unlike England, did not prize the amateur gentleman and that associated a man's accent with his regional more than his social origins.

The structure of the military profoundly affected the nature of colonial rule. According to an aphorism ascribed to Al Capone, a man gets more with kind words and a gun than with kind words alone. The Japanese made no bones about using guns.

In Korea, for example, the Japanese conquerors met bitter resistance. More than 140,000 Koreans supposedly participated in the independence struggle between 1907 and 1911. To break the enemy's will, the Japanese in 1915 increased their initial force of a division and a half to two permanent army divisions, assisted by 13,000 military and regular policemen. Japanese power was reinforced by a highly visible gendarmerie whose senior officers were much better versed in the Korean language and in Korean customs than the other officials; police officers had more contact with rural residents than the remaining civil servants; as Wonmo Dong points out, the ordinary Korean derived his image of the typical Japanese from those Japanese with whom Koreans most frequently came in contact, that is to say from Japanese police officers (and, to a lesser extent, from public elementary school principals heading rural schools).

The government-general of Korea was to all intents and purposes a state within a state where civil and military administration remained closely locked (all governor-generals of Korea were career soldiers). Economic development in Korea owed a major debt to Japanese capitalism. The Japanese bureaucracy served as its chief instrument. A civil servant in Korea was expected, therefore, to serve as a jack-of-all-trades; he lacked the highly specialized skills of a senior civil servant in Japan. Hence, personnel transfers between the Japanese metropolitan bureaucracy and the Japanese bureaucracy were rare; once stationed in Korea, a Japanese civil servant in Korea was apt to end his career there, confirming thereby Korea's separate status.

Japanese military might and Japanese military autonomy played an equally large role in the Kwantung province, where the initial Japanese occupation forces, originally designed to guard the railway, were expanded into an entire army. Taiwan was smaller than Korea; Chinese resistance was not as bitter as its Korean counterpart. But, having

---

also allotted to conscripts, who, having served with the colors, elected to try for commissions, and to selected noncommissioned officers under twenty-six years of age, who were recommended by their commanding officers. Commissioned officers had a choice of higher institutions for specializing or for increasing their general knowledge.

acquired Taiwan by the Treaty of Shimonoseki in 1895, the Japanese required two divisions to put down Taiwanese opposition; more than 10,000 people died on the Taiwanese side.

This impressive military deployment was not hard to achieve. Japanese conscripts, unlike British professional soldiers, were cheap, they were available, and they were used overseas in large numbers. Even in the 1920's, an era of peace, when Russian and German military might had been laid low and when Great Britain and the United States were wedded to disarmament, Japan's military deployment overseas was impressive. Her military establishment in dependencies abroad (already described) was much larger than the forces maintained by Great Britain in the whole of its huge African empire. To give just one example, in the first half of the twentieth century the British ran Northern Rhodesia—a country considerably larger than France, Holland, Belgium, and Switzerland together—with one black battalion of eight hundred men commanded by some thirty British officers and NCOs. A British governor was expected to run his dependency with a minimum of force; promotion came to the man who could govern a dependency without calling on the military and without arousing criticism either in the British press or in Parliament. A Japanese official, however humane, always knew that he could rely on strong military support. For a Japanese governor, the premium on proconsular pacifism was infinitely smaller than for his opposite number in the British service or even in the reputedly militaristic German service.[3]

Comparisons between the civilian administrators who served the various colonial powers are even harder to draw than between the soldiers. When the British acquired their new African empire they had already a long-standing tradition of overseas service, and such service carried with it a good deal of social prestige. British colonial governors were automatically raised to the knighthood; but in Germany, where civil servants were respected, no civilian governor was

---

[3] By 1913, just before the outbreak of World War I, the Germans maintained little more than 6,000 soldiers, mostly Africans, in their entire African *Kolonialreich*, comprising what are now four separate countries: German Southwest Africa (Namibia), Togo, Cameroun, and German East Africa (Tanzania). The Western imperial forces were also minute as compared with the size of the post-colonial military forces. In 1914, for example, the British establishment in Nigeria comprised just under 4,000 men, compared with 231,000 in Nigeria in 1977. The British armed forces in India (including what is now Pakistan) comprised some 257,000 men in 1914, as compared to 1,096,000 men in the armed forces in India in 1977 and 429,000 in Pakistan. The military growth in Japan's former colonial possessions is, of course, equally striking, with 474,000 men maintained in 1977 by Taiwan, 512,000 by North Korea, and 642,000 by South Korea.

ever rewarded for his services with the coveted "von." British administrators as a whole looked on themselves as gentlemen rather than as bureaucratic or military specialists. Unlike their counterparts in continental bureaucracies, they had not been trained exclusively in legal and administrative studies. They had instead taken degrees in a variety of subjects, commonly literary or classical.

The majority of British colonial administrators had been molded by great private boarding schools (misnamed "public schools"), where the sons of merchants and bankers rubbed shoulders with the sons of landowners and professional soldiers and where a classical education was prized above all else. Those who had not gone to public schools had at least attended good grammar schools shaped by the public-school ethos. A high proportion had attended Oxford or Cambridge universities or great military institutions like Sandhurst. Later in life they joined distinguished clubs, where they mingled on terms of social equality with businessmen, senior civil servants, and military officers, an arrangement well suited to a country with the most homogeneous ruling class in Europe. Geographically, they were mainly drawn from London and the Home Counties; the "Celtic fringe" did not go unrepresented, but in no way did it play as important a part as did southeastern England.

There was more social cohesion within the various ranks of the British governing stratum than within those of its continental counterparts. Professional officers did not form a separate caste, as they did in Wilhelminian Germany. Junior clerks in the Upper Division of the Colonial Office one day might head the ministry; assistant district commissioners one day might reside in Government House. They were gentlemen by definition, gentlemen who—on the whole—trusted one another, and with good reason. Personal corruption was almost unknown; tensions between civilians and soldiers were less than among continental colonials. The service was perfectly capable of assimilating some outsiders—Jews, "colonials" recruited in Canada or in Australia—but all were united by a common cult of "good form."

Administrative cadres on the continent were not as tightly knit as those of the British. A good number of colonial dignitaries in Germany were nobles from the more backward rural areas—East Prussia, Pomerania, Bavaria, and so forth. The industrial cities of the Ruhr or trading communities like Hamburg and Bremen, for whose collective benefit the colonial empire had supposedly been built, went unrepresented. The French recruited a considerable number of their colonial officials from peripheral regions like Alsace, Corsica, and Algeria. The Portuguese relied heavily on northern Portugal as an area of recruitment. The Belgians drew many of their administrators from the Ardennes—a French-speaking, poverty-stricken region, but one well supplied with schools. In addition, the Belgian establishment had a strong urban orientation. Brussels played a relatively larger part in furnishing senior officers than did Paris or Berlin. Every exception had its sub-exception, so that sociologists cannot easily establish all-embracing rules with regard to gubernatorial provenance.

Once the pioneering period was over, the "generalists," drawn from the ranks of the army, sometimes from the medical profession and from other occupations, were replaced by trained bureaucrats. On the continent, these senior civil servants were more uniform in their educational background than were their British colleagues; they were trained overwhelmingly in the legal profession and in administrative sciences. Nevertheless, administrative factionalism was more evident on the continent than it was in Great Britain. France, Belgium, and Portugal were rent by quarrels between clericals and anticlericals. In France and Portugal, there was also a sharp cleavage between republicans and opponents of the republican system. These divisions affected a governor's promotion prospects, which they did not in England; they might also plague his professional life in minor ways. The upper ranks of the bureaucracy were also structurally divided. The French and Belgian administrations, for instance, maintained rigidly separate corps, each with a tradition and an ethos of its own. Within the French bureaucracy, the *inspecteurs d'état* formed an elite, many of whose members advanced to high positions. The *inspecteurs* had no counterpart in Great Britain; their role was to assure administrative centralization, to investigate abuses, and to weed out wrongdoers. They operated in a system in which trust was less apt to be taken for granted; they were heirs to an ancient centralizing tradition derived from monarchical governance and to quarrels and mistrust.[4]

The Japanese bureaucracy resembled the French and German civil services more than it did the British. The upper echelons were recruited through a strict examination system that attracted the most

[4] For details concerning the social background of French administrators, see William B. Cohen, *Rulers of Empire: The French Colonial Service in Africa* (Stanford: Hoover Institution Press, 1971); for the British, see Robert Heussler, *Yesterday's Rulers: The Making of the British Colonial Service* (Syracuse, 1963), and L. H. Gann and Peter Duignan, *The Rulers of British Africa, 1870-1914* (Stanford: Stanford University Press, 1978); for the Germans, see L. H. Gann and Peter Duignan, *The Rulers of German Africa, 1884-1914* (Stanford: Stanford University Press, 1977), and for the Belgians, L. H. Gann and Peter Duignan, *The Rulers of Belgian Africa, 1884-1914* (Princeton: Princeton University Press, 1979). Also see L. H. Gann and Peter Duignan, eds., *African Proconsuls, European Governors* (New York: Free Press, 1978).

talented men from Tokyo University. The civil service operated through an intricate system of by-laws and rules; its ethos was rigidly conservative, hostile at the same time to the unrestrained operation of *laissez faire* capitalism and to the labor movement. Senior-level administrators were integrated into the home civil service in a manner unknown to the British; high-ranking Japanese administrators rotated between the colonies and the metropolis. Senior administrators increasingly were drawn from the ranks of diploma-bearing specialists, a development which paralleled the ever-growing reliance of great Japanese business firms on university-trained managers. As Johannes Hirschmeier and Tsunehiko Yui point out in their recent study, the sons of workers and tenant farmers initially had little chance of going to college. As late as 1900 the sons of former samurai still predominated, as did sons of civil servants, prominent businessmen, and the offspring of other great families, preferably based in Tokyo— an arrangement that would in many ways have been familiar to contemporary Englishmen.[5] Gradually the university somewhat broadened its social base so that bureaucratic service became for some a means of social advancement as it did in Great Britain.

The Japanese, like the French but unlike the British, also employed a substantial number of metropolitan-born officials in the lower levels of the administration. These men were apt to stay in the same colony during their working lives; theirs was not a prestige occupation. In Japan, the colonial service as a whole was not an important ladder to social promotion, as it was in Great Britain. In this respect Japan was closer to Germany, where a governor would obscurely end his days in retirement, with a modest bureaucratic title and a minimum of influence. No solid study exists as yet to illustrate the social and geographical origins of Japanese colonial administrators. Investigators will probably find that the Japanese colonial officials, like so many of their German colleagues, were apt to be the sons of military officers, civil servants, teachers, and other professional men, and that in the lower ranks they derived primarily from small towns and villages rather than from major industrial cities.

COLONIAL DOMINATION: FORM AND CONTENT

The phraseology and symbolism of colonial governance varied a good deal from one colonial power to the next. German governors like Major General Leutwein of Southwest Africa spoke unashamedly in

[5] Johannes Hirschmeier and Tsunehiko Yui, *The Development of Japanese Business, 1600-1973* (Cambridge: Harvard University Press, 1975), p. 163.

terms of national self-interest. Their British counterparts, men like Lord Lugard, preferred to justify imperial governance in terms of a dual mandate according to which the imperial power owed a double responsibility, one to the "mother country" and the other to the indigenous people.

During the first decade of the twentieth century, all the major European powers in colonial Africa passed into an era of what might be called capitalist self-criticism; terms like "trusteeship," *política de atracção, moralisation, ethische systeem,* and *Eingeborenenfürsorge* entered the political vocabulary of countries as diverse as Great Britain, Portugal, Belgium, Holland, and Germany, respectively. Essentially, these theories assumed that Africans or Indonesians should no longer be equated with the "idle poor" of eighteenth-century parlance; instead, the "primitive" people—like European workers—should be regarded as economic men, responsive to economic incentives rather than to coercion. Aboriginal institutions hence should be recognized insofar as they were compatible with a market economy as well as with the dictates of "natural law and morality." Workmen should receive a fair wage and cultivators fair prices for their crops. Civil servants should be specially trained in their work. Colonial administration should become humane, orderly, and predictable. The old-style adventurers, idlers, and thugs, of whom there were all too many among the pioneers of colonial administration, should be disciplined or dismissed.

Japanese theoreticians like Nitobe Ināzo fully shared these views and called for a more liberal and humane policy toward Japan's subject peoples. Japanese reformers, like their European counterparts, demanded that Japan's subjects should be introduced to the benefits of modern civilization, that alien rule could be justified only by the positive benefits that the rulers introduced to the conquered lands in the shape of railways, hospitals, schools, roads, and all the other appurtenances of industrial civilization.

In Great Britain, the doctrine of trusteeship came to be linked with kindred doctrines of education for self-government, according to which the "brown" and "black" colonies should ultimately gain dominion status, just as the "white" colonies had done earlier. Power within the British colonial empire ws highly decentralized. Each colony had its own legislature, with some local representation, and governors enjoyed a wide measure of initiative. Correspondence between different British colonial administrations, such as those of Southern Rhodesia and British India, were sometimes conducted with a degree of acerbity that marks the exchange of independent countries on hostile terms with one another. Local pressure groups became increasingly important within the framework of colonial governance. In British India, for instance, the Indian bourgeois from 1923 onward succeeded in effectively protecting Indian manufacturing industries against competition, including British competition by a new system of protective tariffs. Indians increasingly secured appointments to the higher ranks of the ICS (Indian Civil Service), an elite body recruited by stiff examinations. Throughout the empire, moreover, British trusteeship doctrines were supported by vigorous debate in Parliament, by a free press, by an independent judicature, and by the operation of a governing system that took pride in publishing massive and well-publicized reports and commission-of-enquiry findings on all manner of imperial abuse—this in the tradition of the great official Victorian reports that had so well served Marx and Engels.

The Japanese tradition was quite different. Japanese colonial administration was even more centralized than its imperial equivalent in the French and Portuguese colonies. Japanese governors, unlike British viceroys in India, did not have to contend with an independent "native" press; Japanese governors—unlike their British colleagues—did not have to defend their policies in local legislative councils. In the British colonies, local governors enjoyed a wide measure of independence. In Japan, the colonies were ruled explicitly for the benefit of the mother country.

There were also striking differences in the ethos of government. The military remained powerful. (The governors-general of Korea were always soldiers.) The police held powers comparable to those of British district commissioners—policemen in the districts collected taxes, enforced sanitary regulations, provided the public with information on all manner of subjects, supervised public works, gathered political intelligence, performing tasks that were left to civilian administrators in the British African colonies.[6] Taiwan was a perfect *Polizeistaat*, quite unlike, say, Hong Kong or even German-occupied Tsing-Tao. And whereas British colonial policy became increasingly liberal, the Japanese policy at home and overseas became ever more authoritarian. Like the Hungarians in the Austro-Hungarian monarchy, like the Germans under the Kaiser's rule, the Japanese increasingly—and unsuccessfully—attempted to force Japanese customs,

---

[6] I am indebted to the manuscript made available to me by Mark R. Peattie, "The Japanese Colonial Empire, 1895-1945," to be published in the *Cambridge History of Japan*, to be published with Cambridge University Press, 1982, vol. 6. I am equally indebted to Wonmo Dong who has allowed me to read before publication his important essay "The Japanese Colonial Bureaucracy in Korea: 1910-1945: Pattern of Recruitment and Mobility." Social Science Research Council Conference on Colonialism, 1981, held at New York City.

Japanese manners, and the Japanese language onto their subjects in the colonies. During the 1930's the style of Japanese governance became increasingly military, wedded solely to the requirements of defense and imperial autarchy. The requirements of World War II and the need to tie the colonial elites into the war effort somewhat modified Japan's authoritarian approach, but until the island empire faced defeat the Japanese never considered granting independence to any of their dependencies.

Traditional controversy over the cultural policy of the colonizers centered on the opposing concepts of "assimilation" versus "separate development." According to a long-accepted orthodoxy, the French and Portuguese continued the tradition of ancient Rome and aimed at turning their subjects into good Frenchmen or good Portuguese, respectively. The British, on the other hand, reputedly stood for a system of "indirect rule" whereby the subjects were encouraged to stick to indigenous languages and traditions. In practice, this distinction is hard to make. A knowledge of English is far more widespread in the former British countries of Africa (especially in a formerly settler-ruled state like Zimbabwe-Rhodesia) than is a comprehension of French diffused in those black African countries formerly governed from Paris. French assimilation was most effective in Alsace-Lorraine, not in Africa. In Alsace-Lorraine Germans shared with Frenchmen the common experience of the French Revolution, with its beneficent consequences; here Germans were persuaded that "it is chic to speak French."

In theory, the Japanese were committed to a policy of cultural assimilation, though there was a considerable degree of ambivalence in this regard. But whereas the British succeeded in turning English into the lingua franca over a great part of Africa, Asia, and the Pacific, the Japanese failed to implant their own tongue in the lands formerly ruled by the Mikado. The Japanese respected Chinese culture; Japanese rule in Taiwan was far from unpopular, especially at a time when the Chinese mainland was in the hands of quarreling warlords. A good many educated Chinese learned Japanese, or a Japanese of sorts. But the Japanese were in no position to spread their language to the Korean people or to the Taiwanese people at large. There was no equivalent in Taiwan to the great body of men and women who acquired English as a second language in great commercial centers like Hong Kong and Singapore. Few Taiwanese or Korean were ever persuaded that it was chic to master Japanese.

Japanese policy in Korea was even more counterproductive than in Taiwan. With a number of honorable exceptions, the Japanese held the Koreans in contempt; they tried to stamp out the use of Korean much in the same way as the Germans tried to "Germanize" the Polish population of the former Polish Corridor. The end effects of Japanese policy are not easy to assess. Korean labor migration to Japan after World War II had ended probably proved a more effective means of linguistic assimilation than Japanese colonial rule.

In Korea itself, only a small percentage of Koreans managed to acquire a thorough knowledge of Japanese language and culture during the colonial era. It is true that Japanese rule—for all its brutality—was a model of humanitarian governance compared with the German domination of Poland during World War II. The Japanese did not indulge in the planned liquidation of the Korean intelligentsia; neither did they deliberately practice genocide. Japanese scholars made a serious contribution to the study of Korean letters. The educational system of South Korea to this day owes much to the Japanese model. Nevertheless, the Japanese record in Korea was sufficiently harsh to earn for Japan a harvest of hatred that continues to haunt Korean memories.

Had Japanese colonial policy been guided by reformers like Yanahara Tadao, the Japanese would assuredly have learned from their mistakes. Whereas Western, especially British, colonialism became more and more self-critical, the Japanese went in the opposite direction. At its most magnificent, the splendid razzle-dazzle of the *Chant du départ, Preussens Glorie, The British Grenadiers* and *Land of Hope and Glory* could not compare with the Japanese exaltation of the imperial dynasty, its divine links, and Japan's sublime destiny. Even the mystic mumbo jumbo concerning German maids and German honor, German wine and German song—unhappily bequeathed to Germany by the Romantic movement—does not quite measure up to Japan's imperial self-praise.

During World War II, Japanese—like German—nationalism became increasingly radical. The Japanese, like the Germans and Italians before them, proclaimed a new doctrine on the international class struggle whereby nations were equated with social classes; the young, virile, and proletarian nations were supposedly engaged in a struggle for existence against the aging, decadent pluto-democracies of the West. This conflict could be resolved only by a new sharing of the world. But Japanese theoreticians were not consistent. In pursuit of conquest, they also enunciated a new form of pan-Asianism, comparable in certain respects to Russian pan-Slavism of old, proclaiming the unity of Asian interests against the "decadent" imperial powers of the West. Pan-Asianism, however, could not be reconciled with Japanese ethnocentricity, the ardent faith preached in military schools and universities, which asserted that the Japanese race as such had a special historical vocation to become the new *Herrenvolk* of the Pacific.

In the end, nothing survived of Japan's empire or of its imperial ideology. The peoples of Indonesia, Burma, or Micronesia did not thank the Japanese for hauling down the flags of Holland and Great Britain. On the contrary, the Japanese widely earned for themselves a reputation for particular harshness. As a South Sea islander put it in a (probably apocryphal) remark: "We feared the Germans, but did not obey them. We feared the Japanese, and them we obeyed. The Americans we neither feared nor obeyed."

Comparisons between the different forms of colonial rule exercised by the different colonial overlords over their respective subjects are difficult to make. A historian can only compare like with like, and case studies unfortunately are rare. Anthony Asiwaju, a Nigerian scholar, has made an interesting start. According to findings that will be incorporated in his pioneer study *Partitioned Africans* (Lagos University Press), Asiwaju's fellow Yoruba fared better under the Union Jack than under the French *Tricolore*. The Yoruba country, now mainly situated in Nigeria, was divided between the British and the French during the course of the nineteenth century. But the British governed the Yoruba in a manner very different from that used by the French. The British relied on volunteers for their army; the French, on conscripts. The British, through commercial means, encouraged cash crops; the French enforced their cultivation. The British contented themselves with a low rate of taxation; the French insisted on high imposts—and so on.

Asiwaju's findings make good sense when colonial policy is regarded as an overspill of the colonizer's domestic policies overseas. The French drafted their young men at home; hence they saw nothing wrong in drafting young colonials abroad. Despite their revolutionary tradition (or possibly because of it), the French treated their workers with a much greater degree or harshness during the nineteenth century than did the British. The French, for instance, made a practice of using soldiers massively against domestic insurgents and strikers; the British normally used civilian policeman. Until 1890 a French workman was obliged to carry a *livret*, an internal passport comparable in some ways to a similar document compulsory for all Soviet citizens today. Such passes were unknown in Great Britain. Trade unions were legalized in Great Britain between 1824 and 1825, part of a wider reform movement. The French took another sixty years to effect similar changes in the workers' legal rights to establish labor unions.

No one has as yet tried to compare, say, British and Japanese rule in Hong Kong. If such an investigation were to be carried out, the British would surely outscore the Japanese, just as they outscored the French. For all the strictures of British rule that fill the world's library shelves, no reasonable man in any part of the world would have preferred his country to have been occupied by the Japanese army (or for that matter the German, Russian, or Chinese) rather than the British.

EFFECTS OF COLONIALISM

Conquerors throughout the ages have gloried in the splendor of empire. Biblical historians telling of King Solomon's splendor, Viking bards, Zulu praise singers, and *griots* from the Senegal all rejoiced in the great conquests of their respective sovereigns. The moral revulsion toward empire, embodied in activist political creed rather than in religious resignation, is of comparatively recent origin. During their imperial heyday the Japanese, like their competitors, took pride in their imperial power. Japan's defeat in World War II helped to engender a mood of anti-imperial revulsion or even a form of historical amnesia. A modern Japanese who defends any aspect of his country's imperial record risks being called a militarist, a fascist, or worse. The critics have a strong case. Ienaga Saburō, in the new mood of self-criticism engendered by the post-colonial era, provides detailed documentation for the grimmer sides of Japanese rule. Japanese warlords committed all manner of atrocities. They inflicted psychological humiliation on their Korean and Taiwanese subjects; to some extent they attempted to stamp out their national identity. They ruthlessly harnessed colonial economies to the requirements of a Japanese-inspired war. The deeds committed in the name of the "Greater Asian Co-Prosperity Sphere" belied the claims of Japanese pan-Asianists that the Pacific War was fought by all Asians to rid the Far East of Western imperialism.[7]

Japanese rule, with its centralizing tradition, its weakening parliamentary restraints, and its commitments to *étatisme*—the priority of the state over the individual citizen—in some respects followed the French rather than the British pattern.

The economic effects of colonialism are, if anything, even harder to assess than its political impact. Much depended on the social structure of the conquered peoples. Hunters and food gatherers in the Stone Age stage generally experienced tragedy; Iron Age cultivators,

[7] Saburō Ienaga, *The Pacific War: World War II and the Japanese, 1931-1945* (New York: Pantheon Books, 1978).

such as the Bantu-speaking peoples of sub-Saharan Africa, often showed remarkable success in adapting themselves to the new challenges; so did cash farmers and craftsmen in West Africa. Their response, in turn, differed widely from that of highly developed peoples such as the Jews in Mandatory Palestine who considered themselves more highly qualified in a technical sense than their imperial overlords. More perhaps depends even on the condition of the world markets, markets that are no more subject to control by colonial governments than by their post-colonial successor governments. Few experts even know that, as demonstrated by Sir Arthur Lewis, British India during the three decades preceding World War I had a rate of industrial expansion comparable to that of Germany. Fewer still may be aware of Hong Kong's astonishing success story under British governance in the wake of World War II. But to what extent were these economic achievements due to occasioned colonial governance? How far were they occasioned by market forces that the colonizers did not even understand?

Not surprisingly, there is a wealth of interpretations. These include such avowed apologies for imperial rule as the work written by Sir Alan Burns, a British scholar and ex-governor, characteristically entitled *In Defence of Colonies*. Next comes what might be called the conditional defense of colonialism. These derive from the farthermost points of the political spectrum. Marx believed that the British overlordship in India, for all the rulers' rapacity, "objectively" served a progressive historical function by bringing about India's first genuine socio-economic revolution. Engels welcomed the French conquest of Algeria on the grounds that greedy but enterprising bourgeois were to be preferred over tribal chieftains and feudal magnates. My colleague Peter Duignan and I have interpreted Western colonialism in Africa as an engine of cultural transfusion on the grounds that Western conquerors, unlike Zulu, Ndebele, or Tutsi warlords of an earlier vintage, brought to Africa radically new means of production, new forms of administration, new systems of technology, and new systems of thought. During the era of de-colonization these views have fallen into disrepute. Colonialism has widely become a word of abuse. The charges range widely from those of brutal exploitation to the accusations made by Walter Rodney, a black scholar who tried to explain—in the face of all evidence—*How Europe Underdeveloped Africa*.[8]

[8] See Sir Alan Burns, *In Defence of Colonies: British Colonial Territories in International Affairs* (London: Allen and Unwin, 1957). For Marx's and Engels's view, see Shlomo Avineri, ed., *Marx and Engels on Colonialism and Modernization* . . . (New York: Doubleday, 1968). Our own interpretation has been put forward in L. H. Gann and Peter

The literature concerning Japanese colonialism, with which—being unable to read Japanese—I unfortunately have but a sketchy acquaintance, follows a similar pattern. The "imperial benefaction" school has been succeeded, in the wake of Japanese imperialism, by the "nipped in the bud" school of thought, according to which the Japanese overlords actually retarded the development of its dependencies. This interpretation has been broadened by Marxist-Leninist scholars; they try to show how the Japanese bourgeois, like their European rivals, garnered superprofits from their colonies, but fail to explain why Japan should have attained its greatest prosperity after the end of its empire.

Clearly, Japanese rule incurred an extensive debit account, especially during World War II, when the quality of Japanese rule clearly deteriorated as a result of real or assumed military necessities. The Japanese acquired for themselves a sorry kind of distinction for their treatment of captives and subjects; they incurred an odium that had not been attached to Japanese arms in the early twentieth century campaigns in the Russo-Japanese War and in the campaign against German-held Tsingtau in 1914. But Japan's record nevertheless was double-edged.

Whatever interpretation a scholar may choose to follow, he will note certain features that distinguish Western and Japanese colonialism alike. These include, for instance, the relative brevity of colonial experience. For better or for worse, the Japanese empire lasted no more than half a century—only a little less than the life-span of Western European predominance over most of tropical Africa. Secondly, modern colonialism—Japanese and Western alike—was essentially a middle-class achievement. A few titled men made names for themselves in the colonies; a handful of working-class candidates achieved promotion in the empire. But the bulk of civilian administrators and military men were drawn from the middle layers of society. Thirdly, the colonialists—far from creating an integrated system of world capitalism—had little sense of a common interest. After World War I the Allies stripped Germany of its colonies; in World War II the British smashed the Italian colonial empire; the Japanese played a major

Duignan, *Burden of Empire: An Appraisal of Western Colonialism in Africa South of the Sahara* (Stanford: Hoover Institution Press, 1971), and Peter Duignan and L. H. Gann, eds., *Colonialism in Africa, 1870-1960* (Cambridge: Cambridge University Press, 1969-1975, 5 vols.). Anti-colonial works include Paul A. Baran, *The Political Economy of Growth* (New York: Monthly Review Press, 1957); Kwame Nkrumah, *I Speak of Freedom: A Statement of African Ideology* (New York: Praeger, 1961); and Walter Rodney, *How Europe Underdeveloped Africa* (London: Bogle L'Ouverture Publications, 1972). Another assessment is found in Sir (William) Arthur Lewis, ed., *Tropical Development, 1880-1913: Studies in Economic Progress* (London: Allen and Unwin, 1970).

part in dismantling the British, Dutch, and French empires in the Far East. In conquering Indo-China, Malaya, Burma, and the Dutch East Indies, the Japanese regarded themselves as liberators. Initially, their new subjects often accepted the Japanese claim—only to be disappointed as Japanese conduct belied their propaganda. Modern Japan's role as liberator and conqueror, in some measure resembled Napoleon's, whose armies in the Rhineland and parts of Italy were often welcomed by the local people, only to make the foreigners disliked, if not detested, by their practice of conscripting young men, and of injuring trade through the enforcement of Napoleon's "Continental Blockade" of Great Britain. The Japanese, like their fellow colonialists, garnered for themselves a universal harvest of dislike or hatred, a widespread odium that makes any defense of colonialism a perilous undertaking in academia today.

In economic terms, however, colonialism was a qualified success, and in this respect Japanese colonialism was no exception. According to its critics, colonialism is a system of exploitation designed to tie the backward periphery to the imperial metropolis and to syphon off the subjects' surplus wealth. According to Marxist economists such as the late Paul A. Baran, the capitalist system in its various guises has accounted not only for the poverty of the underdeveloped world but also for its stagnation. Capitalism, once a mighty engine of economic development, has turned into a no less formidable "hurdle to human advancement."[9]

The experience of Taiwan and Korea under Japanese domination do not bear out these strictures. Other contributors to this volume, especially Yamada Saburō, Mizoguchi Toshiyuki, and Yamamoto Yūzō, provide detailed information showing how the economies of Taiwan and Korea expanded under Japanese hegemony. In the economic sense, the Japanese tried to extend to the colonies the experiences of the Meiji state in fostering economic development in Japan. The Japanese initially emphasized agricultural production and the creation of a logistic infrastructure. New crops would help to provide local revenue; they would also help to feed the mainland. The Japanese, like their colonial competitors in other parts of the world, built railways, harbors, roads, schools, agricultural research stations, clinics. Government investment played an important part in capital formation. Taiwan had traditionally formed part of China's settlement frontier; much of the island had been developed during the late seventeenth and eighteenth centuries by emigrants from the mainland

---

[9] Baran, *The Political Economy of Growth*, pp. 249-250.

who had built up a market-oriented agricultural system from the inception of Taiwan's modern economy. The Japanese found favorable conditions when they attempted to modernize traditional systems of property rights, to assist cultivators by irrigation works, and to mobilize savings to finance domestic investments. The agricultural growth rate rapidly expanded, and Taiwan became a major producer of sugar and rice. Agricultural development in turn gave a boost to agricultural processing industries like sugar refining, a process familiar to students concerned with the history of advanced African territories like Kenya or Nigeria. Private consumption rose in a striking fashion. At the same time, capital formation proceeded apace, as did the development of an indigenous working class and the expansion of an indigenous bourgeoisie with a stake in both farming and industry.

Korea during the Japanese era likewise experienced the formation of a new working class. Korea also underwent a significant economic growth, especially in the manufacturing field, as did British colonial areas like Southern Rhodesia. In Korea, the Japanese helped to promote modern forestry and to improve agricultural methods. They also created hydroelectric works as well as heavy industries; this development benefitted from a great pool of cheap labor and from Korean mineral wealth, the opening of a wide hinterland in Manchukuo, along with Japanese technical and managerial skill and extensive government aid. Rice production improved. Korea's monoculture economy gradually diversified. The Koreans paid a heavy price for these advances, not merely in terms of political liberty, but also in terms of well-being, since many farmers were reduced to the status of tenants. Nevertheless, living standards for the bulk of the Korean people probably rose, albeit slowly. New industries came into being; most of these new industries were in the hands of local owners, a feature shared by Korea and Taiwan with South Africa. Mizoguchi and Yamamoto indicate that by 1939 Japanese capitalists owned less than half the manufacturing ventures in Korea and less than one-fifth of such undertakings in Taiwan.

Whatever the many political and social failings of Japanese rule, the Japanese thus made a positive economic contribution to their imperial dependencies. The *Wirtschaftswunder* experienced by Korea and Taiwan after World War II had its roots in the Japanese colonial era. On the other hand, Japanese colonization, like that of the Germans, failed to meet the expectations of those who looked to overseas expansion for a solution of the population problem in the metropolis. A substantial number of Japanese went to Korea, Manchuria, and some of the South Sea Islands, but in proportion to the metropolitan population their numbers were negligible. Only a relatively small number of these emigrants made their living by working the land.

What lessons, if any, can be drawn from Japan's imperial experience? The imperial history of Japan indeed has a quality of the melodramatic, the improbable, that makes the futurologists' ambitions seem futile. If we were to step back into the past, to the year 1860 in the twilight days of the Shogunate, we might well have regarded Japan as a potential European colony like Annam. At best, Japan appeared to Westerners to be an exotic island kingdom shrouded in mystery, a land of cherry blossoms and swordsmanship. No political scientist, no economist, no philosopher dreamt that within a generation Japan would have gone through a relatively peaceful revolution, becoming the major industrial power in the Far East. Taking 1890 as his next starting point, a Westerner might then have predicted cautious progress punctuated by constitutional crises fomented within the newly founded Imperial Diet. Few outsiders would have been willing to wager that within less than two decades Japan would have successively defeated both China and Russia, thereby shaking the Ch'ing and the tsarist monarchies to their foundations.

The events of the next thirty-five years would have been even harder to forecast; they would have seemed a tale told by a madman. Japan, from the 1930's, conquered a huge part of China, struck a smashing blow at the United States, and occupied the colonial possessions of the Dutch, the French, and the British, all of whom had humiliated Japan at some earlier stage in Japanese history. But Japan's new empire turned out to be the most short-lived in history. Japan stumbled into total defeat, suffering misery and destruction that not even the gloomiest pessimist would have dared to predict. Again, reality falsified all prediction. Within less than a generation of her unconditional surrender in 1945 Japan had made the most rapid recovery in history. Stripped of imperial and military might, resource-poor and overpopulated, Japan—incredibly—enjoyed a much higher standard of living than ever before. By the late 1970's the gross national product of Japan considerably exceeded the combined gross national product of France and Great Britain, an outcome that would have been as inconceivable to Marx and Engels as it would have been to Prince Bismarck and Lord Salisbury.

To sum up, Japanese imperialism had many similarities with the imperial systems of Western Europe. Japanese colonialism, like the Western, was a powerful engine for cultural transfusion. Unlike so many earlier conquerors in history, protagonists of the new imperialism helped to transmit new methods of production, new methods of administration, new ways of thought. Japanese imperialism, like the Western, was, for all its pomp, essentially a middle-class achievement. It was double-edged in its consequences, creative and destructive at the same time. Japanese rule, like the Western, came to be bitterly resented by its subjects—often by those very middle-class men and women who seemed to have benefitted most from foreign-imposed education and the new economic opportunities that the conquerors had helped to create. The Japanese empire, like the French and the Russian, was built on a centralizing tradition; yet, whatever theorists might say, the Japanese were surprisingly unsuccessful in assimilating their overseas subjects to Japanese ways.

All European imperialists looked to military strength and to military glory as well as to profits. But no empire builders indulged in quite the same spirit of mystical self-exaltation as did the Japanese. No empire was quite as security-minded as Japan's. None crashed in quite as spectacular a fashion. Except for Hitler's short-lived Thousand Years' Reich, none has been more discredited. Whereas Kipling is still read with respect by Africans and Indians, whereas Britain's imperial story may be about to experience a nostalgic revival, Japan's colonial record seems both dead and damned. Yet, unwittingly, the Japanese colonizers helped to mold the shape of East Asia's postcolonial future.

List of Contributors

Ching-chih Chen, Associate Professor of History, Southern Illinois University at Edwardsville, was born in Taiwan. He has conducted research in Japan and Taiwan and has published several articles on Taiwan under Japanese colonial rule.

Edward I-te Chen, Associate Professor of Japanese History at Bowling Green State University in Ohio, has published many articles on Japanese colonialism. He has in preparation an interpretive study on Gotō Shimpei, Japan's civil administrator in Taiwan from 1898 to 1906.

Bruce Cumings, Associate Professor, School of International Studies, University of Washington. Author of *The Origins of the Korean War: Liberation and the Emergence of Separate Regimes, 1945-47*, editor of *Child of Conflict: The Korean-American Relationship, 1945-1953*, and various articles on Korea and China. Currently working on the second and last volume of his Korean War study and a book on the Northeast Asian Political economy.

Peter Duus is Professor of History at Stanford University. He has taught at several other institutions, including Washington University, Harvard University and Claremont Graduate School. He is the author of *Party Rivalry and Political Change in Taishō Japan, Feudalism in Japan*, and *The Rise of Modern Japan*. He is also the editor of Volume VI of the projected *Cambridge History of Japan*.

Lewis H. Gann is a Senior Fellow at the Hoover Institution, Stanford University. He holds his doctorate from the University of Oxford; he is a Fellow of the Royal Historical Society and of numerous other learned bodies. He is author, co-author, or co-editor of twenty-four published works on the history of European colonization in Africa, on the structure of colonial governance, and on various aspects of white settlement in Africa. Before coming to the Hoover Institution, Lewis H. Gann has worked as a historian at the Rhodes-Livingstone Institute (now the Institute for Social Studies at the University of Zambia); he has taught at Manchester University, England; he has served as an archivist in the National Archives of Rhodesia (now the National Archives of Zimbabwe).

Samuel Pao-San Ho is Professor of Economics at the University of

British Columbia. He is the author of *Economic Development of Taiwan 1869-1970, The Small Enterprise Sector in Korea and Taiwan*, and various articles on the economies of China, South Korea, and Taiwan. Before joining the University of British Columbia, he taught at Yale University and was associated with Yale's Economic Growth Center. He has served as consultant to the World Bank, UNDP, and the Government of British Columbia.

Marius B. Jansen, formerly of the University of Washington and now Professor of History at Princeton University, is the author of *The Japanese and Sun Yat-sen, Sakamoto Ryōma and the Meiji Restoration, Japan and China from War to Peace, Japan and Its World: Two Centuries of Change*, former Associate Editor of The Journal of Asian Studies, past president of the Association for Asian Studies, and a general editor and editor of Vol. v of the forthcoming *Cambridge History of Japan*.

Ramon H. Myers is Senior Fellow and Curator-Scholar of the East Asian Collection of the Hoover Institution on War, Revolution & Peace at Stanford, California. He is also the author of *The Chinese Peasant Economy* (1970) and *The Chinese Economy Past and Present*. He was formerly Associate Editor of The Journal of Asian Studies and Editor of *Ch'ing-shih wen-t'i*.

Mark R. Peattie served for nine years with the United States Information Agency in Japan before obtaining a doctorate from Princeton University in modern Japanese history. Prior to joining the faculty of the University of Massachusetts, Boston, where he is currently associate professor of history and director of the Program in East Asian Studies, Peattie taught at the Pennsylvania State University and the University of California at Los Angeles. He is the author of *Ishiwara Kanji and Japan's Confrontation with the West*.

Michael E. Robinson is an Assistant Professor of History at the University of Southern California where he teaches Korean history and culture courses. A product of the University of Washington Korean Studies Program, he is an expert on the Korean Colonial period. He has published articles on the intellectual history of early twentieth century Korea and is currently writing a book on the origins of Korean nationalist ideology.

Yamada Saburō, Professor, Institute of Oriental Culture and Graduate School of Agricultural Economics, University of Tokyo. He is the author of *A Comparative Analysis of Asian Agricultural Productivities and Growth Patterns*, and *A Century of Agricultural Development in Japan: Its Relevance to Asian Development*.

Mizoguchi Toshiyuki is Professor of Economics at the Institute of Economic Research, Hisotsubashi University and author of *Personal Savings and Consumption in Postwar Japan*.

E. Patricia Tsurumi, Associate Professor of Japanese History at the University of Victoria, is the author of *Japanese Colonial Education in Taiwan, 1895-1945*. She has published articles on Japanese colonialism, the history of Japanese education, and Japan's ancient female emperors. Currently she is engaged in a study of Meiji women, education, and industrialization and is also writing a critical biography of Takamure Itsue.

Yamamoto Yūzō is currently Associate Professor in the Jimbun Kagaku Kenkȳujo of Kyoto University. He is co-author of Volume 14, *Estimates of Long-Term Economic Statistics of Japan since 1868: Trade and International Balance of Payments*.

Index

Library of Congress Cataloging in Publication Data
Main entry under title:
The Japanese colonial empire, 1895-1945.

   "Based on a conference sponsored by the Joint
Committee on Japanese Studies of the American
Council of Learned Societies and the Social Science
Research Council."
   Bibliography: p.   Includes index.
   1. Japan—Colonies—East Asia—Administration—
History—Addresses, essays, lectures. 2. Japan—Colo-
nies—East Asia—Economic policy—Addresses, es-
says, lectures. 3. East Asia—Politics and govern-
ment—Addresses, essays, lectures. I. Myers, Ramon
Hawley, 1929- . II. Peattie, Mark R., 1930- . III.
Chen, Ching-chi. IV. Joint Committee on Japanese
Studies.
JV5260.J36   1983   325'.31'52095   83-42571
ISBN 0-691-05398-7